# Psychoanalytic Interpretation in Rorschach Testing

## THEORY AND APPLICATION

Austen Riggs Foundation

Monograph Series

No. 3

# Psychoanalytic Interpretation in Rorschach Testing

## THEORY AND APPLICATION

ROY SCHAFER, Ph.D.

OTHER PRESS
*New York*

International Standard Book Number 1-59051-059-3

Dedicated

to

my father, Abraham

and

my mother, May

# Contents

# Preface

No matter how helpful a clinical tool it may be, a psychological test cannot do its own thinking. What it accomplishes depends upon the thinking that guides its application. This guiding thought is psychological theory, whether explicit and systematized or implicit and unsystematized.

The danger of forgetting this scientific truism is especially great in the case of so complex, versatile and forceful a tool as the Rorschach test. For the novice and the experienced clinician alike, it is steadily tempting to think that interpreting Rorschach test results is simply a matter of reading psychological hieroglyphics. Unaware, we tend to drift into the belief that the interpretations are all there, in the responses and scores, waiting for the sharp eye and quick mind—and rote memory—to make them out.

Of course, this is not the way it is at all. While Hermann Rorschach got his test off to a remarkable theoretical and interpretive start, and left his stamp indelibly on the test's subsequent development, in final analysis he did no more than apply to his protocols the conceptions of personality and psychopathology that were available to him and impressive to him during his time as student and practitioner. This was more than thirty years ago. Rorschach had no developed psychological theory to work with. In many respects his approach was eclectic. His thinking reflects the influence of associationist psychology, Bleuler, and the early Freud and Jung.

Today, great strides have been made beyond the psychological frontiers at which Rorschach conducted his bold, masterful explorations. Psychoanalysis has come a long way since the early twenties. Our general theories concerning the development and organization of personality and the meanings of psychopathology are richer. Our particular theories concerning the workings of perceiving, learning, thinking, drives and affects, and the interrelationships among these and other psychic processes, are more articulated. Through the work of Rapaport, Schachtel and others, much more is known about the Rorschach test too—about its potentialities and its limits. It therefore seemed to me worthwhile at this time to attempt a general formulation of these developments as they bear on current work with the Rorschach test in the clinic and in research. Pulling together these various direct and indirect, actual and potential contributions to Rorschach theory and interpretation should help us to remain the self-conscious masters of this powerful clinical tool.*

I began writing ·this book in the spring of 1951, completed the major theoretical sections by the spring of 1952, the case studies by the spring of 1953, and the polishing of the manuscript by the end of 1953. Not long before I began writing, I conducted a series of workshop meetings in Boston at which I expressed in rudimentary form many of the ideas elaborated in the present volume. In June of 1951 at a workshop in Utah, in January 1952 in several lectures in Philadelphia, and in the spring of 1952 in a course on testing I taught at the Harvard Psychological Clinic, I developed these ideas further. And in symposia on projective testing at the 1952 and 1953 meetings of the American Psychological Association, I presented theoretical paoers on the psychoanalytic study of Rorschach content and on contributio.s of psychoanalysis to projective testing; one of these has since appeared in print [137] and the other is now in press. It took so long to finish this book because of the pressure of routine clinical and teaching duties, my undertaking the previously mentioned time-consuming but personally rewarding workshops, lectures and papers, and the additional harassment of uprooting myself in the middle of 1953 and moving from Stockbridge and the Riggs Center to New Haven and the Yale University School of Medicine.

During these three years many research papers have appeared on topics touched on or developed at length within this book. Earlier, there had been comparatively few pertinent publications. I have tried to take account of these recent contributions, at least by calling the reader's attention to them at appropriate places in the text, but I have attempted neither a survey of the literature nor the compilation of an exhaustive bibliography. My references will, however, be broadly representative of relevant trends in Rorschach practice, research and theory.

This book is written for those who have completed at least their basic clinical training in administering, scoring and interpreting Rorschach test results; preferably the reader should also have clinical testing experience beyond the doctoral level. The traditional, more or less established signifi-

---

* Independently, Holt [79] and Wyatt [154] have put forth formulations that have much in common with some of those to be presented here. This overlap is particularly true of the emphases on "regression in the service of the ego" (see Chapter 3, below) and on cautious, psychoanalytically-oriented content analysis (see Chapters 4 and 5, below). See also an earlier general statement by A. Korner [90]. These various discussions, along with the related but significantly different ones by Phillips and Smith [105] and Beck [11], and many relevant, more or less recent reports of research and conceptual analysis, all reflect the trend of the times of which this book is also a part. It is a trend toward the systematic application of psychoanalytic concepts in clinical testing.

cances of scores and score configurations will not be reviewed here. Rorschach [*124*], Beck [*8, 9*], Klopfer [*86*], Piotrowski [*107*], Schachtel [*129, 130, 131, 132*], and Rapaport [*118*] have all presented major expositions of Rorschach technique. While their many differences in individual points of administration, scoring, and interpretation cannot be overlooked, each presents a broad, helpful introduction to the test. Of all these discussions, Rapaport's—and my clinically focused summary of it [*134*]—provide the best introduction to what follows here. Unless the reader is intimately familiar with at least one of the major expositions listed above, he is certain to be confused by the present work's variations on basic Rorschach themes.

More than a solid grounding in Rorschach principles and technique is required for an adequate reading of this book. The reader should also have had a general introduction to psychoanalytic theory and to the data of psychoanalytic observation. Obviously, a book of this sort cannot at the same time attempt to be a text on psychoanalysis; some background of psychoanalytic study is therefore necessarily assumed, even though the referents of the psychoanalytic conceptions that stand out in this book, such as *defense, primary and secondary processes, regression in the service of the ego,* and *ego identity* will be specified along with the indications of relevant psychoanalytic literature. Rapaport's recent theoretical survey and summary [*113*] is a valuable and convenient source of additional clarification of these and other psychoanalytic concepts as they will be used in the following discussions.

As a theoretical and clinical statement, this book covers only certain normal and psychiatric subjects, namely, those who are (1) white, (2) American or well adapted to American culture, (3) at least average in intelligence and education, (4) from subcultural backgrounds that are not extremely bleak or deviant, (5) in late adolescence or older, and (6) without noteworthy "organic" psychological deficit. The assumptions developed here seem to apply—with appropriate modifications—in other cultural, intellectual, age and neurological contexts, but at present I cannot specify how much they do apply and with which specific modifications and supplementary conceptions.

This book is as much an outgrowth of my supervised experience in psychoanalytic psychotherapy as it is of my continuing experience with clinical testing. To my mind, each has made the other more meaningful, effective and gratifying than it could have been otherwise. I am grateful to the medical directors of the Austen Riggs Center for encouraging my development of psychotherapeutic skills and for providing supervision of my therapeutic work whenever necessary. I am additionally indebted to the directors of the Austen Riggs Center and to its trustees for granting me the invaluable time and clerical assistance to undertake and carry through the main part of this project.

Every book has many authors. Among the silent co-authors of this book are my friends, colleagues, and teachers at the Austen Riggs Center, particularly David Rapaport, Margaret Brenman, Robert P. Knight, Erik Erikson, and, for too brief a time, Merton Gill. The greater part of what I understand about contemporary psychoanalytic psychology and psychotherapy I owe to them. To David Rapaport I am doubly indebted, for he also conveyed to me, in developed and incipient form, much of what I understand about clinical psychological testing. Through the years, continued discussion of psychological problems with my wife and co-worker, Sarah, has also helped develop my understanding of people and testing.

There is another group of co-authors that overlaps the first. These are the critical readers of preliminary phases of this manuscript. For their thorough, challenging, clarifying and enriching reviews of the text I am deeply grateful to Robert R. Holt, now of New York University, and David Rapaport. Many valuable suggestions came from my wife, Sarah. In addition, I owe thanks to David Shapiro, present staff psychologist of the Austen Riggs Center, for his comments, and to Margaret Brenman for her general critique of the early chapters of this book.

Finally, I want to thank the secretaries who prepared this manuscript for publication—Betty Thompson, Betty Smith, and Anne Palmer, with assists from Rena Masiero, Anne Peters and Polly Smith. They were all good, steady, conscientious helpers.

ROY SCHAFER

*New Haven, Connecticut*
*January, 1954*

# 1. Introduction

THIS BOOK WILL BE CONCERNED WITH WHAT seems to me one of our basic needs at this point in the history of Rorschach testing in particular and clinical testing in general—our need for a broad treatment of the contributions psychoanalysis has made and can make to test theory and interpretation. We hear so much these days about the influence of the tester on the test results, the symbolic interpretation of response content, the test indications for therapy, and the like. Psychoanalytic assumptions are almost always involved in these discussions. Obviously, the more we can specify, amplify, appropriately modify, integrate and concretely illustrate these psychoanalytic assumptions and their applications, the more we may hope to improve our work with tests in practice and research. It is to this end that this book is devoted.

This means a journey to the frontiers of Rorschach test theory and interpretation. These have been busy frontiers. The post-World-War-II rapid expansion of clinical psychology as an area of practice and research, and the steadily increasing influence of psychoanalytic theory in psychology have led to the asking of many fresh questions concerning the workings of the Rorschach test. Sometimes, the answers to these questions have challenged basic Rorschach theory and interpretation, as in the studies of reactions to color [2, 22, 28, 94, 99, 127, 147] and in studies and discussions of attitudinal, interpersonal and situational influences on test results and their interpretation [1, 58, 66, 80, 82, 83, 84, 97, 126, 128, 131]. Sometimes, the answers to these fresh questions have contributed directly to test interpretation, as in the many recent studies of the diagnostic, prognostic, and dynamic significance of response content [3, 13, 16, 27, 29, 31, 32, 39, 40, 63, 65, 74, 75, 79, 81, 104, 120, 137, 141, 146, 153, 154]. But whether challenging or contributory each fresh answer raises new questions, and thus the frontiers continue to expand, often faster and farther than we can keep track of. At such a time, we have special need for an explicit and broad psychoanalytic frame of reference. With such a frame of reference, we will be in an advantageous position to comprehend and evaluate each new contribution and challenge; without it, we may easily lose ourselves

1

in wild speculation, impulsive *ad hoc* explanation, doubt, contradiction and disillusionment.*

At least three basic contributions have already been made toward a psychoanalytic orientation to the Rorschach test. First, there are Rorschach's fragmentary but illuminating psychoanalytic conceptualizations of the response process in his posthumously published case study with Oberholzer [124]. Second, there is Rapaport's thorough and subtle analysis of thought processes underlying Rorschach responses [128]. In this analysis, and in his more recent contributions [121, 126], Rapaport makes extensive use of the Freudian psychoanalytic theory of ego development, organization and pathology as these are expressed in memory organization, concept formation, perception and other psychic processes. Third, there are Schachtel's series of perceptive and stimulating papers on "the Rorschach situation" and on the major determinants of Rorschach responses—form, color and movement [129, 130, 131, 132]. Schachtel's discussions significantly advance our comprehension of the interrelationships between the formal and content aspects of Rorschach responses and, along with Rapaport's analysis of verbalization, they open up test attitudes and behavior to psychoanalytic study.†

In this book I shall attempt to fill in, coordinate and extend these (and other) contributions. The plan of this volume is the following: first, to analyze the major dynamics of the test situation and the interpersonal tester-patient relationship, and to cast this analysis in contemporary Freudian concepts. By "contemporary" is meant particularly the genuine appreciation of how ego processes, such as defense, reality testing, and self-integrative efforts, are at least as central in determining behavior as id and superego processes. This ego-oriented analysis will deal with many realistic and unrealistic psychological constants in the interpersonal test relationship as well as with problems raised by the individual personality

---

* Of course, other theoretical points of view than the psychoanalytic are applicable to test data. This is not the place to argue the relative merits of psychoanalytic theory. Its value will be assumed in what follows, despite its many vague, incomplete and conflicting aspects.

† In many respects, Schachtel's conception of personality and pathology is different from Rapaport's, and also narrower, but his approach to Rorschach theory and interpretation remains basically psychoanalytic. Actually, the difference between these two writers is that between the contemporary Freudian and the so-called cultural schools of psychoanalysis. It also seems true, however, that Rapaport tends to emphasize formal, structuralized ego characteristics at the expense of the live situational dynamics and cultural pressures with which Schachtel has been particularly and instructively concerned. On his part, Schachtel follows Fromm, Horney and Sullivan in essentially disregarding the vital need for structural as well as dynamic concepts in psychoanalytic theory. In this regard, see Rapaport's recent theoretical survey and summary [113].

problems of tester and patient; it will also consider the ways in which these constants and individual problems may clarify and obscure the test findings. Particular attention will be paid to the behavorial and attitudinal expression of individually preferred mechanisms of defense.

With this study of reality, conflict and defense in the testing situation as a necessary background for the entire subsequent discussion of Rorschach theory and interpretation, this presentation will move on to an extended analysis of the response process. Here my effort will be to illuminate the preconscious and unconscious as well as conscious processes involved in the coming about of Rorschach responses. This rationale of the response process will rely heavily on Rapaport's analysis of thought processes underlying Rorschach responses and Schachtel's elaboration of the motivational and affective forces behind these responses; it will also depend greatly on Freud's analysis of dreams [43] and Kris's psychoanalytic contributions to the psychology of creativity [92].* In addition, a comparative analysis of dream imagery, daytime imagery and ordinary perception will be attempted, partly to apply what we understand about these phenomena, particularly dreams, to the rationale of Rorschach responses, and partly to clarify the ways in which Rorschach responses are different from other imaginal and perceptual phenomena.

Clinical psychologists' rapidly increasing interest in symbolic interpretation of Rorschach responses—a mode of interpretation that tends to regard Rorschach responses as identical with dream images—makes it especially important that we be clear about the differences as well as similarities between Rorschach responses and dreams. Therefore, after the general analysis of the response process and its detailed comparison with dreaming, two related sets of considerations will be presented: (a) the justification, potentialities and limits of content interpretation; (b) the criteria for sound but searching interpretation—criteria that may simultaneously safeguard us against the hazards of wild and gratuitous interpretation and yet allow us to exploit fully the diagnostically and dynamically valuable material in (1) response content, (2) the vicissitudes of the patient-tester relationship, and (3) the patient's fixed and changing attitudes toward his own responses.

These discussions of Rorschach content and criteria for interpretation will bring us up to the second major section of this book. This section will be devoted to a detailed study of the interplay of impulses, defenses,

---

* The recent contributions of Beck [11] and Phillips and Smith [105] to the Rorschach literature are obviously deeply influenced by psychoanalytic thought, but they are not systematically and explicitly defined in terms of psychoanalytic theory. In fact, they avowedly set "empirical results" with the test before theory as their guide in interpretation. Neither work therefore can be considered primarily a psychoanalytic contribution.

and adaptive strivings in test responses. Most of all, this study will focus on the responses' defensive aspects. Despite Rapaport's major pioneer effort [118], Rorschach theory and analysis have not kept pace with this basic aspect of the psychoanalytic study of the ego [37, 42, 50].* A great deal about preferred defenses may be inferred from the patient's response content, the relationship he attempts to set up with the tester, and his attitudes towards his responses, as well as from his pattern of W, D, M, F and other traditional formal scores. Focusing on defense this way does not mean, however, that analysis of underlying strivings and of adaptive efforts will be ignored.

This second major section of the book will lead off with a general discussion of the theoretical problems surrounding the interpretation of defense. This will be followed by a survey of Rorschach indications of stable and unstable, successful and failing defensive operations. Next, a series of four chapters will take up the following mechanisms of defense: repression, denial, projection, and the obsessive-compulsive defensive syndrome of regression, isolation, reaction formation and undoing.† In these chapters, a brief summary of the psychoanalytic theory of the defense in question will be followed by a review of expected Rorschach test indications of this defense. After the introduction to each defense, a series of four verbatim Rorschach records will be carefully analyzed for indications of that defense in operation, again with simultaneous attention being paid to that which is being defended against and to adaptive efforts.

Throughout these discussions and illustrations of defensive operations and their interplay with impulse and adaptation, I shall steadily emphasize individual differences in defensive style, in defensive success or failure, and in other major personality characteristics. These aspects of the analysis of defense are important for clinical purposes in order that we may describe the patient with some appreciation of his individuality and complexity, with some estimate of his current ego assets and liabilities, and with some understanding of the place his preferred defenses occupy in his total functioning. Analyzing the individual style, relative success and total personality context of defensive efforts is also of theoretical importance since it leads beyond the simple though valuable identification of preferred defenses to confrontation of the intricacies of ego organization and pathology. These are intricacies that may be decisive determinants of overt behavior and social

---

* Beck [11] and Phillips and Smith [105] take up the interpretation of defenses, but, as will be elaborated below, they generally do so in a manner that is relatively cursory or theoretically idiosyncratic.

† For reasons to be detailed later (see pp. 191–2), introjection and sublimation, the two remaining major defense mechanisms according to traditional psychoanalytic theory, will not be given separate attention.

adjustment; they may also be the factors that make much of the difference in response to therapy and in prognosis.

This is the plan of the book. Clearly, it does not exhaust the actual and potential contributions of psychoanalysis to Rorschach test theory and interpretation. It defines and illustrates an orientation; it is not a complete, thoroughly integrated statement. Yet, in conception at least, this presentation does significantly broaden and articulate the psychoanalytic frame of reference for the study of people through the Rorschach test. If, within its limits, it is successful in what it attempts, it will bring Rorschach practice and research into closer relations with psychoanalytic theory and particularly with recent developments in psychoanalytic ego psychology [18, 19, 35, 42, 68, 69, 70, 71, 72, 73, 89, 91, 92, 112, 113, 114, 115]. And the achievement of these closer relations will represent no insignificant advance, for to my mind much of today's most important theoretical and clinical progress in the study of personality is being made through psychoanalytic ego psychology.

# 2. Interpersonal Dynamics in the Test Situation

THE CLINICAL TESTING SITUATION HAS A complex psychological structure. It is not an impersonal getting-together of two people in order that one, with the help of a little "rapport," may obtain some "objective" test responses from the other. The psychiatric patient is in some acute or chronic life crisis. He cannot but bring many hopes, fears, assumptions, demands and expectations into the test situation. He cannot but respond intensely to certain real as well as fantasied attributes of that situation. Being human and having to make a living—facts often ignored—the tester too brings hopes, fears, assumptions, demands and expectations into the test situation. He too responds personally and often intensely to what goes on—in reality and in fantasy—in that situation, however well he may conceal his personal response from the patient, from himself and from his colleagues.

In short, an intricate interpersonal relationship, with realistic and unrealistic aspects, exists during the testing. This is not an evil. It should not be striven against. As in psychoanalytic technique, this relationship must be regarded as inevitable, as a potentially significant influence on the patient's productions, and as a possible gold mine of material for interpretation.

Analyzing the interpersonal relationship and the real test situation may take us out to, or beyond, the borders of "objective" test interpretation—in the narrow and, I believe, superficial sense of "objective" test interpretation. But if we mean, as we should, to track down the origins and vicissitudes of the patient's test responses, we must deal with the total situation in which the responses occur. The inkblot alone, the digit span sequence alone, the picture of a boy and a violin alone, do not totally define the stimulus situation existing at any moment. There are many other more or less uncontrolled but more or less identifiable stimuli in the situation. There are larger situational and interpersonal meanings that surround and invade the simple test stimuli. It is with these meanings that we shall be concerned in this chapter.

First to be considered will be the needs and problems of the tester as these are defined by his professional and personal position and by the

6

realities of the testing situation and relationship. Afterwards the psychological situation of the patient being tested will be considered, and then the implications of the preceding analyses for interpretation of test results.

## A. THE DYNAMICS OF TESTING

The needs and problems of the tester in the testing situation are defined by his historical and social position as a particular type of professional man, by his spontaneous and imposed assumptions as to his professional and scientific responsibilities, by the additional responsibilities he assumes and gratifications he seeks because of his personality make-up, and by the behavior of the patient and the particular conflicts in the tester this behavior stimulates. The tester's needs and problems will be sensed by the patient, the more so the more sensitive, paranoid, overcompliant and/or negativistic the patient is. These needs will, as they impinge on the patient's own needs and assumptions, influence the patient's definition of the testing situation.

As evidenced by the relatively recent papers by Gitelson [60] and Berman [14] among others, it being acknowledged more and more, regarding countertransference in psychotherapy and psychoanalysis, that it is not only futile but psychologically meaningless to set up an ideal of complete therapeutic impartiality or objectivity. Inevitably there are personal reasons why someone chooses to practice psychotherapy. As Fromm-Reichman has described, there are certain gratifications and securities the therapist seeks through his job and through his relationship with patients [56]. The same may be said of the tester. The tester's responsibility, like the therapist's, is not to try to eliminate these needs; it is his responsibility to acknowledge their presence, understand them, keep them relatively unobtrusive, and try to ascertain how they have influenced the patient's productions and his own interpretations of these productions. The last two of these responsibilities are capable of very incomplete fulfillment at best. In psychotherapy, for example, the therapist often discovers only long afterwards that a look, a word, a gesture, made a difference in the patient's definition of the relationship. It would therefore be too much to ask a tester to be altogether clear about his influence on the testing situation. So far as major disruptions of test performance are concerned, however, the tester often can come to tentative conclusions.

In what follows the needs and problems of the tester will be discussed from three points of view—that of his professional situation, that of his role in the test relationship and that of his own personality. It should become progressively clearer as we go on that these three points of view are not really separable. Professional, technical and personal problems are inextricably intertwined.

## 1. The Tester's Professional Problems and the Test Relationship

The following discussion will concentrate on the psychological situation of a tester in a psychiatric hospital or clinic—the situation with which I am most familiar. It seems, however, that a good deal of what will be said is transposable, with appropriate modifications, to most situations in which clinically oriented testing is done. In the end, the reader will have to analyze his own work situation and decide which of the factors discussed here apply and to what extent; he will also have to determine which other factors, not mentioned here, also apply.

The emphasis in what follows will be on difficulties. This should not be taken to mean that the tester's relationships with colleagues and patients are always and inevitably miserable, conflict-laden affairs. They are very often cooperative, secure and gratifying. Therapists and testers can and do work together in the spirit of pooling their approximations in order to understand the patient better, and with an individualized relationship that takes account of the assets, limits and liabilities of each. Similarly, patients usually do have a strong enough wish to get well, a good enough sense of reality, or at least sufficient desire to be liked or to receive attention, that they cooperate adequately throughout the testing.

In the background of the professional problems to be considered are a number of historical and social sources of confusion and anxiety. For one thing, the status and boundaries of clinical psychology as a profession are still unsettled. There is no binding consensus on what is "good practice." There is a lack of firm, professional tradition in clinical psychology. There is, for example, little standardization of basic examination and treatment practices, and it is only recently that any code of ethics has been proposed [76]. Then, there is much leeway left to the psychologist's temperament in defining his "style" of practice. In addition, the relation between theory and practice is often unclear, even though theory in this field usually greatly and immediately influences practice. And very important is the extremely rapid growth of the profession of clinical psychology during and after World War II. Swift growth of a profession inevitably means—for many, if not all—sketchy or inadequate training, and premature assumption of responsibility and status as the "expert" professor, supervisor or private practitioner. Finally, there is the "hot potato" of lay psychotherapy and psychoanalysis; the tensions between psychologists and psychiatrists, and also among psychologists, are constantly felt these days.

Because of its rapid growth, a boom town excitement has characterized clinical psychology until very recently. News of a "good" test, like news of striking oil, has brought a rush of diagnostic drillers from the old wells to the new and has quickly led to the formation of a new elite. The same has been true for new statistical techniques. Checking the claims made for new tests and new statistical techniques has provided many graduate students with dissertation projects, the reports of which have tended to crowd the psychological journals. And the handbooks and source books have been pouring out like maps of the countryside that are sure to lead one to riches.

Almost all that has been said about clinical psychology is true for psychiatry as well. While an older profession by far than clinical psychology, psychiatry has grown rapidly in recent years and has also been having its booms and busts. New treatment techniques (both physical and psychological), new theoretical emphases (particularly the variants of Freudian psychoanalysis), and new personalities and "splinter" groups have appeared rapidly during and after World War II. Being in its own quick flux, psychiatry imposes special burdens and uncertainties on its practitioners. These burdens and uncertainties inevitably intrude into—and to some extent disrupt—the psychiatrist's smooth working relationships with members of other professions, such as psychologists and social workers, who make claims, demand equal status and privileges, and create uncertainties themselves.

All of these social and historical factors combined have kept the tester's professional setting—and his self-concept as a professional—anxiety-arousing, obscure, fluid, doubt-laden and open to opportunistic manipulation. But in addition, these factors have been challenging, exciting and stimulating to exploration and growth. In this uncertain, hectic atmosphere works the tester—whose professional, individual and interpersonal problems we shall now consider.

Ordinarily the tester has a service function. The patient is referred to him for testing by someone—psychiatrist, judge, teacher, social worker or psychologist—who has therapeutic or administrative responsibility for the case. The tester must produce a report that contributes in various measures to diagnosis, comprehension of dynamics, prognosis, and plans for therapy or disposition. Whether he be in private or group practice, the tester's economic and professional status and his self-esteem depend on the value of his reports to the sources of referral. There is therefore every reason to assume that the tester's needs for security and gratification will be intimately involved in each of his testing relationships. Since, as will be discussed later, there is also every reason to assume more or less resistance to the testing in many patients, and therefore more or less apparent threat to the tester's "success," the tester must be on the alert for a significant degree of anxiety, demand and resentment between himself and the patient in the course of the testing.

If the tester is in group psychiatric practice, he often both is put and puts himself on the defensive. As a rule, he tests patients who, for the time being at least, are in the care of or being worked up by psychiatric residents. The residents themselves are often professionally insecure and anxious—not only about their comprehension and handling of their cases, but about their relationships to senior staff members as well. In addition, they are usually essentially unfamiliar with tests and principles of test interpretation. They do not know what to expect from the tester and are unprepared to evaluate what they do get. To them testing may well appear as some strange hocus-pocus or at least as something not immediately comprehensible and therefore to be on guard against. Often, therefore, the psychiatric residents fall in with the attitude toward testing displayed by the chief of their psychiatric section or clinic or by other senior staff members. They assume, not always correctly, that the chief's attitude is informed and trustworthy. If this attitude is hostile and disparaging, as will soon be discussed, the tester is certainly in a difficult position.

But if the prevailing psychiatric attitude is favorable, difficulties do not end; other problems arise. To some extent, and not alway subtly, the residents ambivalently transfer to the tester major or full responsibility for clarification of diagnostic, dynamic, prognostic, therapeutic or dispositional problems in the case. It becomes the tester's "job" to settle the problematical issues. This difficulty becomes especially acute when cases are not routinely tested but are referred for testing only where major confusions or uncertainties exist in the psychiatrist's mind. A heavy and therefore inevitably anxiety-arousing responsibility is thereby imposed on the tester. His way of coping with this anxiety may significantly influence his personal approach to the patient and his interpretive approach to the test results.

Since the tester is, as it were, ambivalently glorified by these high expectations, the combination of glorification and reactive anxiety may facilitate his falling back on the implicitly megalomanic defense of being a know-all. Defensive loss of sight of one's personal and professional limitations—if it works at all—does no more, of course, than afford some relief from *conscious* anxiety; the tester remains fundamentally anxious but now has the added burden of maintaining an especially vulnerable grandiose self-concept. Under these conditions, the patient becomes, in fact, more of a threat than before and is met by the tester with more anxiety, resentment, and demand.

Further unfortunate consequences are possible. The test responses may be overinterpreted. Any new test with a colorful set of interpretive principles may be seized on, especially if seemingly deep or complex interpretations may be arrived at simply or mechanically—as in the case of the Szondi test [26, 136]. The formulation of interpretations may be dramatized by pseudo-literary and pseudo-philosophical metaphor—as is so often evident in Rorschach interpretation. Test jargon may be resorted to more and more. And, in the end, the tester's denial of personal anxiety over inadequacy means denial both of the complexity of human problems and of the uncertainty of human understanding.

"Omniscience," with or without literary and philosophical trimmings, is not the only way out, however. A common alternative solution to the demands and anxieties imposed by the psychiatrist's glorification of the tester is the hedging solution. The hedging does not have to be explicit hedging of the could-be-this, could-be-that variety. More commonly the hedging is obscured in a buckshot barrage of interpretations. Almost every variety of psychopathology is mentioned somewhere in what is likely to be an overly long report. No hierarchy of importance of the variables mentioned is established. In the end the tester will always be able to say— autistically—that the test results reveal the specific problems of the patient. The unsophisticated or insecure psychiatric resident—also autistically— may agree. And a good but profitless time will be had by all.

A further aspect of the ambivalent glorification problem is that the psychiatric resident, in the negative part of his ambivalence, may also fear and resent being "shown up" or at least having his life "unnecessarily complicated" by test findings at variance with his own. The resident may then uncritically accept confirmatory reports or confirmatory parts of reports, and blithely or critically disregard the tester's nonconfirmatory contributions. This internally contradictory position is not infrequently taken by senior psychiatrists who have remained significantly insecure and pretentious. Think what this does to the morale of the tester. He cannot be sure he will be esteemed or appreciated for even his best work. He is naturally tempted to play along with the psychiatrist's impressions in order to protect his job (or referrals), his professional relationships and status, and his self-esteem. By playing along he also may avoid facing the fact that his is actually a "lower" professional status. Or the tester may be driven to rebel, to fight the psychiatrist arrogantly with as many interpretations as possible that clash with or show up the psychiatrist. Then again, he may withdraw his emotional investment in testing, feeling that the condition of his professional acceptance and survival is that he be a yes-man.

More likely than not, the tester will not be characterized by any one attitude, but will shift about among these submissive, rebellious and withdrawn positions, especially during his younger, less secure years. These shifts will often be implicit and covert, but will emerge at times of crisis in professional relationships.

The overvalued tester may—it is common enough these days—be inadequately experienced, trained or supervised. He may then naively or fearfully retreat from human complexity and desperately avoid saying "I don't know" and "I'm not sure." He may manufacture "experience" by recalling previous interpretations as previous interpretive successes; that is, having handled an interpretive problem a certain way one or more times in the past, he may believe that that is *the* way to handle it. An error or a hunch repeated enough times easily gets to feel like a confirmed principle.* And this prematurely independent tester may be driven into all the other misconceptions and misrepresentations discussed above—hedging, etc.

Such pushes and pulls as these—toward grandiosity, hedging, propitiation, rebellion and withdrawal—play on the tester all the time in settings where he is consistently overvalued or inconsistently and opportunistically overvalued. These pushes and pulls are more or less part of the context in which clinical testing is done, and help determine how it is done, how the patient is regarded and related to, and how the results are interpreted and presented.

Of course, the tester usually is not simply the passive victim of the psychiatrist's misconceptions. He may actively contribute to these misconceptions and to the resulting conflicts and anxieties. He may, for example, oversell himself, appearing on the scene like a fortune teller with his Rorschach crystal ball, acting and writing reports as if his tests do say the last word about the patient and, in effect, according the psychiatrist no status at all. This pretentious approach is certain to provoke retaliation, very often in the form of the ambivalent overvaluation just discussed. The tester may also contribute to conflict by writing far-fetched, jargonistic or hedging reports; these may provoke justified skepticism and indifference. Frequently incorrect diagnoses or poorly integrated personality sketches may well lead to a decrease in referrals or to the psychiatrist's filing the test reports without reading them. It is incorrect, therefore, to view either the psychiatrist or the psychologist as the "villain of the piece." The complexities of the professional relationship are such that frequently, in spite of genuine good will between them, both the psychiatrist and the tester may unnecessarily and unwittingly provoke each other and then retaliate.

Of course, consistent or inconsistent overvaluation of the tester represents only one type of difficulty in the tester's professional relationships. This difficulty is mentioned first because, as clinical testing is more and more accepted as part of psychiatry, it is coming to be more typical. A much older but still lively set of problems centers around undervaluation of the psychologist—real and fantasied. It is, for example, difficult for the tester to accept the fact that a non-medical psychologist may be and usually is a second-class citizen in a psychiatric setting. It is additionally difficult

* Instead of repeating one's own errors, one may repeat errors or cling to prejudices of one's teachers. Positive identification with teachers—despite its strengthening aspects—will also limit both one's own capacity to think critically about all aspects of one's work and one's flexibility; negative identifications will be equally—though differently—self-limiting.

because his scientific and psychological training, even if superficial, exceeds that ordinarily encountered in psychiatric residents. The tester can hardly avoid resentment, rebelliousness, withdrawal and the like, when faced with the status of subordinate or technician that is frequently imposed, explicitly or implicitly, by psychiatrists and, to an extent, *implied in the realities of the situation*. He is, after all, performing an auxiliary function.

Matters get still worse when the tester, as he often does, secretly regrets not having an M.D., that is, all the authority, prestige, mobility, responsibility, income-potential and opportunity for therapeutic and psychoanalytic training that in reality go with the M.D. degree in this field, and all the omniscience, omnipotence, and solid living that are associated with this symbol in our magical thinking. The craving for the M.D. may underlie, accompany, or be displaced by the desire to do therapy. Very often testing is regarded as—and in fact is, to an extent—the back door into doing therapy. The tester then submits himself to what he regards as the debasement of his clinical novitiate in hopes of ultimately being appointed a high priest of therapy. In all this, on the side of the physician-therapist and on the side of the psychologist-tester, there are great potentialities for re-enactment of sibling rivalries and propitiations and also father-child rivalries and propitiations.

Another type of devaluation of testing is that common in large hospitals. The tester sends out his report and, because few cases are presented at staff conference, because few detailed case histories are prepared, because the tester is relatively isolated from many of the psychiatrists, and because relatively few, if any, patients enter psychotherapy, he may never know whether the report was read or used or how well it "fit" the case, and he may feel that his work makes little or no difference to anyone. Morale, professional self-esteem, cannot be sustained very well under these conditions.

The feelings of occupational and therefore personal inferiority, of being, so to speak, a clinical eunuch, may provoke the tester to overcompensate. He may feel impelled to "show up" the psychiatrist by proving him "wrong," or to outdo him in depth and breadth of interpretation. Inevitably this solution suffuses his work with further anxiety—about success and failure—and with burdensome, compulsive demands for powers and achievements that are not easily to be had, if at all. The quality of test reports may suffer. In the end the patient may suffer too, because the tester passes the buck to him, and demands of him what he, the patient, may not be eager or able to provide—maximal cooperation and self-revelation.

Thus, undervaluation as well as overvaluation of his work, on the part of both his psychiatric colleagues and himself, may well impose extra, unrealistic demands on the tester, and through the tester on the patient.

This conclusion raises two questions: In what ways will these demands be made on the patient, that is, with what ultimately disruptive assumptions may the tester, under the pressure of these professional problems, approach the patient? And what unfortunate consequences are possible? Five such assumptions or demands will now be considered, along with the complications they create.

a. *The tester wants responses.* He needs them to render service. It is rare that a patient yields no test responses. It is not at all rare, however, that the patient, because of a repressive, depressive, negativistic, or paranoid orientation, or because of psychological deficit, yields minimal responses, that is, responses few in number, brief in extent, and barren in content. This is particularly likely to occur in the Rorschach and Thematic Apperception tests. To the insecure tester, who will regard minimal response as little better than nothing, this may mean defeat at the hands of the patient. As the testing proceeds, anxiety-driven resentment against the "thwarting" patient, and intolerant demand for output, may readily increase. In consequence, the patient's anxiety, resentment and unproductivity may also increase.

In this and in other contexts, each tester will deal with his and the patient's anxiety and resentment in his own way. His "own way" will, of course, be influenced by the type of patient and by his own current personal and professional life circumstances. The tester may become bored and possibly even sleepy; he may become irritable and impatient; his helpfulness may become condescending; his friendliness may break the rhythm and continuity of the total test; his inquiry may become perplexing or humiliating.

A good part of the minimal response problem may reside in the tester's assumption that only *content* really matters. This assumption may be taken over from the psychiatrist who has already been thwarted by the patient's rigidly concealing defensive structure and who has turned to tests as "royal roads to the unconscious." Sometimes the tests do clarify some of the underlying dynamics of these resistant patients, but often they don't. The fact they *do* or *don't* may then itself be more significant than any particular content they may elicit. That is to say, granted that the tester has tried hard but not too hard to break through the patient's resistant attitude, the test results may then offer an independent assessment of the depth and rigidity of the patient's defensive structure. A secure and sophisticated psychiatrist may accept this; an insecure and naive psychiatrist, overwhelmed by his brief acquaintance with the id, may not. In such a way, the competence and personalities of his colleagues may play a large part in the tester's security in his own work.

The rigidly defensive or otherwise psychopathological basis of paucity of responses itself constitutes a finding of the foremost importance in any psychological appraisal. Appreciating the value of analysis of defenses helps avoid the pitfalls of this situation. The desperate alternative of trying by arbitrary, far-fetched, symbolic alchemy to turn leaden test responses into golden content interpretations is hardly satisfactory, though common enough these days. Similarly desperate and arbitrary is the solution of falling back on tests, such as the Szondi [26] and Draw-A-Person [98] tests, with a set of *mechanical* interpretive principles that allow seemingly deep and broad interpretations to be made under any and all circumstances. The Draw-A-Person test is of demonstrated value as a projective technique, but it is no substitute for a psychoanalysis.

On the other hand, while the tester wants responses, he does not want to be swamped by them. Detailed, elaborate and abundant responses require a great deal of time and effort to record, sift, analyze and synthesize. The tester may often justifiably feel, therefore, that the burdens of a long, "rich" record represent hostile demands and subtle obfuscation by the patient. For example, some patients, particularly some obsessional patients, do assault the tester through a relentless "compliance" with the Rorschach test instruction to give all their impressions of each inkblot. The resentment felt by the overwhelmed tester, with developing writer's cramp and a cramped time schedule, can be *used* by him to increase his understanding of the patient's motives and defenses. This resentment may, however, be *abused* by him if he takes revenge on this maliciously "sincere" patient. Very often, the tester's suppressed and obliquely expressed resentment is sensed by the patient, increases the patient's anxiety, and only spurs him on to greater "cooperation."

Much of the difficulty here begins with the tester's assumption that every response is to be valued, and that a patient should never be stopped in the midst of a stream of responses. "Who knows," he may wonder and hope, "the twenty-third response to this Rorschach card may express something of basic significance that was avoided in the twenty-two that came before?" This is, of course, a vain hope. An average of ten responses per card provides more than enough material for description of the major personality characteristics and problems of the patient. Of fine trends there is no end anyway, whether they are seen in the test results or not.

It is important, however, to know whether the patient, if left to his own devices, will run on seemingly endlessly. This may be established in the course of the first two or three Rorschach cards. But beyond that point the problem often becomes one of unrealistic, inhibiting fear on the part of the tester that he will hurt, depress, anger or otherwise disturb the patient—in short, the tester's fear of asserting his authority and responsibility in the testing situation. As in rearing, teaching or testing children, it seems that this *laissez-faire* attitude may well stimulate rather than avoid increased anxiety and distress in the patient.  The *laissez-faire* attitude may be wrongly supported or rationalized by a naive attitude towards standardization of test administration (see section *e* below).

Thus, because he wants responses, that is, because he wants the patient to tell important things about himself, the tester may be at once plunged into a morass of mutual anxiety, demand and resentment.

*b. The tester wants not only responses but, wherever scoring is called for, scorable responses.* But he often receives vague, evasive, fluid or over-abundant material to score. This may apply to the spontaneous responses and to responses to inquiry. *Vagueness* and *evasiveness* are encountered, for example, in patients with low anxiety tolerance and little capacity for reflection and self-confrontation; *fluidity* in schizophrenic settings, where inquiry often leads only to greater confusion than that caused by the patient's spontaneous inadequate communications; *overabundance* in obsessional, pedantic settings, where qualifications, doubts, alternatives, exceptions, and negations thrive.* In this respect too, as in the demand for responses in general, the patient's defensive policy and the tester's "service" needs may easily clash and cause disruption of the testing relationship. It helps to remember that evasiveness, vagueness, fluidity and pedantic outpourings may express character trends and psychopathology of primary significance.

*c. The tester wants frankness.* The patient may, however, be compelled to withhold some responses. The tester, especially if he is naively content-oriented, may then feel he is losing vital material, and may try, by persistent, challenging inquiry, to force the patient to be frank. Here too the defensive aspects of the withholding, particularly its paranoid or obsessional aspects, should be recognized as test findings of major significance. No more pressure should be put on the patient than that necessary to test the rigidity of this defensiveness.

The withholding of responses may, however, be threatening to the tester on another basis. That is when the differential diagnostic problem involves psychosis, and when the tester suspects that the withheld responses are autistic. This problem is not unusual in paranoid disorders and in patients showing remission or "sealing over" of psychotic breaks. In these cases, the tester may at least safely conclude that reality testing is sufficiently well preserved or restored to force self-critical rejection of bizarre reaction tendencies. This conclusion itself will be of the greatest significance for prognosis and therapy. Diagnostically, it will raise the question whether the patient ought not be regarded as a "borderline" or "sealed-over" case rather than fully psychotic; at the same time, it will call attention to pos-

---

* Vagueness, unreflectiveness and fluidity are also often encountered in organic cases and in children.

sible paranoid trends of significance. In short, fluctuations in frankness should be made objects of diagnostic study in themselves, and should not be regarded—as nowadays, in psychoanalysis, resistance is no longer regarded—as an unfortunate interruption of "real" communication.

*d. The tester wants a verbatim recording.* Careful analysis of verbalization is often crucial in understanding the patient. But many patients, despite all reminders of this need of the tester, talk too fast or too long at a stretch for verbatim recording to be possible. If this volubility is persistent, *despite the tester's intervention,* it expresses considerable narcissism, negativism, provocativeness and demandingness on the part of the patient. The patient's "sympathetic" suggestions that a dictaphone would make life easier for the tester only underscore his weak or hampered adaptiveness.

It is never easy to handle this type of situation. There are few situations in testing that are equally exhausting. One great temptation is to retaliate passively, avoiding open conflict, by beginning to abstract the patient's verbalizations or by simply recording, "etc., etc." Some valuable material may, however, be lost this way, particularly material that clarifies the inner structure of responses and the patient's attitudes toward his responses. The loss of such material is against the interests of both the tester and the patient, and this will inevitably cause some anxiety and resentment in the tester. Another great temptation is to comply passively, again avoiding open conflict, by scribbling as fast as one can in order to "get it all down"; although this solution may be successful, disruptive resentment at being rushed so is inevitable. Even if the situation is handled by persistent interruptions of the patient, to allow time to catch up, an unpleasant social demand may still be felt and resented. Unfortunately, the intellectual, professional satisfaction of being able to observe and interpret this *quite significant* narcissistic, demanding, provocative verbal display lessens the tester's tension only a little usually.

In part, it is perhaps wisest to find a position between these three methods of handling the problem—abstracting, writing faster, and reining in the patient. In addition, however, the tester should always feel free to interrupt the testing with open discussion of the problem of the patient's too rapid verbalization. This, reinforced by mild scolding perhaps, often affords a very good release of the tester's tension. Of all solutions, this one is the most likely to pay off. As in the case of overproductiveness, it is safe to assume that the patient will only be made more anxious and be stimulated to increased provocativeness by the tester's passive retreat into *laissez-faire.* True, in response to explicit pressure by the tester, the patient may alter his form of provocativeness, either by then saying very little, in which case the tester will have to intervene again and prod the patient toward a middle position, or by rendering exaggerated, mocking obeisance to the tester's recording needs, in which case the tester has what he asked for and need only note the switch in aggressive and defensive policy.

The patient's talking in a low voice, mumbling and trailing off present similar problems regarding verbatim recording. In interpretation, the aggressively demanding aspects of these types of verbalization should not be ignored in favor of the pathetic manner in which they are frequently expressed.

*e. The tester wants to sustain the "standardized" administration of the test.* This is a worthy ideal and certainly to be pursued with reasonably cooperative patients. Standardized administration is desirable as a way of maintaining a relatively set baseline for the interpersonal comparisons which are so vital in the interpretation of test results. It is also desirable if the tester intends to use his test records in a research project. But it is naive to think that standardization may be maintained by the tester alone. It takes two to keep things standardized. A patient is called "cooperative" when he accepts the tester's assumptions about the testing situation. When the patient rejects these assumptions, the tester will be painfully and unproductively rigid if he does not move away from the routine test procedures, and does not attempt thereby to engage the patient and find some acceptable ground on which the testing may proceed.

One patient, for example, for clearly emotional reasons, may say, "I don't know," in response to intelligence test questions he may safely be expected to know. Another patient may require much help in constructing TAT stories, and may even produce no more than descriptions of the pictures and "guesses" at possible situations depicted therein. A third patient may attempt to reject all or nearly all of the Rorschach cards without producing interpretations, or may, as described above, produce far more than is necessary and convenient. There is no end of these exceptional, unstandardized modes of response on the part of patients. Intervention by the tester is obviously called for in these situations. Insofar as he intervenes, he does alter the test situation, but he gains the important advantages that come with maintaining control over the test situation and with decreasing anxiety and tension stirred up by the test situation itself. The tester's responsibility in these instances is always to be sure of what he gets under standardized conditions before modifying his administration, to record his interventions and to attempt to establish their consequences.

He must ask himself, for example, "Did help with that fourth block design encourage or discourage the patient? Was it appreciated or resented? Could the patient catch on with help and use the help on later problems, or was the help wasted?" "Did special reassurance about the acceptability of certain Rorschach interpretations ease the patient's tension and free the flow of responses? Did it evoke only greater demands for reassurance? Were these demands oblique, as in constant self-disparagement, or childish, as in direct pleas to be told that the answers are 'right' or 'acceptable?'" Similarly, "Did encouraging the patient to give at least one (or more than one) response to each Rorschach card actually increase productivity? If it did, was the result instructive or was it empty? If it did not, was it in spite of real effort on the patient's part or did it only elicit a little token compliance?" These and similar questions are often grossly answerable. The answers, and thereby the deviations in administrative technique, ultimately enrich and clarify rather than impoverish and obscure the test findings.

The preceding analysis has not been exhaustive. It has touched on only some of the common needs and problems that confront the tester as a service-oriented psychologist. It should be clear by now, however, that in reaction to the various stresses existing within his professional context and as a manifestation of his own way of coping with these stresses, the tester may enter the testing situation with quite a number of burdensome assumptions, anxieties, oversensitivities and demands. The manner and extent of the patient's acceptance or rejection of these assumptions and demands, and the manner and extent of the tester's coping with the problems that ensue, together significantly influence the smoothness and instructiveness of the testing and the accuracy and effectiveness of the final test report.

The professional problems just considered constitute only one segment of the tester's psychological situation. There are, in addition, problems inherent in the test relationship itself and problems created by the individual adjustment patterns and difficulties of the tester. We shall now consider these two sets of problems in turn.

## 2. Psychological Constants in the Tester's Role

On the surface it seems adequate to define the clinical tester's role as follows: the tester is a person trained in certain techniques of observation and in certain ways of thinking about behavior, who attempts to perform a helpful, socially useful, auxiliary service to other persons—patients— troubled by adjustment problems. The patient, insofar as he wants help and is in contact with reality, perceives and accepts this role of the tester.

This definition, though valid, is superficial and incomplete. Testers, like patients, have unconscious reaction tendencies. They think and feel irrationally as well as rationally. They respond to certain aspects of their life work and relationships in terms of primitive, magical, dramatized conceptions. However much "ego autonomy" may obtain in the tester's work, that is, however free his work may be from the vicissitudes of unconscious personal conflicts and primitive conceptions, the autonomy or the freedom is always *relative*. We have already seen how problems of professional training, competence, status and role definition decrease the tester's relative "ego autonomy" and foster disruptive behavior in relation to the patient and the psychiatrist.

The channels of communication between daily behavior and deep conflict are never entirely closed. The channels may be more open in some testers than others. Also, in any one tester, these channels may be more open at one time than another. But the unconscious, primitive, more or less rejected tendencies and conceptions are ever present and ever ready to find an opening through which they may gain expression. The play of irrational tendencies and conceptions that underlies and sometimes invades the tester's professional functioning may support and promote his work, undermine and limit his work, or both, depending on the strength of these tendencies and the tester's style and effectiveness of coping with them.

It therefore seems worthwhile to explore some of the implicit, primitive, not so "socially acceptable" aspects of the tester's role. Some of these originate primarily in the tester's personality, that is, they reflect his way of structuring most or all situations he gets into. Others, however, derive largely from certain constants in the situation or role in which the tester functions. Situations and roles play on us, as well as we on them. Situations and roles bring one or another of our partial trends to the fore and obscure others. It is necessary to emphasize this because our growing acquaintance with character analysis and projective test theory tends to intrigue us too much with how we structure situations and to blind us to how much situations structure us. Ultimately, and as usual, the most enlightening approach to the problem is to view it as a matter of interaction, of mutual influence between the demands and implications of the role and situation on the one hand and the specific personality on the other.

It may seem to the reader that what follows confuses the individual psychopathology of testers with the general psychology of testing. This criticism would hold that most testers are essentially normal, objective, professionally detached participant-observers, and are not volatile, childish, erratic and irrational. This criticism ignores the restraining, modulating, buffering influence the defensive and adaptive ego functions exert on volatile, childish, erratic and irrational reaction tendencies. There is no internal contradiction in saying that the most primitively conceived and experienced reactions may occur in the tester without spilling over into his behavior as a tester and utterly disrupting it. Ego barriers and controls stand between these primitive reactions and conceptions on the one hand and conscious experience and behavior on the other. Exploring the primitive aspects of the tester's experience adds depth to our understanding of the tester and the test results and does not devalue the tester as a psychological participant-observer.

At least four constants in the tester's role may be singled out for purposes of this analysis: the role is voyeuristic, autocratic, oracular and saintly. These are constants in the sense that they appear to be present regardless of the personal needs and circumstances of fate that brought the tester to begin with to his professional role, and regardless of the tester's individual response to particular patients or patients in general.

*a. The voyeuristic aspect of the tester's role.* The tester is in the position of a psychological voyeur. He peeps into the interiors of many individuals and never once commits himself, as would be required under normal social conditions, to a relationship. His desk and writing board, his pictures, blots, blocks and stopwatch are doors and windows between him and the patient. All is observed from the safety of psychological distance and transiency of relationship. The tester's human obligations in the testing situation are temporary and usually shallow. Maintenance of sufficient superficial good will to complete the tests is often all that is required. In return for both his deliberate and his unwitting—but sensed—revelations about himself, the patient receives a bare minimum of information about the tester. Equally important, the tester ordinarily need not return any interpretations in exchange for the patient's self-exposures; he leaves that part of the job to the therapist. The tester finds out but tells nothing.

As will be discussed below, this peeping may be used by the tester in various hostile ways. It may also significantly increase the anxiety of the patient. The hostile and anxiety-arousing aspects of the peeping may, in turn, stimulate in the tester anxiety, guilt and desire to atone, or rigid denials of these. There is no clear line between keeping the patient reasonably comfortable during the testing and being ingratiating and overindulgent. There is also no clear line between being reasonably firm with and detached from the patient and being coldly indifferent to his trials and tribulations. The tester's anxious or guilty response to the voyeuristic aspect of his role may further obscure these two lines; it may lead him, depending on his character make-up, his life circumstances, and his response to the particular patient, to feel and behave too close to the patient, too distant from the patient, or in an inconsistent way, both too close and too distant. These excesses may then impair the effectiveness of the testing and the adequacy of the final test report.

Going further, our knowledge of primitive, affect-laden levels of thinking suggests that psychological voyeurism may be unconsciously elaborated as an act of hostile, sexual intrusion. That is to say, even if the tester did not, to begin with, choose testing in part as a more or less sublimated outlet for his infantile voyeuristic inclinations, these inclinations may well seize on the looking-in-secret aspects of testing and thus may invade the professional role. When this occurs in force, further anxiety and guilt about testing may result. This anxiety and guilt may then be manifest in awkward or avoided inquiry into fantasy material and emotional reactions, in atonement through ingratiation or superfluous reassurance, or in rigid maintenance of distance from the patient. On the other hand, the opportunity for voyeuristic intrusion afforded by testing may stimulate too much inquiry, too eager pursuit of "suggestive" details of responses and verbalizations. This will inevitably put the patient on guard and increase the tension in the test relationship. More about the patient's reactions to this psychological and sexual peeping aspect of the tester's role and to the other aspects to be discussed next will be found in Section B of this chapter.

   *b. The autocratic aspect.* The tester not only looks surreptitiously; he also dominates. The autocratic, dominating aspect of his role is implied in the fact that there is little sharing of control in the relationship. Even though inactive for long periods during the testing, the tester is the controlling one in the relationship. The tester tells the patient what to do, when to do it and when to stop, sometimes how to do it. He often demands to know why the patient did what he did, when he did, and the way he did. He brings out anxiety, inadequacy, compliance, rebellion and a host of other reaction tendencies. The tester is, in this respect, a psychological ringmaster. True, patients often fight hard and with more or less success to keep control of the situation themselves, but even then they are still oriented toward the tester's whip. The tester implicitly remains the dominant one. This is so even if he simply tells the patient during the Rorschach test, for example, "It's up to you," every time the patient asks for rules or guidance. In this regard, the situation is reminiscent of the cartoon showing a child in a progressive school desperately asking the teacher, "Do I have to do what I want to do?"

   In a keenly insightful paper—a paper we shall return to frequently—Schachtel has discussed varieties of response to the freedom or lack or rules in the Rorschach situation [131]. However, Schachtel equates complete permissiveness with freedom, and ignores the fact that complete permissiveness and lack of rules is just another kind of demand or control and not an absence of it. This point will be amplified later.

   The tester's conflicts over and guilt concerning domination and manipulation of others—on a more primitive level, his conflicts over sadistic impulses—may therefore easily intrude into the test relationship. This is particularly likely when the patient expresses considerable anguish in the course of and in response to the testing. One tester may well need and enjoy his autocratic powers. He may be unduly threatened, resentful and retaliatively "strict" if the patient resists his domination. Another tester may play down or relinquish his control in order to lighten his guilt or blunt the overt, implicit or potential resentment of the patient. He may even fall back to a masochistic attitude of despair over how "impossible" it is "to handle" this patient. But it is always a reality of the testing relationship that control or dominance is ultimately in the hands of the tester. His way of using, abusing or hiding the ringmaster's whip in his hands may have much to do with the quality and quantity of the patient's productions and his own interpretation of them.

c. *The oracular aspect.* The oracular aspect, like the voyeuristic and dominating aspects, is also a constant in the clinical tester's role. After all, the tester does draw momentous and portentous inferences from signs and symbols. He "sees into" hidden meanings, predicts turns of events, implicitly or explicitly advises. This oracular position may be reinforced if the tester is overvalued by the psychiatrist, as has been already pointed out. It may be further reinforced by the fact that the prescription of tests is often explained to the patient by the psychiatrist as a way of obtaining "objective" evidence as to the type and extent of problems or personality changes. In part, this explanation may imply to the patient *and to the tester* that the psychiatrist or therapist is a fallible, ordinary human being, while the tester cannot possibly be fooled, misled, confused or otherwise troubled by the possibility of error. The tester, it is promised, will come up with *the* answer. Still another contribution to the tester's oracular conception of his role may be made by the patient: patients commonly ascribe magically insightful and influential powers to doctors, therapists and their agents.

The tester, when he chose clinical psychology as his life work, may have been seeking just such an oracular role. Testing—or therapy—may be to him a royal road to omniscience—short, broad, smooth and well-marked. One sees this conception in blatant form in many young graduate students of clinical psychology for whom there is no response they cannot interpret, no contradiction they cannot resolve, no obscurity they cannot penetrate, no integration they cannot achieve. One sees it too in the grandiose claims made about many of the newer projective tests, not to speak of the Rorschach test itself. To those who anxiously lose distance from and cling to this oracular fantasy, the confusing patient—not a rare bird—is a serious threat and is resented. But in all of us, even if well repressed or well controlled, there is this longing for omniscience, for oracular powers, and as testers we must cope with constant stimulation of this longing.

It must also be pointed out that it is easy enough for any tester to feel in instances of clear-cut disagreement between his test report and the psychiatrist's or therapist's opinion that he is right "really," and that his colleague is being misled by superficial appearances or by misconceptions. The line between sticking to one's guns with realistic justification and remaining defensively, megalomanically aloof from contradiction or correction is not a clear one, especially since it often enough does happen that the combination of tests and tester penetrate deeper or more accurately into the patient's problems and present status, or certain aspects of these, than the combination of clinical interviews and psychiatrist.

The tester may, on the other hand, beat a hasty retreat from the oracular implications of his role, responding more to its burdens than to its apparent blessings. He may minimize to the psychiatrist and to the patient the importance of his contribution. He may write reports full of pseudo-objective references to specific intelligence test scores, to specific numbers of *Whole* responses or *Human Movement* responses in the Rorschach test, and the like. He may write reports full of anxious doubts disguised as careful weighing of each point. In the end, he may refuse to take a stand on major points even when the available material is adequate for a strong stand. He will thereby dump all the responsibility for understanding the patient back into the lap of the psychiatrist.

*d. The saintly aspect.* By definition, the tester's role is a helpful one, even if only in an indirect and auxiliary way. The patient comes to the psychiatrist for help and the psychiatrist sends the patient to the tester with the assurance that the tester's report will more or less increase the effectiveness of treatment or the correctness of disposition.

Now, we have seen how, on a primitive level of experience, examining the patient takes on voyeuristic connotations, how instructing and questioning the patient takes on autocratic connotations, and how understanding the patient takes on oracular connotations. In the same primitively conceived way, helping the patient takes on saintly connotations. Is it not so that the tester does his best to help, no matter how provocative or "ungrateful" the patient? Does not the tester give out with all he has so long as he believes it is for the patient's good? Does he not implicitly promise psychological salvation? Will he not subdue his own needs and resentments and selflessly try to understand and feel the tragedy of the patient? Is not this code like that of a saint with a sinner, a slave or a leper? It certainly is— as it is in the case of the therapist too—once we get below the level of objective, logical appreciation of reality and confront some of our magical thoughts and wishes. Often patients tend to cast us in just this saintly role and they find us not altogether unprepared for it.

The obligations of saintly restraint and warmth and of the power of salvation are heavy burdens to bear. Testers will be driven in various directions by these primitively conceived constants of their social and professional role. One way of "coping" with burdens is to drop them and flee. The tester may then be crisp with and overly detached from the patient. He may maintain to himself that his is only a research or theoretical interest in the patient or that the ultimate fate of the patient is no concern of his. He will then steadfastly refuse to exert himself to get a reasonably full record from the patient with a reasonable minimum of pain. If the patient does not spontaneously "come across," the tester will contend, "It's his problem, not mine!" And if the patient makes a move to put himself in the tester's hands psychologically, the tester will take cover behind "standardized administration" more quickly than he needs to. There will be no room in this test relationship for even the little bit of mutuality that is possible.

In contrast, the tester may be seduced rather than repelled by the saintly aspect of his role. As we shall see later, this is particularly likely if his reaction formations against dependent and hostile impulses are rigid and pervasive. He then may go all out to comfort the patient and sell him on the Promised Land benefits of taking the tests. He will go to inappropriate lengths to get the fullest possible record with the least possible pain. At all times, this tester will need to have it perfectly clear to the patient that he is being helpful. But his saintly advances may be spurned by the patient, that is, his reassurances brushed aside, his instructions and explanations ignored, his kindnesses unappreciated, and his urgings ineffective. In this case, he may redouble his saintliness in what will now be a clearly hostile, guilt-provoking maneuver, or he may become impatient, irritable, cold, bored or otherwise unsaintly.

These have been caricatures of reactions to the saintly aspect of testing. Their purpose has been to highlight its most disruptive consequences. No tester plays "saint," but all testers are tempted by their role—and by the patient—to feel saintly and to act accordingly.

The voyeuristic, autocratic, oracular and saintly constants in the test situation must be coped with by every tester, each in his own way. Some of these ways of coping have already been touched on; others will be discussed below. What has not been pointed out so far, and what must certainly be remembered, is that the tester can more or less come to terms with (not escape) these constants in a primarily adaptive manner. He need not invariably be driven to extreme acceptance or rejection of the irrational implications of these constants. He may be relatively free to look searchingly, control flexibly, interpret both imaginatively and soundly, and help out with realistic restraint and self-assertion. He is more likely to do so if he is aware of the complex psychological implications of his job and of his relationships with colleagues and patients. A sense of professional security and self-esteem, based on experience and competence, also helps greatly. With the help of insight, security and self-esteem, the tester is also more likely to find his way again, if, as not rarely happens, he loses it in overreacting to particular patients or to problems in test administration. The tester's competence and humility, his powers of reality testing, his genuine interest in helping others, and his understanding and acceptance of himself will powerfully counteract the irrational conceptions and temptations. And, it must be stressed, the irrational tendencies may not only hinder but also promote testing skills; up to a point they may increase alertness, strength, insightfulness and responsiveness.

### 3. The Tester's Personality in the Test Relationship

Having considered some of the major ways in which the situation and his role play on the tester, we may now round out our analysis of the tester by considering ways in which he, in accordance with trends dominant in his personality make-up, may actively play on or structure the test situation.

Eight types of testers will be discussed: those with an uncertain sense of their own identity; the socially inhibited or withdrawn; the dependent; those with rigid defenses against dependent needs; the rigidly intellectualistic; the sadistic; those with rigid defenses against hostility; and the masochistic. Admittedly, these are "types." They are oversimplified characterizations which will be helpful for purposes of discussion. These eight types are not exhaustive, mutually exclusive or otherwise systematically selected and described. They merely summarize frequent and conspicuous problems of testing and are discussed only to open up the study of the individual aspects of the tester at work. *Ultimately, these types should be thought of as aspects of each tester's personality, one or more of which might usually be dominant, but any of which might become dominant at certain times of crisis in the tester's total life situation or in the tester's relationship with a particular patient.* An effort will be made to point out how each of these major tendencies may facilitate as well as hamper effective testing.

*a. The tester with an uncertain sense of personal identity.* The study of clinical psychology is probably particularly attractive to persons with a chronically diffuse self-concept, persons who are unsure what sort of individuals they want to be, what kinds of relationships to cultivate, which of their impulses and feelings to accept and express and how to express those they can accept, which of their assets to develop and which traditions and values to adhere to. These individuals may be described as having an uncertain sense of personal identity, following Erik Erikson's use of the concept of identity [35]. Psychology may seem to them to offer help in working out their personal solutions to this problem. *Clinical* psychology particularly may have this appeal because it deals with such problems as these all the time, and because, at first acquaintance, it seems to offer all the answers.

To a tester beset by identity problems, testing becomes a means of observing a wide variety of personal identity solutions. By "discrediting" other solutions—often easy enough to do in a clinical setting—the tester may employ his observations to reassure himself either as to his "normality" or as to the acceptability of his "abnormality." He may also use his test observations to pick up such fragments from the total personality pictures of various patients as seem usable in his personal integrative efforts. We do, after all, observe traits in our patients which we admire or envy, such as charm, wit, verbal facility, forcefulness and imaginativeness. As a way of finding out how other persons manage or mismanage, testing is therefore relatively safe and inexpensive, even though not too personally rewarding in actuality. Insofar as this identity orientation involves direct or indirect self-confrontation, it may imbue testing with considerable anxiety. Insofar as the identity orientation exists within a predominantly narcissistic setting, it may lead the tester to demand richly self-expressive material from patients incapable of giving it, and to manifest excessive favoritism in his dealing with patients—love flowing to the instructive or admired ones, for example, and boredom and disgust to the barren, obscure, or challenging ones. This identity orientation may also lead the tester to lose himself in his case material, and weaken or obscure whatever sense of identity he has to begin with.

On the positive side, the tester's search for an identity may increase his perceptiveness of just how the patient is trying to solve his problems, just how the patient does try to conceive of himself. Uncertainty about one's self may contribute significantly to a capacity to see the great variety of solutions available to others and the subtler aspects of the way others flounder around among these solutions. It may thereby foster a feel for uniqueness and a tolerance for and constructive use of ambiguity and apparent contradiction in the implications of test findings. Also, insofar as it involves self-confrontation, this orientation may contribute to the personal and professional growth of the tester.

*b. The socially inhibited or withdrawn tester.* To this tester, testing may become an avenue toward human contact, and in some respects toward interpersonal intimacy. At the same time, however, testing offers this tester the defensive advantage of reassurance against the dangers and the pain of ambivalence in relationships; it does this by guaranteeing that there is nothing binding in these moments of intimacy, that there is little danger of control of the relationship slipping out of his hands, and that the flow of intimacies will be in one direction only—towards him. The controlled, temporary, one-way intimacies in the tester's professional life will have appeal to the extent that the tester's personal relationships are fraught with compulsive, schizoid or paranoid anxieties and inhibitions.

Under these conditions, difficulties may develop in the test relationship if the patient vigorously attempts to wrest control of the situation from the tester, and to move in on him in a "too personal" way, demanding more human response and involvement than the tester is prepared to give. Considerable anxiety may ensue in the tester. This anxiety may lead him to become cold, brusque, irritable or more withdrawn. Ultimately the testing may become a painful and unprofitable experience for both participants.

On the positive side, social inhibition is often accompanied by hypersensitivity to emotional nuances in relationships. This hypersensitivity may add to the tester's perceptiveness—provided that the tester is not overly paranoid or arbitrary in his perceptions to begin with.

*c. The dependent tester.* As an expression of a dependent orientation, testing may be viewed as a means of obtaining receptive gratifications. These receptive gratifications are of the sort that are implied in esteem and appreciation the patient expresses to the tester as a professional helper, and in the major share of the work of personal communication assumed by or imposed on the patient in the course of testing. The tester asks, the patient gives. In this respect, the tester's looking and controlling become a kind of feeding on the patient. The demanding or ungiving patient—another common bird—may easily stir up disruptive resentment in such a tester. To the extent that his own passivity leads the tester to misconstrue (and mishandle) the testing situation as one in which he may regularly enjoy free receptive gratifications, to that extent will his testing relationships be tense, cold, hostile, and frustrating.

This tester may, for example, fear displeasure or resentment in the patient. He will want to stay on the patient's good side, i.e., his generous, indulgent, supportive side. In response to discomfort in the patient, the dependent tester may not press inquiries or demand for continued effort even though such pressure is clearly indicated. He may defensively rationalize this gingerly policy by asserting the necessity of maintaining good rapport. That this is a defensive rationalization is attested to by the unnecessary sacrifice of dynamically or diagnostically significant material that may have been entailed by his kid-gloves approach. Good rapport is not, after all, an end in itself; it is a way at getting at the material we need to write worthwhile reports and thereby help the patient. To a degree, rapport must often be sacrificed in order to clarify crucial problems in the course of administration and inquiry. (Here again is a parallel to therapy.) One may easily hesitate, for example, before inquiring into a possible contamination in the Rorschach record of a suspicious, hostile patient. It is easy to feel, "What a mess I'll get into if I inquire into this! Is it really worth it?" When passivity and fear that the patient will withdraw his "supplies" are strong enough to interfere persistently with thorough test administration, some active self-confrontation on the tester's part is obviously in order.

*d. The tester with rigid defenses against dependent needs.* Defenses against dependent needs, perhaps particularly reaction formations, often play a vital part in the clinical psychologist's choice of profession. The psychologist tends to the needs of others and, in his professional role at least, denies his own. Unconsciously, through identification with the cared-for patient, the tester may derive some indirect gratification to balance his conscious "sacrifice." The repressions of and reaction formations against dependent needs may, however, be too rigid or too weak. If too weak, the type of behavior described under the heading "the dependent tester" may well occur. If too rigid, that is, if the tester's entire life is dominated by a defensive imperative always to give and never to receive, then the tester will in a too cold, too maternal, too saintly or too syrupy way try to force the patient into a passive receptive role. Patients long for this role but are typically terribly afraid of it. Consequently, the test relationship may suffer in response to the "all-giving" tester.

If the tester's defenses against dependent needs are neither too rigid nor too weak, that is, if dependent needs are well integrated into his character structure, then he will be a very good tester indeed. At least, his moderate and flexible defenses and his self-tolerance will limit the demands he makes on the patient and increase his empathy for the patient's needs and his tolerance of the patient's need-denying defensive tendencies.

*e. The rigidly intellectualistic tester.* To an extent an intellectualistic bent is necessary and probably present in all psychologists. So long as it remains under some control, this bent is, of course, an important asset. Insofar as it involves isolation of affect, intellectualizing makes it possible to deal with what is often very highly charged and potentially disturbing material in the patient's responses. It also helps to maintain due caution in interpretation, it supports reasonable skepticism, it opposes mechanical interpretation, and it increases alertness to the infinite variety of shifts in emphasis or meaning of responses in different configurations. The intellectualistic bent can be the driving force behind thoroughly exploring the implications of test results in daily clinical practice, and it can be the driving force behind using tests to refine and develop theoretical hypotheses.

Against the background of a rigidly intellectualistic character makeup, however, testing may tend to become too much of a detached, "logical," verbalistic, puzzle-solving affair. In his test report, the rigid intellectualizer may use his findings in a provocatively "informed" manner to complicate the case unnecessarily; he will interpret everything in sight, and substitute quantity for quality, doubt for responsibility, and overabstractions for descriptions. He may go blithely and pretentiously on and on about castration fears, incestuous wishes, sadistic fantasies, phallic mothers and what-not without the least twitch of personal anxiety and with absolutely no "feel" for the unique, emotionally tangible qualities of the specific patient. Insofar as the tester's intellectualizing is tainted by underlying grandiose aspirations, the tester may use his test reports to reassure himself that he indeed "sees all and knows all."

Something of this intellectualistic detachment and omniscient pose will certainly be communicated to the patient, who will understand it—in part, correctly so—as coldness and narcissistic self-absorption. Many of our gratifications as testers come from cases we find interesting and instructive, but there is hardly an easier way to irritate a patient than to convey to him the feeling that you view him as "an interesting case." Patients fear and resent being reduced to the level of laboratory specimens; they insist on being recognized as unique human beings.

*f. The sadistic tester.* Out of a sadistic social orientation, testing may become a means of ferreting out the "weak," "debasing," "humiliating" aspects of the lives of the hated Others. As has been described in connection with the autocratic aspects of the tester's role, testing does facilitate safe and socially sanctioned tyranny or domination of the relatively helpless "sick one." When, in addition, inner scorn and subtle humiliation of the patient are dominant tendencies, the test relationship may become clearly sadistic. Deeper transference implications of dominating, shaming and proving one's self superior to parents and siblings may easily find a place within this testing orientation. To the extent that the patient's illness itself constitutes a sadistic assault on others—and the intrusive tester will certainly be no exception to the patient's sadism—to that extent will the testing settle down to a war of attrition. The tester who, within this orientation, sets himself up as the Chief Inquisitor will tend to write one-sided reports that sound like exposés or denunciations; he will be insensitive to or ignore signs of strength, adaptability and appeal in the patient.

On the other hand, test reports often do have to deal with serious psychopathology and "base," unpleasant impulses and feelings. A capacity for forthrightness of description is required to write good test reports. In a test report, as anywhere else, it takes a certain aggressive freedom to call a spade a spade. If the tester can tolerate some awareness of inner, irrational hostility—even toward the patient he is testing and describing— and if he can get some pleasure out of competition and "overwhelming" his opponent, he will be freer to call a schizophrenic a schizophrenic and a psychopath a psychopath. It will be easier for him to see and handle the sadism in the patient's masochistic maneuvers and the burdensome mockery in the obsessional neurotic's conscientiousness and compliance. He will not be too eager to be taken in and manipulated by tears, smiles and groans. He will not have to undo every "malignant" interpretation with a benign one, and he certainly will not have to avoid "malignant" interpretations.

*g. The tester with rigid defenses against hostility.* Like defenses against dependent needs, defenses against hostility probably also play a vital part in the clinical psychologist's choice of profession. Conquering hatred and fear of others by devoting oneself to their welfare is an old and honored way of achieving adjustment and surviving in society. When repression of, reaction formation against, and undoing of hostility are crucial defensive aspects of the tester's personality, testing may easily signify atonement through good deeds. Through transference on the tester's part, testing may further signify forgiving or curing parents or siblings by whom the tester has felt abused or neglected. Like the therapist in the same dynamic position, the tester may then narcissistically hate patients when, by not exposing themselves to him, they resist his desperate efforts to be "good" to them.

If this tester's reaction formations are corrupted by unsuccessful warding off of hostility, he may behave much like the sadistic tester toward the patient, but with the difference that his manner and his inner feeling will be one of tender loving care. In this there will be a masked "return of the repressed"—a hallmark of weak reaction formation. A saintly attitude, as has already been discussed, will justifiably put the patient on guard in the test relationship and will very likely increase his sense of guilt. This too-benign tester conveys to the patient the guilt-provoking and irritating attitude, "I am being so patient, tolerant, understanding and helpful, and you ungratefully refuse to cooperate." In this way, saintliness can be a powerful sadistic weapon.

Finally, while rigid defenses against hostility may, on the one hand, blind the tester to malignant implications of the test results or lead him to minimize them or undo them by qualifications, they may, on the other hand, contribute to his perceptiveness of strengths, adaptive potential and constructive strivings in the patient.

*h. The masochistic tester.* In the setting of a passive masochistic social orientation and adjustment, a tester may thrive on the great portion of his daily life he spends arduously in contact with human beings whose capacity to give warmth and support and to tolerate anxiety and frustration is seriously limited. In other words, the tester may relish the patient's narcissistic demands, abuse and non-compliance. He may even do much to exacerbate such behavior. He may, for example, let control of the testing slip out of his hands and allow the entire situation to become relatively disorganized. His pleasure in testing may derive from the anxiety he unconsciously engenders in his patients and the resulting difficulties he creates for himself. Inasmuch as masochism has its accusing, hostile aspect, his pleasures in interpretation may consist in exposing just how "bad" people "really" are.

In one respect, the masochistic orientation may be a help to the tester, and that is in its making it bearable to spend a great part of his waking life with patients. A masochistic streak, especially if coated with humor, increases ability to take punishment.

Other orientations and their consequences could very well be added to the eight described above. Those that have been mentioned and others that may be conceived of should not be thought of as mutually exclusive by any means. Various combinations and layerings of these are likely to be the rule among testers, just as among any other group of human beings. It is worth repeating that these orientations might best be thought of as different facets of every tester's personality, any one or combination of which may stand out under the impact of different crises in the tester's life and of patients different in personality type.

Under favorable conditions, that is, with a cooperative patient, with no major crises in the tester's life, and with the tester reasonably well integrated, none of these orientations may become disruptively prominent or dominant. The entire testing may be carried out in the setting of well-sustained mutual good will and collaboration. This is often the way it is. The importance of this entire discussion does not lie in any contention that patients are consistently very difficult to test; it lies in the fact that where difficulties arise, the basic assumptions of the interpersonal test relationship are shaken up and rise to the surface. The psychological complexity of the test relationship must be recognized and clarified—generally, for a theory of testing, and specifically, for the successful administration and interpretation of tests.

## B. THE DYNAMICS OF BEING TESTED *

### 1. Constants in the Patient's Psychological Position

The situation to be analyzed below is primarily that of a patient taking psychological tests during a period of initial psychiatric evaluation. A

* Phillips and Smith [*105*, Chapter 7, pp. 162–191] have recently offered a detailed interpretive treatment of a wide variety of patients' test attitudes, behavior and verbalization. As in the case of content analysis (see below, p. 118, footnote), and total qualitative and quantitative analysis of the record (see below pp. 142–3 footnote), the reader will find considerable overlap between their presentation and this. There is much of interest in their discussions. Yet, their material is presented from a significantly different point of view, and this point of view is bound to have different consequences in individual cases. Phillips and Smith are basically test-centered and they attempt fixed, elaborate interpretations of each stylistic indication. In contrast, this book is centered on personality theory and on the concepts or categories emphasized by theory and general clinical experience; here, interpretation is limited and is directed at integrating observation of test attitudes and behavior according to clinical and theoretical psychoanalytic thinking. The difference is

patient taking tests under other circumstances, such as during therapy or upon its completion, and any person taking personality tests for other than psychiatric reasons, such as for vocational guidance or occupational screening, will experience the situation somewhat differently. Yet, many of the considerations to be advanced below appear transposable to any situation where a person knows that his personality is being investigated.

In what follows, attention will be centered on the irrational, primitive, usually implicit attitudes and conceptions in the patient being tested. It will be assumed that to some degree the patient consciously accepts the idea of testing, that he takes on faith its helpfulness and the tester's helpful intent, and that he is pleased and reassured to be in the process of being helped. These conditions do not always obtain, of course, but the value of the following discussion lies in its clarification of why and how it comes about that ostensibly positive and cooperative conscious attitudes towards testing—as well as adequate test behavior itself—may be disrupted. As in therapeutic technique, clarification of disruptive forces within the clinical relationship is a central aspect of understanding the patient's illness.

What follows is, however, in no way a manual of testing technique. It is assumed that the reader is sufficiently familiar with clinical phenomena to be able to identify various types of emotional reaction without having these described in great detail in this text. It is also assumed that the reader is sufficiently experienced to have worked out his way of handling the problems of test administration he typically encounters—and creates. The center of interest in this chapter is on what goes on below the surface

---

reflected in organization of material: Phillips and Smith's headings pertain to test behavior and the elaborating paragraphs to interpretations of this behavior; here, the headings pertain, for example, to defense mechanisms and the elaborating paragraphs present a variety of relevant behavioral and attitudinal test indications.

Ultimately, Phillips and Smith's approach runs the risk of leading to what may be called a Rorschach theory of personality—an intra-test, closed system of inferences that presumes to encompass the total personality. This is evident in their presenting their empirical observations of dynamic relations as independent of and to be compared to the system of psychoanalysis. A more moderate instance of this trend is evident in Beck's recent statements [11]; he, for example, implicity advances a new theory of defense in which anxiety, fantasy, and "self-reinforcing" are basic "defenses," while projection, isolation, etc. are either combinations of these or a group of secondary "tactics." It is recognized within psychoanalysis that psychoanalytic theory and concepts can stand clarification, coordination and revision, but it is difficult to see the place of unexplained modifications, such as Beck's, based on a single and limited—though valuable—approach to the study of personality and psychopathology. The fact that Beck's case studies are often penetrating and instructive does not, of course, prove the value or correctness of his departures from accepted theory.

of the testing relationship and what is implied in its disruptions. No one style of testing will be recommended. The following discussion is intended merely to help clarify and make diagnostic capital of the dynamics of different types of test relationships.

   a. *Self-exposure in the absence of trust; violated privacy.* It was said of the tester that he is in the position of a psychological voyeur. It now may be said of the patient that he is in the position of the voyeur's passive victim. Of course, some patients relish the opportunity afforded by being tested to exhibit themselves psychologically and, unconsciously, sexually. These patients do eagerly "expose" themselves and are not passive victims of the tester's voyeurism. Also, other patients are made anxious by the test situation's stimulation of their ego-alien and repressed but strong exhibitionistic tendencies. These patients are caught betwixt and between the temptation to welcome the intrusion and show all and the defensive imperative to repel the intrusion and conceal all.

   As a rule, however, it would be incorrect to refer to the patient's role as that of a psychological exhibitionist. It is generally true that the testing situation is not spontaneously sought out by the patient and that the process of self-exposure is not relished. The patient's position, therefore, is usually passive, not active. It is that of being peeked at rather than eagerly showing. The problem to the patient is all the more acute because he knows he is being peeked at, because he feels to some extent that he ought not (though some patients do) pull down his psychological window shade, and because he does not know for sure just what is being seen and is not even certain that he ever will know. Being left in ignorance thus, he may easily begin to fear the worst. In this respect he is in the position of the "innocent" victims of the practical joke, each of whom received an anonymous note saying, "Flee! All is discovered!" and all of whom left town at once.

   Not only is the patient confiding innermost matters, but he is confiding them in a stranger, in someone whom it may not be safe to trust. Impaired capacity for trust is common in psychiatric patients. It may exist alongside both a more or less realistic acceptance of the tester's professional detachment and helpful intent and an unrealistic projection onto the tester of magically omniscient and influential powers. The mistrust, like the ascribing of magical powers, need not be at all conscious, but it is likely to show in test behavior, attitudes and verbalizations. The patient in the test situation has no way of knowing whether, and to what extent, the tester will understand, accept, defend and help, or misunderstand, condemn, slander and punish. Whereas we ordinarily spend a great part of our social lives seeking out people with whom it seems safe to begin preliminary explorations of tentative testing-the-limits of possible confidences, in the testing situation all at once the patient feels himself stripped bare before an unknown, and therefore quite anxiety-arousing, psychological intruder. In this respect the testing is a violation of one of our usually highly valued social interests: privacy.

On his side, the tester reveals next to nothing of his inner self. He does not thereby at least render himself equally exposed and vulnerable as the patient. Of course, testers vary amongst themselves in how much they indicate or frankly reveal about themselves in their dress, language usage, manners and expressive movements. But ordinarily the intention of each tester is to keep his own personality in the background of the test situation and to draw out the patient. This inevitably makes the tester somewhat unnaturally reserved from a social point of view, even if he feels appropriately friendly, interested and responsive. More conspicuous and often more alarming to the patient is another aspect of the tester's reserve, namely, his ordinarily inscrutable reaction to the *content* of the patient's responses. Even if the tester is otherwise friendly and supportive to the patient, in the interest of good testing he intends to give the patient no cues as to how he feels personally about this or that response. The especially mistrustful patient, worried about his response but confronted by this tight-lipped, inscrutable, prying but self-concealing stranger, typically feels the tester to be cold, aloof, scornful and even displeased or antagonized. More or less delicate and taxing rapport problems frequently result.

On the other hand, several factors seem to diminish the patient's anxiety over this violation of his privacy. For one thing, it usually affords the patient some relief, on a conscious level, to remain unaware of much of what he is communicating or exposing, and to anticipate that he may never know. At least he will not have to confront consciously that intimate, potentially threatening material before he is ready for it; perhaps he may never have to confront it (see also *c,* below). For another thing, the patient, like the tester, may be reassured by realizing that the relationship is transient. It is typically easier for the wary patient to be spontaneous, warm and frank with a passive stranger than with someone closer, someone who may become the object of deep and lasting involvement. In this respect the tester is a "safe" confidant. Of course, the patient knows that his therapist will have the information derived from the tests; the test report may then become a focus of anxiety in the therapeutic relationship. But the relationship with the therapist is usually so fraught with anxiety about self-exposure anyway that the anxiety stimulated by the test report usually does no more than take one place in a long list of the patient's fears.

In its essentials, the patient's exposed, vulnerable, anxious psychological position during the testing parallels the position of a child who feels that his parents are omniscient, are persons from whom no secrets can be protected. This parallel is likely to stimulate the development of transference feelings toward the tester. The transference reaction to the tester will also be stimulated by the fact that the patient comes for help to the tester as an agent of the therapist and puts himself in the tester's hands temporarily. As a result, the tester may be experienced by the patient as if he were an omnipotent as well as omniscient parent. For these reasons, fears of condemnation, rejection and withdrawal of parental love may be revived or intensified, and the patient's anxiety over violation of his privacy may be all the greater.

Realistically as well as neurotically or autistically, the patient's distress may be further increased by his anticipation that the test results will influence decisions concerning his need for therapy. In this respect, insofar as transference is already established toward prominent figures in the therapeutic setting, the presumably utterly revealing test results do threaten loss of "parental" love. In schizoid cases particularly, but probably to some degree in all cases, as Bergler has argued [12], the opposite fear may also be stimulated, namely, fear of "parental" love itself—the patient being driven, for sado-masochistic and defensive reasons, to stimulate parental rejection repeatedly.

Thus, the situation of being forced to confide blindly and without trust is fraught with considerable anxiety, both on the real interpersonal level (in terms of accustomed modes of social relationship and privacy, and in terms of treatment recommendations) and on a transference level (in terms of fearing the love and hate of the omniscient and omnipotent "parental" therapeutic figures).

*b. Loss of control in the interpersonal relationship.* During the testing the patient surrenders a considerable portion of his control over the situation he is in. This is threatening to him. Psychologically disabled or not, each of us relies heavily on his ability to keep control, or at least to share control, in interpersonal relationships and social situations. Emotionally, the patient being tested is very much on the defensive: he must function in situations not of his choosing, must cope with problems and another person that are strange or that he might ordinarily avoid, must remain in a situation that is more or less threatening and unpleasant, and must stay on good terms (which some refuse to do from the outset) with a seemingly demanding and remote stranger. The balance of power seems very much on the tester's side. We assume, usually correctly, that the patient will "submit" on the basis of his intact appreciation of the possible therapeutic advantages to be derived. An autocratic problem inevitably exists, however, because of this unequal balance of power. The autocratic aspects, like the omniscient aspects, will contribute to the patient's transference reaction to the tester. The patient's realistic and transference modes of coping with the problem of authority will be highly instructive (see *e*, below).

What must be further emphasized here is that to maintain or share control in interpersonal situations appears to serve as a major buttress of a person's intrapsychic defensive strategy. By choice and avoidance of situations, topics and relationships, by tactical shifts in the balance of power within relationships, a person may guarantee that he will not suddenly find himself in a situation where provocations, opportunities or objects are present that would seriously threaten his defensive strategy. For example, a prudish spinster may in daily life avoid consciously erotic situations, and thereby support a defensive "pure" self-concept, but in the test situation she will have to deal in some conscious way with erotically tinged TAT pictures. A man of limited endowment (or organic deficit) may in his daily life avoid encounters in which he would be forced to face his intellectual limitations openly, but he will have to cope in some way with a test of intelligence or concept formation. A young woman in mortal terror of her hostile impulses may maintain a rigid pollyannish outlook and live in superficial peace with the world, but she will have to do something with the bloody red colors in the Rorschach test, pictured physical assault in the TAT, and Word Association test stimulus words like *fight, bite, cut,* and *gun.*

In short, by depriving the patient of control over choice of situations, we undermine some external props of his defensive structure. The result appears to be an intensification of the patient's defensive efforts, a vigorous try to reinforce his defensive outposts. This increased defensiveness does not *interfere* with the testing; it *enriches* it. The testing situation in this respect may contribute greatly to an understanding of the patient's defenses. From the psychoanalytic point of view, this *defense* aspect of the "projective hypothesis"—the active structuring of the world according to inner requirements and outer demands—is of crucial significance.*

* Related to this is an interesting point made by Baer [5]. Writing from a psychoanalytic point of view, Baer maintains that the "loss of form" in the perceptually unstructured Rorschach test is unconsciously experienced by the subject as a traumatic "loss of objects," and that the subject's basic anxiety in the test situation derives from just this fact. The subject's responses must then be understood as efforts to restore objects by restoring form. Baer further maintains that (a) the content of responses, especially of movement responses, expresses the individual content of this trauma; (b) shading and color responses—other than the form-color responses—express disorganized reactions to this trauma; (c) form responses, when they are of good quality *(F+)*, express restoration of objects; (d) shifts among the determinants reflect waxing and waning success or failure in this struggle to restore objects and thereby master the trauma. Of particular interest here is Baer's point regarding the "loss of objects." This point indicates how, in addition to the general aspects of the test situation we have been considering, the nature of the Rorschach test stimuli themselves removes the individual even further from control over objects. While Baer treats this trauma from the

*c. Dangers of self-confrontation.* It is becoming increasingly clear that testing represents and is felt by the patient as an assault on his defenses. Anticipating that he may consequently have to confront rejected, perhaps repressed, aspects of himself, the patient responds with anxiety, and is forced into an acutely ambivalent position: to the extent that there is some intact ego that desires help and cure, and perhaps with the additional impetus provided by the "need to confess" that has been emphasized by Reik [119]*, the patient will want to cooperate by responding fully and openly, come what may; on the other hand, because of his neurotic anxieties and his masochistic need to suffer, the patient may fear to stick his neck out and may be reluctant to help himself. The patient being tested does not even have the support for self-confrontation that he might gradually develop in a therapeutic relationship, where similar anxiety is experienced but rendered tolerable as a satisfactory relationship with the therapist develops. Such support as the patient may get from the total hospital organization, from other patients, and from the psychiatrist working him up, though often considerable, cannot entirely dispel this anxiety over defensive security in the test situation.

Thus, because his defenses are threatened by the tester, the patient may be exposed to premature self-awareness. In addition to the dangers of being seen through by the omniscient, voyeuristic tester, there are the dangers of seeing into one's self. The tester is not the only interpreter of what is going on; we must assume that the patient also preconsciously or consciously interprets his responses—before, during and after their coming to consciousness and to expression.

The entire problem of self-awareness is heightened by two factors: (1) immediately, the psychiatric history taking that is concurrent with the testing; (2) broadly, the context of life crisis in which testing usually takes place, this context fostering intense hope and despair in the patient concerning each possible "solution" to the crisis. For these reasons, the patient may be unusually sensitive to what his test responses and attitudes "reveal" concerning his past and also what they "forebode." Premature— as well as incorrect and unrealistic—self-awareness and anticipations lurk behind every inkblot.

With respect to primitive, rejected drives and feelings, the premature awareness may pertain to hatred, infantile dependence, incestuous or homo-

_____

point of view of threatened libidinal relationships, it may also be viewed from the point of view of defenses. In this regard, we see that the individual is deprived by the test stimuli of external defensive props to which he is accustomed. The limitation of Baer's argument is that he jumps too quickly to id interpretations and slights ego processes and interpersonal dynamics, even though he does not ignore them entirely.

* F. Wyatt called this variable to my attention.

sexual desires, and the like. Fantasies that touch on these usually threatening topics, even if only obliquely, are likely to stir up painful anxiety. Or the premature awareness may pertain to denied, painful feelings such as those of despair, fear and shame. The premature awareness may pertain to superego-defined moral shortcomings: being "tested," the patient runs the serious risk of being "found wanting"—wanting in Goodness, Purity, Sincerity and Selflessness. The threatening awareness may pertain to the image of one's self in relation to reality; for example, disturbing awareness of intellectual and emotional limitations in coping with problem situations. In these connections, precarious self-esteem may be given some painful blows during testing.

In short, the patient not only wants to hide things from others but to hide them from himself as well. In these desires he is no different from any of us, but, because typically he is in a life crisis, and because his overall integration is more or less precarious, he is likely to be especially threatened and defensive in the test situation. How threatened he is by self-confrontation and how he copes with this threat are central aspects of his personality and pathology and will certainly be crucial factors in his response to therapy.

*d. Regressive temptations.* Asking for and receiving help are difficult and painful to patients. Typically, the patient feels utterly baffled and defeated in his efforts to find a workable solution to his life problems. Filled with feelings of futility, he is tempted to give up the struggle, regress to an overtly passive and helpless position, and demand that some real or fantasied strong figure in the environment "nurture" and "save" him. At the same time, out of pathological pride and mistrust, he feels incapable of delegating such power to anyone. He therefore needs to defend against these regressive impulses, as by denying them and by driving away potentially helpful persons through arrogant or rebellious provocation and through discouraging inflexibility. Except in extreme cases, however, he will not go too far in driving away help, because he feels desperately in need of it too. In addition, the desperate but proud and mistrustful patient needs to feel that he can magically control and manipulate his nurturant saviour. Otherwise he would be too much at his saviour's mercy—an intolerably humiliating and vulnerable position. He thus tries simultaneously to get help and to spurn help, and also to be "taken over" and to "take over" himself. Such contradictions are the essence of psychopathological behavior. They become particularly clear in the patient's relationship to his therapist.

These conflicts or contradictions will also be brought into the test situation by the patient, even if not as prominently or strongly as into the therapeutic situation. The tester as a therapist-surrogate—and ultimately as a parent-surrogate—will become the target of the patient's pathologically regressive and pathologically counter-regressive impulses and maneuvers.

(There are, of course, non-pathological counter-regressive processes too—as in growing up healthily.) If the patient is not able to keep these fantasies and wishes controlled or buried, he will try to seduce the tester into "taking over," into being the big, helpful, indulgent and reassuring papa or mama; simultaneously or alternately he will try to repel the tester and to nip in the bud any emotionally felt acknowledgment that the tester's help is desired, being sought, or taking effect; and, not rarely, seduction and repulsion will intermingle to the point where the tester does not know whether he is "in" or "out" from one moment to the next. The tester may then feel—in a sense, correctly—that he is dealing with an impossible child, that is, a child who wants all sorts of protection, reassurance and indulgence, but only on his own unpredictable, tyrannical, internally contradictory terms.

Every patient strikes his distinctive balance between accepting and rejecting regressive temptations, and we may expect him to strike this characteristic balance in the test relationship. Also, the same balance may be struck with varying degrees of adaptiveness. For example, utterly dependent test behavior may be quietly compliant or loudly demanding, and utterly independent test behavior may be efficient and cooperative or inefficient and rebellious. The kind of balance struck and its degree of regressiveness are therefore well worth careful definition by the tester; they express crucial aspects of the personality and pathology of the patient.

*e. The dangers of freedom.* The patient is given considerable freedom to respond as he wishes in the testing situation. Schachtel [131] has emphasized the absence of rules in the Rorschach situation in particular, and has well demonstrated the value of analyzing the patient's response to this freedom—actually, his "escape from freedom" [54].

However, this freedom is not so great in the Rorschach test as Schachtel implies, since "no rules" also imposes a demand of a sort. It imposes a demand in the sense that it forces on the patient an obligation to make *all* the decisions as to what is to be acted on or expressed and what is to be inhibited. The demandingness of this freedom-in-a-vacuum is nowhere clearer than in the burdens and anxieties imposed on children by "nondirective," noncontrolling, noncollaborating parents. The Rorschach test type of freedom imposes a demand by omission rather than by commission, but a weighty demand it imposes nonetheless. And the Rorschach test type of freedom is by no means representative of that obtaining in healthy human relationships in our culture—which are characterized by *mutual* regulation and intimacy. Even in well-adjusted persons, therefore, this limitless freedom cannot be simply the skylark affair Schachtel would have us believe.

On the other hand, the patient not only fears, resents and flees from freedom, as Schachtel has described, he reacts similarly to rules and highly structured demands. In other words, both loss of control and gain of control have positive and negative valences and the patient's test behavior will reflect his vacillation between these two poles as much as it will his coping with either extreme alone. We have already considered reactions to loss of control (see particularly *b*, above). What follows next is a summary of Schachtel's discussion of reactions to freedom or gain of control. There is no contradiction in saying that in the Rorschach situation the patient both gains and loses freedom; as in any complex situation, we must be prepared to find a distinctive pattern of gain and loss of control in different areas of that situation. Schachtel's discussion overlaps much of what has already been discussed or will be discussed later, although his psychoanalytic orientation is somewhat different.

Schachtel approaches this problem with the concepts of Fromm [*54*] and Sullivan [*142*]. He defines "the subjective definition of the Rorschach test situation" as the testee's total experience, conscious and unconscious, of that situation. This subjective definition may be inferred from the testee's reactions to the common, standardized elements of the situation. These include two persons being together, one giving a task to the other, the task being understood to be one which allows conclusions to be drawn regarding the personality of the testee, and the task being distinguished from usual tasks by its relative lack of rules and the great freedom of approach that it allows the testee. Schachtel then describes three common types of subjective definition encountered in Western civilization: the authoritarian, the competitive, and the resistant. Actually, as will become evident, all three are basically authoritarian definitions.

*The authoritarian definition,* fostered particularly by the testee's past experience with the typical tests and tasks imposed throughout life in Western civilization, is characterized by ". . . fear of, admiration for, or rebellion against irrational authority . . . and all the various forms which an inner dependence on such authority may take." The testee feels that the test results will render him vulnerable to external and internal (superego) approval and condemnation. He feels he must work to meet certain demands. Finding no specific demands imposed, and being deeply frightened of freedom, he invents demands. He transforms the test into a school examination. He then concentrates on meeting these actually self-imposed and ultimately self-limiting demands, expectations and prohibitions.

*The competitive definition* is closely related to the authoritarian definition in that it is also oriented toward powerful, culturally defined parental images, but whereas the authoritarian definition leads to emphasis on winning the approval of authority and to restriction of performance in order to comply with imagined rules and demands, the competitive definition leads to competition with the imagined performance of others, in order to defeat all rivals, and to restriction of performance according to these fantasied standards.

*The resistance definition* is the rebellious negative form of the authoritarian and competitive definitions. It is distinguished by a conscious or unconscious reluctance to see anything or to be interested, and may even include the intention of doing the opposite of what, according to imagined demands or standards, seems to be expected. If the patient is especially concerned with status rather than achievement, this definition may lead him to conceive of the test situation as a battle in which the tester must be defeated by some form of noncompliance. If the patient feels intensely weak and guilty, this definition may lead him to conceive of the testing situation as a "trial" and to clam up in response to his fear being "found out." If intense rebelliousness toward authority accompanies dependence upon it, a generally negativistic response to the test and tester may ensue.

Schachtel goes on to describe various effects these definitions may have on the Rorschach performance. His discussion instructively emphasizes that the same general definition may have superficially opposite effects. For example, *quantity ambition* and *quality ambition,* manifest perhaps in high $R$ and low $R$ respectively, may both result from an authoritarian definition of the test situation. He concerns himself with nine aspects of the performance: the number of responses, initial reaction time and total reaction time per card, sequence, form level, modes of apperception, content, the determinants, general test behavior and turning of the cards, and response to inquiry.

Throughout his discussion of these nine aspects, Schachtel contrasts those persons, like pedants and depressives, who take the test too seriously, make work out of it, and constantly feel under the pressure of demands deriving from their authoritarian and/or competitive orientations; those who respond in terror of being "found out" and who try persistently to cover up; and those, such as the ones who enjoy fantasy or are elevated in mood, who take pleasure in the freedom of fantasy afforded them by the absence of rules in the test situation. It is characteristic of the first two of these three groups that they feel a lack of relatedness to the world around them: they experience the outer world as a great force with which they must cope, against which they are in opposition, of which they are not a part, and with respect to which they are passive and helpless rather than active and potentially effective. For these reasons they are incapable of spontaneously relating themselves to the blots and of being freely interested in them. They frantically search for order, rules, methods, and are the most vulnerable to the various types of "shock" which may be observed in the test—"shock" being essentially an indication of the absence or breakdown of rules and methods by which the anxious patient hopes to be able to cope with this threatening situation.

Thus, some aspects of the Rorschach situation may offer the patient more freedom than he can tolerate. His response to this freedom will probably clearly indicate how he handles one broad and vital problem in our culture—coping with real and fantasied authority, present and absent.

We have now considered five major constants of the patient's position in the test situation and relationship: intimate communication and violation of privacy without a basis in trust, loss of control of the interpersonal relationship, exposure to the dangers of premature self-awareness, regressive temptations, and dangers of freedom. Under these challenging, anxiety-arousing conditions, it seems inevitable that definite defensive and transference reactions to the tester will be stimulated or exacerbated. Analysis of these transference and defensive reactions may contribute significantly to our understanding of the patient.

We shall soon consider some of the ways in which defensive reactions may be seen in the interpersonal relationship. Schachtel's discussion has already provided a beginning for this, and will not be repeated in what follows. His paper should be read carefully. Before getting into the analysis of defensive behavior, however, it is in place to consider briefly another aspect of the patient's definition of the test situation, namely, the psychosexual aspects of his attitudes toward his responses.

## 2. The Patient's Psychosexual Orientation Toward His Responses

The previous and following sections of this chapter draw heavily on Freudian psychoanalytic understanding of the vicissitudes of the therapeutic relationship. This understanding has been transposed, with modifications appropriate to the changed reality situation, from the therapeutic relationship to the test relationship. This transposition has provided a frame of reference within which a wide variety of behavior by both tester and patient can be interpreted. In important respects, the transposition has had and will continue to have a speculative aspect. After all, the patient's associations to and elaborations of his test behavior are ordinarily not immediately accessible to the tester, though they often do become available later through the therapist.

The present section on the patient's psychosexual orientation toward his responses will be the most speculative in this chapter. *Direct* support for this specific transposition from the therapeutic to the test situation can come only from classically psychoanalytic or psychoanalytically-oriented therapeutic interviews. Informally collected impressions from the therapy of patients who have been tested tend to support this transposition, but cannot be offered as well-established evidence. Some *indirect* support for the transposition may be found in two considerations. First, it is reasonable to expect some continuity of subjective experience from one clinical situation to the next. The patient telling the therapist about himself cannot feel too differently about both the *fact* of telling and the *content* of telling than he feels telling the tester about himself. The fundamental context of these communications is much the same. Second, indirect support for the transposition may be derived from the analysis of other aspects of the test results. That is to say, the formal and content aspects of the test results may point clearly in the direction of the type of hypotheses to be presented here. As will be discussed in Chapter 5, such convergence of inferences drawn from different aspects of the test record should be a prerequisite of any major conclusion about the patient. All roads should lead to it, so to speak. Although admittedly speculative, therefore, the following considerations may provide us with concepts and reference points which will further clarify the psychology of the test situation and relationship.

In psychoanalysis it has been found that analysands often have definite infantile, irrational psychosexual conceptions of and attitudes toward their associations. These conceptions and attitudes may be clearly specific to the content of the associations, as in certain phases of analysis when material of a particular sort is being worked through. Often, however, these concepts and attitudes are generalized and structuralized. They are organized into a relatively fixed and pervasive orientation and remain prominent regardless of the content of the associations. Gross has used the analysis of such conceptions and attitudes in elucidating the psychology of telling secrets [64].

Whether as a transient reaction or as a fixed orientation, the patient may conceive of his associations, for example, in predominantly "oral" terms— as nourishing supply, as life-giving substance, as a flowing-out. In response to this "oral" conception, the patient may devalue or overvalue his supplies, may feel drained by the analyst, may supply unnourishing stuff (barren associations), may cut off his supply and try to structure the situation so that supplies will be flowing in *from* the analyst and not out *to* the analyst. The analysand may, on the other hand, gush out associations in order to deny (and vicariously satisfy) his own hungers. Which way the patient will handle or react to his "oral" conception of his associations will depend on many other trends in his personality.

The associations may be conceived primarily in "anal" terms—as dutiful and submissive delivery of internal products, as a letting-go or a giving-in. In response to this "anal" conception, the patient may fear to let go, especially if dominated by a hostile, evil conception of his internal products, and he may therefore withhold associations; or he may withhold associations out of stubborn defiance. On the other hand, he may hostilely deluge the analyst with his waste products, with scattered, affectless, valueless associations or with "dirty" thoughts and fantasies.

The associations may be conceived primarily in "phallic" terms—as a means of seduction, as a submission to psychological rape, as an exhibitionistic exposure or as a hostile intrusion. In response to this "phallic" conception, the analysand may resist or else invite and surrender to the analyst's "sexual" assault, may tease with hints and not "come across," may make of his associations an isolated masturbatory affair; he may be actively seductive or intrusive to conquer or debase the analyst, or may strive to be repulsive in order to preclude the possibility of mutual attraction and intimacy.

It should be noted that within all of these psychosexual orientations there are greater or lesser sadistic, masochistic, narcissistic and sensual emphases, and more or less prominent feelings of pride or shame, guilt or accusation, inadequacy or competence, and the like. The psychosexual ladder—oral, anal, phallic—is after all but one aspect of the complex configuration of drives, drive derivatives, attitudes, defenses, etc. that constitute the personality. It should also be emphasized that "oral," "anal," and "phallic" are gross temporal as well as dynamic abstractions. These phases of infantile development overlap greatly and no person should be thought of as totally fixated on or regressed to just one of the levels.

With these reservations and qualifications in mind, we must now ask what there is in common psychologically among these various psychosexual orientations and behavior trends. It seems that they all involve at least the following four major components: (1) associations are regarded and handled as objects; (2) these objects are felt to be parts, extensions, or externalizations of oneself; (3) these objects or parts of oneself, because they are felt to be given to or withheld from the analyst, take on an aspect of interpersonal currency; (4) these objects are evaluated and manipulated by the patient as he evaluates and manipulates the bodily and social aspects of himself to which they correspond, in accordance with their current place and past history in his total psychic structure.

It is very likely that the same four components are actively involved when the patient is delivering his test responses. As with free associations, the psychosexual attitude toward any test response may be largely determined by the content of the response or it may be generalized to the point where it is brought to bear on most or all responses. In any event, there is a second order of test response—the patient's subjective reaction to the test response he is forming or communicating. Prominent in this second order of response are primitively conceived psychosexual attitudes.

The relationship between self-evaluation and response-evaluation will vary from one patient to the next in the following three ways: (1) in the extent of the patient's awareness of the relationship itself: some patients seem altogether unconscious of their identification with their responses, while others seem to use their responses as pretexts for deliberate and relentless self-evaluation or self-exposure; (2) in the degree of generalization and rigidity of particular types of evaluation: some patients do nothing but disparage or praise their responses from beginning to end, while other patients may become self-critical in some contexts and pleased with themselves in others; (3) in the extremeness of their evaluations: some may be persistently yet mildly critical of their responses, while others may be in complete anguish and despair over their "foolish" and "horrible" responses.

These three types of variation apply not only to the relationship between self-evaluation and response-evaluation, but also to the interpersonal currency aspect of the test responses. (1) Patients vary in their degree of awareness of this giving-something-away-to-the-tester aspect of their responses: some deliberately devalue their responses through provocative facetiousness directed at the tester, while others devalue responses as if it were principally a matter of their failure to meet internal standards. (2) Patients vary in the degree of generalization and rigidity of their attitudes toward giving responses to the tester (or to the figures behind the tester: the therapist, and ultimately the parental figures): some remain fixed in an attitude throughout, such as sullen submission, while others shift their ground depending on *how* things are going or *what* things are going at the moment. (3) Patients vary in the extremeness of these attitudes; to some it is a major issue, to others not.

It therefore seems important to note whether and to what extent the patient is kind or cruel to his responses, proud or disparaging, orderly or sloppy, generous or stingy, trivial or ambitious, flashy or drab, driven or inert, optimistic or pessimistic, and the like. How he presents, evaluates and treats his responses reflects how he presents, evaluates and treats himself inwardly and in his relationships. For purposes of test reports we need not and generally should not speculatively push our way down to the level of unconscious psychosexual attitudes toward responses; higher level, ego-oriented description of how the patient presents, evaluates and treats his responses and himself is clinically more to the point and much less inferential. But for purposes of a theory of testing, it is necessary to take account of the psychosexual origins of the patient's orientation toward his responses as well as the relationship of these origins to the formal and content aspects of the responses themselves.

### 3. Defensive Aspects of the Patient's Test Behavior

Thus far in considering the dynamics of being tested, we have concerned ourselves chiefly with certain constants in the patient's role, such as violation of privacy and loss of defensive control, and briefly with the influence of one or another dominant psychosexual orientation on the patient's attitudes toward his responses. Throughout, there have been numerous references to the assault the tests make on the patient's defenses and to the patient's increased defensiveness in the face of this assault. In the present section we shall consider more systematically a variety of defensive responses in the test situation. Some of these modes of defense, such as projection, will fall under the heading of classical mechanism of defense. Others, such as ingratiation, will be defensive only in a broader sense, that is, they will represent patterns of behavior which *from one point of view* may be regarded as defensive operations. This section will be concerned with defense mechanisms and defensive operations as they are expressed in *test attitudes and behavior*. The expression of defensive emphases in *test responses proper* will be discussed in the later chapters on specific defense mechanisms.

Before going on to consider specific defensive test behaviors, it is necessary to say a little more about the theory of defense implied in this discussion. This theory will be discussed more fully in Chapter 6. Here we shall anticipate only two of its major aspects.

First, *defenses vary in complexity.* Some seem to be relatively simple, like repression; others are relatively complex, like regression; and still others, not on the list of classical defense mechanisms, such as masochism and homosexuality, are extremely complex in that they involve subtle hierarchies and synchronizations of a variety of libidinal and aggressive drives, defense mechanisms, superego demands and prohibitions, modes of adaptation, values and social orientations. The more complex the behavior in question, the more desirable it is to speak of it as having a defensive aspect, rather than to call it a defense. Simply to call it a defense is to ignore its psychological intricacy. For example, homosexuality may be conceived of as a defense against sadistic impulses, but homosexuality is so many other things psychologically that it would be better to speak of "the important but not all-embracing *defensive aspect* of homosexuality." Brenman's treatment of the masochistic character well illustrates this point of view [18].

The second important aspect of the theory of defense we must consider here is the assumption that *every defensive behavior has a potential or actual adaptive aspect.* To put it more precisely, behavior of any complexity can be shown to have a potential or actual adaptive aspect, even if its defensive aspect is outstanding. Intellectualization, for example, may be highly adaptive in many respects even while it defends against feeling and impulse to a pathological degree. By "adaptive" is meant more or less need-implementing in accordance with prevailing inner conditions (id, ego and superego harmonies and conflicts), and prevailing outer conditions (needs, demands, limits of others and of the physical and social environment generally).* It is therefore by no means stigmatizing to refer to this or that

---

* See in this regard Hartmann's discussion of "rational and irrational action" [68].

behavior as a defense or as defensive. Up to a point, even the capacity to be defensive may be adaptive; there are times when restraint of potentially disruptive impulse and feeling, even if it means constriction of the personality, is a help in maintaining inner and social integration. There are also instances, as we shall see, where restrained use of a defense mechanism, like projection, may be adaptive and enriching rather than impoverishing or constricting [87].

Bearing in mind that defenses do vary in complexity and that they may have important adaptive aspects, we may now consider the expression of defense mechanisms and defensive operations in test behavior and attitude.

*a. Projection.* A moderate amount of projection—projection as a mechanism of defense—seems to be necessary for a productive performance on tests like the Rorschach test and Thematic Apperception test. The patient may more freely produce richly self-expressive responses if he can externalize some of the responsibility for these responses. This externalization places the responsibility for the patient's reactions on the tester and his test materials. This is not altogether unrealistic, of course, since to some extent the test materials do favor some types of response over others. It becomes *projection* when the patient loses sight of the fact that his response is a result of *interaction* between the stimulus and himself. The stimuli are typically not *that* compellingly hostile, sexual, morbid, gay, deep, or enchanting. Still, a limited amount of projection or externalization of responsibility beyond what the stimuli objectively justify cannot be considered pathological. It is with the projections that have more or less pathological implications that we shall now be concerned. The normal use during testing of the defense mechanism of projection will be discussed in more detail in Chapter 3 on the response process.

Projections are commonly divided into id projections, that is, projections of unacceptable erotic, hostile and dependent impulses, and superego projections, that is, projections of intolerable superego commands and criticisms. This is not an easy distinction to maintain and it has been criticized as not sufficiently comprehensive. Here is not the place to attempt to formulate a theory of projection that will embrace all the possibilities. Accordingly, three types of projection will be discussed below—superego projection, id projection, and—as a catch-all—unclassified or mixed projection.

(1) *Superego projection* is common in the responses of psychiatric patients to testing. Schachtel ascribes this fact to our culture's authoritarian emphasis in general and its authoritarian definition of tests in particular [131]. So far as testing is concerned, as has been already pointed out, this point of view puts too much of the burden on the patient and on society. It ignores some of the psychological realities of the test situation, such as the

intrusive and dominating role of the tester and his relative uncommunicativeness.

In any event, all sorts of moral judgments and criticisms may be unrealistically ascribed to the tester by the patient. The tester's relative detachment may be interpreted as coldness, disapproval and scorn. The patient may be excessively guarded and legalistic in his formulation of responses, as if he were "on trial," as if the tester were "out to get him" and would use the test findings "against him." Or the patient may be excessively apologetic and prone to make excuses for his "poor" performance, projecting onto the tester his own superego-based condemnations of this performance. In extreme form, the patient may conclude that any test item with "bad" connotations implies that the tester thinks or "knows" these "bad" connotations apply to him. On this basis, for example, a paranoid schizophrenic went into a temporary panic upon hearing the Word Association test stimulus word *homosexual*. A milder form of this last projection is seen in the paranoid patient conveying the feeling, "What must you think of me to show me this horrible picture?"

(2) *Id projection* commonly takes the form of exaggerating the externalization of responsibility for responses. The essential point the patient makes is, "Were it not for your instructions or lack of them, and were it not for the nature of the test items, I would never have reacted this way. It's really your impulse, not mine!" It is particularly paranoid if this reaction occurs during the Rorschach test. There is considerably more—though not complete—reality support for such thoughts in the Thematic Apperception test, where some of the pictures do push one strongly in the direction of some kind of sexual or destructive story. In the Rorschach test, the paranoid patient may end up, for example, with the idea that the test is "designed" to elicit sexual thoughts. In somewhat milder paranoid form he may think that he is "supposed" to find some sex responses. Or, still milder, he may say, "The red looks like menstruation, *if you want that sort of thing.*"

When the externalizations of responsibility are numerous, even if not extreme, a pervasive paranoid orientation is implied. The patient may clam up suspiciously in response to his projections, but he also may comply with his projected demands and pour out a stream of the "wanted" material, i.e., lots of sex and gore in the Rorschach and Thematic Apperception tests. The latter reaction seems to be becoming more common as public acquaintance with "psychoanalytic" ideas increases. The tester should not be misled by the faddish tone some paranoid patients give to such responses; this tone is usually a rationalization that covers an underlying paranoid projection. Often, this blend of projection and rationalization is encountered in persons of precarious, at least borderline psychotic, ego status.

The id projection may become more personal than this. Evil, hostile, or perverse interests and tendencies may be ascribed to the tester because so many of his test items are "evil," "hostile" or "perverse." In milder form, the personal projection may simply take the form, "You don't like me" or any of its many variants, when it is the patient who resents and dislikes the intrusive, autocratic tester.

(3) *Unclassified and mixed projections.* A very common expression of a pathological projection is the patient's idea that the tester is somehow "playing tricks" on him. In mild form it appears in such questions during the administration of the Wechsler-Bellevue Scale as, "Can this really be done?" "Is there really an answer?" "Are there enough blocks here to do it?" In more extreme form it appears in definite negative answers to these questions: "It can't be done!" "There is no answer!" "There aren't enough blocks!" Sometimes patients explicitly ask if there are "trick questions" in the Arithmetic subtest or Picture Completion subtest. This implicit projection of responsibility for difficulty or failure stems from and is a denial of painful inability to face one's limitations, and may involve various id and superego components.

In the Rorschach test, in mild form, patients may project onto the tester demands, for example, for *many* responses or for *Whole* responses. Insofar as the emphasis is on what *should* be done, these may involve superego projections; insofar as the emphasis is on the tester's insatiability or cruelty, these may involve id projections. Paranoid patients may take any inquiry into a response as a clear indication that the response was wrong, significant, baffling or unique. They may conclude that they are "not supposed to" see sex or so many animals; or, once finding a sex or blood response, they may conclude that they are "supposed to" find them. They may immediately generalize from their responses to Cards I and II that all the cards will look alike and elicit the same responses. In general, when the verbalizations of the patient continuously or dramatically contain inferences about what is expected or discouraged, favored or disliked, "good" or "bad," hinted or impending, it is implied that the patient's adjustment efforts are characterized by steady or extreme paranoid projections or both.

*b. Isolation.* It was said above that a modicum of projection is necessary for the production of richly self-expressive test responses. The same may be said of the defense mechanism of isolation. Isolation of affect renders tolerable the communication of highly personal material, of a recognized and unrecognized sort, to a psychological intruder, in the absence of a well-defined, trustworthy relationship. In fact, it even seems reasonable to say that a modicum of isolation is a necessary attribute of normal everyday functioning. We often do better not to feel the full extent of our emotional involvement in a situation. The capacity for logical thinking itself seems to depend on powers of isolation [50].

Like projection, however, isolation may be used too rigidly and pervasively by the patient in the test situation. He may maintain an utterly detached attitude toward the entire proceedings. He may manifest a minimum of involvement in the situation, the tester and his own responses. One Rorschach card is the same to him as the next; and the Word Association test stimulus word *bowel movement* is responded to with as much aplomb as *lamp*. This detachment must not be confused with mature poise. Its defensive meaning is established by our appreciation of how emotionally strange, varied, complex and surprising the test requirements are and how inappropriate perfect composure is under these circumstances.

Often we see the opposite extreme of rigid, pervasive isolation, that is, extreme failure of isolation and the domination of all or most responses by anxiety and emotional lability. In these instances of utter failure of isolation, the patient's handling of test problems will be quickly and pervasively invaded by personal conflict. Ego autonomy is at a minimum and almost everything seems to be a "hot issue." Care must be taken, however, to distinguish the failure of isolation and consequent suffusion of most or all responses by anxiety and affect from the histrionics of persons who are not deeply involved with the test items, but who feel they *should be* responsive and are driven to make these outward shows of affect. The latter are often hypomanics whose parade of affect follows a route all its own, ignoring the lines laid down by the test stimuli. If not hypomanic, these patients are likely to have cultivated a pseudo-responsiveness as a fashionable denial of narcissism, inhibition or withdrawal.

*c. Intellectualization.* According to theory, intellectualization is a variant of defense by isolation. Like isolation, its purpose is to seal off affect. Its distinctive feature is its shift of emphasis from immediate inner and interpersonal conflict to abstract ideas and esoteric topics. Intellectualization, like projection and like isolation of affect in general, can be a help in taking tests. It can add zest to problem solving, interest in one's own thought processes, and pleasure in the discovery of new facts and relationships.

When the intellectualizing is too rigid and pervasive, however, the patient may displace all his anxieties onto the intellectual implications of the situation, and particularly onto the possibilities of success and failure. This reaction also implies an authoritarian or competitive orientation, as discussed by Schachtel, but from a defensive point of view it may be characterized as overintellectualized. In milder form, the patient may make an intellectual game or contest out of the test situation, taking the tests very much like an eager or bored student being quizzed by a teacher. If his intellectualizing is fraught with aggression, the patient may define the test situation as an intellectual battle between himself and the tester; he may then challenge and criticize many of the test items. He may, for example, hotly deny that there can be any similarity between *praise* and *punishment,* since strictly speaking these are not opposites; that is to say, an answer would be possible if the item read *praise and criticism* or *reward and punishment,* etc., etc. He may scold the tester for asking such vague questions as, "Who invented the airplane?" since any fool knows that such inventions evolve through the work of many people, that da Vinci did in one sense, that the Wright brothers merely made the first successful flight, etc., etc.

If psychologically "sophisticated," the overintellectualistic patient may blithely produce a flood of psychoanalytic jargon; in the Rorschach test he may dwell at length on "lurid" content and "interpret" many of his responses. This patient in one respect may be making a verbal, affectless game of his lostness and unhappiness, and in another respect may be desperately trying to maintain conscious control over everything he communicates.

*d. Compulsive perfectionism.* Perfectionism seems to be a behavior based on a blend of the compulsive defense mechanisms of isolation, reaction formation and undoing. Its undoing aspect is seen in its guilt-reducing potential. Its reaction formation aspect is seen in its substitution of excessive order and restraint for excessive disorder and impulsiveness. The isolation aspect of perfectionism will become clear shortly. Since perfectionism is a very frequent test manifestation of these compulsive defenses, it merits separate consideration.

Within limits, like the previously discussed defenses, perfectionism may be an asset to the patient. A perfectionistic tendency facilitates careful reality testing, full development of responses, clarity of communication, and the maintenance of some orderliness and consistency of approach to the test problems.

When the perfectionism is extreme, its affect-isolating aspect becomes prominent. The patient seems then to be trying to avoid all emotional reactions by concentrating entirely on fine detail, formal order and logical consistency. He may maintain great critical distance from the stimuli and "judge" them rather than allow himself to react to them directly and spontaneously. He may, for example, emphasize the lack or presence of symmetry in the Rorschach inkblots and the artistic merits and demerits of the TAT pictures. He may take a long time before giving his responses, substituting caution for spontaneity and control for affect. He may work long, hard and obnoxiously on "perfecting" his responses, specifying in the Rorschach test, for example, those details of a response that are good and those that are poor, giving slightly different interpretations as alternatives, and generally covering all possibilities so as not to run the risk of appearing careless, disorderly and impulsive to himself or anyone else.

This painful, perfectionistic elaboration of test responses is to be distinguished from a kind of pseudo-creativity shown by some persons who, upon finding a Rorschach response they like and which is plastic, cling to this response frantically and go into a theme-and-variations routine. They may, for example, see the popular figures on Card III first as dancers, then as waiters, then as cannibals, porters and chickens. The criterion for this pseudo-creativity is the low number of other responses, particularly imaginative responses, to the card. Such persons tend to be those who are so insecure with respect to their "good ideas" that they run each one they get deep into the ground before they leave it be. It makes no sense, therefore, to score each of the variations as a separate response.

In some precariously integrated compulsive patients we observe sporadic or frequent decompensations of perfectionism and consequent eruptions of sloppy and impulsive responses.   The inconsistency in the daily behavior of so-called anal-compulsive characters, such as overt hypercleanliness and covert dirtiness, is often paralleled in the test behavior of these patients. They may greatly emphasize the precision and orderliness of their responses, and yet, in the Wechsler-Bellevue Scale, for example, may suddenly fit an Object Assembly item together quite sloppily, or in a Block Designs item they may ignore a gross error they would never have committed in the first place if they had sustained their usual cautious checking and evaluation of responses.   In the Rorschach test they may dwell at great length on the fine detail of one obvious response and then give a strained or arbitrary response with no cautious qualification whatever. Or suddenly, after perfectionistic straining, they may be emotionally overwhelmed by the "messiness" of Card IX or the "chaos" of Card X and react in an inadequate, "disorderly" manner.

*e. Repression.* Indications of a strong repressive emphasis appear not so much in the patient's relationship to the tester as in the test responses and test patterns proper. These responses and patterns are discussed in detail in Chapter 7. Only a few general points will be made here.

First, as in normal everyday functioning, repression is an indispensable defense and is in some respects an adaptive asset during testing. The tests should not and do not break down basic repressive barriers. The patient is not ordinarily flooded by awareness of primitive desires, feelings and fantasies in response to the test stimuli. While the tests do in a sense circumvent repressive barriers so that often the tester may infer unconscious content from the patient's responses, the patient himself is not ordinarily keenly aware of this circumvention, even though he may fear it. The patient is therefore considerably less threatened than he would be otherwise.

Second, *flexible* and *limited* relaxation of repressive barriers also seems to play a crucial part in the elaboration of expressive test responses. Vivid Rorschach test imagery and imaginative TAT stories are creative acts which depend on somewhat freer access of preconscious and unconscious content to consciousness than is ordinarily the case. This relaxation of repressions is discussed more fully in Chapter 3 on the response process.

The patient who is over-repressed or whose repressive barriers are precarious cannot tolerate free fantasy and spontaneity in thought. To him the entire world of ideas is threatening. Accordingly, the tests, which again and again demand fantasy and reflection, will seem especially dangerous to this patient and will provoke an intensification of his repressive efforts. His spontaneous verbalizations and his responses to inquiry will tend to be naive, egocentric and unreflective. In his eyes the tests and/or his responses will be unpleasant, morbid, weird, crazy or silly. Being unable to accept the fantasy aspect of the Rorschach test, the repressive patient may cling to the idea that the blots are pictures and are to be recognized rather than interpreted. This form of naive realism is to be distinguished from that of the paranoid patient who also may treat his responses as if they are entirely external objects: in paranoid projection, the emphasis is distinctively on inferring relationships and smoking out hidden meanings rather than on simple "recognition."

Failure of repression in the test situation usually reflects acute or chronic general ego weakness. When repressions fail, perverse, morbid and fantastic thoughts and fantasies tend to flood consciousness. Themes of murder, torture, rape, incest, mutilation, sexual aberration and frustration, freakishness, and the like pour out—explicitly in the TAT and more or less implicitly or symbolically in the Rorschach test content. Depending upon the total context of the ego weakness, the gush of primitive content that comes with failure of repression may elicit considerable anxiety, may be a blandly regarded "external" event, or may be dressed up in hostile rationalizations about "wanting to shock" the tester (or therapist). As a rule, the greater the anxiety about the primitive, bizarre content, the more likely it is we are dealing with a decompensation into a borderline psychotic or fully psychotic state; the greater the blandness, the more likely it is we are dealing with a more or less stabilized character disorder with borderline psychotic or fully psychotic trends; the "desire to shock" is often encountered in borderline psychotic cases who are enough in touch with reality to know that the content of their responses is bizarre but who cannot genuinely respond otherwise and who therefore try to make an act of "free choice" out of their psychotic necessity.

*f. Denial.* Narrowly defined, "denial" means the defensive refusal to acknowledge the existence of disturbing external realities. The concept is, however, often used in a broader sense to include refusal to acknowledge the existence of inner disturbed reactions to the external provocations. It is in the broader sense that the concept "denial" will be used here.

A modicum of denial helps one take tests as it probably helps daily adjustment. It is very difficult, as we see in some obsessional cases, to take into account all problematical details of all daily situations or test situations. In the TAT, for example, it is sometimes necessary to disregard one or another element of a picture in order to tell a story. In the Rorschach test, it is often necessary to ignore one or another aspect of an inkblot that conflicts perceptually or emotionally with a more general impression. Moderate and flexible use of denial prevents getting bogged down in detail and contradictions, and it facilitates decisiveness and smooth responsiveness.

Overemphasis on the mechanism of denial is routinely prominent in the test behavior of hypomanic patients and sometimes prominent in addicts with psychopathic trends. The following is a composite of expressions of denial in test behavior. The patient glosses over anxiety-arousing and depressing aspects of his present life situation in general and of the test situation in particular. By ingratiation and affability, he tries to deny his intense underlying rage and his irritation over having to take the tests. He relentlessly strives to remain self-propelled and high-spirited throughout the tests, easily taking a great liking to the tester, getting a big kick out of the tests, and emphasizing his agreeableness to any of the tester's suggestions or requests. All evidence of underlying depressed, needful, hostile feelings tends to be minimized and concealed, although it is more than likely to be prominent in the formal and content aspects of the test responses. In fact, these repudiated feelings are usually obliquely expressed in test behavior itself. Thus, while on the one hand the patient will be exaggeratedly self-confident, will frequently overestimate the quality of his responses, will desperately avoid confronting inadequacy, and will impatiently discourage the tester's instructions and reassurances, on the other hand he will aggressively and demandingly ignore some test instructions, such as not to talk too fast and not to make his TAT stories too long, will subtly define the relationship as one in which the tester is too demanding, and will comply irritably when restraints are imposed by the tester. Typically, blithe denial and aggressive negativism and demandingness are opposite sides of the same coin.

In exaggerated form, denial may be expressed in flightiness, the patient not staying with any response long enough for its importance to be recognized, felt and acknowledged. In true flightiness all details are equally unimportant, just as in true obsessional meticulousness all details are equally important.

In hypomanic settings, the denials are often unstable. The "good cheer" and "confidence" may then alternate rapidly with tears, despair and clinging to the tester's reassurances. Sometimes, as in sun showers, the sunniness and storminess even seem to co-exist.

Other forms of expression of denial in test behavior also occur, such as pollyannish denial of gloom and hostility via serene, optimistic, pleasant, "trustful" docility, and masochistic denial of good cheer and hope via loud and long lamentations, complaints, and self-flagellation. These will be referred to in more detail elsewhere in the text.

*g. Reaction formations against hostility.* The patient with strong but not extreme reaction formations against hostility will usually be very easy to test. He will be considerate, cooperative, calm and everything else the tester's heart desires. He will find the tests interesting, will be certain they will be most helpful, and will be explicitly grateful for the tester's time, effort, interest and patience. He will anticipate the tester's needs, as by spontaneously noting the location and determinants of his Rorschach responses. His point will be: "See how harmless and kindly I am." This manner of response, like the too detached poise of the patient who rigidly isolates affect and the too serene pleasantness of the pollyanna, should not be confused with healthy maturity. A little irritability, impatience and non-compliance should be expected if there is any genuine freedom of expression of hostility, or in other words, mature self-assertiveness. The tests *are* a nuisance in some ways. The mature self-assertions will be adaptively expressed as a rule, as, for example, with a humorous twist or with a verbal or attitudinal indication of having retained some distance from the modulated, well controlled hostility. It is sometimes worthwhile to test the rigidity of prominent reaction formations by encouraging the patient to complain a little, as, for example, by saying upon completion of the testing, "That finishes the tests. I won't be bothering you any more." Perfectly sustained serenity and good will should be considered suggestive of rigid reaction formations against hostility. Of course, paranoid wariness and excessive denial may also account for such attitudes and behavior.

When extremely rigid, reaction formations lose even their pseudo-adaptive quality discussed above. They culminate in a sticky sweetness and a saintly benevolence that are often emotionally inappropriate and are difficult to endure. Other aspects of the patient as a real person are then unreachable for the time being.

*h. Reaction formations against dependent needs.* In the test situation and relationship, rigid reaction formations against dependent needs tend to lead to all types of concealing of need by the patient. The rigidly defensive patient of this sort is the one who typically not only refuses a cigarette and a light offered by the tester, but insists that the tester try one of his cigarettes. Of course, a modicum of this defense is a help in self-reliantly weathering the difficult occasions that arise during the testing.

There are four general courses of action open to the patient who is intolerant of and bends over backwards to minimize his dependent needs: (a) he may sullenly, grudgingly, sarcastically take the tests, making no bones about his resenting this "kid stuff" or "foolishness"; (b) he may, as

in the example of the cigarette, make a big show of his supplies and benevolence, striving to be the nurturant one in the relationship; similarly, he may
show much sympathy about "all that writing," all that the tester has to "put
up with," and the tester's "boredom" with his tests; (c) he may quickly
and vigorously try to establish an informal, chummy atmosphere, and a
definition of the relationship as one between equals or as one that is more
of a lark than anything else; (d) he may displace the reaction formation
emphasis onto the test responses, repeatedly making a point of his control
over what comes out of him; he will say in the TAT, for example, "I'll
make it a happy ending," or "Let's have him get killed"; in the Rorschach
test, upon completing his responses to a card, he will say, "That exhausts
that one," or "I could go on far into the night." In all these instances, two
major points are being made: "I don't need anything from anyone!" and
"I've got more than enough for everybody!" Implicitly this patient is also
saying: "I'm not really a patient; I don't need help!"

*i. Passive demandingness.* In passive demandingness, and in the next
four modes of response to testing to be discussed (counterphobic, masochistic, ingratiating, and rebellious operations), we will be dealing with complex
behavior which has defensive aspects but which cannot simply be called
defensive. In other words, while defensively colored, the behavior serves
many other purposes than that of defense. Because these five remaining
modes of response are commonly encountered in testing, and because they
are defensively colored, they will be considered in this section on defensive
attitudes and behavior, even though that does some violence to their
psychological complexity.

Passive demandingness commonly involves defensive regression from
adult, more or less self-contained and directly assertive modes of coping
with problems to passive, infantile, "helpless," demanding modes. The
demandingness will be particularly prominent when the regression is primarily oral in nature. Passive demandingness stands in contrast to the
defensive behavior just discussed in the paragraphs on reaction formations
against dependent needs. It is no psychological contradiction to say that
both the warding off and the expression of the same needs and impulses may
be used for defensive purposes.

A slight tendency in the demanding direction during the testing may
indicate some freedom to relax and some healthy acceptance of dependent
and inadequate feelings. Some patients, however, unceasingly emphasize
their helplessness. They cannot tolerate anxiety and delays in getting
gratification of their need for support. They desperately avoid difficult
situations and explicitly demand reassurance, praise, comfort and help.
Loud cease-and-desist pleas may be made, the patient declaring himself
incapable of continuing or unwilling to continue with a particular test or

any of the tests. Passive demanding women are nowhere more draining as a rule than during the Arithmetic subtest of the Wechsler-Bellevue Scale. The passive demandingness may also be expressed in symptom flare-ups of the sort that interrupt testing, such as dizziness, headaches, pains or tearful depression. In the Rorschach test, the patient may also sullenly refuse to apply himself, that is, to "give out," and he may try to get by on minimal response, both spontaneously and in inquiry.

*j. Counterphobic defense.* Although not included in standard lists of defense mechanisms, counterphobic behavior is generally spoken of as a defense. It would be more correct, however, to speak of it as a behavior pattern and orientation with a prominent and complex defensive aspect. Defensively, counterphobic behavior can be shown to involve at least projection (of inner, threatening impulses), denial (denial in deed of the projected threat), and reaction formation (against impulses to regress to a weak, helpless, dependent position). But more generally and simply, counterphobic defense refers to the characteristic of attacking or daring in situations where one is most afraid. The rationale of this behavior seems to be that the best defense is an offense. One combats a fear of crowds by becoming a leader; one combats a fear of physical injury by climbing mountains, fighting wars or starting brawls; etc.

In the test situation, exaggerated counterphobic defense may take the following forms: (a) exaggerated criticality and querulousness; (b) scornful amusement in the face of the supposedly weird, frightening or otherwise distressing test stimuli and response content; (c) unyielding determination to persist at problem-solving or productive attempts despite all discouraging difficulty encountered and encouragement by the tester to give up. Obviously, the dogged aspect of the behavior described under (b) and (c) can be a big help in taking tests, as in adjusting to daily life, so long as it does not become inflexible or autistic.

*k. Masochistic operations.* The defensive aspect of masochistic operations includes maintaining control over the situation and relationship, preventing the development of feelings of need, and masking both the expression of considerable hostility toward the tester and the projection of considerable hostility onto the tester. The hostile and paranoid implications, as well as the adaptive aspects, of moral masochism have been described recently by Brenman [*18*].

In the test situation, the masochistic patient may fall back on frequent self-criticism, proclaiming himself an unimaginative moron and apologizing for not knowing the answers, for experiencing difficulty in producing responses, and in a way even for being alive. In addition to persistently disparaging himself and his responses, he may rebuff all reassurance, obviously inviting the disappointment and displeasure of the tester and being satisfied with nothing else and nothing less. He may put on great shows of anguish which ultimately take the form of oblique accusations that the tester is a sadist; thus, he may characterize *all* the stimuli as horrible, warn that they will stimulate nightmares, and insist that the tests only make him feel worse. Through these oblique accusations and attacks, the patient appears to be trying to provoke the tester and thereby to "bring out" his sadism. The masochistic patient provocatively defines this entire situation as one of torture and disappointment.

In somewhat more adaptive form, the masochistically-oriented patient may persistently make fun of himself and his responses. At his most adaptive, he will be funny but will not overdo it. When he is in a poorly integrated state, his joking will not be funny; it may become relentless, manneristic, and even pathetic.

It is not a pathological masochistic maneuver when a patient acknowledges anxiety about the tests, some aversion to them, or some dissatisfaction with some responses. As a rule, this should be considered appropriately free expression of feeling. After all, it is more or less unpleasant and painful for psychiatric patients to take the tests; also, not all of their responses are adequate, imaginative or otherwise "good." It is when the patient's implicit emphasis falls heavily on mutual torture and disappointment or on persistent self-abuse, humorous or otherwise, that the pathological sado-masochistic component may be said to be present.

*l. Ingratiating maneuvers.* The defensive aspects of ingratiating maneuvers stand in superficial opposition to those of the sado-masochistic operations just described. The ingratiating patient tries to sell himself to the tester on a personal basis, hoping thereby to pull attention away from what might be "coming out" in the test responses proper. His general strategy is to deny and obscure his resentment of the testing and tester, his negativism, suspiciousness, withdrawal or unpleasantness; it is also part of his strategy to present himself as charming, witty, super-conscientious or however else it seems to him he will make a "good" impression on the tester. Implicit hostility may, however, usually be discerned in these instances, particularly in the form of mockery. Up to a point, of course, ingratiation may be a useful component of a cooperative test attitude.

The form of expression of the exaggerated ingratiating maneuvers will depend on the general personality context from which these maneuvers emerge. The following discussion therefore overlaps with discussions elsewhere of reaction formation, passivity, rebelliousness, etc.

In a setting that includes prominent psychopathic tendencies, great emphasis may be put on being Sincere, Earnest and Industrious; yet, response output will tend to be limited to evasions and to the sheerest banalities trimmed with fabulations. In this same context, the ingratiation may also take the form of deference exaggerated to the point of burlesque. For example, upon being asked to read aloud the last two arithmetic problems on the Arithmetic subtest in the Weschler-Bellevue Scale, this patient may read the numbers of the problems, "Number 9" and "Number 10," and may even go so far as to read them "Problem number Roman numeral nine" and "Problem number Roman numeral ten." During the Rorschach test inquiry, the same type of patient may pick up clues as to what the tester is interested in and then mercilessly "spontaneously help out"; for example, he may say of each new response, "It's blue (or red, yellow, black, etc.) but that had nothing to do with it." This burlesquing patient will be the one who in daily life will always provoke censure and rejection and will always feel unfairly treated in view of his having been "trying so hard."

Where reaction formations against hostility are central, the ingratiation may be heavily colored by strivings toward impeccable conscientiousness, helpfulness and good manners.

In a strongly passive receptive context, the ingratiation may take the form of superficially trying to be pleasantly obliging. Upon finding few dependent gratifications as the testing proceeds and no cessation of demands, this kind of patient often becomes increasingly petulant, demanding and negativistic. The defensive aspect of this maneuver begins to fail. In these cases, the tester's words of praise, encouragement and reassurance are at best only briefly effective and tend to become even less effective as time and demands go on.

On the part of the promiscuous patient who relies on sexual currency to establish and maintain relationships, we may observe ingratiating, though again implicitly hostile, erotization of the test situation. When the tester and patient are of opposite sexes, the patient may resort to various means of flirtation. The patient may be flattering, cute, coy or suave. Women patients of this sort often tend to expose themselves physically in the way they dress, sit or change positions. Homosexual men not infrequently dress in a way that leaves them looking partly undressed—a lot of chest may show because their shirts are too open or a lot of leg may show because their trouser legs are pulled too high when they sit.

*m. Rebellious operations.* What is meant here is a relatively explicit and sustained rebellion, since some degree of rebellion appears to be implied in many of the defensive operations thus far discussed. Rebellious maneuvers more or less fall under the heading of the *resistance definition* of the testing situation described by Schachtel. The common denominator of these maneuvers is a provocative, negativistic approach to others, usually with an underlying strong authoritarian orientation and a desperate need to defend against inner desires to seek out and submit to powerful authority.

Rebellion is defensive in its warding off desires to surrender entirely to the much needed but feared powerful parental figures.

The rebellious patient may talk too fast when the recommendation is to talk slowly. He may stubbornly refuse to tackle some test problems or answer some test questions. He may vigorously dispute some questions, such as the meaningfulness of "Why should we keep away from bad company?" He may be persistently facetious and mocking, belittling the tests, poking fun at the test questions and the tester, telling ribald jokes in the TAT. This patient may give sloppy responses, as by haphazardly fitting together the Object Assembly items. He may respond in a minimal way, as by superficially complying with the TAT instructions, making up stories that include all the specified essential elements, and yet somehow not telling stories at all. Similarly, he may give one response to each Rorschach card and not really try to form other impressions no matter how persistently the tester "keeps after him." He may deliberately avoid any sign of initiative and may require constant prodding. He may be irritable, arrogant and sarcastic. He will be difficult to test.

Up to a point, a capacity for rebelliousness may make a positive contribution. It may foster reasonable and adaptive self-assertion during the testing, as in deciding when to give up each Rorschach card and what kinds of stories to tell in the TAT.

We have considered thirteen defensive modes of response to the test situation and test relationship. These thirteen modes are not systematically coordinated, they do not exhaust the range of possibilities, they are not mutually exclusive, and they more or less overlap each other. Again, as in the consideration of the tester's mode of defining the test relationship, it is best to think of these defensive modes as different facets of each patient's personality. In any individual case, most of these modes may be consistently of negligible significance while one or two may be consistently very prominent. Sometimes a number of these defensive modes are prominent, one or another coming to the fore and fading out in accordance with the vicissitudes of the testing as a whole. Ingratiation may, for example, soon give way to projection of hostility, which in turn may be replaced by a mixture of rebellious and masochistic operations. The choice, extremeness and interplay of defensive modes are data of primary significance in interpreting the test material fully. The analysis of defensive modes in the test relationship should, of course, be integrated with the analysis of the defensive modes in the test responses proper. Insofar as they are separable, these two sets of data—the test responses proper and the patient's test attitudes and behavior—confirm, amend and amplify each other. In the end, the tester who achieves an integration of these two sets of data will be closer to the possibility of describing a living person in his test report and further away from playing with jargon and disembodied abstractions. He will also more fully understand the coming about of the diagnostic test responses.

## C. IMPLICATIONS FOR INTERPRETATION

The preceding section on the patient's defensive test behavior concludes this direct analysis of the dynamics of the test situation and test relationship. Thus far we have surveyed professional, situational and personal aspects of the psychology of the tester, and situational and personal aspects of the psychology of the psychiatric patient being tested. It remains for us to consider what the entire foregoing discussion implies for the interpretation of test results.

The implications of the foregoing discussions branch off in three directions. (1) *Distortion of the test responses.* By "distortion" is meant emphases in the patient's test responses and test behavior which do not correspond to his usual mode of responding, but which result from the unique dynamics of the test situation and of the interpersonal relationship established between the specific tester and specific patient. In short, the question is whether and how the test situation may make the test results misleading. (2) *Distortion of the test interpretations.* Here the question is whether and how the test situation may mislead or bias the tester. (3) *Enrichment of interpretation.* Through integrating observations of the test relationship into the total analysis of results, the interpretations may be enriched. The question here is how an understanding of the test situation may make the patient more comprehensible. Actually, these three sets of implications have already been touched on repeatedly in this chapter. The task remaining is therefore largely one of summary and definition of problems.

## 1. Distortion of Test Responses

The following proposition is fully in accord with the basic assumptions of projective testing: those major components of the patient's personality that go into his definition of the test relationship will, in all likelihood, also express themselves in the formal and content aspects of his test responses proper. Interpretation of test results would be considerably more reliable, however, if we could assume that it is only the patient who defines the relationship. This is a common enough assumption. Even Schachtel, who analyzes with great sensitivity and thoughtfulness the patient's definition of the Rorschach situation, assumes that ordinarily the tester's personality plays a negligible part in shaping the test records. According to Schachtel, for example, the patient with an authoritarian orientation will simply invest the neutral tester with authoritarian values, and, having thus established a familiar structure in the test situation, will "know" how to act and respond from then on.

Yet there are many patients, perhaps particularly those encountered in a psychiatric hospital setting, with whom the tester must actively enter into some type of immediate social give-and-take. The tester must do this in order to carry out the testing without major disruptions. The more this active role is called for, the more reason there is to question the assumption that the tester's personality and *his* definition of the test relationship are relatively unimportant. While it is true that the patient brings certain readinesses for response into the test situation, it is also true that the tester, if he is at all actively engaging the patient (and he usually is), stimulates certain of these readinesses and blocks others. To a significant extent, the relationship is actually *mutually* defined. This is certainly true in psychotherapy. From this point of view it may be seen that Schachtel approached this problem like an old-fashioned psychoanalyst. His conception of the test situation is modeled on the original—but now greatly modified—conception of the classical psychoanalytic situation. He concerned himself only with pseudo-relationships, that is, relationships defined solely by the patient and with no real support in the tester's behavior. But the growing psychoanalytic literature on countertransference problems in the psychoanalytic relationship clearly corrects the classical picture of the analyst as simply a *tabula rasa* on which the patient writes his own pathology.

It therefore seems more realistic to say that the patient responds to the definition of the test situation that is worked out jointly by himself and the tester. Depending upon the tester's own personality and emotional state, his reaction to the patient, his usual method of administering tests, his talents and sensitivities and articulateness, and other trends and circumstances, the tester will contribute more or less to this definition. He will never be a nonentity in the situation. The patient may exaggerate and overreact to what he sees, but he sees a real person and not, as Schachtel implies, a shadowy authoritarian figure. There are, for example, authoritarian testers. There are competitive testers. Previously, in Section A-3, we considered a variety of "types" of testers. The tester's authoritarian, competitive or other tendencies may be for the most part latent so long as the patient is submissively and quietly cooperative, but they may show themselves prominently, even if obliquely, once real interaction is required. It is with these real as well as fantasied or pseudo-interactions that we have been concerned. The distinction between real interactions and pseudo-interactions is important for interpretation since we must disentangle the patient's *spontaneous* contribution to the definition of his relationships from the *reactive* elements in his definition of his relationship to the specific tester. But both aspects of the patient's behavior—spontaneous and reactive—will be instructive, especially if the tester is aware of those aspects of himself that tend to become prominent in his relationships with patients.

In the preceding sections of this chapter we have been concerned with the effects these interactions have on the test situation's total atmosphere and on the varieties of ways patients behave in it. We have considered various effects the situation may have on the quantitative and qualitative aspects of productivity, on persistence, on compliance with test instructions, on responses to inquiry, and on manner of delivery and treatment of responses. These effects will not be restated here.

Little has been said, however, about the effects on the Rorschach test record proper. For example, will anxiety *stimulated by the test situation itself* increase the patient's use of the shading in the Rorschach inkblots? Will inhibition *induced by the test relationship* increase the *Form per cent?* Here the reader must be disappointed, for at the present time there is little to say in answer to such questions. Although there is some evidence that different testers tend to get different average distributions of Rorschach scores from the cases they test [*58, 97, 126*], these remain obscure matters. We lack criteria and analytic techniques by which to distinguish what the patient is ready to express and conceal in any event from what he expresses and conceals specifically in response to the particular type of relationship that has crystallized between himself and the tester. All we are sure of is that we should establish and maintain "good rapport," in hopes of getting a maximally representative test protocol from the patient. But this consideration only leads right back to our problem: the ways of establishing and maintaining good rapport vary according to the patient and the tester. We still must analyze not simply the "goodness" of rapport, but the *kind* of rapport, that is, the interpersonal assumptions on which rapport was established or not established.

Experimental clinical psychology provides only a little help. It has been experimentally demonstrated, for example, that imposing frustration in conjunction with the administration of the Thematic Apperception test tends on the average to increase the number of themes of aggression and punishment [*24*]. The results of experiments of this sort have, however, been analyzed in terms of group averages and not in terms of meaningful individual variation, that is, the effect of the frustration on particular types of personality has been disregarded. Also the frustration has not been an intrinsic and subtle part of the test situation and test relationship.

Systematic experimental investigation of this problem is difficult. Repetition of tests under altered experimental conditions, such as altered tester's attitudes, would yield ambiguous or inconsistent results [*97*]. For one thing, the internal conditions in the patient would no longer be the same: (a) the patient would be familiar with the test; (b) if an alternate form of the test were used, the patient would be familiar with the type of test; (c) he would remember some of his previous responses; (d) he would know the tester; (e) if a new tester were used each time, it would be arbitrary to maintain that all the testers were "equivalent" in all aspects except their major attitudes; (f) it is not so easy to define precisely the major attitudes of each individual tester.

Suppose, however, tests were not repeated and alternate forms were not used. Suppose instead a group of patients with similar personality configurations was divided into "equivalent" subgroups, each one to be subjected to different attitudes on the part of the same tester. The results would probably be more instructive though still ambiguous: (a) the "equivalence" of patients would be no more than gross at best; (b) the convincingness of artificially adopted attitudes in the same tester would certainly be questionable; (c) the tester's private definition and private reaction to each of his various psychodrama-like roles would intrude into the test atmosphere; the "rest" of the tester could not remain constant; it would be a hotbed of unknown variables. An additional difficulty is that a prohibitively large number of patients would have to be screened in order to set up these "equivalent" subgroups.

Ingenious and prolonged research in this area is obviously called for.* We are in essentially uncharted territory. From what has been said so far in this chapter, however, there is good reason to think that tests may show up the patient at his "worst," that is, at his most anxious, defensive and regressed. After all, we ordinarily do function with external props and cues, with some measure of control, with some safeguards of secrecy and with some choice of relationships. Taking tests is being severely put to the test. It is, however, particularly the projective tests that are so taxing, and most of all the Rorschach test. The Rorschach test introduces the greatest loss of reality support, or, as Baer has put it, "loss of objects." In contrast, the Thematic Apperception test at least shows relatively familiar situations, and the stories are subject to conscious and unconscious manipulation on some basis that satisfies the patient to some degree as to their safety or appropriateness. It follows that test interpretation must be incomplete unless we use additional tests, tests which are less "projective" than the Rorschach. We need material that will help us approximate both the "best" functioning of the patient and his functioning under "average" or "usual" conditions.

For this reason the TAT, which comes closer to real-life situations and fantasies than the Rorschach test, and which is better structured at the same time as it remains quite personal, is valuable in a test battery. By putting the patient in a situation more like those he encounters in daily life,

* See in this regard the recent work of Sanders and Cleveland [126].

and in which he has more or less well established modes of response, the TAT helps us get a balanced picture of the patient's adaptive and defensive assets and strengths. These assets and strengths may well be minimized or obscured by the Rorschach test.

For the same reason a test like the Wechsler-Bellevue Scale is valuable in a test battery. The items of this test are relatively objective, impersonal and structured. It is a "test" of the sort one would feel familiar with from school experience. And, as Rapaport has shown, it is a test that taps a variety of intellectual functions that are usually relatively remote from internal conflict and therefore relatively stable—even though they do vary in vulnerability to emotional stress [110]. Excepting anxiety over intellectual success or failure, the prominent and explicit intrusion into the intelligence test situation of personal preoccupations and interpersonal problems strongly suggests significant chronic ego weakness or overwhelming of the ego by the patient's conflicts.

In the testing of borderline psychotic patients, for example, it is not unusual to obtain perfectly orderly intelligence test results, TAT stories that are pathologically perverse, morbid and eerie in content but logical, well organized and verbally faultless in form, and a Rorschach test replete with Confabulations, Peculiar verbalizations, arbitrary forms, pure C and the like. Schematically, one may say that the Wechsler-Bellevue Scale brings out such a patient's non-psychotic side—his more or less preserved capacity for realistic, objective thought and action, that the Rorschach test brings out his psychotic side—the underlying chaos and virulent autistic potential, and that the TAT brings out the in-between or borderline forms of autistic-realistic thought and action that characterize the patient's spontaneous, personal but socially oriented responses in daily life. Thus, the three tests together show us the patient's range, from "best" through "usual" or "average" to "worst," with a clarity and forcefulness that no one test alone could achieve.

This discussion of distortion of test responses has moved away from the test situation and relationship to the nature of the tests used. But there is actually no sharp line between the test and the situation that surrounds it; each defines the other. If the Rorschach test, with which we are particularly concerned, creates difficult response problems for the patient and tends in many ways to show him at his least adaptive, this will have repercussions in his test behavior. And, if the test situation is responded to with intense, disruptive affect and anxiety, this may well have repercussions on the test responses proper. In both ways, therefore, the Rorschach test results may be distorted.

But the distortion is likely to be one of degree rather than kind. During the testing, the patient may be more hostile, inhibited, suspicious, self-concealing, self-absorbed or meticulous than usual. Simultaneously, his *Form level* may be unrepresentatively low, his *Form per cent* unrepresentatively high, his use of color unrepresentatively primitive. But even if exaggerated, these behaviors and scores will reflect the direction his preferred or uncontrollable reaction tendencies take. The tester must bear in mind that the test results reflect the typical *direction* of response more reliably than the typical *intensity* of response, that they accurately reflect *what* the patient tries to be or seem and *how* he tries to accomplish this, and also *what* the patient has trouble being or seeming and *how* he fails at this. Except in extremely sick cases, Rorschach results alone ordinarily do not pinpoint *how much* the patient usually succeeds or fails in what he does try. Usually, the test results only give us a gross—though still useful—estimate of the patient's range. Further research into the positive, healthy aspects of test responses undoubtedly will make it possible to narrow this estimate. But the estimate can never be very precise because the patient's successes and failures of defense and adaptation in daily life do not depend solely on his personality and current adjustment status; they depend just as much on what is independently going on in his daily life, on how others who appear on the scene react to him, on sociological forces influencing his social, occupational and familial stability, etc. Circumstances may help him rise to new heights of health or they may force him down to the depths of incapacity and misery. Good and poor therapy may also have such effects.

In any event, the tester should be cognizant of the relative unreliability that pervades quantitative estimates based on projective test results. Regarding the Rorschach test and the Rorschach situation particularly, he should carefully avoid the constant risk of overestimating sickness and underestimating health, and should be more emphatic in specifying the typical direction of response than in specifying the typical degree or intensity of response. Future research may increase our sensitivity to indications of strength in severely maladjusted Rorschach records.

## 2. *Distortion of Test Interpretation*

As a result of the various stresses and strains under which he functions, the tester may easily lose distance from the test report. He may make it serve his personal needs instead of the patient's best interests. Honest self-confrontation concerning his test reports will easily convince any tester that this is so. There is already a little experimental evidence for this point [66]. The stresses and strains that tend to distort interpretation stem from three sources: (a) the tester's professional problems; (b) his problems in relating to patients; (c) his own interests, aptitudes and sensitivities. A broad treatment of these problems has been given in Section A of this chapter. What follows is only a brief summary that centers on the writing of the test report.

   *a. The tester's professional problems.* The tester may compete excessively with his psychiatric colleagues or may retreat from competition with them. If he competes, his competition often takes the form of trying to outdo the psychiatrist in depth, breadth, and all-around fanciness of interpretation. Very often this form of competition boils down to a demonstration that either the tester remembers more of Fenichel's protean psychoanalytic text than the psychiatrist does or has a more vivid imagination (or literary style), or both.

   In contrast, the tester who flees from competition with his psychiatric colleagues may do this by hiding behind test jargon and score recitations, at the same time seeming oracular and super-scientific. Or he may retreat into hedging, either through presenting too many interpretations or through presenting too few interpretations to which he commits himself, or both. Then again, he may avoid competition, and may also protect his job, by ingratiating the psychiatrists. The ingratiation may take the form of trying to anticipate the psychiatrists's impression of the patient. In various measures this tester will base his anticipation on the patient's test behavior, whatever clinical information about the patient is available, whatever remarks about the patient the psychiatrist has made, and what he knows about the psychiatrist's general approach to psychiatric problems and particular approaches to "types" of patients. The tester may then slant his interpretations accordingly. *It is easy to engage in this opportunistic slanting without being aware at the time that one is so doing.* In this respect, slanting reports is not so much an ethical problem as it is a problem of human fallibility in observing, understanding and reporting behavior. When slanting occurs frequently, grossly, and possibly even consciously, an ethical problem does, of course, exist.

   *b. Problems in relating to the patient.* A variety of these problems have been described previously. Passing reference has been made to the tester's countertransference reactions to the patient. These may play a considerable part in his formulation of test findings. Hovering images of "good" and "bad" mothers, fathers, brothers, sisters, children, and externalized aspects of himself may all powerfully influence the tester's interpretations of the test results. Of course, not all of the tester's reactions to the patient are necessarily countertransference reactions. Some may be quite appropriate and realistic on a social level; but even these are inappropriate as hidden influences on interpretation. If used in interpretation at all, the tester's emotional reactions should be used explicitly, and then only as guides to understanding the kinds of relationships the patient characteristically tries to set up. All inferences derived from the tester's reactions to the patient should be well supported by test scores and test content before being used. Otherwise the tester autistically implies that his emotional reactions are infallible diagnostic indicators.

The general feeling tone of the test relationship is a powerful factor to contend with during the drafting of a report. If the tester finds the test relationship predominantly hostile and frustrating, he will be tempted to write a vindictive test report, emphasizing particularly the "bad" implications of the record—the patient's narcissism, demandingness, suspiciousness, negativism and the like, and minimizing or ignoring indications of the patient's potential or actual inner resources and adaptiveness. Out of professional insecurity or out of an underlying vindictive orientation to patients, the tester may do the same sort of thing with the idea of "exposing" the patient.

If the tester'~ reaction formations against hostility are rigid, he may, under the same conditions as those just described, or under any conditions, write "kindly" reports. This tester will consistently emphasize the patient's "valiant" efforts to persevere in the face of stress, the basic will and need of the patient to "reach out to others" and "grow." He may ignore not only conspicuous evidences of hostility and self-destructiveness, but may, out of "kindness," minimize diagnostically malignant findings. This benevolent soul may feel it harsh or not truly empathic to call someone schizophrenic or paranoid unless absolutely forced to by overwhelming diagnostic data. He may find all sorts of "nice" reasons to explain away clear-cut diagnostic findings of this probably malignant sort.

A tester may do all of the "nice" things just described simply because he likes a particular patient and wants to do that patient a favor, although it should not be overlooked that at the same time he thereby justifies or rationalizes his own positive response to the patient. While the liking may be appropriate, the too favorable test report is, of course, no favor at all to the patient. Also, as a result of narcissistic identification with "colorful," "talented," "sweet," or otherwise "appealing" patients, the tester may grossly underestimate or underplay pathology.

These have been only a few possible types of distorting influence the test relationship may have on the tester's interpretation of results. A number of other such influences have been anticipated throughout the discussion of the dynamics of testing in Section A of this chapter. The important thing is not to catalog these phenomena exhaustively but to alert the tester to the important, though usually neglected, personal problems inherent in his work.

*c. The tester's interests, aptitudes, and sensitivities.* These also may influence interpretation and formulation. Each tester has his personal and theoretical conflicts, preoccupations, preferences and securities. As an expression of these, he may overemphasize certain types of findings and may be insensitive to or neglectful of others. His selective emphasis may fall on hostility, passivity, anxiety, intellectual assets, masculinity-femininity, and the like. Testers may too readily find their own conscious and/or unconscious problems in the test results of their patients. In this respect, test analysis has its own "projective" aspect.

Then again, the tester's selective emphasis may fall on a certain test that interests him most or with which he feels most secure. It is easy to feel that a certain test reveals the essentials of "all that really matters," and that other tests merely provide confirmation, minor additions or wasteful ambiguity. It is especially easy to feel this bias if one has intensive training and experience with that test, if one has a "natural feel" for it, or if one has a special stake in its development. Of course, so long as it remains within bounds, this preference for one test has its justification in the fact that sensitive handling of any technique is increased by training, experience, "natural feel" and personal investment in its development. Not only that, but this sort of bias may foster the clarification of important general theoretical issues by leading to intensive consideration of rationale and principles of interpretation and to active research and communication of results. Even so, this championing of one technique has its narrow, scientifically arbitrary aspect; it tends to confuse what the test and tester are especially sensitive to with what is important in the theory of personality.

If the tester's grasp of theory is insecure or weak, he may mechanically use a different set of concepts in writing up the results of each test in his battery. As a result, he may even write a test report full of implicit internal contradictions. The fact is that the traits and dynamics emphasized by Klopfer discussing the Rorschach test [86], Deri discussing the Szondi test [26], Murray discussing the TAT [102] and Rapaport discussing the Wechsler-Bellevue Scale [117], even though they overlap, do not stem from identical assumptions about personality and psychopathology. The eclectic tester is inevitably test-centered in his reports rather than patient-centered. The sections of his test-centered reports will, like freight cars, each loaded with a different type of goods and each headed for a different ultimate destination, be hitched together to make up a cumbersome train of ideas and dispatched on their creaky journey together.

The tester's potential and actual development as a human being, as a scientific psychologist and as a professional helper, all color his conception of the patients he examines and the instruments he uses.

Thus, the tester's professional problems, his problems in relating to patients, and his interests, aptitudes and sensitivities may all powerfully distort his interpretation of test results. In some respects, as we have seen, these problems and trends may also sharpen interpretation, but they simultaneously tend to bias it. Like the paranoid patient whose hyper-alertness always finds at least a small reality peg on which to hang his paranoid idea, the tester's individually conditioned hyperalertness may lead to interpretations which seem correct if viewed narrowly but which are obviously overweighted, one-dimensional or nonspecific if viewed broadly.

## 3. Enrichment of Interpretation

One major implication of this entire chapter has been that no sharp line exists between the test record proper and the patient's part in the real and fantasied interpersonal relationship in the testing situation. It follows that the richest interpretation of results will be based on the patient's total behavior in the test situation, that is, his behavior from the time he first enters the tester's office until the time he leaves there upon completion of the last test. It is not, however, a matter of interpreting responses *and* behavior. It is a matter of interpreting test responses in the light of be-havior, and interpreting behavior in the light of test responses. As will be discussed more fully in Chapter 5, the implications of these two types of material are in some instances congruent, in some instances superficially antithetical but fundamentally expressive of the opposite sides of ambivalence, and in some instances just different and supplementary.

Consider the following five cases:

| Case | Test Behavior | Use of Color in Rorschach |
|---|---|---|
| 1. | Egocentric, demanding | Emphasizes FC |
| 2. | Egocentric, demanding | Emphasizes pure C |
| 3. | Egocentric, demanding | Emphasizes CF |
| 4. | Compliant, submissive | Emphasizes CF |
| 5. | Inhibited, stiff | Emphasizes CF |

Cases 1, 2 and 3 behave similarly, but each uses color differently. Cases 3, 4 and 5 behave differently, but each uses color similarly. In each of these instances, the interpretation should embrace and, where necessary and possible, reconcile the implications of these two types of material. Although it is an oversimplification to draw conclusions from so little information, the following conceivable interpretations are presented to illustrate the present point.

*Case 1:* Relationships tend to be unreliably adaptive, being funda-mentally passive and clinging, with adaptiveness breaking down when de-mands are made on him. (This pattern is often encountered in settings of acute conflict between rebellious and submissive tendencies.)

*Case 2:* Tends to be fundamentally withdrawn and regressed to "in-fantile," fluid, unmodulated modes of response in relationships. (This pattern is often encountered in borderline or full schizophrenics.)

*Case 3:* Relationships tend to be characterized by childlike over-responsiveness, emotional lability and egocentricity; only weak adaptive efforts are made. (This pattern is very frequently encountered in child-like, hysterical women.)

*Case 4:* Relationships tend to be characterized by superficial ingratiation of "powerful" figures, but are basically narcissistic. (This pattern is often encountered in cases with psychopathic tendencies.)

*Case 5:* Relationships tend to be characterized by suppressed emotional lability, noteworthy resulting tenseness, and possibly a special readiness to react somatically to stress. (This pattern is frequently encountered in poorly integrated or decompensating compulsive personalities.)

Similar interpretive exercises could be carried out to interrelate high or low $F\%$, high or low $M$, or high or low emphasis on shading on the one hand, and various types of behavior expressing particular definitions of the test relationship on the other.

Observations of test behavior should never be construed so as to negate certain general implications of the test responses proper and *vice versa.* It is tempting, once interpretation of behavior is woven into the interpretive process, to throw out consciously or to neglect unconsciously certain test findings that seem to contradict striking aspects of test behavior. It is similarly tempting to disregard certain aspects of test behavior that do not appear to fit the test findings proper. Continuing with the example of interpreting the patient's use of color: we may be taken in by the "sincerity" of a psychopath, and disregard his narcissistic use of color; we may be overwhelmed by the tearful, suspicious, demanding behavior of a depressed, aging woman, and disregard evidences of underlying preserved adaptiveness; we may be blinded (perhaps through our own rage) by the provocativeness and negativism of a rebellious patient, and minimize the tempering dependent and compliant implications of numerous $FC$ responses; or in any of these three instances we may attend too much to the use of color and neglect the test behavior. The question is never which type of material is more reliable or deeper in implication. The question is always to what extent does one type of material confirm the other, bring out the opposite, possibly latent side of ambivalence, or shed altogether new light on the intricacies of the patient's relationships and emotional experiences.

There are those who would object that this total-situation approach violates the objectivity of test interpretation. Only in the narrow and false sense in which objectivity has usually been conceived is this true. The ideal of objectivity requires that we recognize as much as possible what is going on in the situation we are studying. It requires in particular that we remember the tester and his patient are both human and alive and therefore inevitably interacting in the test situation. True, the further we move away from mechanized interpretation or comparison of formal scores and averages, the more subjective variables we may introduce into the interpretive process. The personality and personal limitations of the tester may be brought into the thick of the interpretive problem. But while we thereby increase the likelihood of personalized interpretation and variation among testers, we are at the same time in a position to enrich our understanding and our test reports significantly. The more data we use, after all, the greater the textural richness and specificity of our analyses— and in the long run the more accurate we become.

We do risk personalizing our interpretations if we strive after increased richness and accuracy in our reports. Depending upon the congeniality of our professional relationships, upon our temperaments, stability, training, and talents, and upon the particular material we are dealing with, it may be wise or foolish to attempt analysis and synthesis of the dynamics of the total situation. But all this views the problem solely from the *practical* side, which is not our only concern here.

*Theoretically,* it seems that the proponents of the narrow definition of "objectivity," the proponents of conservative, score-bound interpretation, misconstrue the situation. From what has been said throughout this chapter, it follows that to comprehend fully the meaning of various scores or score patterns we must simultaneously comprehend the dynamics of the total situation, including the interpersonal relationship. Everyone would agree that one *FC*, for example, does not necessarily mean the same thing as the next; and that when twenty *FC* are present in one record, they cannot be thought of as individually no different in psychological significance from the solitary *FC* given in the next record. To be consistent, the same principle that the "objective" interpreters emphasize to cope with this problem, namely, interpretation of the record as a whole, must be extended to include interpretation of the situation as a whole. *The more material relevant to the formation and delivery of responses we obtain, the more we comprehend the response and—through the response—the test, the patient, and personality and psychopathology in general.*

# 3. The Response Process

PEOPLE CARRY WITHIN THEMSELVES A NETWORK of self-expressive imagery culled from the surrounding world and from social and bodily experience. In psychoanalysis, this imagery has traditionally been treated as a problem of symbol-formation and of substitute-formation by condensation and displacement. For a long time the approach to these images as symbols and substitute-formations involved the assumption that what was being represented was some primitive, infantile, id impulse alone. In recent years, particularly with the advent of psychoanalytic ego psychology, it has been re-discovered that ego strivings also have their imaginal language. This imagery, as it occurs in dreams, for example, has been found to express such ego phenomena as defenses, values and anticipations.* In fact, it seems necessary and profitable to assume that id, ego, superego and reality pressures are simultaneously expressed in dream imagery. The dream image of a *devil*, for example, would potentially have id implications concerning hostile impulses, superego implications concerning sin and punishment, ego implications concerning social and religious values, and reality implications concerning problems of current interpersonal relationships. Such multiple determinations may be assumed to underlie all personally important images.

At the same time, in the course of development and in the interest of general reality adaptation, people also accumulate many impersonal images and neutralize many once highly charged ones [112]. While normally the impersonal and neutralized images far outnumber the personal, conflict-laden images, they will not be given proportionate attention in what follows. This is because the former type of image is static and psychologically opaque and therefore teaches us less about hitherto neglected aspects of the Rorschach response process.

As a rule, the charged, personal, multiply determined imagery is kept in a carefully locked book which is opened up only in the privacy of fantasy and dream life. In more or less controlled, subtle forms, however, these images are expressed in our style of verbalization, wit, play of fancy in social interchange, and in our conceptions of and responses to social, political and esthetic objects and events. Insofar as personal imagery comes to expression in these ways, it tips others off as to what is contained

* See, for example, Erikson's study of Nazi imagery [34].

74

between our covers. We may not, however, be consciously aware of these cues we constantly give as well as respond to. In this regard, psychoanalytic interpretation only makes conscious and explicit what ordinarily remains (together with expressive movement and its corollaries) the implicit communication that goes on outside conscious awareness.

It will be a major thesis of the following presentation that the Rorschach test often briefly unlocks the book of our private imagery, and renders the images in it amenable to partial psychoanalytic interpretation.* We shall be concerned with the process whereby this becomes possible and with the bearing this thesis and its development have on interpretation of Rorschach test records.

## A. The Test Instructions

To begin at the beginning we must consider the test instructions. In the preceding chapter, in considering the situational and interpersonal forces in the test situation, we more than once touched on the impact these forces have on the response process. In fact, the preceding chapter made it plain that the "beginning" long antedates the test instructions; it more or less coincides with the patient's first psychiatric contact. But for a close-up study of the response process, the beginning will be considered the time of the test instructions.

In the instructions, the patient is told by the tester that he will be taking a personality test, one that will help his doctor—and the staff—understand better what he is like personally and what his problems are.† There is no passing or failing this test, he is reassured; the ultimate purpose of the testing is to help us arrive at the best possible recommendations for him. With no further orientation, with nothing at all said about the specific nature of the test stimuli or about how people usually respond to these stimuli, the patient is then confronted with Card I and asked, "What could this be? What might it look like?"

If the patient gives only one response to the first card and indicates that

* Phillips and Smith [105] venture some explicit psychoanalytic formulations of test interpretation (typically in footnotes), but the nonspecific, over-abstract and sometimes seemingly circular aspects of these formulations raise doubts as to their validity or clinical utility. For example, after describing $M$ as being normally related to self-control, to sensitivity to others as individuals, and to freedom for self-expression in conformance with long range goals, they say, "Psychoanalytically, $M$ in a normal context implies that 1) desexualized drives freed from their original instinctual components are at the disposal of the ego, as a consequence of which 2) the individual will show a pattern of behavior marked by sublimation rather than symptom formation and 3) object relations rather than identifications will be maintained." (page 69).

† Actually, since a battery of tests is ordinarily administered, the instructions speak of "a number of tests."

he believes he has complied fully with the test instructions, he is asked, "Is there anything else it might look like?" If he then hastily decides he can respond no more, he is encouraged, "Take your time; maybe another possibility will occur to you." The tester's aim in doing this is to encourage freedom of response as well as to see if the patient can shift from his initial impression and give at least one more response. Once the patient has given a second response, or after one or two minutes, the tester no longer urges the patient to keep working on the card. This requirement of a minimum of two responses or one or two minutes of application to the card also guides the administration of the remainder of the Rorschach cards.

After Card I is given up, the tester explains, "It will be the same with the rest of these cards. On each one, tell me everything you see that might look like something. As soon as you think you are finished, say so and I will take the card back." If the patient was unproductive and hasty in giving up Card I, the tester ordinarily adds at this point, "But please take your time on each card. If you rush it, you will spoil the test." Following this explanation and before going on to Card II, the tester carries out indicated inquiry into the responses to Card I. Inquiry is routinely carried out after each card and not at the end of the test.*

These instructions have manifold implications. Some, such as the relative lack of rules in the situation, have been considered in the previous chapter; others, such as the assumption that the patient has a wish to respond, will be considered later in this chapter. For the present only a few major implications of these instructions need be considered. (1) The instructions indicate that the responses should fit the configurations and properties of the blots. They thereby define the situation as perceptual and "objective." (2) The instructions imply, however, that resemblance or approximation is called for and not necessarily exact correspondence with real objects. They thereby encourage relaxation of self-critical striving for objectivity. (3) Since, in addition, the blots are clearly not pictorial—though some normally and pathologically naive or concrete persons assume they are "pictures"—the instructions also implicitly ask the patient to summon up consciously his images of things and to rely heavily in forming responses on his reorganizations of these images and of the stimulus field. The instructions thereby introduce into the response process a major element of "subjectivity," imagination or fantasy, as well as of memory and concept

---

* For a detailed discussion of the rationale of this style of Rorschach test administration, see Rapaport [118]. The present instructions and their follow-through deviate somewhat from those described by Rapaport, but on the whole his discussion of administration is still relevant. The verbatim Rorschach records presented in Chapters 7, 8, 9, and 10 of this book indicate further details of this style of test administration.

formation.* (4) By emphasizing self-expression rather than achievement —even though emotional factors prevent some patients from grasping this distinction—these instructions reinforce the inward-turning, imaginative orientation stimulated by the non-pictorial stimuli and by the need to search for approximations and resemblances.

Thus, these instructions encourage responsible reality testing and free fantasy to mingle and interact during the formation of each response. They pull the patient out of himself by directing his attention to the ink-blots, but they simultaneously push him back into himself by directing his attention to the images, memories and concepts that make up a large part of his inner life. The instructions stretch awareness both ways at once— toward what is "out there" and toward what is "inside." By encouraging the intensive interplay and intermingling of imagination and perception, the instructions also tend to obscure somewhat the line between subject and object, self and not-self, or image and percept. As a result, the instructions tend to evoke subtle, complex, transitory shifts in the patient's level of psychic functioning. Depending upon many conditions, a number of which will soon be discussed, the level of functioning may range from the developmentally advanced, realistic, differentiated and hierarchically organized to the developmentally primitive, physiognomic, autistic, diffuse and syncretic [150]; or, as Freud conceptualized the difference, from thinking characteristic of the "secondary process" to thinking characteristic of the "primary process" [45]. Secondary process thinking is predicated upon delay of immediate, direct, unmodulated discharge of impulses; it seeks such detours toward gratification as are appropriate to the individual's total prevailing life situation; it is selective and modulating. Also, secondary process thinking is oriented toward reality and logic; it is reflective and forward-looking; it maintains the boundaries between self and not-self. Primary process thinking, in contrast, is indifferent to reality and logic and is organized around the vicissitudes of drives; it is oriented toward immediate, direct, and uncontrolled discharge of impulse; it is fluid, undiscriminating, and unreflective; it ignores relations of time, place, identity and causality. In addition, primary process thinking tends to fuse self and not-self; and it teems with condensations, displacements, physiognomic impressions and magical notions.

It is with the description and rationale of the fluctuating level of psychic functioning during the Rorschach test performance that we shall be particularly concerned in the following discussion. In this realm lie new clues to understanding the psychological processes underlying Rorschach responses specifically, and perhaps even clues to the theory of thinking and of the ego generally.

* For discussion of the memory and concept formation aspects of the response process, see Rapaport [118].

## B. Shifts in the Level of Psychic Functioning

We must at once pause, however, to clarify what is meant by "level of psychic functioning" and by "shifts" in this level; these concepts will recur frequently in what follows. The views to be presented are those put forth in their original form by Freud [45] and subsequently elaborated and extended by Kris [91, 92] and Rapaport [112, 113, 114] particularly. These views can only be briefly and incompletely presented here. Study of the original sources is necessary to do justice to the intricacy of the existing discussions of these matters.

First of all, there are the distinctions already mentioned above between primary and secondary process thinking. Each level of psychic functioning will be characterized by its relative position with respect to the two poles described. At each position or level, both the primary and secondary processes will ordinarily be discernible upon close analysis, but their relative weights will vary. In states of fatigue and intoxication, for example, the relative prominence of primary process thinking will increase, while in states of intense and efficient concentration on an intellectual problem the relative prominence of secondary process thinking will increase [114].

Secondly, to each level of psychic functioning there corresponds a particular configuration of id, ego, and superego relations, that is, of relations between (1) unconscious, infantile, rejected impulses and their derivatives in fantasies, wishes and feelings, all of which constantly seek to become conscious and to be acted upon; (2) defensive ego operations which aim to ward off these eruptive, primitive, id expressions; (3) adaptive ego operations which seek to articulate, regulate, and coordinate a wide variety of inner (id, ego, superego) demands with each other [68, 103] and to integrate these with the opportunities, dangers and limits in the surrounding physical and social environment; adaptive ego operations also seek to manipulate and alter these external opportunities, dangers and limits; and (4) primitively conceived and expressed self-judging, self-disciplining and self-rewarding superego activities. On the primitive psychic levels, unmodulated id and superego forces tend to prevail more than on the advanced levels where the supremacy of the defensive and adaptive ego functions is characteristic.

Beside the relative importance of primary and secondary process thinking on each level of psychic functioning, and beside the unique configuration of id, ego and superego relations—the so-called structural relations—that corresponds to each level of psychic functioning, there also seem to be configurations within the ego specific to each level. On the advanced levels, thought functions (such as concept formation), thought content (such as images), and psychic energy (such as that used in attention) tend to be characterized by "relatively autonomous" [115] or "conflict-free" [70]

modes of operation and expression. On the primitive levels, thought functions, content and energy tend to lose their autonomy; they are invaded
by conflict and affect, and take on major aggressive and libidinal qualities.

How are these changes of level manifest, for example, in the three
instances mentioned above—concept formation, images and attention?
On the lower levels of performance where the primary process dominates
the secondary, *concept formation* tends to be organized around drives
conflicts, fears and the like rather than around relations that exist in
reality among objects and their properties. A group of tools in the Object
Sorting Test of Concept Formation may then be conceptualized as "piercing
and stabbing instruments" or a group of white objects as "they can all be
consumed—by eating or fire." *Images* expressing infantile drives, conflicts,
fears and the like tend to crowd out of consciousness those of relatively integrated, neutral, reality-reflecting character. Card I of the Rorschach test
may then immediately elicit the image of "an evil, hovering bat-woman"
rather than "a bat," "a butterfly," or "a dancer." And *attention* will be disrupted because the neutralized energy required for sustained attention
will be available in very limited quantities at best. On the primitive levels
of psychic functioning, most or all energy normally available for the
advanced, adaptive thought functions is tied up in aggressive and libidinal
urges and conflicts. Thus it is that performance on tests of attention, such
as Digit Span, will ordinarily be poor under primitive-level conditions
[117], and the patient may be unable to give more than one response to
certain Rorschach cards because an aggressively or libidinally charged
image may be stimulated and may so "capture" attention that a shift of
interest to other response possibilities is impossible.

In summary, it may be said that on the advanced levels of psychic
functioning the reality principle and the secondary process prevail over the
pleasure principle and the primary process; delay, indirectness, and modulation of discharge of tension take precedence over immediate, direct,
uncontrolled discharge; logic and reality testing overshadow autistic
thought; and clarity and organization of subjective experience replace
fluidity and diffuseness of experience, loss of the "self," and minimal
reflective and selective capacity.

It must be added that the primitive levels of psychic functioning do
not go out of existence with the attainment of advanced levels [150].
They co-exist with and are always ready to replace the advanced levels.
They frequently co-determine responses with the advanced levels, putting a
personal stamp—possibly a too personal stamp—on would-be impersonal,
objective reactions. Also, it seems that throughout the day and night each
individual's level of psychic functioning varies—sometimes greatly, as in
dreaming, and sometimes slightly, as in fleeting daydreams. It is here
that the concept "shifts of psychic level" becomes relevant.

By "shifts in the level of psychic functioning" is meant changes in the balances just described—in the relative weights of primary and secondary process thinking, in the mutual relations between id, ego, and superego processes, and also in the relations among ego processes. These changes may be subtle and brief, as in ordinary daytime experience, or gross and more or less fixed, as in severe schizophrenic conditions, but they are a constant aspect of psychic life. Whether stimulated by outer duress and temptation or by inner privation and conflict, these shifts reflect the individual's never ceasing and never altogether resolved—though not necessarily always tumultuous—striving for adaptation and gratification. The shifts in the level of psychic functioning are never total shifts but rather vary in scope; even the most regressed schizophrenic, for example, retains capacities and abilities—in motility, perception, verbalization and thought—characteristic of his premorbid level of functioning. The always incomplete nature of these shifts seems to be due in part at least to the autonomy certain ego functions and contents achieve from the conflicts out of which they originated and by which they were once dominated. When the shifts are in the direction of primitive levels of function, they are termed "regressed" or "regressive" because, as we have seen, functioning then becomes more archaic both in a developmental and organizational sense.

There is one type of shift of level of functioning that has been particularly emphasized by Kris—that of "regression in the service of the ego" [*92*]. Taking his cue from Freud, Kris applies this concept particularly to creative processes. His use of this concept will have considerable importance when we analyze the creative aspects of the Rorschach response process. By "regression in the service of the ego" is meant a partial, temporary, "inspiration" seeking shift to a more primitive level of psychic functioning than that typical of the individual's normal waking state. In its relative position to the poles of primary process and secondary process, the normal waking state of consciousness varies inter-individually, and, from one time to the next, intra-individually, but there are gross individual and group norms around which waking states of consciousness cluster. It is from the gross intra-individual normative position that the creative regression is assumed to take place. On the primitive psychic levels reached by this "regression in the service of the ego," thinking and feeling characteristic of the primary process are relatively freely admitted to consciousness. This increased openness of consciousness requires relaxation of the defensive, regulatory and organizing ego attitudes that normally screen unconscious material seeking passage from the unconscious to the preconscious and from the preconscious to the conscious.

This creative regression, when it is truly creative and not predominantly a disguise for psychotic trends or for unsocialized daydreams, remains essentially under the control of the ego. It is primarily or largely an *active* process of taking imaginative liberties and not an altogether *passive* process of being overwhelmed by alien forces. Its active rather than passive nature is demonstrated by the fact that the creative regression is always accompanied or succeeded by critical, reality-oriented and communication-oriented evaluation and modification of the primary process material. The creative process thus involves a more or less oscillating and partial abandonment and re-instatement of higher level controls and critical attitudes.

I am not aware of the concept having been used before in this sense in psychological discussions—although the phenomenon is certainly well known—but "progression in the service of the ego," or, more correctly, "progression of psychic functioning" to a level more advanced than the individual's usual level may also be involved in the creative process. The progression of psychic functioning will be evident in the critical, elaborative, analytic and synthetic manipulations of artistic images, scientific concepts, or any creative material demanding intense, hyperacute concentration, rationality or sensitivity. We do rise above ourselves at times too.

The final creative product may be seen therefore to represent a synthesis of relatively regressive, developmentally and organizationally primitive, unreflective and autistic material and relatively progressive, developmentally and organizationally advanced, self-critical and reality-oriented material. This *spread* of reference in the final product—from the regressive to the progressive—is one manifestation of creative "regression in the service of the ego" and its consequences that will figure prominently in the analysis of the Rorschach response process to be resumed soon.

Of course, this spread is not restricted to the products of the creative process; it seems to be an aspect of all human thinking and behavior. *From the point of view of psychoanalytic ego psychology—which is the point of view of this theoretical approach to the Rorschach test—all thought and behavior must be understood in part as an expression of a particular balance of ego dynamics and id dynamics, that is, of progressive, adaptive trends and regressive, autistic trends.* Nevertheless, the spread of psychic levels in creative activity seems clearer and perhaps broader than that usually encountered or discernible in more routine daytime thought processes and actions. The outstanding place of the Rorschach test and Thematic Apperception test among personality tests seems to derive to a great extent from the prominence and resulting instructiveness of creative work they require in the response process.

It must not be thought that the regressive alterations of functioning involved in creative work amount to total personality upheavals and reorganizations such as may be seen in psychotic disorders. These creative regressions are circumscribed, small-scale affairs. They may parallel gross, psychopathological regressions in many respects, and may reflect the play of large scale forces within the personality, but typically they are limited to expression in thought and feeling. They do not result in stormy, primitive, impulse-ridden action. The regression remains "in the service of the ego."*

Thus far, in considering only a few implications and effects of the test instructions, we have inevitably and inextricably become immersed in the general problems of psychoanalytic ego psychology and the particular problems of levels of psychic functioning and of creativity. More psychoanalytic spade work is required, however, before we can fruitfully return to direct dealing with the Rorschach response. At this point it should help our inquiry if we direct our attention for a while to the levels of psychic functioning characterizing dreaming, daydreaming, purposeful visualizing and normal perceiving. Each of these four common processes typically occurs on and reflects a different level of psychic functioning, even though it often overlaps and merges into the others, and even though its level varies more or less from one individual to the next. Dreams, daydreams, purposeful visualizations and normal percepts do not exhaust the varieties of conscious experience and corresponding levels of psychic functioning. They are merely modal points on a conceptually gross continuum ranging from the most advanced to the most primitive psychic levels. They have the advantage—particularly dreams do—of having been intensively studied [43]. Also, as will become clear later, all seem to share important properties with Rorschach responses. They constitute therefore a convenient and illuminating frame of reference within which to analyze the Rorschach response process.

## C. Dreaming, Daydreaming, Purposeful Visualizing and Normal Perceiving

In what follows dreaming, daydreaming, purposeful visualizing and normal perceiving will be treated as points along a continuum from the more primitive to the more advanced levels of psychic functioning, from the regressive to the progressive, from the dynamics of the id and the primary process to those of the ego and the secondary process. But, it must be repeated, these processes are not sharply demarcated from each other; their boundaries often overlap. In fact, each represents a highly complex response to a variety of forces and therefore cannot be systematically and exhaustively fitted to one continuum. In addition, there are varieties of conscious experience, such as synesthesias, that do not neatly fit this continuum at all. Still, the notion of a dream–percept continuum does seem to capture certain aspects of psychic functioning that are both generally important and specifically relevant to the Rorschach response process.

* See pp. 105–6 for a related discussion of the microcosmic nature of the creative regression involved in the Rorschach response process.

In considering each of the four processes mentioned, we shall be concerned with two general sub-headings: (1) the process as a response to certain stimuli, and (2) the properties of the psychic level on which these responses commonly seem to occur. The treatment of these processes will continue to express the Freudian psychoanalytic orientation to psychic functioning. A presentation of the Freudian position that is both brief and thorough is not possible. This presentation will be brief. It will select for emphasis only certain highlights of the psychology of dreams, daydreams, purposeful visualizations and percepts. These highlights will be those most relevant to the psychology of the Rorschach response.*

## 1. Dreaming

a. *Dreaming as a response.* Dreaming is essentially a response to urgent internal promptings. These promptings are usually needs or tensions which have not been adequately discharged during the day and which have become attached to and derive their urgency from unconscious, infantile wishes and unresolved conflict. Dreaming is at the same time a protective response to the organism's wish to sleep. Sleep would be disrupted if these reinforced residual tensions were experienced directly and in full force. Even when physical stimuli "trigger" dreams, it is assumed that there would be no dream without a wish on the part of the organism to preserve sleep. In other words, the disturbers of sleep may be internal or external stimuli, and the internal stimuli may be physical, such as hunger or thirst, or emotional and anxiety-producing, but *the prerequisites of the dream are the day's residual tensions, the unconscious infantile tendencies that reinforce them, and the wish to sleep.* The successful dream simultaneously involves sufficient expression of the reinforced, residual tendencies to ease existing tensions, and sufficient disguise or primitivized (and therefore obscured) expression of the objectionable aspects of these tendencies to avoid anxiety on the part of the sleeping but not defunct ego. The successful dream is a great compromiser, achieving relative and temporary tranquility on all the psychological fronts.

b. *The level of psychic functioning in dreaming.* Dreams occur on regressively primitivized levels of psychic functioning. As a shorthand reference, this regression will often be spoken of from now on simply as "regression"; its meaning will remain that described in the preceding section of this chapter (see pp. 78–82). There are three major aspects to this regression.

(1) Although an image, the dream is typically experienced as a percept.

* The reader interested in extensive, general treatments of these matters should see especially Chapter 7 of Freud's *The Interpretation of Dreams* [43], Chapters 1, 13 and 14 of Kris's study of art [92], and Part 7 of Rapaport's study of thinking [113].

Dreams, even those that label themselves "absurd" by certain contents, have phenomenal reality. In them, the line between self and not-self is obscured. Ordinarily a person has distance from his daytime imagery. He knows that the image is in him and not "out there." In the altered state of consciousness characterizing sleep, this distinction is almost always lost. The dream in this regard is a full projection and a close relative of the hallucination.

Unawares, that is, preconsciously, the dreamer knows that he is dreaming, however, and that the channels to motility are sealed off. Otherwise the dream itself would disrupt sleep—as it sometimes does when motility is invaded by the dream and we make, for example, abortive, spasmodic movements and then awaken. At times, in the background or foreground of the dream, there may seem to be the conscious notation: "I am only dreaming this." But even then, this reflective taking of distance from the dream is typically poorly sustained and the dream becomes "real" repeatedly or remains "real."

(2) The loss of conscious distinction between self and not-self is only one of the ways in which the dream regression manifests itself. There is also a relaxation of defensive ego functions. In this state of relaxed defense, representations or derivatives of unconscious, rejected infantile tendencies more easily and openly come to conscious expression than is possible in the normal waking state. The relatively high level of daytime defensive vigilance is not maintained, and forbidden thoughts and wishes press their claims with often alarming vigor and success. In one respect this defensive let-down protects sleep: by opening consciousness somewhat to the unconscious tendencies, the defensive let-down allows small amounts of sleep-disturbing tension to be discharged in a safe—that is, immobile—way.

(3) Beside the projective loss of distinction between self and not-self or image and percept, and the temporary weakening of defensive ego functions, there is a third major regressive aspect of dreaming. This is the archaic mode of dream thinking. Dream thinking, in both its expressive and defensive aspects, shares many of the characteristics of the thinking of children, psychotics, and members of primitive cultures [150]. Freud [43] has discussed these characteristics partly in terms of the already described primary process thinking (Chapter VII, especially pages 524–540) and partly in terms of the "dream work" (Chapter VI, especially pages 319–368). We shall not review the description of primary process thinking here.

The dream work is the means by which compromise expression of impulse and defense is achieved so as to elude the "censorship" partially and yet insure sleep. Freud lists four major aspects of dream work: displacement, condensation, regard for representability, and secondary elaboration. (1) By "displacement" is meant the transfer of energy from one idea to an associated idea whereupon the latter comes to "stand for" the former. (2) By "condensation" is meant the concentration on one idea of the energies belonging to several ideas, whereupon the single idea comes to "stand for" all the ideas and may become especially forceful and vivid. (3) "Regard for representability" refers to the relative restriction of dream content to thoughts and feelings that lend themselves to representation in concrete terms and particularly in visual terms. Concrete, visual images constitute the greater part of dream vocabulary. Regard for representability is a major determinant of the absence from the dream of explicit, verbalized logical relations, such as cause, sequence and contradiction, and also of abstract concepts, such as "guilt," "faith," and "conflict"; the latter are typically expressed implicitly in formal (spatial, temporal, etc.) peculiarities of the dream or in already existing unconscious symbols.* (4) By "secondary elaboration" of the dream is meant the post-dream, preconscious tying together and rational re-representation of the remembered dream fragments so that in a misleading way "the dream loses the appearance of absurdity and incoherence, and approaches the pattern of an intelligible experience" (page 455).

Thus, the dream work, with the exception of the secondary elaboration, freely violates the rules of logic and ignores or alters patterns of relationships existing in reality. In the end, an object or quality may be represented directly or by its opposite; a person may be represented by one of his parts or by several persons, while several persons may be represented by one person; causal relations may be represented by simple temporal sequence or by reverse sequence; mutually exclusive alternatives may be simultaneously represented in an "and" rather than "either . . . or" fashion; as already mentioned, abstract ideas may be represented by concrete objects or spatial and temporal positions; objects may be conceived animistically; and physiognomic renditions of objective qualities may be numerous and conspicuous.

The dream work seems therefore to use mechanisms peculiar to primary process thinking as described previously. In this regard the dream work seems to be a close relative of the "regression in the service of the ego" that we considered earlier in discussing creativity and levels of psychic functioning: both the dream work and the creative regression *use* the primary process for their own purposes and do not simply *submit* to it; both are active rather than passive processes; both remain largely under the control of ego functions; one may yield a tension-reducing but safely

---

* Additional major determinants of the dream's preponderantly visual character are, according to Freud. (1) the temporal aspect of the dream regression, that is, the prominence in the dream of wishes and memories from childhood which are themselves couched principally in visual terms, and (2) the typical closing off of the "sluices of motility" during sleep.

disguised dream, the other a piece of art; and when ego control over the regressive process weakens beyond a certain point, then the dream and the artistic creation are disrupted and we have neither dream nor art, but only anxious wakefulness or unsocialized daydreaming.

Finally it should be re-emphasized that the dream we have been discussing is a gross abstraction. Dreams actually seem to spread over a continuum from the most regressed (and usually intensely anxiety-arousing) to those, as in light sleep or dozing, that border on daydreams. Also, any one dream may not remain on the same level of psychic functioning throughout: parts of it may be archaic and parts of it daydream-like, parts fragmented and vague and other parts clear and with good narrative continuity. The same amount of dream work is not always attempted or accomplished. There are slow-downs and speed-ups, and successes and failures in the dream work, depending on various psychic conditions.

In brief summary, the regressed level of psychic functioning characterizing dreaming is evident in the hallucinatory, defensively weak, and archaically, autistically conceived and expressed aspects of the dream. Yet, this regression is usually not altogether uncontrolled. During dreaming, the strong grip of the ego is relaxed but not released.

## 2. Daydreaming

a. Daydreaming as a response. Like dreaming, daydreaming is essentially a wish-fulfilling but defensively disguised and limited response to inner urges and conflicts. Its important difference from dreaming in this regard is that it is not in the service of a wish to sleep. The daydream seems to function more as a safety valve, a fantasy consolation, a soothing self-feeding during the day by which we escape from, deny, and make up for the harsh, frustrating aspects of life, the externally and internally imposed failures and deprivations we experience.* Although we may adaptively envisage our goals in daydreams, we unadaptively tend to take short cuts toward these goals. Like the dream, the daydream may have its external precipitating stimuli, but these stimuli cannot themselves produce a daydream. Frustrated wishes or conflicts must also be present. They are the driving forces of the daydream as of the dream.

b. The level of psychic functioning in daydreaming. The daydream, like the dream, occurs on a regressively primitivized level of psychic functioning. Although daydreams vary considerably in this respect, some (or parts

* There are, of course, unpleasant daydreams too, but the daydream's wish-fulfilling, consoling aspects cannot be assessed simply on the basis of its conscious hedonic tone.

of some) being dream-like in quality, the usual extent of the daydream regression is less than that of the typical dream.

(1) The daydream is, for example, ordinarily fairly well distinguished from reality. We know that our daydreams originate within ourselves and somehow express our needs and feelings. Our daydreams are not hallucination-like projections. At the regressive extreme of daydreams, the distinction between self and not-self does become blurred; at the progressive extreme of daydreams, where adaptive and planful imagining begin, this distinction is relatively clear. Although the usual daydream resembles the dream in relying heavily on visual imagery—a developmentally relatively primitive form of expression—it tends to be more realistic than the dream in its imagery, though still often replete with autistic distortions.

(2) In the typical daydream, there also seems to be less relaxation of the defensive ego functions than in the dream. Despite the daydreamer's waking state, there does occur a decrease in the usually dominant ego functions of outwardly-oriented, selective attention and of maintenance of some defensive boundaries between preconscious and conscious processes in the interest of adaptation to reality. Also, narcissistic, egocentric wishes more or less dominate the daydream. Yet, such wishes as come to expression are usually more or less syntonic to the conscious self-image. Except in incipient or fully psychotic states, there is in the ordinary daydream no serious breakthrough and elaboration of unconscious, archaic content which is then experienced as terribly threatening or intolerable.* Ordinarily we enjoy our daydreams, though conscience may punish some of us for this self-indulgent departure from "duty."

(3) Thus far we have seen that the daydream is not so regressed a response as the dream in that it is neither a blatant projection, nor as daringly expressive of unconscious, rejected, infantile tendencies. The third regressed aspect of the dream pointed out above is its being dominated by primary process thinking. Here again the daydream is ordinarily less regressed than the dream. Even at its most regressed, the daydream remains under stricter control than the dream. Normally, it is more "in the service of the ego" and may be abruptly suspended or redirected if it becomes at all anxiety-arousing. In contrast, as we know from "normal" nightmares, the dream may get altogether out of hand.

Also, daydream thinking is typically closer to logical, secondary process thinking. True, in daydreams we may fly like a bird, be elected president or crowned king, seduce or be seduced by the most desirable

---

* Well-isolated obsessions may have a primitive and ego-alien daydream quality, but they seem to differ so from daydreams in their origin and function that they cannot be considered under the heading "daydreaming." During psychoanalytic treatment, when defenses and controls may be weakened somewhat, deeply disturbing daydreams may occur in the absence of psychotic trends.

men or women, and make spectacular ninety-yard touchdown runs; true, in other words, that reality is usually grossly overruled. Upon closer analysis of daydreams, we may also discern condensations and displacements in the "daydream work." But simultaneously, certain realistic, logical and narrative interests tend to be respected at least a little. For example, temporal and causal sequence, avoidance of gross contradiction, and verbal coherence and relevance characterize many a daydream. Individuals vary and daydreams vary: there are the dream-like daydreams and the realistic, planful daydreams; there are colorful chronic daydreamers and dull, inhibited daydreamers; there are long story-tellers and abstract form-and-color daydreamers; etc. But the daydream described above is a common, intermediate type. It seems to represent grossly what we usually have in mind when we say someone is "daydreaming."

From this brief and incomplete description of daydreaming we may conclude that daydreaming is also a regressive response in that it is commonly concerned rather with imaginary narcissistic gratifications than with reality adaptation, is more or less colored with autism, and employs pictorial and otherwise relatively archaic modes of thinking. Daydreams are not, however, products of so regressed a psychic level as dreams in that they are typically distinguished from reality, are better protected against representation of infantile, unconscious tendencies, and more or less partake of the characteristics of secondary process thinking.

It was said of dreams that they spread out over a continuum, ranging from those most openly and archaically expressive of basic impulses to those most defensive and secondarily elaborated (the so-called "waking dreams"). And it may now be said of daydreams that they too spread out over a continuum: on their most primitive, regressed level, they reach and possibly extend a bit beyond the point where highly defensive and secondarily elaborated dreams end, and at their most advanced level the point where conscious, realistic, adaptive planning and anticipation begin.

### 3. Purposeful Visualizing

*a. Purposeful visualizing as a response.* Purposeful visualizing as conceived here is distinguished from wishful, defensive and adaptive daydreaming in its being prompted by requirements of adaptation to immediate reality situations. When, for example, in trying to remember the face of an acquaintance so that we may describe it to a third person, we visualize that face, narcissistic and egocentric impulses ordinarily play a lesser part in this psychological process than in daydreaming. The same is true when we are planning, through a visual and perhaps auditory rehearsal, how to handle a situation that is coming up, say a discussion of some minor professional problem with a colleague. Narrow situational or interpersonal requirements and anticipations are conspicuous in this type of imagery, though to be sure upon close analysis the part played by our deeper, narcissistic interests may also often be discerned. In other words, in purposeful visualizing, we are more interested in how that scene *will* take place and what its real result *will* be, and how that face *does* look, than in our preferences in the matter, even though preferences do shape anticipations and memories to some degree.

  b. *The level of psychic functioning in purposeful visualizing.* Purposeful visualizing does not typically occur on a significantly regressed level of psychic functioning. Ideally, the secondary process holds forth over the primary process in it, the defenses against unconscious, rejected strivings are not relaxed, and the distinction between what is seen and what is imagined is sharply maintained. Purposeful visualizing, when it is not disrupted, is a consciously directed, reflective, self-critical process. It is adaptive in orientation. It does not suspend active dealing with immediate reality problems—it *is* active dealing with these problems. In purposeful visualizing we keep more or less distance from ourselves and from the problems with which we are coping. But like the dream and daydream, this type of imagining might best be thought of as spreading over a range: at one end are near-daydreams in which the voluntary image merges with the involuntary image, plan merges with wish, memory with attitude, and possibility with impossibility; at the other end are moment-old percepts, vivid instances of recognition and recall, and accurate spatial and temporal orientations.

  4. *Visual perceiving.* Visual perceiving is ordinarily a process similarly directed, voluntary and adaptive as purposeful visualizing in the sense just described. Under ordinary circumstances, visual perceiving occurs on the usual level of psychic functioning characterizing the individual's waking state, that is, on a relatively advanced level. In perceiving we are ordinarily vitally concerned with and relatively successful in distinguishing self and not-self, excluding unadaptive impulses from participating roles in the response process, and establishing congruences between percepts and objects. Perceiving occurs while such critical ego functions as judgment and concentration are in full play.

  There is reason, however, to maintain that lower and higher order impulse-defense struggles and compromises find expression even in "normal" perception. To a greater or lesser degree, depending upon many circumstances, these conflicts and compromises may significantly influence the selection, organization and subjective experience of visual stimuli [15, 101]. This influence is especially obvious in—but not restricted to— states of great need, ambiguous and marginal perceptual situations, and situations where fatigue, toxicity or other causes weaken the integration of functioning. Klein has even adduced evidence for the propositions that

each individual is characterized by a general "cognitive style," one manifestation of which is his style of perceiving, and that this more or less
selective, organizing and distorting style reflects relatively stable character
trends that have grown out of conflict and compromise [15, pp. 328–355].
Ordinarily, however, with the real object immediately available for
reference, perceiving is even less vulnerable to narcissistic distortions than
purposeful visualizing, which has no such external anchor.

For our present purposes, perceiving may then be thought of as a
process at the opposite end of the continuum from dreaming, so long as
we bear in mind that perceiving itself spreads out on this continuum from
the most inaccurate, fluid, impulse- and conflict-determined perceiving,
through the relatively stable, stylistic and still more or less biased forms
of perceiving, to the most accurate, autonomous, conflict-free and impersonal perceiving.

To summarize briefly the discussion thus far we may say that these four
processes—dreaming, daydreaming, purposeful visualizing, and visual
perceiving—do not appear to be sharply demarcated from each other;
they share many attributes, even though to different degrees. And in a
rough sense they appear to reflect a continuum of levels of psychic functioning, dreams falling at the subjective, archaic, internally-driven, and in-
ternally-oriented pole, and normal daytime visual percepts at the relatively
objective, logical, externally-sustained and externally-oriented pole.*

## D. The Rorschach Response and the Dream–Percept Continuum

What of the Rorschach response? Where does it fall on this continuum?
This is an inadequate question. It must first be specified which Rorchach
response we are talking about. There are some responses—for example,
the popular animal on Card VIII—that seem very close to normal daytime percepts. There are others—for example, all of Card X seen as
human anatomy—that seem very close to dream images both in the
part narcissistic strivings play in their formation and in the weakness of reality testing they involve. These considerations seem at
first to lead to the following overall view of the situation: Rorschach
responses may be individually located along a continuum, with the objective,
realistic, percept-like responses at the progressive, secondary process pole,

* Other varieties of conscious experience along and around this continuum,
such as reveries, hypnogogic imagery and *déjà vu* experiences, and the levels
of psychic functioning to which they correspond, will not be considered here,
since we are concerned only with developing a gross framework for analyzing
the Rorschach response process and not with an exhaustive catalogue and
ordering of psychic processes and conscious experiences. For discussion of the
latter see Rapaport [114]. The present discussion also slights the role of
memory and concept formation in the processes under consideration, for which
see Rapaport [113].

and the subjective, unrealistic, dream-like responses at the regressive, primary process pole. But is this view adequate? A few considerations will show that it is not.

Consider first the popular animal on Card VIII: some call it a rat, others a coyote or weasel, and others a chameleon; some call it a wolf and others a wolverine; some see it with four legs, some with three legs (one "missing") and a tail, and some with three legs (one "missing") and a penis. Then, too, some do not see the animal at all. Obviously, each of these variations must have its own emotional, more or less personal connotations. These observations make it impossible to continue to regard the popular animal on Card VIII simply as an objective, perceptual response to a well-structured stimulus. What we seem to have here instead is a perceptual situation with sufficient plasticity so that in it progressive and regressive tendencies may be and often are simultaneously at play in the response process.

Does this progressive-regressive spread characterize our perception of the usual things about us? Not ordinarily—at least, not to the same extent. At first glance this spread does seem to characterize perception in ambiguous or unstructured situations. A bush beside a road on a dark night may seem—with good justification—much like a man. Yet, this is not quite the same kind of ambiguity or unstructuredness that obtains on the Rorschach card. There is little doubt what you see on the Rorschach card: the inkblot is before you; it is static; its shape, shading and coloring are clear and fixed. In the darkness of night or of the experimentalist's room there is ordinarily no such sharp delineation of the properties of the visual stimulus: there we are not certain where the shadow bulges, where the smudge is lighter, what the relative sizes are. In what then does the Rorschach ambiguity or unstructuredness consist? Let us put this question aside for the moment—we shall be better prepared to consider it later*—and return to consideration of the inadequacy of locating single Rorschach responses along a simple dreaming–perceiving continuum.

In considering the response in which all of Card X is seen as human anatomy—the apparently opposite extreme of the popular animal on Card VIII—can we say that this response is equivalent to a dream image simply because it is so grossly incongruent with reality and seems so narcissistic in origin? On second thought, although it is poor in form and organization, this anatomy response also shares some properties with realistic percepts: it is a response to an external stimulus, which is correctly recognized as external by the patient; it does not simply stem from internal tendencies; and as a rule it contains within it reflective attempts at its own logical justification.

* See pp. 114–7.

Thus, both the popular animal on Card VIII and the anatomy response to the whole of Card X seem to combine properties of processes occurring all along the dreaming–perceiving continuum of levels of psychic functioning as previously described. Each Rorschach response may thus be said to represent a syndrome of variables rather than any single variable. It seems futile therefore to try to locate Rorschach responses at points along this continuum. The continuum itself does not include only one variable. As we have seen, "level of psychic functioning" is a complex concept that refers to many processes simultaneously; these processes can only be moderately intercorrelated. The continuum concept will, however, prove to be valuable if we use it more appropriately as a gross frame of reference within which to analyze the construction and properties of Rorschach responses.

From what has been said so far, we may now formulate a major characteristic of the Rorschach response: *by virtue of its spread along the dreaming–perceiving continuum, the Rorschach response may and often does simultaneously bear the imprint of primitive, unrealistic, unconscious processes and articulated, realistic conscious processes.* In the former respect, Rorschach responses may depart greatly from ordinary percepts, and in the latter respect from usual dream images.

Of course, most responses reflect the primary and secondary thought processes to varying degrees. Thus, simply "animal" to the lateral pink on Card VIII is almost altogether perceptual, while "snarling, ravenously hungry wolf" to the same area has, in addition to realistic perception (since the form *is* accurate and well articulated), a large admixture of the infantile or archaic. And all of Card VII as "a vagina," being an unarticulated and overimpressionistic response, has a minimum of realistic perception and reflective, self-critical, secondary process thinking, and a maximum of physiognomic, drive-centered, primary process thinking.*

Thus far we have spoken only of the two extremes—dreams and percepts—of the continuum. What about daydreams and purposeful visualizing? The latter can be taken into account relatively simply: checking nascent responses against images of real objects—images summoned up specifically for purposes of this comparison—seems to be an essential part of the development of most Rorschach responses [118]. This comparative process is logical, adaptive, directed, purposeful visualizing as described before, although it may take place on the fringe or even outside the realm of awareness. There are, of course, responses that are blurted out impulsively or, from the present point of view, prematurely, without adequate reflective, comparative, purposeful visualizing; these responses are consequently vague or inaccurate in form as a rule.

* See in this connection the note by Goldstein and Rothman [62].

The relevance of daydreams to the Rorschach response process is a more complex matter. It was maintained above that the content of even popular Rorschach responses may express highly personal, primitive tendencies as well as the successful operation of realistic daytime perception. It was assumed then that this brought the Rorschach response into clear relationship with dreams. But why dreams rather than daydreams? Daydreams too may be highly personal, emotional and conflict-laden, and they are often fantastic. Qualification of the earlier statement is required. It now seems more correct to say that not only may the response simultaneously reflect the most primitive and most advanced levels of functioning, but any level along this continuum as well. We may, after all, *daydream* about snarling wolves.

But what of a patient who sees "an infant with fangs protruding from its mouth" in the bottom red on Card IX? Does this sound like daydreaming in any usual sense? Rather it strikes us as dream-like in its condensed and bizarre aspects. We expect such content in the daydreams of psychotic individuals, that is, individuals whose conscious thinking is dream-like in many essential respects. Yet even this *fanged infant* response, for all its dream-like quality, involves accurate, adaptive perception—it will be scored $F+$ according to Rorschach norms—and in all likelihood realistic, comparative imagery was invoked in its development. In this response we see a truly wide spread over the psychic continuum. We may conceive of this patient as having been responding on several levels of psychic functioning simultaneously. As noted previously, the primitive levels co-exist with the advanced and often co-determine thought and behavior—sometimes subtly, and sometimes (as in this perceptually sharp but bizarre *fanged infant* Rorschach response) grossly.

It was noted earlier in this chapter that all thought may be regarded as bearing the imprint of both polar types of processes—the primary and the secondary—although the relative prominence of each of the two may vary considerably in different instances. Sometimes the imprint of one may be so slight as to be neglected without risk of serious error in our analysis. But in any event, the spread of the Rorschach response is not in itself unique; it is perhaps the frequent obviousness of its spread that is unique. It is this obviousness, the palpability of the Rorschach response's spread, that so often allows the Rorschach tester to penetrate into the patient on several levels simultaneously and to evolve a hierachically organized conception of his character and his illness.

At this point, the earlier discussion of creativity is relevant.* There we noted that the creative production is often characterized by a relatively conspicuous spread of levels of psychic functioning. We see now how

---

* See pp. 78–82.

Rorschach creativity is a special instance of creativity in general, and we can better appreciate how it is that the test's exploration of the individual's personal imagery is so penetrating.

In considering the psychology of the Rorschach response process, we have thus far concerned ourselves with its place on the dream-daydream-purposeful visualization-percept continuum, and have seen that it typically does not fall at one or another point along this continuum, but spreads out along it, sometimes ranging from one extreme to the other and including major points in between. We have also touched briefly on, but have done nothing to resolve, the problem of defining the special nature of unstructuredness or ambiguity in the Rorschach situation. Let us at this point return to the psychology of dreaming for further comparison of the dream and the Rorschach response. Additional distinctive characteristics of the Rorschach response process will be highlighted by this specific comparison.

### E. FURTHER REMARKS ON THE DREAM AND THE RORSCHACH RESPONSE

In what follows, the Rorschach response will be likened to and contrasted with the dream in a number of key respects. The comparison will focus on the role of the external stimulus, degrees of narrative continuity and autobiographical specificity, requirements of interpersonal communication, and types and degrees of regression in the level of psychic functioning. The dream is used in this comparative analysis for two reasons, first because it is also a dramatic means of expression of basic personal patterns and conflicts, and second because the careful study to which the dream has been subjected by Freud and others provides a good frame of reference within which to study the properties of the Rorschach response.

It is not intended, however, to show that the Rorschach response is either *the same* as the dream or *altogether different*. Neither objective would be psychologically meaningful or productive. It is intended rather to see what the existing conceptualization of dream phenomena can teach us about the Rorschach response. Even the differences we establish between the two should therefore help us understand the Rorschach response better.

### 1. The Role of the External Stimulus

Both the Rorschach response and the dream depend for their content on accumulated images and their modifications, but the Rorschach response depends at the same time on an immediate, external inkblot stimulus. The Rorschach response therefore prominently involves giving meaning as well as, like the dream, recalling and revising already meaningful images. The inkblots should not, however, be thought of as utterly formless or meaningless. As wholes and in their parts, and also in their colors and shadings, these blots coincide to greater or lesser extents with conformations and qualities of real objects. Hence the continuum from *Popular* to *Absurd* and *Original*—. In short, each Rorschach response is not a creation from scratch; it combines finding meaning with giving meaning. This combined giving meaning to and finding meaning in the external stimulus is one feature that distinguishes the Rorschach response from the dream, since the dream to begin with works with already meaningful images and adapts itself to no external stimulus.

There is a second major aspect of the role of the external stimulus in this dream–Rorschach response comparison. The dream is burdened by minimal commitments to reality; ultimately it is limited in its choice and manipulation of content only by the dreamer's experience, creativeness and defensive requirements. The Rorschach response is subject not only to these limits but to the additional and weighty obligation to stand in some objective relationship to the inkblot. This external reference point, if attended to at all, inevitably limits the variety of images that can be brought into play in the Rorschach situation. Even though the blots elicit amazingly varied responses, they are not infinitely plastic, and for any one person their plasticity is definitely limited.

Thus, even though the Rorschach situation's external stimulus and reference point add a creative dimension to the Rorschach response not present in the dream, that of giving and finding meaning, the physical properties of the test stimulus tend to limit the variety of content in Rorschach responses in a way not true for the dream. Yet both the dream and the Rorschach response may be viewed as creative acts and in both the potential variety of content is very great.

## 2. Narrative Continuity and Autobiographical Specificity

Dreams frequently have narrative content and sequence, however abrupt their transitions, and they often deal with specific objects and persons out of the patient's real life experiences. Rorschach responses, on the other hand, ordinarily constitute a set of isolated, static, generalized images that do not explicitly express *specific* content drawn from the patient's real life. In fact it is a malignant sign when narrative qualities and self-references are conspicuous in a Rorschach record; they indicate that autism or self-absorption is overwhelming logical thought and concern with reality.

The Rorschach communications, when they are not confabulated, are more abstract and fragmentary than the typical dream communications. They often state problems but cannot articulate them, at least not to any significant degree. Moreover, they often merely state problems that are ubiquitous, for example, concern with masculinity and femininity, and do not allow us to do what as testers it is our foremost aim to do—to distinguish this individual sufficiently from enough others that he takes on some psychological identity. Lacking the orientation provided by narrative continuity and autobiographical specificity, the Rorschach tester must always be on the lookout for frequently recurring, intense, elaborate, and individualized expressions of unconscious, essentially ubiquitous tendencies within the record he is analyzing. Only when he has found such distinctive features may the tester then say that such and such an unconscious trend or conflict is of relative importance in this case. One incomplete figure in a set of responses, for example, tells us nothing of value; but when the figures repeatedly lack arms, legs and heads, when the animal skins are ragged and worn and the butterflies tattered and torn, we have reason to suspect that anxiety over bodily integrity, probably based on castration fantasies, is crucial in the determination of these Rorschach responses, and that this anxiety is probably especially significant in the patient's present life role and illness.

*It follows that insofar as the Rorschach response expresses unconscious, infantile tendencies, it is ordinarily a guidepost to these tendencies and not a highly articulated map of the unconscious terrain.* If, however, we "go by the book" and attempt mechanical reconstructions of how these tendencies or conflicts originated, we may end up with what appears to be a full psychoanalytic genetic study of the individual but is in fact only a demonstration that we have read a psychoanalytic text and have either accepted tentative genetic formulations as final truths, or opportunistically used often inconsistent texts to support our immediate thesis. It is said that the devil can cite scripture for his purpose; Fenichel's monumental text [37] lends itself to similar abuse. We should not forget Freud's dictum that even where the most compelling symbol-like content occurs in the manifest dream, we should be cautious about interpreting it fully before we collect the free associations that lead to the latent dream thoughts. To spin out complex, genetic interpretation of unconscious trends based on Rorschach responses is "wild analysis." To interpret this way also naively underestimates the role and power of ego processes in the coming about of the Rorschach response.*

The usual absence of narrative continuity and autobiographical specificity in the Rorschach response is probably a major condition of its frequently highly revealing content. Ordinarily, the isolated, static, generalized Rorschach image seems so impersonal, emotionally remote or emotionless to the patient that he feels considerably less anxiety and defensiveness about it or involvement in it than he otherwise would. He can then more easily become conscious of the revealing image and verbalize it.

Yet, the difference in narrative quality and autobiographical specificity between the Rorschach response and the dream, while important, is only

---

* For detailed discussion of this problem, see Chapter 5.

relative. It must be remembered that the verbal protocol of the dream, which is after all our chief source of raw data for dream psychology, is itself already severely fragmented in some respects and secondarily elaborated in others. The verbal protocol of the dream usually represents a selection rather than a full report of all that is retained of the dream. Transitions, spatial positions, relative sizes, details of dress and decor, and the like, may or may not be verbalized when the dream is reported. There is a teller between the dream and the analyst. In organizing his report, the teller follows certain selective principles that are themselves highly revealing of his personality. These selective principles are no doubt closely related to the selective principles operating in the Rorschach situation. In addition, autobiographical specificity is frequently concealed, if not lacking, in the manifest content of dreams out of defensive necessity—the same necessity that seems to play a part in the lack of such specificity in Rorschach test content. Seen from the point of view of the dream, therefore, there is significant overlap between the dream and the Rorschach response with respect to narrative and autobiographical qualities.

Looked at from the point of view of the Rorschach test, further overlap becomes evident. It is not uncommon that one or more responses in a Rorschach record are sensed, if not explicitly labeled, by the patient as autobiographically specific. He may at least see resemblances to real, personally meaningful individuals in cultural and political history, such as Shakespeare or Teddy Roosevelt, or even occasional objects reminiscent of specific objects in his past or present life, such as a dress his mother wore or an X-ray he has recently had taken and seen. At times, even real persons in his life may be introduced, such as a crabby aunt or an impish child. Similarly, narrative qualities of a limited, non-malignant sort are frequently encountered in limited or rudimentary form; for example, the "proud show dog" on Card X, the "hungry chicks in a nest" on Card I, and the "stalking wolf" on Card VIII. It might well be that systematically collected associations to or reflections on Rorschach responses by patients would bring forth many instances of unverbalized autobiographical and narrative elaboration [81].

It is at this point that sequence analysis of the Rorschach responses becomes especially relevant. Sequence analysis, particularly when it includes analysis of imagery and of test attitudes and behavior, often uncovers meaningful continuity from one response to the next. This continuity may not tell an imaginative story such as the dream may, but it does tell a true story of conflict and of success and failure in resolving this conflict. When, for example, the first response to Card II is "blood" and nothing further follows except demanding and evasive test behavior, one type of story is being told; when the first response is "blood" and the next (tranquilly) is "a cathedral," and the third (delighted) "a sweet little lamb," quite another story is being told. *Bearing in mind that these examples are grossly oversimplified,* the first story may be read as follows: I am beset by hostile images, feelings and impulses; I am unable to keep them out of consciousness; all I can do is either try to flee from the situation in which they arise, which dooms me to perpetual fear, flight and ego-restriction, or fall back into an infantile, helpless, passive role, which dooms me to perpetual humiliation, disappointment, and further rage; there is no good, peaceful way out. In contrast, *and again grossly oversimplified,* the second story, told by the blood-cathedral-lamb sequence, may be read as follows: I do what I can to conquer the rage within me by devoting myself to what is pure, good, innocent and gentle in human relationships; although anger may erupt at times, my saintly ideal will help see me through these crises.

*These are the same stories dreams tell.* On a different level of functioning and in a somewhat different language, the Rorschach response sequence may take up the same themes as the ordinarily more narratively continuous and autobiographically specific dream. But whereas dreams tell these stories all the time, Rorschach responses do not. Although not rare, Rorschach response sequences of a dramatic and dynamically transparent sort are not the rule, except in certain psychotic and near-psychotic conditions. And the sequences should be dramatic and dynamically transparent, and also well supported by other test data, before we make much of them interpretively. Otherwise, since we do not have the associations the analyst uses to back up similar interpretations he may make, we are carrying on "wild analysis" and may be utterly misled by our own preconceptions, misconceptions and personal problems.

In summary of this section of the dream—Rorschach response comparison, it may be said that the Rorschach response ordinarily seems to have significantly less autobiographical specificity and narrative continuity than the dream, and that much of what it does have is likely to remain unverbalized or hidden in sequences of apparently discontinuous responses. Yet, these seemingly impersonal, remote, fragmentary, static aspects of the Rorschach response allow it an expressive freedom that is rare in normal states of waking consciousness. This freedom helps make the Rorschach test, if not handled in a "wild" analytic manner, the unusually sensitive and valuable instrument of clinical examination it is.

### 3. Interpersonal Communication

Dreams are dreamt when the dreamer has withdrawn his interest from the outer world to a striking degree. Typically the dreamer is oblivious of his immediate surroundings and does not verbalize his dreams as they are spun out. Yet, dreams have two striking interpersonal aspects, one being that they deal intensively with interpersonal problems, and the other that the dreams we know the most about have been dreamt in the context of a psychoanalytic relationship and therefore inevitably have a prominent communication-to-the-analyst aspect. In the first respect, the dreamer is not as asocial and withdrawn as might be thought, for the interpersonal problems he deals with in the dream may be as real and forceful to him as when he is awake and actively engaging others. In the second respect, the analysand soon comes to appreciate that his dreams will be studied and remembered to some extent by his analyst; dreams then soon become another level of discourse on which the analysand can convey his concerns and attitudes to the analyst. In one extreme form this latter appreciation may result in what have been called "compliance dreams," that is, dreams triggered and directed by a wish to gratify or pacify the analyst. Compliance dreams tell the analyst what the analysand fancies the analyst wants them to tell—usually something in line with the analyst's latest interpretation. In the same general class are other dreams apparently designed to mock the analyst. As with all thought processes, therefore, dreams may be approached and partially understood from the aspect of efforts to communicate (and master) interpersonal problems.

The Rorschach response, in contrast to the dream, is formed and delivered in the context of an immediate interpersonal relationship. The patient is obviously in relationship with the tester throughout the testing, and, as we have seen in Chapter 2, through the tester he may be in relationship with the therapist and the family. But once we acknowledge that the patient may be implicitly, if not explicitly, in relationship with the analyst throughout his dream, we see that this difference between the Rorschach response and dream is relatively superficial. In fact the difference may be greater in the opposite direction; that is to say, even though the tester and patient are closer together in time and space than the dreaming analysand and his analyst, the test relationship is more emotionally remote and transient by far than the analytic relationship. Still, as we have seen in Chapter 2, the test relationship is of a piece with any therapeutic relationship. Again, we are dealing with relative emphases and not clear-cut dichotomies.

It does make a big difference, however, that Rorschach responses must be verbalized as they develop, whereas dreams carry no such social obligation. In this respect the requirement that the patient verbalize his images has the same effect on Rorschach responses as the previously discussed requirement that the patient relate these images to an external reference point (the inkblot): both requirements tend to subordinate the response to reality requirements and to mold it into more or less conventional forms. The dream is under no such social pressure. In the dream you can shoot first and ask questions later, so to speak, whereas in the Rorschach test you must carefully respect the requirements of due process of law. In the Rorschach situation you must see describable things; preferably you should even be able to name them. This imposes demands on the responses for sharpness of boundaries and articulation that the dream is free to ignore. Many aspects of dreams—forms, meanings, atmospheres—often cannot be put into words at all. In addition, the dreamer may count on his analyst's taking time to "figure out" the obscurities in the dream, and also having the background data to do it with, while the patient being tested cannot so freely and confidently impose such "puzzles" and "riddles" on the tester.

Of course, many dream images are clearly formed and named. Also certain patients try to ignore the interpersonal communication requirements in the Rorschach situation by transforming the response process into something that combines "inspiration," "free association," and "dreaming," and by concentrating on expressing the resulting "inexpressibles." Despite these instances of overlap, there can be little question that the immediacy and transiency of the Rorschach relationship tend to limit regressive forms of communication, while the dream is a prime example of freely regressive communication. Still it must be remembered that both dream and Rorschach responses, as they are encountered and studied clinically, are heavily interpersonal in subject matter and have a more or less prominent communication aspect.

## 4. Levels of Psychic Functioning

Earlier in this chapter it was pointed out that the dream is a regressive phenomenon, occurring on a relatively primitive level of psychic functioning. The dream regression is evidenced (1) by the dream's hallucinatory quality, the distinction between self and not-self usually being lost, (2) by the dream's relative openness to expressions of normally unconscious, infantile, rejected tendencies and their derivatives, this openness reflecting relaxation of defensive and synthesizing ego functions, and (3) by the dominance of the archaic, fluid, drive-oriented primary process mode of thinking.

The Rorschach response process seems to stand in clear contrast to the dream process in these respects: (1) it is not hallucinatory, the distinction between self and not-self usually being well maintained; (2) it occurs in the waking state when defensive ego functions are ordinarily fully mobilized and when expressions of unconscious tendencies are carefully restricted; and (3) the Rorschach response is controlled by the orderly, logical, reality-oriented secondary process mode of thinking. An additional difference is that the patient in the Rorschach situation is encouraged to remain realistic, even if imaginative. He is asked, "What could this look like?" and not "What occurs to you?" Of course, the patient may depart from this instruction, the more so the more autistic he is. For the most part, however, patients attempt to respect this requirement to be moderately realistic, a requirement that does not obtain with any force in the dream.

From these considerations it would seem that the patient's level of psychic functioning during the Rorschach test is vastly different and far more advanced than that during the dream. We have previously noted, however, important similarities between dreams and Rorschach responses, particularly in their creative aspects, that is, the "regression in the service of the ego" both entail and the "spread" from relatively regressive to relatively progressive levels of functioning that may be discerned in both. At this point a more detailed comparison of the regressive shifts in dreams and Rorschach responses is in order. This is because the rationale of the variety and depth of personality trends commonly discernible in Rorschach responses is still far from completion. To elaborate this rationale further we must focus particularly on *similarities* between the regressive shifts in dreams and Rorschach responses, for the dream is a regressive phenomenon outstanding in its variety and depth of personal expressiveness.

*a. The motivation of the regressive shift.* What sets the dream going and keeps it going? We have noted before that it is assumed to be the combination of residual tensions of the day, unconscious infantile tendencies associated with these day residues, and the dreamer's wish to master these tensions and preserve the state of sleep. These are the basic motivations of the dream. The motivations of the Rorschach response seem to be of quite another sort.

Why does the patient respond or wish to respond to the inkblot stimuli? It will be better to concentrate on the *wish to respond* rather than on responsiveness itself since defensive requirements may severly limit responsiveness despite a strong wish to respond, just as little may be remembered of dreams despite intense psychic activity during sleep. The wish to respond in the Rorschach situation seems to derive basically from (1) the patient's realistic therapeutic zeal, that is, his awareness of illness and his healthy desire to do all that is necessary to get well, including taking psychological tests if indicated, and (2) the patient's desires to submit to, confess to, gratify, overwhelm, defeat, establish contact with or otherwise interact with or control the tester and therapist. These motives have been considered previously in Chapter 2 on the interpersonal test relationship. These motives may possess great force and, it seems reasonable to assume, may be reinforced by unconscious, infantile tendencies coming into associative contact with thoughts and images stimulated by the inkblots. This last assumption is reasonable because it is a special case of the one that helped Freud decipher the dream, and because Freud's assumption has become a cornerstone of the psychoanalytic theory of psychic functioning and psychopathology, namely, that unconscious, infantile, rejected tendencies are always ready to seize any opportunity to express themselves, and freely use even far-fetched and trivial connections as pretexts to gain expression. The so-called psychopathology of everyday life—the slips of tongue, of memory and of motility—provides no end of examples to support this assumption [44].

Imaginative productions are particularly vulnerable to such "returns of the repressed," and the Rorschach response, like the dream, is certainly no exception. Even when the Rorschach image is to begin with nearly purely perceptual, as in the case of the popular animal on Card VIII, it may be elaborated in content so as to express something of these rejected tendencies. The perceptual core of the response may be impersonal, yet its development may be highly personal. The freedom or autonomy of the most clearcut percept from unconscious exploitation is thus only relative and not absolute. Of course, in the waking state, these invaders from the unconscious are strenuously opposed by defensive ego functions and under ordinary circumstances achieve limited and sporadic success at best.

Also, the Rorschach response process may be influenced somewhat by tensions of the day such as hunger, disappointment and resulting low mood, irritation, and others that also make up the day residues that stimulate the dream. Finally, intellectual curiosity, desire for play, pleasure in being creative and similar motives may be brought into action by the test situation and may significantly increase the impetus and zest of the response process.

Thus, the Rorschach response process may be assumed to be set off and sustained by inner urgency that quantitatively and in some ways qualitatively differs little from the urgency of the dream. In important respects the wish to respond in the Rorschach situation may be considered the counterpart of the wish to sleep in the genesis of the dream.

*b. The facilitation of the regressive shift.* It has been maintained so far that an important, if only relative, difference between the dream and the Rorschach response is that the dream is not at all committed to being realistic while the Rorschach response that takes into account its external reference point and the test instructions is so committed. However, closer scrutiny of this proposition will indicate that the difference is in some important respects less than this.

Although required implicitly to be realistic by the test instructions and external stimulus, the patient in the Rorschach situation is deprived to a significant extent of means by which he may assess the safeness or conventionality of the content of his responses. He has no idea what others usually see in the blots. More than that—and here we come to one of the most crucial aspects of the Rorschach response—*the patient is to a significant extent relieved of responsibility for being realistic as to content, even though not as to form.* The tester relieves the patient of responsibility for the lack of content-congruence between his responses and the usual details of the real objects to which they refer. After all, the whole test is his idea, not the patient's. If, for example, the patient sees a figure with breasts *and* penis on Card III, he is in a sense entitled to feel and often does feel that he did not put them *both* there; the tester did. It's just a sad commentary on the psychologist. Significant relief from anxiety and threat of superego punishment appears to result for the patient.

In dream analysis we can always tell the patient, "It's your dream." In his own self-perceptions the dreamer knows this to be the truth. Having inwardly accepted responsibility for his dream in the first place, he had automatically tried his best to obscure the "reprehensible" in the dream. In the Rorschach situation the patient may feel more protected, because to a limited extent he can turn the tables and say, "It's your test, doctor!" Patients say this in a thousand different ways. We must agree. The breast-penis combination, for example, is not simply a spontaneous image, and the patient may claim with justice that he has found *external resemblances of accurate form.* But we agree only in part, because we also know that not all patients see this *content,* and we therefore safely reassign a good part of the responsibility for the response to the patient.

Thus, by a kind of deception, we relax the patient's defenses without creating anywhere near the sense of threat in him that he would experience were he to relax his defenses spontaneously and allow an image of a figure with breasts and a penis to come to consciousness in the absence of an external justification. This is only a relative deception, however, for a degree of taking responsibility for responses is present in every patient in the Rorschach situation, even if only implicitly. The fleeting smile, the slight hesitation, the blocking, the guarded verbalization, all betray this taking responsibility. Most of the responses are not that exact a copy of nature or that compelling, and patients shed only part of the responsibility for the content of their responses. What is striking in the Rorschach situation is the relative calm with which patients frequently consciously experience intimately self-expressive and highly conflict-laden imagery. The opportunity afforded the patient to externalize the responsibility for his responses appears to play a great part in this relative increase in his sense of security. The externalization of responsibility thereby facilitates a regressive shift in his level of psychic functioning. The creative regression doesn't seem so dangerous after all.

It may be seen therefore that even though the patient's waking state and realistic orientation do limit the content that can come to consciousness during the Rorschach test, the psychic regression stimulated by the patient's wish to respond, and furthered by his being relieved of much of the responsibility for the content of his responses, seems to restore a good deal of the imaginal freedom that is ordinarily lost during the waking state. The previously discussed usual lack of explicit narrative continuity and autobiographical specificity in the Rorschach response appears to further this restoration and increase of imaginal freedom.

*c. The nature of the regressive shift.* It was previously noted that people seem to shift along a continuum of levels of psychic functioning throughout the day and night. The dream is not equally regressive throughout, for example, and the waking state is not equally progressive throughout. It was also suggested above that a regressive shift seems to occur during the Rorschach test as a result of the test instructions' implicit emphasis on mingling imagination and fantasy with realistic perception. Without this regressive shift the patient could do little more than describe the blots as blots or at most give only a few popular responses. It is not, after all, our usual state of waking consciousness to look at things for what they remind us of but for what they are. Thus, in complying with the test instructions to tell what the inkblot "might look like," even though still reality-oriented, the patient must to an extent relax his usual standards of waking perception and thought. This regressive relaxation of standards entails increased permeability of consciousness with respect to ordinarily preconscious and unconscious images. The patient will relax his standards and controls this way if his wish to respond is intense enough and his sense of defensive security strong enough. When, as an expression of rebelliousness or defensive insecurity and rigidity, the wish to respond is weak or absent, or, as Schachtel has termed it [131], when the "resistance definition" of the Rorschach situation prevails, no such regressive shift occurs, and meager, banal, "perceptual" records result.

We should not, however, settle for the static notion that now presents itself to the effect that one regressive shift occurs at the beginning of the test, goes only so far, and then stays put until the end of the test. Just as the level of psychic functioning shifts throughout the day and night, so does it seem to during the Rorschach test—and for some of the same reasons. In the dream, for example, some parts may have a higher degree of secondary elaboration, while others may be fragmented and vague, and still others so weak in their defensive aspects that we wake from them in anxiety. Similar shifts appear to occur during hypnotherapy, the depth of the hypnotic trance varying with the prevailing balance of psychological forces in the therapeutic situation [19]. It seems useful to think of the up-and-down shifts that occur during the Rorschach test as also reflecting shifting balances of forces: now drive representations come to the fore; now anxiety is felt and defensive processes are intensified; now anxiety is minimal, defenses are secure, and impersonal, relatively conflict-free attitudes and images prevail; etc.

Rorschach [124], speaking of this shifting balance of forces at a time when psychoanalytic ego psychology and the theory of defenses were in their infancy, commented with remarkable insight as follows: ". . . we are able by means of the test to follow the conflict between the repressing conscious and the repressed unconscious, and observe how the neurotic repressions narrow the productive sphere and see how freedom of 'inner life' is completely stifled by conscious restraints (corrections) and by compulsive super-criticism" (page 203).

As already anticipated in the earlier discussion of creativity in general (see pp. 78–82), it is not implied that the total personality is actively involved in these shifts of psychic level during the Rorschach test. Otherwise, of course, the patient would be racked by total upheavals of his adjustment and would suffer numerous schizophrenic episodes and other gross alterations in his state of consciousness in order to complete the test. The Rorschach response process must be thought of as being like the dream, the artistic creative process, or any thought process in this regard: it is an experimental and tentative form of action using small quantities of energy. This means that to a great extent it ordinarily works with relatively remote derivatives of basic needs and drives, such as attitudes, values and interests of an everyday, individually characteristic sort. Such attitudes, values and interests may even have achieved relative autonomy from the basic drives and conflicts from which they arose, although grossly or subtly they will still bear the stamp of their origins, and in a crisis may still be sucked back into the vortex of conflict and lose their autonomy. This designation of the Rorschach response process as a special case of thought processes in general also means that the Rorschach response process ordinarily works to a great extent with relatively obscure, as well as remote, derivatives of basic personality forces, such as symbols, screen memories, idiosyncratic metaphor, and verbal clichés.

In other words, dreams and Rorschach responses are or may be microcosmic expressions of the macrocosmic trends and conflicts in the personality. The same may be said of any creative production. When, for example, the patient sees "blood" on Card II of the Rorschach test, he is in a sense expressing a hostile theme, but he is not being hostile; when he sees a "monster devouring a person" on Card V he may be expressing the theme of intense devouring impulses, but he is neither devouring nor fleeing from the office in terror in response to this projection. In small ways he may react to his themes as he does to the real forces or events to which they allude. Thus, he may become anxious upon seeing "blood" and may become especially deferent toward the tester, as if to deny or make up for the "hostile" expression; similarly, while he may not flee from the office in response to the "devouring" image, he may flee from the card by rejecting it at once with more or less overt uneasiness and possibly even a touch of fright. At times, particularly in psychotic cases, apparently genuine changes in states of consciousness occur, the Rorschach responses become briefly "almost real," and intense emotional reactions result, but this is not typical. At times too the patient's conscious experience of the response process may not be too different from his experience of daydreams and dreams: images may just well up in him and he may feel himself to be only a passive observer of the stream of images. But the patient is neither dreaming nor daydreaming: he is awake and ordinarily is in close touch with reality at the moment or soon afterward.

Thus, when it is said in connection with the Rorschach test that a regressive shift in the level of psychic functioning has occurred, or that a new balance of id-ego-superego forces has been struck, or that defenses have been broken through by repressed impulses, it is meant that these dramas are being enacted on a small stage and by actors who stand for real forces but are not the forces themselves. *This is what thought is.* Yet this remote microcosm will parallel the macrocosm, and the Rorschach record will therefore help us understand the total personality crises and resolutions that are occurring in the patient's real life. On this level of analysis there is every reason to apply the same analytic concepts to the Rorschach response as to the dream and the work of art. We should not forget, however, that the Rorschach response is not a dream. It is produced by an awake subject and must be understood as a variety of waking conscious experience. Above all, it is an experience controlled by the ordinarily relatively strong waking ego.

*d. Evidence for the regressive shift.* What evidence is there that the level of psychic functioning does fluctuate during the Rorschach test? There are at least four classes of relevant evidence.

(1) There are the observations first described by Rorschach himself of the subject's general orientation or attitude toward the test stimuli [*124*]. Rorschach contrasted those subjects who think of the inkblots as depicting something real and therefore of the responses as simple perceptions, and those subjects who are more aware of the interpretive process, that is, of their part in selecting and defining responses. In this connection he says, ". . . it is apparent that the difference cannot be said to be due only to associative processes; emotional factors may also shift the boundary between association and perception" (page 18). Patients appear to spread out all along this continuum between naive realism and self-consciousness, between the "perceptual" attitude and the "interpretive" attitude.

More than that, the same patient often does not maintain the same attitude toward the inkblots all through the test. At times he will be pre- nantly blot-conscious and at other times predominantly self-conscious.

Rorschach touches on this in his discussion of alternating "coartation" and "dilation" during the formation of responses (pages 202-203). Rapaport, using the concepts of "closeness to" and "distance from" the stimulus, has discussed this process at length [118]. These shifts within one patient between the poles of self and external stimulus, as well as the distribution of patients along this continuum with respect to their dominant attitude during the test, may be conceived of not simply in the descriptive terms *introversive, extratensive, coartated,* and *dilated* as Rorschach did, but, as is being attempted in this chapter, in psychoanalytic structural and dynamic terms as well.

From the point of view of thought organization, these changes from the "perceptual" to the "interpretive" attitude or *vice versa* appear to involve shifts of the line between reality and fantasy. Consider the example of a patient who, from the beginning of the test, has been cautious and critical of his responses, who has been working hard to be "objective," and who suddenly sees "a stern old man" in the red on Card IX. Here is a clear-cut shift deeper into fantasy, evidenced by the fact that the "stern" characterization is not repudiated or even commented on by this otherwise meticulously "perceptual" patient. The patient seems to have lost distance from his response, presumably in reaction to the emotional charge of the image.

In the more striking shifts that usually occur in schizophrenic records, we may encounter on one card an unembellished common response, followed by a *DW* response, followed then by a contamination with perverse sexual content, then a witty *Original+* that includes an *FC,* and finally another unembellished common response. In this instance, the patient's self-critical distance from the inkblot, his conceptual level of thinking, his momentary defensive and adaptive status as expressed in his accepting or repudiating, mastering or being overwhelmed by his autistic tendencies, and other aspects of his relation to internal and external reality are all altered from one response to the next. It is as if there is a new definition of the test situation and of his role in life with each response. It is these varieties of definitions, as expressed in different types of thought organization involved in each response, that indicate the shift of the line between fantasy and reality, and the corresponding shift in level of functioning. These shifts may be benign or malignant, of course, depending on how far they go and in what direction. They are nowhere clearer and more dramatic than in schizophrenic records [118, 124, 134]; but then such astonishing shifts in level of psychic functioning are almost distinctively schizophrenic.

(2) As further evidence of fluctuating psychic levels in the response process, there are the shifts back and forth between banal and highly

original, self-expressive images. From these shifts we may often infer changes in the boundaries of unconscious, preconscious and conscious processes, and associated changes in the mutual relations of id, ego, and superego. In particular we may see in these shifts waxing and waning of defensive efforts.

(3) Also relevant in this regard are the shifts back and forth between accurate and inaccurate form, between form and movement, between color and form, between whole responses and tiny detail responses, and the like. From these shifts we may often infer changes in the patient's relationship with reality as well as changes in his inner experience. At one moment external reality may dominate the scene $(F+)$, and at the next idiosyncratic preoccupation may blur and distort perception of reality $(F-)$; at one moment maintenance of control may be of primary concern $(F)$, in the next a rich fantasy $(M)$, and in the third a warm affect $(CF)$.* These shifts often have regressive and progressive aspects.

(4) Finally, fluctuating levels of functioning are evidenced in changing emotional reactions throughout the test. As already mentioned in Chapter 2 on interpersonal dynamics, and as will be extensively illustrated in Chapters 6 through 10 on defensive operations, the patient's feelings about and attitudes toward the stimuli and his own responses may change subtly or radically as he goes along. Each such change betokens a reorganization of the psychological forces in the field or a shift in their balance, and many of these reorganizations and shifts involve regressive and progressive movement.

Considering these four types of evidence, it seems justified to maintain that shifting levels of psychic functioning do characterize most patients during the Rorschach test. The regression during the Rorschach test is not held at one point but is a fluctuating one, as in any creative act, in dreams, and in hypnosis. Too great relaxation of controls threatens breakthrough of material difficult to cope with, in which case anxiety signals are sounded or guilt is felt, and a flight from this regressed position occurs.

In the Rorschach situation, the anxiety or guilt and resulting flight from regression are seen in various ways: the patient may block, retreat to banal content or tiny details or pure form, give up the card, begin describing the inkblots instead of interpreting them, ask for further instructions, criticize his responses, engage the tester in some social interchange, etc. If we were to represent these alterations of functioning from one response to the next diagrammatically, each response being represented by a vertical line, they would look something like Figure 1.

* Baer has put forth an intriguing, but somewhat mechanistically conceived, method for schematizing these shifts on a Rorschach psychogram [5]; see also above, pp. 37-8, footnote.

*e. Individual differences in regressive shifts.* Patients respond in individually characteristic ways to the regressive aspects of the Rorschach test situation.

(1) *Patients differ in the extent to which they must regress before they can respond imaginatively.* The extent of the regression required will be determined by the general rigidity, weakness or flexibility of prevailing defenses, by the ego-syntonicity of primitive and creative tendencies, and by the wit available to effect disguises of objectionable tendencies. Some patients start responding at the drop of a Rorschach card, as if they are accustomed to doing precisely this sort of thing all day long; others labor mightily to achieve the necessary imaginal freedom required to form and accept each response, as if habitually they carefully avoid any temptation to engage in idle or busy fantasy.

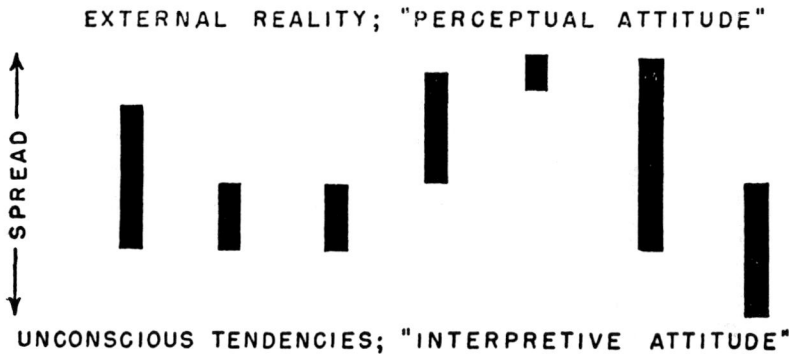

EXTERNAL REALITY; "PERCEPTUAL ATTITUDE"

UNCONSCIOUS TENDENCIES; "INTERPRETIVE ATTITUDE"

FIGURE 1

(2) *Patients differ in the extent to which they can regress.* The extent of regression possible will depend upon anxiety tolerance and capacity for self-expression and self-confrontation; it will also depend upon the pressure and strength of certain mechanisms of defense. The patient who can count on his powers of isolation of affect, for example, can let himself see most anything in the blots; the patient who relies heavily on paranoid projection can find much personally taboo material in the blots; and so on.

(3) *Patients differ in the ease and extent of regression in different emotional areas.* In different cases, anxiety will ordinarily be greater concerning some types of buried material than others. Some patients produce dramatic imagery that extends only or mainly to their major defensive operations and not at all to their primitive impulses; some patients express mainly their problems concerning hostility, while others may express mainly their problems concerning dependency; etc.

(4) *And patients differ in the extent to which they recover from their temporary regressions.* This recovery may be gauged by the final formula-

tion of the response—its accuracy, its subtlety of disguise, the patient's maintenance of composure and possibly even pleasure in this creative process, the adequacy of subsequent responses, and the stability of the patient's attitude toward the test situation and relationship.

In this section we have considered five aspects of the regressive shifts in the level of psychic functioning during the Rorschach test. In order, these aspects have been the motivations of these shifts, their facilitation, their inner structure, evidence for their existence, and individual differences in their occurrence. These various considerations make it plain that the Rorschach response process is a process of considerable complexity. The preceeding discussions have merely scratched the surface of this complexity. Only by penetrating this intricate response process can we hope to arrive at better Rorschach theory, and through that at better Rorschach interpretation.

## F. Summary

What understanding have we gained of the Rorschach response process? How is it, to return to the opening proposition of this chapter, that the Rorschach test does unlock the book of our private imagery and render the images in it amenable to partial psychoanalytic interpretation?

An attempt has been made to understand the Rorschach response process within the framework of psychoanalytic ego psychology in general and the psychoanalytic theory of thinking and of creativity in particular. This analysis has treated the Rorschach response process as a creative thought process often characterized by a relatively obvious and vital spread of reference from the primitive to the advanced levels of psychic functioning. This spread over different levels of psychic functioning brings the theory of Rorschach response into relation with the theory of dreaming, daydreaming, purposeful visualizing and normal perceiving, since the latter processes appear to be high points on a gross continuum of levels of psychic functioning, ranging in the order given from the primitive to the advanced. It has been brought out that functioning on the primitive levels is characterized by inadequate maintenance of the boundaries of the self, weakened defense, and domination of thought and action by the primary process, that is, by impulse-oriented, diffuse, fluid, archaic, undiscriminating and unreflective tendencies and features; functioning on the advanced psychic levels is characterized by adequate maintenance of the boundaries of the self, relatively strong defense, and domination of thought and action by the secondary process, that is, by reality-oriented, articulated, hierarchically integrated, selective and reflective tendencies and features. The creative spread of the Rorschach response has been held capable of simultaneously encompassing properties of functioning on many psychic levels, although individual Rorschach responses vary in the amount of spread that may be discerned in them.

Not only do the individual Rorschach responses seem to vary in the amount of spread they contain, but total Rorschach records vary in their general breadth of reference to the various psychic levels, and the same record may vary dramatically in this respect from one part to the next. In this last regard we have spoken of *shifting* levels of psychic functioning during the test, and have assumed that this shifting is dynamically on the same order as the regressive and progressive shifting that ordinarily occurs throughout the day and night, and that has been particularly observed in dreams, therapy, and creative work. Dynamically, the Rorschach shifts of psychic level appear to reflect shifting balances of psychological forces within the patient, and the shifting balances of forces in turn appear to reflect the vicissitudes of the test relationship and of the response process itself, that is, the type of imagery that comes to consciousness and patient's reactions to this imagery.

The imagery that comes to consciousness is assumed to be that stimulated by the inkblots and their partial or total resemblances to real objects, that pushed forward by the patient's infantile conflicts and tendencies, and that ordinarily readily available in impersonal dealings with the environment. Depending directly upon how anxiety-arousing these images are, or in other words how obviously the images express impulses, fantasies and feelings difficult to tolerate in consciousness, the level of psychic functioning will fluctuate. Accordingly, the least psychic regression has been found to occur where there is the least tolerance for and the most rigid defense against conscious *fantasy,* that is, in pathologically repressive persons, or the least tolerance for and the most rigid defense against conscious *feeling,* that is, pathologically inhibited and compulsive persons.

The shifting levels of functioning in the test and the corresponding shifting balances of forces are necessarily to be thought of as microcosmic and not macrocosmic. They involve remote, obscure or greatly attenuated expressions of the basic personality forces to which they refer. In this respect the Rorschach response is no different from the usual dream or from other imaginal productions, and ultimately no different from any form of thought.

Such shifts as occur during the test may be discerned in (1) fluctuations between the "perceptual" and "interpretive" attitude toward the test stimuli, that is, altered definitions of one's momentary relationship with reality as evidenced in shifts of the line between reality and fantasy, (2) fluctuations between originality and banality, (3) fluctuations between accuracy and inaccuracy, and variations in the size, location, and determinants of responses, and (4) changing attitudes toward the responses, the test and the tester.

The regressive aspects of the Rorschach response process have been particularly emphasized since they seem to heighten greatly the self-expressive nature of the responses. These regressive aspects appear to be expressions of "temporary regression in the service of the ego," that is, regressions in which the ego actively and adaptively exploits the primary process tendencies for creative purposes and is not passively and unadaptively overwhelmed by these tendencies, as happens in unsocialized daydreams and in pathological phenomena generally. This temporary regression in the level of psychic functioning is assumed to be a prerequisite of achieving the imaginal freedom and expanded consciousness, that is, the conscious access to normally preconscious and unconscious images, necessary to respond to the inkblots with more than descriptions or simple popular images.

The coming about of this psychic regression has been considered to be due basically to the patient's wish to respond to the stimuli in accordance with the test instructions that he find resemblances. In turn, the wish to respond appears to derive from a combination of (1) realistic therapeutic intent, (2) irrational or transference reactions to the tester—to his role as tester *per se,* and to his role as agent of the therapist and ultimately of the family, (3) to the constant pushing of unconscious, rejected, infantile tendencies and their derivatives toward conscious expression, (4) miscellaneous motives such as intellectual curiosity, the desire for play, creative zeal, and need to discharge residual tensions of the day.

The temporary creative regression appears to be encouraged and facilitated by (1) the test instructions' calling for mingling of realistic perception and free fantasy, (2) the opportunity afforded the patient to externalize the responsibility for the content of his responses, (3) the absence of external reference points to help the patient keep the content of his responses safely conventional, and (4) the usual absence of explicit autobiographical specificity and narrative continuity in his responses, the responses superficially seeming fragmentary, isolated, static and impersonal, even though response *sequences* may implicitly tell dramatic stories of conflict. These features of the test situation and the test responses facilitate the temporary creative regression because they tend to reduce the anxiety and its counter-regressive effects the patient would otherwise feel in reaction to the more primitive or transparently self-expressive of his images.

Nevertheless, counter-regressive forces seem to be active during the response process. These include (1) the external reference point—the inkblot—with which the response is expected to stand in some objective relationship, (2) the patient's need to verbalize his responses as he forms them, (3) the partly eluded but very much on guard defensive ego functions and the anxiety signals from which they take their cue, and (4) the persisting adaptive, synthesizing ego attitudes and functions.

In this regressive situation, individuals vary in (1) the extent to which they must regress before they can respond freely, (2) the extent to which they can in general regress for creative purposes, (3) the ease with which and the extent to which they can regress in different dynamic areas, and (4) their ability to recover from temporary creative regressions in their level of functioning.

It is through this complex process that the patient's network of both self-expressive, conflictful imagery and impersonal, conflict-free imagery is exposed to and interacts with the test stimuli. This network of imagery is played on by the forms, colors, and shadings of the inkblots, but also it selectively emphasizes certain of these forms, colors and shadings. The response process is therefore one that is the reverse of that described in Freud's formula for repression—the push from above (from the repressing ego) and the pull from below (from the repressed memories and tendencies). Here there is a pull from above (from the inkblots and the wish to respond) and a push from below (from the impulse- and affect-charged imagery). The defensive ego functions are operating all the while to maintain basic repressive security; the adaptive ego functions are operating simultaneously to find, shape, formulate, and revise responses; and the inkblots contribute to and limit the possibilities. Rorschach responses appear to be the final precipitates of all these partial processes. It is for reasons such as these that the Rorschach test is so often so dramatically revealing of the adaptive and defensive strengths and weaknesses of the patient, his pathological trends, his conscious and unconscious values, yearnings, fears, wrath, guilt and joy, and the overall color and tone of his personality.

# 4. Thematic Analysis

P REVIOUSLY, WE CAME UP TO THE POINT OF critically reexamining the concept of the relative ambiguity or unstructuredness of the Rorschach inkblots. It was said then that in a literal sense the blots are not unstructured. They have definite, easily perceivable shapes, colors, textures and configurations. In other words, if we did not leave patients on their own, but instead we simply asked them all the same direct, detailed questions about these properties of the blots, they would manifest little individual variability of response, except perhaps in style of verbalization. Having arrived at the question, "In what then does the stimulus unstructuredness consist?" we deferred further investigation of that point in order to give more consideration to the place of the Rorschach response on the percept–dream continuum, and to the similarities and dissimilarities between dream images and Rorschach responses.

## A. UNSTRUCTUREDNESS IN FORM AND CONTENT

Returning now to the problem of unstructuredness, we must first of all reexamine the concept "unstructuredness" as it applies to the Rorschach test. While it is probably true that patients would agree to a great extent in describing the properties of the blots, *provided that they were asked detailed questions,* it is also probably true that if the patients were initially simply asked to describe the properties of the blots *and were then left entirely on their own,* they would differ a great deal in their reports. Some would mention color first, and others form first; some would give overall descriptions first, and some would start with details and perhaps never give overall descriptions; some would be sensitive to certain types of "enclosing," *V*-like and *O*-like configurations, and others would be sensitive to "protruding" or "intruding" configurations; etc. We would see here the operation of relatively automatized perceptual principles or "cognitive styles" [85] which themselves have evolved from, were shaped by, and are expressions of major personality trends. These perceptual principles would select and organize certain properties of the blots, and ignore or minimize others. The blots are sufficiently complex that such self-expressive, relatively stable, selective principles of perception would have relatively free play in this situation. Thus, when we say that blots are "unstructured," we mean this mainly with respect to a perceiver who intends to describe or interpret the blots more or less freely. In other words, unstructuredness is defined largely by the perceiver's attitude or intent. We also mean by "unstructured" that the blots are plastic rather than unclear or elusive.

Yet it seems unwarranted and ultimately unproductive to think of the structure-giving perceptual principles or "styles" as having meaning only in a formal sense and not in a dynamic or content sense as well. It seems more fruitful to regard these perceptual "styles" as enduring, integrated response tendencies which have remained in the service of and reflect enduring configurations of drives, defenses, and adaptive efforts, and the imagery with which these are associated. From this point of view, enclosures and projections, forms and colors, totalities and details, or rough and smooth edges matter to us because they are congruent with dominant, affect-charged images, even when this congruence and its associative links are unconscious. This implies that the perceptual organizing principles do not achieve complete autonomy from emotional life. These principles might best be thought of as automatized rather than autonomous, as trusted and well-trained slaves rather than emancipated freemen. Schachtel's analysis of "dynamic form perception" in the Rorschach test [129] and Erikson's analysis of the use of space in play constructions [33, 36] appear to be based on similar interpretative assumptions.* Structuring the Rorschach stimuli is as much a matter of content as of form, and the dominant imagery of bodily and social experience is a major aspect of our perceptual organizing principles.

We know, for example, that the combination of pedantic aggressiveness, flight from affect and anxiety because of their potentially "messy" and "violent" eruptions, subjective feelings of being lost in a basically unmanageable big world, and defense by compulsive perfectionism may all rigidly restrict a patient's attention to tiny details of the blots. Here is a perceptual "style" that clearly derives from and reflects a total personality configuration. Similarly, we know that megalomanic defense, with its inherent high level of ambition, may underlie a relentless drive to perceive the blots in their entirety only, to be "all-seeing," as it were. We know too that in one individual a combination of intense sadistic impulses and megalomanic defense may lead to the delivery of many *Whole* responses which in their content emphasize weapons, wounds, deformities and explosions, and that a combination of intense sadistic impulses and finicky compulsiveness may lead to an emphasis on the very same content in tiny areas. A final example, this one working from the Rorschach record back to the patient's personality : colors and shadings may be completely avoided, and only form-determined responses offered. Here is a "formal style" of perception from which we commonly infer great emphasis on intellectual

* For related discussions, see also Booth [17], and Bruner [21].

control, on inhibition, minimization, isolation and avoidance of affective experience. But "affective experience" is not a one-dimensional, irreducible concept. To one patient—judging from the results of a battery of tests— affective experience may mean principally dirty, defiant, "anal" attitudes and behavior that are totally incompatible with his severe superego dictates and reaction formations, while to another patient affective experience may mean principally yielding to passive, feminine, "self-castrating" tendencies that are incompatible with maintenance of masculine self-esteem and counterphobic defense. In either case, however, perceptual "style" and dynamic orientation seem to be two aspects of a general personality configuration.

It must be added that while they are instructive, these examples have been somewhat artificial. Not that the test patterns described are never encountered clinically; they are, but they are not the rule. They represent relatively extreme, clear-cut, "pure" cases. Usually we encounter varieties of locations, determinants and content in each record. Such "style" as is ordinarily evident is more in the nature of a trend than an all-embracing pattern. Also, more than one such trend is commonly found in each record. The trend may be toward $W$ and $F$ or toward $W$ and $C$; it may be toward $W$ and $F$ and *Animal*, $W$ and $F$ and *Art*, $W$ and $C$ and *Animal,* or $W$ and $C$ and *Art*, etc. The combinations and permutations are virtually infinite—a fact that also helps account for the Rorschach test's great usefulness in establishing significant individual nuances of adjustment and pathology.

Of course, a goodly amount of perceptual structuring will ordinarily be relatively impersonal and conflict-free, or, as Schachtel has put it, "detached" perception rather than "dynamic" perception [*129*]. This is partly because ordinarily many essentially neutral images are available to the ego functions of reality testing and purposeful visualization and hence to the Rorschach response process. It is also partly because, as has been mentioned already, many of the areas conform rather closely to the configurations of real objects, animals and persons. The popular responses and the many near-popular responses, unless given with an individual twist, are the best examples of relatively "detached" perception. In these responses the perceptual organizing principles that bear the individual's distinctive stamp ordinarily play a minor or obscure part. Of course, since capacity for relatively "detached" perception plays so major a part in our everyday functioning, the presence or absence of these "detached" responses is a matter of utmost importance in the interpretation of adaptiveness, adequacy of contact with reality, and strength and efficiency of defenses.

The further we move away from these more or less compelling, realistic, "detached" responses, however, the more it seems that the same principles that regulate the perceptual structuring of the blots will regulate the selection of content to be introduced into the blots. With increasing distance from "detached" perception, shifting levels of psychic functioning and corresponding shifting balances of impulses, defenses, adaptive strivings, etc., will be increasingly prominent in the perceptual approach to the blots.

In summary of this section it may be said that creating perceptual structure and creating content seem to be two aspects of the same process. The simultaneous study of the perceptual structuring principles and of content tells us a good deal about what matters to the patient and what he does about it. Complex configurations of impulses, defenses, adaptive strivings and other major aspects of personality may be expressed in the perceptual organization and in the content. Neither structuring nor content is the exclusive property of any one psychic system such as the *id* or the *ego;* both are multiply determined. Both also have their relatively neutral, impersonal, conflict-free, "detached" aspects. The case studies to be presented later will amply illustrate these points.

But while the dynamic interpretation of perceptual behavior has received a fair amount of theoretical attention, notably by Rorschach [*124*], Schachtel [*129*] and Rapaport [*118*], and while Rorschach content interpretation is freely practiced in clinical work these days, the theory of dynamic interpretation of content has been pretty much ignored. In theoretical discussions, the perceptual ambiguity of the situation has been favored over the content ambiguity; in clinical work, the need for theory has been virtually unrecognized. Yet, as we have seen above and will also see later in this chapter, not only should the analysis of content or imagery play a major role in Rorschach interpretation, but this analysis must be clear on what it assumes about personality and about the psychology of the Rorschach response process. Otherwise, serious confusions and distortions in Rorschach research and interpretation may result.

## B. Static and Dynamic Content Categories

All of the foregoing considerations confront us with the inadequacy of the content categories now in use, such as *Animal, Human, Object, Anatomy, Nature,* etc. These categories are of some demonstrated value, particularly with respect to estimating breadth of interests and identifying specific preoccupations, such as bodily or sexual preoccupations. Nevertheless, their value is limited because they are static categories. They reflect Rorschach's original disparagement of content analysis. The psychology of personality has long since abandoned strict adherence to such *class* concepts and has shifted emphasis to *functional* or *dynamic* concepts. For example, a lamb, a sleeping infant, and a cradle have much in common thematically, although they represent three different static content categories, i.e., *Animal, Human* and *Object* respectively. They may be said to deal with the theme of infantile innocence, or perhaps the need for care and protection, or both.

Similarly, a worn-out bearskin rug, a withered leaf, a crumbled wall, and a toothless old man have in common the theme of decay or deterioration although they represent four different traditional content categories, i.e., *Animal detail, Plant, Architecture* and *Human*.*

We are led now to see that *thematic analysis,* in much the same sense as that applied to the Thematic Apperception test stories and to free associations and dreams in psychoanalysis, can be a basis of meaningful study of Rorschach responses. In its broadest sense, thematic analysis should and can include all aspects of the responses—those covered by the customary location, determinant, and content scores and their sequences, those included under test attitudes and behavior, and those implied as dynamic themes in

* Compare the recent publications of Beck [*11*] and Phillips and Smith [*105*]. In line with their general emphasis on the empirical approach to Rorschach testing, these authors list specific classes of content (e.g., Anatomy, Architecture, etc.) and give the psychodynamic significance of each. Of the two publications, Beck's is by far the more conservative. Beck properly insists that these content significances be used only as "leads" for subsequent clinical investigation; also, he keeps his interpretations relatively close to the manifest content of the responses; finally, he does include thematic *classes* of content in his list (e.g., Oral). In contrast, Phillips and Smith present a long list of specific images (e.g., Bat, Beetle, Butterfly, Food, Peninsula, etc.) and elaborate extensively the implications of each (pp. 119–153). These elaborations are said to be based purely on normative Rorschach data and not on psychoanalytic theory or clinical experience; they refer with astounding specificity and breadth to the patient's past experience and relationships as well as to present total patterns of functioning. Moreover, Phillips and Smith insist that each specific content must be assigned a fixed significance, regardless of context, unless good evidence to the contrary can be established by research. So long as they support their claims by reference to data, these authors cannot be criticized for carrying on "wild analysis," but one wonders at the nature of "normative data, however unrefined" (p. 119) that can organize such a multiplicity of complex and elusive trends and observations around single response categories.

At the extreme of this type of "empirical" content analysis is that advocated by Lindner [*96*] and more recently by Brown [*20*], in which not simply narrow classes of content are interpreted elaborately but single responses to specific areas; that is to say, individual responses, such as "cat's face" given to all of Card II *and not to any other card or area,* are held to represent more or less complex configurations of the patient's past experience and present organization and functioning. In all these publications the reader will encounter instances of overlap with content significances suggested in this volume. It should be remembered, however, that here the basic emphasis is on themes, not content categories, and that these themes, while they reflect the phenomenology of Rorschach responses, depend on contemporary psychodynamic theory and observation. As much as possible, the dangers of test-centered principles of interpretation are avoided and the test is kept subordinate to theory and clinical data. Also, the content interpretations here remain relatively general and modest, and they are in keeping with the level of analysis employed successfully in recent experimental studies of content significance [*3, 16, 27, 31, 63, 65, 146*]. See also pp. 32–3, footnote, 142–3, footnote, and 147–8.

the content. With respect to sequence analysis of scores, for example, thematic analysis would not only ask, What is implied by the sequence of locations and determinants? Thematic analysis would also ask, How is this sequence an expression of the same problems and means of coping with problems as are expressed in the dynamic themes in the content and in test attitudes and behavior? In this chapter we shall be concerned with thematic interpretation of the content alone. In the next two chapters and in the later case studies, the broadest application of thematic analysis will be discussed and demonstrated.

To a significant extent, identifying the most fruitful content themes to emphasize, and specifying the referents of these themes, are matters for future systematic research. But more important, these content themes are largely reflections of one's theoretical point of view or conceptual framework. How we formulate what matters to the patient depends greatly on what matters to us theoretically. Obviously, the final choice of major themes will be decided not by Rorschach research, but by the general development of the theory of personality and psychopathology—to which Rorschach research may make a contribution if, as advocated here, it is conceived of within the mainstream of clinical and theoretical thought. For the time being, however, we are left with the combined advantages and disadvantages of great—almost literary—flexibility in the concepts we may apply. Our themes—see *Section H* below—will be drawn chiefly from contemporary Freudian psychoanalytic psychology.

## C. What Matters to the Patient?

An individual's drive, defense, and adaptation problems, his image of himself and of others around him, his primitive morality and refined values, and his general outlook on life are identified to a large extent by the attributes of persons, objects and events that matter to him. These attributes have a way of coming to the fore in his perceptions, fantasies, memories, anticipations and dreams. For this general reason, and for the particular reasons elaborated in the previous chapter, these attributes also tend to come to the fore in his Rorschach test responses. The tester can tune in on these expressions of personal and social orientation by listening not only to the content proper of the responses but to the patient's descriptions, elaborations and evaluations of this content and of each response as a whole. Sometimes the self-expressions are more explicit, as in the response "a lovely flower," and sometimes more implicit, as in "a snowman." Sometimes they are closer to home, as in "an ugly person," and sometimes more remote, as in "a coat of arms" or "a withered leaf." In whatever form they come to expression—and within records of any richness the forms of expression may be extremely varied—these self-expressions are often statements of basic personal and social orientation points of the individual.

There is, of course, a close parallel between what matters to a person about himself and what matters to him in the world around him. We see and evaluate others much as we see and evaluate ourselves. This age-old insight does not, however, imply that the inward and outward views have equal access to consciousness or equal prominence in it. Often, particularly in psychopathological settings, one or the other is mostly outside the realm of consciousness. Depressives, for example, unconsciously condemn others who have "abandoned" them, but consciously condemn only or mainly themselves. Some paranoid patients, in contrast, righteously condemn all the world and remain unaware that they judge themselves just as harshly, if not more so. In more attenuated and balanced forms, these depressive and paranoid prototypes are popular maneuvers in the normal range. It is said, for example, that we especially dislike faults in others that remind us of our own faults, and that we like our virtues in others. The mechanisms in the normal and pathological ranges are much the same—some degree of reality distortion or psychological obtuseness being inevitably involved— although differences of degree should certainly not be minimized.

For purposes of the following analysis it is also important to note that unconsciously, in line with the characteristics of primary process thinking, these personal and social orientations also tend to be conceived of in terms of absolute dichotomies. There is, for example, Good and Bad and nothing in between. Moreover, someone or some activity is either All Good or All Bad; there is no middle ground, no continuum, no allowance for the context of past and present circumstances. If you are not strong now, you are weak, always have been and always will be, and are to be despised. If your friend lets you down once, you were a fool to have ever trusted him, and obviously should trust neither him nor anyone else ever again. Neither you nor anybody else can be manly *and* sentimental, courageous *and* fearful, kind *and* selfish, etc. In short, you cannot be all the things that people generally are. This stark black-and-white psychology appears to persist to some extent in all of us, more or less unconsciously and not without some effect, but ordinarily it is rejected by our more rational, articulated, realistic principles or modes of self-regard. In times of life crisis, of being threatened in areas of particular personal vulnerability, these primitive conceptions are likely to become more apparent and dominant than during relatively tranquil times. Greater acceptance of or domination by these archaic dichotomies than this usually implies basic character disorder.

## D. THREE BRIEF EXAMPLES

The considerations in the three previous sections of this chapter— *Unstructuredness in form and content, Static and dynamic content categories,* and *What matters to the patient?*—will be more meaningful if we now consider some concrete examples. Our interest will be in interlocking implications of form and content, in dynamic interpretation of content, and in the clarification of what matters to the patient about himself and in the world around him. Like most examples, these will be oversimplified. The interpretations to be presented should always have multiple support before much is made of them.

*Example 1.* A seemingly hard-headed, hard-driving, rigidly compulsive, grumpy, highly successful but recently somewhat anxious and depressed businessman sees "a beautiful sweet pea" at the bottom of Card VIII. Since this is a nice $FC+$ response, it implies some interest in good rapport with others. But is this all it implies? Certainly not. In fact, even the correctness of this routine interpretation depends upon a number of implications more intimately bound up with the response.

The patient tells us first that he knows something about flowers. *Sweet pea* implies an articulated concept of flowers that comes only with interest in and some kind of appreciation of them. By certain widely held "masculine" standards in our culture, this is not manly; flowers are appropriate matters of concern only to the fair sex, connoting as they do gentleness, sentimentality, free play of affect. But our grumpy gentleman not only does not blush to see a flower, but twice affirms his acceptance of this complex of emotional experience, first by calling the flower specifically "a sweet pea," and second by declaring it "beautiful." All that has been said of the *flower* stereotype applies doubly to so extravagant and free an emotional response as is expressed in the word "beautiful." Altogether this is quite a luxury for such a big success in the world of men to allow himself. Yet he does indulge himself, and in so doing tells us that his compulsive need for order and control is not so rigid and pervasive that he rejects all sentimental experience as disorderly, non-utilitarian, weak, feminine, and a matter of fear and shame. He declares that there is a place for sentiment in his life.

*Assuming that the rest of the Rorschach record and the other tests in the test battery are in line with these inferences,* this patient would therefore seem to be characterized by noteworthy flexibility, by a healthy degree of balance between controls and spontaneous experience. In this setting a man may be free to engage in—and we could reasonably expect him to be interested in—closeness with others, for closeness means affect and sentiment, even if these are compulsively starched. By this route we arrive at a particularized version of the routine interpretation of the strong, good $FC$ —an interest in good rapport with others—but what we have learned along this route adds all the richness of understanding that context and specificity provide.

*Example 2.* A compulsive, ambitious, aggressive, well-endowed, Jewish man of 50 had risen from a poverty-stricken childhood through training at Annapolis to subsequent success in business. He progressively elaborated an ostentatious, lavish style of life. In World War II, as a high-ranking naval officer, he achieved considerable status and responsibility. He was, however, eased out of his position once the fighting was over. Deeply hurt by this rejection and no longer satisfied with his former civilian status— in fact, having great difficulty in re-establishing it profitably—and having no constructive outlet for his intense aggressiveness and need to control and dominate, he began to decompensate into a state of anxiety and depression. The advent of the Korean crisis re-awakened his hopes of achieving naval glory and intensified his feeling that life was passing him by.

In the upper middle area of Card V, he gives as his first response, "A man wearing a helmet or a derby." We score this response $Dd$ $F+$ $Hd$. None of these scores alone or in combination with others tells us even a small fraction of what he is probably communicating through this response. The response appears to set forth a complete identity problem. "What shall I be," he seems to be asking, "an ostentatiously elegant civilian or a daring man of action?" On another level, he seems to be asking, "Shall I be refined or tough?" and "Shall I subdue my antagonisms or shall I be destructively belligerent?" And he is very likely telling us that *attacking* and *elegance* are what matter to him in his self-image and his social relationships. It is with these variables in relationships that he has probably identified himself. Implicit to these values are fears of their opposites—being weak, defenseless, crude, poor and alien—all the fears a poverty-stricken Jewish childhood can instill. We need not have had the biographical information about his current and past life dilemma to have arrived at the essentials of these inferences. The biographical details were given above to demonstrate how accurately the results of thematic analysis may point to major life problems. Naturally, we should not draw major conclusions of this sort from one response alone.

*Example 3.* An extremely passive, dependent, demanding schizophrenic young man who has never succeeded in any school or job undertaking, and who has for many years tyrannized his parents through his withdrawn, helpless position, gives as his first response to Card V, "Two, no, three, no, four crocodile heads" (right, left, upper middle and lower middle pairs of projections). What is he telling us? In this simply an indication of anxiety and low anxiety tolerance, in that there is a disturbance of the manner of approach (giving $D$ and $Dd$ instead of a $W$ to begin with), and a flight to peripheral detail (edge projections emphasized rather than the large, dark, shaded areas)? Does it reflect an inability to see things conventionally (missing the popular response)? It would be a shame to be satisfied with so little interpretative yield. Most important of all, we see that apertures almost indiscriminately mean *mouths* to him, and that mouths mean *destructive, cruel engulfing*. This is what he is on the alert for, what he is ready or set to see. If devouring is so prominent in his stock of readily available ideas and images, then it must be an important dimension of his self-evaluation and his evaluation of significant figures in his environment.

Very frequently we find particular emphasis on *devouring* in the records of schizophrenic young men who have been more or less withdrawn and passive for many years; and invariably in their therapy the oral-destructive aspects of relationships become very prominent. Unconsciously or consciously, "Devour or be devoured!" is a basic tenet of their schizophrenic dogma. Devouring is what goes on in the world and what matters in the world. From this point of view, the present response may be seen to express the intent of confronting the world with a rapacious mouth—in front, behind, to the right and to the left.

This patient, who sees four crocodiles on Card V, sees on Card II "two bloody animals that must have been biting each other" (black and lower red) and "two bloody human heads that must have been biting each other" (upper red). Significantly, during the inquiry, he explains the latter response as follows: "I thought they were fighting because they are facing each other." He seems to imply by this that direct human contact is to him inevitably a mutually destructive, oral-sadistic affair. This entire outlook implies, in turn, that to himself he is all that *crocodile* stands for. Clinically this young man was characterized among other things by fascination with crocodiles and also with sharks—the *shark* preoccupation also manifesting itself prominently in his Rorschach imagery. These various oral-aggressive responses have been cited to indicate *the internal cross-validation or convergence of lines of reasoning and association that is often possible and always the goal in thematic analysis of Rorschach content.* The criteria for adequate, conservative, yet penetrating interpretations will be considered in detail in Chapter 5 to follow.

### E. The Place of Interests

The objection might be raised at this point that too big an interpretive jump is being made from Rorschach imagery to major dynamic formulations. It might be argued that the content is first of all an expression of interests. This argument would be consistent with the traditionally cautious handling of content as mainly an expression of breadth of interests.

To this objection we must say, Yes and no—*yes* in that often it is true that first of all imagery does reflect interests, as in the case of some physicians seeing more than the average amount of anatomy, but *no* for four reasons. (1) Interests themselves must be regarded as aspects, expressions, derivatives, or implementations in reality of major dynamic trends. We become interested in what matters to us for deeply personal reasons. In this respect the interpretive jump is not so big as it seems. In all three of the preceding illustrations, the mediating role of interest has been at least implicitly recognized, but has been used as a stepping stone to interpretation of deeper dynamic trends. (2) If we shift our attention from the range of content to specific instances of content, from the general to the particular, we must explain why certain images are available to express interests and not others. An interest in nature might as well be expressed in a hawk as a butterfly, in a rocky chasm as a grassy knoll, in a thunderstorm as a lovely sunset. This question leads us into an examination of the individual's selective principles of imagery, and thereby into an examination of his drive, defense, and adaptation problems and solutions. (3) The emphasis on interest places too great stress on sheer familiarity with objects; often, esoteric objects that are not part of organized interests are used for the most intimate self-expression. (4) Not all content expressions may be regarded as expressions of interests in any usual sense of the term *interest.* "A withered leaf" cannot be taken simply as an expression of interest in the condition of leaves. This response appears to express concern with wholeness and vitality. The leaf is merely a prop for the expression of this concern. Also, it does not seem very meaningful to say that there is an *interest* in wholeness and vitality. It seems more meaningful or at least clearer to say that wholeness and vitality are themes of significant concern to the patient. To avoid confusion, the term *interest* should be restricted to its traditional, primarily intellectual meaning.

Thus, while the role of interest will be acknowledged in the following discussions, it will take second place to or be used as a stepping stone to consideration of more central or disruptive dynamic problems.

### F. Life Context and Thematic Analysis

It might be further objected that the thematic approach to Rorschach content analysis ascribes invariant meanings to specific images. That is to say, such factors as differences in age, sex, cultural background and pathological syndrome are ignored. This is by no means the case.

1. *With respect to age differences,* for example, one might ask, If a 20-year-old girl and a 50-year-old woman both see several sets of ovaries in the blots, are they communicating the same concern? The answer to this question is, It depends on your level of interpretation. It seems correct to say on a general level that both women appear to be concerned with reproductive organs and functions. This is perhaps the level on which the Rorschach interpretation proper should remain. To say more is to go beyond the Rorschach test itself and to adorn the response with probably or possibly correct clinical insights into the meaning of concern with reproduction at different stages in the life cycle. There is much to be said for the conservative position in daily clinical work. From the point of view of Rorschach theory and the ultimate enrichment of clinical Rorschach interpretation, however, it will be worth our while to examine these specific qualitative variations of general themes.

It is reasonable to assume that throughout life there occur significant relocations of particular images in the individual network of imagery. With regard to the ovary example, we may say that what at 20 was probably an expression of hope, fear, and/or curiosity about child-bearing, is at 50 very likely an expression of some dismay and grief at what is regarded as loss of vitality, attractiveness, and opportunity to play a nurturant role. Perspectives on ovaries are significantly different in anticipation and retrospect.

Similarly in the cases of an 18-year-old boy and a 40-year-old married man and father, both of whom see a threatening, gigantic figure on Card IV. On a general level this response appears to express fearfulness, a self-image that emphasizes smallness, weakness and vulnerability, and an image of others that emphasizes bigness, violent strength and overwhelming powers. But for a boy in late adolescence who is probably trying to come to terms with the challenges of young adulthood—becoming a man among men, loosening bonds with parents, competing with and submitting to new father-figures—this anxious outlook is quite a different thing from that in a man in immature "maturity" with a long life-history of occupational, community, and familial demands, privileges and supports. *To get at the immediate relevance of the Rorschach imagery, we must be oriented to such modal crises throughout the life span.** This principle is no different from that which guides good dream interpretation or therapy in general. No better treatment of this problem may be found than Erikson's [35].

2. These considerations apply just as well to *sex differences*. Suppose a male patient and female patient both see many small, incomplete or otherwise minimized and imperfect male figures in the blots. From this, both patients appear to be concerned with the general theme of masculine inadequacy or "castration." In the case of the man, however, this imagery probably expresses an intensely anxious, weak, regressive self-image and orientation, while in the case of the woman this imagery probably expresses a competitive, disparaging orientation toward men. Even though the woman's hostile orientation may be largely a counterphobic maneuver and a denial of her own anxious, weak, regressive self-image and orientation, her use of the imagery appears to express the outcome of the denial and the counterphobic defense and not what is covered up thereby. Other women, for example, often express the anxious self-image directly and betray thereby quite a different general solution—or lack of solution—of their conflicts over feminine identity.

3. *With respect to cultural differences,* the immediate implications of Rorschach imagery also vary. Consider the example of the naive, poorly-educated rural woman and the sophisticated, well-educated urban woman,

* For a similar emphasis, see Vorhaus [145].

both of whom see "sexual intercourse" on Card IX. In the former case, considerably more serious or malignant failure of defense is suggested— though not established—than in the latter. The sophisticate has behind her a cultural pattern that sanctions the response to an extent, while the farm girl seems to be overthrowing her traditions to an alarming extent. Similarly, the naive, devoutly religious person and the highly intellectual, militant atheist, both of whom see a crucifix at the top of Card VI, express somewhat different problems, even though on a general level both indicate that they are concerned with religious issues. The believer is probably expressing an image of accepted faith, while the atheist appears to be expressing unstably, ambivalently rejected faith. The instability of the rejection in the latter case is suggested by the fact that many non-believers see no religious imagery at all in the test; religion seems to be too much on this patient's mind.

4. Finally, *with respect to differences in pathological syndrome,* we may contrast the passive, alcoholic, chronically failing man of 40 who sees numerous mouths and food objects, with the currently anxious and de-pressed but normally hard-driving, ascetic, chronically successful, com-pulsive man of 40 who sees the same things. Both men seem concerned in their imagery with oral, passive, receptive needs. Yet in the former case, these needs may be presumed to be largely ego-syntonic and relatively freely acted upon, while in the latter case these needs are likely to be mainly ego-alien but breaking through reaction formations and other defenses and stirring up considerable internal distress thereby. In one case the attitude is accepting and in the other rejecting. The first man's meat is the second man's poison.*

Thus, *thematic analysis of Rorschach imagery need not and should not assume invariant meanings of images except on a general level of interpre-tation.* On this general level, the interpretations are ordinarily so lacking in specificity that their clinical usefulness is greatly limited. Thematic analysis is especially penetrating clinically, and less likely to go off half-cocked, if it is elaborated in the context of age, sex, cultural and educa-tional background, pathological syndrome, and such other relevant aspects of any patient's existence as marital status, number and ages of siblings and children, recent traumatic breaks in relationships through death or conflict, chronic physical defect, and previous or current therapy.

It cannot be overemphasized that thematic analysis stands in constant danger of becoming "wild analysis," and that many safeguards are required to keep it within bounds. Additional safeguards and dangers will be dis-cussed below and particularly in the next chapter, after we have considered the kinds of themes that may be inferred from Rorschach images. The

* See in this regard the discussions of ego identity, pp. 158–9 and 172–3.

previous considerations make it plain that inflexible, one-to-one correlations between images and specific themes are theoretically unsound and therefore inevitably misleading clinically.

### G. Some Dangers of Thematic Analysis

There is no one thematic frame of reference that will adequately embrace all possible implications of Rorschach content. This is because the tester's choice of themes follows largely from his explicit or implicit theoretical definition of important, useful variables. This holds true not only for different theoretical orientations but for the variations of emphasis within any one general orientation. Within the psychoanalytic frame of reference, for example, the same content may be looked at from different points of view. We may consider what a particular response implies regarding drives, defenses, adaptation, superego pressures or such derivatives of these as values, self-concept, interpersonal orientation and mood.

For purposes of research, it is necessary to decide beforehand which variables are to be systematically investigated in each Rorschach record. In daily clinical practice, however, as contrasted with systematic research, it seems more economical to follow the patient's lead to a great extent, and to see around which of many possible themes his images cluster—provided, of course, that we at least remain within one theoretical framework, such as the psychoanalytic, and do not eclectically run hither and yon among theories for our concepts. In one record, for example, "anal" imagery may cluster around a specific homosexual theme and in the next around a general obsessional theme; there may be a cluster of "authoritarian" images in one record and none in the next; etc. We stay more in tune with the individual patient if we try to clarify *his* themes than if we inflexibly impose *our* themes on his responses.

To follow the patient's lead does not imply, however, that the themes he brings forward in his record are necessarily the most disturbing, most basic, most pervasive, most conspicuous or most anything else. On some level, we may be relatively certain, these themes are *important*. In view of the readiness and forcefulness with which they came to expression, these themes are also likely to be *pressing* and in some respects *relatively easily amenable to verbalization* or *relatively easy to infer from overt behavior*. More than that we cannot say with confidence about conspicuous themes at the present time. When sufficient research has been done in this area, we may be in a position to be more specific in our predictions. Aside from the limitations of prediction, however, an element of uncertainty will always persist in thematic analysis because part of the problem—that pertaining to the best way to conceptualize themes—is theoretical rather than empirical in nature.

Despite these problems of conceptualization and prediction, and despite the general absence of systematic, validating research, it will be worthwhile to list and exemplify a number of dynamic themes that have seemed useful in daily clinical practice.* No effort will be made to be exhaustive or rigorously hierarchic. The general categories will not, therefore, be mutually exclusive or subordinated one to the other. Sometimes the same example will be used in more than one context. The foregoing discussions should make it clear that repeated examples are not oversights, redundancies or contradictions. It is just that the same content may be looked at from different points of view and may enter into different thematic clusters. For example, the response "peg-leg sailor" might refer to the following themes: castration fantasy (the missing limb standing for the missing penis specifically and the impairment of masculinity generally), rebellious fantasy (the peg-leg sailor image commonly pertaining to antisocial pirates), sadistic fantasy (the cruel pirate in vicious combat), childish adventure fantasy (running away from home to sea; being kidnapped; seeking buried treasure), and masochistic fantasy (the idea of the painful amputation and the distorted, repulsive consequences on appearance). Which particular connotation of the peg-leg sailor image to emphasize in individual clinical workups will always have to be settled by the total context of test results, while in research investigations the connotation to emphasize will be decided by one's experimental hypothesis.

If anything, therefore, the reader should pay special attention to recurrence of the same image under different thematic headings. A list of the sort that follows always carries with it the danger of being applied dictionary-style to each new record encountered clinically. While this is not sufficient reason to refrain from setting up lists, it is sufficient to warrant repeated emphasis on theoretical variations on themes, multiple determination of responses, complex meanings that shift with context, and whatever else underscores the tentativeness and the flexibility required to use such lists productively.

In this connection it will be well to consider briefly the method of content analysis described by Lindner [96]. Lindner states: "Those of us who have worked in the content area have come to accept the following propositions: (a) that certain responses reflect basic processes within the personality; (b) that certain responses are characteristic of various diagnostic groupings; (c) that certain responses indicate essential motivants and dynamisms within the patient; and (d) that certain responses 'act as road markers and signposts along the difficult path of clinical differentiation.' Up to the time of this writing, 43 responses that are consistent with the above propositions have been isolated" (page 77). Thus, Lindner

---

* A rapidly growing number of publications indicates the fruitfulness of thematic analysis; see, for example [3, 13, 16, 27, 29, 31, 32, 40, 63, 65, 74, 75, 120, 146, 153].

correlates single, specific responses with major pathological trends and diagnostic categories. He says, for example, that the response "tomahawk" to the central light grey detail on Card I is given "chiefly by aggressive psychopaths" (page 79); similarly, "gorilla" to all of Card IV "is found among depressives and ruminating obsessives who experience strong guilt reactions and self-recriminations" (page 84).

This is a naive, overly empirical approach to content analysis. It works with highly specific images and not with classes of thematically and theoretically related images, and it therefore allows no generalizations and transpositions. What if the central area of Card I is seen as a "spear head" instead of a "tomahawk" or all of Card IV as a "monster" instead of a "gorilla?" Do Lindner's conclusions apply to these thematically closely related images? One would expect so, yet Lindner's method of analysis provides no answer; in fact, it obscures the question. His findings lack theoretical rationale, and, because they involve isolated responses, they virtually preclude any rationale other than untrustworthy even if shrewd *ad hoc* explanations.

Another unfortunate result of Lindner's approach is the inapplicability of its findings to individual cases, since these findings are based on no more than simple enumerations and are merely statements of relative frequency. While relative frequencies are theoretically interesting, they are clinically of limited usefulness. Even if the differences in relative frequency are statistically significant (Lindner provides no specific data), there is bound to be much overlap between groups with respect to the occurrence of any single image. For example, of the *gorilla* on Card IV, Lindner could have added—according to my experience—"This response is also found in the records of anxiety hysterics, conversion hysterics, schizophrenics, relatively normal secretaries, and sundry other groups as well."*

Without theoretical rationale there can be no flexible, sound, and clarifying application of statistical trends to fresh individual cases. A content choice, after all, is an expression of a dynamic trend on some level, and dynamic trends are not the sole property of any one clinical group, whether conceived diagnostically or dynamically. Aggression, orality, anality, sexual conflict, defense mechanisms, etc. may be found in everyone, even though not to the same extent and not in the same total context. Existing to different extents in different contexts, these tendencies take on more or less individualized colorings or "styles." Lindner tends to ignore problems of degree and context, while in daily clinical work we would be lost if we

---

* Lindner does preface his diagnostic remarks about the *gorilla* response with the statement that it "signifies the projection of the self in an effort to depict the baser side of the personality" (page 84). Although one might take exception to this dynamic formulation, it would have been methodologically sounder if Lindner had stopped at this point.

ignored them. In the end, Lindner's one-to-one correlations foster diction-ary-style diagnosis and research. These have never worked and never will. They get the wrong answers or spoiled answers because they ask the wrong questions.*

The thematic approach to be illustrated below appears to avoid the pit-falls in Lindner's method of analysis. The inferences from content pertain only to dynamic trends and are not tied rigidly to any specific pathological syndrome. Oral-aggressive imagery, for example, may be conspicuous— and understandably so, according to the psychoanalytic conception of adjust-ment and illness—in the records of alcoholics, depressives, and schizo-phrenics; it may even be conspicuous in the records of certain well-functioning normals.† What is important is that the imagery is oral-aggressive in implication and that one major trend within a total context has been identified.

## H. THEMES AND VARIATIONS

In what follows, some major themes will be formulated on significantly different levels of generalization or subtlety than others. Also, some sub-themes will seem at best loosely connected to their major theme; similarly, some concrete examples of sub-themes will seem relatively remote or obscure. In these instances, identifying or explanatory footnotes or parenthetical remarks will be appended. Altogether lacking will be notations of the weight that may be assigned to each image as an instance of a theme, even though some images seem clearly more emotionally charged than others. Weighting is partly a matter to be established through research, and partly a matter for detailed discussions of individual context such as will be presented in the later case studies. Here our concern will be with images only. Finally, by way of introduction, this categorization is not meant to be systematic or hierarchically integrated, and there is nothing mutually exclusive about the categories. This is merely a tentative list that seems to help organize experience meaningfully.‡

* The recent statement by Brown appears subject to these same criti-cisms [20].

† In this regard it is well worth while to consider Erikson's discussion of psychosexual "zones" and "modes" in personality development and pathol-ogy [35].

‡ While many of these categorizations overlap with those recently set forth by Phillips and Smith [105, pages 107–161], the approach here is not simply empirical as theirs is represented to be. It also takes into account what is understood of symbolism and substitute-formations in psychoanalysis, and what is directly evident in some of the images cited. It is, accordingly, considerably more flexible and context-oriented. The approach of Phillips and Smith is subject to some of the criticisms levelled at Lindner previously. See also pp. 32–3, footnote, 118, 142–3, footnote, and 147–8.

1. *Dependent Orientation; Orality; Preoccupation with Supply and Demand.*

  a) *Supply; oral-receptive orientation.*
    1) *Food*: meat, vegetables, candy, ice cream, boiled lobster.
    2) *Food sources*: breasts, udders, nipples, corn field.
    3) *Food objects*: syrup jar, frying pan, decanter, cornucopia, table setting.
    4) *Food providers*: waiters, bakers, cooks, mother bird with worm.
    5) *Passive food receivers*: chicks with open beaks, nursing lambs, fetus, fat person, big belly, pig, person eating.
    6) *Food organs*: mouth, lips, tongue, throat, stomach, umbilical cord, navel.
    7) *Supplicants* (if thematic context is conspicuously "oral"): beggar, person praying, hands raised in supplication.
    8) *Nurturers, protectors*: nurse, cow, mother hen, bird on nest, Good Fairy, protective angel.
    9) *Gifts, givers*: Santa Claus, Christmas tree, Christmas stocking.
    10) *Good luck*: wishbone (other than near-popular middle orange on Card X), horseshoe.
    11) *Oral erotism*: figures kissing or nuzzling, lips, lipstick.

  b) *Demand; oral-aggressive orientation.**
    1) *Devourers*: birds, beasts and persons of prey and their oral and clawing parts, such as lion, tiger, shark, crocodile, vampire, Dracula, wolf, coyote, vulture, octopus, wild boar, tapeworm, crab (other than the popular side blue "crab" and the common side gray and upper gray "crab" on Card X), spider, spider web, claws, teeth, eagle's beak, fangs, tusks, jaws, cannibals. Tomato worm, mosquito and the like may be regarded as defensively minimized "devourers."
    2. *Devouring*: carcass; animals clawing, biting, chasing or eating other animals or persons.
    3) *Engulfing, overwhelming figures and objects*: woman with enveloping cloak, witch, octopus, pit, vise, trap, spider.
    4) *Depriving figures and objects*: breastplates or brassiere (in heavily "oral" contexts these seem to stand for barriers in the way of the desired object—the breast), flat-chested (i.e., breastless) woman, witch.
    5) *Deprivation*: beggar, scarecrow, emaciated face, wasteland,

* It is unusual to find emphasis on *supply* only or *demand* only. Usually, if oral themes are emphasized, both the receptive and aggressive images will be conspicuous, although one type may predominate.

steer skull in desert (if prevailing emphasis is on "oral" rather than "decay" themes; see also 3-c and 13 below).

6) *Impaired or denied oral capacity*: mouthless face, toothless face, false teeth, dentist's tools.

7) *Oral, verbal assault*: persons or animals arguing, spitting, yelling, sneering, sticking tongues out.

8) *Burdens* (if "oral" themes are emphasized, these images may relate to feelings of being "drained" or "sucked dry"): ox, yoke, camel, mule, man weighted down by pack, Atlas.

2. *Anal Orientation and Preoccupation.**

   a) *Direct anal reference*: anus, rectum, colon, buttocks, feces, toilet seat, person or animal defecating, bustle, rear ends of creatures.

   b) *Anal contact and perspective*: figures seen from behind or with backs turned, buttocks touching or bumping, persons back to back.

   c) *Dirt*: mud, dirt, smear, stain, splatter.

   d) *Assault; explosion*: bleeding rectum, creature with talons around anus, erupting lava, flaming tail of rocket or jet plane, gas mask.

3. *Sado-masochistic Orientation.†*

   a) *Sadism*: *emphasis on hostility, attack, violence, destructiveness.*

      1) *Oral attack*: devouring, stinging, biting, tearing objects or creatures, as in the oral-aggressive examples cited in Section 1-b.

      2) *Anal attack*: bombs, explosions, torpedoes, volcano, poison gas, gas mask (see also 2-d above).

      3) *Phallic attack*: piercing, cutting, bludgeoning, shooting objects and creatures such as arrow, spear, cannon, rifle, knife, hatchet, saw, pliers, shears, club, stinger, horns, rhinocerous, centaur, charging bull.

---

* Whereas Category 1 (Dependent Orientation) is very broadly conceived to include emphasis on oral impulses and objects and on many derivative attitudes, Category 2 (Anal Orientation and Preoccupation) is limited to a great extent to direct "anal" reference or implication. This is an empirically determined inconsistency. Experience seems to indicate that these anal images may occur in a variety of contexts and yet form a cluster within each context; for example, within the homosexual orientation (see 7-g) and within the sadistic orientation (see 3-a-2). Attempts to set up common denominators for all these contexts seem at this point too speculative and too general to be justified and clinically useful.

† The three main sub-themes of this heading—Sadism, Protection, and Masochism—commonly are emphasized together, often in the same image. Like the simultaneous oral-receptive and oral-aggressive thematic emphases previously noted, this common emphasis seems to be an instance of the general human tendency to think and react, unconsciously or consciously, in terms of opposites or dichotomies (see page 120). Compare De Vos [27] and Elizur [31].

4) *Aggressive, primitive men*: Mr. Hyde, cavemen, Ku Klux Klan figures, Prussian, savages, demon, devil, King Kong, Joe Stalin.

5) *Aggressive, primitive women*: shrew, witch, Amazon, Medusa, Charles Addams' cartoon woman, menacing female figure.

6) *Miscellaneous*: blood, tank, steam roller, animals colliding head on, legs smacking together, persons fighting or wrestling.

b) *Protection, defense.*

*Examples*: shield, armor, shell, camouflage, visor, helmet, hip guards, shoulder pads, breastplates, moat, fortress, turrets, porcupine, sheltering features of the terrain such as valleys or thickets.

c) *Masochism*: *emphasis on victimization, damage, punishment, defeat.*

1) *Deprived, devoured, burdened*: see examples in Section 1-b on Demand.

2) *Mutilated*: mangled wings, bleeding leg, squashed tomcat, bleeding vagina, peg-leg sailor, headless woman, split-open skull, person being torn in half.

3) *Worn, diseased, ruined, dead*: tattered clothes, falling bird shot in flight, mummy, inflamed tissue, gangrenous tissue, pus, ruined wall, bombed building, war-torn and devastated terrain, eroded pelvis, rubble, withered leaf, autumn leaf, stagnant water.

4) *Oppressed*: slave, climbing animal being pushed down or held down, ox, yoke.

5) *Punished*: Hell, fire and brimstone, person on a rack.

4. *Authoritarian Orientation.**

a) *Authority.*

1) *Power*: God, Jehova, king, queen, crown, throne, scepter, general, admiral, Napoleon, Prussian, policeman, Ku Klux Klan figures, seal of state, fierce or huge or otherwise threatening figure, person giving orders or addressing a multitude.

2) *High social status*: crest or coat of arms, derby, top hat, mink coat, castle, palace, butlers; references to the pride, elegance, richness and formality of figures and objects.

---

* The authoritarian orientation is here considered a special case of the sado-masochistic orientation. "Authoritarian" is a concept on a different level than "sado-masochistic," the latter being more impulse-oriented and therefore socially relatively non-specific, and the former concept presupposing a sado-masochistic emphasis but being explicitly oriented toward modes of interpersonal relationship and cultural values. "Authoritarian orientation" is listed separately because it refers to a tightly knit and frequently encountered cluster of themes and images. In turn, both the authoritarian and the sado-masochistic orientations are likely to involve prominent "anal" elements, even if these are not conspicuous in the Rorschach imagery.

b) *Subjugation.*

  1) *Submission*: slave, servant, kneeling or servile position, squashed or crushed figure, chains, prison bars, yoke, robot, parrot, chess pawn, trained seal or monkey, marionette, clipped French poodle (regarded as the utterly and humiliatingly domesticated beast).

  2) *Low social status*: torn or ragged clothing and objects, hut, beggar, slave, servant, peasant; references to the coarseness, dirtiness and clumsiness of figures and objects.

c) *Rebellion*: Liberty Bell, and other references to the American Revolution; Confederate flag or hat and other references to the rebellion of the South; American Indians and other references to defiance of white man's authority; hammer and sickle and other references to the Communist revolution (overthrow of established social and economic authority); devil, Loki and other references to religious and mythological figures of rebellion; gangster, person sticking tongue out, cracked yoke, broken chains.

5. *Superego Conflicts.*

a) *Guilt*: Hell, Purgatory, Satan, cloven hoof, fire and brimstone, black sheep, stain.

b) *Morality*: Jehova, prophet, Puritan, policeman, Decalogue, Inquisitor.

c) *Projected superego*: pointing finger, eyes, ears.

d) *Innocence; denied guilt*: Jesus, Madonna, saint, angel, cherub, nun, monk, cathedral, halo, Good Fairy, Alice in Wonderland, lamb, bunny, "snow-white buttocks," Snow White.

e) *Masochism*: see 3-c.

6. *General Weakness and Strength.*

a) *Weakness.*

  1) *Inadequacy, impotence*: straw man, scarecrow, jellyfish, body without a backbone, "ghost without muscles," drooping arms, wings too large or heavy for body, birds without wings, dunce cap, dangling legs, "mice barely hanging on"; emphasis on "bad" construction or preparation, as in a badly tied bowtie, badly smeared slide, crudely skinned animal, badly baked cookie.

  2) *Fearfulness*:* ugly, weird, loathsome, huge, menacing, sinister, frightening or frightened figures such as gorilla, ghost, Dracula, dragon, monster, dark cave, fleeing deer, dog scampering away, "bat coming toward me."

* *Among other things,* conspicuous statements of fearfulness imply the taking of a weak, helpless position and so presenting oneself to others—or being so tempted.

3) *Need for support and guidance*: beacon, handles, lighthouse, cane, crutch.
   b) *Strength.\**
      1) *Physical power; potency*: powerful wings, muscular figures, lumberjack, truck driver, Atlas, Hercules, stag, charging bull.
      2) *Wisdom*: Socrates, Buddha, Christ, Shakespeare, Lincoln, Einstein.
      3) *Leadership; forcefulness; heroism*: Napoleon, George Washington, Teddy or Franklin Roosevelt, king, crown, Norseman, warrior.
      4) *Counterphobic attitude*: toy gorilla, comic book monster, "ridiculous ghost," "an ancient tribal mask that once was frightening," and similarly belittled phobic images (see 6-a-2).

7. *Fear of and Rejecting Attitude Toward Masculine Identity; Feminine Identification in Men.†*
   a) *Reversal, combining, blurring and arbitrary assignment of sex characteristics*: middle figure on Card I as a man, popular figure on Card III as a woman or bisexual, lower middle of Cards II and VII and upper middle of Card IV as a penis, lower middle of Card I and upper middle of Card II as a vagina, upper middle of Card IV as an ambiguous sex organ; men in gowns, such as mandarins and monks; change of sex originally specified; symmetrical figures seen as one man and one woman; mixed-species figures such as mermaid or centaur. (Mixed-species figures may refer to feelings of being part man and part woman. They may deny sexual identity by eliminating human sex organs. Such images may state a more general theme regarding impulses, however, such as half-human and half-inhuman or half-good and half-bad).
   b) *"Feminine" emphasis*: brassiere, bed jacket, corset, stockings, gowns, materials and textures (silk, taffeta, tulle), jewelry, perfume bottle, cosmetics, pregnancy; decorative objects and plants such as vases, chandeliers, candelabra, pretty flowers; careful attention to details of dress of female figures.
   c) *Reference to perversions*: lesbians embracing, men embracing, woman masturbating man, bestiality, man with cosmetics, frank transvestism, androgyny.
   d) *Hostile, fearful conception of masculine role; phallic-aggressive emphasis*: gigantic penis, bleeding hymen, club, arrow, drill, caveman, apeman, fighting cocks, double-barrelled shot-gun; see also

---

\* An accumulation of these images usually implies passive, submissive longings toward such figures and/or megalomanic denial of such longings.
† Compare Bergman [13], Due and Wright [29], Fine [40], Reitzell [120] and Wheeler [153].

subsections (3) and (4) in Section 3-a on the sado-masochistic orientation.

e) *Hostile, fearful, rejecting characterizations of women*: Amazon, witch, Medusa, shrew, gossip, "old hen," web, trap, vagina with hooks in it.

f) *Equating passivity and/or exhibitionism with femininity; preoccupation with feminine bodies and pleasures*: woman reclining, sunbathing, sleeping, eating, having gay time; chorus girls, ballerinas, nudes.

g) *Anal perspective and preoccupation*: see Section 2.

h) *"Castration" emphasis*: amputated, crippled, stunted, withered, deformed or missing limbs or head; nutcracker, pliers, tweezers, truss; stump of tree, dead branch; cuts, wounds, scars, missing or blind eyes; unfinished figures; see also subsection (1) in Section 6-a on the theme of weakness.

i) *General increase in sexual, anal and oral imagery*:* penis, testicles, vagina, womb, sexual intercourse, anus, colon, mouths, food, breasts, devouring, etc.

8. *Fear of and Rejecting Attitude Toward Feminine Identity; Masculine Identification in Women.*†

a) *Reversal, combining, blurring or arbitrary assignment of sex characteristics*: see Section 7-a.

b) *"Masculine" emphasis*: mechanical objects, especially if specifically named, such as "wings of a DC-3" or a mechanical governor; athletic objects and figures, such as baseball bat, umpire, bowling pin, ice skaters, mountain climbers.

c) *Reference to perversions*: see Section 7-c.

d) *Hostile, fearful conception of masculine role; phallic-aggressive emphasis*: see Section 7-d.

e) *Warding off intrusion*: shield, dragons at the entrance to a building, gargoyles over a doorway.

f) *Disparagement (symbolic castration) of men*: gnomes, dwarves, gremlins, dunces, boys, Little Lord Fauntleroy, Andy Gump, man with no chin or receding chin, dandies, little man, artificial antlers, deer without antlers.

g) *Disparagement of maternal figures*: flat-chested woman, bony chest.

h) *Rejecting attitude toward "conventional" feminine role and status*: women engaged in trivial gossip, vacuous looking woman, revulsion in response to "menstruation" or "vagina" images.

---

* This trend appears to reflect the preoccupation with varieties of sensual experience commonly encountered in homosexual men, which in turn would partly be a reflection of their sexual "role diffusion" [35].

† Compare Fromm and Elonen [55].

i) *"Castration" emphasis*: see Section 7-h.

j) *Sensuous attention to physical, feminine detail*: fine descriptions of the dress, grooming, shapes and attractiveness of female figures.

k) *General increase in sexual, anal and oral imagery*: see Section 7-i.

9. *Rejecting Attitude Toward Adult, Nurturant, Parental Role.*

a) *Regressive preoccupation with childhood imagery\**: witches, dragons, wizards, elves, ogres, Alice in Wonderland, Snow White, children bundled up, cradle, bunnies, leggings, circus, fireworks, candy, ice cream.

b) *Devouring characteristics of children*: baby crocodiles, little demons, fat-bellied devils, tiny lions, fat-cheeked pussy cat, lizards.

c) *Feelings of being devoured*: bone or chicken neck with the meat removed; "the skin eaten away by bugs"; mice tearing down a house; emaciated cow head.

d) *General oral emphasis*: see Section 1.

10. *Negative Identity: Defiant, Ostentatious, Chronic Failure and Inadequacy as a Life Role.*

a) *Weakness*: see 6-a.

b) *"Castration" emphasis*: see 7-h.

c) *Subjugation*: see 4-b.

d) *Masochism: emphasis on victimization, damage, defeat, punishment, ruin, etc.*: see 3-c.

e) *Deprivation*: see subsection (5) of 1-b.

f) *Decline*: see Section 13 below on *Concern with Aging and Death.*

11. *Body Narcissism; Sensuality*: jewelry, dress form, hairdresser's head rest, perfume bottle; clothing and other decorative objects, especially with emphasis on their sheen, iridescence, fragility, delicacy and texture; peacock, exotic scenes, persons or objects from *The Arabian Nights;* chorus girl, sunbather.

12. *Concern with Reproduction or Generativity* †: ovaries, uterus, womb, swollen or pregnant abdomen, egg, stork, fetus, semen, stamen, pistil, pollen, seed, woman in delivery position, umbilical cord; emphasis on big, hollow, "empty" or "cleaned out" internal spaces; worn, broken, distorted pelvic anatomy.

13. *Concern with Aging and Death*: worn, torn, decayed persons, anatomy, animals, plants and objects, as in a withered leaf, old post, worn-out

---

\* A moderate amount of this imagery in an otherwise relatively healthy record, and if not accompanied by many images from subsections (b), (c), and (d), indicates acceptance of one's own childhood residues, empathy for the feelings and needs of others, capacity for playfulness and whimsy—in general, relaxed adult-ness and parental orientation.

† See Erikson for discussion of the concept "generativity" and its application to the early middle years in the life cycle [35].

skin, mangy fur, eroded pelvis, ragged boot, frayed garment; see also examples in Section 3-c on masochistic imagery.

14. *Emotional Tone; Interpersonal Atmosphere.**

a) *Sad*: tears, crying, mourning; desolation, ruins, decay.

b) *Gay, warm*: carnival, circus, clown, frolic, dance, embrace, snuggling, kissing, toy, childhood references as in Section 9-a.

c) *Cold*: Eskimo, ice, iceberg, snow, polar bear.

d) *Barren, lonely*: desert, little island, wasteland.

e) *Controlled*: governor on steam engine, anemometer, wall, shell, geometrically precise objects.

f) *Cautious, timid, slow*: turtle, snail, rabbit, mouse, mask.

g) *Turmoil*: thunderstorm, high wind, storm cloud, lightning, fire, explosion, volcano, chaos.

h) *Active*: leaping, springing, dancing, playing, pushing, charging.

i) *Inert*: lying or sitting down, resting, sleeping, snail, sloth.

## I. Postscript

This categorization of themes should be regarded merely as an illustration of a way of thinking about Rorschach responses. There are two basic questions with which each category may be challenged. One is, In what ways and to what extent is this category useful? As already indicated, this question must be dealt with largely in terms of personality theory and not simply in terms of the Rorschach test. However, the usefulness of the categories will also be decided by research. In research, these categories may be tied to hypotheses or invoked in predictions and their instructiveness decided thereby.

The second challenge which may be directed at these thematic Rorschach categories is, How valid is each example as an instance of the general theme under which it is subsumed. A corollary of this question is, What other examples, with what validity, may be added to the list? These are as much research problems as theoretical problems. From a research point of view, the problems center on how well each of the "items" (images) correlates with the "total score" (overall thematic emphasis). From a theoretical point of view, the problems center on systematizing the empirical observations and working out their rationale. Many of the image-theme correlations cited above are well known in clinical psychoanalysis from its study of dreams, phantasies, free associations, art, and cultural symbols

* Emphasis on any one or combination of the sub-categories in this area does not necessarily imply that that emotional tone will be most conspicuous in the patient's behavior and relationships. The imagery emphasis suggests only that the emotional tone in question is one that matters to the patient particularly or is one he is especially sensitive to, whether he usually shows this outwardly or not.

and rituals. It is for this reason largely that the preceding categorization has seemed useful in clinical Rorschach practice.

Carried out with due caution—with life context taken into account, with the rest of the Rorschach record and the results of other tests carefully scrutinized, and with the fact that there are no guaranteed image-theme correlations borne in mind—thematic analysis of the Rorschach content may often greatly enrich our understanding of individual patients. If we consider next the general criteria for judging the adequacy of interpretations, we will see how we may strengthen our safeguards against too naive, mechanical, far-reaching, dictionary-style application of the preceding categories and examples. One major safeguard, of course, is constant concern with theoretical rationale. Chapter 3 on the psychology of the Rorschach response process is in this respect an indispensable preparation for the present chapter on thematic analysis, just as the next chapter on interpretive safeguards is an inevitable sequel to this chapter.

# 5. Criteria for Judging the Adequacy of Interpretations

IN THE PRECEDING CHAPTER ON THEMATIC ANALY-
sis, exemplification of themes was carried out in a one-dimensional manner,
that is, in terms of image-to-theme correlations. The ramifications of each
image in depth and breadth were not explored. But, as already indicated
in previous discussions of the multiple determination of responses and the
conceptual complexities of thematic analysis, thematic analysis of any image
may be pursued on various levels and in various directions.

"An explosion," for example, suggests (1) intense hostility; (2) appre-
hension that defenses and controls will not contain this hostility; (3) an
expectation that upon failure of containment, a violent and indiscriminate
outburst will ensue; (4) an unconsciously carried definition of hostile
impulses in primitive, destructive, anal-expulsive terms.

"The Liberty Bell with a crack in it," given by a 25-year-old patient
belonging to an aristocratic Philadelphia family, appears to imply: (1) concern with independence, (2) which involves noteworthy rebelliousness,
(3) and possibly death wishes (armed rebellion), (4) and which is
probably directed against conservative, authoritarian, aristocratic parental
images and traditions; (5) the image therefore suggests a generalized
adolescent outlook and sense of crisis. Since this special concern with independence, rebellion and parental domination usually is a one-sided representation of intense ambivalence concerning these dimensions of experience,
the theme therefore suggests that we also be on the alert for indications of
strong dependent, submissive, conciliatory tendencies. As chronic adolescents frequently do, the patient may be vacillating between "surrender"
tendencies and "revolt" tendencies. (6) Two aspects of the image may well
pertain to the "surrender" side of the ambivalent rebellion: (a) "the
crack" in the bell suggests a feeling in the patient that revolt has failed or
will fail, or at least that it does not "ring true," and (b) the very symbol
of rebellion, the Liberty Bell, like the Mayflower, has a genteel, conformist
aspect, being sanctioned by generations of tradition, being a symbol of the
"right kind of revolutionary spirit," and being linked to an extent with
American aristocracy as well as to rebellion against hostile, absolute
authority.

These examples indicate that exploring the subtleties of images and

140

themes may lead us some distance from the raw responses. Our conclusions may be "fascinating," "deep" and "brilliantly explanatory," but they may have little or nothing to do with the specific patient. How are we to decide whether our explorations have led us home or astray, whether we have glittering gold in hand or just glitter? And how are we to distinguish between thoroughness and recklessness? We need criteria for judging what will be called the "adequacy" of interpretations. The following six criteria, to be considered in detail below, deserve particular attention: (1) there should be *sufficient evidence* for the interpretation; (2) the *depth* of the interpretation should be appropriate to the material available; (3) the *manifest form* of the interpreted tendency should be specified; (4) an estimate should be made of the *intensity* of the interpreted tendency; (5) a *hierarchic position* in the total personality picture should be assigned to the interpreted tendency; (6) both the *adaptive and pathological aspects* of the interpreted tendency should be specified. An interpretation need not meet all these criteria to be adequate or useful. It is the ideal interpretation that does meet them all. *But an interpretation should meet enough of these criteria to make sense psychologically and to represent a stand by the tester that is definite enough to be open to verification or refutation by carefully gathered clinical material.*

## A. There Should Be Sufficient Evidence for the Interpretation

What constitutes *sufficient* evidence is not easy to specify. With reference to the interpretations of the two preceding examples—the explosion and the cracked Liberty Bell—it might be objected that there is no justification for making so many inferences from single responses. Agreed. Fortunately, however, patients usually help us out by giving not one but a number of images, score patterns and attitude expressions that confirm, modify, offset or de-emphasize the interpretive leads provided by one response. The crocodile example in *Section D* of the previous chapter illustrates this massing of evidence. Apropos of the cracked Liberty Bell example, records with rebellious, adolescent imagery often also contain prominent images of power, status and authority on the one hand and of passive submission on the other; they also often contain similarly authoritarian, rebellious and submissive test attitudes, and prominent emphasis on both *Space* responses (negativism, rebellion) and *Form-Color* responses (conformity, submission). In short, the case for any major interpretation must and ordinarily can be built on a number of pieces of evidence. One clue is never enough to establish a major trend.

This does not mean, however, that it is foolhardy to explore all possible implications of each response. The more such implications or hypotheses we detail as we go through the record, the more adequate our frame of reference for evaluating each new response and for achieving a final synthesis of interpretations. With respect to the explosion example, for instance, the charged imagery through the test may be mostly explosive (volcano, jet plane, fireworks, etc.) and may be compatible with all the implications of an explosion elaborated previously. But the charged imagery in the record may be mostly of a different sort; for example, although hostile on the whole, it may not be particularly explosive (blood, spear, trap, cannon, demon, etc.). In the latter instance the interpretive emphasis shifts from *explosive attack* in particular to *hostile attack* in general, the forms of expression of which may be quite varied, i.e., explosive, engulfing, piercing, and so on. In these two instances we see how different contexts may support different implications of a response, and we see thereby the value of initially spelling out as many reasonable implications of each response as possible.

Of course, when a response and its possible implications stand isolated from the bulk of the test material, they should be handled cautiously. There are instances, however, where only one or two responses express a certain trend but do so dramatically, as, for example, in the case of a sudden *M—* or *Confabulation*. These isolated but dramatic responses should as a rule be given careful interpretive attention.

Returning to the interpretation of the two examples that opened this chapter—the explosion and the cracked Liberty Bell—it might also be objected that there is no justification for assuming that the tester's associations to these images necessarily parallel those of the patient. Agreed again. The same counterargument holds, however, as has already been presented, namely, the final interpretation should ordinarily represent the *convergence* of several or many paths of associative elaboration. This principle of convergence is essentially no different from that which guides both dream analysis in psychoanalytic therapy and thematic analysis of Thematic Apperception test stories. Another counterargument, however, is that surprisingly many images conform reliably in their implications to popular stereotype and/or psychoanalytic experience in interpreting symbols and substitute-formations. These images are often not such unique or subtle creations as we might at first think. *More often it is the choice and patterning of these images that carry the patient's individual stamp.*

As a first general rule of evidence for thematic analysis, the following may therefore be stated: *the security with which we may formulate an interpretation is a function of the extent to which there is a convergence of the imagery themes, the formal scores, and the patient's test attitudes— considered singly, in relation to each other, and in sequence.* The case studies to be presented later will illustrate the application of this rule.

* This type of total analysis of Rorschach results is not new. Rorschach's case study with Oberholzer attempted it [*124*]; Schachtel [*131, 133*], Schafer [*134*] and Beck [*11*] have applied it too. The latest statement on it has

Of course, other tests are indispensable in the search for secure interpretations that are at the same time specific and penetrating. Also, there are larger order convergences and complementary emphases to establish *among* tests. An entire volume would be needed to analyze and apply the principles and techniques of integrating Rorschach interpretations with interpretations based on other clinical test results; this cannot be undertaken here.

Genetic reconstructions based on Rorschach test responses deserve some attention in connection with the criterion of sufficient evidence. An example of what is meant by "genetic reconstruction" is the following: "Our experience with this card (IV) suggests that the use of the choices, 'giant' and 'a big gorilla' is frequently indicative of a disturbed relationship with the father. It suggests in view of the previous projections, that the individual has a negative attitude toward a domineering, criticizing and overwhelming type of father-figure. *To speculate further, the need to prevent fear and annihilation has led to introjection of the ambivalently regarded father as a superego figure which now operates as a criticizing and devaluating force against his own drives and strivings to be an individual*" (italics mine) [*67*, pages 227–228]. While it is admittedly speculative, the last part of this interpretation infers complex genetic sequences from only one or a few isolated end results. The interpretation might well be valid in this instance, but psychologically it both presumes too much and is gratuitous.

The genetic reconstruction *presumes too much* because the person in question might very well have arrived at these response choices by quite a

---

come from Phillips and Smith [*105*], who refer to it as "Type II sequence analysis" (pp. 243–256). However, Phillips and Smith base their interpretations and integrations of scores, content and attitudes not on established theory and clinical observation, but on unreported data and on their own experience with "types" of patients. On this basis, they present far-reaching interpretations of almost every detail of every response; for example, they find profound significance for the total personality even in the incidental use of the first person pronoun (p. 244), in the "could be" preface to a response (p. 272), and in differences between beetle and bug (pp. 272–273; see also p. 120). In these extreme respects, this approach gives little or no recognition to external reality, the ordinary requirements of verbal communication, and the existence of relatively autonomous, conflict-free thought; it implicitly dispenses with the ego and with regard for contexts of meaning, and it treats single response fragments as dynamically discrete, highly overdetermined, elaborate but transparent dreams or infantile fantasies. The authors cite genetic Rorschach data in support of some of their interpretations, but the gap between the data and the conclusions often seems great. The fact that some of the author's inferences are plausible, convincing or even valid, does not, of course, justify their total approach. It only means that sharp observation or reasoning is combined with theoretical and methodological arbitrariness (see also Thiesen [*144*] and footnotes on pp. 32–3, 118, and 130).

different genetic route. The father, for example, instead of being over-whelming in reality, may have actually been passive and ineffective on the whole. He may have become overwhelming only after considerable projection of hostility onto him by the child had occurred. He would then be a hostile father-figure, as inferred, but the superego structure of the individual in question would be quite different in this instance.

Other complicating considerations are these: (1) often, ambivalence felt toward both parents is split so that in the end one parent is all "good" and the other all "bad"; (2) often, a feeling is displaced from one parent to the other because it is less dangerous to feel that way about the latter parent; (3) often, in regression from problems in the relationship with one parent, problems in the relationship with the other parent are reacti-vated and possibly even dramatized to call attention away from the original, "trigger" problem. From a genetic point of view, how are we to know then whether the "overwhelming" Rorschach figure is necessarily the father, the true father or a fantasied father, only the father or hardly the father?

The genetic reconstruction cited is *gratuitous* because it is nothing more than a statement of a psychoanalytic proposition concerning the genesis of overwhelming father-figures. It is in no way derived from the Rorschach test responses. The Rorschach record can neither support nor refute the interpretation. The interpretation in effect does no more than remind the therapist to whom the report is submitted what Freud, Fenichel *et al.* have said about overwhelming father-figures.

Distinction between two types of genetic reconstruction is called for at this point. One type is that already discussed: it infers sequences of early relationships and details of the personalities involved from what the patient emphasizes at present. It thereby neglects the inevitable selectivity, distor-tion and other retrospective falsification in current representations of remote experience. How a patient spontaneously represents his past tells us how he needs to see that past *now*. At best this account is only fairly well correlated with the actual past. It is by no means identical with it. The present "autobiography" cannot therefore be taken at face value. Often it is only late in treatment before certain vital corrections are introduced into the patient's initial account of his past. The case history at the beginning and end of treatment may therefore read quite differently. A "horrible" mother may prove to have been an early Good Fairy, or a brother to whom one was "indifferent" may turn out to have been a key, positive or nega-tive identification figure, even if from afar. For these reasons and those mentioned earlier, Rorschach images cannot be considered reliable indi-cators of the actual past. They reflect only the currently emphasized views of past relationships. Future research may establish that certain images or thematic categories may be safely taken to indicate actualities of early relationships and experiences, but the above considerations suggest that these findings will be at best in the nature of "trends," more of theoretical interest and orienting value than of immediate, individual clinical utility.

The other type of genetic reconstruction, and one which is sound, pertains to the evolution of character structure. These reconstructions are usually only implicit in test reports. When, for example, we say there is evidence of a compulsive character structure, we refer to certain personality characteristics which we assume could not exist in their present form and intensity unless they had been evolved through a long history of trial and error, choice and rejection, modification and extension of certain modes of defense and adaptation. By definition, a character structure is a life work and is enduring. It is not built overnight, and, once established, can be modified only slowly and with great difficulty. Similarly, if we say that repressive defense appears to occupy a basic position in another patient's strategy of adjustment, we imply a relatively stable, crystallized or structuralized personality feature which must have a long and central history. In no event, however, does the interpretation say how the patient got that way. The reconstruction therefore is formal and not etiological. This type of reconstruction is safer than the first type because it is general, and it is sounder because it is in line with all major current personality theories.

A third major and meaningful type of reconstruction may be mentioned, although it is not "genetic" in the usual sense of applying to the earlier years of life. This type of reconstruction concerns itself with the relatively recent past. It makes inferences concerning the patient's premorbid personality or about differences between his current state and one in the not too distant past. For example, it is often possible to discern diagnostic evidences of a recent psychotic break now "sealed over"; it is also often possible to estimate the premorbid I.Q. level when the I.Q. has been lowered by illness, or to speak of certain premorbid defenses that are now decompensated or in vestigial form. Reconstructions such as these are like the implicit reconstructions and interpretations of character structure. Often they appear to be the only hypotheses that can reconcile apparent contradictions in the findings or can integrate seemingly scattered trends.

As a second rule of evidence for thematic analysis, the following may now be stated: *since at present there seems to be no evidence in Rorschach test records to support or refute genetic reconstructions concerning specific, important, early experiences and relationships, and since current representations of the remote past are historically unreliable even though revealing of current pathology, interpretation can and should pertain only to the present personality structure and dynamics of the patient or to changes in these in the relatively recent past.*

A last application of the criterion of *sufficient evidence* is that pertaining to the assignment of fixed symbolic meanings to the Rorschach blots themselves. Card VII, for example, has been held to represent the mother-figure, and all responses to this card to represent therefore conceptions of and attitudes toward the mother-figure [*125*]. Often, however, there appears to be no way of establishing from the record in hand whether and to what extent this symbolic, unconscious apperception of a mother-figure has occurred. Of course, if the responses to this card deal with "nasty old hags" (upper ⅓ or ⅔ or *W*), we have something to go on. But if the responses are remote from "mother" themes, if they include, for example, only clouds (*W*), a map (*W*), an animal head (middle ⅓), a butterfly (lower ⅓) and a vagina (lower middle), how are we to know that these responses are in reaction to or in any way involve a latent mother image?

It is of some theoretical and practical interest that the configurations, colors, shadings and popular content of certain cards and certain areas of certain cards commonly elicit psychodynamically meaningful and seemingly symbolic responses. The upper projection on Card VI, for example, is often seen as a penis and is also often reacted to with what seem to be symbolic variations on the penis theme (e.g., club, fist, rattlesnake, beacon, decanter). Similarly, the lower middle of Card VII is often seen as a vagina and is often reacted to with what seem to be symbolic variations on the vagina theme (e.g., church, haven, Madonna, gun emplacement, wound, chasm). A third example is responding to the area on Card III popularly seen as men with such variations as marionettes, devils, lambs, clipped French poodles or women. In these instances, there is warrant to assume that unconscious or preconscious apperception of sex organs or male human figures, as the case may be, has probably occurred. There is independent psychoanalytic evidence from the study of dreams, symptoms, parapraxes and free associations to support this assumption. Here, as in the case of the "nasty old hag" on Card VII, we have responses that seem to stand in some clear, if speculative, relation to the assumed latent meaning of the area in question. We are not flying blind.

When, however, it is assumed that the card or area in question *must* mean penis, vagina, man, etc., no matter what responses the patient gives to these areas, we are flying blind. We are, in fact, committing serious psychological errors. The errors lie in reasoning (1) as if no adaptive and defensive ego functions stand between the stimulus and the deep dynamics of the individual, (2) as if there are no relatively neutral images available to the patient in his efforts to cope with the stimuli, (3) as if there could be only one dynamic meaning in the card or area in question, (4) as if a statistical trend is the same as a perfect correlation, and (5) as if all we have learned about personality-rooted individual differences in perceptual thresholds and perceptual organizing principles were still unknown.

It is a different matter if one of the "symbolic" areas mentioned above is obviously avoided or obviously disturbing in some other way. Unusual behavior with respect to a certain card or card-area ordinarily suggests that an anxiety-provoking response has been stimulated, even though this response may not be in consciousness. Hasty dismissal or ignoring of an area in a way that is out of keeping with the patient's usual test attitude is an instance of such disruption or "shock," even if none of the images offered seems to express anything significant. In other words, if test attitudes and behavior are included within the concept *response*, then we need not have a "symbolic" image before we may infer that a certain area with a common meaning has had a disturbing effect on the patient.

It is, however, a far cry from this position to that recently taken by Phillips and Smith [105]. They first disclaim attaching any fixed symbolic significances to the Rorschach cards. They claim only to be reporting research findings. Yet their reasoning makes it plain that they regard at least six of the cards as invariably conveying a basic theme to test subjects. Those subjects who show "shock" in reaction to these cards—"shock" being defined by such criteria as delayed reaction time, negative attitudes, and paucity or stereotypy of response—are said to be characterized by certain current dynamics and behavioral trends and by certain relatively specific past experiences and relationships which determine the present trends. For example:

"Shock on Card I is evidence for an unresolved and intense relationship with a mother or nurturing figure which appears to have permanent derivatives in the subject's current behavior. The mother may have been punitive and rejecting or dominating and overly concerned. In men, shock on Card I is associated with economic incompetence, a poor work record and psychosexual immaturity. Many of these men show generalized attitudes of resentment and hostility and a chip-on-the-shoulder manner by surliness, arrogance, provocativeness and apparently insatiable demands. Men who show this adjustment complex often express (or 'act out') their dependency problems quite directly: assault, heavy drinking, temper tantrums, and stealing (which presumably reflects the theme 'I'll take by force that which is not given') are common. Suicidal gestures occur in this group, but seem to be intended primarily as threats. In women, and less frequently in men, the most common behavior pattern associated with shock at I involves seclusiveness and suicidal threats or attempts which imply 'Look what you've done to me.' Usually these patients complain of feelings of loneliness and depression. Often they are characterized by excessive passivity and submission; by whining or nagging and consistent querulous demands; sometimes by listlessness, apathy, or even lethargy and apparent relinquishment of all self-assertion and initiative; sometimes by verbalizations which connote 'I am only a child'; sometimes by jealousy of siblings, children and other competitors for nurturance.

"It is not possible to assign the subject to one or another of these groups simply from the evidence of shock at Card I" (page 201).

These remarks are distinguished by the absence of explicit rationale of the reported correlations, and by the presence of an *implicit* double rationale of fixed, symbolic card meanings on the one hand and the acceptability of far-reaching genetic reconstructions on the other. Card I emerges as the dependency-on-a-certain-kind-of-mother-figure card. Shock at Card I indicates intense, unresolved, infantile, behavior-dominating conflicts in this dynamic area. Whether the absence of such shock implies no great conflict and past traumata in this area is not discussed, but this implication would follow inevitably from the authors' underlying mechanical conception of the response process. No evidence is offered and no argument elaborated that Card I in any way stimulates articulated or physiognomic images pertaining to mother, child, mother-and-child, "leaning" or "clinging," or any other response or theme relevant to the reported correlation. Unless a plausible—if not convincing—rationale can be elaborated, and unless strong evidence for frequent or individually revealing, mediating imagery reactions (such as to the phallic configuration on Card VI) can be marshalled, this approach fosters mechanical interpretation by rote memory rather than flexible, psychological interpretation.*

There follows a third general rule of evidence for thematic analysis: *symbolic inferences should be based on actual responses, on clear-cut avoidance of responses, or on disruption of the response process ("shock") in reaction to cards or areas that commonly elicit emotionally charged images; symbolic inferences should not be based on fixed meanings assigned to certain cards and areas of cards, which meanings are assumed to hold for all patients and to explain ultimately all responses to the cards and areas in question.*†

To summarize briefly the answer to the question, "What constitutes sufficient evidence for an interpretation?", it may be said that at least several lines of inference should converge on the same interpretation, and that the starting points of these lines of inference should be actual images, scores, test attitudes, and behavior, and their interrelationships and sequences. For genetic reconstructions there can be no direct or reliable evidence in the test responses, and for fixed symbolic card-meanings there is at best suggestive and certainly not universal support in the test responses. Unless we see something of the process leading to the end result, we are safer and wiser to avoid genetic speculation and symbolic forcing. And, again, we are always safer and sounder if we base our final interpretations on the results of a battery of tests.

* In view of the looseness with which the authors discuss some dynamic relationships (as that between dependency and assault), it begins to seem that theirs is the plight of the factor analyst desperately seeking a common denominator in highly diverse trends, and resorting to oversimplifications and overabstractions in this search.

† For discussion of a similar psychological error involved in the rationale of the Szondi test, see Schafer [136].

## B. The Depth of the Interpretation Should Be Appropriate to the Material Available

The term "deep" in psychoanalytic lingo has been used to refer to archaic, primitive, infantile, instinctual, usually rigidly repressed tendencies and conceptions. Sadistic impulses, castration fears, oral impregnation fantasies, death wishes against loved ones and the like may, in this sense, ordinarily be said to be "deep." What is not "deep," instinctual or archaic follows less the primary process (drive-dominated, magical, fluid, irrational) and more the secondary process (drive-regulating, realistic, orderly, logical). It is more a part of the ego than of the id. It includes such more or less rationalized, stabilized, conventionally conceptualized and reality-oriented derivatives of the archaic tendencies and conceptions as attitudes, overt style of interpersonal relationships and daydream content.

In the case, for example, of a Rorschach record with frequent references in it to food, mouths, teeth and devouring creatures, it seems legitimate, though not exhaustive, to apply the "deep" drive concept *oral* to these images. In the case of a record with frequent references in it to buttocks, feces, dirt, channels and explosions, it seems legitimate to apply the concept *anal* to these images. If the oral images deal mainly with food, open mouths, stomachs and infants, it seems legitimate to speak of themes of *passive, receptive orality,* while if the oral images deal mainly with teeth, jaws, webs, fangs and devouring creatures, it seems legitimate to speak of themes of *aggressive, demanding orality.* It must be remembered that unless we describe the manifest form of appearance of the trends in question, their relative intensity, how they are controlled, etc., these archaic, instinctual concepts tell us little about the patient. In all of us, presumably, there are noteworthy amounts of orality, anality, and other instinctual trends.

Around the middle position on the continuum of depth, as defined above, there are such responses as Christmas tree, Santa Claus, hands raised in supplication, reclining or sleeping person, wishbone and lucky horseshoe. These responses bespeak a passive, receptive orientation without explicitly involving orality. It is likely that these images and this passive, receptive orientation derive from a basically oral emphasis, but we cannot say we have evidence for this inference in the test responses.

In contrast, records that contain relatively few responses, all of which are popular, near-popular or vague, and none of which is elaborated in detail or quality, allow chiefly or only interpretation of defenses and controls. These constricted records are at the opposite extreme of those that contain numerous references to infantile tendencies and conceptions. The defensive picture inferred from the constricted record may be one that is ordinarily associated with certain infantile trends—as in the case of defensive compulsiveness and anality. If, however, anality is not more or less directly implied in the test imagery or attitudes, the test interpretation proper should not push below the level of defense. The psychoanalytically-oriented therapist will know that marked compulsiveness, for example, is likely to represent to a large extent a defensive coping with tendencies that on their most primitive level are anally conceived and expressed. It is misleading to write test reports as if this anality is "seen" in the test record when actually only a common derivative of and defense against anality is seen.

As a rule, therefore, the depth to which interpretation may be carried should be determined by the material available in this and the other tests. From this point of view, as from the point of view of sufficiency of evidence elaborated in the preceding section, genetic reconstructions and fixed symbolic card meanings are arbitrary, presumptuous efforts to deepen interpretation *in spite of the patient.*

## C. The Manifest Form of the Interpreted Tendency Should Be Specified

This criterion of an adequate interpretation is far easier to mention than to meet. It is always difficult to be specific, let alone exhaustive, in regard to phenotypical expression. Often, we are able to infer the presence of a powerful trend but cannot say which of several possible manifest forms it tends to assume. For example, a strong homosexual trend may be indicated in the records of two male patients without there being additional evidence to indicate that one patient ends up heterosexually inhibited in behavior and the other ends up a Don Juan. Perhaps in part this is a matter of our still being insensitive to subtle cues in the records that could tell us which manifest form of expression to expect in certain cases. But undoubtedly the problem derives to a great extent from limitations of the Rorschach test as an instrument. Manifest behavior of any importance is, after all, invariably highly overdetermined; that is to say, it is a resultant of numerous interacting determinants. It cannot usually be explained by reference to one underlying trend. In the case of the two patients with strong homosexual trends, such other factors as specific identification figures, superego attitudes, social and cultural settings and values, type and strength of defenses, traumatic sexual experiences, and possibly constitutional predispositions would all have a great bearing on their ultimate overt pattern of sexual behavior. Some of these factors might also be indicated by the test results, but we would hardly be justified in assuming either that *all* relevant determinants are indicated or that we can always and with confidence so interrelate the indicated factors as to predict very specifically the final outcome in overt behavior. This is one respect in which a battery of tests can be an enormous help. But considering the Rorschach test alone, we see now why it is much easier to insist that the manifest forms of interpreted tendencies be specified than it is to meet this demand.

As a rule, the deeper interpretations go, the more of this difficulty we meet. Interpreting defensive tendencies, for example, often allows (and includes) rather precise specification of manifest form, while interpreting drive tendencies often does not or cannot. For example, we may be rather specific about just how a compulsive person behaves compulsively, but we may be unable to say just how an anal instinctual emphasis is expressed in behavior.

It might be objected that if the manifest form of a trend cannot be specified, then the interpretation is not subject to tests of validity and is not therefore psychologically and scientifically meaningful. This objection is too hasty, however. For one thing, while one specific form of appearance of the trend might not be predictable, a limited variety of possible forms might be specified. To return to the example of the strong homosexual trend, certain forms of behavior are more likely to express this trend than others. We might predict, for instance, sexual inhibition or impotence or Don Juanism or eruption of homosexual feelings into consciousness or some meaningful combination of these. Yet, this buckshot predicting cannot be entirely satisfactory for it actually boils down to a prediction that some disturbance of heterosexual adjustment will be evident. If such disturbance is evident clinically, the fact of *a* disturbance does not directly validate the *homosexual* basis of the disturbance. Other pregenital problems, such as oral-dependency problems, could just as well "account for" the disturbance.

There is, however, another and more important rejoinder to the objection that no prediction of manifest form precludes scientifically necessary tests of validity. That is that the clinical material or other criterion might itself imply the same trend as the test material. The dreams, free associations, transference reactions and life history of the patient might all point *independently* in the direction of a strong homosexual trend. If two independent lines of inference—from test results and from clinical data—converge, then a test of validity has been carried out. Overt behavior has not been ignored but has been used as a stepping stone to this test of validity.

From all of these considerations it would seem unwarranted to insist that one criterion of an adequate interpretation is that it specify the manifest form of the interpreted trend. On the contrary. The difficulties in the way of reaching this ideal have been discussed first in order to demonstrate the complexity of the interpretive problem. There are in fact good reasons to support the inclusion of this criterion, particularly if we modify it so: "*Whenever possible,* the manifest form of the interpreted tendency should be specified."

For one thing, as has been mentioned already, interpretation of defensive operations usually allows specific description of overt behavior—for example, the meticulousness, conscientiousness and pedantry associated with compulsive defenses, and the guardedness, suspiciousness and implicit arrogance associated with paranoid defenses. The same may be said of adaptive operations such as striving for rapport and for accurate reality testing.

For another thing, it is often possible to say something about the manifest form of a dynamic trend, particularly if the formal score patterns and test attitudes and behavior—*and the results of other tests*—are taken into account too. In the Rorschach test itself, the Don Juan type of overcompensation for homosexual tendencies might be expressed during the testing in an effortful, exaggerated poise and "manly," "clear thinking" efficiency, and in denial of anxiety through denial of shading in responses and through counterphobic imagery. The sexually inhibited patient with a strong homosexual trend might, in contrast, be timid, deferent and ingratiating during the testing, and might give numerous anxious, phobic responses (using diffuse shading frequently and seeing fearful things in the blots).

These oversimplified examples indicate that interpretations which include emphasis on drive, defense and adaptation may more easily be brought into connection with overt behavior than one-dimensional interpretations. The drive, defense and adaptation interpretations require, however, scrutiny of all aspects of the Rorschach record and the consideration of these in the context of other clinical approaches to the patient.

As another example of anticipating manifest form, we may consider two records full of oral imagery, one of which is characterized by relatively arbitrary form, numerous color and shading responses that are weak in form, and demanding test attitudes, and the other of which is characterized by precise form, exaggerated emphasis on form as a determinant, and cold, impersonal test attitudes. In the former case we might expect rather open, ego-syntonic expression of oral, passive, dependent tendencies in interpersonal relationships, while in the latter case we might expect conspicuous efforts to stave off any feelings or relationships that smack of oral, passive, dependent tendencies. Both patients will be concerned with passivity in overt behavior, but one will be for it and the other against it. More about all of this will be discussed in *Section 5* below on hierarchic location and integration of interpreted trends.

For the time being it may be said that: (a) because all important overt behavior is multiply determined in a complex fashion, the Rorschach test cannot always be expected to provide sufficient information to allow very specific prediction of the manifest forms of indicated trends; (b) interpretations simply of genotypic trends *are* subject to clinical validation because similar inferences concerning genotypic trends may be made independently from clinical data and the two sets of inferences subsequently compared; (c) defensive and adaptive manifestations are typically easier to specify than drive manifestations; (d) if on the one hand we pay close attention to scores, images and test attitudes, and on the other hand we think in terms of configurations of drives, defenses, and adaptive efforts, we will be in the best position to make fairly specific predictions of patterns of manifest behavior and we will have achieved fairly rich understanding of these patterns; (e) if we follow these principles and employ a battery of tests instead of the Rorschach test alone, we will be in the strongest position of all.

Yet, however strong our interpretive position, we must be careful not to overestimate or overstate our ability to understand and predict from test results. The patient's limits and resources with respect to adaptive, sublimatory activity and achievement are often difficult to estimate. They depend so much on situational supports and threats, and on significant events over which the patient may have little or no control. Also, these limits and resources are not easily definable inasmuch as one personality context or identity may foster a productive application of what might otherwise be a starkly pathological trend, while another might not. Of these matters we still know very little.* "Expert" dispositional recommendations on the basis of test results *alone* is therefore unsound and to be avoided.

## D. The Intensity of the Interpreted Trend Should Be Estimated

Because so many of the trends we infer from test results are very widespread if not universal, it is highly desirable to be able to estimate the strength of each trend we interpret. Otherwise our interpretations may become largely gratuitous. Borrowing a didactic device wittily employed by Holt with regard to the same problem in Thematic Apperception test interpretation [78, page 457], one might compose the following test report on a patient without ever having seen his Rorschach test results: "Although narcissism and hostility are indicated and there is at times a tendency to withdraw if frustrated, there are also longings for closeness to and dependence on others. Strong emotional stimulation tends to produce anxiety and to lower intellectual efficiency. Ambivalence toward parental figures is also suggested. (Etc.)" Because it applies to everyone, this report applies to no one. Its validity is perfect but perfectly spurious. The tester has not taken a stand on a single interpretation that would enable us to distinguish this patient from many or most others.

The tester's report would be useful and meaningful, though still not complete, if he had instead written the following: "This is an intensely narcissistic and hostile person who withdraws deeply in response to relatively slight frustration. Such longings for closeness to and dependence on

* See pp. 158–9 for further discussion of this problem.

others as are indicated appear to be overshadowed by the narcissism, hostility and withdrawal tendency. Extreme anxiety results if feelings are even moderately stimulated, and intellectual efficiency declines markedly. There are indications of ambivalence toward parental figures, but not sufficient basis in the test data to estimate the intensity of this ambivalence. In view of the preceding description of this patient, however, the ambivalence is likely to be extreme and conspicuous." *Intense, marked, extreme, slight, moderate* are at best only gross estimates, but the usual validating criteria —estimates based on clinical judgment—are no finer. Gross distinctions between patients are possible on this basis and so are gross checks of the validity of the interpretations. In effect, interpretations should cover a five-point rating scale: extreme (intense)—strong (marked, conspicuous)—moderate—weak (slight)—negligible.

As in the case of the three preceding criteria—sufficient evidence, appropriate depth, and specification of manifest form—this quantitative criterion of an adequate interpretation is not sufficient in itself to pinpoint a distinctive trend in the patient. It helps, of course. For example, if the manifest form of an infantile, instinctual trend such as oral aggressiveness cannot be specified, it is better at least to be able to say that the oral aggressiveness appears to be an extreme or strong trend. This gross quantitative specificity at least implicitly predicts that derivatives of this trend should not be difficult to discern clinically. Ideally, however, all six of the criteria being discussed should be met.

### E. The Interpreted Tendency Should Be Given a Hierarchic Position in the Total Personality Picture

This criterion in some ways subsumes the previously discussed criteria of sufficient evidence, appropriate depth, specification of manifest form, and estimate of intensity. It requires that, insofar as possible, each trend interpreted be explicitly or implicitly related to other major trends. The trend in question may stand in relation to other trends as a defense, as that which is defended against, as an attitude that reflects a compromise between certain drives and defenses, as an overcompensation, as an emotional reaction (including anxiety and guilt), and the like. The point is to avoid chain-like interpretation in which each trend is simply juxtaposed to other trends, and no hierarchy of importance, generality, stimulus and response, push and restraint is established. A battery of tests is invaluable in organizing hierarchic test pictures; on the basis of the Rorschach test alone one cannot do a thorough job in this respect.

The two following brief examples of test reports should illustrate the difference between the chain and the hierarchy. (1) *Chain-like interpretation*: "The patient is very hostile. He also appears to be markedly anxious. He is compulsive but his efficiency is impaired." (2) *Hierarchic interpreta-*

*tion*: "Strong hostile impulses are indicated. The patient appears to try to defend himself against these hostile impulses by heavy reliance on compulsive defenses. At the present time the compulsive defenses appear to be relatively weak or ineffective. The intense anxiety that is also indicated is likely to be largely in reaction to this impulse-defense instability." The latter interpretation is, of course, much bolder than the former, but it is not free improvisation. It applies certain clinically well-established dynamic patterns to the findings in order to synthesize them; it is not simply an *ad hoc*, meaningless dynamic integration of the interpretations. Such arbitrary *ad hoc* formulations are not uncommon in test reports. Words like *although, however* and *in addition* are used to give a semblance of integration to the interpretations; the end result is usually psychological nonsense. For example: "Although stereotyped in outlook, the patient is adaptive. In addition, however, he is very anxious."

Hierarchic integration is not, however, only a matter of applying well-established dynamic patterns to the test interpretations. *Such integration as is attempted should be based on sufficient evidence in the actual test responses themselves.* In the case of the hierarchic interpretation of hostility and compulsiveness presented above, we should have some supporting evidence, such as the following, in the record proper: (Card IX) "This is very messy: the colors run into each other and they don't go together anyway. I see a face here but the nose is too long (tiny edge detail). This looks like a pelvis (green; poor form). The whole thing could be an anatomical drawing (poor form; artificial color). Of course this part could look like the explosion of the atomic bomb (midline and lower red): I thought of that before but didn't mention it because the color is all wrong and the shape is too regular." In this sequence of responses we see first an anxious attempt to stave off a hostile image by resorting to unproductive compulsive criticism; then adaptively weak rare detail, poor form and artificial color; and finally the emergence of the hostile, explosive image—which by now, however, is under a rather sterile compulsive control. This sequence points toward just such an integration of interpretations as was offered above: hostility opposed by shaky compulsive defense with resulting anxiety.

Of course, assigning hierarchic position to interpretations presupposes a hierarchical personality theory. While it leaves much to be desired in this regard at the present time, Freudian psychoanalytic theory appears to be the theory best suited for this task. Such sets of concepts as drive-defense-adaptation, id-ego-superego (the "structural" concepts), unconscious-preconscious-conscious (the "topographic" concepts), and the interpersonally and culturally oriented attitudes-values-identity, all of which have a place in Freudian psychoanalytic theory, greatly facilitate hierarchic ordering of interpretations.

In these integrative efforts as nowhere else, what the tester brings to his work in the way of background and talent becomes centrally important. How ably he analyzes and synthesizes his clinical data will be determined by his general sophistication in the liberal arts and sciences, his study and understanding of the theoretical and clinical aspects of psychodynamics, the richness of his experiences with colleagues (in staff and individual conferences, etc.) as well as with patients, his self-awareness, sensitivity and perceptiveness, his tolerance for the error and ambiguity that so often and inescapably permeate clinical thought, and his wit, verbal facility and imaginativeness on the one hand balanced by his skeptical demand for solid evidence on the other.*

All these requirements for meaningful hierarchic interpretation also act as safeguards against persuasive, tightly integrated personality pictures that are, however, glibly elaborated and have little to do with the particular patient. This misleading glibness is a steady danger in ambitious test interpretation. A capacity on the part of the tester to say "I don't know," "I'm not sure," "I can't tie it together but . . ." can be, if not overworked, an invaluable asset.

To return to our interpretive criteria and problems, hierarchic integration of interpretations according to a more or less definite body of psychological assumptions and findings avoids another type of psychological nonsense besides the already mentioned *ad hoc* improvising, namely, juxtaposing dynamically contradictory interpretations. To say of a patient that he has "a strongly dependent, oral character" but that he has "basically healthy heterosexual drives" is an instance of this error by internal contradiction. To say in one paragraph of a report that the patient is "psychopathic" and in the next that he is "compulsive" is another such instance. Interpretations like these typically stem from a mechanical, chain-like handling of test signs and from the naive assumption that whatever "the test says," goes.

Actually, many seeming contradictions are reconcilable if appropriate integration of them is carried out. For example, the juxtaposed compulsive and psychopathic trends might be handled in at least two meaningful ways: (a) a psychopath may, for ingratiating purposes, assume a compulsive manner that, upon close examination, is found to be essentially empty and opportunistic; or (b) the patient may have been unable to integrate adequately a rebellious, impulsive, somewhat psychopathic trend and a submissive, conformist, compulsive trend, with the result that he may vacillate

* We are in this respect dealing with a problem of fundamental importance for the teaching of clinical psychology. We cannot, of course, turn out psychologists like automobiles on an assembly line, each identical in mode of operation, horsepower and miles-per-gallon. Even so, we still understand very little about how to teach in a systematic manner the fundamentals of this complex technique of hierarchically integrating clinical data. Our psychiatric and psychoanalytic colleagues are in no better a position.

—like many an adolescent—between these two positions. Both of these patterns are frequently encountered and are dynamically meaningful. Seemingly contradictory trends in the test results may often express identical contradictory trends in the personality of the patient. It is a help therefore, when it is at all appropriate, to think of the patient as being on a continuum between two contradictory poles with respect to each dominant trend indicated, and to try to ascertain his usual position on this continuum and the degree to which he shifts about on the continuum. Of the patient with prominent compulsive and psychopathic tendencies, we might say, for example, that his shifts of position on the *rebellion-submission continuum* appear to be frequent in occurrence and wide in amplitude.

Thus, giving each interpreted trend a hierarchic position in the total personality picture not only helps avoid psychological contradictions but may even capitalize on seeming contradictions and bring out basic patterns of conflict or contradiction within the patient. This hierarchic integration should be based on a personality theory and its body of findings and not on *ad hoc,* test-centered and sign-centered improvising.

## F. THE ADAPTIVE AND PATHOLOGICAL ASPECTS OF THE INTERPRETED TENDENCIES SHOULD BE SPECIFIED

It is as vital to a good test report to assess the adaptive strengths of the patient as to assess his pathological tendencies. Very often, in fact, the same trend will have both adaptive and pathological aspects. Consider the defense of rigid reaction formation against hostility, for example. On the pathological side it involves, among other things, retarded development of an important aspect of the personality—appropriate, aggressive self-assertiveness. It also involves a basic lack of freedom in human relationships, and a saintly and sugary righteousness that justifiably alienates others. On the adaptive side, however, rigid reaction formation against hostility may involve noteworthy, even if superficial, tolerance, gentleness and helpfulness toward others. Or in the case of schizoid withdrawal into fantasy life, we may have, on the pathological side, deep mistrust of human relationships and passive aggressiveness against others, and, on the adaptive side, a rich cultivation of artistic creativity. Of course, neither the pathological nor the adaptive aspects of these trends are fully accounted for by the trends themselves. The trends in question may, however, be focal points of one section of the personality analysis.

In other words, test interpretation should take account of the fact that people do not achieve complete sublimation of all infantile trends, complete security in all interpersonal relationships, complete resolution of all conflicts between drives or values or goals in life. It is only against this fundamentally neurotic ideal of health that compulsiveness, repression, dependence, aggressiveness, narcissism and the like may be thought of as invariably pathological. If real human beings are our measuring sticks, then compulsiveness, dependence, etc., must be viewed as trends that have their more or less constructive and limiting or destructive aspects. In some cases the constructive aspects may predominate, in others the limiting or destructive may predominate. But with respect to each patient we should try to establish in what ways and to what extent a certain trend helps and hinders his adjustment efforts.

We are at a point now where the concept "ego identity" may help us a great deal [35]. This concept promises to extend our understanding of the organizing functions of the ego by pointing up and clarifying how complex configurations of drives, defenses, capacities, attitudes and values, may be organized around privately and usually unconsciously conceived social roles and expectations and self-images. The ego identity concept helps us see how the interaction of culture, bodily experience, and infantile as well as later relationships provides themes around which to organize experience and action. It shows how what may be a pathological trend in one identity configuration may become an asset in the next, because the latter gives it a new meaning and value. The ego identity concept also provides a key for understanding how formal aspects of functioning may express the content of major fantasies about the self—how, for example, in one instance meticulousness may represent a living out of the identity of an aristocrat (the clean, impeccable one) and in another instance the identity of a slave (the conscientious, subservient one).

Turning specifically to the Rorschach test, in one case the dominant approach to the inkblots may be artistic, while in the next it may be pseudo-masculine, anti-aesthetic and anti-intellectual. In each case the place of affect and hence the significance of color responses will be somewhat different. To the "artist," a shaded *Color-Form* response may stand for a positively valued, creative, integrative experience of affect, while to the pseudo-masculine patient it may stand for frightening, disorganizing, "feminine" affect. Also, at certain points of the response process, these dominant identity statements will be more prominent or better integrated than at others. The rise and fall of their prominence and integration will often mark areas of special adjustment difficulty or adaptive resources.

In addition, the emotional tone and/or intellectual evaluation with which the patient conveys his Rorschach images may be accepting in some instances and rejecting in others. This differential treatment of images may reflect major rejected as well as accepted identity solutions—what the patient dares not become as well as the role to which he must cling or in which he may take great pride. In one man's Rorschach test imagery, the passive, virginal little girl may come forward as the preferred, secretly maintained, "good" identity and may be associated with aesthetic sensitivity and cultural aspiration, while the sadistic, adult, heterosexual male figure may emerge as the rejected, "bad" identity and may be associated with the patient's inability to consolidate his accomplishments and use his assets productively. In another case, no identity may be treated favorably and negative images and themes of ruin, decay, and failure may predominate.*

Projective test interpretation oriented to ego identity problems requires taking into account the context of age, sex, educational and familial status, and cultural background. As these vary, the identity themes and problems vary. But in any case, identity solution or lack of solution appears to have a major bearing on the fate of various drives, defenses, abilities, etc.

It appears therefore that defining identity problems and solutions in test results may put us in a good position to recognize and weigh the adaptive aspects of major personality trends, pathological though these trends may seem in other respects. It is a major weak point in the interpretation of test results that we are often so much better at identifying pathological potentialities and weighing pathological trends than we are at identifying and weighing healthy, self-integrative "normal" trends. These problems will come up again in the next chapter. Some guiding interpretive principles will be proposed then, but meanwhile it is important to note Erikson's theoretical lead concerning ego identity and its possible major contribution to rounded test interpretation.

## G. Summary

We have considered six general criteria for judging the adequacy of an interpretation. In summary it may be said that ideally an interpretation, if based on sufficient evidence, should push as far down to deep, archaic, infantile, instinctually-colored material as is appropriate and as far up to manifest, highly socialized forms of functioning as is appropriate. Equally important, the interpretation should include an estimate of the strength of the interpreted trend, should locate it hierarchically in the total personality picture, and should develop its adaptive as well as its pathological aspects. The more of these six criteria any actual interpretation meets, the more adequate and useful it will be. In every case, however, the interpretation should always be rooted in actual responses given by the patient. It should not derive simply from a textbook of psychoanalysis or from mechanical, symbolic interpretation of everything in sight. The interpretation should also always be oriented toward how people are actually put together and not toward *ad hoc*, test-centered improvising. When these conditions are more or less met, the interpretation ought to be open to at least a gross test of its validity—provided, of course, that the validating clinical material is sufficiently rich and meaningful to be used for validation purposes.

* The TAT stories should certainly be scrutinized for support and qualification of such interpretations.

# 6. Introduction to the Interpretation of Defenses

"DEFENSE" HAS COME TO BE ONE OF THE KEY psychoanalytic concepts. It has been found invaluable in the theory of adjustment and maladjustment, in comprehending general and individual trends in personality development, and in elaborating therapeutic rationale and technique. For these reasons, it is a challenge to the psychoanalytically-oriented tester to integrate test theory with the theory of defenses, and to set forth principles of defense interpretation of test results. In the preceding theoretical discussion of the response process, some account has already been taken of the psychoanalytic theory of defense, and more will be said about this theory throughout the remainder of the book. At this time, however, it will be well to focus our attention chiefly on general principles of defense interpretation. As a preface to doing so, it will be helpful to review the general outlines of the psychoanalytic conceptualization of defense.

## A. THE PSYCHOANALYTIC CONCEPTUALIZATION OF DEFENSE *

In the course of growing up, people learn to fear certain of their impulses. Realistically and unrealistically, they come to anticipate that discharge of these impulses will result in their losing the love of important persons in their lives and possibly being punished by these persons as well—punished in the form of deprivation, physical attack or moral condemnation. Realistically and unrealistically, people also come to anticipate that certain of their impulses, if given any opportunity for discharge, will get altogether out of hand. They then fear a traumatic state of pent-up need or excitation, consequent disorganization of highly prized, security- and gratification-

---

* The major treatments of the concept "defense" will be found in Freud's *The Problem of Anxiety* [50], Anna Freud's *The Ego and the Mechanisms of Defense* [42], and Fenichel's *The Psychoanalytic Theory of Neurosis* [37]. The genetic and metapsychological aspects of the theory of defense will receive minimal consideration here since we are concerned with the clinical evaluation of the adult patient's already more or less crystallized defenses. For pertinent genetic and metapsychological considerations, see Freud [50], Rapaport [113], Fenichel [37], Hartmann [69, 70], Hartmann and Kris [71], and Hartmann, Kris and Loewenstein [72, 73].

insuring, adaptive ego functions, and ultimate destruction of needed external figures and of themselves.

The pressure of these threatening impulses and the prospect of discharging them stimulates reactions of anxiety. After the formation of the superego, reactions of guilt may also be stimulated or at least anticipated in connection with these rejected impulses. Other painful feelings, such as shame and disgust, may also be involved. Preliminary phases of these distress reactions, particularly in the form of mild anxiety, may then be used as indications by the ego that a crisis over impulse control is developing, and as signals of the necessity for starting or reinforcing defensive action. Whereas, originally, archaic, automatic anxiety reactions are passively and painfully experienced by the relatively weak infantile ego, later on these anxiety reactions are used by the stronger ego for its own purposes. "The ego's judgment of impending danger brings the organism into a state similar to that of a trauma, but of lower intensity" [37, pages 132–133].

People cannot flee from their impulses as they can from a storm or a snake. Accordingly, they must rely on intrapsychic maneuvers or operations by means of which they may block any and all discharge of the threatening impulses. These operations usually entail denying conscious representation to ideas, affects and other impulses associated with the threatening impulses, as well as blocking discharge of the threatening impulses themselves. Otherwise, if these impulse representations gained consciousness, they would bring the individual that much closer to being dominated by the rejected impulses themselves, and would tend to stir up intense anxiety, guilt, and other painful feelings.

The operations by which impulses and their representations are blocked from expression in consciousness and action are known as defenses. Defenses differ from controlling or regulating ego functions in that the latter are relatively autonomous, conflict-free functions facilitating the discharge of impulses, even if in partial, modulated or indirect form. In contrast, defenses ultimately are desperate, thoroughgoing, uncompromising attempts to "eliminate" the rejected, threatening impulses and their representations. Of course, a defensive operation may fail partially or totally, in which case more or less discharge and conscious awareness of the rejected impulse result along with more or less anxiety.

In brief, defense is understood to refer to any psychological operation that is intended to block discharge of threatening, rejected impulses and thereby to avoid the painful emotional consequences of such discharge.

Defensive operations may utilize thoughts, perceptions, feelings, attitudes, actions and even impulses other than those being defended against, as in the case of regression to passivity in defense against hostile impulses. It is obvious, therefore, that we ought not think in terms of any finite number of defenses. In our clinical material we encounter an endless variety of defensive operations, ranging from some that are so extensive as to involve total, enduring personality configurations (as in severe regression) to others that are small-scale, circumscribed and transient (as in "symptomatic" forgetting of a name). Also, any categorization of defenses will reflect the conceptualizer's general theoretical and clinical orientation. Consequently, there cannot be any one "correct" or "complete" list of defenses, but only lists of varying exhaustiveness, internal theoretical consistency, and helpfulness in ordering clinical observation and research findings.

In Freudian psychoanalysis, particular attention has been paid to certain "mechanisms of defense," namely, denial, repression, introjection, projection, isolation (and its common variant intellectualization), reaction formation, undoing and regression [42].* Operating either singly or in complex, layered configurations [18], these defense mechanisms have been found to be major aspects of psychopathological phenomena. They have also become basic reference points for understanding the phenomena of personality development and organization in general and of thought processes in particular [112, 113]. These mechanisms of defense will therefore command particular attention in the chapters to follow.

The conceptual separation of the defensive aspects of behavior from its impulse aspects, while useful and justifiable, should not be misunderstood to imply that there is such a thing as defense in itself. All human behavior must be thought of as multiply determined, as being the resultant of a number of psychological forces. In the case of any psychological phenomenon, defensive efforts may constitute some of the forces behind it but certainly not all of them. Consequently, we cannot say of any behavior item or trend simply that it is "a defense"—except as a shorthand way of saying that its defensive aspect is particularly striking, relevant or crucial.

Consider in this regard defensive "intellectualization." Ordinarily, intellectualization is spoken of as "a defense." This formulation is based on the proposition that intellectualization represents a flight from spontaneity in general and from feared hostile and/or libidinal impulses in particular, and a rigid clinging to a consciously overdetached and over-controlled, strictly logical, overabstract, verbalistic, affectless and therefore seemingly impulse-free, anxiety-free and guilt-free approach to important life problems and relationships. Yet, intellectualizing also is likely to have its impulse-discharging aspects (intellect used aggressively

---

* Sublimation has also been called a defense, although a "successful" one as opposed to the "pathogenic" ones listed above [37]. For many reasons that cannot be gone into here, it seems confusing rather than clarifying to consider sublimation together with the other defense mechanisms.

as a social weapon; intellectual pursuits unconsciously conceived as feeding or sexual peeping), its superego aspects (dutiful submission to incorporated, perfectionistic standards of accomplishment; self-punishment through the ascetic aspects of diligent study), and its adaptive aspects (mastery and improvement of external reality; development and use of one's own assets; rewards for intellectual accomplishment in money, self-esteem and the esteem of others, and the variety of biological and social gratifications these facilitate). Thus, when we say intellectualization is a defense, we mean—or should mean—merely that we are concerned with *the defensive aspect* of intellectualization. Similarly, regression is not *a* defense: it is a complex change of personality organization and behavior one very prominent aspect of which is defensive, namely, the warding off of threatening impulses associated with one level of psychic functioning by retreating to a genetically earlier and less threatening level.

Defenses or defensive operations are therefore abstractions we make from total, multiply determined behavior. Of any piece of behavior we may ask: In what ways, to what extent, and how well does it serve a defensive function? Seen in this way, the genesis and current status of any defense are problems of the total personality; they are not isolated problems of a limited segment of the ego or even of the ego as a whole. Nevertheless, as the psychoanalytically-oriented clinician observes the patient's behavior during a therapy session, he cannot but be compelled to think in terms of defenses as something apart from and in opposition to impulses. In therapy, irritation in the patient followed by apologetic undoing, repressive "forgetting" of a loaded topic brought out into the open the day before, partial insight into antagonism followed by projection, and the like, are familiar enough phenomena. The play of impulses and defenses in test responses has received far less attention than it has in therapy. Yet it is often equally prominent, dramatic and instructive in the Rorschach situation as in a therapy hour.

In addition to the impulse and defense aspects of behavior, it is also conceptually compelling and useful to distinguish the adaptive aspects of behavior. Although a clear distinction between what is defensive and what is adaptive is frequently difficult to draw—the two often merging into each other—the following definitions are helpful: insofar as operations are defensive, they seek to obstruct discharge of rejected impulses totally; insofar as operations are adaptive, they facilitate discharge of accepted impulses, although they may also greatly delay, refine and limit expression of these accepted impulses so as to insure maximum gratification consistent with the individual's total life situation. The "total life situation" is understood here to include inner as well as outer conditions; and among the inner conditions, it includes the intensity of the impulse and its representations, the superego and ego ideal positions with respect to the impulse, and the individual's ingrained defensive modes and strivings toward self-consistency. A repudiated hostile impulse, for example, if handled defensively and if the defense is successful, will not be felt internally and will be blocked from discharge; a state of unconscious, pent-up hostility will result. An accepted hostile impulse, on the other hand, if handled adaptively and if the adaptation is successful, will be felt by the individual and will be discharged at an appropriate object, in appropriate form and with appropriate intensity. What is "appropriate" and what is "accepted" and "repudiated" will be defined in terms of the current external situation, the inner conditions listed above (superego position, etc.), and the reasonably foreseeable external consequences of the hostile behavior (counterattack, abandonment, etc.).

Even the traditionally listed "mechanisms of defense" have potential adaptive value. Projection and introjection, for example, have been shown to be intimately involved in empathic response [87]. In Chapter 2 on the analysis of the test relationship, repeated reference was made to the possible adaptive aspects of certain defensive operations.

Thus, according to the theoretical position taken here, the separation of adaptive and defensive operations is as abstract a distinction as the previously discussed separation of impulse and defensive operations. Impulse, defense and adaptation are all aspects of or abstractions from observed total behavior, including inner experience such as thought and feeling. It is actually the patient's shifting position with respect to these three basic reference points—impulse, defense and adaptation—that catches, holds and rewards the attention of the psychoanalytic observer. Therefore, if applied cautiously and with awareness of its abstract nature, this separation of the impulse, the defense and the adaptation aspects of behavior may be expected to provide a useful frame of reference for comprehending the psychological movement of a patient in the course of a test.

Our focus in what follows will be on defensive operations. To begin with, it will be helpful to list and illustrate a variety of ways in which defensive operations may be evidenced in Rorschach test responses and a variety of ways in which the relative effectiveness of defensive operations may be assessed. This introduction should facilitate transition to the detailed case studies that are included in the following chapters on specific mechanisms of defense.

## B. DEFENSIVE OPERATIONS IN THE RORSCHACH RESPONSE PROCESS *

Defensive operations may be expressed in various aspects of the Rorschach record. These aspects may be divided into three categories:

* Beck [11] touches briefly on some of the specific indications of defense that will be considered systematically in the following chapters. His remarks

scores, themes and test attitudes. As a rule, major operations are indicated in all three categories. This interpretive consideration has been elaborated in Chapter 5—"Criteria for Judging the Adequacy of Interpretation." We may now add another interpretive consideration, one which is consistent with the previously taken theoretical position that defense is merely one aspect of behavior and not a thing in itself: *often, different aspects of the same Rorschach response seem to express similar or opposing aspects of the interplay of impulses, defensive operations and adaptive operations.* For example, the gleefully verbalized response, "A wicked ghost on tiptoes," scored $D\ M+\ (H)$, is frightened in theme (impulse aspect: hostility, phobically projected—first defensive aspect), counterphobic in attitude (second defensive aspect) and adaptive in organization and accuracy $(M+)$ and possibly feeling tone as well (pleasure at mastery of neurotic fear). Other mutually supporting and opposing aspects of responses will be illustrated below.

In all, seven general and thirty-six specific types of expression of defense and/or the defended against will be distinguished and illustrated in what immediately follows. Although these types often overlap each other and also often accompany each other, each of them seems sufficiently unique to warrant separate classification. To highlight the distinctive features of each type of expression of impulse, defense and adaptation, all illustrations of imagery will pertain to the same situation—coping with Card II. *The illustrations do not, of course, necessarily always have the same significance and never have only the simple significance implied in this presentation. The total record and the results of other tests may modify and even significantly transform any of the following interpretations.* Possible adaptive aspects of these responses will not be emphasized here, as a rule.

Some of the illustrations have been made up in order to sharpen a contrast or underscore a similarity. Those that have been made up have, however, been selected so as to conform to the spirit of actual, dynamically equivalent responses. Because at this point the objective is to sketch the phenomenology of defensive operations and to indicate how we can spot these operations and their disruption, the specific defensive operations involved in the illustrations will often not be discussed or even named. Later chapters will tie specific defenses to specific response trends. Wherever appropriate, however, mention will be made of whether the type of response being considered usually implies weak, rigid, unstable, or strong and flexible defense.

---

are particularly relevant to the discussion of projection (Chapter 9) and the obsessive-compulsive defenses (Chapter 10). Earlier discussion of these matters will be found in Rapaport [118], Schachtel [131], and Schafer [134].

1. *Defensive Operations Expressed in the Scores.*

   a) *Locations.* A string of forced *W,* for example, may indicate the pathologically high level of ambition that is one prominent aspect of megolomanic, paranoid defense. A string of *Dr* and *De* may indicate the hypermeticulousness that is a prominent aspect of the compulsive defenses of reaction formation and isolation.

   b) *Determinants.* A relative emphasis on *F* and *FC,* for example, may indicate the overcontrolled, overadaptive mode of interpersonal approach that is a prominent aspect of reaction formation against hostility. A relative emphasis on *F/C* and *C/F* may indicate the forced rapport and simulated spontaneity that are prominent expressions of hypomanic defense by denial.

   c) *Content.* A relative emphasis on animal content (*A%*) and/or popular responses (*P%*), when it is out of keeping with the patient's intellectual level, may reflect overreliance on repression or on submissive conformity. A relative emphasis on anatomical content by a physician may reflect a defensive tendency in interpersonal relationships to hide behind the role and status of the impersonal medical authority.

   d) *Converging score implications.* Relative emphases on the scores *Dr* and *FC+* often converge to indicate obsessive-compulsive defense by reaction formation against hostility and by isolation of affect. In these instances, the *Dr* emphasis suggests conscientiousness and meticulousness, the *FC+* emphasis suggests overadaptiveness, and the preference for handling only specks of color suggests a wary, inhibited approach to affect and impulse in general. In contrast, relatively great emphases on *S* and *CF* often converge to indicate weak defense against negativistic, impulsive, narcissistic tendencies.

   e) *Opposing score implications.* The implications of *FC* and *S* tend to clash—the former emphasizing adaptiveness and compliance and the latter negativism and rebelliousness. Yet, both may be conspicuous among the responses given by an obsessive-compulsive person whose reaction formations against hostile, defiant, negativistic impulses are shaky. Similarly, the implications of tiny *Dr* and *F—* may clash—the former usually emphasizing meticulousness and the latter poor or careless reality testing. Nevertheless, both may occur together frequently among the responses of a poorly integrated obsessive-compulsive person. Particularly if *R* is high, the contrast of *Dr* and *F—* suggests vacillation between dutiful, submissive conscientiousness (reaction formation against hostility) and rebellious, disorderly narcissism (the defended against impulses). In this instance, defensive operations seem to be relatively unsuccessful, whereas in the instance of the converging implications of *Dr* and *FC+*, defensive operations seem to be relatively effective.

2. *Defensive Operations Expressed in Images.*

    a) *Simple images.*

        (1) *Impulse expression: hostility.* "People fighting and bleeding" (*W*). "Explosion" (lower red). "Spearhead" (upper middle gray).

        (2) *Defense expression: reaction formation against hostility.** "Puppies nuzzling each other" (dark areas; popular). "Pretty butterfly" (lower red). "Sunrise" (lower red). "Pixie heads" (upper red).

    b) *Sequences of images.*

        (1) *Impulse sequence: relatively weak defensive efforts.* "People fighting and bleeding; explosion; spearhead."

        (2) *Defense sequence: relatively rigid defensive efforts.* "Puppies nuzzling each other; pretty butterfly; sunrise; pixie heads."

        (3) *Impulse-defense sequence: breakthrough of impulse followed by reinstatement of defense; possible defensive flexibility or resiliency.* "People fighting and bleeding; puppies nuzzling each other; pretty butterfly."

        (4) *Defense-impulse sequence: relative defensive weakness behind fragile "good front."* "Puppies nuzzling each other; people fighting and bleeding; explosion."

    c) *Dynamically alternative images: relatively unstable defense.†* "Puppies nuzzling each other or they could be fighting over this red meat up here." "Two people fighting or dancing." "Puppies or wild boars."

    d) *Changing images.*

        (1) *Involuntary changes: relatively unstable defense.* "It looks like two people dancing. . . . The more I look the more it looks like they're fighting." "Two clowns. . . . Now, all of a sudden, they look more like witches."

        (2) *Deliberate changes: defensive stability or rigidity.* "Two people; the red at the bottom looks like blood, like they have been fighting. You could also make it two red boots, in which

---

* To illustrate the oversimplification involved in this presentation of indications of defensive operations, it should be mentioned that the examples in this paragraph might express other defensive modes of handling hostility, such as repression and denial, and that the examples need not have important defensive aspects at all. These might be primarily adaptive, relatively conflict-free responses. It is the especially or relentlessly sweet, tender, affectionate, benign aspects of these images that *may* express reaction formations against hostility.

† See pp. 180–2 for other possible aspects of these dynamic alternatives.

case it would be two clowns dancing. I'll stick with the last idea."

e) *Condensed images: relatively unstable defense.* "The face of a clown who's been crying and the paint has run" (*WS*). "A stingray coming to the surface" (middle space). "A ray of light shining through the darkness" (dark areas and middle space). The first of these examples appears to express reliance on the mechanism of denial (gaiety concealing depression) and a feeling that the denial has failed; the second example suggests the feeling that attacking impulses may be breaking through defenses and coming to expression; the third suggests underlying feelings of gloom and/or being lost, and attempts at denial of these feelings through forced optimism.

f) *Internally contradictory images: relatively unstable defense.** 

(1) *Implicit contradictions:* "Clowns fighting." "Wild boars nuzzling each other."

(2) *Explicit contradictions:* "Puppies nuzzling each other; the red makes it look like their paws are bloody but that doesn't fit—they look friendly." "A penis . . . but it is pointed like a spear" (upper middle gray). "A butterfly, but there is this big, empty hole in the middle of it" (*WS*).

g) *Delayed images: relatively unstable defense.* "The way these things come together here (lower middle) and here (upper middle). . . . I don't know. . . . They look like things in opposition. . . . Could be two people pushing against each other" (*W*). "Two people; a butterfly; a steeple; two more butterflies; those two people I mentioned at first look like the witches in Macbeth."

h) *Blocked images: relatively rigid defensive efforts.* 

(1) *Implicit blocking:* avoidance of certain outstanding areas and/or colors, such as the red areas, which frequently suggest hostility, and the upper middle gray and the lower middle, which frequently suggest sex.

(2) *Explicit blocking.* "Two people. . . . I don't know what this red would be down here or how it would relate to them. . . . It doesn't mean a thing to me." "A splattering of something; I don't know what it would be" (lower and upper red).

3. *Defensive Operations Expressed Through Test Attitudes.* These have been discussed in some detail in Chapter 2 on the psychology of the testing situation and will be touched on later in the chapters on specific defenses.

* See pp. 180–2 for other important aspects of these responses.

4. *Defensive Operations Expressed Through Combinations of Scores and Images.*

   a) *Converging implications of scores and images: relatively stable, unstable or rigid defense.* "Ashes," based solely on the dark color and scored $C'$, has depressive implications both in its determinant score and its content. The implications of the score and the image converge. Similarly convergent in score and image is "peppermint sticks," based on the fine, lower red projections and scored $FC+$. This response has a playful, receptive note in its content and a successfully adaptive note in its determinant score. "Hunks of raw meat," based on the upper red and scored $CF$, has, in contrast to the previous food response, relatively primitive, unmodulated implications of hunger or need in its content, and emotionally diffuse, narcissistic implications in its determinant score.

   b) *Opposing implications of scores and images: relatively unstable defense.* "Butterfly wings, flesh-colored as if the outer skin has been ripped off," based on the upper red areas and scored $FC\pm$, is an image that has a notably cruel thematic implication even though its determinant score has a notably adaptive implication. It should be added, with respect to formal thought organization, that the response is bizarre. This response was given by a patient prominently characterized both by severe obsessive-compulsive features and by near-psychotic weakness of integration. In a poorly disguised way the response seems to suggest a blend of overadaptive compliance (based largely on reaction formation) and sado-masochistic orientation, a blend that characterizes severely obsessive-compulsive behavior.

   Another example of opposing or at least mutually modifying implications of scores and images is "a clown's face" $(WS)$, scored $F/C-$, which in its content suggests gaiety and playfulness and in its determinant score suggests that adaptive efforts have a forced and out-of-tune quality—in short, that such gaiety and playfulness as are felt or expressed are shallow and involve defensive denial. Such would be the case clinically in a hypomanic setting, for example.

5. *Defensive Operations Expressed Through Combinations of Scores and Test Attitudes.*

   a) *Converging implications of scores and attitudes: relatively stable, unstable or rigid defense.* An arbitrary $F-$ given hastily and confidently illustrates such convergence, as does a very sharp $F+$ given carefully and responsibly.

   b) *Opposing implications of scores and attitudes: relatively unstable defense, or insincerity.* An arbitrary $F-$ given meticulously and responsibly and a *CF* nearly rejected because of the weakness of its form element are instances of opposing implications of scores and test attitudes. In the former instance we might be dealing with a psychopathic show of conscientiousness designed to obscure a basic poverty of response, or with an unsuccessful effort to maintain compulsive defenses against affect and impulse. In the latter instance—the nearly rejected *CF*—we might be dealing with enfeebled compulsive defense which inadequately staves off impulsiveness and conscious affect and which is rushed into action late.

6. *Defensive Operations Expressed Through Combinations of Images and Attitudes: Response to the Formed Image.*
   a) *Accepting attitude toward image: relatively stable or rigid defense.*
      (1) *Pleasurably accepting:* "A very pretty butterfly." "A gay picture of dancing clowns."
      (2) *Counterphobic pleasure:* "Two gorillas fighting: that's very good!" "The blood makes it look real gory!" (pleased tone). "Clowns dressed up to look frightening and pretending to fight; it's very humorous." "Ferdinand the Bull: poor creature!"
      (3) *Excitement:* "Two dogs kissing: this test is fascinating!"
   b) *Rejecting attitude toward image: relatively unstable defense.*
      (1) *Negation of a response\*:* "It doesn't look like blood: it's too red."
      (2) *Flight from a response:* "It looks like blood and that's all!" (card emphatically rejected).
      (3) *Negative attitude toward a response:* "Gorillas: I don't like to think about such things." "Blood: do I have to look at it?"
      (4) *Negative attitude toward the card:* "There is something sinister about it, something I want to get away from!"
      (5) *Negative attitude toward the test:* "Menstruation. I hate this test!"
      (6) *Negative attitude toward the tester:* "Menstruation. Everything you show me is so ugly! Why don't you show me pretty things! This will give me nightmares!" "A penis and here's a vagina. . . . You must want me to find sexual things in these."

---

\* According to psychoanalytic understanding, negation is a form of verbalization that implicitly admits what it is denying [49]. Its earmark is the spontaneous introduction of the idea to be negated. It would not be negation if the tester asked if the red looked like blood and the patient said it did not; it is negation if at one and the same time the patient introduces the idea of blood and rejects it. Defensively, negation appears to involve partial failure of repression (the thought becomes conscious) and subsequent reliance on isolation (the thought occurs affectlessly with no sense of subjective conviction or of responsibility for it) and denial (the thought is contradicted).

"Blood: is that the kind of thing you want? I wish you would say something instead of just sitting there!"

(7) *Explicit repudiation of a formed response\*:* "Blood: no, it really doesn't look like that!" "At first I thought the people were fighting, but they're not."

(8) *Implicit repudiation of response†:* "*If you wanted to,* you could say this looked like blood." "It looks like blood. . . . *Really, I don't see anything in this.*" "Blood. . . . They're all so symmetrical *they don't look like anything except inkblots.*" "*If it weren't so symmetrical,* it would look like blood." "Two people fighting and the red might be blood—*symbolically, I mean.*"

7. *Defensive Operations Expressed in Configurations of Scores, Images and Test Attitudes.* Illustration of these operations—which take in all aspects of the test record and all six of the preceding general types of expression of defensive operations—will be the main subject matter of the following chapters. There these illustrations will be preceded by summaries of the rationale of various defense mechanisms; the illustrations will be more meaningful then. It will be better therefore to postpone elaboration of this most complex form of configurational analysis.

At the present stage of introduction to the problems and techniques of interpreting defensive operations, it remains to outline systematically common indications of the relative success and failure of defensive operations. These indications have been touched on in this section in the various passing references to defensive instability, rigidity, resiliency, etc. More can and must be said about this most important problem before we can move on to the detailed case studies of defensive operations. It is impossible, however, always to separate neatly test indications of successful and failing defensive operations from test indications of successful and failing adaptive operations. At least, it is impossible for me to do so at the present time. The next section will therefore deal in general with defense *and* adaptation, although in some instances one or the other may be relatively weak or absent.

## C. Defensive and Adaptive Success and Failure

Discussing indications of successful and failing defensive and adaptive operations runs the risk of becoming an oversimplified, mechanical, mis-

---

\* This reaction is related to negation (see paragraph 6-b-1 above) but differs from it in that negation never explicitly accepts the response in the first place. Repudiation of a formed response may represent either more poorly integrated defense than negation or more security with respect to the ultimately repudiated content.

† See preceding footnote.

leading listing of "signs" of good or poor adjustment. For reasons given in the following theoretical and empirical preface to this section, this "sign" approach must be carefully avoided and a flexible, reflective approach maintained.

Many types of personality are "workable." Some personalities are characterized by greater overall defensive and adaptive security than others, and some show greater security in certain problem areas than others. Some personalities are characterized by striking imbalances or excesses—of aggressiveness, inhibition, tenseness, etc.—but are nevertheless "workable," that is, more or less productive, subjectively tolerable or gratifying, at least partially socially acceptable, and grossly stable through time.

The growth and organization of personality appears to require that certain of each individual's potentialities be cultivated and others neglected or even plowed under. Normally, the potentialities to be cultivated are those supporting the development of an integrated, effective social role and personal "style" of living, while those to be neglected or plowed under are irrelevant to or clash with the guiding themes of the personality. This differential development of potentialities occurs in a process of interaction between the individual and his familial and larger cultural surroundings. In society there are many roles to be played or avoided, and many talents to be exploited and deficiencies to be accommodated to or even made into virtues.

Erikson's use of the concept "ego identity" is relevant in this regard [35]. "Ego identity" is understood to refer to the guiding themes, self-concept and social role that form the core around which the individual, with the support and pressure of his culture, attempts to integrate his drives, defenses, capacities, deficiencies, values, interests, and the like. Put differently, "ego identity" sums up what the individual is trying to become, remain or return to in his past or the past of his family or culture, how he is trying to accomplish this, and in what context of biological, familial and cultural forces. Ego identity formation is inevitably a selective affair.

Since many types of personality are "workable," and since the requirements of personal and social development and integration appear to foster considerable individual variation in personality organization and ego identity, it is impossible as well as incorrect to define only one "optimal" personality or identity. The question must always be asked, "Optimal for what?" Recognizing this, we cannot very well specify only one "optimal" pattern of Rorschach test results. Theoretically we must be prepared to accept—and empirically we find—that within one culture, subculture, family and even single life history there is a *range* of possible optima. There are many kinds of effective balance and tolerable imbalance in personalities, expressing themselves accordingly in Rorschach records of considerable variety.

For example, what is optimal for a leader is not altogether so for a follower; what is optimal for a laborer is not altogether so for a salesman; similarly for a child and an adult and for a dull person and a gifted intellectual. The place of impulsiveness versus reflectiveness, assertiveness versus submissiveness, narcissism versus adaptability, and the like, varies in these different contexts. What is personally gratifying, situationally useful and socially esteemed is for the most part not the same from one of these contexts to the next. Accordingly the place of $F$, $M$, $FC$, $Dr$, $P$, etc., will vary with the prevailing ego identity problems and solutions, even though each score may retain something of its general significance in all settings.

Turning to concrete Rorschach patterns, a special emphasis on $FC$, for instance, will somehow pertain to striving for rapport with others, whether expressed by a child or an adult, a laborer or a salesman. In the child, however, this strong $FC$ emphasis may indicate premature socialization that severely restricts social spontaneity and flexibility, while in the adult it may indicate useful and gratifying adaptability. In the laborer the strong $FC$ emphasis may reflect a submissive, ingratiating social manner that promotes his being picked on, while in the salesman it may reflect a smooth social versatility that promotes sales.

The upshot of these generalizations and examples for the present discussion is this: estimating the success and failure of adaptive and defensive operations is always a relative matter; it must therefore take into account the total Rorschach record, the results of other tests, and the past and present general life circumstances of the patient, such as his age and sex, his subcultural, educational, socio-economic and religious background, his occupational history and present status, and his past and present family constellation (number and ages of siblings and children, if any; parents living or dead; patient single, married, divorced, etc.). On the basis of these test data and biographical orientation points, we may be able to sketch out the patient's prevailing problems and achievements in ego identity formation. With the help of this identity sketch, we may then best understand what is defensively and adaptively workable for the patient and what is not. And with this understanding we may be able to estimate the relative success or failure of the patient's adaptive and defensive operations.

Yet, there are certain broad Rorschach test limits beyond which white adults of at least average intelligence in American (if not Western) culture may not go without indicating thereby serious weakness or disruption of defense and adaptation. It is with these broad limits that we shall be concerned in what immediately follows. It must be remembered, however, that even these broad limits may be inapplicable in certain cases.

In the Rorschach test, indications of the overall success or failure of defensive and adaptive operations may be found in at least six general aspects of the test performance: its *emotional tone*, the extent to which the patient emphasizes *specific, articulated form* in his responses, the extent to which he achieves *accurate form,* the *integratedness* of the score, image and attitude aspects of the responses, the degree of *thematic moderation and balance* maintained, and the extent to which *formal thought disorder* is indicated by the scores, images and attitudes.*

Certain imbalanced or extreme score patterns not covered in the following survey but usually indicative of adaptive and defensive instability will be encountered in many clinical records. Such, for example, are records with extreme emphasis on *W* (more than 20) or *S* (more than 10% of *R*) among the locations, or extreme emphasis on movement only or color only in the *Experience Balance* (10 *M* : 0 *sum C* or 1 *M* : 20 *sum C*). Covering all these specific overemphases and imbalances requires a general survey of diagnostic indications—a survey that obviously cannot be undertaken here.†　A number of these diagnostic patterns will, however, be touched on throughout the discussion of pathological defenses in the later case studies.

*1. Emotional Tone.* When defensive and adaptive operations are relatively successful (in the sense of staving off anxiety and guilt, and expressing impulses and impulse representations constructively and with release of some tension), the patient's emotional tone will generally be calm, relaxed and more or less positive. Humor, interest in the responses and sustained cooperation with the tester will be more or less available. The patient's responsiveness may be more varied than this in emotional tone, or somewhat different and still be essentially adaptive and well defended but even so his emotional position will not be extreme and it will be appropriate to the content of the problems encountered. He may then manifest mild flurries of anxiety, a dash of gaiety here and there or even a constant playfulness, a passing or persisting light sadness, some flippancy, boredom or irritability, moderate satisfaction and dissatisfaction with responses, and so forth.

In the type of relationship he attempts to set up with the tester, the patient may, for example, be submissive but not abjectly, embarrassingly, provocatively so; he may be domineering but not incapable of general compliance with the test instructions; he may be detached but not to the point of indifferent, minimal, bored responsiveness; he may be intensely involved but, except for brief and moderate lapses, he will not lose sight of the line between fantasy and reality.

When defensive and adaptive operations are relatively ineffective, we are likely to encounter any extreme of submissiveness, efforts to take over

* Compare Beck's recent discussion of "the insufficient ego" and of "bound" and "free" anxiety in the Rorschach test [*11*].
† For such a survey, see Schafer [*134*].

control of the situation, boredom, frequent tears, forced laughter, inappropriate jokes and facetiousness, intense anxiety and its bodily manifestations, irritability, querulousness, painful tenseness, apathy, histrionics, exultation, suspiciousness or evasiveness, or any combination of these. Actually, many of these behaviors may be seen, from one point of view, to be exaggerated or last-ditch-stand defensive expressions. Defense in these instances is, however, relatively primitive in form and utterly unproductive in outcome, in contrast to smooth defense that is built right into the response and does not disrupt the test atmosphere and relationship.

The distinction between well-defended, adaptively modulated responsiveness and poorly defended, unmodulated responsiveness is not always clear, of course, but insofar as the distinction can be made with confidence, it provides a useful index of the effectiveness of defense and adaptation. One patient, for example, might casually see a "threatening" figure on Card IV and point out with some amusement the incongruity of the large feet and the small arms. The next patient might see the same figure but find it "horrible" and quickly give up the card. In the first case defensive and/or adaptive operations seem relatively successful, and in the second not.

It is not self-contradictory, it should be noted, to speak of relatively successful defense and adaptation in the responses of psychiatric patients Psychiatric patients spread out over a wide range of maladjustment and each one is not equally sick in all areas of functioning. Many have relatively minor adjustment problems or else are reacting strongly but transiently to an external psychological trauma. In these instances the patients' basic adaptive and defensive positions may remain relatively secure and their test records may be indistinguishable from those of "normal" subjects.

*2. Emphasis on Specific, Articulated Form.* The best estimate of relative emphasis on form is provided by the *extended F%*. The *extended F%* is the percent of $R$ made up by $M$, $FM$, $Ms$, $FC$, $F(C)$, $FC'$, $FCh$, as well as by pure $F$—in short, by all responses with a primary or major form component.* An $FC$ butterfly, after all, is as formed a response as an $F$ butterfly, just as an $M$ human being is as formed as an $F$ human being. Therefore the usual $F\%$ alone does not reflect the patient's total emphasis on form. For example, if the *extended F%* is 95%, an $F\%$ of 50% is misleadingly low as an index of emphasis on form. Consequently it is the *extended F%* to which particular attention must be paid in this regard. In the following, the *extended F%* will be considered relatively low when it drops below 80%–85% and relatively high when it rises above 90%–95%.

A relatively low *extended F%* usually indicates more or less failure to take hold of the problem situations represented by the ten Rorschach cards and impose articulated, meaningful structure on them. *Blood, explosion,*

---

* For scoring criteria, see Rapaport [118].

*smoke, dough, mud, water* and *darkness* are the types of images, and *CF* and *C, C'F* and *C', ChF* and *Ch,* and *(C)F* the scores that reflect this failure to impose form. Baer, conceiving the Rorschach inkblots as threatening because they stimulate infantile anxiety concerning loss of objects, has spoken of this failure as a failure to restore objects through form [5]. As a rule, the more these weakly formed or unformed responses preponderate in the record, the more severe the paralysis, feebleness or overwhelming of ego functions concerned with restraint and modulation of impulse and affect. The patient's emphasis on form usually parallels his emphasis on self-control. Where *CF* and *C, C'F* and *C',* and similarly weakly formed or unformed responses dominate the record, the patient is likely to be flooded with diffuse, intense affect and anxiety, and to be either extremely tense or severely impulse-ridden. When form is under-emphasized, therefore, weak defensive and adaptive efforts are likely to characterize the patient's present status.

There is more involved, however, than is conveyed by the *F%* and *extended F%*. Many responses are scored *F* more by default than by any achievement of specific, articulated form. For example, a "map" on Card IV will be scored *F* if no shading determinant is elicited in inquiry; similarly, "anatomy" without color on Card VIII and "islands" without color or shading on Card X will be scored *F*. Responses like these are usually more or less vague, haphazard, inert, impulsive, physiognomic, or otherwise unarticulated and unspecific. They are minimally formed and it is almost charitable to score them *F* as we do. They are not "wrong," so to speak, but they are not "right" either. They do not stand for con-trolling, delaying, modulating efforts made by the patient.

It represents a significant step forward when the "map" becomes "a map of the United States," when "anatomy" becomes "a diagram of the anatomy of the thorax and abdomen," and when islands become "Sardinia" and "England." In these responses an attempt is usually made to achieve specific, articulated form. The patient is actively and responsibly engaging the stimuli and attempting to make good use of their potentialities as well as his own. This active approach to the test situation and the availability of energy for carrying it through ordinarily indicate some strength in the patient's present psychological status. Thus, this consistent search for specific, articulated form—not just any vague form impression—is a necesary, even if not sufficient, indication of well-maintained adaptive and defensive efforts.

Sometimes, an adaptively and defensively stable patient might momen-tarily be driven at first into a color or shading response with little or no form, but he will then show significant resiliency by pushing his way into the areas involved or into other areas on the card and imposing form on them. For example, Card VI might at first be seen as a vague map with the resilient patient then successively pointing out such details of the map as a river, elevations and depressions, fertile and infertile areas, and the like; similarly, Card VII might at first be seen as clouds with the resilient patient then pointing out the popular heads, the butterfly at the bottom, the vagina in the lower center, and perhaps finally even seeing the entire blot as dancers. The defensive and adaptive efforts of patients such as these have bounce in them despite initial shakiness or vulnerability.

More adaptively and defensively stable patients than these might not even see the global, amorphous images at all, or might give then only within a sequence of more or less formed, articulated responses to a card. In the latter instance, the patient might include the more or less formless response as one among several possibilities, and may be neither flustered by it nor dominated by it. The relatively formless response may then merely represent a let-up of effort and a healthy acceptance of the need to relax, or it may represent an instance of the sporadic, limited defensive or adaptive failures that mark even the best adjustments. In contrast, a patient with seriously impaired defensive and adaptive effectiveness gave the following response sequence on Card X: "This is . . . a design. Somebody got wild with a paint brush. . . . Something like Salvador Dali might do to represent spring (C). . . . This way (sideways) it's a fireworks display (CF). Here again (upside down) is another design, symbolizing perhaps spring or undersea life a couple of fathoms down (CF)." On Card X, another such patient may just see "an anatomical chart because of the color" or "chaos" and let it go at that.

An intense sense of precariousness may lead the patient to go too far in his efforts to maintain control. His excessive emphasis on control may be manifest in a very high $F\%$ (above 75%–80%) and *extended $F\%$* (above 90%–95%). In this case, defensive operations are likely to be too rigid and severe, adaptiveness limited, and feeling and fantasy stifled.

*3. Achievement of Accurate Form.* In the immediately preceding paragraphs on emphasis on specific, articulated form, nothing was said about the accuracy of the form responses evolved. Actually, a response may be specific and articulated and yet the area referred to may not be congruent with the real object to which the response refers. For example, patients sometimes maintain that half of Card VI (sideways) looks like "a map of the United States"; Florida, Texas and the Gulf of Mexico may be specifically pointed out; shading may even be invoked as a determinant. Here is a concrete, differentiated image and yet it is for the most part grossly inaccurate and will be scored $F-$. Similarly, Card II is not infrequently said to look like "a cat's face" with the upper red areas "the eyes," the upper middle grey "the nose," and the middle space "the mouth." Even though specific and somewhat articulated, this is another $F-$ response.

Thus, the patient may try to impose form but may do so only at the expense of quality—in this respect, accuracy. While, as a rule, it is more adaptive to try to impose form than not, a try is not synonymous with successful adaptation. When the failures in accuracy are quantitatively or qualitatively extreme, as in a preponderance of inaccurate form over accurate form or in *absurd F−*, reality testing may be said to be significantly impaired.

The best single estimate of the extent to which accurate form is achieved is the *extended F+%*. The *extended F+%* is the *F+%* that takes into account not only the form level of the pure *F* responses, but of the *M, FM, Ms, FC, F(C), FC'* and *FCh* responses as well.* The basic *F+%*, which is the percent of all pure form responses that are accurate in form, is not as good an estimate of overall perceptual accuracy as the *extended F+%* because, as was mentioned in discussing the *extended F%*, responses like *M* and *FC* are as formed as any *F* response, and their accuracy is therefore just as important to estimate and take into account. It may happen, for example, that the *F+%* is 55% while the *extended F+%* is 80% : it would be incorrect to speak of impaired reality testing in this case, but only the *extended F+%* indicates this. Again, the *F+%* may be 75% and the *extended F+%* as low as 50% : only the latter figure indicates that reality testing may be significantly impaired. In the following, therefore, the *extended F+%* will be particularly emphasized. It will be considered relatively low when it drops below 70%–75%, and it will be considered relatively high when it rises above 85%–90%.

The achievement of accurate form indicates adequate reality testing. Adequate reality testing presupposes a relatively secure defensive and adaptive position. "Ego strength" is ordinarily defined by effective defensive and adaptive operations. It is probably for these reasons that maintaining an adequate form level has been held to be good index of "ego strength" [10]. When defensive and adaptive operations are effective, the patient ordinarily maintains an adequately high form level even when he is dealing with content that is highly emotionally charged or conflictful. For example, on Card VIII a male patient might see: "Stalking tigers (*P*) ; teeth (middle space) ; a corset (middle blue)." All are *F+* responses although all may be assumed to be significantly emotionally charged or conflictful.

If the patient is adaptively and defensively less stable than this, one or two poor forms might appear first and then several adequate and/or superior forms, the latter indicating noteworthy resiliency. With increasing defensive and adaptive failure, whether or not the content is clearly emotionally charged or conflictful, the form level tends to fall off (*extended*

---

* For criteria for scoring form level, see Rapaport [118].

INTRODUCTION TO THE INTERPRETATION OF DEFENSES

$F+\%$ below 70%–75%). For example, the following sequence of responses was given to Card VII by a severely schizoid, very precariously integrated male patient of 30: pelvis ($W$ $F-$), mask ($WS$ $FC'-$), kittens tumbling ($D$ $FCh\mp$), marine form ($De$ $F\mp$), and caterpillar ($Dr$ $F+$).

Actually, nonspecific form and inaccurate form frequently accompany each other when defensive and adaptive ego functions are weak. A typical sequence is that given by the same schizoid patient to Card VI: sound track ($W$ $F\mp$), map of terrain ($W$ $ChF$), feathery wings ($Do$ $FCh+$), spinal column ($Dr$ $F\mp$), texture of stone ($D$ $Ch$), X-ray ($D$ $C'F$), male figure ($Dr$ $F+$), penis ($D$ $F+$), and womb ($D$ $F-$).

The failure to achieve accurate form may be underscored by occasional or even frequent *absurd F—* responses, that is, responses so inaccurate that they seem almost altogether arbitrary and betoken total momentary collapses of reality testing. Calling all of Card VII a "snake" is such a response. In the other direction, some $F+$ responses represent greater integrative and imaginative achievements than others. Card IV as a "skin" is $F+$; as a "worm's eye view of a man sitting on a stump" it is $M+$. No distinction is drawn in the form level scoring between the superior accuracy and integration of the latter and the simplicity and obviousness of the former. Recognizing the existence of the *absurd F—* at one extreme and the superior $F+$ at the other, we must attend to the qualitative as well as quantitative aspects of success and failure in achieving accurate form. The $F+\%$ and the *extended F+%* are merely general orientation points for this aspect of our investigation and do not tell the whole story about reality testing.

For example, an adequately high $F+\%$ might be based on an utterly banal, limited record consisting mostly of popular and near-popular responses. If the patient is above average in intelligence, such a record indicates defensive rigidity and impoverishment of adaptiveness and inner experience rather than the defensive and adaptive flexibility and stability and the corresponding richness of inner experience that are important aspects of ego strength. To take another example, an adequately high $F+\%$ might be found in the record of a paranoid schizophrenic most of whose responses are $F+$ although one is a *confabulated M—*. While it is very likely that this patient will manifest "toughness" or stability and preservation of assets in his paranoid integration, his high $F+\%$ suggests strength of somewhat different sort than that implied when we speak of ego strength without further qualification, that is, as synonymous with an adaptive, adequately realistic, resilient personality, defended well but not rigidly. Again we must conclude that the $F+\%$ and *extended F+%* cannot be taken at face value, useful though they often are as indices of adaptive and defensive stability.

The *extended F+%* may be too high (above 85%–90%) as well as too low or misleadingly "adequate." This, like the too high *extended F%*, suggests rigidity of defense and limited adaptiveness. In particular, it suggests inability to relax sometimes and perform casually or impulsively rather than dutifully, cautiously or perfectionistically. Such defensive rigidity precludes the spontaneity and self-assertiveness that allow a normal amount of irresponsibility, laziness and self-indulgence.

It should be said at this point that the estimates "too high" and "too low" as applied to the emphasis on specific form and on accurate form do not necessarily imply *pathologically* high or low. Many a person gets along with little more than average discomfort despite rigid or weak controls and despite unduly cautious or relatively poor reality testing. "Too high" and "too low" imply rather that large segments of experience and personal potential may be sacrificed and that significant limits may be put upon the depth, stability, and gratifying consequences of relationships.

It should also be emphasized at this time that we cannot expect perfect accuracy in our generalizations from Rorschach test results to life situations. We can achieve gross accuracy, particularly if we use a battery of tests, but we must always assume that the tests have not revealed all major personality variables and their patterns of interaction. We must also always make the limiting assumptions that fate often tips the scales of external circumstance one way or the other regardless of the individual's character structure and intentions, and that to a significant extent the prominence of character features and pathological trends depend on external circumstance. Predicting behavior in therapy from test results, for example, can hardly be expected to be very accurate so long as the personality, competence and technical approach of the therapist, and the way these play into the specific patient's problems, are not taken into account.

*4. Integratedness of Scores, Images and Attitudes.* Types of opposing score, image and attitude aspects of responses have been listed and illustrated in *Section B,* above, on the expression of defensive operations in Rorschach responses. The more these opposing aspects or implications of response are present and the more dramatic they are, the greater the patient's adaptive and defensive instability and/or failure. The better integrated the score, image and attitude aspects of the responses, the greater the patient's defensive sturdiness and adaptive flexibility. "A pink polar bear" (Card VIII, *P*), for example, is adaptively and defensively weaker than "a polar bear, but it's the wrong color," and the latter is weaker than "a polar bear" or "a polar bear on ice with reflected sunlight giving it a pinkish hue." "A horrible monster with shriveled arms" (Card IV, *W*) is adaptively and defensively weaker than "an animal with ineffectual flippers," which in turn is weaker than "a skin" or "a worm's eye view of a man sitting on a stump." In both sets of examples there seems to be a gross sequence from least to most integrated and realistic response, or, dynamically, a sequence from weakest to strongest adaptive and defensive position.

With defenses working well and adaptability not highly restricted, the patient will more or less successfully rationalize or weed out the frequent, almost inevitable more or less incongruous elements of his images. Thus, if the popular men on Card III are seen, the projections on their chests will be ignored or called "dickies" and the projections at their knees will be ignored or called "coattails"; even if these figures are seen as women with the projections on their chests interpreted as "breasts," the projections at the knees will then be disregarded or perhaps made into "skirts." In any event it is unlikely, when adaptive and defensive stability obtains, that they will be seen as "persons with breasts and penises." Effective adaptive and defensive operations tend to eliminate such incongruities.

Poor integratedness of the elements of an image often involves expression of the defense on the one hand and the defended against on the other in a way that might be characterized as a "returning of the repressed" and a failure of adaptation. Other responses illustrating poor integration of image components are "An infant with a fang" (lower red, Card IX), in which aggression seems to intrude into a regressive theme of helpless passivity; "A gay celebration only it's spoiled by a dark brooding figure over it all" (Card X, W), in which depression appears to break through a defensive denial; and "Two men bowling but they couldn't be facing each other that way" (Card III, P), in which assaultive intent apparently invades a theme of playful competition.

Defensive and adaptive stability in the Rorschach situation is not, however, simply a matter of avoiding responses that are poorly integrated and internally contradictory. A stable defensive and adaptive position makes it possible, given adequate intelligence, to elaborate more or less complex responses in an imaginative, internally consistent way. Not only that, but the well-defended and adaptive patient is often able to call up concepts or images that make virtues out of what would otherwise be flaws in his responses.

For example, the well-functioning, superficially normal, intelligent, obsessive-compulsive man to be discussed in the chapter on the obsessive-compulsive defenses, saw a face in the outer half of the lower pink on Card VIII: a light spot in the upper outer corner was the eye and a projection from the lower outer corner was the nose. Left as such, this would have been a moderately poor Dr F— response. The subject went on to say, however, that the face was like one by Pieter Breughel. Anyone who has seen Breughel's fantastic renditions of people in his religious, moralistic engravings will appreciate the aptness of this characterization of the response.* The response thus became Dr F+. The subject had sufficient

* See, for example, The Fantasy of Pieter Breughel [6].

intelligence and cultural interest to have acquired and retained the Breughel image or a schema of that image; and he was sufficiently secure and cool in his adaptive and defensive position to be able to manipulate the percept and to delve into his store of imagery until an idea was formed that put the faults in the face response to good use. In the end he had made a silk purse out of a sow's ear. This is the *positive* form of expression of secure defense and adaptiveness, just as avoidance of internally contradictory or loose responses is the *negative* form of expression of secure defense and adaptiveness.

A "poor relation" of the type of response just cited is that in which certain formal inadequacies of the response are included in its verbalization; for example, "A face but the nose is too long," "Just at first glance it looks like an airplane," and "If there were another arm and leg it might look like a dancer." If not overdone, this type of response may indicate noteworthy ability to take self-critical distance from oneself, which in turn may imply a relatively secure emotional position. If persistent, however, this self-critical emphasis may represent unproductive pedantry that is intended to mask anxiety-induced inefficiencies or hostile and/or passive inertia and disorderliness.

*5. Thematic Moderation and Balance.* In Chapters 3 and 4 on the psychology of the Rorschach response process and on thematic analysis of imagery, it was maintained that the appearance of richly self-expressive imagery in Rorschach responses is due to a great extent to nonpathological relaxation of defensive barriers against normally preconscious and unconscious images. Thus, there may appear images that are predominantly hostile in theme, such as explosion, cannon and spear, or predominantly passive in theme, such as nipples and chicks being fed, without it being implied that the patient is necessarily overwhelmed by hostile or passive tendencies.

It is not usual, however, when defense and adaptation are relatively secure, that the Rorschach record is overrun with images pertaining to primitive impulse and conflict; nor is it usual, under relatively stable conditions, that imagery of violence and destruction is qualitatively extreme. With respect to hostile imagery, for example, a split-open bleeding skull, a shredded leg, and a face peering out from the ruins of a bombed building are images so intense and/or bizarre in their violent, destructive aspects that even one of them in a record strongly suggests serious defensive and adaptive instability. A spate of milder hostile images such as spear, teeth and blood suggests shaky defense and adaptation more because of quantity than quality. And an occasional, moderate hostile image is in itself diagnostically valueless in this regard; in fact, it may well imply healthy freedom of awareness and expression of impulse and feeling, and may thereby indicate desirable defensive and adaptive strength and flexibility. It is not unusual, for example, that such moderate aggressive images appear or increase in frequency in the retest records of patients whose general security and stability have increased during therapy, and who were, to begin with, troubled by too rigid defense against hostility.

Turning to passive imagery, a Christmas tree here and a dish of ice cream there may reflect balanced defense against and adaptive freedom of expression of passive, receptive impulses, while many such images imply precarious defense and adaptiveness, and "a mountainous breast" and "an inflamed open mouth" suggest very weak defense and seriously limited adaptiveness.

These contrasts among hostile and passive images parallel in implication the differences between $CF$ and $C$ responses, and between poor $F-$ and *absurd* $F-$ responses. That is to say, some (but not too many) $CF$ and $F-$ are ordinarily desirable or at least acceptable, but $C$ (except with high $R$ and numerous other color responses) and *absurd* $F-$ are not. Similarly, some expressions of hostility, passivity, sexuality, anxiety, etc., may be present in the images without carrying ominous implications, but quantitatively and qualitatively extreme expressions of these may not. When qualitatively extreme themes prevail, it is strongly suggested that the patient's consciousness is flooded with normally unconscious, threatening thoughts, fantasies, feelings and impulses, and that a psychotic breakdown or primitivization of defense and adaptation has occurred. Then the Rorschach record is likely to be overflowing with gore, devastation, filth, decay, lust, sexual perversity, devouring, mutilation or horrible deformity, or any combination of these. These extreme thematic emphases will almost always be accompanied by numerous other indications of undermined defense and adaptation, such as disruption of emotional tone, pathologically poor reality testing, and formal indications of thought disorder.*

There is, however, more to look for among the themes when assessing defensive and adaptive effectiveness than moderation alone. There is also the matter of balance. As already mentioned, some freedom of awareness and of expression of impulse and feeling is a mark of secure adjustment. But, in addition, the secure person is not likely to be limited to the images that convey more or less implication of need, anger, threat and conflict. He is also likely to use images that are more or less positively toned, images that express themes of gratification, peace and security. These

* Up to a point, patients who have been in psychoanalytic therapy and who, as a result, may be characterized by nonpathological openness of consciousness to normally unconscious content, are exceptions to this rule; so are some psychoanalytically-oriented psychiatrists and psychologists. In the records of all these subjects, however, other possible indications of severe adaptive and defensive failure should not be present if the primitive content is to be regarded as not ominous.

are the playful or affectionate images of dancing, embracing, toys and games, prosperity and abundance, liberty and dignity, decorations and celebrations, entertainers and benevolent figures. Clowns, dancers, people drinking a toast, rocking horse, garden flowers, green fields, coral, candy, fireworks, merry-go-round, ice skaters, W. C. Fields, Andy Gump, Skeezix, Abe Lincoln, Statue of Liberty and cornucopia are examples of such benign imagery.

A liberal amount of these benign, optimistic images interspersed with the common *bats, butterflies, skins, dogs* and *bears*, and the occasional *explosion, gorilla, breasts, withered leaf, raincloud* and *headless figure* gives balance to the thematic statements in the record. This balance ordinarily suggests that the patient can feel and acknowledge the "bad" things in life and yet enjoy the "good" things in life too; that he neither dwells on misery masochistically nor engages in extensive pollyannish denial of problems; that he neither flees in terror from his primitive or tender impulses nor surrenders to them completely; and that he is capable of creative "regression the service of the ego" without losing control and being swept along on a flood of primary process material.

Of course, these conclusions are merely suggested rather than established by the images and themes alone. They should be amply supported by the implications of the scores and test attitudes, and by the results of other tests, before they are considered sound. But it is often the case that within broad limits *thematic moderation and balance* characterize the records of patients and normals whose defensive and adaptive operations are relatively effective.

*6. Formal Thought Disorder.* It is self-evident that as indications of formal thought disorder increase quantitatively and qualitatively, they bespeak increasingly severe undermining or collapse of the patient's adaptive and defensive status. Confabulation, contamination, peculiar verbalization, autistic logic, perseveration, extreme concreteness of conceptual orientation, blocking and retardation, and other manifestations of formal thought disorder are predicated upon pathologically regressive shifts in level of functioning, that is, retreats toward primitive, minimally socialized modes of defense and adaptation.*

We have considered six major sources of indications of adaptive and defensive success and failure—the record's *emotional tone,* its emphases on *specific, articulated form* and on *accurate form,* the *integratedness* of the score, image and attitude components of responses, the maintenance of *thematic moderation and balance,* and the presence or absence of indications of *formal thought disorder.* All these, considered together with

* For a rationale and classification of these indications of formal thought disorder in the Rorschach test and for numerous examples, see Rapaport[*118*].

diagnostic patterns of extreme score emphases or imbalances, with pertinent indications provided by other tests, and with orienting biographical data, provide a frame of reference within which it is usually possible to estimate grossly the effectiveness of the patient's defensive and adaptive operations. These estimates have the advantage of not being chained to specific, normative "signs." They are based on individual psychological analysis of the patient's entire mode of functioning.

## D. In What Follows . . .

A great deal of theory lies behind us by now. Ahead lie the theoretical summaries and case studies of specific defensive operations. Before moving onward, a number of orienting remarks are called for. These remarks answer some questions that are bound to arise in the reader's mind as he goes along.

*1. The General Plan of Presentation.* The following chapters are organized around specific "mechanisms of defense"—repression, projection, denial, and the obsessive-compulsive quaternary of regression, isolation, reaction formation and undoing. Each chapter will begin with a brief summary of theoretical psychoanalytic propositions about the defense in question. Following this there will be a discussion of a variety of expected Rorschach test indications of this defense mechanism. Finally, a series of four illustrative records will be analyzed.

Discussion of each record will center around indications of the defense under consideration but will not be restricted to these indications. Consistent with the general view advocated here that defense is only one aspect of behavior and that impulse and adaptation are equally significant aspects of behavior, the analysis of the records will consider indications of impulses and adaptive operations as well as defensive operations. Considering all three aspects of behavior at once tends to increase our understanding of each aspect separately. In addition, superego pressures and both ideal and rejected self-concepts will also be examined so far as they are interwoven with the defense mechanism in question. It is therefore misleading in an important way that defensive operations should be so emphasized in the following chapter headings. Actually the analyses are analyses of total behavior. Yet, without a focus the analyses could become chaotic, and defense is the focus of the analyses; the chapter headings therefore are not inappropriate.

*2. The Treatment of Scores.* While attention will be paid in the case studies to scores, test attitudes and imagery, the scores will often be relatively underemphasized. This is because I hope to show how much we can understand the Rorschach record without referring to scores. This is not for the purpose of a *tour de force.* I believe that the development of

Rorschach technique has tended to restrict attention to scores and their sequences to the point where scores often become barriers between the tester and the patient. Theory and interpretation suffer as a result, becoming mechanical and jargonistic. Rapaport's emphasis on analysis of verbalization represents an important break with the score-oriented tradition [118]. Schachtel's discussions of the test relationship [131], "dynamic form" [129], and varieties of significance in $M$ responses [132] have also helped restore the flesh-and-blood patient to Rorschach theory and to make testers the masters instead of the slaves of scores.

Another reason for my relative neglect of scores in what follows is that the standard principles for interpreting scores, score sequences and score patterns have been set forth in detail by a number of writers [8, 9, 86, 107, 118, 124].

The score summaries will frequently be touched on only briefly and only after the response-by-response part of each analysis is complete. The scores will be checked then chiefly to see where and to what extent they reflect the already inferred trends. This didactic technique is used to demonstrate what is new and not to disparage what is old and well established. It should not be construed to imply either that scores are of secondary and limited significance or that this relative neglect of scores is the best way to approach a Rorschach record. There is no "best" way to begin. Each record extends a different helping hand to the tester—one in an unusual score pattern, one in a dramatic image, one in a sudden change of attitude, etc. It also seems to be the case that different testers vary in what they find most helpful in a record. Once the helping hand has served its purpose, however, we must systematically explore and try to interrelate all aspects of the scores, images and test attitudes.

*3. The Scores.* Despite this didactically required de-emphasis of scores, a brief summary of the scoring system is necessary. This is because the scoring system, which is virtually identical with that set forth by Rapaport [118], is not widely used.

*Area of Response*

W :        all or nearly all of the blot.
D :        portions of the blot which are relatively large, clearly set off and
           frequently interpreted.
Dd :       small but not tiny areas, clearly set off from the bulk of the blot.
Dr :       tiny areas, or relatively large areas which are neither clearly set
           off nor frequently interpreted.
De :       interpretation of a contour line.
S :        a relatively large white area in or around the blot.
s :        a relatively small white area.

Do: interpreting an area frequently seen as a part of a larger area, and retaining the same content for the smaller area as it would have in the larger, frequent interpretation.

Do-tendency (additional score only): initial or partial fragmentation of responses, even if they are not common responses.

DW: reasoning from a part of the blot to the entire blot without checking the conclusion against the actual appearance of the entire blot.

*Determinants*

F: an interpretation based solely on the formal configuration of an area; all F responses (also *M, FM, Ms, FC, F(C), FC'* and *FCh*) are scored for form level, as below.

F+: a form response of acceptable or superior accuracy.

F—: a form response of inferior accuracy; may be vague or arbitrarily organized.

F±: a basically acceptable form response with some minor inaccuracy.

F∓: a basically inaccurate form response with some saving features.

M: a response in which a complete or nearly complete human figure is seen in action or in some position of tension.

FM: an *M* response with weak emphasis on motion or tension, with animal-like features stressed, or with animals in human-like activity.

Ms: an *M* response using a relatively small area.

FC: a response using form and color, with color subordinate or equal to form as a determinant.

CF: a response using form and color, with form subordinate to color.

C: a response based on color alone.

F/C: a response using form and color, based primarily on form and with color added artificially, e.g., "A colored map of Norway."

FC arbitrary: assigning inappropriate color to a form without rationalizing it as artificial, e.g., "A blue horse."

C/F: a response using form and color, based primarily on artificial use of color, e.g., a vague "colored map."

F(C): a form response in which variations of shading are important in defining the outline or important inner details; may also signify the use of the texture in colored areas.

(C)F: a vague *F(C)*, i.e., one with nonspecific or poorly articulated form; may also signify the use of the texture in colored areas.

FC': a response based on form and black, gray, or white color, with these colors subordinate or equal to form as a determinant.

C'F: a response in which black, gray or white color is dominant over form.

C′:     a response based on black, gray or white color alone.

FCh:    a response based on form and shading, with shading subordinate or equal to form as a determinant.

ChF:    a response in which shading outweighs form as a determinant.

Ch:     a response based on shading alone.

Combined scores: where more than one score is applicable, they will be combined, the dominant or diagnostically more significant determinant being listed first. Thus, "smoke and fire" on Card II might be scored $CC'F$, signifying that it combines a $CF$ and a $C'F$, and "dancing Negroes" on Card III might be scored $MC'$, signifying that it combines an $M$ and an $FC'$. Scores listed after the first will be tallied "additional" in the score summary.

*Content*

| | | | |
|---|---|---|---|
| A: | full animal figure | Cg: | clothing |
| Ad: | animal detail | Dec: | decoration |
| H: | full human figure | At: | anatomy |
| (H): | human-like figure | Geog: | geography |
| Hd: | human detail | Geol: | geology |
| (Hd): | human-like detail | Arch: | architecture |
| Obj: | object | Ldsc: | landscape |

*Miscellaneous*

P: popular responses, given by at least one out of every five subjects; (P) denotes a minor variation in a popular response.

Orig: original response, found no more than once in every hundred records. This score will not be used in the following analyses.

Combination: combination response in which two or more interpretations are meaningfully related.

Fabulized Combination: combination response in which two spatially contiguous interpretations are arbitrarily (but not elaborately) related.

Fabulation: feelings, motives, qualities or events are alluded to with marginal support in the blot.

Confabulation: extensive and arbitrary associative elaboration without objective support; also includes some of Rapaport's "Reference Idea" verbalizations.

Confabulation tendency: extreme Fabulations or minor Confabulations, and full Confabulations verbalized with a trace of self-conscious, critical distance.

Contamination: two interpretations fused into one, or the same area simultaneously stands for two interdependent but logically separate interpretations.

Peculiar: verbalization of response is unsuccessful communication because of illogical, cryptic, or incomplete formulation; also manifestation in the response of unrealistic evaluation of the role of subjective processes or of the objective stimulus. This category will include Rapaport's "Queer" verbalizations, which essentially are exaggerated "Peculiar" verbalizations.

Deterioration C: pure C responses using bland pink, orange or yellow colors or involving "morbid" content.

Absurd: form aspect of response is extremely arbitrary.

Symbolic: explicit use of form or other determinant to represent an abstract idea.

Confusion: severe breakdown or fluidity of orientation to the perceptual, associative and/or recall aspects of a response.

Fluid: lapses of train of thought or verbalization, and distorted recall of responses and blots.

Reference Idea: arbitrarily setting up or emphasizing formal relationships between different areas of an inkblot or between different inkblots; these will be included under Confabulation or Confabulation tendency in the following records.

Autistic logic: illogical, autistic efforts to derive a response or a meaning "logically."

## Summary Scores

R:       total number of responses.

EB:      ratio of M+FM+Ms to FC+CF+C (*sum C*) with weights of .5 given to FM and FC, 1 to M, Ms and CF, and 1.5 to C. F/C and C/F are added secondarily onto the basic *sum C* score; thus, in a record with 2M, 3CF and 1 C/F, the *EB* will read 2–3(4).

W%:     percent of W responses in entire record (R).

D%:     percent of D responses in entire record.

DR%:    percent of Dr+De+S+s in entire record.

F%:      first part expresses percent of all pure form responses in entire record; second part expresses percent of responses with strong form (F, M, FM, Ms, FC, F(C), FC', FCh) in entire record.

F+%:    first part expresses percent of all pure form responses scored F+ or F±; second part expresses percent of all responses with strong form scored + or ±.

H%:     percent of A+Ad responses in entire record.

A%:     percent of H+Hd responses in entire record; this is secondarily extended to include the (H)+(Hd) scores.

P% :        percent of popular responses in entire record; this is secondarily
            extended to include (P) scores.

Orig% :     percent of original responses in entire record; this summary
            score will not be used here.

The verbalization scores, such as *Confabulation* and *Peculiar*, are often
based on subtle deviations in word usage. Because it would require lengthy
discussions that would obstruct developing the main theses in the following
case analyses, the justification of these scores will ordinarily be omitted.
Rapaport's numerous examples should be consulted by those unfamiliar
with this clinically vital technique of inferring thought disorder from
Rorschach responses [*118*].

*4. The Exhaustiveness of the Analyses.* The analyses to be presented are
not intended to be complete. Only certain outstanding implications of each
record will be discussed in detail. Some possibly highly significant responses
or aspects of responses will be ignored because they do not contribute to
the development of the major interpretations. It is not implied that these
responses should be ignored under routine clinical circumstances. This
restriction of interpretive attention was dictated by a striving toward clarity
of presentation and by a desire not to overburden the reader. Thus, not all
evidence for the interpreted trends will be cited, as in the case of the under-
emphasized scores, and not all interpretable trends will be interpreted, as
in the case of those that do not add to the chief points under consideration.
Responses that seem to clash with the major interpretations will not be
ignored, however.

*5. The Format.* Interpretive remarks have been set just beneath each
response considered significant. This form of presentation was chosen
for several reasons: (a) to spare the reader the taxing necessity of referring
back from discussion at the end of the record to responses in the midst of
the record; (b) to help re-create the often exciting experience of discovery
as one begins and carries through an analysis; (c) to highlight the process
of setting up and then confirming, revising or abandoning hypotheses about
the patient. These advantages seem to me to outweigh the disadvantages of
some redundancy and fragmentation of interpretation.

The records, including inquiry, will be verbatim, except when a key word
of routine, easily reconstructible inquiry seems adequate. The standard
opening question in inquiry is, "What made it look like a . . .?" and the
standard follow-up question is, "Was there anything else to make it look
like a . . .?" In the case of a *fire* response, for example, the abstracted
record of the tester's inquiry might then merely read, "Fire?" and "Anything else?" Locations, scores and inquiry will be given response by re-

sponse, and the scores and interpretations will be summarized at the end of the record.

*6. The Absence of Detailed Clinical Case Summaries.* Only a little will be told of the life histories and clinical pictures of most of the patients under discussion. This is sure to disappoint many readers. If nothing else, the reader will want to know more about what kind of person could give this or that set of responses, or if I was "right" in all my interpretations. It will be as if I were telling the reader jokes and leaving out the punchlines. For this disappointment I apologize in advance. Yet, I have omitted clinical detail advisèdly. My point in presenting these analyses is to illustrate *a way of thinking* about Rorschach test records and to demonstrate that this way of thinking leads to personality descriptions of individual patients that are well in accord with the general psychoanalytic theory of that patient's illness. I would therefore regard it as unfortunate if the reader paid too much attention to whether I was "right" or "wrong" in each single interpretation. The presence of detailed clinical information would tend to direct attention toward rightness or wrongness of individual interpretations. The validity or usefulness of the approach would not be established by any such casual proof of "rightness."

Also, I will not use this "case history method" of persuasion here because I am too well aware of the possibilities of unwitting opportunistic selection or editing of clinical material in order to "prove" a point or create an illusion of understanding. Validation should be systematic and rigorous and not impressionistic and literary. The systematic, rather than anecdotal, coordination of clinical data and test data is a task for which principles have not yet been worked out. For these reasons, I have avoided detailed clinical summaries. Some clinical information, even if only the diagnosis and major symptoms, will be included, however, along with age, sex, and other orienting biographical data.

*7. Some Omitted Defense Mechanisms.* In what follows the defense mechanisms "introjection" and "sublimation" will not be considered separately. "Introjection" will not be considered because all I now know about its indications may be summed up in one sentence: when *oral* themes are outstanding in the content of responses, oral-incorporative modes of handling or defending against interpersonal conflict are likely to be emphasized, and introjection as a defense is likely to be prominent.

"Sublimation" will not be considered because, first, it extends into too many other aspects of behavior to be considered in a chapter by itself. It will, however, receive some individual attention in the discussion of the obsessive-compulsive defenses in Chapter 10. Second, the theory of sublimation *as a defense* is by no means clear nor, to my mind, satisfactory, but this is not the place to pursue such questions further. The third and last justification of the omission of a chapter on sublimation as a defense is that sublimation is expressed in responsible, flexible, productive adaptiveness, and this type of functioning will be attended to in the following case studies.

*8. The Range of Pathological Defense.* Finally, and very important, the records presented in illustration of the operation of each defense mechanism will usually spread out over a continuum of ego-integratedness—rigidly or precariously defended normals or clear-cut neurotic patients toward one end and borderline or fully psychotic patients toward the other. Over this continuum, the forms of appearance of the same defensive operation vary in some ways and remain constant in other ways. Also, the relative success of the defensive operations decreases as a rule as we progress from the normal end to the psychotic end of the continuum. In psychotic records we often see the smooth defensive operations of the neurotic break down into their components and go off in all directions. Discussing these changing ego contexts with their varying degrees of defensive success and their varying forms of defensive expression should foster an appreciation of the complexity, uniqueness and drama of individual Rorschach records, and of the invaluable contributions psychoanalytic thought can make to comprehending this complexity, uniqueness and drama.

# 7. Repression

F ENICHEL DEFINES REPRESSION AS FOLLOWS ". . . unconsciously purposeful forgetting or not becoming aware of internal impulses or external events which, as a rule, represent possible temptations or punishments for, or mere allusions to, objectionable instinctual demands" [37, page 148; see also 47]. In the background of this definition are the following considerations: (1) the basic aim of repression, as of all defenses, is to block discharge of objectionable instinctual demands; (2) the repressed continues to exist outside conscious awareness, however, and to seek conscious representation and discharge through derivatives, that is, through associatively connected impulses, thoughts and feelings; (3) the individual's defensive requirements may then necessitate repression of these derivatives along with the original objectionable instinctual demand; (4) the instinctual demand and its derivatives are "objectionable" because the prospect of discharging them or even becoming aware of them stimulates fear of super-ego punishment, fear of painful consequences in external reality, such as destruction of relationships, or—because intense, unchecked impulses threaten to overwhelm highly valued ego achievements and functions— fear of the intensity of the impulses themselves.

Repression holds a special position as a defense, namely, it appears to be ubiquitous and prominently so. That is to say, everyone seems required to expend a more or less significant amount of psychic energy ("counter-cathexis") in keeping inevitably persisting and disturbing infantile strivings and their derivatives out of consciousness. Psychoanalytic theory and observation indicate that repressive defense is to be accepted as a part of normal development and normal adult personality organization. As a rule, people differ from each other much more in their selective emphasis on other defense mechanisms than they do in their reliance on repression. Also, repression appears to be more or less built into most other defenses. The ubiquitous prominence of repression has led to its being spoken of as the basic defense [57].

Like any defense, however, repression itself may become the over-riding aspect of the individual's defensive strategy. This is usually true, for example, of persons clinically described as hysteric. Repression characterizes functioning of these individuals in a wide variety of situations and with respect to a wide variety of thoughts, fantasies, feelings and impulses that are actual or potential derivatives of forbidden, threatening impulses. It is with the manifestations of this *generalized repressive strategy* that we shall be particularly concerned in this chapter. Specific, relatively isolated instances of repressive operations may be found in many test records; these will be frequently pointed out in the case studies in this book even when other defensive operations than repression are the chief focus of interest.

Another major dimension of repressive strategy, besides its generality, is its relative strength or success. Extensive reliance on repression may be found throughout the normal and neurotic ranges and, in shattered form, even in the psychotic range. At the extremes of the neurotic range, among the so-called "borderline" cases, we usually encounter glaring evidence, clinically and in the test results, that repressive defense is failing, that threatening impulses and their derivatives are consequently invading consciousness, and that archaic defenses, such as projection and denial, are being called upon for a last ditch stand against the invasion.

## A. Generalized, Chronic Repressive Defense

Any act of repression cuts off a part of the personality from growth toward maturity. The successive modifications and redefinitions of impulse derivatives that normally take place during latency, adolescence, early adulthood and maturity cannot occur. Being cut off thus from ego-regulated participation in life experiences, the repressed retains its original infantile character. Up to a point—a point which seems to vary with intellectual endowment, cultural traditions and values, and early family experiences—some reliance on repressive defense is necessary in anyone's development. When, however, a generalized emphasis on repressive defense develops early in life and persists, it inevitably results in severe restriction of the ego and conspicuous immaturity in later years.

Indeed, highly repressed adult personalities typically present a child-like appearance, some glaringly, others subtly. Their emotional experience, for example, tends to remain relatively diffuse and labile; their action tends to be impulsive; their anxiety has a naively fearful or phobic quality; and their relationships tend to be narcissistic and childishly clinging and/or unstable though intense. Also, because the world of ideas has been and always remains so terribly threatening—any thought or fantasy being a potential channel of expression of the rejected impulses—and because intellectual curiosity and mastery are thereby continuously discouraged, their thinking tends to be naive, egocentric, unreflective, affect-laden and cliche-ridden. As a result, these people somehow strike one as novice thinkers, as babes in the woods, or as "bunnies." Altogether then, those who have chronically and extensively relied on repressive defense give the appearance of grown-ups with the egos of children.

This explanation of the child-like ego functioning of the over-repressed

adult looks at the problem only from the point of view of defense, however. Viewed broadly, these child-like qualities seem to have major impulse-
expressing aspects too. For example, in a woman, these qualities typically
signify unconsciously clinging to the identity of a little girl, maintaining
her infantile, Oedipal attachment to and yearnings toward her father-
figure, and defining and experiencing her current "adult" relationships
accordingly. Relatively mediocre or limited intellectual endowment along
with familial and subcultural discouragement or nonsupport of intellectual
activity in the early years of life also appear to be relevant factors in
understanding the genesis and workings of generalized repressive defense,
just as superior endowment and an intellectually stimulating early environment appear to favor defensive intellectualizing. It should be remembered,
therefore, that we are always dealing with total personality configurations
and not just with defenses. But our present focus is on adult defensive
operations and it is chiefly to these operations that we shall relate pertinent
patterns of psychic functioning in the Rorschach situation.

## B. Test Expectations

What then might we expect in the Rorschach records of people who rely
heavily on repressive defense? First of all, those aspects of the record
that indicate an active, ego-syntonic interest in ideas and fantasy will
probably be underplayed. In particular, the total number of responses $(R)$,
the number of human movement responses $(M)$, and the number of content categories included should all tend to be relatively low or at most
average. In addition, the absolute number of whole responses $(W)$ and
rare and tiny detail responses $(Dr)$ should not be high. High $R$, $M$, $W$, $Dr$
and variety of content all tend to issue from an active ideational life, from
a significant investment in the abstract and the creative, from a highly
articulated, broad and searching pattern of intellectual functioning. Repressive personalities are notoriously weak in these respects. They are particularly threatened by the creative regression in the service of the ego
called for in the test situation. In fact, long reaction times and card rejections are not unlikely, since in non-psychotic, non-depressed, non-organic
and non-defective contexts these delays and rejections usually represent
massive repressive reactions to anxiety-arousing feelings or fantasies stimulated by the inkblots.

Turning from score patterns to attitudes toward the test, the tester, and
the test responses, we should expect to find these attitudes more or less
naive, unreflective, concrete, egocentric, insecure, vague, impulsive and
emotionally-toned. The over-repressed patient's unreflectiveness may be
particularly evident in his responses to inquiry, emphasis being put on subjective conviction or past experience rather than on present articulated,

perceptual experience ("It just did"; "Because I like flowers"; "I once saw one in *Life* magazine"; "We had a bearskin rug at home"; etc.). His intellectual insecurity may ʋe particularly evident in his needing the tester's reassurance that his responses are adequate, realistic, acceptable ("It looks like a bat, doesn't it?"). His naivete and concreteness may be evident particularly in a "realistic" or "perceptual" test attitude ("I don't know what it *is*."). In these test attitudes we see in action what we see already structuralized in the record's pattern of formal scores (relatively low $R$, $M$, etc.). Typically, these lines of evidence converge.

Secondly, we may expect those aspects of the record that pertain to affect and anxiety to be more or less conspicuous. In particular, relative emphasis on color and shading should prevail. Whether, with respect to color responses, the form-color ($FC$) or color-form ($CF$) responses will predominate depends on the relative weight of submissive, clinging, ingratiating tendencies ($FC$ emphasis) as opposed to impulsive, volatile, labile tendencies ($CF$ emphasis). Similarly with shading ($Ch$): where anxiety tends to be diffuse, unarticulated, "free-floating," $ChF$ and $Ch$ will be likely to prevail over $FCh$; where this is not so, $FCh$ will probably prevail. Simultaneously, the emotional toning of the patient's test attitudes and responses is likely to be relatively diffuse in quality. Naive verbalizations that emphasize the "weird," "horrible," "scary," "lovely," "beautiful" qualities of the blots are likely to be conspicuous.

When repressive defense that has been heavily relied upon begins to fail, we may anticipate the following changes in the record: imagery that is experienced as threatening will increase in frequency and intensity; the formal specificity, articulation and accuracy of the responses will decrease; the inner integration of the responses will suffer; emotional lability will increase; and the test atmosphere will become more and more one of trepidation, panic, inadequacy, bewilderment, antagonism or misery, or any combination of these. At the extreme, other and more malignant defense mechanisms, such as projection and far-reaching regression, will come to the fore, and autistic modes of response and communication will appear.

The pattern that has been described is that expected of the severely repressive patient. Of all patients, this is the one most likely to develop hysterical symptoms. It does not follow, however, that every patient presenting this pattern is beset by hysterical symptoms. The patient may have come for examination and treatment because of anxiety attacks, depressive spells, alcoholism, fits of rage, insomnia and many other complaints that are not peculiarly hysterical—though they may have major hysterical components. Also, not all patients with hysterical symptoms present over-repressed character pictures. Many present mixed character pictures, including compulsive as well as repressive features.

These areas of diagnostic overlap, ambiguity or seeming inconsistency need not dismay us, however. Ultimately it is more important for therapy and prognosis to define the personality context out of which the patient's symptoms have developed than to classify or predict his particular symptoms. Thus, it is more helpful to be able to identify extensive reliance on repressive defense or on mixed defense than to predict the clinical diagnosis "hysteria." On the other hand, while the present emphasis on defensive structure cuts across traditional diagnostic boundaries, it does not discard much of value that has been learned by studying diagnostically defined groups of patients.*

## C. Case Studies

In the following we shall consider the Rorschach test records of four patients manifesting prominent, pervasive repressive emphases. These patients are all women and are also all primarily hysteric, the first being a conversion hysteric and the last three being anxiety hysterics, i.e., phobic.† It is no accident that all the repressive patients are women and hysteric. As already noted, because repression is the major defense in hysteria, its operation will be seen most clearly and pervasively in the records of hysterical patients as a rule. Also, in present-day American culture at least, repression tends to be favored as a major, pervasive defense by women much more than by men. Hysteria is certainly encountered more frequently among women than men in our culture.

### Case 1

The first patient is a 41-year-old, married, childless woman with three years of high school education and an IQ of 110.‡ She was born into an old, aristocratic Southern family and long played the role of the Southern belle. The clinical diagnosis was "conversion hysteria in an hysterical and narcissistic character." Among other symptoms, she had developed localized abdominal pain which seemed to involve hysterical identification with her long-ailing, semi-invalided husband—a man many years her senior and several times close to death not long before the patient's symptom appeared.

---

* For an extensive psychoanalytic summary according to diagnostic categories, see Fenichel [37]; for a test summary, see Rapaport [118] or Schafer [134].

† For a sample record of a repressive, relatively normal woman with hysterical trends, the reader should turn to the first record discussed in Chapter 8 on the mechanism of denial (pp. 234–42). That record well illustrates both repression and denial in action.

‡ All IQ's recorded are total IQ's obtained on the Wechsler-Bellevue Intelligence Scale [149]. The Vocabulary subtest score is substituted for the Digit Span score in calculating the IQ.

CARD I        REACTION TIME: 3″.        TOTAL TIME: 25″.

> *1. (W F∓ Plant,Dec) That looks like an orchid.* [What made it look like an orchid? *It could be.* How was it like one? *I think the shape of it.* Anything else? *No.*]\*

(a) As the opening response, this unusual image forcefully suggests emphasis on narcissistic-decorative values. (b) The orchid image also seems to include noteworthy passive-receptive connotations: to a woman an orchid is something she *gets* as a tribute to her attractiveness. (c) Note the utterly unreflective initial response to inquiry.

> *2. (D F± Ad) And it looks like elephants too, with long ears (upper side D).*
>
> *3. (D F+ Cg) And I see a woman's dress (middle D).*

The emphasis is on the dress (the outside) and not the equally or more often seen woman (the inside or substance). Thus, the opening narcissistic-decorative theme (I-1) seems to be restated.

> *That's all.*

CARD II        REACTION TIME: 6″.        TOTAL TIME: 35″.

> *1. (D F+ A P) It looks like a bear to me.*
>
> *2. (D F(C)+ (Hd)) Looks like two little dwarfs or something on top of the bears' heads (upper red).* [Dwarfs? *They had little caps on their heads and they remind me of the seven dwarfs in Snow White.* What made them look like caps? *Just the head.*]

(a) Dwarfs, like gnomes, leprechauns, midgets, Pinocchios, male puppets or clowns, commonly suggest disparagement or mockery of men. (b) Introducing the idea of Snow White and the seven dwarfs suggests, in addition, the fantasy or hope of being the lovely, innocent, virginal (sexually repressed) little girl who is waited on hand and foot by gallant, sexless and somewhat foolish, depreciated beaux. In these respects, the psychology of Snow White and that of the Southern belle are not far apart. (c) In this record, and as is common in hysterical settings, childhood fantasy and story are major sources of non-banal Rorschach imagery.

> *That's about all I see.*

CARD III        REACTION TIME: 10″.        TOTAL TIME: 35″.

> *1. (D Ms+ H) It looks like two people taking exercise—the little red spot (upper red).* [Exercise? *They're on their back with their feet in the air.*]

(a) This is the only *M* in this quite repressed record and it is a moderately uncommon *M*. Its occurrence is all the more striking because the most com-

---

\* In these reproductions of Rorschach records, inquiry, if any, immediately follows the response to which it pertains, even though inquiry ordinarily takes place after each card. For purposes of this discussion, this temporal violation of the record offers the important advantage of allowing on-the-spot discussion of complete responses. Inquiry and the patient's response to it are set apart in brackets, and the tester's questions are distinguished from the patient's responses by being set in Roman type rather than in italics. The tester's occasional questions and comments *during the patient's spontaneous responses* will be set

mon *M*—which is on the same card—is not seen. The image and its theme
are likely therefore to have originated from an especially important value or
source of anxiety. Also, the image shows us she has the ability to see the
popular figures here. The failure of these figures to appear suggests the operation of repression—perhaps in response to the breast-phallus, masculine-feminine problem of integration often posed by this popular *M*. (b) The image
itself suggests concern with physical condition, which in turn could refer to
narcissistic interest in appearance (see I-1, I-3, II-2), or to preoccupation
with physical symptoms, or both.

> 2. *(W F∓ A) I don't know what these black spots remind me of;
> maybe of beetles or something (all black).* [Beetle? *It looks like an
> enlarged picture of a fly or something.* How? *Just the feet (P leg)
> and the head (lower middle).*]
> *That's all.*

CARD IV     REACTION TIME: 35″.     TOTAL TIME: 1′.

> *It doesn't mean a thing to me.*
> 1. *(D F+ Cg) This . . . (shakes head) . . . looks like a pair of big
> feet (lower side D).* [Any particular kind of feet? *Sort of a boot.* Can
> you say any more about it? *It just looked heavy to me. It looked like
> a boot would look it if was drawn by me, for instance, who cannot
> draw a line.*]
> *That's all I can see. (Anything else?) No. I'm afraid my imagination
> is not very good.*

Emphasis on the bigness of these feet, while not rare, is noteworthy. It seems
to express feelings of smallness and inadequacy. In the coming about of this
"big feet" response, it is likely that first the entire blot is seen as or sensed
to be a large, threatening figure, then the anxiety stimulated by this forming
image leads to its partial repression or to disruption of its crystallization, and
finally the relatively innocuous "big feet" response forms and is accepted as
safe. Three aspects of her response to this card lend support to this inference:
(1) the delayed reaction time of 35″ (previous reaction times were only 3″,
6″, and 10″) suggests an initial anxious, repressive response to the blot; (2) so
do her repressively-toned opening comment and her hesitation in verbalizing
the response; (3) her spontaneous self-disparagement after the response and
her self-disparagement in inquiry appear to parallel the implication of feelings
of smallness and inadequacy in the "big feet" image itself, and could well
have issued from the same source.

CARD V     REACTION TIME: 1″.     TOTAL TIME: 30″.

> 1. *(W F+ A P) That looks like a bat to me. That's all. (Make sure.)
> No, that's all that means to me. . . . Nothing else.*

CARD VI     REACTION TIME: 20″.     TOTAL TIME: 50″.

> 1. *(W F+ Ad P) It could be a bearskin or some animal skin—I don't
> know what. It could be anything. It looks like some taxidermist has been*

---

apart in parentheses but will remain italicized; parentheses and italics will be
used similarly in describing the patient's expressive behavior, locating responses
and, just prior to the response, giving the response's scores.

*at work here.* [What made it look like a skin? *Have you ever seen—you have, of course—a skin stretched out? You see the feet and the tail.* Anything else make it look like that? *No. Just the shape of it.*]

*(Anything else?) No, that's all. All animals!*

Possibly more self-derogation, or else uneasiness about the possible unconscious, instinctual significance of her "animal" fantasies.

CARD VII     REACTION TIME: 25".     TOTAL TIME: 55".

1. *(D F+ Hd P) It just looks like two figures of two women (upper ⅓), two heads facing each other, with some kind of exaggerated hairdo (rejects card).*

*(Keep on.) . . . Nothing.*

CARD VIII     REACTION TIME: 10".     TOTAL TIME: 35".

1. *(D F+ A P) More animals! It looks like a rodent of some kind to me; a rat.*

*(Anything else?) No. . . .*

2. *(D CF Rock) A rock at the bottom (lower pink and orange).* [Rock? *Just the color and the way it's shaped. Coral or. . . .*]

CARD IX     REACTION TIME: 15".     TOTAL TIME: 1' 20".

1–2. *(Dd F± Ad; Dd F± Plant) I would't know what that was, unless it's some kind of beetle on top there (upper middle orange projections).* [What made it look like a beetle? *The antennae; maybe the head. Could I see it? (Card shown.) No, not a beetle. It could be a stick, a branch of a tree, a dead branch.*]

(a) The appearance of the dead branch image only during inquiry, as well as the long pause between #1 and #3, suggests that this image may have been repressed to begin with. (b) This dead branch image appears to express the theme of the male figure's death or impotence through age. In turn, this inference suggests intense ambivalence, anxiety and repressive efforts in the area of fantasy and feeling about her husband's age and illness.

*I couldn't tell you. (Nothing else?) No. (Take your time.) . . .*

3. *(D F± Cg) It looks like a . . . it could be an armor too. You know, knights in armor: the helmet and steel (lower center is helmet; lower red areas are steel shoulder plates).*

(a) This response, like Snow White and the seven dwarfs in II-2, sounds the theme of gallantry, ladies fair and damsels in distress. This is hysteric imagery, Southern-belle style. (b) It is also conceivable that this image was partly determined by the patient's own need to ward off hostile intrusion.

CARD X     REACTION TIME: 15".     TOTAL TIME: 1'.

1. *(D F+ A) I see a dog (middle yellow).*

2. *(D FC+ A) And some caterpillars (lower green).* [What made it look like a caterpillar? *It was long and green and I just despise them.*]

Her volunteering "I just despise them" appears to have two major implications: (1) it is a naive, egocentric response to inquiry in that she gives a feeling as a determinant of the response instead of a perceptual aspect of the blot. It is not unusual for repressive, hysterical women to respond in this egocentric manner during the test; (2) the verbalization may have phobic implications, and, because phobias typically develop where strong repressive emphases prevail, it suggests noteworthy repressiveness. This is not to say that all people with bug-phobias are primarily repressive in their defensive strategy. The phobic and repressive inferences derive their chief support from this patient's naive, egocentric and spontaneous style of verbalizing this fear.

    3. *(D FC+ Plant) And maybe a flower bud (side yellow with gray base).* [Flower bud? *Just the shape: a half of it, not a full. . . .* Anything else? *The coloring: the yellow and the . . . I think it was green. I'm not sure; I can't remember.*]

The theme here is one of birth and youth, a theme that may in one respect express concern over her childlessness and in another respect nostalgia for her youth and worry over losing her youthful charms.

    4. *(D F+ A) At the top it looks like some more bugs, beetles or something (upper gray).*

    *That's all.*

All through the test the patient has been in great haste to give back the cards. Her average total-time-per-card is only 46″, despite relatively strong pressure from the tester that she take her time. Like delayed reaction times and card rejections, short total times frequently betray a repressive (and avoidant or ego-restrictive) defensive emphasis. The repressive person flees from this situation because he is deeply afraid of free fantasy, that is, of relaxing repressive barriers in the interest of imaginative, creative, self-expressive responses. This patient leaves the game while she's ahead, so to speak.

SUMMARY OF SCORES

R: 19        EB: 1–2

Average Total Time: 46″

| W | 4 | F+ | 9 | A | 7 | W% | 21 |
|---|---|---|---|---|---|---|---|
| D | 14 | F± | 3 | Ad | 3 | D% | 74 |
| Dd | 1 | F∓ | 2 | H | 1 | | |
| | | Ms* | 1 | Hd | 1 | F% | 74–95 |
| | | FC | 2 | (Hd) | 1 | F+% | 86–89 |
| | | CF | 1 | Plant | 2 | | |
| | | F(C) | 1 | Cg | 3 | A% | 53 |
| | | | | Dec | 0+1 | H% | 11–16 |
| | | | | Rock | 1 | P | 5 |
| | | | | | | P% | 26 |

In summary, thematic analysis suggests that this is a naive, egocentric, repressive, narcissistic woman with significant feelings of smallness and inadequacy. She appears to try to view herself as a fair, innocent, virginal

---

  * Unless otherwise indicated, the responses other than *F* that are scored for form level are + or ±.

damsel in distress who needs somewhat depreciated and sexless but attentive beaux to admire her and minister to her, and who also needs a hero to save her. Also suggested is noteworthy anxiety over physical status, aging, infirmity and death, particularly that of the male figure but possibly her own as well. A phobic trend may also be present.

The summary of scores strongly supports the inference of heavy reliance on repressive defense: $R$ is relatively low; there is only 1 $M$ and that is a small one ($Ms$); the variety of content is limited and the responses generally banal ($A\%$, $P\%$ high); she spends short total-times-per-card despite the tester's pressure; and the low $W$ and $Dr$ are consistent with this repressive picture. The relative absence of emotional lability and anxiety in her manner of taking the test is paralleled in the scores by the absence of shading responses, the relatively low $sum\ C$, the prevalence of $FC$ over $CF$, the adequate $F\%$ and the moderately high $F+\%$. We may infer therefore that this patient's repressive and narcissistic defenses and her symptoms are working fairly well to seal off anxiety; however, her eagerness to get rid of the cards and the breakthrough of anxiety-arousing images (or its clear imminence) suggest that her defenses are by no means invulnerable.

The role of the patient's intellectual level in this test picture is, of course, relevant. Her level—IQ of 110—is not high enough to allow for a rich record.* But this consideration only leads us into the problem of the genetic interrelationship between endowment and choice of defenses. As a rule, repression seems to be favored for defensive purposes by those who are intellectually mediocre or relatively limited, just as the obsessive-compulsive defenses seem to be the defenses of choice among those who are intellectually precocious. We do not seem to be dealing with an *either-or* proposition. More or less limited endowment seems to favor turning away from mastery of reality and conflict through intellect and tends to foster repressive solutions to problems; in turn, these repressive solutions may lead to neglect and even devaluation of such intellectual assets or potentialities as are present. In the end the IQ is the resultant of interaction of, on the one hand, the limits set by endowment, and, on the other hand, the defensive and adaptive solutions which produce significant variation within these limits. Early environment also seems to play a major part in this interaction.

The question of the evidence for neurosis must also be considered. A repressive emphasis is clear in this record, but experience with relatively well-functioning women of average intelligence indicates no distinctive

* Certain forms of pathology—particularly those involving psychotic features —may enrich the Rorschach records of patients with average or lower IQ's; in these instances, defensive collapse and the flood of consciousness by usually unconscious, primary-process-type content seems to give the Rorschach records a malignant bloom.

features in this record that *prove* that this woman now has a moderately disabling hysterical symptom requiring psychiatric treatment. Narcissistic character features are also plain but there is no evidence that these extend outside the normal range. In fact, some warmth and adaptiveness is implied by her *FC-CF* distribution and by the content of her color responses. Of course, if we define "neurosis" very broadly, we could say that a neurotic pattern is evident, but this definition probably would bring most everyone into the domain of neurosis. Moreover, it still would not differentiate the relatively well-functioning, asymptomatic, non-patient "neurotic" from the poorly functioning patient with symptoms. It can only be concluded therefore that this Rorschach record shows neurotic hysterical-repressive *trends*.

## Case 2

This patient is a 36-year-old, unmarried woman, a college graduate and formerly active athlete with an IQ of 118. The clinical diagnosis was "hysteria with phobic and depressive features."

CARD I     REACTION TIME: 7".     TOTAL TIME: 1'.

    *1. (W F+ A P) It could look like a butterfly.*

    *Do you want more? (That's up to you.) The whole thing or parts? (However you like.)*

"Do you want more?" suggests she is beginning to structure the test relationship as one in which she is being burdened by the demands of the tester. Also, both questions tend to set the tester up as an authority figure who must take responsibility for her responses.

    *2. (Do F+ Hd) Well the center part could be the torso of a woman (middle of middle D).*

If this area is seen as a woman's torso, it is usually part of a full female figure or dress outline. Also, if just part of the figure is seen, it is usually the legs and not the torso. Hence, the *Do* score. The relatively unusual restriction of the response to just the torso may be based on one or both of two possibilities: (1) anxiety-produced interference with or repressed perception of the lower part—the "sexual" part—of the figure, with the implication of fear and rejection of sexuality; (2) selective preoccupation with the upper part—the bust or "feeding" part—of the figure with the implication of significant oral-passive trends. Both suggestions are not strong but in the general dynamics of anxiety hysteria, repression of sexual problems and regression to a passive, clinging, demanding, essentially oral orientation are prime factors. The implications of this torso response seem in line with this dynamic formulation and also with the earlier impression that she was beginning to define the test relationship in terms of demands.

    *3. (D F+ Obj) And the wing part could be airplane wings (upper sides). It looks a little like a DC-3.*

Noteworthy masculine interests are suggested by her casually "expert" identification of the type of plane for which the wings are appropriate. A relatively strong masculine identification may therefore play a distinctive part in her dynamics. If so, we should encounter more indications of this identification.

> *That's all I see.*

> 4. *(Dd F+ Ad) (Additional response given during inquiry while pointing out previous response.) I also see some crab claws too (upper middle projections).*

(a) This is a common response and therefore ordinarily unrevealing. Its late emergence suggests, however, that it may have been anxiety-arousing and consequently temporarily repressed, suppressed, or impeded in its crystallization. (b) Symbolically, claws appear as a rule to represent extensions of teeth, that is, organs used for grabbing hold, tearing and bringing to the mouth. Claw responses therefore may be thought of as expressing an oral (attacking) theme —a theme already suggested (see I-2). In turn, the theme of oral attack may be a regressive expression of castrating attitudes. There is no evidence present to support any of these possible meanings of her delay in giving this response. These archaic meanings are mentioned only to indicate likely sources of anxiety concerning this response and to provide reference points for analysis of later responses.

CARD II     REACTION TIME: 3". TOTAL TIME: 1'.

> 1. *(DS F∓ At, Sex) (Sigh) I see a woman's pelvis there (dark areas and middle space).* [What made it look like that? *I don't know. It just sort of looked like it. I don't know. It just looked sort of like the shapes of them I've seen in medical books.* Anything else? *No.* Was there something about it to suggest a *woman's* pelvis particularly? *No, I suppose it could be anybody's.*]

Pelvis responses often express concern with bodily status in general and reproductive powers in particular. They are common in the records of aging women, for example. Also, they are often veiled sex responses. The latter is especially likely if the pelvis is designated "male" or "female." On Card II, sexual implications are all the more likely because of the often seen female genitals (or menstruation) in the lower middle and/or womb in the middle space. This patient is probably consciously suppressing rather than unconsciously repressing the genital aspect of her response—note her floundering response to inquiry— but suppression of response, unless it is a paranoid maneuver, is quite common in repressive settings, being the logical next step if repression has not successfully kept a threatening image or theme out of consciousness. When pressed in inquiry, the patient appears to abandon the female quality altogether, rather than "confess." These inferences overlap those drawn from the woman's torso response (I-2).

> 2. *(D F± A) And a dog (dark area; nose is middle of upper edge).* [*A Scotch terrier (while tracing).*]

> 3. *(W F± A) I still see butterflies.* [What made it look like a butterfly? *The whole thing looks sort of like a butterfly.* How? *I suppose because it sort of had wings.* Anything else? *No.*]

Note the unreflective initial response to inquiry.

> *That's about all.*

CARD III    REACTION TIME: 20″.    TOTAL TIME: 2′.

   *1. (D F+ A) Oh! (Nervous laugh) There's another butterfly in the middle (middle red). [Butterfly? Because it had wings again. Anything else? No.]*

   *2. (D FM± H (P)) And two men (P area, but usual arm is leg and usual leg is excluded).*

The delayed appearance of the popular response, as well as her inability to bridge the gap between the torso and the usual leg, suggests a repressive emphasis. The few *M* that repressive persons give are usually weak in some way: they tend to be small, incomplete, relatively statically described, late, uncertainly verbalized, partly animal, etc. The first patient considered had only one *Ms* —and that on Card III; this patient, in addition to distorting these common figures, goes on to make them animals in her fifth response to this card.

   *3. (D FC′Ch± Plant) And some sticks of wood (usual P leg). [What made it look like that? It just looked like it. I don't know why. It just looked like sticks with bark on it. Bark? Because it was shaded black and gray.]*

Further striking unreflectiveness.

   *Should I look at it other ways? (However you wish.)*

As on Card I, she seems to be shifting responsibility to the tester-authority.

   *4. (W F∓ A) ∨ This way it looks something like a crab (all black) with claws going out here (usual P leg).*

Again the oral-attacking theme is suggested (see I-4).

   *I can't see anything else.*

   *5. (D F± A) ∧ These look something like chickens too, dressed up in men's clothes (same as #2).*

(a) Changing the men (#2) to chickens may have a belittling implication. Indications of masculine identification (see I-3), fear of men, and disparagement of men often go together in Rorschach test imagery. (b) The appearance of this chicken-man response as an afterthought—she had already said once she was through—underscores both the conflictful implications of the response and what appears to be her repressive, defensive style of handling conflict.

   *That's all.*

CARD IV    REACTION TIME: 10″.    TOTAL TIME: 1′.

   *1. (D F+ Ad) (Long sigh) Down here I see a cow head (lower middle).*

Specifying that this commonly seen animal head is that of a cow suggests the oral (milk-giving, milk-receiving) theme already noted. The thematic emphasis this time is peaceful and receptive rather than hostile and grabbing.

   *2. (D F+ Hd) And a couple of feet turned sideways (lower sides).*

   *3. (D F+ Ad) A snake's head (upper side D).*

Snakes have prominent phallic connotations. In a setting of noteworthy oral-regressive trends, such as the present setting seems to be, the biting, poisonous, oral-aggressive aspects of the snake image may become dominant, however. Patients with strong oral problems frequently see cobras, asps, rattlers, and the like in the inkblots, along with vultures, sharks, crocodiles, etc.

   *∨ . . . < ∧ That's all.*

CARD V     REACTION TIME: 1″.     TOTAL TIME: 1′ 30″.

*1. (W F+ A P) Butterfly (weary, drawn-out, facetious pronunciation).
I bet you get tired of hearing butterflies.*

The patient's ennui may be approached from four directions, all pertinent to
dynamic trends already indicated: (1) the ennui may reflect the dulling of her
intellectual and emotional life brought about by intense, pervasive repression.
The general banality of her response content is relevant in this regard; (2)
her ennui may convey a masked demand for richer fare from the tester;
(3) she may be covering up anxiety that she is not meeting demands she has
projected onto the tester-authority; (4) she may be obliquely expressing dismay
at the self-limiting aspects of her illness which the test is forcing her to confront.

*2. (W C′F Cl) ∨ ∧ I haven't thought of black clouds yet either. I
could think of a thunderstorm. [Thunderstorm? Because it was black
and blurry. Blurry? Just opaque; not opaque, I don't know, just blurry.]*

Ordinarily black clouds and thunderstorms in the Rorschach test carry fearful
and depressive connotations. When, however, the patient says, "I could think
of . . . ," she indicates some taking of distance from these disturbing connotations.
This combination of fearful theme and detached attitude typically reflects noteworthy counterphobic and/or counterdepressive attitudes, although the strongly
counterphobic patient frequently goes on to poke fun at or minimize the phobic
images as well. The counterphobic interpretation here ties in with the previous
suggestion of noteworthy masculine identification (DC-3, chicken-men) and
with her history of strong athletic interests. It is implied that this patient may
not be surrendering to her phobic inclinations and may be actively combating
them. Similarly, the counterdepressive implication might well reflect efforts to
contain the depressive trends noted in her clinical diagnosis.

*3. (D F+ Ad) ∨ . . . ∧ Sort of looks like a pig's foot (side projection).*

In general, pig images have prominent gluttonous implications. The fact that
this leg is typically seen as a woman's leg suggests that the patient may unconsciously equate femininity with gluttonous passivity and that she may view
herself (particularly the "feminine" aspects of herself) as piggish, i.e., as
unacceptable, dirty, indiscriminately gluttonous and beastly. The general oral
(aggressive and receptive) emphasis in the record seems to reflect tendencies
which would contribute to such a self-concept.

*4. (Dd F+ Obj) Ice tongs (lower middle).*
Possibly an oblique oral reference.
*That's all.*

CARD VI     REACTION TIME: 18″.     TOTAL TIME: 1′ 20″.

*(Patient begins to sigh frequently while responding to this card.) Oh,
dear! They all look alike! I'm so tired of them!*

(a) Heretofore the patient has overtly criticized herself for being banal or for
not meeting standards she probably projected onto the tester. Now she seems
to abandon this relatively depressive position and to begin being demanding
toward and critical of the tester. Hostility seems now to be directed outward
rather than inward.

(b) Her claim that the blots "all look alike" is probably an outgrowth of the
rigidity of her defensive repressive policy. That is to say, just about any situa-

tion may pose the same set of threats for her. But now she attacks the tester's blots and no longer her own "butterflies."

(c) It is noteworthy, however, that this disruption of the response process occurs on Card VI—the card that has the compelling phallic configuration at the top. We are therefore likely to be dealing with a threatened reaction to this particular card as well as a cumulative threatened reaction to the test. In other words, it is likely that the suggested intensification of her repressive efforts, abandonment of her depressive position, and the emergence of open demanding-ness, all represent reactions to unconscious recognition of the phallus. We may be seeing here in test behavior what we previously surmised from imagery (see I-2; IV-3): regression from sexual conflict to orality. Her frequent sighing may reflect tenseness associated with this defensive struggle.

(d) It is also noteworthy that on this card and throughout the test the patient has been able to hold together well enough to respond relatively quickly and more than once to each card. Some adaptive and defensive resiliency is implied and this tends to support the counterphobic and counterdepressive implications of her thunderstorm verbalization in V-2. She goes on to give two responses to this card, for example, the first after only 18″, and she does not need to avoid the upper area altogether (see #1).

> *1. (D F+ Ad) Birds' feathers (upper wings).* [Feathers? *I don't know. It just looked like birds' feathers.*]

Note how utterly unreflective her response to inquiry is in this and in the next response. Very likely this unreflectiveness is another reflection of intensified repressive efforts. To reflect at all deeply now might well upset her presumably precarious defensive position.

> *2. (D F+ Ad P) It looks like a squirrel's skin after it has been skinned and spread out (lower D).* [Skin? *Well because it was all stretched out and the legs were sticking out.* Anything else? *No.* Why a squirrel? *It could be any animal's skin only more like a squirrel because I've probably seen squirrel skins more than any others.* Any other reason? *I just imagine because that's what I've seen more.*]

Inquiry runs into a stone wall of unreflectiveness.

> *That's all.*

CARD VII     REACTION TIME: 30″.     TOTAL TIME: 1′ 15″.

> *1. (S F± Harbor) Well, I see a harbor (middle space).*

The harbor image usually implies safe, passive retreat. In this respect it is consistent with the previous passive, regressive themes.

> *2. (Dr F∓ Hd) And a couple of fingers (upper projections).* [Did you have a particular finger in mind? *The index finger.*]

Pointing fingers frequently suggest paranoid sensitivity to accusation, or, in other words, a predisposition toward superego projections. This may relate to previous suggestions in her test attitudes of projection of demands (or high standards?) onto the tester.

> *3. (Dr F+ Arch) Down here: a church (lower middle).* [What made it a church particularly? *Because it had two steeples and a doorway.*]

Her seeing a church in an area frequently seen as female genitals suggests she may need to maintain a sexually pure and inviolate self-image. Such a need would be of a piece with the previous indications of tendencies to reject and repress sexuality and femininity and to emphasize masculinity on the one hand and passivity on the other.

*That's all.*

CARD VIII     REACTION TIME: 30".     TOTAL TIME: 1'.

*I'm glad to have a different color for a change. (Patient uneasily notes that this comment is recorded.)*

(a) Another expression of ennui by the patient and a thinly veiled complaint as well. (b) Her reaction to the recording of her remark may have paranoid implications (see VII-2).

1. *(D F(C)+ Obj) These are pillow cases hanging out to dry (middle blue). [Pillow cases? They look as though the wind was billowing in them.]*

(a) A doubly passive theme is suggested—sleeping and also passively dangling in the wind. (b) Also suggested is a guilty sexual theme, i.e., soiled bed-linens that need to be cleaned. In this regard, the church in VII-3 would be the "positive" form of expression of sexual conflict and guilt of which this is the "negative." (c) That this response precedes the exceptionally popular animals (#2) tends to underscore its content significance.

2. *(D F+ A P) And this is an animal. [Any particular animal? Possibly like bears.]*

*That's all.*

CARD IX     REACTION TIME: 10".     TOTAL TIME: 1' 15".

1. *(D FM± (H)) This looks like an embryo a little (lower red). [Embryo? I just saw one embryo: the head on the right (outer right section); the feet are tucked up in here (outer left section)—you can't see them. What made it look like an embryo particularly? I don't know; it's more in that position, and it was one solid mass.]*

The thematic implications of the embryo image ordinarily extend in two directions, both of which seem relevant to this case. (1) The embryo image is likely to imply concern with reproduction and childbearing, a concern that is probably great in this woman. She is a 36-year-old spinster whose time is running out with respect to marriage and motherhood. In retrospect, the female pelvis in II-1 may state the same theme. (2) The embryo image also often states a regressive, passive, oral theme, a theme that has been repeatedly suggested throughout the record. In this regard, the embryo is a curled-up, warm, protected, relatively inert, completely passively fed figure (see also the harbor in VII-1).

*I'm getting awfully tired trying to figure out anything about them.*

The fact that this implicitly demanding, complaining statement of fatigue or boredom follows the embryo response strongly suggests that that response stirred up significant anxiety in the patient and a consequent repressive, rejecting attitude toward the test. We might again (as at the beginning of Card VI) have an instance of disruptive and regressive test behavior in reaction to a fantasy with sexual, reproductive and/or oral content. The patient continues responding, however.

2. *(D C Water) This looks something like the color of the water off Bermuda (green).*

(a) A pure *C* at this point is in line with the interpretive remarks just made. It represents a passive letting herself go, a temporary abandonment of ego controls.

(b) The content too may well have passive—i.e., vacation—implications. (c) It is also possible, however, that the content is associated with a latent romantic, sexual fantasy, and that the rejecting attitude toward the test expressed just before this response represented a passive, regressive attempt to ward off this sexual theme.

　　　*Okay.*

A simultaneously masculine and bored closing.

CARD X　　REACTION TIME: 13″.　　TOTAL TIME: 45″.

　　　*Is this the last?*

Another oblique complaint and demand.

　　　1. *(W CF Plant) That looks like a flower garden.* [Flower garden? *Because it had a lot of colors in it.* Anything else? *Well the shapes were something like flowers.* Any particular flowers? *No. Maybe daffodils— the yellow ones.*]

This global, intrinsically affect-laden response is followed by a retreat to the gray area (see #2) and then by hasty rejection of the card. Beginning with Card VI, her productivity has fallen off. On Cards I through V she averaged about four responses per card, while on Cards VI through X she averaged about two. It seems likely that relatively strong anxiety—engendered by the assault the test has been making on her repressions, and probably particularly on her sexual repressions—has led to intensified repressive efforts and to increased regression to a passive, demanding, complaining position. Increased repressiveness would certainly reduce the number of responses.

　　　2. *(Dr F± Obj) This looks like the stem of a microscope (upper middle gray shaft).*

　　　*Okay. (Anything else?) No.*

SUMMARY OF SCORES

R: 30　　　　EB: 1–2.5

| | | | | | | | |
|---|---|---|---|---|---|---|---|
| W | 6 | F+ | 15 | A | 8 | W% | 20 |
| D | 17 | F± | 5 | Ad | 6 | D% | 57 |
| Dd | 2 | F∓ | 3 | H | 1 | DR% | 13 |
| Dr | 3 | FM | 2 | (H) | 1 | | |
| S | 1+1 | CF | 1 | Hd | 3 | F% | 77–90 |
| Do | 1 | C | 1 | Obj | 4 | F+% | 87–89 |
| | | F(C) | 1 | Plant | 2 | | |
| | | FC′ | 1 | At-Sex | 1 | A% | 47 |
| | | C′F | 1 | Misc. | 4 | H% | 13–17 |
| | | FCh | 0+1 | | | P | 4+1 |
| | | | | | | P% | 13–17 |

In summary of the thematic analysis, it appears that this is a woman whose rigid repressive policy toward sexuality is failing somewhat, and who is consequently intensely anxious, somewhat guilty and depressed, and inclined to regress to an orally-conceived passive, demanding, complaining position. In this position she tends to set others up as unsatisfactory authority figures who do not take enough responsibility for her and who are too demanding. The pressure of sexual thoughts and feelings may be increased by concern with her spinsterhood and childlessness. Although there are suggestions of some resiliency, doggedness and counterphobic strengths, probably associated with what appear to be noteworthy masculine strivings, at the present time she appears to be too threatened to sustain an active, productive role for long. Under stress she does little more than go through the motions of compliance and activity. Her depressive inward-turning of hostility appears to give way before long to thinly veiled complaints and noncompliance; a full-fledged depression is therefore not likely to be present. Some reliance on projection as defense, involving projection of demands particularly, is also suggested.

The summary of scores bears out the impression of a special repressive emphasis: $R$ is average, $M$ is low and weak, the emphasis on color exceeds that on human movement, content is relatively limited in variety, her total time per card is relatively low (average 72″), and $W$ and $Dr$ are not high. The emphasis on $CF$ and $C$ among the color responses parallels her present narcissistic, usually obliquely demanding, weakly adaptive style of interpersonal relationship. It is noteworthy that in her color scores the patient previously considered emphasized $FC$ more than this patient and in test behavior was, on the surface anyway, considerably more compliant, restrained and undemanding. This patient's defensive position seems somewhat more precarious than that of the previous patient, but she gives no evidence of defensive collapse and falling back on autistic modes of solution such as will be seen in the next two cases. Her $F+\%$, for example, is 87–89 and she gives no peculiar verbalizations.

## Case 3

This patient is also phobic, but, unlike the previous patient, her defenses and neurotic symptoms appear to be failing badly. For example, she recently has been spontaneously becoming aware of sexual desires for her father; also, her phobic symptom is itself a focus of constant torment and preoccupation.

The patient is a 26-year-old, married, childless woman, recently separated from her husband after six months of marriage. She is a high school graduate with a total IQ of 117 (verbal IQ 111, performance IQ 121). The original clinical diagnosis was "severe anxiety hysteria in a narcissistic, masculine character disorder." The revised diagnosis, after some months of therapy, included mention of borderline psychotic features.

Because it will be relevant to the content of the patient's phobic reactions and paranoid projections, it should be added that her life history has been characterized by noteworthy masculine strivings (among other indications,

she now masturbates by making masculine copulatory movements) and by
alternating periods of rebelliousness and conformity (her rebelliousness
taking the form of unruliness, aggressiveness, dirtiness and strong sexual
tensions and preoccupations; her conformity taking the form of prudish-
ness, hypercleanliness, driving herself into hard work, and feeling isolated
and depressed). As is usual in anxiety hysteria, the present phobic developments brought with them or exaggerated a passive, demanding, controlling
orientation to interpersonal relationships.

CARD I      REACTION TIME: *22"*.      TOTAL TIME: *1' 20"*.
    *I can't tell.*

    *1. (W FC'— A DW-tendency, Confabulation tendency) It looks like it
    might be a spider or something but it couldn't possibly be.* [What made
    it look like a spider? *The head and those little things on each side.
    I hate spiders and it had that black forbidding look about it. Something
    sinister about it, I guess.*]

(a) This is a grim opening. That an overvalent, relatively primitive image
breaks through in her first response with so little reality support (very poor
form) and so diffuse a perceptual organization (DW-tendency) suggests impaired
reality testing and seriously weakened repressive barriers. The patient's reality
testing is sufficiently well preserved, however, for her to reject the response
spontaneously. Yet, in all likelihood it is her need to reject the threatening
*content* of the response that provides the power for her critical rejection of the
*accuracy* of the response (see I-2 below). (In this regard, it would have been
helpful to inquire why it could *not* be a spider.)

(b) Although the patient's style of verbalization in inquiry—"I hate spiders"—
is characteristic of phobic patients, her additional emphasis on the "forbidding,"
"sinister" aspects of the image suggests that considerable paranoid projection is
also involved. This is because the external justification for her anxiety is too
specifically elaborated and too detached from herself. That is to say, verbalizations like "weird," "ugly," and "I hate them," which tend to stand out in phobic
responses, are implicitly, if not explicitly, pinned to physical or physiognomic
qualities of the objects seen; they also imply some taking of responsibility for
the emotional response to these external qualities; and they do not—as paranoid
verbalizations of the "sinister" type do—first ascribe to the objects specific
motives or feelings for which there is minimal perceptual justification in the
inkblots and then express utterly righteous, unreflective, un-self-critical reactions
to these projections.

(c) The content of what is projected and then feared—as indicated by the
spider image—would probably be the hostile, evil, devouring aspects of her
self-image and/or her image of her mother. Strong and poorly defended against
oral tendencies are implied.

    *2. (W F+ A P) It also looks like it might be a bat but it couldn't
    possibly be that either. It has that spread-out look.*

(a) By ordinary standards the bat response is relatively easy to accept. Bats,
however, can partake liberally of the sinister oral aspects of spiders (see #1).
This overlap may be what leads her to reject the bat response too. (b) But by

rejecting this popular response after forming it, whatever the motivation of this rejection, she gives another indication of severe perceptual diffuseness and weakened reality testing.

> *3. (W F∓ A) It looks like a crab but it couldn't be that either because the outside is undefined.*

(a) Again the content of the image may be oral and hostile in implication (see also II-2 and VII-2 below), and again the image is ostensibly rejected on perceptual grounds. (b) ". . . the outside is undefined" suggests, in addition, anxious feelings of weakness of ego boundaries or defensive perimeter. Judging by the perceptual vagueness and associated poor reality testing as well as the apparently pathological projection running through her responses to this card (and to the rest of the cards as well), the patient has good reason to feel threatened in this way. (c) It is possible that instead of or in addition to the trends already mentioned, her relatively rapid rejection of these responses and of the card involves a negativistic, obliquely hypercritical maneuver.

CARD II     REACTION TIME: 32".     TOTAL TIME: 1' 15".

> *Oh gosh! (Nervous laugh) I can't tell which end is which.*

"Oh gosh!" and nervous laughter suggest that something is up. Her emphasis on problems of spatial organization suggests that we are not dealing with color shock. This verbalization lends itself to the following speculations: since the lower middle of this card is fairly often seen as a vagina and the upper middle as a penis, and since indications of masculine strivings are relatively conspicuous in this record (see below), it is not inconceivable that her immediate problem—which end is which—derives from a repressed recognition of these sexual organs and expresses intense ambivalence toward and confusion about her sexual role. Continuing to speculate, it is also conceivable that the contrast is between the (oral) claws in the upper red (see II-2, below) and the (repressed) vagina in the lower red, and that her dilemma—which end is which—expresses a significantly oral conception of sexuality, i.e., mouth equals vagina. This speculation would fit with the previous (and later) suggestions of intense orality. There is, of course, no way of verifying these speculations from the present meager material. The speculations are presented because they fit other inferences from her responses, because they indicate the type of crucial unconscious meanings that may underlie problems in spatial organization and styles of verbalization, and because they provide us with hypotheses to check against subsequent responses.

> *1. (W F— A) It looks like something that creeps or crawls.*

(a) In the Rorschach situation, aversion to creepy and crawly things is found chiefly in the records of phobically-inclined patients. (b) The diffuseness of the response is particularly striking. The handiest explanation of this diffuseness is that it reflects primitivization of perceptual organization under the impact of the anxiety evident in her opening verbalization. But the explanation must be carried further, since this initial anxiety must reflect a defensive struggle. We may suspect that repression has been hard at work here and that the appearance of a vague phobic image signifies partial failure of repression; that is to say, repressive efforts may have sufficiently impeded the free flow of ideas that a more specific and articulated impulse-expressing image could not be evolved, but they could not block the response altogether. At the same time, this diffuse-

ness suggests the weakened reality testing (blurred perception of situations) that
has already been noted.

> 2. (D CF Ad DW-tendency) These two red things look like lobster
> claws (upper red). [Lobster claws? Because they were pink and had
> a vague shape like lobster claws, and the way they stick out from the
> body.]

Claws being functionally extensions of teeth, they ordinarily have unconscious
oral, biting, hanging-on implications. Thematically, this inference matches previous inferences concerning special unconscious emphasis on devouring.

> 3. (D C'F Ad Confabulation tendency) The black stuff has a sinister
> look about it again: wings or whatever they might be (dark areas).
> [Did you think of something else those wings might be? I don't know.
> It didn't really look like wings. It could look like a butterfly.]

(a) The "sinister" emphasis, like that in I-1, appears to combine phobic and
paranoid qualities.

(b) A momentary strengthening of defense and adaptation is suggested when,
in inquiry, she discards this "sinister" theme and forms a butterfly response.

(c) It is noteworthy that all six responses to Cards I and II have dealt more or
less explicitly with ugly, frightening, evil themes. It is also noteworthy that all
these responses have been diffuse, arbitrary or weak in form, including even
the popular bat on Card I since she did not appreciate its adequacy as a response. These two trends—ugliness, etc., and inadequate form—suggest that
repressions, general ego controls and reality testing are all in a precarious state.
The patient's adaptive and defensive position seems to be in serious danger of
being overwhelmed.

> That's all I see.

CARD III     REACTION TIME: 15".     TOTAL TIME: 1' 30".

> 1. (D M+ H P Peculiar) That looks like nothing at all to me, except
> it looks like two little men here in a modernistic water color (lower
> middle excluded). It looks like it might be a dance or something like
> that.

(a) "Little men" is likely to be condescending in implication and suggests noteworthy masculine strivings and rivalry with men.

(b) Her peculiar negative introduction of this response ("like nothing at all")
may reflect a defensive need to "take back" the response. If so, the total response
could indicate conflict between accepting and rejecting her masculine strivings.

> 2. (D F/C∓ At) This red part in the center looks like some colored
> pictures you might see of internal organs of the body; lungs or what
> have you (middle red).
> I think that's all.
> 3. (D F∓ A) This section at the base looks like it might be a crab
> (lower middle gray).

Giving this response after saying "that's all" suggests abandonment or failure
of a repressive effort. The crab image, distinguished more than anything by
claw-like legs, again suggests the oral-aggressive theme. In II-1 a similar response was strikingly vague; here it is delayed. In both instances a strong
repressive orientation is suggested.

CARD IV    REACTION TIME: 15″.    TOTAL TIME: 30″.

*1. (W C′F A Confabulation tendency) This again has a sinister look about it. It looks like some sort of insect, something which creeps or crawls, something horrible to look at! (Look of revulsion) Take it away! (Very anxious) That's all. (Is it too hard to keep looking at it?) Yes. I don't like it. [Why was it hard to look at it? It reminds me of something I might see, like a horrible spider: something dirty, poisonous, ugly. I keep using the word "sinister." Did it look like a spider? Yes, a little bit. Not so much the shape but because it had the same things about it I just mentioned—ugly things.]*

(a) The intensity of her anxiety and revulsion, and the response's consequent perceptual diffuseness indicate again this patient's defensive and adaptive instability. (b) Again both phobic and paranoid qualities seem to blend in her reaction to her response (see I-1, II-3). The additional emphasis now on poison adds to the paranoid quality. (c) Most telling regarding the paranoid trend, however, is the fluidity of ego boundaries implied in her response. So completely does she lose sight of the fact that what is out there on the card is really mainly a thought of hers that she reacts as if the tester has just plunked a live, hairy, bobbing tarantula in front of her. There is more involved here than simply great emotional lability and the tendency toward naive realism (the "perceptual attitude") often encountered in repressive records. This patient's horror at her "evil," instinctual tendencies appears to be so great and her repressive efforts so ineffective that she must also fall back on paranoid projection of the intolerable, bursting-out content.

CARD V    REACTION TIME: 8″.    TOTAL TIME: 50″.

*I'm beginning to dread every one!*

She said this as the card was being put before her and prior to seeing it. Her anxiety is obviously mounting and so is her implicit complaintiveness and demandingness. By now it seems that she is transforming the test situation into a phobic, real-life situation, parading her misery before the tester to rebuke him obliquely for assaulting her with his "dirty," "poisonous" pictures, and, through this conspicuous misery, implicitly demanding a cessation of testing. This extreme position is outside the limits of how phobic patients ordinarily respond to the test. It implies considerable masochistically-colored paranoid projection of hostility, i.e., transforming the tester into a first-class sadist.

*1. (W FC′+ A P Confabulation tendency) This looks like a bat. It's got horrible feelers. It looks dirty. [What made it look dirty? I don't know. I just don't like to look at them. I think of the bat as dirty. Was there nothing on the card to make it look dirty? No, it was just the association.]*

(a) More of the same. (b) Her assertion in inquiry that the bat does not actually look dirty and that the dirtiness was just an association cannot be taken at face value to indicate restoration of awareness of the boundaries between self and not-self. It is more likely that her explanation represents a need to avoid visualizing and reflecting upon the anxiety-provoking blackness of the card. The response is therefore scored FC′. (c) Her emphasis on dirtiness (see also IV-2) and her revulsion suggest that anal tendencies may be important sources of conflict along with the disturbing oral and phallic tendencies already inferred. Anal imagery is not uncommon in paranoid Rorschach records. Also, severe defensive and adaptive instability tends to be reflected in threatening and disruptive Rorschach imagery pertaining to all types and levels of impulse and impulse-expression. It is as if no workable and secure hierarchy of motivations and defenses has been worked out. This may well be the case here.

> *Another reason I don't like these: they look dead; they look preserved, like they were spread out in a museum. Are they going to get worse? (I don't know how the rest will seem to you.)*

(a) More of the same; i.e., misery, ugliness, implicit complaints and demands, and—in "Are they going to get worse?"—a thinly veiled, paranoid accusation of sadism on the tester's part. (b) "Are they going to get worse?" may also express a need for reassurance or an effort to brace herself for further "assault," but in either of these instances her basic assumptions and orientation would probably be those referred to in (a).

CARD VI    REACTION TIME: 30″.    TOTAL TIME: 1′ 30″.

> *(Patient shies away from card.) I don't like any of them! (She turns her head away.) I can't look! (Try.)*

The patient's anxiety appears to be approaching panic. However, the extremeness of her response is beginning to suggest histrionic exaggeration of anxiety (see also beginning of Card V). Unless she were flagrantly psychotic—and she does not seem to be—she could not truly lose distance from the cards to this extent. The tester therefore continues to press her for responses.

> *1. (W C'F A Confabulation tendency) It looks like all the others except it has a different shape. I don't know what the shape is. [Did it suggest something in particular? No. A vague indistinct shape; something unpleasant. Why unpleasant? I don't know. I guess these things all remind me of something dead or on exhibition. I just hate to look at something dead or mutilated. I hate to kill anything—a spider, a bug, a caterpillar—and yet I hate to see them running around.]*

(a) Her spontaneous verbalization indicates that the problem is not simply the sameness of all the blots. The blots have been similar in their dark, shaded aspects and to these aspects she has indeed reacted intensely, even if histrionically. As she now acknowledges, however, this one is different in shape. The problem seems to be largely that the total Rorschach situation constitutes a serious threat to what are obviously already very shaky repressions. From this defensive point of view, the blots are all alike—they are all threatening.

(b) Inquiry into the response brings out the most explicit evidence thus far that her revulsion and fear pertain to her own hostility to a significant extent: the projection breaks down partly and she refers the hostility back to herself ("I hate to kill . . . I hate to see . . ."). The sequence through the record seems to have been: (1) generalized external threat (sinister, forbidding, dirty, and poisonous things); (2) emerging destructive implications (death in Cards V and VI); and now (3) partial failure of repression (mutilation and killing). Her defensive failures are characterized as partial because the killing involves only insects and because even that is still partly ego-alien.

(c) The theme of mutilation and the revulsion it arouses also suggest the presence of the complex of disturbing castration fantasies, rejecting attitudes toward the feminine role, and masculine strivings. Patients with anxiety-ridden castration fantasies frequently emphasize torn, incomplete, mutilated, deformed and similar aspects of objects, animals and people in their Rorschach imagery.

It is in accord with the psychoanalytic theory of homosexuality that the men who emphasize this imagery frequently are characterized by strong feminine trends and the women by strong masculine trends. Her belittling of the male figure on Card III would be another form of expression of this problem in sexual identification. That all of this occurs on Card VI—the "phallic card"—underscores the inference at the beginning of this paragraph.

> . . . *(Anything else?)*
>
> *2. (D F+ Ad) That up there looks like feathers, bird feathers sticking out (upper wings).*
>
> *3. (Dr F+ Ad) The two little things up front look like feelers (fine projections near upper tip).*
>
> *There is just something awful about it! I'm afraid to look at the next one!*

In #2 and #3 the increased articulation and specificity of perceptual organization and her neutral emotional tone reflect some recovery from her anxiety, but soon again, in her closing remark, the patient re-emphasizes her dread. Her taking time out, as it were, to give two adequate responses and then becoming intensely "phobic" again constitute another indication that she may be prone to dramatize her anxious suffering for demanding and hostile purposes. This type of dramatization is of a sort commonly encountered in the behavior of "moral masochists," i.e., persons whose character structure and way of life are more or less conspicuously organized around the themes of suffering, deprivation, mistreatment, self-abasement, etc. The paranoid aspects of masochistic operations, such as were pointed out on Card V, have recently been clarified [*18*].

CARD VII    REACTION TIME: 23".    TOTAL TIME: 1' 40".

> *That's not so bad. I don't know what it looks like. It's much less sinister than the others, less bad looking.*

Apparently she does not initially experience the blot as unpleasant or threatening. Most likely the lighter-toned and more spread-out quality of Card VII as compared to the preceding six cards accounts for much of her feeling of relief. Nevertheless, she couches this reaction of relief in negative terms, i.e., "not so bad," "less sinister," etc. It is as if everything *must be* bad or sinister and it is only a question of *how* bad or *how* sinister it is. This style of verbalization strongly reinforces the masochistic impression that began to crystallize on Cards V and VI.

> *1. (Do F± Ad) The center part looks like part of an insect but I don't know what—perhaps a butterfly's body or something (lower middle).*

This is a relatively unusual *Do* response. Her fragmentation of the fairly common butterfly response to all of the lower one-third of the blot may well be based on an anxiety-arousing and repressed perception of the lower middle as female genitals, since this area relatively frequently elicits "vagina" responses. Anxiety and intensification of repressive efforts may have blocked further development of this butterfly response, or her attention may have been so riveted to the central area because of repressed recognition of its sexual possibilities that in the butterfly response she could not give adequate thought to the wing area.

> *That's all. (Nothing else?) No. That's all. (Try a while longer. Something may occur to you.) No, there's nothing else!*

Her desire to give up the card so quickly (after 45″) tends to reinforce the previous inference concerning a repressed sex response. Her initial "not so bad" reaction to the card apparently has already succumbed to a new sense of threat. Her calmness on Card VI was similarly short-lived. All three responses to this card are fragmented, relatively inadequate productions.

> 2. *(De F— Ad) These little things where it is uneven around the edge almost look like the edge of a crab . . . and the shape almost looks like a crab without claws (lower and outer edges of lower 1/3).*

(a) In this response and the next the patient returns to the previously much-emphasized crab image and is again concerned with the claws. The crab image has already been interpreted as probably expressing an oral-attacking theme. In the sequence of the first two responses we may well be witnessing an instance of a perceptual and associative shift of a sort that reflects proneness to regress from sexual (female genitals) to oral (claws) problems. As has been pointed out already in the discussion of the preceding two patients, regressive tendencies of this sort are common in female hysterics. (b) "Crab without claws" may represent a denial of the oral-aggressive theme and hence of her own demanding, "devouring" inclinations. In this respect, this clawless crab image would parallel images of false teeth, toothless faces, mouthless faces, miniature dragons, mosquitoes and others that delete or minimize oral-aggressive characteristics. (c) But since it emphasizes incompleteness and, implicitly, immobilization and helplessness, "crab without claws" may also involve a regressive (oral) statement of the theme of castration (see VI-1 particularly). Both interpretations—(b) and (c)—are in line with previous inferences, but both are, of course, highly speculative.

> 3. *(Dr F∓ Ad) These at the end (upper projections) almost look like crab's feelers because of the roughness on the outside of the shell.*

Further preoccupation with the creepy, crawly, clawing crab.

> *I can't see anything else.*

Card VIII     Reaction Time: 10″.     Total Time: 2′ 30″.

> 1. *(W C A) The first thing I thought of is a lobster. I don't know why. It doesn't look like a lobster. I suppose because of the color in it.* [What about the color? *It was pink, and the green stuff in the lobster.* Anything else? *Not the shape.*]

(a) This diffuse response is probably due to a great extent to the impact of the colors, just as the previous diffuse responses seem to have been due largely to the shading and darkness of the earlier cards. At present, her controls and adaptive resources seem quite weak and limited. (b) Yet she spontaneously reflects on the determinants of this response, probably trying to anticipate inquiry (see also VII-3). Considering the general tone of this record, this reflection seems to be another indication of adaptiveness, even if a weak one. She is probably not so totally overwhelmed by and histrionic about her fears as she appears at first glance. (c) The content of the image may have oral implications of two sorts: (1) lobster is often just a variation of the crab image (or *vice versa*); (2) the image implies that this is a lobster to be eaten, the colors being those of a cut-open lobster as one might view it on a plate. (d) That this image precedes the popular, perceptually compelling animals reinforces the above inferences.

> *Are you supposed to look at it this way? (However you like.)*
> 2. *(D F+ A P)> This looks like an animal. I don't know what kind.*

*It's not a fox. Some kind of little animal that was in the woods. Do you call them woodchucks?*

This response appears to contain a significant instance of negation, that is, verbalization of an association in negative form. In telling what the animal is *not*, she indicates what she has already thought it *could be*. The image of the fox—the expert barnyard plunderer—implies crafty, stealthy oral-aggressiveness. Oral-aggressiveness has been conspicuous throughout the record, although usually in projected form. Here it seems to be defended against differently—by negation and also by minimization (see also VII-2—the "crab without claws"). In all instances, the oral-aggressiveness is carefully excluded from her self-concept.

*3. (D F+ At) ∧ This looks a little bit like ribs or something in there (usual middle ribs).*

*4. (Dr F± Sex) (Patient laughs nervously and obviously suppresses response.) (What were you thinking?) In pictures of anatomy or books about sex: this part looks like a picture of a vagina, a womb (lower middle). That's all.*

(a) Suppression of a sex response by a patient being tested as part of his clinical evaluation is most often a repressive and/or paranoid maneuver. This patient has given strong indications of both repressive and paranoid trends already. Once she comes out with the sex response, the patient subtly "blames" the response on books; that is to say, the point of her verbalization seems to be that sex is not the sort of thing that could occur to her spontaneously. It seems more likely now that there is something to the speculations on Card II and VII regarding repressed sexual perceptions.

(b) That she could have denied this response even when she was questioned but did not, again indicates some tolerance for anxiety (see the brief interlude of calm productiveness on Card VI and the discussion of VIII-1).

CARD IX      REACTION TIME: 15″.      TOTAL TIME: 1′ 35″.

*1. (W CF A) That again either looks like a lobster or a crab or something. This arch at the top reminds me of a crab, and then again the colors.*

(a) Another diffuse, poorly controlled initial response to color, and (b) another image of the lobster and crab variety. By now this response is almost perseverative. Perseveration in this context would probably represent extreme and potentially malignant repressive efforts, i.e., attempting to blot out almost everything from consciousness and yet having the blotting-out efforts invaded by the repressed content.

*I guess that's all.*

*2. (Dr F± Sex) This at the bottom (lower middle) looks like what I told on the last one: the vagina. Not really very much.*

(a) In milder form, this seems to be a repetition of what occurred in the previous vagina response (VIII-4). Here the patient first says, "That's all," apparently intending to avoid crystallizing or verbalizing the subsequent sex response, but then volunteers it even though she seems at first inclined to avoid using the word "vagina." (b) In view of her apparently anxious reaction to sexual images, her ability to volunteer this response might be another late indication of some adaptive and defensive resources and of associated tolerance for anxiety. It is also possible, however, that she was merely beating the tester to the draw, since the tester had in a sense forced the sex response out of her on Card VIII. She might well have anticipated a recurrence of this "grilling" on the present card. We already have evidence of efforts to anticipate inquiry (see VIII-1). Yet, because the record is so generally disturbed, it is especially important neither to be carried away by pathological indications nor to overlook indications of strengths and resiliency. The first, strength-oriented interpretation may well have something to it.

> *I don't see anything else.*
> 3. *(Dr F± Hd) These on each side look like eyes (in green-orange shading).*

Eyes seen in isolation almost always suggest a paranoid orientation. Of all eyes seen in isolation in the Rorschach test, however, these are perhaps the most frequent. In itself, therefore, this response could not indicate a paranoid trend. Yet the response is of a piece with the paranoid indications and images that pervade the record. Its appearance after she says she is finished underscores this possible content significance.

CARD X    REACTION TIME: 10″.    TOTAL TIME: 2′ 15″.

> 1-2. *(W F— A DW-tendency; D F+ A P Contamination tendency)* *This again looks like an insect or something that crawls, like a crab or something (W; #1). A variety of them, several (points particularly to side blue; #2). Not really, but I think of them. Not the shape; just the feelers sticking out here and there. It looks like an indistinct picture of a crab or insect. [Crab? It had feelers and claws. That was all. The little blue things almost look like crabs (in themselves) except that it had too many claws.]*

(a) Instead of a diffuse color response as on Cards VIII and IX, the impact of the colors on Card X seems to produce first a diffuse form response. The content—crab or crabs—is, however, virtually identical with the opening content on the previous two cards. (b) The *Contamination tendency* is scored because it is unclear whether the side blue crabs stimulated the perception of the entire blot as a crab, and the *DW-tendency* because the extensions on various parts of the blots appear to have been her main basis for characterizing the entire blot as a crab. These near-autistic responses, like the previous ones, further indicate the impairment of reality testing associated with her intensely anxious, emotionally labile, and consequently perceptually diffuse responsiveness.

> 3-4. *(D F+ Ad P; D F± (Hd))* *This green thing at the bottom (all lower green) looks like a weird picture of some kind of animal. The face part could look like anything: a rabbit or a mule (#3). These green things that come down on the side remind me of curls the judges in England wear (#4). [Did you think of the curls as being on the animal head?* No, it was separate. I thought of the very, very old things they used to have on tapestries or coats of arms with the curls and then I thought of the curls separately as being on a judge's wig.]*

(a) These two responses, like the previous two, are related in a vague, fluid manner that again indicates a relatively poorly organized response to this card. (b) Typically, "weird" is a recurrent word in the records of phobic patients. (c) The rabbit-mule alternative in #3 suggests a contrast of overt fearfulness and underlying stubbornness—especially since the mule image is rarely invoked in this popular response. The inflexibility of this patient's emotional orientation may well involve significant stubbornness. (d) The judge image is a common superego representation and probably states the theme of guilt and fear of (or desire for) punishment. (e) Her mention of the coat of arms in inquiry suggests that preoccupation with social status may be significant.

      5. *(Dd F± (Hd)) The center part down the middle here looks like the top of a totem pole or a caricature of a man (upper gray shaft).*

The "caricature" concept suggests belittling of the male figure (see III-1).

      6. *(D F+ A) The two things on each side look like some kind of crabs or animals trying to crawl up (base of upper gray).*
*That's all.*

SUMMARY OF SCORES

R: 30          EB: 1-3.5(4)

| | | | | | | | |
|---|---|---|---|---|---|---|---|
| W | 10 | F+ | 8 | A | 14 | W% | 33 |
| D | 12 | F− | 3 | Ad | 8 | D% | 40 |
| Dd | 1 | F± | 6 | H | 1 | DR% | 20 |
| Dr | 5 | F∓ | 3 | Hd | 1 | | |
| De | 1 | M | 1 | (Hd) | 2 | F% | 67–80 |
| Do | 1 | F/C | 1∓ | At | 2 | F+% | 70–67 |
| | | CF | 2 | Sex | 2 | | |
| | | C | 1 | | | A% | 73 |
| *Qualitative* | | FC′ | 2(1−) | | | H% | 7–13 |
| DW-tend. | 3 | C′F | 3 | | | P | 6 |
| Confab. tend. | 5 | | | | | P% | 20 |
| Contam. tend. | 1 | | | | | | |
| Peculiar | 1 | | | | | | |

     In summary of thematic analysis, it appears that these responses have been given by a woman whose repressive barriers are dangerously weak and whose consequent intense anxiety and emotional lability seriously interfere with articulated, accurate reality testing and effective adaptation. The patient seems to have been forced to fall back on intertwined phobic and paranoid mechanisms by which she projects—not always successfully —extremely threatening, attacking, devouring, "dirty" and destructive fantasies and impulses. Rigid but unsuccessful repressiveness in the realm of sex, masculine strivings (involving highly charged castration fantasies), and regression from sexuality to orality are likely to be of major significance in her dynamics. In her test attitudes the patient seems to manifest in relatively extreme form the histrionic, accusing and demanding maneuvers typically encountered in the clinical behavior of masochistically-oriented and/or phobic patients. Only traces of anxiety tolerance and adaptive efforts are evident at present. While obviously seriously disturbed, this patient may be obscuring more adaptive resources by her dramatization of fearfulness and misery. Diagnostically this appears to be a case of severe anxiety hysteria with borderline psychotic trends.

The summary of scores indicates the repressive emphasis in the average *R*, only one *M* as compared to four responses involving *C* and five responses involving *C'*, the relatively low *F%* (67–80) and the severe restriction of variety of content (*A%* 73). The virtual absence of *FC* among her color responses indicates the dominance of narcissistic, demanding, immature, unadaptive reaction tendencies in her emotional experience and interpersonal relationships. So many poorly controlled dark-toned responses underscore the impression that she is in a dangerous state of vulnerability. Because of their primarily paranoid and phobic content, these dark-toned responses do not suggest major depressive trends in this case. The *F+%* falls around the lower limits of adequacy (70–67) and suggests the weakness of reality testing, though by no means as strongly as the tendencies toward *DW, Confabulation* and *Contamination,* and the preceding qualitative analysis.

The relatively high *W* (10) and *DR%* (20%) do not conform to the typical repressive score-pattern. The high *W* is understandable mainly in terms of the diffuse, global, phobic-paranoid responsiveness evident during the test. Not one of her *W* is a well-articulated and well-integrated response. The high *DR%* may derive from her projective inclination—paranoid persons often have a high *DR%*—or it may derive from a compulsive streak in her character make-up that has been otherwise obscured by her regressed, diffuse, anxious responsiveness. Of all hysterics, it is typically the anxiety hysterics and not the conversion hysterics who manifest compulsive tendencies clinically and in the tests.

Comparison of this record with the previous two records makes it clear that (1) this patient's defenses and neurotic symptoms are considerably less successful in staving off intensely painful fantasies and feelings, (2) this patient is considerably less adaptively oriented or successful than the others at the present time, but (3) like the other women, she relies heavily on repressive defense, even though in desperation she apparently has had to fall back on supplementary severe paranoid projection and passive regression as well.

*Case 4*

This record was also obtained from a phobic patient—a 48-year-old, twice married, childless woman with two years of college education and a total IQ of 108 (verbal IQ 117, performance IQ 99). In this case, however, the clinical picture is one of long-standing, multiple phobias in a severely regressive context. The clinical diagnosis was "borderline psychosis with recurring phobic states in an immature, inadequate character with narcissistic and paranoid features." The record is of interest in demonstrating how regressive trends may greatly exaggerate the qualitative indications of heavy reliance on repressive defense. In particular, this patient's naivete, unreflectiveness, fuzziness and fragmentation of thinking, and her intellectual as well as emotional clinging are outstanding. The patient's "bright normal" verbal IQ of 117 must be borne in mind to appreciate these features.

CARD I     REACTION TIME: 5".     TOTAL TIME: 1' 10".

> *1. (W F+ A P Do-tendency) A moth. An eagle. Or are you supposed to give one thing? (Not necessarily.) First I thought of wings. An eagle. A moth. Then you keep looking.*

In these naive, fragmented, repetitive comments, the patient resembles a little girl talking to herself as she performs a task or plays a game. Such verbalization is utterly inappropriate coming from a 48-year-old woman of bright normal verbal intelligence. It immediately suggests extreme repressive and regressive tendencies. This is obviously not a reflective, mature woman.

> *2. (W F— Geog) It could possibly be a map, the edge of it, jutting out to the water, couldn't it?* [What made it look like a map? *Nothing inside of it. On the outside it could be: irregular, jutting out. But my first thought was not that. You're not allowed to ask any questions?* What do you have in mind? *Has anybody ever said that: a map or a moth or an eagle?* We can't talk about that during the test; ask me after it's over.]

(a) ". . . couldn't it?" indicates both utter insecurity regarding independent thought and an intense need to cling to others for support, reassurance and guidance.

(b) In inquiry, "But my first thought was not that" implies that she feels it necessary to choose between her responses, which in turn implies the naive realism or "perceptual" approach to the inkblots that is common among unreflective, repressive persons.

(c) In inquiry, "You're not allowed to ask any questions?" seems to be more than simply a naive question or even a naive authority-oriented question. By its extremeness, it also seems to state implicitly a deeply mistrustful part-conclusion and part-anticipation that it is forbidden to ask for anything—information, orientation, help, or any other form of consideration. In other words, a suspicious attitude may well be expressed in this sugar-coated, naive, unprotesting manner.

(d) "Has anybody ever said that?" is a type of question that usually implies another question, namely, "How deviant from convention am I?" or "Am I crazy (or dangerous, horrible, doomed) or not?" In addition, because it actually concerns a popular response and a vague (map) response, both of which, if they are seen, ordinarily have an immediate convincing or at least plausible quality, this question indicates deep insecurity about her powers of reality testing. Neither response needs elaborate or brilliant justification. It is not as if she had given an intricately or daringly organized response in an unusual area and with esoteric content. Good and secure reality testing involves at least the capacity to accept a banality, even if its banal quality is unrecognized.

> *Do you still want me to give other suggestions? (Do you think of anything else?) No. I don't think so.*

The patient seems to be casting the tester in the role of a strict authority who, in answering her frequent questions about what is expected of her, must continually reassert his authority. The tester attempts to avoid taking this role. This trend of the patient's continues throughout the record and will not be commented on further except when it becomes grotesque or otherwise striking.

CARD II     REACTION TIME: 5″.     TOTAL TIME: 2′ 45″.

> *My goodness!*
> *1. (W C Art 2-Peculiar) A futuristic painting. Yet in a way it has a similarity to the first, doesn't it? Only in the outside. First I thought of a futuristic painting and then. . . . Just making the design, doesn't it, when you say futuristic painting, leaving it to your imagination?* [*Futuristic painting? It was something abstract. I have been to the museums. It just looks like putting colors and lines together.*]

(a) The "futuristic painting" concept is an instance of empty, vague, culturally pretentious rationalization of a repressive response to the card. In effect she says, "There is no content. However, I am not vague; the card is vague. In fact, I am sophisticated enough to recognize the meaningfulness of the vagueness." Actually this seems to be simply a global response to color and possibly also a repressive response to the compelling hostile (bloody, explosive) and/or sexual (penis, vagina, womb) implications of the inkblot's configuration.

(b) Her verbalizations become especially fragmented and, in the last sentence of the first response, almost incoherent. Fuzziness and looseness of thinking of severe proportions are suggested.

(c) The "similarity to the first" comment has, in addition, a paranoid implication, and is scored *Peculiar*. Emphasis on the physical similarities and differences among the blots is particularly encountered in settings where paranoid trends are conspicuous. The rationale of this finding seems to be (1) that the patient is searching for inter-card relationships as if she assumes there is a common, hidden theme to be discovered, and (2) that in this quest the patient's perceptions may become so arbitrary that gross differences between cards are ignored and minor or vague physiognomic similarities are overemphasized. Paranoid impairment of reality testing is implied. See also Chapter 9 on projection.

> *2. (W F∓ A Peculiar) It could be some sort of animal here too: prongs here (upper red), tail (lower red).* [*Any particular sort of animal? Well, it certainly would be one that flies.*]

A rather vague response, peculiarly verbalized since she probably meant *insect* when she said "animal."

> *(Peculiar:)\* It's something you wouldn't want to look at very long: it's not very inspiring as far as beauty goes or telling a story—not to me.*

(a) In this verbalization, the patient clearly expresses a phobic, repressive, denying orientation: one must turn away from and blot out what is unpleasant or conflictful. (b) In "it's not very inspiring as far as beauty goes," she also seems to put on airs and to criticize subtly the tester's taste and sensitivity, if not his motives. (c) The "telling a story" idea is scored *Peculiar*.

---

\* Whenever a *Peculiar, Confabulation* or other scorable verbalization occurs outside the context of a numbered response, the qualitative score will be given in parentheses before the verbalization.

CARD III     REACTION TIME: 30″.     TOTAL TIME: 2′.

> *1. (W F+ A (P) Do-tendency, 2-Peculiar) Sort of a disjointed*
> *. . . . Oh heavens! . . . It looks like a half. . . . At first I thought it*
> *was a distorted face of a person (P head) and yet the legs are of an*
> *animal (P leg and combined P arm and lower middle D). That's the*
> *foot of an animal (P shoe). That's about all. First I thought of a face:*
> *distorted, you know. The longer you look, the more it's an animal.*
> *Fantasy, you know. An animal. [Any particular sort of animal? A frail,*
> *delicate . . . usually a sheep or a lamb; nothing wild. What made it*
> *look frail? It just did. Perhaps it didn't bring to my mind anything*
> *like a lion or rhinosceros. It's an animal, isn't it? (Nervous laugh).]*

(a) Her difficulty in bridging the gap between the torso and leg of the popular figure is one that is frequently experienced by repressive persons. Her shift from human to animal content during this response also reflects repressive inclinations. In both respects she indicates inability to develop an *M* response, that is, an imaginative response involving human activity and motivation. Fragmentation of perception occurs that matches the fragmentation of her verbalizations throughout the test.

(b) In inquiry, we have an instance of negation in her "nothing wild" statement. By spontaneously ruling out *wildness,* she rules it in and indicates instability of defense in this area. The substitution of "frail, delicate . . . lamb" for "wild . . . lion or rhinosceros" suggests a policy of rigid repression of hostility and of regression to the "safety" of a weak, fragile role. This suggestion well matches one prominent aspect of the clinical dynamics of phobic patients.

(c) As a further suggestion of defensive instability, her contemplating the aggressive alternative content (lion, etc.) apparently leads to further repression in the form of questioning the animal image altogether—"It's an animal, isn't it? (Nervous laugh)."

(d) Her unreflectiveness in inquiry is also striking and again points to an extreme repressive orientation.

(e) Another important aspect of this entire response is her passive, vaguely puzzled experience of the shift of the content from human to animal—"The longer you look, the more it's an animal." While from a defensive point of view, as was indicated in (a) above, this is understandable as a manifestation of repressive operations, from the point of view of contact with reality this appears to be further evidence of weakness of ego boundaries verging on the psychotic. Weak ego boundaries are suggested by the extent to which she lacks or loses awareness of her part in defining the responses. She externalizes the entire response process to the point where she reacts as if she were watching a movie.

> *(Peculiar:) They have this design running through all of them (mid-*
> *line reference). I wonder why. . . . They're supposed to show some-*
> *thing more or less; isn't that it, sir?*

(a) Her comment in II-1 regarding the similarity of Cards I and II suggested the possibility of a search for hidden meanings in the test and led to the inference of a noteworthy paranoid trend. Now the search for hidden meaning is even more strongly suggested: the midline "is supposed to show something" on each card. As in her "naive" question on Card I—"You're not allowed to ask any questions?"—she tends to express her paranoid orientation with disarming naivete.

(b) Addressing the tester as "sir" when he is about twenty years her junior indicates both the "little girl" self-concept previously noted (see I-1) and also an unconsciously mocking caricature of a submissive authoritarian orientation, i.e., casting the tester in a powerful, dominating, parental role (see end of Card I).

CARD IV     REACTION TIME: 20″.     TOTAL TIME: 3′ 15″.

> 1. *(Dd F± Plant DW-tendency) I don't know. This looks more like an old plant growing in the forest. Something up here makes me think of a leaf (upper middle), and yet this tail (lower middle) isn't it. . . . It would be something . . . an old formation. This part made me think of a leaf (top) and the bottom part looks like a heavier substance though.*

(a) Extreme fragmentation of percepts, ideas and verbalization runs through all three responses to this card. This quality persists in more or less extreme form throughout the remainder of the test and it will not be commented upon further except in special instances. (b) The "old plant" in this response and the "ice formation in caves" in the next, considered together with the patient's age of 48 and her childless status, suggest concern with childlessness, sexual frigidity or menopause, or any combination of these. (d) The "leaf" reference suggests some vestige of sensitivity—an $F(C)$-tendency—which, however, cannot be integrated. (Inquiry may have even been able to elicit the $F(C)$ aspect of the response.) The relatively high number of *Dd* responses in this record also suggests some sensitivity.

> *For that matter I've never seen anything like these drawings before, from all the exhibitions I've gone to.*

Repressive impoverishment of response covered with a pretentious overlay is again suggested (see II-1 and end of Card II).

> 2. *(W F— Ice DW-tendency) It could also be like those ice formations in caves. This part right here reminds me of a leaf (reference to #1). Could be an ice formation or it could even be a stone formation. [Ice formation? All of a sudden I remembered being in a cave: associations of what I once saw. How did it look like it? That part of the top that comes down (upper side D). Anything else? A little on the sides but not too much.]*

> 3. *(Dr F+ Ad) Of course, it has feet here (tiny bottom projections on lower middle). It has a little bit of everything. Of course that might just be a formation (#2) that represented it (feet). [Any particular sort of feet? Of an animal. How many feet? Four, weren't there?]*

CARD V     REACTION TIME: 5″.     TOTAL TIME: 1′ 40″.

> 1. *(W F+ A P) That's just the same miller moth effect; butterfly. No, that's not a butterfly; it would come to a point more. I just get the impression: something that flies.*
> *(Anything else?) No. (Are you sure?)*

> 2. *(D F+ Hd Peculiar) You mean I ought to say that (side projection) looks like a leg? But that's . . . (That's what?) Well no cloud ever looked like that; no tree. . . . I'm just eliminating.*

The tester's pressure on her to keep looking at each card apparently paves the way for a pathological projection: she baldly externalizes responsibility for seeing the common side leg.

> (Between Cards V and VI, the patient is told: "Take your time on these. You don't have to see more things but you might." She replies, "Evidently I'm not seeing as much as I should.")

CARD VI     REACTION TIME: 1".     TOTAL TIME: 2'.

> 1. (D F± Obj Peculiar) Isn't that funny! I thought of a violin right away. This part (entire middle section) reminded me of it. It was my first. . . . Something about the center of that.

Note the passive, somewhat puzzled experiencing of her own thought processes. As was discussed in connection with III-1, pathological weakness of ego boundaries may be implied. Hints of her slipping into this altered state of consciousness occur throughout the test.

> 2. (D ChF Geog Peculiar) Sometimes on a map it's variegated, you know, the shading or darking showing different types of soil or whether it's high (lower D). The shading, different types of shading: it isn't as solid.

In this peculiar word-usage—"darking"—the disorganization seems to be attacking the elements of speech as well as, throughout the test, its continuity.

> 3. (D F∓ Geog Do-tendency, Peculiar) All of them you've showed me jut out. Maybe if you took the half of it (1/2 lower D). . . . But this has more shading in it. [What were you thinking in connection with half of it? It would remind me of a map if I didn't see the rest. Why a map? Only on the side, the edging of it.]
> I'm through.

CARD VII     REACTION TIME: 10".     TOTAL TIME: 1' 15".

> 1. (W ChF Cl) This reminds me more of clouds, floating clouds. [Clouds? Certainly not the color, but just the foamy lightness of it. I can't. . . .]

Except for popular and near-popular images, her responses have consistently been more or less unarticulated, nonspecific, fragmented, inaccurate, and, in the case of the map image, rather repetitive. These formal features underscore the defensive and adaptive weaknesses implied in her verbalizations.

> 2. (Dr F± Arch Peculiar) This looks like an entrance into something (lower middle). [Did you have any thoughts as to what it might be an entrance to? To a house.]

Conceivably, this peculiar, initially abortive image or verbalization results from (1) her nearly completely repressing recognition of the lower middle "vagina," (2) her tendency to fragment ideas, and (3) her general intellectual and emotional inertia.

> That's . . . I really haven't anything else.

CARD VIII     REACTION TIME: 13".     TOTAL TIME: 1' 20".

> 1. (D F+ A P) Well, these two look like animals.
> 2. (D F+ Plant) That looks like the top of a Christmas tree shape

*(upper gray-green). . . . First I got the impression it was like a fir tree; not the color but just the line, the way it went up to a point.*

Images pertaining to Christmas commonly have passive, receptive implications.

*3. (D CF Gem, Dec) The bottom part looks like it might be a lovely gem, stone; a pretty stone. It don't have to be precious but . . . (lower pink and orange). [What made it look like that? Why? I used to have a collection of different colored stones and they reminded me of one I once had. It had a very odd color. Anything else? No.]*

Some sensitivity and warmth are implied, but the narcissistic connotations of the "gem" and the egocentricity of her response to inquiry suggest that these positive reactions may be limited to situations involving narcissistic gratification primarily. The minimally adaptive quality of this record as a whole supports this inference.

*That's about all.*

CARD IX    REACTION TIME: 20".    TOTAL TIME: 2' 30".

*1. (D (C)F Vista Do-tendency, Peculiar) Hmm! There's more of a vista in this. I mean to say, in this picture I'm looking back and that might be some sort of a stone formation, part of a mountain: just the center (around the lower, brownish part of center). The perspective is different in this. [Vista? Just the center, I think (patient vague in pointing out location).]*

*(Peculiar:) But it doesn't particularly remind me of anything. (Take your time.) I'm not rushing myself. I feel very relaxed. Maybe I don't appear that way. Just that someone wanted to draw some odd shapes with colors. The colors are lovely. If I were looking at this, I would be looking at the colors, the lovely shading. I love colors. These colors appeal to me. (Peculiar:) Is that all right?*

(a) Her asking if it is all right for her to express liking for the colors is an even more extreme instance of burlesquing a submissive authoritarian orientation than her addressing the tester, "Sir" (see end of Card III). Again, however, the anticipation that her pleasure might not be "all right" strongly suggests an underlying paranoid attitude (see I-2). The tester would have to be a brute to forbid her this moment of pleasantness and spontaneity. (b) Her attitude toward these colors may be regarded as the positive form of expression of a repressive orientation, of which her last comment on Card II ("something you wouldn't want to look at very long") would be the negative form. Actually, denial of a pollyannish sort also seems to be involved—seeing only what is pretty and serene in the world. The *repressive* aspect of the response lies in its emphasis on affect and its ideational emptiness. (c) Again some sensitivity and warmth are suggested in her positive response to color and shading, but again the childish, egocentric, fuzzy and empty qualities of the response are dominant.

CARD X    REACTION TIME: 35".    TOTAL TIME: 4' 35".

*1. (D F+ A P) Well those might be crabs (side blue). They (projections) give you the feeling of legs of a crab.*

*2. (WS C Floating 2-Peculiar) This gives me a feeling of things floating. Lovely colors . . . with things sort of floating. [Floating?*

*Sort of not one solid thing, not one big. . . . Can you explain that further? Of course, the peninsulas (#4, see below) aren't floating. It gives me the feeling it's surrounded by water but in some parts it didn't. The reindeer (#7, see below) wouldn't be in water. At the end I was just looking for things but it wasn't my first impression.]*

(a) From the formal point of view, this response sums up very well what appear to be the fluid, blurred, amorphous aspects of her perception of the surrounding world—a kind of perception that seems to be compounded out of repressive and pollyannish ego restriction, regressive primitivization and peculiarity of psychic functioning, and a little-girl self-concept and social manner.

(b) From the content point of view, the image seems to state the theme of abandonment of the self to an utterly passive, drifting role (see also the "floating" emphasis in the clouds of VII-1). The theme parallels the perceptual organization here. Her response is so poorly integrated that it is nearly incoherent.

*3. (D F± Ad) This (all lower green) couldn't be a wishbone because it has two prongs going the wrong way (usual rabbit ears) but this part (the rest of it) is kind of like a wishbone.*

Except for the nearly popular wishbone in the middle orange on Card X, wishbones commonly have childish, passive, receptive connotations. This image parallels her relative emphasis on Christmas imagery (see VIII-2 and also X-7, below).

*4. (D F∓ Geog) This part looks like the way a peninsula might be drawn (red).*

*Anything that might come to your head? (Yes.) That gave me the feeling of the wishbone (#3), a peninsula (#4), a crab (#1).*

In the first two responses to this card and now again she speaks of having the "feeling" of something—crab legs, things floating, and a wishbone. This "feeling" style of contact with reality seems to be uncritically accepted and used by her. We are apparently observing in operation a deeply ingrained, ego-syntonic, passive, affect-laden, "floating" mode of functioning. Similarly "floating" in psychic quality is the "entrance into something" in VII-2.

*5. (Dd F+ Obj,Dec Do-tendency, Peculiar) This is the queerest thing: it could be like the bottom of a vase (upper gray shaft).*

*Do-tendency* is scored because this area, if seen as a vase, is typically seen as a complete one. *Peculiar* because of the inappropriate use of "queerest thing."

*6. (Dd F± Obj) Or a thermometer (upper gray shaft).*

*(Peculiar:) Holding something, I mean (reference to vase in #5). . . . This, the more I look at it, it could be like. . . . All of these things, most of them. . . : That seems to have movement to it (the crabs in #1) and this does (side gray). (Fluid:) I did say that in the beginning, didn't I? (Say what?) Floating, movement.*

Further near-incoherence and fluidity.

*7. (D F+ A Peculiar) It could be like reindeer floating through the . . . I mean this brown part (side gray). [What made it look like reindeer? I've just been looking and looking. How did it look like one? Like before Christmas, they show reindeer with legs up and flying.*

*A very small one, of course. The leg part of it did.* Anything else make
it look like that? *No.*]

(a) The Christmas theme is again introduced (see VIII-2). This strongly
suggests passive, receptive yearnings. These yearnings would be related to the
generally regressed quality of the entire record (see X-2, for example). (b)
Along the same passive line, this is also the third reference to floating. (c) Her
first verbalization in inquiry is superficially irrelevant and is scored *Peculiar.*
(d) Her second verbalization in inquiry—"like before Christmas"—is pathetically infantile and foggy.

*Oh, I am just. . . . That's all I can think. No more suggestions there.*

### SUMMARY OF SCORES

| | | | | R: 26 | | | EB: 0–4 | | | |
|---|---|---|---|---|---|---|---|---|---|---|
| W | 9 | F+ | 9 | | A | 7 | | W% | 35 | |
| D | 12 | F− | 2 | | Ad | 2 | | D% | 46 | |
| Dd | 3 | F± | 6 | | Hd | 1 | | DR% | 8 | |
| Dr | 2 | F∓ | 3 | | Obj | 3 | | | | |
| S | 0+1 | CF | 1 | | Dec | 0+2 | | F% | 77–77 | |
| | | C | 2 | | Plant | 2 | | F+% | 75–75 | |
| | | (C)F | 1 | | Geog | 4 | | | | |
| *Qualitative* | | ChF | 2 | | Misc. | 7 | | | | |
| Peculiar | 20 | | | | | | | A% | 35 | |
| Do-tend. | 5 | | | | | | | H% | 4 | |
| DW-tend. | 2 | | | | | | | P | 4+1 | |
| Fluid | 1 | | | | | | | P% | 15–19 | |

In summary of thematic analysis, it may be said that this seems to be an
extremely immature, repressive, pollyannish and regressively passive,
receptive woman who probably has been hovering on the brink of psychosis
for some time. Her thinking and perceiving seem to have remained strikingly childish, naive, vague, physiognomic, fragmented and fluid. A culturally pretentious overlay utterly fails to conceal the underlying impoverishment and chaos. The patient seems deeply insecure regarding her powers
of reality testing and for good reason. We do not, however, see Rorschach
evidence that normally unconscious, archaic thoughts and impulses are
invading consciousness.

Such sensitivity and capacity for warmth as are suggested seem restricted
to the context of narcissistic gratification and seem relatively shallow or
child-like anyway. In addition, the patient persistently seems to caricature
an authoritarian orientation. Her role is that of the submissive, clinging,
inadequate, "frail," helpless babe-in-the-woods. Implicitly, the tester's role
is that of an inconsiderate, suppressive, coercive, harsh figure. In this
definition of the test relationship there appears to lurk noteworthy paranoid
projection. Her test attitudes and implicit conception of the tester have
relatively little to do with the tester's real personality and behavior as a
tester, although they do seem to crystallize certain primitive conceptions

to which the tester's role lends itself.* The tester's prodding her for more responses hardly warrants his being addressed, "Sir."

The summary of scores captures the high points of this personality picture. The patient's qualitatively prominent repressive efforts are indicated by an average $R$ and an $EB$ of 0–4. The five $Do$-tendencies and two $DW$-tendencies indicate the tendencies toward fragmentation, fluidity, and arbitrariness of percepts and ideas. The distribution of color responses—0 $FC$, 1 $CF$ and 2 $C$—indicates her primary narcissistic, immature, unadaptive, regressive emotional responsiveness. The two $DW$-tendencies, two $C$, one *Fluid,* and twenty *Peculiar* point up the psychotic trends.

Comparatively, this patient seems the most loosely integrated of all the repressive patients considered in this chapter. The previous patient, although obviously in an acute state of neurotic decompensation and already showing some autistic tendencies, was on the whole capable of clear, organized communication with the tester. When disorganization invades and pervades verbal communication, an ingrained mode of disorganized functioning and a chronically weak ego are strongly suggested. As regards the overall success of defensive and adaptive operations, this patient's record is certainly a far cry from the first record considered.

* See Chapter 2, especially pp. 19–26.

# 8. Denial

T HE DENIAL OF FACTS AND FEELINGS THAT WOULD be painful to acknowledge consciously has been referred to as a preliminary stage of defense in the normal development of children [42]. The basic formula for denial is simple: there is no pain, no anticipation of pain, no danger. As applied to the past, the formula is: it did not happen that painful way at all. Denial is typically carried beyond the point of turning away from painful reality in the past, present and/or future. Denial is completed and confirmed by reversing the painful facts in fantasy; for example, in fantasy, weakness may be transformed into strength, fear into courage, and passivity into activity. Moreover, this reversal in fantasy may be carried over into speech and action, as in the imaginative play of children.

Normally, denial is most prominent during the early years of life before the ego and superego are fully formed and at a time when adults encourage the child's use of denial in their play with and manipulation of him. In normal development, as the highly prized ego function of reality testing is established, as real ability to avoid or transform painful external situations develops through maturation and learning, and as defenses characteristic of later stages of development crystallize, the archaic defense of denial is necessarily more or less abandoned. The fact that denial ordinarily has more the quality of a temporary pain killer than a lasting defensive solution—reality sooner or later breaking through denials—also accounts for its relatively early abandonment. Denial in fantasy, word and act tends to be superseded by repression, reaction formation, sublimated interest in active mastery of reality, etc.

Crises in later life may, however, force people to fall back regressively on defense by denial. Reliance on denial may even persist into adult life as a steadily operating, prominent character trait. When, as a character trait or as an emergency reaction, denial is rigidly, pervasively and extravagantly brought to bear on problem situations, the ego's powers of reality testing are inevitably sacrificed. Estrangement from reality becomes manifest.

Denial is involved in neurosis in general, in that neurotics invariably act as if certain realities do not exist [53]. *Massive* denials are not characteristic of neurosis in general, however; other defenses often take precedence over denial, as in the case of repression in hysteria and the combination of regression, isolation, undoing and reaction formation in obsessional neurosis.

231

Pathological denial has been noted particularly in hypomanic character disorders and hypomanic states [37, 95]. The hypomanic's ego regression to defense by denial appears to be the counterpart of his outstanding libidinal regression to orality. In both regressive respects his orientation is archaic, magical, narcissistic. In other words, the hypomanic simultaneously regresses to infantile (oral) modes of gratification and to infantile modes of defense.

Besides being characteristic of hypomanic pathology, denial is also grossly apparent in some psychosomatic cases, namely, those who report no conflict, no psychic pain that amounts to anything. In fetishism [51] and in homosexuality [48], denying that women lack a penis is generally a central defensive effort. Denial in fantasy is often a major aspect of schizoid persistent daydreaming. Denial in word and act seems to be part of counterphobic daring and recklessness, the outer danger and inner apprehensiveness being denied and reversed. More or less on the borderline between character disorder and so-called normality—an elusive borderline, to be sure—denial may be seen in the context of pollyanna-ism. Within the normal range, denial may be seen in everyday functioning in the form of unconsciously ignoring disturbing details of situations and in some transient self-consoling or self-reassuring daydreams.

## A. General Test Expectations

What then should we expect in the Rorschach records of those who rely heavily on defense by denial? Obviously, much depends on the content of the denial. For example, high ambitions, intended to deny one's own limitations and the discouraging complexity of reality, may push the number of $W$ up, while lowlier aspirations, intended to deny one's assets and the opportunities to influence reality, may push the number of $W$ down. Similarly, emphasis on tiny detail may involve denial of larger, more threatening issues, while gross inattention to tiny detail may involve denial of complexity, inconsistency and irregularity in reality.

Much depends also on the context of the denial, in particular on the other defensive operations emphasized by the individual. In a predominantly obsessive setting, denial may be expressed through the content of the $M$ responses, since $M$ is likely to be a particularly important determinant in this setting. The human motivations, actions, feelings and interactions in these $M$ responses may then be exceptionally warm, peaceful, gay, and the like. In contrast, in a hysterical-repressive setting, a setting in which $sum\ C$ tends to outweigh $M$, denial may be expressed rather through the content of the color responses. Much emphasis may then be put on pretty, soft, gay, warm, colorful things.

Thus, *the context of denial* and *the content of the denial* may influence the Rorschach test locations and determinants variously. Consequently, we should not expect to find *specific* indications of defense by denial in the location and determinant scores, even though we may learn much from these scores about the forms taken by denial and the position it occupies in the total personality.

The specific indications of defense by denial should most of all be found in the dynamic aspects of response content and in the individual's test attitudes, including his attitudes toward his own responses. We should expect these images and attitudes to be diagnostic in this regard because the test has its major perceptual aspect (threatening things may be "seen" in the cards and denial is largely denial of threatening perceptions) and because the test also has its major emotional aspects (various disturbing emotional reactions may be set off and denial is directed against painful feelings as well as external facts). For example, images of dependence, guilt and gloom may well up within the patient in the relatively unstructured Rorschach situation. To express these images in responses and thereby to acknowledge to oneself at least partly that one is concerned with such problems may be subjectively intolerable. Those who rely heavily on denial will then be in the position of having to deny the existence of these imagery reactions and possibly even to reverse the quality of the images and of the feeling tone associated with them. They will then strive to find angels instead of devils, buxom figures rather than emaciated, open-mouthed figures, gay and serene colors and configurations rather than dark and depressing ones, and the like. One hypomanic patient, for example, saw a battleship in the middle space of Card II "heading right toward me," and then quickly added, "But it has too much hope in it to be that," referring here to the optimism suggested by the white color.

A third major influence on the way defensive denial is likely to be expressed in the Rorschach test must be mentioned. Besides the context of denial and the content of the denial, there is the matter of the relative success of the defensive operation. For example, on the clinical side, sustained euphoria in a hypomanic condition is not possible if the patient's denials of depressive, emotionally needy and hostile feelings and their external referents are unstable. Similarly, sustained pollyanna-ism is not possible if the patient's denials of inner irritability and external provocation or gloom are unstable. On the test side, dynamic content and test attitudes and behavior are sensitive to the effectiveness of defensive operations and, as will be demonstrated below, vary with it.

Two major forms of expression of heavy reliance on defensive denial will be considered in this chapter: pollyanna-ism and hypomania. With respect to each form, a review of the expected test patterns will be presented first and then some illustrative, verbatim protocols. Pollyanna-ism will be illustrated by two records, one of a relatively normal, well-functioning woman and one of a woman with chronic, multiple psychosomatic symptoms. Two cases will illustrate hypomanic denial. Both of them are more or less unstable in their hypomanic state—a fact which is valuable for purposes of this presentation since the hypomanic's instability not only tends to force his denials into extreme, unmistakable forms, but simultaneously tends to throw that which must be denied into clear relief as well.

## B. Pollyannish Denial

When defense by denial is a rigid, pervasive, enduring character trait, a pollyannish orientation will very likely prevail. The patient will make persistent efforts, through selective perception, minimization, and reversal in fantasy, to be conscious of only cheerful, optimistic, benevolent, pretty, sincere, innocent, untroubled and otherwise positive aspects of experience, relationships, and behavior.*

In such a setting, pollyannish imagery should be readily available to the ego in its efforts to cope with the forms, colors and shadings of the Rorschach inkblots, and pollyannish attitudes should be readily effective in prettying-up and sentimentalizing responses during and after their formation. Ideally, flowers, dawns and sunsets, small, gentle animals and benign persons should abound in the test imagery. These responses should tend to be experienced and characterized as sweet, lovely, delicate and the like. The ideal manner of taking the test should be serenely obliging, trusting and appreciative, the denials "insuring" that there are no dangers to worry about and possibly even much to be grateful for; that is to say, implicitly the denials should thoroughly purify the responses, the test situation and the tester of hostility, demandingness, "dirtiness," ambivalence, indifference, anxiety, etc.

With increasing instability in this defensive position, however, the Rorschach content should more and more reflect underlying tensions in the areas of dependency, hostility and sex, and the serene test attitudes and behavior should be invaded by subtle rigidity, negativism, irritability and even mockery.

## C. Two Case Studies of Pollyannish Denial
### Case 1

The following Rorschach record is a good example of pollyannish reliance on denial. It is the record of an essentially well-functioning though immature, repressive woman of 34, married, childless, and a high school graduate with an IQ of 115, bright normal range.

* Pollyanna-ism also seems to involve massive repressions and reaction formations, and some projection of unacceptable impulses, the projections subsequently being denied by what may be called a counterparanoid (i.e., too trusting) outlook. In clinical as well as test material, the indications of these other defenses may overlap those of denial.

CARD I    REACTION TIME: 5".    TOTAL TIME: 1' 45".

>    *1. (W F+ A P) Looks like a bat to me. Are you supposed to describe . . . ? The wings . . . (What did you start to say about the wings?) They are pointed and the body resembles a bat.*
>
>    *It probably isn't that at all. (Anything else?) I can't think of anything else it resembles.*

When this subject says, "It probably isn't that at all," she appears to convey several things: (1) noteworthy naivete and unreflectiveness (implied in the simple realism of her approach to the card); (2) insecurity about her independent intellectual adequacy and retreat to a self-disparaging position; (3) possibly a repudiation of the content of the response. It is in this last respect that we may be observing an instance of denial. It is too early to be certain that this is denial, but if we bear in mind her naivete and self-disparagement, the submissiveness implied in her earlier question, "Are you supposed to describe . . . ?" and her giving only one response to this card, we have a context in which it would be particularly unpleasant to see a bat—even this "popular" one—and particularly compelling to reject or deny the possible interpretation.

CARD II    REACTION TIME: 80".    TOTAL TIME: 2' 30".

>    *Is it supposed to be something in particular or just whatever it looks like to me? (Whatever it looks like to you.) It looks like dabs of red here and there: I don't know what it would suggest.*
>
>    *1-2. (S F± Expl; D C'F Water) It looks like, I've seen pictures of the atomic bomb. It might be the bomb in the center (middle space) and this would be water (dark areas). [What made it look like that? I've seen the movie of just as the bomb was dropped. There was a center that was perfectly plain and black on the outside. That was because I was trying to find something. Anything else make it look like that? The darker area and the calm center.]*

(a) The sequence of verbalizations in these responses probably represents a defensive rearrangement of the actual sequence of inner reactions. Some such scrambling is suggested already by the long reaction time and by her opening question. A dynamically meaningful reconstruction of the sequence of her reactions would be: (1) strong reaction to the explosive configuration in general and red color in particular; (2) anxiety at the threatened breakthrough of a hostile image followed by a struggle to reinforce repression and denial of the threat (long reaction time and emphasis on the meaninglessness of the red areas); (3) further retreat to a submissive position and thinly veiled externalization of responsibility for the hostile image (the subject asks for permission and reassurance in her opening question); (4) a compromise-formation image from which the most intense, explosive, gory, unformed aspects have been deleted (the red), and the bomb has been brought under control ("calm," well-shaped, not intensely colored explosion); (5) during inquiry, a further externalization of responsibility for the finished response ("That was because I was trying to find something" probably meaning "You made me see it; this sort of thing doesn't come natural to me.")

(b) Regarding denial in particular, the fourth aspect just noted is most significant. The subject finally responds as if the red were not there at all. Yet there is every reason (from general experience with this card and from her concern with the red areas) to expect that the red color played a vital part in the development of her response. In addition she makes the explosion as serene and static as can be. The distinction between repressed perceptions and denied perceptions is not clear, but the general context of *reversal*—from the threatening to the benign—helps establish the presence of denial here.

(c) It is interesting to note, however, how the defensive operations of repression, projection and regression to a passive position seem to play their part in the crystallization of this response. All of the defensive operations together make it possible for her to express the response: violence is minimized, responsibility externalized, and reassurance gained.

(d) We might ask now, since the response was not altogether staved off, whether it is to be regarded as an instance of relative failure of defense, that is, as an instance of ineffective effort to ward off an obviously threatening, violently hostile fantasy. In one respect the answer must be yes: the subject seems too threatened by the response for us to regard this as a relatively secure acceptance and expression of a hostile theme. Everything points to her preferring not to think along these lines at all. The response's weakness of form and the fact that the subject does not begin with the popular or common response also suggest defensive instability. In another respect, however, the answer is that the evaluation of defensive failure is not that simple. The extent of the failure cannot be gauged from the material thus far discussed. For one thing, the subject was not overwhelmed with anxiety as she gave the response, as many patients are whose defenses are seriously failing. This is evident in her relative composure (signs of anxiety would have been noted in the record). For another thing, she was relatively effective in muting the response. In these respects she did succeed in defensively mastering the breakthrough to a significant extent. Thus some instability rather than failure of defense, and also some defensive resiliency, seem to be indicated.

> 3. (D F+ A) *These things look like some kind of animal there (upper red) but I wonder what kind. . . . A bird: feet and beak and wing.*

Continuing her mastery of the hostile breakthrough, the subject goes directly back to the red areas. While she is still unsure of herself (". . . animal . . . I wonder what kind"), she slowly imposes good form on the upper red area, seeing it as a clearly articulated bird. Thus, she halts her retreat from the red areas and makes a new and successful attack. (Inquiry for color could have established whether her recovery was complete enough to enable her to use and control the color by integrating it with form.) In addition, the image is neutral, if not positive, and the new mastery may well still involve denial and repression. The resiliency indicated in this response suggests that such failure of defense as occurred in the first response was moderate and short-lived. In the end, the subject's defensive structure appears to have stood the pressure fairly well even if not excellently.

CARD III    REACTION TIME: 10″.    TOTAL TIME: 2′ 45″.

> 1. (D FC(C)+ Cg) *It looks like a bow tie in the center (middle red) but I wouldn't know.* [What made it look like that? *It could have been a hair ribbon.* What made it look like a bow tie or ribbon? *The color? (musing naively) It was red and shaded.*]

The subject is again strongly responsive to the red color, her first response being to the middle red area. This time, however, her coping with the color is faster and more effective, probably on the basis of the ease with which the middle red area lends itself to a well-structured and neutral or positive interpretation (bow, butterfly, and the like). When the subject turns her attention to the much more amorphous upper red areas shortly afterwards, she can do nothing with them.

> 2. *(D F(C)+ Hd,Cg Peculiar) The way this is shaded it could resemble the human top of a woman (lower middle).* [What made it look like that? *The way you draw a bathing suit. It looks like she had a bra on.*]

(a) In spontaneous verbalization it sounds as if the subject sees breasts, whether covered or not. Her overgeneralized and gingerly wording of the response suggests intense embarrassment in connection with this image and it is probably this embarrassment that underlies the verbalization's peculiar redundancy. By the time inquiry is begun, she seems to have recovered control and she makes the image acceptable by explicitly emphasizing the coveredness of the breasts, by making it a "drawing," and by making it a bathing suit rather than an "unmentionable" brassiere. These defensive transformations of the image smack of denial and repression. (b) This largely oral image is both unusual and direct and suggests strong passive, receptive tendencies. (c) The *Peculiar* score suggests that malignant potentialities may exist despite some evidence already of defensive resiliency. It is possible, however, that this *Peculiar* may merely be an instance of the occasional, non-malignant disruption of communication that occurs in some normal and neurotic records.

> *I don't know what these (upper red) would suggest.*

> 3. *(D F± Ad) They look like a wooden animal or some such caricature of animal to me (popular figure, leg area excluded).* [How much of the animal did you see? *Just the upper part.* What sort of an animal did it look like? *I thought it looked something like a dinosaur but I don't know, like you see in museums.*]

(a) This response, particularly as it is elaborated in the inquiry, seems to represent another instance of defense by denial. The dynamically meaningful sequence appears to have been: a threatening dinosaur, a safe dinosaur (dead, preserved in a museum), it is not even a dinosaur (just an animal, a caricature, and made of wood at that). Denial of a potentially threatening image is thus clearly implied. Again, as in II-1, the threatening image is not altogether repressed, however. It comes to expression and then is dealt with in a relatively adequate though highly defensive and inhibited way. It should be noted that in this response, as in II-1, a sequence of reaction is assumed that is almost the reverse of that conveyed by the subject's verbalization. On the surface, the subject's sequence seems to go from complete denial and repression to partial denial and repression. Actually, the sequence is probably more intricate, the image forming and being manipulated preconsciously and consciously until a thematically limited, subjectively tolerable and socially expressible form has been evolved.

(b) Dinosaurs often state the theme of primitive, aggressive impulses. In view of the fact that the area involved is so often seen as men, the theme suggests fear (denied) of the primitive hostility of men.

> 4. *(D F± Pl) This could look like a twig of a tree (P leg).*

This area is usually called a branch rather than a twig, if it is interpreted in that connection at all. A tendency to see things as small and even minute seems to characterize the Rorschach responses of those who rely heavily on denial. Perhaps this minimization of size reflects a defensive denial that one feels small (like a child or infant) and that things around seem huge and frightening.

*As a whole, I don't think it looks like anything.*

CARD IV     REACTION TIME: 27".     TOTAL TIME: 2′ 30″.

1. *(D F± Ad) These look like the horns of a mountain goat (upper side projections) but the animal itself doesn't . . . or whatever it is, I don't know. I don't know where to start on this one.*

(a) These are anxious, flustered reactions, as indicated by the delayed reaction time and the expressions of uncertainty and feelings of inadequacy. (b) Horns may state a phallic-aggressive theme, i.e., the piercing, intruding, masculine organ (see III-3).

2. *(D FCh+ Ad (P) Do-tendency) Looks like an animal put on the wall (all but lower middle and upper side projections). I wouldn't know what kind though.* [What made it look like an animal on the wall? *It seemed like a bearskin but the horns don't belong.* What made it look like a bearskin? *The big feet coming out.* Anything else? *It was spread out and furry.* What made it look furry? *The shading up at the top.*]

(a) Resiliency of a limited sort is again evident in the subject's evolving the popular response and in her being able to verbalize the influence of shading in inquiry. (b) Denial is suggested, however, in her ignoring the gross heavy shading of the blot and acknowledging only the more refined, delicate upper middle shading.

*I don't believe I can make too much out of it.*

CARD V     REACTION TIME: 3".     TOTAL TIME: 1′ 30″.

1. *(W F+ A P) That reminds me of a butterfly. The body would be very similar. This (wings) is a different shape.*

A relatively unimaginative, unproductive conscientiousness is evident in her critical examination of the parts of her response. The *Do*-tendency in IV-2, the concluding comment on Card III, and her general cautiousness have similar implications. Note particularly how she spontaneously begins conducting inquiry more and more as the test proceeds—especially from Card VIII on. She already strives to be a "good girl" and seems on the whole to succeed. She does not behave like a woman of 34 with some rights and privileges in the world.

*I wouldn't know what else it would suggest.*

CARD VI     REACTION TIME: 11".     TOTAL TIME: 1′ 30″.

1. *(D F+ Obj) The upper part looks like an Indian totem pole but I wouldn't know in what way it would be connected with that part (rest of card).*

*I can't make anything out of the bottom.*

Her avoiding the bottom, massive area of this card may reflect difficulty in coping with its prominent shading (see also IV-2). If so, we might be dealing with a denial of either anxiety or sensuality. Her docile, naive, repressive manner thus far suggests poor integration of sensual needs into her character structure as well as relatively low anxiety tolerance.

CARD VII    REACTION TIME: 8".    TOTAL TIME: 2' 20".

*1. (W ChC'F Cl) If they weren't joined together, they would look like fleecy clouds to me; they seem to have that whiteness in the shading.*

Denial is vaguely suggested in the emphasis on the fleeciness and whiteness (rather than darkness) of the clouds, an emphasis that gives the clouds a cheery quality. Yet, the clouds on Card VII lend themselves relatively easily to this benign construction, so that in this instance a distinctive reliance on defensive denial is not clear. We can at least say that in the total context the subject is responding consistently.

*Do you have to take them as a unit or can you take them individually? (However you like.)*

*2. (WS ChC'F Ldsc) It reminds me of space somehow (middle space). This could be like down in a valley: this could be part of the terrain (dark areas) and this a small object (lower center). The way things look: sort of minute. There could be a house down in the valley (lower center). [What made it look like terrain? Like when you look from the top of a mountain. It (dark areas) looks more like water than land. Why? It has different shading. Water is apt to have that.]*

(a) Optimistic themes of tranquility and being sheltered are suggested by this image. (b) Both responses to this card are heavily shaded and for the most part weakly formed. This suggests that the subject is open to relatively strong, diffuse anxiety reactions. At the same time, the cozy content of both images indicates her defensive, pollyannish means of coping with anxiety. In this respect, these images are better defended versions of the disruptive atomic bomb theme in II-1. With greater defensive instability she could well have seen some storm clouds or a reef on this card, or even what would be for her the very distressing "female genitals." (c) This response includes further emphasis on minuteness (see III-4).

CARD VIII    REACTION TIME: 25".    TOTAL TIME: 2' 45".

*1. (D F+ A P) Oh dear! I must be animal-minded but these look like animals to me, but they're pink. I never saw pink ones. Does it have to be color or is shape all right? (Either way.) Looks like a racoon or ground hog but the color isn't right.*

(a) There is again an increase in reaction time and an exacerbation of uncertainty, submissiveness and conscientiousness (see Cards II and IV). This time, however, nothing ego-alien is exposed. Her interpretation of the popular animal is peaceful. This animal lends itself just as well to hostile constructions (wolf, coyote, etc.). As in the case of the fleecy clouds in VII-1, all we can say is that the subject remains consistent in her benign orientation.

*The coloring is lovely.*

Another positive, accepting, uncritical comment. Before we can infer genuine warmth and adaptiveness from such remarks, we need evidence that the subject can use color warmly *within responses.*

*2. (D C Dec) Looks like different stones I used to hunt: amethyst (lower pink and orange) and turquoise (middle blue). Not the shape;*

*just the coloring. Are you supposed to go by the shape? (That's up to you.)*

(a) Here she does use color prettily within a response. This indicates that her general comments about color are not empty pretenses at affective response. Yet, both the egocentricity of the response's content and the pure *C* score suggest that the warmth of this response may be too diffuse and narcissistic to represent significant adaptive potential. (b) From here to the end of the test, the subject's reliance on denial becomes progressively more apparent.

*I can't think of anything this straight line suggests (mid-line).*

3. *(D F+ Ad) This looks like a fish bone (usual ribs).*

CARD IX    REACTION TIME: 20″.    TOTAL TIME: 2′ 30″.

1. *(D F+ Emblem) Just the formation looks something like the coat of arms of England (orange). Like on pins you bought during the war, with crossed. . . . Just the way they sat there.*

(a) The subject remains consistent, avoiding the possible implications of hostile interaction in the orange areas. (b) Some social status consciousness may be implied in the coat of arms image, but her quick emphasis on the smallness and non-aristocratic connotations of the object (a war-time, commonly worn pin) suggests that denial may be at work even here. She ends up an unassuming, undistinguished citizen. (c) It is conceivable that at the end she meant to say "crossed swords" or something similar before she cut herself short in what could therefore be a defensive avoidance of a hostile theme.

*They all have straight lines in the center but I don't know that it suggests anything to me; just joining things.*

2. *(D CF Ldsc) This beautiful color (green) reminds me of Lake Louise in Canada; emerald color.* [Did anything beside the color suggest Lake Louise? *The shape, but it is particularly the color.*]

She is emotionally and defensively consistent in finding beauty in the green color and elaborating it with pleasant, if not sentimental, memories.

3. *(D CF Food) The pink doesn't remind me of anything. Strawberry ice cream, but it doesn't look like it.* [What suggested strawberry ice cream? *I was trying to think of something. It's that color.*]

In this food response, a sweet, self-indulgent, childhood, receptive oral theme is first opposed by what seems to be a repressive maneuver ("doesn't remind me of anything"), then is expressed, and finally is rejected by denial ("doesn't look like it"). This sequence recalls particularly her uneasy, defensive, awkward handling of the breasts-bra image in III-2 and the dinosaur image in III-3. This "girl" apparently is made quite anxious by her passive-receptive tendencies, which do seem strong.

CARD X    REACTION TIME: 17″.    TOTAL TIME: 3′ 30″.

1. *(D F∓ Snow) The shape of these (side blue) looks like snow flakes but not the color.*

2. *(D F+ Pl) And this (upper gray) looks like a tree with the roots coming out, perhaps like flowers growing up the side of it.*

*Once again the pink doesn't seem to suggest anything to me; just that it is shaded into lovely colors there.*

3. *(D F± A) This reminds me of that sea horse they have at Jones*

*Beach. It's their trade mark (lower green).* [What made it look like a sea horse? *Just the head and . . . I don't remember . . . long ears? A rather odd looking creature.*]

*4. (D FC+ Pl) This could look like a flower coming out of a bud there (side yellow and gray).* [What suggested a flower? *A yellow flower, like the ammon lilies I have right now.*]

*5. (D F+ Ad) This almost looks like a wish-bone (center orange). We will say it looks somewhat like it, if we have to find it.*

Her lapsing into the editorial "we" has a lofty aspect and recalls the coat of arms in IX-1 and the lofty position of the viewer in VII-2. Together, these responses suggest—and dynamic theory and clinical experience would support this—that below her submissive, "good girl," self-effacing tendencies lie significant imperious and self-righteous tendencies. She would not have to go to the humble lengths she does were it not for her fighting an inner battle with expansive tendencies.

*6. (D CF Cl) The pink could look something like clouds, sunset clouds, except the dark color wouldn't be there.*

Snowflakes, flowers, buds, "shaded into lovely colors," wishbone, sunset clouds which have no darkness in them at all (see also VII-1)—on the whole, a steady stream of sweetness and serenity pours forth on Card X. On Cards VIII, IX, and X the subject appears to have fully regained her defensive stride even while continuing to respond strongly and more or less diffusely to color. She did the same with shading on Card VII. She does not falter once in her delivery of benign imagery. The external world and the world of affect are gentle, serene, pleasant. Denial (plus repression) reigns supreme.

### SUMMARY OF SCORES

R: 26                    EB: 0–5.5

| | | | | | | | |
|---|---|---|---|---|---|---|---|
| W | 4 | F+ | 9 | A | 5 | W% | 15 |
| D | 21 | F± | 5 | Ad | 5 | D% | 81 |
| S | 1+1 | F∓ | 1 | Hd | 1 | DR% | 4 |
| | | FC | 2 | Obj | 1 | | |
| | | CF | 3 | Cg | 1+1 | F% | 58–73 |
| *Qualitative* | | C | 1 | Plant | 3 | F+% | 93–95 |
| Peculiar | 1 | F(C) | 1+1 | Ldsc | 2 | | |
| Do-tend. | 1 | C'F | 1+2 | Cloud | 2 | A% | 38 |
| | | FCh | 1 | Misc | 5 | H% | 4 |
| | | ChF | 2 | | | P | 3+1 |
| | | | | | | P% | 12–15 |

Altogether we seem to see a relatively pervasive and rigid defensive policy in which denial figures prominently although it is synchronized with repressive, passive-regressive and mild projective defense. This defensive policy appears to culminate in a relatively stable pollyannish orientation. Although the subject occasionally falters in her defensive operations, and responds anxiously and with diffuse affect, she possesses sufficient resiliency to effect fairly good recovery *within the limits of her overall strategy.* The overall strategy is, to be sure, an ego-restrictive one. It should also be noted, on the adaptive side, that the subject's defensive operations do not result in clearly forced or inappropriate "loveliness" such as is present in the record of the next case to be considered. The general success, resilience and appropriateness of her defensive operations, all suggest a relatively stable though limited, immature, dependent, anxious and emotionally labile style of adjustment. This indeed was characteristic of this subject in daily life.

No peculiarities or other indications of autistic trends emerged except for the peculiar verbalization on Card III. This finding, as well as the absence of other psychotic indications in the score summary, makes it plain that we are probably not dealing with a malignant process.

The distribution of scores indicates chiefly the repressive and hysterical trends in this subject's character structure (average $R$, low $W$, no $M$, relatively strong emphasis on color and shading, relatively low $F\%$). The relative emphasis on $CF$, $C'F$ and $ChF$ among the colored and shaded responses, and the relatively low $F\%$ of 58–73 indicate sufficient anxiety and emotional lability to warrant the conclusion that the subject's defenses (repression and denial particularly) work only fairly well. But at the same time, the presence of 2 $FC$, 2 $F(C)$ and 1 $FCh$ and the high $F+\%$ indicates that adaptive and controlling resources and resiliency are probably present to a noteworthy even if not altogether adequate extent. The high $F+\%$ also suggests that conscientiousness and meticulousness may be prominent in her adaptive efforts.

In general, these inferences from the scores parallel or supplement inferences drawn from the thematic analysis of the record. *The thematically prominent and relatively effective pollyannish denials could not, however, have been inferred from the scores.*

*Case 2*

This pollyannish record issues from a pathological context. The patient is a 58-year-old married woman with one child, a college graduate with an IQ of 135, very superior range. The clinical diagnosis was "rheumatoid arthritis, hypertension, dermatitis and mild depression in a compulsive character." In this record we will see the extremes to which denial may be carried without becoming psychotic.

CARD I    REACTION TIME: 5".    TOTAL TIME: 1' 45".

> 1. (*W FC'+ A P*) *It could look like a very beautiful butterfly, with all the bright spots.* [Bright spots? *Those four white spots: they were symmetrical and butterflies are generally marked symmetrically.*]

This is a masterpiece of denial. This butterfly is rarely referred to as beautiful. If the inner spaces are noted, they are ordinarily "holes" in the wings. Subjects not characterized by feelings of being torn, worn or imperfect usually prefer to ignore the spaces as part of the butterfly. It takes a pollyanna to make them "bright spots" and to make the butterfly exotic.

> *(Anything else?) Oh! Do I have to make a choice? No, a butterfly.* . . .

> *2. (Ws F— Geog) Well, as far as that's concerned it might be a perfectly symmetrical island with lakes in it, promontories, little islands outside, nice little bays.*

Another benign, sentimental touch is added in her making the ragged edges into "nice little bays." Already pathologically rigid defense by denial is suggested, the patient tending toward extremes from the very beginning. In this respect she differs from the relatively normal subject previously discussed. Here elements of forcing and inappropriateness begin to creep in.

> *Do I have to keep on going? (That's up to you.) My imagination? I think that's all I can possibly see. My imagination stops working very quickly.*

In her two questions pertaining to "choice" and "keep on going," the patient seems to be beginning to structure the situation as a demanding one. Both times the emphasis is on "Do I *have* to . . .?" The patient rather quickly gives up the card, possibly refusing to comply with the projected demands. She falls back on isolation of "imagination" from the rest of her personality. "My imagination stops working" can be translated "I want to stop thinking about this." It is also possible that anticipation of a breakdown of her pollyanna constructions forced her to this passive retreat. In any event, more could have been expected from this woman in view of her very superior IQ and the fact that she is able to give as many as five human movement responses in the test as a whole.

CARD II     REACTION TIME: 2″.     TOTAL TIME: 1′ 50″.

> *1. (W M/C+ H P) Now these are two people playing pattycake. They must be at a masquerade. They have on red masks. They are down on their knees.*

(a) The image is playful but—like the fleecy clouds on Card VII and the unthreatening popular animal on Card VIII in the previous record—it is not unusual. We need only note the patient's consistency, for here the two figures are also often seen in conflict. (b) The patient ascribes the masquerade idea to the red masks, but it is not unlikely that the primary source of the masquerade idea was a feeling that such play and amity as she describes can only be a pretense, a mask for hostility, as it were, and that this moved her to capitalize on the mask-like appearance of the faces and to make it all a masquerade. It is consistent with this line of reasoning that playful but only artificial use is made of the red color.

> *2-3. (S FC'+ Dec; D C'F Dark) Also there is a chandelier hanging from the ceiling (middle space); I guess a dark background (dark areas).* [Did you have a particular background in mind? *A dark wall.* What made it look like a chandelier? *It was just like a chandelier.* How? *The shape and it was light.* Light? *I suppose the dark background made the white look light.*]

These two responses seem to represent another good instance of denial, this time accomplished through a figure-ground reversal. The dark (unpleasant, anxiety-arousing area) is relegated to the background, the space (bright, light, decorative, well-formed) is called into the foreground, and the disturbing, potentially hostile red is not used at all. In this instance the perceptual figure-ground reversal would seem to correspond in part to the mood reversal—good spirits covering over depression—which is common in settings where denial is heavily emphasized. The usual negativistic or stubborn connotations of S might very well be present as well.

> 4. (D F+ Ad P) I think I see some bears kissing each other too with their forepaws up (dark areas). Of course they might be dogs.

The patient continues on her serene course, emphasizing the most affectionate version of this popular response.

> I don't see anything else.

CARD III     REACTION TIME: 5".     TOTAL TIME: 1' 50".

> 1. (W M+ H P) If one had his head bowed, it would look like "After you, Alphonse and Gaston." It looks like two men leaning back and bending forwards. They have on high collars. I don't know what they have in their hands—dust mops, maybe. I don't believe that's right though. [What made it look like a dust mop? It was fuzzy (nervous laugh); one of those dust mops you put on your hands, one of those glove things. Fuzzy? I guess they sort of spread a little bit. . . . They have long ends (reference to edges).]

(a) The pollyanna consistency is maintained in the emphasis on politeness and gentility. An element of mockery creeps in, however, Alphonse and Gaston being ridiculous figures. The mockery is increased by the reference to dust mops which exaggerates the effeminate quality of the men. It is probably because the patient senses the hostile overtones of the response that she retreats quickly into a denial: "I don't believe that's right," or, in other words, "Oops! I take it back. It isn't so."

(b) The distinction between denial of feared masculine aggressiveness and hostile, castrative devaluation of men is not always easy to make. We must remember, however, that men may be seen in neutral or positive activity (e.g., working, playing, being affectionate) that is still respectably masculine. It is when the "beast" is tamed too much and deprived of some or all of his masculinity and basis for self-respect that the operation of more than defensive denial must be suspected. Then, noteworthy hostile, castrative, devaluating intent is implied. Persistent and/or extreme or dramatic emphasis on the smallness, incompleteness, inadequacy or ridiculousness of men is bound to be multiply determined; that is to say, it will be serving numerous instinctual and defensive needs. Denial may be only one of these.

> 2. (D F+ Cg) There is a bow tie here in the red, between them (middle red), but it has nothing to do with them (the men). [What made it look like that? It was tied together here and went out on each side like a bow. Anything else? Nothing else.]
> I see too much of the symmetry of it rather than being able to. . . .
> I notice the men (#1) have beards. . . . I don't see anything more.

CARD IV     REACTION TIME: 7".     TOTAL TIME: 3' 20".

> 1. (W M+ H, A) There is a boy having a lot of fun sitting on a water plug, I mean fire plug. His feet are out in opposite directions. His head is back: I think he is laughing. He has on too-large shoes, of course.

> *Oh mercy! I can't think of things. Also could be an animal of some kind with a funny beak face. I don't know what kind of an animal it could be. It looks like ears out of the sides. It might be playing leap-frog over something (nervous laugh); why it would, I don't know.*

(a) This is another triumph of pollyanna-ism. Here is no monster, ape, giant, menacing figure at all. It is only a playful little boy, harmless as can be, "having a lot of fun." Moreover, here is no weird, dark, possibly Oriental face. The boy is laughing. This is a relatively rare construction put on this blot. Ordinarily, if the figure is not seen as threatening to some degree, it involves a more or less static perspective view of a seated or reclining figure of neutral or unspecified emotional quality. Here, as in the case of the beautiful butterfly (I-1), a reversal by denial is strongly indicated.

(b) As the patient goes on, however, and refers to the oversized shoes, mockery of men again seems to creep in (see III-1). On this card, even the "little boy" image can be seen as a devaluation of the male. And again, presumably anxious because she senses the hostility in her response, she retreats: "Oh mercy! I can't think of things," appears to mean "I haven't seen anything so far (a denial of the previous response) and I had better watch my step." The patient, now flustered, changes the content to an animal and makes the response altogether ridiculous by attempting to maintain the now clearly inappropriate playful activity. In all likelihood she is fleeing from the hostile potentialities of the response.

> *I'm not very successful at these. I can't see too much.*

There follow self-disparagement and indication of wanting to give up the card, which at the same time may retroactively deny what has already been said on this and the previous cards.

> 2. *(Dr FCh(C)± At) It might be an x-ray of a spine, I don't know, down the middle (upper midline area), but I don't know what you'd do with the rest of it. It might be a few ribs jutting out (shading along midline).* [What made it look like that? *I don't know. It just looked like it.* How? *Maybe the light and the few little things running off from it.*]

She now falls back on anatomical content.

> *I can't think of anything more. That was working the imagination over-time at it was.*

Finally she obliquely expresses resentment at the demands of the tester ("working overtime"). The sequence through the card seems to have been: successful denial, threatened failure of denial, flustered intensification of denying and repressive efforts, depression, bodily preoccupation and retreat to passivity along with projection of passive-demandingness. This sequence is a meaningful one in psychopathology and is in accord with the dynamics of the particular patient as they were evident clinically.

CARD V    REACTION TIME: 1".    TOTAL TIME: 1' 20".

> 1. *(W F+ A P) There is another butterfly. Definitely! Another pretty one! It has feelers and a tail and the tips of the wings are split.* [What was pretty about it? *I have forgotten the name, but it's a butterfly very much that shape. It has long feelers and a tail. I don't know if it is tropical; I think it should be tropical.*]

This butterfly, like the butterfly in I-1, is rarely described as pretty. Again we seem to have a somewhat forced, inappropriate instance of denial. Similarly, her firmly classifying it at the end of inquiry as tropical, makes the butterfly distant, exotic, and possibly attractive in its ugliness.

> *I wish they weren't symmetrical. That's the trouble with me. I think I could see more if they weren't symmetrical. I really don't see anything but a butterfly.*

(a) The patient vacillates between overtly criticizing herself and implicitly criticizing the tester and the test for her difficulty in dealing with the symmetry. (b) Note that mostly she is spending less than two minutes on each card and also that she relatively often answers questions quite unreflectively. She seems to be a woman who is quite uncomfortable with her intellectual assets and her fantasy life and who tries to be minimally introspective.

CARD VI    REACTION TIME: 1".    TOTAL TIME: 3'.

> 1. *(W FCh+ Ad P) Somebody's pinned up a skin to dry, nailed it on the barn. I don't know what kind of a skin it is. It could be a fur rug very easily.* [What made it look like that? *The shape: it had arms and legs and a tail; and the skin.* What about the skin? *It had a mottled effect, as though there might be different colorings.*]
>
> 2. *(D FCh(C)± Ldsc) This (lower D) could be a small portion of an aerial view: higher land on the sides, and lower land (inside), and a canal dug across (midline). I don't know why it would be that shape but I can see a straight canal across that portion of country. The canal it quite a bit lower than the immediate surrounding country, and these are higher peaks out around the outside. This reminds me of a very boring, very straight road through the Everglades in Florida. The darker bumps on each side would be little islands where trees grew out; the rest would be saw-grass. Do you want me to get the whole shape into it or just what I see in the middle? (Whatever occurs to you.) That would be a very good explanation then. I think that's all.*

(a) The neutral image (aerial view) turns into an unpleasant one, the Everglades being a swamp and saw-grass easily cutting people if they brush against it. Here then her denial fails her, and the resulting anxiety apparently has to be dulled by a retreat to boredom. Boredom can be one form of expression of denial, although not a very successful one. The insufficiency of defense, suggested first by its inappropriate application (see I-1, V-1), now becomes somewhat more directly apparent.

(b) It is possible that this image of terrain is connected with an unconscious or preconscious response to the aspects of this area that resemble female genitalia. Such features of terrain as canals, grass and rolling land are often used in dreams as female sex symbols. If this is so in this case, we could speculate that this woman has a hostile, ugly conception of her sexuality (swamp, saw-grass) and that she defends against this by adopting a bored attitude, i.e., by denying any noteworthy "exciting" sexual feeling or impulse. This highly speculative interpretation should receive strong support before anything is done with it.

CARD VII    REACTION TIME: 6".    TOTAL TIME: 1' 45".

> 1. *(WS F± Geog) I think that's an atoll, with the protected lagoon in there. I think they've made a canal through here (lower middle) to get out to the Pacific Ocean over here (below).* [Atoll? *Just looks like an*

*atoll.* How? *Generally it's a coral formation.* Anything else? *A nice little harbor in there.* Anything else? *Like water all around it.*]

The "protected lagoon" and "nice little harbor," like the earlier "nice little bays" (I-2), suggest a strong need for a passive, protected retreat. This need has already been evident in her reactions to threatened emergence of hostile imagery and test attitudes. Passive-regressive defense works together with denial in this case.

> 2. *(D F+ Hd P) I see two girls with horses' tails (hair-do's) making faces at each other (upper 1/3).*
>
> 3. *(D F+ A) I see two small elephants standing on their hind legs with their trunks up in the air (upper 2/3, facing out).*

Because the elephant's long trunk is a compelling phallic symbol according to clinical observation, the denial ("small") in this response may concern particularly masculine power. Minimization of men may well have both hostile and defensive significance to this woman (see also III-1, IV-1, VI-2). The suggestion in the elephants' positions that they are trained animals going through a routine adds to the devaluation of the male figure. In the end, these elephants are not so different from Alphonse and Gaston in III-1.

> *But I really think it looks more like a Pacific Island, a coral formation (#1). I can't see any more.*

CARD VIII     REACTION TIME: 22″.     TOTAL TIME: 3′.

> 1. *(D F+ A P) I see two bob-tail cats stalking something.*

Since she later refers correctly to "bobcats" (see below, after #4), her saying "bob-tail cats" now seems to represent a verbal condensation of a sort that expresses a feared impulse (bobcat = wild cat = vicious, predatory animal) and defense against this impulse, in this instance principally denial of danger (bob-tail = tail cut short = deficient, incomplete, or domesticated).

> 2-3. *(D FC(C)+ Plant; D C(C)F Dec) I think this is a flower down here, sort of a petunia effect (lower pink and orange).* [Petunia? *The rippled-y feeling of the petals and the colors. You get some of those combinations: orange-y and pinkish tones. The upper portion left me completely cold. The blue didn't look like anything, unless it might be a piece of material. It was a pretty color and had a nice texture.*]

(a) There follow a benign image and a "cute" style of verbalization in inquiry ("rippled-y," "orange-y").

(b) A further instance of denial is suggested in inquiry when the patient considers the cooler colors: "This upper portion left me completely cold," followed by a pleasant interpretation of that area. In effect the patient seems to be saying, "Unless I can find something pleasant to say about that area, I won't deal with it at all."

> 4. *(S F± At) Well, it looks like another picture of lungs or something (usual rib area). I don't know what part of the anatomy it is. I don't know if it's lungs or not. It might be brain. I've never seen pictures like that. I believe that's sweetbreads.*

She has given only one other anatomy response and that was a spine (IV-2): ". . . another picture of lungs" therefore suggests that anatomical content has been hovering about preconsciously or even consciously but has been left unverbalized. More bodily anxiety and preoccupation than she may care to admit are suggested. Her floundering about among different anatomical possibilities also suggests noteworthy anxiety concerning her body.

> *There's a very nice feeling of those bobcats (#1) stalking, stepping with long steps very carefully. I don't see anything else.*

CARD IX    REACTION TIME: 10".    TOTAL TIME: 2' 15".

> *1. (D M± H) Two girls dancing with very full skirts. Their hair is blowing back from their heads. Their heads are back so you can't see any . . . (green).*
>
> *2. (D M+ H) Two people drinking out of a bottle (orange).*

(a) The possible and often seen hostile interaction of the orange figures is ignored. This is consistent with the patient's overall defensive policy. Conceiving the orange figures as boys, as she does in #3, implicitly makes even the drinking harmless. It may be noted now that all five of her M have been images of gaiety and play (masquerade, game, dance), considerateness (Alphonse and Gaston), and gratification (having a good time, drinking). She has scrupulously avoided possible hostile implications in these M (fighting in III, pulling in III, threatening on IV, clawing, dueling or chasing on IX).

(b) The oral gratification in this response again suggests the passive thread that is intertwined with the thread of denial.

(c) Devaluation of men may again be attempted in her transforming the men into boys.

> *3. (D FC(C)+ Obj) This must be a candle between these two dancing girls and the two boys above: a hand-dipped candle, quite irregular (mid-line). [Candle? Through the center. It has a slightly irregular shape. It is a very large candle. At the top is sort of like a bluish flame. What did you mean when you said it was "between the boys and girls?" I suppose they could be dancing around it.]*

(a) The hand-dipped candle indicates a special sensitivity to decorative values that has already been evident throughout the record although not commented on specifically. The decorative sensitivity can be seen to be meaningfully related to the heavy reliance on denial. Great concern with superficial decorative order, charm and cuteness may serve as a massive denial of the "ugly" insides and interactions of things and people. (b) The hugeness of the candle, which also seems to be a compelling phallic symbol, may derive from her fearful conception of men that appears to underlie her devaluations and denials.

> *4. (D F+ Hd) I can see a man lying down here, asleep, with a moustache (outer lower pink). There would be two of them that way, I guess. I don't see anything. . . .*

This head, though usually seen sideways, is infrequently interpreted as that of a man lying down. This patient's literal interpretation of spatial position in this instance may reflect another criticism or devaluation of the male figure. Here the man is passive, inert, possibly weak or ineffective.

CARD X    REACTION TIME: 7".    TOTAL TIME: 2' 30".

> *1. (D F+ A P) I see some land crabs (side blue).*

The land crab image has connotations of vicious, devouring attack. The remainder of the responses to this card all have passive, receptive, gratified oral implications either in the spontaneous response or in inquiry; they possibly convey denial of underlying, orally-conceived feelings of deprivation.

*2. (D F+ A) I see some beetles eating (upper gray).*

*3. (D FC+ A) And a couple of worms eating (lower green).*
*Oh! This is all nature (pleased laugh).*

*4. (D FC+ A) This could very easily be some of those caterpillars too (pink). [Caterpillar? It looked like feet along . . . how their feet look. You do get such different colored caterpillars—down in Florida, for instance. I've seen pink and all colors and they are generally fat. The symmetry on all of these made it difficult to interpret them, but I guess I shouldn't say that. I shouldn't criticize. I saw so few things. I have no imagination.]*

In her final remarks during the inquiry (the last she made in this test) the patient takes a last, implicit stab at expressing hostility. Her symmetry comment implies that the tester put her in an unfair position. Thus, she externalizes the responsibility for her relatively limited productiveness. This unproductiveness is essentially a reflection of her defensive policy of denial, avoidance and regression to passivity. However, on some level, the patient seems to sense the hostility quickly, and she retreats to apologetic self-criticism. She also continues to divorce her imagination from her desires, feelings and attitudes (see also end of Card V).

*The beetles (#2) are definitely eating a stem. These (#3) are definitely green worms.*

*5. (D F+ A) I get a stylized deer here (side gray). Maybe one of Santa Claus's reindeer, only it doesn't have any antlers.*

Another devaluation of the male figure is obliquely suggested, both in the stylized quality (see Alphonse and Gaston, III-1) and the "castrated" quality (without antlers).

*I see nothing but little bugs and worms and land crabs in this.*

A final suggestion of denial (of the scope of the orality) is present in her needlessly characterizing all the creatures on Card X as "little."

### SUMMARY OF SCORES

R: 29                    EB: 5–3(3.5)

| | | | | | | | |
|---|---|---|---|---|---|---|---|
| W | 8 | F+ | 9 | A | 9+1 | W% | 28 |
| D | 18 | F− | 1 | Ad | 2 | D% | 62 |
| Dr | 1 | F± | 3 | H | 5 | DR% | 10 |
| S | 2+1 | M | 5 | Hd | 2 | | |
| s | 0+1 | FC | 4 | Obj | 1 | F% | 45–93 |
| | | F/C | 0+1 | Dec | 2 | F+% | 92–96 |
| | | CF | 1 | Cg | 1 | | |
| | | F/C | 0+4 | At | 2 | A% | 38–41 |
| | | (C)F | 0+1 | Plant | 1 | H% | 24 |
| | | FC' | 2 | Geog | 2 | P | 9 |
| | | C'F | 1 | Misc | 2 | P% | 31 |
| | | FCh | 3 | | | | |

In general the picture emerges of a woman strenuously attempting to stave off open expression of hostility and oral and sexual needs. Only brief, abortive breakthroughs of sexual and hostile representation appear to have occurred during the testing and from these she quickly retreated. The underlying oral needs show themselves rather conspicuously, however. She seems to rely heavily on defense by denial, by passive regression, and by some projection of the resulting demandingness. She appears to try to consolidate her pollyannish position by elaborating superficial decorative interests and sensitivities and by limiting her responsiveness to outside appearances, particularly to "beautiful" appearances. It is suggested that she is particularly fearful of masculine hostility and devotes many of her denials to this problem area. It even seems that she goes beyond denial of danger; in "good-natured" ways she actually devaluates and mocks men.

The distribution of determinants in this record is in accord with the foregoing interpretations. Outstanding is her emphasis on $FC$ in her use of color (4 $FC$, one $F/C$, and only one $CF$), and her emphasis on $FC'$, $F(C)$ and $FCh$ in her use of shading (2 $FC'$, 4 $F(C)$ and 3 $FCh$ versus one $C'F$ and one $(C)F$), and her emphasis on popular and near-popular images in her choice of content (9 $P$ and very few responses out of the ordinary). Her orientation seems to be steadily "adaptive," "tactful," and "sensitive," but it overemphasizes control (relatively high *extended F%* and $F+\%$) and superficial passive compliance (too few indications of spontaneity, particularly $CF$). The presence of 3 $S$ in this record calls attention to the possibility that a significant negativistic, stubborn, rebellious streak shows through her defensive overadaptiveness.

Also noteworthy in the record is the presence of five $M$, a relatively high number considering the strict scoring standards employed. The five $M$ suggest richer imaginative potentialities than are actualized in the record. As has been emphasized, however, defense by denial is an ego-restrictive solution. The contrast between the excellent resources of this patient (IQ of 135 and 5 $M$) and her relatively limited responsiveness and role underscore this point. Thematic analysis suggests that this patient may even tend to conceal her assets for defensive purposes, as she does her emotional neediness and hostility, and yet be capable of shrewd, sensitive, strong neurotic maneuvers.

### D. Unstable Hypomanic Defense by Denial (and Projection)

Hypomanic denials cannot be discussed without frequent reference to the defense mechanism of projection. In many hypomanic cases, projection and denial obviously work hand in hand to keep the self-concept and the surrounding world "pure" and above reproach. For one thing, the expansiveness associated with hypomanic euphoria and that associated with megalomanic paranoid pathology are very similar in their formal aspects, even though they emerge from different pathological contexts. Also, both involve thought disorder characterized by reference ideas and implications of omnipotence and omniscience.

It seems that persons predisposed to hypomanic reactions not only deny what is painful, but freely and conveniently project their own unacceptable impulses and derivatives of these onto painful situations. Then, in addition to accomplishing this purification of the self like a paranoid person, they adopt a counter-paranoid attitude. They deny the now externalized threat.* Thus, unacceptable, threatening, guilt-laden tendencies are projected and the projections then denied. When the superimposed denials are unstable, this defensive strategy is exposed and the projections tend to emerge more or less clearly. One often wonders then whether the basic pathology is not paranoid rather than hypomanic, with the hypomanic features representing secondary defensive operations.

Once the defensive operations begin to fail, the inadequately denied projections may be left exposed as such, or, as is not uncommon, they may be taken back into the self in the following manner: the externalized "fact" is regarded as a magical sign or omen of one's inner state or fate and it is reacted to in the same manner as the original impulse would be reacted to were it to be acknowledged directly. For example, such a defensively unstable patient may come to the painful conclusion that he is "horrible" because, by projection, he has "perceived" irritability in someone close to him. Were he defensively stronger, he could have successfully denied this paranoid perception and thereby staved off the feeling of guilt and the indirect acknowledgment of his own hostility; perhaps he would even be struck by the "wonderful" unaggressiveness of that person. Thus, in the unstable hypomanic state we find not only denials and failures of denial, but paranoid projections and failures of these projections as well. Generalized fluidity of ego boundaries is implied.

Schematically, the typical unstable defensive sequence in these cases will be: (1) I am in trouble and am showing up unacceptably and inadequately in coping with the trouble (original problem); (2) I am in trouble because they (other people) are unacceptable and inadequate while I am showing up very well (partial denial of problem; projection); (3) I am not in trouble because everything and everybody, including myself, is wonderful (complete denial of problems; denial of projection); (4) they are horrible and making trouble for me (denial of projection failing); (5) I am horrible and in trouble because I see horrible things in them (partial failure of projection and denial; only the external shell of these defenses is preserved).

What is it in the hypomanic setting that must be denied to begin with or

---

* In this respect their dynamics seem to be continuous with those of the pollyannish person.

else projected first and then denied? Psychoanalytic study of hypomanic patients indicates that what is denied and projected usually derives from and reflects the following configuration: a painful life situation that stimulates and/or frustrates strong narcissistic, oral-aggressive and oral-receptive impulses and accompanying demanding attitudes and feelings of helplessness and neediness. The patient reacts to these impulses, attitudes and feelings with intense anxiety, guilt and depression. He then tries to deny everything: the disturbing life situation, the threatening or thwarted impulses and their derivatives, and his painful reactions to these impulses. He typically behaves as if he has completely solved all his life problems or at least now has the key to their solution; thereby the painful reality and feelings of helplessness are denied. He also behaves as if he is happy, untroubled and self-accepting, and not at all guilty, anxious and depressed. Acting out the fantasy of possessing unlimited oral supplies, he puts on a grandiose show of generosity, nurturance, self-sufficiency, good will, good ideas and love of life. Thus the hostile, demanding, narcissistic orality is denied.

Often, the oral emphasis is displaced to the sexual sphere. In these instances, sexual desire or potency may come to stand for denial of hostile, passive, helpless impulses and feelings, while dependence and sexual inactivity or unresponsiveness may come to stand for these unacceptable impulses and feelings.

Actually, careful observation of this entire behavioral and experiential configuration usually reveals that it is by no means free of expression of the denied impulses and the painful reactions to them. Frequently the defense is "invaded" by the defended-against impulses and feelings. The hypomanic's "good spirits" then take on a relentless, unilateral, taxing, overwhelming quality. He becomes irritable if even slightly challenged, ignored or confronted with a show of spirits lower than his; and he demands of his captive audience that they reassure and gratify him through their steady attention and appreciation. Similarly evident upon close scrutiny is the depression and mirthlessness underlying the hypomanic's driven (though possibly very witty) euphoria.

When the hypomanic defense is strikingly unstable, as in the sudden development of a psychotic or near-psychotic hypomanic state or in the decompensation of a chronic hypomanic character, the anxiety, guilt and depression and the hostile, narcissistic, oral impulses and feelings lurk around every corner. Under these circumstances, the patient must constantly overextend his resources to block perception of the real external and internal crisis. In fact, his defensive ego operations are often one desperate jump behind the erupting painful feelings and perceptions. Mood and self-regard then typically fluctuate rapidly and extremely.

## E. Text Expectations in Hypomania

Rorschach content and test attitudes are particularly sensitive to such defensive struggles and instability. In content and attitudes we may therefore expect to observe a more or less rapid shifting back and forth between expressions of denial and expressions of the denied. According to the psychodynamic rationale of hypomania, we might expect the following types of imagery to be readily available to the patient's ego in its efforts to cope with the inkblots and the test situation.

*1. On the side of the denied,* images of guilt (hell, devils, demons, fire and brimstone), oral-aggressive and oral-receptive images (food and food objects, open mouths, breasts, teeth, jaws, crocodiles, wolves, whales, pigs), aggressive, erupting images (bombs, explosions, fires, storm clouds), and images of helplessness, gloom and despair (worn, torn, broken, destroyed, empty, barren, ugly objects).

*2. On the side of the denials,* images of innocence (cathedrals, angels, cherubs, lambs), images of abundant supply and potency (waiters, fat persons, breasts, semen, erections), benign, serene images (gentle clouds, beautiful flowers and landscapes), and images of gaiety, abandon and hope (springtime, festivals, laughing and playing figures, children and toys).

*3. As a reflection of defensive instability,* all through the test the denied may invade the denials and the denials may be rushed in to repudiate eruptions of the denied. As a result, changing characterizations and reinterpretations of single responses and single cards should be common, along with response sequences that range from Heaven to Hell, Darkness to Light, etc.

Among the various specific forms this instability may take, the following are common. (a) *"Magical" use of color.* For example, "I would say a small demon on each side (Card III, upper red) except red is a good color and makes me feel cheerful so I know what they are! They are disguised! They are really cherubim blowing trumpets!" "Reminds me of the alimentary canal or intestines, snow-white, all cleaned up and free and open" (Card V, space between side projections). "A battleship (middle space, Card II) only it's too hopeful for that. (Hopeful?) It's white and that's a hopeful color."

(b) *Shift of attention from content to form.* For example, "Witches (Card I, side D). They are very good witches!" Here it seems that the patient praises herself on her perceptual accomplishment in order to gloss over potentially threatening content. The following shift of attention from content to spatial position suggests failure of denial: "It could be a pedestal with the world turning . . . only it's upside down" (projection on lower edge of Card I). As a rule, spatial literalness occurs only occasionally and in each instance probably has specific dynamic implications; in this example, the patient's original image suggests an attempt at expansive, world-embracing denial of need and fear, while her subsequent altered relation to this image suggests a breakthrough of feeling that the world is actually topsy-turvy, that is, a confusing, uncontrolled and threatening place.

(c) *Confabulation.* Confabulations for purposes of denial often involve magical use of color, as described above, along with flat assertions concerning what "should" or "should not" be in the picture and insistence on personal feelings being more important than objective perceptual details. For example, "It's a bat (Card V, *W*). It really isn't a bat after all! It's an insect with two little horns, and in spite of its color it's a nice insect! It has a slight growth on the right wing. The growth is grayer than the rest which is a sign that it will disintegrate and go away and it will be a free moth which will not die in the candle-flame!" "This looks like a little animal (Card VIII, *P*). . . . It's pulling, both animals are pulling a gray mass (upper gray-green) away from here (midline) so it will be nice and white (internal spaces). That's beautiful! It's an inkblot but it's a creative inkblot! . . . The gray mass doesn't belong there! It's not truthful! It should be an entirely cheerful picture!" "A beating heart (Card III, lower middle). (What made it look like a beating heart?) Because I wanted it to be a beating heart, because I *know* it's a beating heart!"

(d) *Overemphasizing specific responses.* For example, after seeing several disturbing responses on Card IV, including an instrument of sexual torture, one hypomanic patient went on to see a baby elephant from the *Just So* stories and then asserted "And this is such a nice thing to find in this sinister picture which is no longer sinister!"

*Typical hypomanic test behavior and attitudes toward responses* have already been touched on in Chapter 2 on the psychology of the testing situation (see page 55). In general, the hypomanic may be expected to be emotionally over-responsive to the tester, to the inkblots, and to his own responses. He will run the gamut from interest, gaiety, excitement and pleasure to intense anxiety, self-reproaches, irritability and possibly even tears. When euphoric features are prominent, the record should contain, in addition, puns, quips, self-references, and rambling tending toward irrelevancy and chain-thinking. In general, there should be a driven outpouring of words, associations, digressions and emotions. This out-pouring itself may represent a denial of the patient's intense oral need to take in. Hostile noncompliance and demandingness, basic detachment from the tester, and a sense of desperation will probably run through all of this as it does through most hypomanic behavior. In short, test behavior and test attitudes, explicit and implicit, should betray the same instability and the same warring factions as the shifts in content previously described.

With less certainty, we may expect certain scores to be emphasized: high *W* (grandiose aspirations) and/or numerous tiny *Dr* and *De* (scattered, fragmented, restless, undisciplined intellectual approach to prob-

lems); high $S$ (negativistic, rebellious undercurrents); forced and artificial use of color, as in $F/C$, $C/F$, $FC$ *arbitrary* and $C$ *symbolic* (driven,
empty, dramatized emotional responsiveness and "adaptiveness"); emphasis
on black and white as colors (black being associated with guilt, ugliness
and disaster, and white with innocence, loveliness and hope); relatively
low $A\%$ (flighty, scattered thinking); and among the scores of verbalization, *Confabulation* (blurred or lost line between reality and fantasy), *Self-
reference, Symbolic,* and *Fluid* (flightiness).

## F. Two Case Studies of Hypomania

### Case 1

The first hypomanic patient to be considered is a 54-year-old, married,
Catholic woman with four children. She had two years of college education.
Her total IQ is 121, superior range. The clinical diagnosis was "decompensated hypomanic and compulsive character disorder with psychotic features,
depressive and paranoid trends and symptomatic alcoholism." The patient
had been acutely depressed a few weeks before she was seen for psychiatric
evaluation; however, at the time of testing, she was for the most part
moderately elated.

From the standpoint of estrangement from reality, this is a borderline
case. Concerning her dynamics, as revealed by the tests, *in the denied* the
themes that will stand out are aging and decay, fears of loss of control, an
orally hostile, deprived, guilt-ridden self-concept, and a combination of
masculine identification and mixed disparagement and paranoid fear of
men, while *in the denials* the outstanding themes will be control, innocence,
optimism and maternal benevolence.

CARD I   REACTION TIME: 8".   TOTAL TIME: 2′.

> 1. *(W Ch(C)F At)* Part of one's anatomy. [Any particular part? *No.*
> What made it look like anatomy? *When I first looked: the shadows at
> first looked like anatomy, looked like bones, particularly across the chest.
> I thought you wanted a snap impression at first. Sort of like an x-ray.*]
> *I don't like it; I mean, I don't like blots.*

(a) The patient seems to feel threatened almost at once and to try to deal with
this threat by rejecting inkblots altogether. Inquiry into the first response elicits
no specific content that clearly explains her anxiety, but it does elicit externalization of responsibility for the response ("I thought you wanted a snap impression at first."). This defensive reaction to inquiry suggests that she feels she is
being criticized. It is probably no accident, however, that the externalization
of responsibility involves the notion of "snap impression"—snap impressions
being particularly attractive to elated, hyperactive persons.

Of course, the patient's anxiety may have been stimulated by the formation of
this vague anatomical response, since anatomical content may be linked to
anxiety about her bodily status. The theme of physical decay is prominent
throughout the record. It is also possible, however, that her anxiety is in reaction

to the test situation as a whole, and that she has staved off awareness of this reaction only long enough to form one poor response. Still another possibility is that this anxious reaction is related to her third response ("something rather sinister about it"), the sinister element having been obstructed until after her second response (bat). That is to say, preconscious perception of the forming of the third image could have been the source of the initial anxiety and the subsequent rejecting attitude toward the test. In this case, "I don't like blots" would mean "I don't like what I am beginning to think of and am trying not to think of as I look at the blots."

2. *(W F+ A P) Or a bat; never having seen a bat, but . . .*

3. *(D M+ H Confabulation tendency) There's something rather sinister about it. A figure in the middle with hands up (middle D).* [Sinister? *A small head, a big body, and short hands lifted up like this, as though he needed elongation for strength. Mostly a body with a small head, muscular but with no mentality: that's why you could go back almost to prehistoric ages with it. A for effort (laugh) or E for nonsense!*]
*Do I give multiple responses?*

4. *(Ws ChF Geog) A map.*

5. *(Dr F(C)— Ad Peculiar) Eyes of elephants over here on the left (in side shading); sort of the animal kingdom to it.*
*It's a fairly identical, it's divided in halves with the exception of the dots. That's why I say a map (#4), because the spaces could be lakes and the shadows mountains. But in the whole, I don't like it! To me it would represent the worst . . . (laughter).*

6. *(W C' Inferno Symbolic) If you were thinking of a poem, it would look like Dante's Inferno. It certainly wouldn't be anything bright and lovely!*

(a) Response #3 has a number of possible implications: (1) Ordinarily this area is seen as a woman. The sex reversal suggests a strong element of masculine identification in this patient. (2) "Muscular but with no mentality" suggests fears of loss of control of impulses. (3) By making him into a dumb brute, this response also suggests a devaluating orientation toward the male figure. (4) At the same time it suggests fear of this dumb brute. (5) That the figure needs strength contradicts the rest of the impression, however, and suggests something unstable in the patient's conception of masculinity. She may be unsure whether masculinity implies strength or weakness, i.e., whether to be awed by it or to sneer at it.

In any event, the image, as it occurs spontaneously, seems to be anxiety-arousing. Not only is it "sinister," but it leads her at once, in her next verbalization ("Do I give multiple responses?"), to question whether she should have given more than one response. Here she shifts her position with respect to the test responses, her question implying anxious regret that she did go beyond the first response.

(b) The anxiety involved in this "sinister" response is soon dealt with by denial. The patient suddenly increases distance from the response during the inquiry, disparages it as a response, no longer reacts to it as a psychological reality, and laughs at herself. Her laughter itself suggests a falling back on hypomanic denial of the threat. These defensive maneuvers seem to be ineffective, however, the patient returning to the "sinister" impression in her sixth response. She again declares her dislike of the blot, forces laughter, indicates by her reference to Dante's *Inferno* that guilt has been too strongly stimulated, projects the responsibility for her entire immediate psychological problem onto the card, and finally makes a bald statement of her heavy reliance on denial: "It certainly wouldn't be anything bright and lovely" apparently means "It should be; it must be; I can't take this kind of thing for very long!"

(c) It is worthwhile to think back at this point to the previously discussed pollyannish patient with multiple somatic symptoms (see pp. 242–50). That she was a much better, though extremely rigid, denier than this patient is evident in her having transformed Card I into something light and lovely (a beautiful tropical butterfly). It is implied that the present patient's ego status is too unstable for her to accomplish such a masterpiece of pathological denial. Although she would obviously like to, she cannot fend off hostile, guilt-laden imagery and is forced to fall back on increased projection, criticism of the card, defensiveness toward the tester, forced laughter and the like.

CARD II    REACTION TIME: 15″.    TOTAL TIME: 4′.

> *1. (W CC' Fire Peculiar) Well, fire and brimstone, the fire being the red and the brown or black being the brimstone.*

> *2. (Dd F+ Arch) Right here sort of a cathedral idea; a little steeple (upper middle).*

Response #1 provides a classical statement through test imagery of guilt and anticipation of punishment (see I-6). This becomes her problem on Card II, and the patient turns at once, in her second response, to religious, "pure" imagery. In particular, fire and brimstone suggests the destruction visited upon the immoral and faithless in Sodom and Gomorrah.

> *3. (D F+ Ad P) The figures here are like two Scotties, the heads of two Scotties, not the whole body.*

> *4. (D F± Sex) This part here is like a sexual organ (all lower red).* [What made it look like that? *I think the division and the curve.* Anything else? *No.* What kind of organ do you mean? *A woman's.*]

> *5. (S FC'+ Obj) This middle part, the light: a bright light (middle space).* [What made it look like that? *The center part was so white in comparison to the blackness around and rather perfectly done in comparison with the ragged edges of the entire blot.*]

> *6. (S FC'+ Dec) The same (middle space) would be a pendant from a chain, a piece of jewelry.*

> *7. (S C'F Dec) Or it might be a piece of marble (middle space): the contrast with the black.* [Marble? *Something pure; something rather lovely. And the shape, the pendant idea: it looks like it could be hanging from a chain like a stone. It has lightness.*]

In #5, #6 and #7 the patient seems to continue elaborating her denial of guilt by emphasizing the purity theme—something light, pure, lovely, etc.

> *8. (Dr F+ Obj) Way down here, this little tiny—should I call it blot? —looks like one of those bowling pins in a bowling alley (lower middle; usual vagina area).*

> *9. (Dr F± Hd) The two parts up here, the top, look like parts of the joint of the finger, your thumb rather (top of upper red).*

*10. (D F(C)+ Hd) And taking the red as a whole you could see faces of little children with snow hat or scarf around the neck (upper red).*

*The Scotty puppies (#3) could also look like wild boars. If you wanted to civilize it, it could be a Scotty, but if you wanted it wild, it would be a wild boar.*

(a) At this point, denial seems to be working well, the patient coolly manipulating the popular animal response, and thereby implicitly stating that the problem of primitive impulses versus civilized restraint is perfectly under control. We have here a defensively secure self-representation as opposed to the defensively insecure "muscular (figure) but with no mentality" in I-3. (b) The wild boar image is also noteworthy for its attacking, tearing, gluttonous aspects.

*11. (s F± H) And then this figure could be an umpire in a baseball game with a breastplate on and a cap (tiny space in lower middle); the eyes there (specks).*

CARD III     REACTION TIME: 15".     TOTAL TIME: 2' 45".

*1–2. (W M+ (H) P; D C Fire Confabulation tendency) Well, my first quick impression (laugh) . . . is witches over a caldron, this being the caldron down here (lower middle). [Witch? The caldron and the red affair over it. I just think of witches . . . witches. What about the red affair? It looked like fire, coming out of the caldron. . . . But they look more like hobos or caricatures (see after #5, below).]*

(a) The witch symbol generally expresses a hostile, evil, powerful conception of the mother. When her magic flying broomstick is emphasized, the phallic aspects of her hostility and power are underscored; when her ensnaring, depriving, devouring qualities are emphasized, the oral aspects of her hostility and power are underscored. In this image the caldron, with its implication of magically potent or poisonous brew reinforces the oral aggressive implications. (b) This response is also noteworthy for the reversal of the usual sex ascribed to the popular figure. This is another indication of prominent masculine identification elements in this woman's character (see I-3). On this level of analysis, sex reversals in either direction indicate uncertainty as to one's own sexual identity and this in turn suggests noteworthy identification with the opposite sex. (c) After #5, and in inquiry into this first response, the patient changes the popular figures back into men, possibly attempting thereby to deny the "evil, oral woman" theme. The denial of the original image seems to go even further, however: these are not orally hostile figures; these are poor, dilapidated, ineffective failures. In one respect the patient may be saying, "It is not that I am a hostile, demanding, controlling, poisonous creature; men (my father? my husband?) are weak and totally inadequate providers." In another respect she may be emphasizing deterioration of the male figure.

*3. (D FC'± Plant) These two (P leg): limbs of trees. [What made it look like that? Like just looking out that window (of tester's office): a certain. . . . It's in winter. It's dead limbs of trees, not summer limbs of trees. Dead? It had no leaves and it looked dead. How? It looked charred. Charred? It looked like you might put it right into a fireplace.]*

The theme of masculine deterioration is again suggested, symbolically, in the image of the dead, wintry, burnt-out limb (see #2).

*4. (D FCh+ Cg) These two (lower middle D): fur mittens. [Fur?*

*There seemed to be more depth to those two blots, as though it could be a fur. It doesn't look quite as flat as the rest of the blot.]*

There is an accumulating emphasis on decorative images, images that could represent the fruits of her denial-oriented search for "bright and lovely things." On Card II there are the cathedral, bright light, pendant and marble; on Card III there are the fur mittens and the vase (# 6, below).

*5. (D FC'— Plant) This could be part of trees, limbs of an old tree (P arm, torso, head).*

More emphasis on masculine deterioration (see #2, 3).

*And this whole thing (#1) could be either a caricature or an old hobo. I say hobo on account of this (chest area) gives the impression of rags and tatters.*

Raggedness around the chest area may suggest particular concern with the theme of the poor (oral) provider. There may be a complaint in this response that the male figure is inadequately nurturant, and underlying this may be concern with loss of her own capacity to provide as a woman—in which case the complaint against the man becomes partly at least a projection.

*6. (D F+ Dec) This could be a vase, this center part (lower middle light gray).*

*7. (D FM+ A) And . . . these things (upper red) don't seem to mean a thing to me, unless it's something hanging by its legs: a monkey—but the color distorts it for a monkey—hanging from a tree.*

CARD IV     REACTION TIME: 40".     TOTAL TIME: 6' 40".

*1. (W MCh± H Confabulation tendency) My first impression of this— except the heads always seem so small: there's no head to this—but it could be somebody who is dressed all up in part fur and yet the arms are exposed, the feet are terribly large, and yet there is no head. That's the whole thing, with this (lower sides) as the feet. The upper part of the body here, the arms (upper sides) and head (upper middle) being emaciated. [Fur? Like sort of mangy fur; the depth every so often. It looked like an old, moth-eaten, bearskin coat. With the boots (see #3 below), it could be Puss-in-the-Boots. And it could be some mythological or strange creature wandering through the lands with no head.]*

This image seems to restate the themes of I-3, III-3, and the "hobo" postscript to III-1. We now have both a large figure with no head (threat of losing control), and a mangy and emaciated figure (deteriorating, starved).

*2. (D F(C)+ Hd Confabulation tendency) Then there is a face here (upper middle shading): not a true face because the nose is enlarged, but I would rather say a villainous character (laugh) with long eyebrows, yes, and going up so toward the temples, and half-closed eyes, but no mouth at all. It looks more like a wrinkle from the mouth or a deep line or even a moustache. It looks just like a villain to me! I wouldn't like to meet him in the dark, or in the daytime either! That's off the record (laugh); just to you!*

(a) The patient apparently attempts to deny the anxiety in this response by shifting her attention to her relationship with the tester: getting chummy and making a joke out of the response. In itself this joking could be a positive sign, implying ability to laugh at herself in an engaging way. However, within a total context that includes many marked instances of denial, its positive implications are questionable. (b) Preoccupation with the absence of the mouth of this figure suggests specific denial of oral aggressive and receptive impulses—a denial that is central in the dynamics of the hypomanic state.

> 3. (D F+ Cg Fluid) Then if you just wanted to take one of these or one of these: like the fairy story of the old boot (lower side D). [Which story? Puss-in-the-Boots.]

Age is again emphasized ("old boot"), but in the inquiry into the first response we see that the "old" is denied by a complete reversal. The boots are now the magically powerful boots of Puss-in-Boots. At the same time, the inadequacy of the mangy, emaciated figure in #1 is partially denied. What seems to occur is a condensation of ineffective aspects (puss, mangy, old) and a denial of these (magic powers).

> 4. (Dr M— (H) Fluid, Contamination tendency) This section here might be a mermaid. There's no tail and the head is disfigured (outer portion, lower side light gray). [How did it look like a mermaid if there was no tail? I think of the rest (of the mermaid) going down under the water. Was the mermaid related to the peninsula (#6)? The mermaid is the whole thing but the lighthouse (#8) gave me the idea of the mermaid.]

(a) This response, an image of an asexual though alluring female figure, again suggests an uncertain sense of sexual identity and thereby noteworthy repudiation of the feminine sexual role (see I-3, III-1).

(b) The absence of a tail is denied in inquiry but the spontaneous verbalization (no tail, disfigured head) again sounds a note of feelings of inadequacy and dilapidation.

> 5. (Dr F+ A) Might be an animal of some kind (same area as #4).
>
> 6. (D F∓ Geog) And then it might be a peninsula (same area as #4).
>
> 7. (Dr F— A) And these two little things here: if you wanted to think of it in a northern clime, you could think of seals (tiny projection on upper edge of lower side "shoe" projection).
>
> 8. (Dr F— Arch) Or think of lighthouses (same area as #7).
>
> 9. (Dr F+ Geog) This portion looks like the southern part of Africa (dark in lower side D).
>
> 10. (Dr F— Arch) And these two places here and here look like citadels or churches in the distance (tiny projection on upper edge). That little spiral going up could be a citadel or fortress or church in the distance.

One possible implication of her doubt as to whether the structure is a fortress or a church is that her religious faith may represent a major alternative to (and defense against) hostility.

> 11. (Dr F(C)— Hd) There's a man here: two eyes; rather wavy hair; shadowy, of course. He looks like a warrior; old (full-face; left of upper midline).

The male figure is both hostile and aging, but #12, on the opposite side of the card, denies this characterization.

> 12. (Dr F(C)+ Hd) There's a profile on this side (right of upper midline) of a rather esthetic person with a long aquiline nose.

CARD V     REACTION TIME: 5″.     TOTAL TIME: 2′ 45″.

*1. (W F+ A P) This again looks like a bat or an animal; a flying creature.*

*2. (Dd F+ Hd) These two little figures look like two different, look like little gnomes (upper middle). Or if you took them individually and not looking at each other, they could be ancient priests of the Greek church with the tall hats.*

(a) She again disparages men (gnomes) and emphasizes their age ("ancient"), but simultaneously indicates idealization of them (priests). (b) Religious preoccupation is also suggested again.

*3. (Dr F(C)— Hd) A horrible old man down here. He has bushy hair (in lower outer wing). [What was horrible about him? He had a very large mouth.]*

This response again pertains to a hostile and aging man. In this instance, the hostility seems rather clearly to be orally conceived.

*4. (D F∓ Geog) If it weren't formed so almost identically, it could be an island (each half). [What made it look like that? You could think of crags and . . . or . . . that white space, if I use my imagination. . . . That's just half of it. How did it resemble an island? The juttings and promontories.]*

*5. (Dr F+ Hd) And these faces are almost comic. Here is the hair. They have prominent noses and very little mouth and a large head.*

A mouth is again almost eliminated (see IV-2). This is especially noteworthy since inquiry into #3 elicited emphasis on a "very large mouth." The contrast of a large mouth in a horrible face and a small mouth in a comic face suggests that horror is associated with ravenous, hostile orality and gaiety with denial of orality. This inference is in accord with the psychoanalytic theory of hypomania.

*I don't like it (laugh). [Why didn't you like it? I didn't like the shadows and blackness.]*

Anxious and depressive feelings are stimulated by the dark colors. The general run of responses to Card V appears to be in line with this unpleasant global response to the dark colors. We shall see more of this aversion to darkness as well as her attraction to light after Card VI. Note how she laughs after "I don't like it"—a likely denial of the critical attitude she is verbalizing.

CARD VI     REACTION TIME: 35″.     TOTAL TIME: 3′ 50″.

*1. (Dr F+ (Hd)) This looks like a weird figure here (upper tip): here are the eyes, a dark nose, no mouth; just in caricature, of course. [What sort of figure? A totem pole.]*

Again we have a face with no mouth, only this time it is "weird" and therefore may contradict the interpretation of V-5.

*2. (Dr FC′∓ Obj Peculiar) Then, it doesn't look like a river to me, but this entire thing—except that it's split down here—could be a lamp post (midline without upper tip). [Lamp post? It gives off indirect lighting.]*

Further emphasis on light (see II-5, 6, 7 and end of V).

> 3. *(D ChF Geog) And there's a vague suggestion of maps on account of you can see mountains in it and valleys and desert (lower D).*

Introducing the theme of a desert in this landscape is unusual and revealing. In the desert image there are likely to be thematic implications of barrenness and oral deprivation (see her elaboration of III-1 following III-5).

> 4. *(D FCh± (Hd) Confabulation tendency, Peculiar) And a figure here (each ½ of lower D). It looks like old stone, like the Old Man of the Mountains carved out in the rock, not by a good sculptor. It looks ravished by age. [Ravished by age? It looked ragged and not perfect. It looks as though storms or winds or the sea had done something to it, because it is very irregular. And it was done by an ordinary person, not a sculptor.* What made it look like stone? *I think the shadows in it: they just look like rocks to me.*]

(a) Here is another reference to a deteriorating old man ("ravished by age") and a disparagement of the male figure (a poor specimen to begin with).

(b) Her peculiar verbal substitution of "ravished" for *ravaged* may indicate that she somehow connects sexual abuse with the feelings of deterioration she has been emphasizing.

> 5. *(Dr FC'+ Obj) This part from here down could look like a thermometer (midline in lower D).*
>
> 6. *(D ChF Cl) And this can, in spite of the fact that that odd figure (#1) looks horrible—if you wanted to separate that—could look like clouds in the sky (upper wings).*
>
> 7. *(D ChF Geog) Or a map again (upper wings).*
>
> 8. *(Dr F+ Hd) And if you cover it all up. . . . I sort of like those (outer edges of upper wings). You see hands, fingers I should say (patient demonstrates graceful hand position).*
>
> 9. *(Dr F+ Ad) Cat's whiskers (on upper tip).*
>
> 10. *(Dr C' Light) But there's a light here (base of upper D). I sort of like that! [A light? It looked like a light below the shadow.]*

The graceful fingers in the eighth response and the pleasing light of this response indicate efforts to deny the unpleasant imagery previously stimulated. In particular, the "light beneath the shadows" may be an attempt to deny the significance of the shadows by making them superficial.

CARD VII    REACTION TIME: 20".    TOTAL TIME: 3' 35".

> 1. *(D F— Geog) This is a—do you have children?—this is a child's version of a map of America, North and South America (laugh), slightly overexaggerated but . . . (upper ⅔).*

Note the motherly tone in her verbalization.

> 2–3. *(D F+ Ad; D F+ Hd P) These two figures just look like either little mad dogs, or a—I was just thinking of my little girl's drawing— she's nine—like a little girl who is going to have her hair shampooed, with soap suds, and she always puts suds way up like that and looks at herself in the mirror.*

(a) In "little mad dogs" we have a classic instance of denial and that which is being denied being simultaneously expressed. (b) The oral aggressive, rabid emphasis in #2 is quickly denied in #3 in which her motherliness begins to be precious. A pseudo-maternal, "mouthless" role that denies her intense oral impulses is suggested. (c) Underlying projection of oral aggressiveness onto her daughter may also be reflected in the sequence-transformation of the mad dog into her daughter. The patient's affectionate manner of verbalization strictly denies this projection. (d) In #s 1, 2 and 3, she seems to be implicitly criticizing the inkblots as poor (childish) representations (see also X-10).

4. *(D F+ Geog) A map of Spain (right middle ⅓).*

5. *(Dr F+ Arch) This right here—as though I were seeing it from a distance—could be a temple (light lower middle).*

6. *(Dr F+ (H) Confabulation tendency) And all out of proportion to the size of the temple would be a statue of, oh, a particular saint, the Blessed Virgin . . . (dark lower middle, above #5).*

The fifth and sixth responses elaborate a religious image with particular emphasis on the pure, saintly woman and mother—the Blessed Virgin. Because it occurs in an area relatively frequently seen as female genitals, the image is especially striking. It seems to imply self-purification, rejection of the feminine sexual role, and glorification of maternity (see IV-4, and also VIII-2, 3, below). The way that the patient has the Madonna towering over everything in this image suggests that she grandiosely identifies herself with this figure.

7. *(Dr F∓ Mt) And it would be in mountainous country: there are mountains here (upper middle edge, lower ⅓).*

8. *(Dr ChF Cl) And a cloud idea in the background (upper edge, lower ⅓).*

But now in #7 and #8 an ominous element creeps into the holy, virginal, exquisitely maternal image: its surroundings are cloudy and mountainous. It is as if the patient is saying, "My defense by denial, through religion and identification with pure, maternal figures, is surrounded by dangers."

9. *(Dr F— Ad) And also those two little—a terrific contrast, I'll admit—look like two lions facing each other (upper middle edge of lower ⅓). [Lions? They looked like male lions. There's the mane. They're in profile, of course.]*

(a) As suggested by her concern with the "terrific contrast," this response is likely to be meaningfully related to the previous few. In particular, some breakdown of the denial elaborated in the four previous responses now seems to occur. The lion—an orally-attacking, primitive, masculine image—is seen very close to the vaginal-virginal-maternal area. This lion image may well represent what is specifically feared and denied by these "pure" images. (b) Note again the tie-up of masculinity and oral-aggressiveness (see V-3).

10. *(W ChF Putty) It looks like putty a child would try to mold together into a figure—the whole thing. And then they'd make something out of it. [Putty? I was thinking of what we'd gone through over Christmas with all this putty around. She had little pieces all around and starts making the state of Maine, let's say, and puts mountains and valleys in it.]*

Very likely the anxiety stimulated by the previous response leads to this formless,

shaded response. In the inquiry, true to her policy of denial, the patient "dresses up" this momentary decompensation with a conspicuous display of motherliness.
*I don't think there's much else.*

CARD VIII     REACTION TIME: 12".     TOTAL TIME: 2′ 45″.

*1. (W F/C∓ At) The first is anatomy again.*
See inquiry into #6 for basis of *F/C* score.

*2–3. (Dr F— A; Dr F+ Pl) Then it suggests mythological figures, fairy-tale figures, because they're all out of line. Here are two animals going up here (sides of upper gray), their heads buried in a fir tree (middle of upper gray).* [Fir tree? *Just the design of it and the pointed top; it was cone-shaped.*]
Further playful, motherly emphasis.

*4. (D F+ A P) Here are two more animals.*

*5. (S F+ Hd) There's a face in here (middle space; rib area). This (midline) obliterates part of it. The mouth is turned down once again. There's sort of a turban on his head.*
Another hostile, oral masculine image (see V-3, VII-9).

*6. (D CF At) And this (lower pink and orange) sort of looks like part of the body. I haven't looked at a medical book for forty years but it looks like one we had home; some part of the bawdy-er-body.* [What made it look like part of the body? *Once more (reference to #1) the sort of vertebri and the lower part in color looks like an organ of the body. I wouldn't know which one, but I remember these pictures in a book.* How was it like an organ? *The pinkness of color in all probability, and the shape.*]

A significant slip occurs; the patient is being vague about her anatomical impression and then says "bawdy" instead of *body*. This suggests that the not infrequently seen vagina in the lower middle was being inadequately repressed or consciously suppressed. The probable content of the slip—i.e., sex is bawdy —suggests strong sexual guilt. This is in line with the implications of the Blessed Virgin in VII-6 and the Sodom-and-Gomorrah perverse connotations of the fire and brimstone in II-1.

CARD IX     REACTION TIME: 18".     TOTAL TIME: 3′ 50″.

*1. (D F/C+ Obj) This is a small candle but it burns a green light instead of a yellow one (midline).*

*2. (Dr F∓ Ad) Like a cat over here (orange-green shading; full-face).*

*3. (D FC∓ A) These two look like fish (inner sections, lower pink) with little fins out here (streaks up to green).* [What made it look like that? *They looked like shellfish or blowfish of some sort, and they are pink too.*]

*4. (Dd F+ Ad) A crab up here (upper middle projections).* [Crab? *It had scraggly little claws.* Anything else? *Mostly the claws.*]
*There's something nice about this part up here, as though you were going into something rather nice (upper middle space). I can't tell what. (Patient demonstrates ascending, curving, graceful movement.)*

*5. (D FM+Hd,Ad) Face of a baboon—or a prehistoric man rather (green). He has wild hair (upper outer edge) and a short arm (stub on outer edge): that's why I say prehistoric.* [Prehistoric? *He had a prominent chin, almost like a monkey or gorilla.*]

This image and its alternative formulations appear to combine the previously noted fearful conception of men (prehistoric, wild gorilla) and disparaging and fear-denying defense against this conception (baboon, monkey, short or "castrated" arm).

*6–7. (S C'F Light Confabulation, Peculiar; S F∓ Ldsc) I wish I could see something I really liked, except I like the color up here very much—soft green going into pale orange-y shades. There seems to be a feeling of light (upper middle space), almost a temple for the gods with this curve up here (upper edge of middle space); something rather mythological. And if you wanted to take this part (middle space proper): it could be sort of a lake or a mountain. There is something way at the height of it, the top of it (tiny projection, upper center).* [What suggested a temple for gods? *That tiny section in between.* Which section? *(Card shown.) Oh, this candle glowing (#1) and all this light up here (upper middle space), as though it were lighting up a temple for the gods.* Did you see a temple? *No.* Did that thing at the top suggest something in particular? *It's a statue up here and then there's light; this (space) is just the essence of light going up. (Card removed.)* What did you mean by "essence of light"? *It wasn't pure, unadulterated light. It was just a glow from behind something.*]

The theme of religious exaltation which began after #4 ("going into something nice") is now elaborated in #6 and #7. It is instructive to note how the image is essentially unformed at first and is crystallized only after the unpleasant fifth response. At that point, in line with her strategy of denial, the patient declares that she is going after something she likes. She then meanders among the colors for a while, rapidly picks up the theme of light, and autistically confabulates a temple for the gods suffused with the pure, unadulterated essence of light. Grandiose religious fantasies, possibly reaching the point of delusion, are suggested (see also VII-6). This response sequence represents one of the few flagrant breaks with reality in the record. It could easily have occurred in the record of a clear-cut psychotic patient. Its relative isolation in this record— her other confabulations are mostly not so full-blown—and the patient's rationalization of this response as "mythological" combine, however, to give the response (and the total record) no more than a borderline psychotic quality.

CARD X     REACTION TIME: 20″.     TOTAL TIME: 5′.

*1. (D F+ A P) If they were the right color, they'd look like crabs to me or an octopus (side blue).*

*2. (D FC+ A Peculiar) Either two animals, sitting, the brown figures here . . . (upper gray).* [Particular animal? *No, but I don't like the color of them so I don't like them.*]

*3. (D F+ A) Now these green ones are two animals, but they're the wrong color (upper green).* [Particular animal? *Sort of like enlarged mice.*]

(a) In the first three responses the patient tries, mostly unsuccessfully, to force adaptive (*FC*) color responses. (b) A moderate failure of denial is evident in #2.

> *4–5. (D FC+ A; D F± Hd) . . . Could almost be snakes (lower green), with a Hindu figure in back of it (lower middle rabbit head without the ears).* [Snakes? *I should change my mind and say caterpillars.* What made them look like that? *The color and the crinklyness of them, and I hate them.* Hindu? *This part of the face is blocked off (lower part) but I saw eyes and a turban.*]

(a) A mouth is again eliminated. It should be noted at this point that the missing mouth as well as the aggressive mouth has always been elaborated in connection with a masculine image (see V-3, VII-9, VIII-5). Considerable projection of orality onto the male figure may be implied. (b) Changing snakes to caterpillars may be a form of denial, i.e., denial by minimization, as in the frequent use of "small," "little," "gnome," etc., that tends to characterize the records of rigid deniers. Also, of course, caterpillars do not bite, poison, swallow whole or crush. (c) Implicitly, the total image is that of a snake charmer, an image that suggests the theme of denying fear of masculine hostility (the snake in this instance possibly representing the phallus), and even reversing the situation ("taming" the phallus). While quite speculative, this last inference is consistent with numerous other inferences from her responses.

> *6. (D F+ A) Dogs of the . . . Phoenician Age, from way back (middle yellow).*

> *7. (W CF Art) It may mean something but it looks to me like just a child's painting, the whole thing, just a blot painting.*

Denial of all previous responses to this card is implied.

> *8. (D FC+ Obj Confabulation) This, these two little things here (side yellow and gray base) look like torches going (extending) out. They're being carried by a man but the man is not here, but a man ready to go out to see the way.* [Would you explain what you meant? *I was thinking of the days of Charlemagne (French accent) or King Alfred. It could be made from the bark of a tree or bronze; and the flame coming out.* Flame? *A pink or yellow at the bottom and then it faded out, against sort of a bronze container, and I liked the color.*]

(a) This response has the confabulated flavor of the "essence of light" response in IX-6, 7 and also the "sinister" response in I-3. Its theme is one of hypomanic exaltation: a feeling of starting anew and discovery. The positive emphasis on light as contrasted with a negative attitude toward darkness parallels the cyclic mood problem (see also II-5, 6, 7, VI-10, and IX-6, 7). (b) Note too the recurrence of imagery with grandiose overtones (see also VII-6, IX-6). (c) Also significant is the relatively obvious, though implicit, representation of herself as a man in this response.

> *9. (D FC(C)+ A)< If you turned them that way—are you allowed? —these look like figures out of stone again (lower outer orange).* [Figures of what? *I've forgotten. (Patient shown card.) Sort of a Saint Bernard. And this is dark brown here on top and lighter underneath.* What suggested stone? *The ruggedness of it.*]

The Saint Bernard is an image with strong motherly, nurturant, saintly connotations. The fluidity in recall suggests again instability in this defensive position.

*I didn't know you were allowed to turn them.*

Such bland comments often convey denied resentment at having been misled, neglected, "tricked," or put in an unfair position.

*10–11. (D F∓ Arch; D FC(C)+ Plant) I think if it were a child's drawing, this could mean going into a large house (usual rabbit head) with hedges (lower green), but the house is too small; or a temple, I should say. This (lower green) would be all the trees. [Hedges? The color and a certain depth in that green blot.]*

(a) If we interpret these two responses symbolically, the sequence appears to be the following: receptive feminine position (large house with hedges), rejection of the receptive feminine position (the house is too small), concealing the rejection by a religious emphasis (it is a pure, holy house—a temple). This is mechanical symbolic interpretation and could not and should not stand by itself. It is mentioned here because in this instance the interpretation coincides with the gist of the entire record. (b) The "child's drawing" theme in this record may obliquely express criticism of the blots, as already noted, but its pervasiveness also begins to suggest defensiveness—in particular, externalization of responsibility for what is gross, inaccurate or revealing in her responses.

*I think the colors are lovely, all except that (upper gray): I don't like that. Beautiful pastels.*

*12. (Dr FC'+ Obj) Just here it could be just an old post. [Old? The color. What about the color? It was faded, gray. Any particular kind of pole? It might be an old telegraph pole that was partly cut down and grayed with age; not painted the way modern ones are.)*

After rejecting the dysphoric gray, as in Card V, she now uses it for what seems to be a last statement of male (phallic) deterioration.

*There isn't much more (laugh).*

### SUMMARY OF SCORES

R: 86                  EB: 5–8(9)

| | | | | | | |
|---|---|---|---|---|---|---|
| W | 11 | F+ | 26 | A | 14 | W% | 12 |
| D | 37 | F− | 6 | Ad | 7+1 | D% | 43 |
| Dd | 3 | F± | 4 | H | 3 | DR% | 41 |
| Dr | 26 | F∓ | 6 | (H) | 3 | | |
| De | 2 | M | 4 (1−) | Hd | 13 | F% | 49–83 |
| S | 6 | FM | 2 | (Hd) | 2 | F+% | 71–72 |
| s | 1+1 | FC | 6 (1−) | Obj | 7 | | |
| | | F/C | 2 (1−) | Dec | 3 | A% | 24–26 |
| *Qualitative* | | CF | 2 | Cg | 2 | H% | 19–25 |
| Confabulation | 2 | C | 2 | At | 3 | P | 7 |
| Confab. tend. | 6 | F(C) | 6+2 (3−) | Plant | 4 | P% | 8 |
| Contam. tend. | 1 | (C)F | 0+1 | Geog | 8 | | |
| Peculiar | 5 | FC' | 7 (2−) | Sex | 1 | | |
| Fluid | 2 | C'F | 2 | Arch | 5 | | |
| Symbolic | 1 | C' | 2+1 | Misc | 11 | | |
| | | FCh | 2+1 | | | | |
| | | ChF | 7 | | | | |

In summary of the thematic analysis, it may be said that this woman seems to be in a borderline psychotic, hypomanic state. She is apparently beset by strong feelings of oral need and deprivation, by intense oral-aggressive impulses, by fears of losing control of hostile and libidinal impulses in general, and by intense guilt, anticipation of punishment and underlying depression. These pressures she appears to cope with principally by denial, but also by projection. Instead of being the oral, needy, wicked, attacking glutton, and possibly the evil, faithless sexual transgressor, she seems to emphasize the role of the motherly, eagerly nurturant, innocent Madonna and Saviour.* Instead of being depressed and guilty, she is gay and full of religious exaltation. Instead of being weak and hostile, she is, in a grandiose way, strong and pure. If anything, it is the male (husband? father?) figure who is oral, weak, improvident, deteriorating and yet hostile and fearsome too. It is not unlikely that through the Madonna role she also tries to settle the problems of her rejection of femininity and her guilt over sexuality. The autistic aspects of her denials and projections, while not quantitatively or qualitatively overwhelming, are conspicuous enough to indicate that her hold on reality is tenuous at best.

Considering the formal scores in this record, the outstanding features are emphasis on $FC, F/C, F(C), FC'$, and $FCh$. Twenty-three of her responses involve at least one of these scores, while other responses, such as the abortive $FC$ ("but it's the wrong color"), strain in this direction. From this finding we may infer that this woman is characterized by an exaggerated, driven, anxious adaptiveness. Eleven responses involve $Ch$ and $C'$ with little or no form. These indicate that intense anxiety and dysphoric feelings, and probably a helpless passivity in the face of her moods, underlie her adaptive efforts.

## Case 2

A second hypomanic record will now be considered in order to illustrate some of the forms of appearance of denial in a male patient. Thus far all of the records illustrating denial have been those of women. The present record is instructive particularly with regard to failure of denial of hostility. While this will be evident in the test imagery, it will be most conspicuous in the way the patient relates himself to the tester and to his responses.

The patient is a 50-year-old, successful business man from Texas. He is a college graduate with an IQ of 128, very superior range. He is married

---

* On the face of it, this seems typical of reaction formation. The role of reaction formation has been ignored in this analysis because it appears that such reaction formation as is involved in this patient's character structure is in a state of decompensation at present. Instead we see frequent empty, forced maternal posturing that seems at the present time largely one form of denial.

and has two children. The clinical diagnosis was "recurrent and alternating depression and hypomania."

A special problem arises from the patient's Texas background and his frequent use of mannerisms and colloquialisms of Texas speech. Even when casually used, these verbalizations have a flip, "masculine," counterphobic quality that tends to deny involvement, anxiety and sensitivity. From the standpoint of analysis of *distinctive* or *pathological* defenses, it is therefore necessary to watch for increased frequency of these verbalizations, for elements of strain and inappropriateness in them, and for shifts in their content. Also, we must assume that to some extent his selection of Texan cliché and metaphor bears the stamp of his impulse, defense and adaptation problems. In other words, it is legitimate to analyze *his version* of his cultural background and milieu—which of many emphases and shadings of emphases he has internalized, and into what hierarchic organization of drives, defenses, values, etc.

CARD I    REACTION TIME: 3".    TOTAL TIME: 1' 20".

> 1. *(W F+ A P) Oh, something like a bat.*
> 2. *(W F— Geog) The continent of Australia after an atom bomb hit it.*

The theme of devastation is introduced. Explosive hostility is named as a pressing problem. The particular image might pertain to a self-image ("I have been devastated") or to world-destructive wishes, or both. At least we can say that, as he senses it, somebody is destroying somebody.

> *. . . Oh, you mean keep on? (Does anything else occur to you?)*
>
> 3. *(W F∓ A) Some semblance of a crab.*
> 4. *(W ChF Geog Confabulation tendency) Almost could be a map of Shangri-La or something.* [Why Shangri-La? *I was being facetious.* Was there anything on the card to suggest it? *Not a thing.* What made it look like a map? *Because it looked like a map (impatient tone).* How? *Like a contour map to some degree, showing the elevations, bays and inlets and what-not. It could well be it.*]

(a) This is an instance of unreflective, anxiety-denying, aggression-denying but provocative facetiousness. (b) The facetiousness uses for its content the highly significant image *Shangri-La.* The Shangri-La fantasy seems to have at least two outstanding aspects: (1) reassurance against anxiety over aging, the world of Shangri-La being incredibly youth-preserving (the patient is 50 years old and may well be beginning to be concerned with the problems of aging); (2) passive, regressive gratification, the world of Shangri-La being one of peace, plenty, warmth, serenity and quiet contemplation. The fantasy of the warm, secluded niche surrounded by stormy, icy, jagged, perilous mountains, and of the rapid aging that ensues on leaving this shelter, gives the image a strikingly womb-like quality. Thus, in the very act of facetious denial of aggression and anxiety, the patient uses content that suggests both a wish to deny aging and intense passive, regressive wishes. (c) The fact that for purposes of facetiousness he dragged in Shangri-La without perceptual support in the card can be considered indicative of a relatively forced, inappropriate, confabulatory mode of response. (d) Note the extreme contrast of mood between #2 and #4.

> *That's about the crop for me on that one. Is it desirable to see as much as I can in a reasonable length of time? (Not necessarily.) I pass.*

Attempting to structure the situation as a game—"I pass"—is in a way a denial, too, that this is serious business, as well as obviously an ingrained character defense of pseudo-casualness and "informal good fellowship."

CARD II     REACTION TIME: 5″.     TOTAL TIME: 1′ 5″.

> *1. (D F+ A P) That looks like a, like two bears rubbing noses, or two Scotty dogs.*
>
> *2. (DS C′F Cave) Or the entrance to a cave (dark areas and middle space).* [What made it look like that? *For instance, the B— Grotto has an entrance: when you're inside looking out, it looks something like that. The red splashes don't ring any particular bell with me.* How does it look like that? *Just a spot of light in the midst of a black figure.*]

Conceivably, the image of being inside a cave looking out might be related to the haven-womb theme suggested in the Shangri-La image (I-4).

> *To be facetious: which one has the Toni (reference to #1)? And that's about it.*

The content of this facetious, anxiety- and involvement-denying remark suggests preoccupation with genuine quality versus cheap imitations, that is with integrity versus fraud and ultimately perhaps with innocence versus guilt.

> *3. (D F— Hd Confabulation tendency) Eskimos rubbing noses, I guess (same area as #1).* [What made it look like Eskimos? *Just a custom, isn't it? Eskimos rub noses instead of kissing.* Did they look like Eskimos? *No. (At this point the patient picks up the tester's cigarette as if he had been smoking it and puts it out.)*]

(a) The Eskimos rubbing noses, like Shangri-La (I-4), are not perceptually rooted in the card but represent a confabulatory elaboration of a response. Again a quality of inappropriate, pathological use of the defense of denial is implied. (b) The content of this denial—Eskimos—suggests that coldness and possibly a rejecting attitude toward sexual intimacy may underlie a superficially affectionate manner. (c) Not infrequently, patients struggling particularly with oral problems express this struggle in their "cigarette behavior"—offering cigarettes or a light, smoking the tester's cigarette or putting it out, bumming cigarettes from the tester freely, etc. In this instance, the patient may have been expressing his irritation with the tester in oral terms.

CARD III     REACTION TIME: 15″.     TOTAL TIME: 1′ 35″.

> *1. (W F± A) This looks like two grotesque birds with boxing gloves on (P area).*
>
> *2. (W M+ H P) It could be two ballet dancers in some . . . not grotesque, some costume similar for instance to the costume for* Coq D'Or—*in the field of that.*
>
> *The heads (of #1) suggest more of an ostrich to me than any other animal and once again the red doesn't bring on anything.*

Hostility in interpersonal relationships seems to be expressed and denied in the first response and then denied altogether in the second and third. First it is a fight but only between birds and only of the "boxing match" variety. Then it is a ballet boxing match—about as unaggressive a fight as there can be. Finally, the ostrich theme is introduced, the ostrich being a figure of denial par excellence. (b) It is also noteworthy that on Card III, as on Card II, the patient explicitly shies away from the red areas. This suggests that direct dealing with strong affect, perhaps particularly hostility, is significantly anxiety-arousing.

*That's the punch line on this-y. That's about it.*

With a Texan flourish, the patient concludes his remarks by denying the situation's seriousness, i.e., it's all a gag (see also the "I pass" remark at the end of Card I).

CARD IV    REACTION TIME: 10".    TOTAL TIME: 1' 20".

*1. (W FC'+ Ad P) That looks like a bearskin rug that was salvaged from a fire. [Bearskin? It had a head and a form not unlike a bearskin rug spread out on the floor with a head on it. Had it been charred in a fire and the feet bound up it wouldn't be too unlike that. Anything else? The general form of it: arms and legs; what was left of it. Charred? It was black. Where was the head? Between the shoulders and arms, of course (combined irritation and smirk); on top (of the card).]*

The theme is that of devastation, as in the atom-bombed Australia of I-2. The recurrence of this theme in the present form suggests that inner feelings of devastation are probably of more immediate significance in the formation of this image than outwardly directed destructive impulses. The patient appears to feel in ruins. Increasing irritation during the inquiry, thinly veiled as facetiousness, suggests either that this image was particularly anxiety-arousing or that the tester's persistent questioning provoked resentment at the tester's "demandingness," or both (see end of Card II).

*V Can I look at it either way or just one way? (However you like.)*

*2. (W F— A) ΛV Some form of sea life, of the crab family.*

*3. (W F+ A) Could possibly be some odd type of bat as well.*

*4. (W F± Emblem) Could be some shoulder emblem of some military organization: from Mars, I guess.*

(a) The patient apparently resorts to mockery ("from Mars"). (b) He seems, however, preoccupied with irregularity and relative formlessness, but inclined or able only to rationalize this problem weakly (and critically). Instead of articulating accurate and specific form, for which he has the intellectual equipment, he invests his responses with an out-of-this-world quality that externalizes responsibility for their imperfections. Passivity and inadequacy seem to be masked by pretentiousness and critical remarks. More or less in this same vein are the images of atom-bombed Australia, Shangri-La, grotesque costume, charred skin, and odd bat (see also V-1, V-2, etc. below). (c) In content, the military emblem suggests either a hostile conception of the masculine role (see III-1, 2) or preoccupation with masculine and social status, or both.

*And that's about the crop.*

In one respect, he may be saying in this Texan closing that he is being overworked by the tester (slaving out in the fields). In another respect, he may be expressing a primarily oral conception of the response process (crop = food = oral supply). In a third respect, he may be expansively maintaining that he has exhausted this card's potentialities (he has picked it clean). All three inferences are in line with inferences from other outstanding responses and verbalizations, but it is particularly the last that bears on this patient's pathologically expansive denials.

CARD V    REACTION TIME: 10".    TOTAL TIME: 1'.

    *1. (W F+ A P) ∨ Damn, someone must have designed these in Carls-bad Cavern. Once again a bat.*

The patient sees another bat, apparently feels that this is a demonstration of inadequacy, and promptly externalizes the responsibility for the response: the designer of the blots is at fault.

    *2. (W F∓ A) ∧ Could be some microscopic animal.*

This "safe" response is another form of passive, unproductive, even irresponsi-ble—but pretentious—coping with the inkblots.

    *3–4. (W F∓ Ad; Dd F— A) Or it looks like two Scotty dogs (side wing) that both were chasing the same butterfly (upper middle) and had a head-on collision (midline). [What made it look like that? Just like the heads: ears (upper middle bump on wing), tongues (lower middle projections).]*

(a) This image strongly suggests important feelings of competitiveness. The butterfly might represent any prize in general or, symbolically, a woman in par-ticular. The theme of hostile competition is the most important inference to be derived, however. The specific referents of this competitive image could only be established by clinical data. (b) It is significant that the tongues of the dogs are hanging out. This is an unusual and perceptually arbitrary interpretation of the lower middle projections and one that suggests an important oral empha-sis in the competitiveness.

    *>∨ That would be about enough on that one.*

He seems to have to deny that he may have run out of ideas. This is a variation on the theme discussed at the end of Card IV.

CARD VI    REACTION TIME: 20"    TOTAL TIME: 1' 30".

    *1. (W F+ Ad P)∨∧ Again it could be a rug made of the hide of some animal, flattened out on the floor. What animal I wouldn't know. It has the four legs and the head to it, with a spine in the center. [What made it look like that? If you've ever seen a hide spread on the floor (impatient tone), that's the general contour of a hide, having a head, two feet and two rear legs. Anything else? No.]*

The patient's impatience with inquiry into this response again suggests resent-ment of the tester's "demands."

    *2. (D FC'∓ At, Sex) ∨ The central part of it looks like an x-ray pic-ture of some of the abdominal organs (middle section of lower D). [Did you have a particular organ in mind? It could be a female organ, a uterus there. How was it like an x-ray? Well it's a poor answer, but, like a woman says, "Because it does." Largely because it's black and white like a photograph negative and so is that. How was it like a female organ? I've seen some drawings of the uterus and that part of a woman's paraphernalia. It doesn't look exactly like that but it's the closest thing I could think of: some abdominal gadget.]*

The evasiveness in this response becomes particularly clear during inquiry. The patient sees a "uterus," which could imply concern with reproductive powers, but he might very well mean "a vagina," since his whole attitude seems to be that a man shouldn't take—or express—any particular interest in such details, that that is "women's business." That is to say, he appears to have felt it necessary either to play dumb during the testing or to have stayed dumb all along. To be sure, this is partly a culturally reinforced prejudice, but the patient's driven disparagement of the feminine image ("paraphernalia," "gadget") seems to indicate particular anxiety about his masculine status. Further support for this inference is found in his simultaneous talking like a woman ("like a woman says") and his direct disparagement of them ("it's a poor answer").

The patient appears to be defending his threatened masculinity by simultaneously disparaging the feminine organ, disparaging the response, and disparaging women. This recalls the inference of sexual coldness drawn from the Eskimos rubbing noses on Card II. The patient is so busy and uneasy defending his masculinity that tender, affectionate relationships with a woman are likely to be very difficult for him. Seen in the light of these inferences, the previously noted theme of devastation (I-2, IV-1) might well be a generalized statement of fears of loss of masculinity associated with advancing age (see VII-3, below).

∧ *That one doesn't conjure up very many things in my imagination.*

By externalizing the responsibility, he again avoids acknowledging that he is "giving up" or is in any way not adequate to the occasion.

CARD VII      REACTION TIME: 15″.      TOTAL TIME: 1′ 35″.

*1. (D F+ (Hd) Confabulation tendency) It looks like the little—I don't know—cherubim and seraphim in the clouds with a new hair-do (upper ⅓). I've never seen one with hair like that.* [What made them look like cherubim particularly? *That's in the celestial league: I don't know, I haven't dropped in lately (sarcastic).* What made them look like clouds? *They actually didn't look like clouds. They look more like the cherubs and that occasioned some clouds, so I had to stretch my imagination.* Anything there to suggest clouds? *Except that little heads are always in clouds.*]

(a) Denial of guilt seems to emerge clearly for the first time—cherubim implying innocence and heavenly bliss—but even here the sentimental-feminine aspect of the response must be denied, as it is in the facetious reference to the new hair-do and in his facetiousness and irritability during inquiry. (b) Again, in reference to the cloud, we seem to have an instance of a confabulatory elaboration without articulated perceptual support in the card (see I-4, II-3).

*2. (WS F∓ Geog Fluid) Again it could be a map of an island.* [What made it look like that? *Because islands can be almost any form on earth so anything can look like that, I guess.* Map? *I've forgotten which picture we were on now. . . . It looked like drawings I saw in the navy that had to do with safe landing and so forth and this had a harbor (middle space) and what might be a safe anchorage (lower middle).*]

(a) Inquiry into this response brings out the theme of a safe haven that was noted in the earlier images of Shangri-La (I-4) and the interior of a cave (II-2). (b) Characterizing this commonly recognized vaginal area as a haven possibly expresses strong, unconscious, passive-regressive wishes with respect to women—wishes that he seems driven to deny in his disparagement of women and all things feminine (see VI-2).

*3. (D F∓ At, Sex) And one part of it could be a bony structure such as a portion of an eroded pelvis (lower ⅓).* [*Eroded? On account of the edges were. . . . It looked aged, like part of it was decomposed . . . the bone partly gone. Whether bones do that or not, I don't know.*]

Here is good confirmation for previous inferences (see especially VI-2). This image baldly states insecurity regarding sexuality, concern with aging, and feelings of decay and devastation. The image of the eroded pelvis, taken together with the pertinent previous images (I-2, IV-1, VI-2), strongly suggests that the patient feels he is aging and losing his effectiveness and potency. In these "castrated" circumstances, he could be expected to feel especially threatened by passive-feminine wishes and then be driven to defend himself against this threat by denials in the form of an exaggerated masculine pose and disparagement of women.

4. *(D F± A) You turn it over this way and you get what? The bottom part of it here (upper ⅓) looks like two fish snarling at each other, if fish snarl. That's it.*

Oral-aggressive emphasis emerges clearly in the content for the first time. The patient is facetious about it but the response suggests not only the previously inferred tendency to conceive of interpersonal relationships as hostile, but a primarily oral definition of his irritability ("snarling"). Later on, he almost does snarl at the tester (see Card IX).

CARD VIII     REACTION TIME: 10″.     TOTAL TIME: 1′ 50″.

1. *(W F/C+ Emblem P Peculiar) Well it could be the great seal of some place: having on either two sides of it two animals, red animals. Damned if I know which animals they look like particularly. I have to stretch my imagination but it could be a dog of some species.* [*What made it look like a great seal? Not infrequently crests or seals have two rampant—or otherwise—lions or animals on the sides: that's the principal reason. For the rest you have to draw on imagination. Anything else? The general sweeping . . . the ensemble of things, the general composure (patient means composition) of this proposition of a seal.*]

The previously suggested concern with status (IV-4) is expressed more clearly now. An emphasis on status is common among the euphoric denials of hypomanics. Clinically, this status consciousness tends to be expressed in exaggerated conceptions of wealth, influence, social and political "connections," and the like. One major function of these expansive self-concepts is to deny feelings of emotional neediness and helplessness and associated feelings of mistrust of and resentment toward others.

2. *(W FC′− A) We have many forms of marine life: it could be a microscopic form of marine life. And it generally looks more like some infinitesimal thing that's blown up rather than something of actual size. It has the appearance of something you are looking at through a microscope.* [*Infinitesimal? Having looked through microscopes in laboratories a few times, it brought that to mind, and it didn't compare with any actual thing I know of. Also its transparency made me think of a microscopic unicellular organism. Transparency? You see light through it. You can see the white of that card for instance.*]

(a) Now it is as if the grandiose bubble created in the first response is pricked. This is, after all, an inflated image of a minute, insignificant thing. Response V-2 ("could be some microscopic animal"), also conspicuously emphasizing the theme of magnified smallness, is a relatively rare response to that card. In retrospect that response appears to state the same theme as this one. Intense underlying feelings of smallness, inadequacy and insignificance are suggested. (b) But note how in attitude he sustains the expansive denial: the editorial "we" has a decided grandiose ring. (c) This remains, however, one of his basically passive, irresponsible, unformed responses. Thus, one aspect of his personality and pathology is highlighted by the formal inadequacies of the response, while others are highlighted by the expansiveness in the way he deals with the response's inadequacies through the content and in the way he relates himself to the tester.

*That about does it.*

CARD IX    REACTION TIME: 90".    TOTAL TIME: 3' 45".

*(Long sigh) They're all first cousins of these things. < Oh, let's try one this way . . . ∨ or that way. . . . I believe I'm like little Johnny at the birthday party: I'm tired of playing games (irritable tone). I guess there must be a saturation point. Let's just flunk one completely on account of it doesn't remind me of a damn thing! It doesn't bring to life a single thing, so we might as well say so!*

The patient's opening remark ("all first cousins"), meaning that the blots are all much alike, indicates his extreme defensiveness. References to the similarity of all the cards can almost always be translated to mean, "No matter what the real situation is, the same old threats exist in it and my defensive problems are exactly the same." The patient obviously has trouble coping with this card (reaction time 90", card turning). His response to the resulting feelings of inadequacy seems to be partly to project onto the card responsibility for his difficulty, partly to deny the situation's seriousness ("games"), partly to deny expansively his inadequacy feelings (the editorial "we"), and partly to become increasingly irritable and querulous. The test is just a silly game now and he is fed up with amusing the tester.

The patient is certainly disenchanted at this point. Yet, he cannot allow himself to give up, that is, to acknowledge and accept the inadequacy feelings which still persist. The projection of responsibility and denial of seriousness have apparently not been too effective. He goes on to give three responses. There is strength and adaptive potential in this persistence, even if it is closely tied to pathological conflict. A less resilient patient might have quit without responding.

*1–2. (D F/C∓ Hd, Dec; D F/C(C)+ Cg) It could be two people, a contorted or distorted drawing of two South Sea island natives (green, facing in) with their face and hair painted green and two pink ostrich feathers (lower pink) on the head, but I'll be damned if that's not going out of my way to say something. [South Sea natives? They had great big Negroid lips drawn up, smacking (kissing) the other one. Ostrich feathers? Airy, fluffy things that reminds me of them somewhat and they are worn as a headdress—or they were when grandmother was a girl. It could well be worn in that part of the world by a native because that's where the little ostrich makes his home.]*

(a) He forces out one response of a festive sort, making only artificial use of color (i.e., affect), however. (b) On inquiry he indicates that he has again seen a kiss (see II-1) and he again (implicitly) devaluates it: the idea of "great big Negroid lips" to such a stalwart Texan probably has a particularly hostile, sexually abandoned, gluttonous, ego-alien set of implications. (c) The ostrich plumes add a feminine touch to the image and this suggests the common equation of oral-passive and feminine wishes. (d) The ostrich—the classic animal symbol of denial—reappears (see after III-2).

> 3. *(D F/C∓ (Hd), Dec Confabulation tendency) It could be two people in a Mardi Gras or holiday costumes (orange; usual gargoyle articulation), putting on a skit entitled, "We're forever blowing bubbles" (reference to upper middle projection). (Patient comments while tracing response: "It has a pot belly.")*

(a) The patient forces out another response, this one again festive, but artificial in color and triply artificial in content ("costumes," "skit" and "bubbles"). (b) Festivity—particularly Mardi Gras festivity—tends to imply denial of all problems (need, hostility, sexual frustration and inhibition, guilt) and to assert a completely superego-free interest in sexual and oral excitement and abandon. Note the pot belly (voracious) emphasis in inquiry.

> *I don't know whether I'm a clown or not. You'd be amazed how few of these things I run across in my daily work. How is everything in Mars these days? I haven't been up lately. (Patient's tone is increasingly irritated.)*

Apparently, his continuing anxiety over inadequacy, his increasing resentment of the demands of the tester, and apprehensiveness concerning the content of his responses, all result in a momentary decompensation of his flippant role and almost open snarling at the tester. Even this snarling has an element of denial in it, however, the content of his responses being labelled as Martian and therefore utterly irrelevant to the patient's earthly existence and problems.

CARD X    REACTION TIME: 20″.    TOTAL TIME: 2′ 30″.

> *My God! They finally blew one apart here! Let's see.*

(a) The patient's aggressiveness at the end of Card IX seems to be expressed immediately via a variant of perceptual experience rather than a test attitude. He apparently over-reacts to this blot's bright colors and expansive aspects, and expresses this reaction in the language of hostility. (b) "They finally blew one apart" is a hostile, critical characterization of the stimulus (i.e., a mess), but it also projects the responsibility for the hostility (*they*, not *he*, blew it apart). (c) The devastation theme (I-2, IV-1, VII-3) is also suggested by this verbalization.

> 1. *(D FC+ A P) Well I see two blue, two large blue crabs (side blue).*
> 2. *(D FC+ A) And two medium-sized brown ones (upper gray).*
> 3. *(D FC+ A) And two small brown ones (side gray).*
> 4. *(D FC± A) And a couple of snails, green snails (lower green).*

While crabs often appear to have oral-aggressive implications in Rorschach test responses, the popularity of the crabs (#1) ordinarily does not allow any inference of oral-aggressiveness. Seeing them as "large" does, however, indicate that this compelling, percept-like image has touched on live problems in the oral area. (b) The crabs mentioned in #2 and #3, while not as popular as those in #1, are relatively common. Each in itself therefore would also not convey anything significant in the oral realm. But the rapid sequence of three crab responses, like the "large" in #1, points to specific oral content significance. Even the banalities can be exploited for intimate self-expression. (c) The colors, while not purely arbitrary, do sound forced as he names them. This impression is reinforced by his continuing to name color almost automatically in #4 (green snails), #5, (pink meat), and, clearly arbitrary, #6 (blue hyphen).

*I'll be seeing pink elephants here in a minute.*

*5–6. (D CF Meat Fluid, Confabulation tendency; D FC arbitrary Hyphen Fabulized Combination) The crabs (#s 1, 2, 3) might well be feeding on this, this pink piece of meat here (middle red) that's joined together with a blue hyphen (middle blue).* [What made it look like meat? *That's not the same picture is it?* Yes. *Meat is pink and crabs wouldn't be gathered around nothing; it would be something they're eating on.*]

(a) An explicit oral theme emerges and seems to verify the inference of significant oral fantasy or conflict underlying the first three banal crab responses. (b) It is striking how, in its thought organization and perceptual organization, this first clear-cut oral response is also one of the most arbitrary and mixed-up in the record. On a microcosmic scale, we seem to be seeing here a decompensation of defenses and an emergence of threatening material in primary process form.

*7. (DS F/C– Ad,Dec Confabulation tendency)* ∨ *Once again the whole business could be a horse's head dressed in a fancy parade costume, probably allegorical in nature (upper gray is nose, face is space between middle red areas, eyes are middle blue, ears are middle yellow); let's say drawing a float in a Mardi Gras in the center of the parade.* [Parade costume? *All of the blue, goggle-like harness, you might say, around his eyes, or the plumes on top of his head and pinkish flary pieces on either side of the head like extra-fancy trappings on a horse's head.*]

Now there is a return to festivity (Mardi Gras) and status ("center of the parade"). In Cards IX and X particularly we see how the patient's original flippancy is flimsily disguised snarling and how the flippancy gets out of hand as emotional demands (to give responses, to use colors, to respond to inquiry, etc.) increase. At the same time the patient indicates—in his use of color and in his imagery—his solution to this problem of poor control, namely, forced, artificial and even arbitrary high-spirited emotional responsiveness that involves orally and sexually abandoned, exhibitionistic, status-claiming fantasy and/or behavior.

*That's about enough on that one.*

### SUMMARY OF SCORES

#### R: 35                EB: 1–3(6)

| | | | | | | | |
|---|---|---|---|---|---|---|---|
| W | 17 | F+ | 5 | A | 15 | W% | 49 |
| D | 17 | F– | 4 | Ad | 4 | D% | 49 |
| Dd | 1 | F± | 4 | H | 1 | | |
| S | 0+3 | F∓ | 5 | Hd | 2 | F% | 51–91 |
| | | M | 1 | (Hd) | 2 | F+% | 50–53 |
| | | FC | 4 | Dec | 0+3 | | |
| *Qualitative* | | F/C | 5(3–) | Cg | 1 | A% | 54 |
| Fab. Comb. | 1 | FCarb | 1– | At-Sex | 2 | H% | 9–14 |
| Confab. tend. | 6 | CF | 1 | Geog | 3 | P | 9 |
| Fluid | 2 | F(C) | 0+1 | Emblem | 3 | P% | 26 |
| Peculiar | 1 | FC' | 3(2–) | Misc | 2 | | |
| | | C'F | 1 | | | | |
| | | ChF | 1 | | | | |

In general, we have a picture of pathologically heavy reliance on defense by denial. This man appears beset by intense feelings of devastation, decay, impotence, smallness and guilt, and by pressing passive, "feminine," regressive oral impulses. He seems to cope with these feelings and impulses largely by exaggerated, implicitly grandiose pseudo-masculinity—Texas-style and Mardi-Gras-style. Also present are suggestions of noteworthy coldness, incapacity for tenderness, narcissistic ungivingness, passive irresponsibility, competitiveness and rage. He seems to attempt to coat these qualities and tendencies with a thin, patchy veneer of affability and jocularity, all the while projecting responsibility for his inner sense of threat, his inadequacy feelings, and his haphazard output. Often he desperately falls back on what is at its best a culturally defined and reinforced style of masculine brusqueness, facetiousness and "good humor," but is at its not infrequent worst either inappropriate and somewhat autistic "masculine" posturing, or else irritability approaching the point of snarling. Such adaptive assets as he possesses are barely reflected in his test performance, except perhaps in some resiliency and doggedness that contrast with his currently dominant unproductive, evasive passivity.

Most conspicuous in the score pattern in this record are the artificial use of color, the low form level, the high number of *Whole* responses and the *Confabulation tendencies*. Six responses of the *F/C* and *FC arbitrary* variety (four of them poor in accuracy) are present as compared to four *FC* and one *CF*. From these scores we may infer that the patient's adaptive efforts are to a great extent forced, off-key, sometimes even autistically defined. The high *W* (17), considered in the context of the low $F+\%$ (50–53) and the relatively numerous *Confabulation tendencies* (6), suggests an expansive, possibly megalomanic trend. The moderate emphasis on *C'* hints at underlying depressive aspects in the case. The presence of only one *M* points to the unreflectiveness and intolerance of fantasy and self-confrontation that are qualitatively so glaring.

# 9. Projection

THE CONCEPT OF PROJECTION AS A DEFENSIVE operation that will underlie the following presentation may be stated in a series of propositions. These propositions derive largely from the discussions of Freud [46], Anna Freud [42], Fenichel [37], Knight [88, 89], Gill [59], and Rapaport [116].

1. Projection is a process by which an objectionable internal tendency is unrealistically attributed to another person or to other objects in the environment instead of being recognized as part of one's self.

2. The objectionable tendency that is projected may be either an id impulse and any of its derivatives or a superego attitude and any of its derivatives. Projection need not be, as Freud originally maintained, essentially a defense against homosexual tendencies. It may also be a defense against other libidinal tendencies and against sadistic, destructive id or superego tendencies. There is even some evidence that homosexuality may be used as a defense against paranoid tendencies [59].

3. The projection of the id impulse or superego attitude substitutes apparently objective fear of an external danger in the place of anxiety or guilt associated with intrapsychic conflict.

4. This externalization of internal problems offers the projector two advantages: (a) he may now flee from, deny the existence of, or righteously retaliate against the "external" threat or enemy; (b) by projectively purifying himself, he avoids the especially intense subjective pain that would accompany the intrusion of the objectionable material into his self-concept.

5. The projection is typically not indiscriminate but has as its object someone or something whose impulses or qualities meet it part way. These impulses or qualities make up the screen on which the projection is imposed. They serve as "evidence" that the projection is not that at all but a keen perception of "the truth." In all significant relationships, there is sufficient ambivalence of the love-hate, active-passive, masculine-feminine varieties that the projector ordinarily finds some evidence for his projections readily available.

6. Since the projection may involve reversal (e.g., changing the emphasis from love to hate), displacement (e.g., changing the object of the projection from a man to a woman), denial (e.g., behaving as if the projected danger does not exist), and other modifications and disguises, the end result of

projection is not likely to be a simple, naked externalization of the objection-able tendency.

7. Projection involves a blurring of the boundary between fantasy and external reality. With this boundary blurred, externalization of internal tensions is facilitated. This alteration of reality testing has a definite regres-sive quality. Accordingly, the more extensive or extreme the projections, the more far-reaching the ego's reorganization along archaic lines. At the extreme of projection, in paranoid syndromes, thinking and perceiving are often clearly autistic, magical, fluid and egocentric (primary process thinking) instead of more or less objective, organized and logical (sec-ondary process thinking).

8. A continuum of projections must be recognized [116]. At the benign pole, projections are occasional, tempered, well rationalized, tentative and subordinated to the requirements of effective social adaptation. In fact, these benign—and also widespread—forms of projection are not particu-larly defensive. They overlap a great deal with what is implied by the term *projective* in "projective testing," namely, externalized expression of one's private inner world through selective perception and organization of the surrounding world [41]. These benign projections also seem to foster alert, empathic recognition in others of some of our own tendencies [87]. In these respects, projection is not only an integral part of perception in general but it may sharpen rather than impair reality testing.

Pathologically defensive, but retaining noteworthy adaptive potential too, is the constant, hyperalert search for flaws and misleading clues. On the one hand this orientation expresses paranoid mistrust of others and on the other it may contribute to striving for precision and sensitivity to logical, procedural or emotional inconsistency. A relatively unadaptive but moderate instance of defensive projection is such a reaction as "I think he dislikes me" in the absence of sufficient observational support. This is not a rare type of reaction among essentially normal people who, either in a crisis or chronically, feel uncomfortable with their negative feelings toward others.

As we approach the pathological extreme, the projections become more frequent, raw, arbitrary and/or rigid. As an unshakable conviction, "A Communist spy ring is trying to kill me," is an extreme instance of pro-jection; it is likely to occur in the context of paranoid schizophrenia. Diagnostically, our terms range from "paranoid trend" through "paranoid state (or reaction)" and "paranoid character (or personality)" to "par-anoia" and "paranoid schizophrenia." These diagnostic terms reflect clinical awareness of the range of severity over which projections spread.

9. It must also be recognized that pathological projections may occur within varied ego contexts, and that their forms of appearance—their content, obviousness, rigidity, pervasiveness, etc.—vary with these ego

contexts. Projection is rarely used alone as a defense, and the other defenses surrounding it are different from one patient to the next. For example, one paranoid patient may also rely heavily on denial, while the next may be strikingly compulsive.* Also, we often encounter clinical and test pictures in which alternating or simultaneous depressive (introjecting) and paranoid (projecting) solutions are conspicuous. The entire level of maturity and the general intactness of ego also vary greatly among pathologically projective patients. Paranoid pathology is therefore by no means an all-or-none affair; neither can the term "paranoid" serve by itself as an exhaustive description of ego status.

10. Pathological (paranoid) projections generally have both suspicious and megalomanic aspects, although one or the other of these aspects may predominate in any given instance, the other remaining more or less implicit.

## A. Test Expectations

With these propositions in mind, we are in a position to ask what we might expect in the test records of those who rely heavily on defensive paranoid projection. As usual, the pertinent test indications will be found in the distribution of formal scores, in test attitudes, and in thematically significant test content. Since the term "paranoid" covers a broad range of phenomena (propositions 6–10 above), the expected pattern of test findings will necessarily be complex and varied.

### 1. Test Scores

(a) Locations. Megalomanic tendencies imply a pathologically high level of ambition. Accordingly, when megalomanic tendencies are dominant, the number of whole responses ($W$) may be, in absolute terms, very high. More than 10 $W$ in itself may suggest lofty ambitions. More than 15 $W$ and particularly more than 20 $W$ suggest grandiose assumptions or fantasies.† Even when $W$ is very high, however, the pathology may still not be psychotic in nature. Very high $W$ may reflect a character trend which tends towards the grandiose only under certain forms of stress and which is ordinarily manifest in great but realistic integrative efforts in the intellectual realm. When this is the case, we may expect the $W$ to be mostly well organized and accurately seen. When flimsy, unorganized pretentiousness veering toward the grandiose characterizes the patient, we may

---

* It does seem to be the case, however, that more often than not compulsive character features are prominent in paranoid cases.

† For scoring criteria, see Rapaport [118]. Rapaport opposes separate scoring of responses that are minor variations on the same theme. Thus, bat, butterfly and bird on Card I would be scored together and would be represented by only one $W$. Klopfer's scoring of responses—and therefore of $W$—is more liberal than this [86].

encounter numerous vague, noncommittal, empty $W$ (see Case 1 below). When gross megalomanic pathology exists, many of the $W$ are likely to be arbitrarily organized and inaccurately seen. Actually, it is unusual to get many $W$—more than 15 or 20—without a significant number of them being $F-$.

Suspiciousness, in contrast to grandiosity, is typically expressed through hypersensitivity to and overelaborate interpretation of minor details. Accordingly, when paranoid suspiciousness is prominent, the number of tiny detail responses ($Dr$) may be very high (above 20% of $R$). In itself, a high $Dr\%$ may also reflect the meticulousness and pedantry of an obsessive-compulsive syndrome. Indeed, paranoid pathology is very often found in predominantly obsessive-compulsive contexts. The high $Dr\%$ will take on specifically paranoid coloring when the interpretations are over-elaborate, as, for example, when the specks at the bottom of Card I or the tiny projections on the side blue on Card X are interpreted as figures of highly articulated form. Even if the $Dr\%$ is not high, overelaborate interpretation of any tiny detail may still indicate a paranoid tendency. Quality is at least as important as quantity in this respect.

Suspiciousness also implies a tendency to miss the obvious and even to reverse the obvious. The mistrustful person who becomes more wary than ever in the face of kindness and affection is a case in point. Accordingly, frequent figure-ground reversals, expressed in interpretations of the white spaces ($S$), may occur on the basis of a suspicious orientation. More than a few $S$ in the record should be sufficient to alert the tester to possible paranoid pathology. More than 5 or 6 $S$, unless the record is very long (R greater that 50–75), strongly suggests excessive reliance on defensive projection.

Another form of missing and reversing the obvious is the large $Dr$ that is arbitrarily wrenched out of the inkblot in defiance of the blot's natural articulation and organization. Such a response would, for example, encompass one half the side blue on Card X or a large section within the side shading on Card I. Frequent perceptual performances of this sort suggest an inclination in the patient to "see through" or "not be taken in by" obvious appearances, and to ferret out "concealed" relationships and signifi-cances. Accordingly, we may expect this type of response to stand out in paranoid contexts.

Thus, among the location scores, high $W$, high $Dr\%$, overelaborate or arbitrary $Dr$, and high $S$ may all point to significant paranoid pathology. Of course, a diagnosis cannot be made from the locations alone. But then, it never must be. As previously discussed, the use of locations is gov-erned by the same general principles that govern the use of determinants, the selection of content, and the manifestations of test attitudes. Consequently, many lines of inference should converge on the basic test interpretations.

*(b) The determinants.* The paranoid solution is necessarily an uneasy one. It is like maintaining a police state within one's self. Careful watch must be kept over expression of impulse and feeling. Spontaneity must be stifled in the interest of self-justification and social invulnerability. External and internal stimuli must be carefully screened lest they touch off expression of intolerable impulse and feeling. Rigid restraint and watchfulness of this sort are necessary to preclude conscious experience of feelings and behavior which would give the lie to the paranoid projections. For these reasons the paranoid solution is often a constricting one.

In the Rorschach responses of pathologically paranoid persons of the constricted sort (we shall consider the expansive sort below), we might therefore expect overemphasis on form as a manifestation of need for control (high $F\%$); particular emphasis on good form in the interest of realistic self-justification and social invulnerability (high $F+\%$); underemphasis on color paralleling stifled expression of affect and impulse (low *sum C*); often, particular underemphasis on relatively uncontrolled color in the interest of avoiding impulsive warmth or anger (low $CF$); possibly a light, scattered emphasis on $FC, FC', F(C)$ and $FCh$, reflecting cautious, hypersensitive, playing-it-safe compliance and adaptability.

At times, only $M$ of all determinants other than pure form may escape this constrictive, overalert orientation. Partly this seems to be because an $M$ response is still basically justified by its form and therefore involves no direct threat to control. Partly $M$ may persist because paranoid projection is an ideational symptom and ideational symptoms are predicated upon a certain freedom of fantasy about human beings and their feelings and motives. It is this freedom that contributes significantly to the capacity to elaborate $M$ responses in the first place. In the paranoid context, this asset of free fantasy is transformed into a combination of shield and weapon, and it loses its adaptive potential. Since it combines the qualities of $M$ and overelaborated $Dr$ interpretations, the $Ms$ response (small $M$) may be particularly emphasized. Since thinking about and perceiving human feelings, motives and action are regressively, autistically distorted in paranoid contexts, the $M-$ is likely to be encountered relatively more often there than in other pathological settings. Such a response, given to all of Card VII by a severely paranoid man, is "A woman lying down with crooked legs, ready for action" (each side being one leg and the lower middle the genital area). Depending, however, on various nuances of paranoid attitudes and on other defensive and adaptive trends, we may expect many $M, Ms$ and $M-$ or few.

At the extreme of paranoid wariness, we may encounter refusal to take this (or any) test, or, what is not much more than this, numerous card rejections and limitation of response to a few popular and near-popular form responses—responses that are clearly "perceptual" rather than "interpretive."

Thus, one ideal paranoid pattern of determinants includes a high $F\%$ and $F+\%$, restricted use and gingerly handling of color and shading, and either an entirely constricted experience balance $(EB)$ or one weighted on the side of $M$ (and $Ms$) rather than $sum\ C$. But paranoid defense (a) does not exist in isolation, (b) varies in severity and (c) varies in success. Accordingly, this ideal paranoid score pattern may be only moderately and perhaps only barely approximated in actual paranoid test records. For example, some paranoid patients who also rely heavily on repressive defense and who concomitantly show strong hysterical features may use much shading and color and relatively little human movement and form. Others, with strong narcissistic features, may emphasize color, particularly the $CF$ response. Yet others, who are so poorly integrated defensively that they are unable to stave off eruptions of threatening feelings and impulses even while they are desperately projecting and constricting, may make much use of color and shading in addition to emphasizing $M$. The more severe the psychic regression and the resulting generally autistic mode of functioning, the more poor form $(F-)$ will prevail over good form $(F+)$. Specifically, global, physiognomic or partial resemblances will be treated as good total likenesses. A chronic deteriorating schizophrenic may even lose his capacity for $M$ and better than average $F+$ and may be limited more and more to $pure\ C$ and $F-$.

These variations on the paranoid theme could be continued at some length. Those variations that have been mentioned so far indicate clearly enough that we cannot diagnose paranoid pathology simply by the ideal use to which the paranoid patient might like to put the determinants. More often than not, we may expect to see both the struggle toward this ideal and the obstacles, setbacks and failures that attend this struggle. Thus, despite an atmosphere of caution, involving careful checking of verbalization and accuracy, some arbitrary (not merely poor) $F$ and $M$ responses should be encountered. It could hardly be otherwise in the Rorschach test, since some impairment of reality testing is implied in any pathologically projective context. Paranoid patients often do give a whopping $F-$ or $M-$ without awareness that this response does not meet their constrictively high standards of control and objectivity. This internal inconsistency parallels their overelaborate interpretation of tiny detail, which itself is an arbitrary flight of fantasy masquerading as a microscopic sensitivity to detail. The inconsistent $F-$ or $M-$ also parallels the paranoid overabundance of $W$ responses: because megalomania is a desperate and autistic solution, an absolutely high number of $W$ typically includes arbitrary forms $(W\ F-)$.

What the patient considers ideal may itself vary, however. For example, the constrictive ideal associated with suspiciousness may be replaced by an expansive ideal associated with grandiosity. Megalomanic trends may be expected to promote rich and varied responsiveness. $R$, $W$, $M$, $sum$ $C$, $Ch$, ($C$) and $C'$ may all be emphasized or increased by the grandiose orientation. At the same time, however, the arbitrary $W$ and $M$, and the occurrence of arbitrary forms throughout the record, should indicate that we are dealing with a defensively grandiose pose in which reality testing is impaired by a blurring of the distinction between fantasy and external reality.

In general, the use made of determinants may contribute to an understanding of the type, severity and success of defensive paranoid projection and of the total ego context in which paranoid projection is occurring.*

*(c) Other scores.* Secondarily, the traditional content categories may be sensitive to paranoid pathology. Cautious constriction may increase the $A\%$. Suspicious overattention to fine detail may increase $Ad$ and $Hd$. Paranoid somatic delusions are sometimes covertly expressed through hypochondriacal concern. In these instances the $At\%$ may increase. The number of anatomy responses may also increase as an expression of an autistic expectation that these *must be* pictures and that the pictures *must have* special medical significance. Hypochondriacal trends may prompt this particular delusional approach to the test. If paranoid ideas involving sex are clinically prominent, the number of sex responses is likely to increase, unless these sex responses are suspiciously withheld or their crystallization forestalled by initial refusal to respond freely to the stimuli. General evasiveness may increase the number of geographical and anatomical references. But none of these findings in itself will be diagnostic of paranoid pathology.

Perhaps as a reflection of his alertness for magical signs, signals and omens, deriving from omniscient and/or persecutory delusions, but also as a reflection of his arbitrary perceptual tendency to overabstract forms from the inkblots, the paranoid patient is typically the one who will find regular geometric shapes (such as "triangles" in the inner spaces of Card I), letters of the alphabet (such as an "H" in the middle red of Card III), punctuation marks (such as "a question mark" in a speck around the lower edge of Card I), and other abstract or symbolic notations and figures.

*(d) Qualitative aspects of thought and verbalization.* Confabulatory elaboration of responses is predicated upon the blurring of the line between fantasy and external reality that is a prominent aspect of pathological pro-

---

* Recognizing this shifting state of interpretive affairs complicates the tester's diagnostic frame of reference, of course, but it enriches his work immeasurably. Recognizing and specifying complexity is objectionable only to those clinicians who cling to mechanical "sign" interpretation, and to those score-oriented researchers who naively expect that dumping all patients described as "paranoid" (or "anxious," "schizophrenic," "well-adjusted," etc.) into one group will consistently yield highly instructive means, variances or correlations and whose conception of test theory and research stops right there.

jection. Also, confabulatory elaboration frequently requires setting up arbitrary connections between details of the blot. Paranoid patients, in their efforts to ferret out hidden or obscure meanings and to avoid being taken by surprise, as well as to reorganize reality along lines that are not intolerable, typically do relate things to each other—or to themselves—arbitrarily. Consequently, *Confabulations*—as scored and amply illustrated by Rapaport [118]—may be expected to occur relatively frequently in severely paranoid contexts. For the same reasons, we may also expect peculiar notions concerning resemblances and common meanings among the cards or parts of the cards, and wary remarks concerning hidden or obscure meanings in the blots. Actually, thoughts about one part of a blot having originated from another part, about two parts that were once joined but have now been separated, and the like are encountered fairly often in paranoid records.

The paranoid patient is, however, simultaneously striving toward super-objectivity in order to avoid socially vulnerable positions. As a result, his attitudes toward his autistic, confabulatory or otherwise "revealing" or "dangerous" responses may be expected to shift dramatically from moment to moment. His responses may then take on a fluid, elusive quality. In inquiry, the patient may reject a previous response and may even deny that he gave it. For example, one paranoid patient, when asked to explain why he had said the popular figures on Card III could be "men or women," flatly and icily denied that he had said this and insisted that he had only said they looked like "people."

## 2. Test Attitudes and Behavior*

The relative unstructuredness of the test situation and of the test stimuli creates a major problem for the paranoid patient. He is put in a position where he cannot be sure of the significance of the stimuli and of his responses. Consequently, he will be unconsciously terrified of being "found out." Consciously, he is likely to experience this terror mainly in terms of being "misunderstood." He may be afraid the tester will mistakenly draw this or that terrible inference from the responses. If his mistrust is extreme, he may be afraid that this error in inference will not be a mistake at all but a deliberate, hostile act on the part of the tester. The more acute the paranoid problem, that is to say, the more desperately the patient relies on defensive projection, the more we may expect him to freeze, clam up, go into hiding. He may then reject possible responses as inadequate, be over-cautious about obvious responses, and withhold others out of paranoid apprehensiveness. As expressions of rigid unconscious and conscious screening of responses, his reaction times may be long and/or his total

* These have also been discussed in Chapter 2 on the psychology of the testing situation; see pp. 48–50.

times per card short. As already indicated, in the end his total number of responses ($R$) may be strikingly low, and his meager supply of responses mostly flat and unrevealing.

Suspiciousness may take many specific forms: (a) intense interest in what the tester records; (b) anxiety over verbatim recording, particularly verbatim recording of asides, interjections, sighs and the like; (c) evasive, querulous, elusive, defensive responses to inquiry; (d) continued demands for more explicitness in the test instructions; (e) emphasis on similarities and differences between the cards and on the lack of perfect symmetry between opposite sides of single cards; (f) legalistic documenting or critical evaluation of each detail in each response; (g) preoccupation with what the tester is "really" after (e.g., sex, gore, morbid matters). This preoccupation may appear indirectly in overconcern with the problem of *why* the cards are symmetrical or *why* they are black and white or divided in the middle, but it may also be expressed point blank. The themes of all these behaviors and attitudes seem to be, first, that everything the patient says will certainly be used against him and that he had best avoid being pinned down, and, second, that he is being put in an unfair position, possibly even being misled and tricked (by false appearances of perfect symmetry, for example), and that he had best watch his step and not fall into any traps.

The expansive effects of megalomanic features should more or less counteract all these constrictive effects of suspiciousness. Megalomania has its proud, self-assured, self-righteous aspects which, among other things, deny vulnerability and minimize the effectiveness of criticism and attack by others. The predominantly megalomanic patient may therefore be expected to go through the test without being obviously guarded, legalistic and constricted in attitude. In fact, in ways that are entirely inappropriate in the test situation, he may strike a benign, patronizing pose, or an inscrutable pose that combines a frozen smile with steely eyes, or a supremely self-assured pose that is saturated with a holier-than-thou loftiness, disdain and even disgust.

Because suspiciousness and grandiosity typically co-exist in paranoid syndromes, we are most likely to find intermingling expressions of both constrictive and expansive paranoid test attitudes and behavior.

### 3. Thematic Analysis of Content

Because projection results in a sense of surrounding danger and thereby fosters feelings of needing protection, the imagery of external threat and of self-defense may be expected to stand out in the test content of paranoid patients. In addition, the content should indicate something about the types of threat (erotic, hostile, accusing, etc.) and modes of self-defense (flight, hiding, power, etc.) particularly emphasized by the individual patient. These expectations assume, of course, that the patient is yielding more than a few banal responses.

(a) *The paranoid experience of external threat.* Superego projection commonly is expressed in fear of being exposed to hostile scrutiny, seen through, incriminated, or pointed out accusingly. Accordingly, eyes, pointing fingers, blood stains, fingerprints or footprints, detectives or policemen, leering faces and the like may stand out in the content. In contrast, projection of hostility is commonly experienced as apprehensiveness regarding being assaulted, evilly influenced, snared, overwhelmed or deceived. Accordingly, fierce, threatening, sinister, evil, approaching or hovering figures, faces or global physiognomic qualities may be conspicuous, along with traps, webs, pits, poison, electrical or radio waves, concealing darkness, and hidden or partly concealed or obscured figures. Of all the content themes to be discussed in this connection, those of external threat seem to be the most specific to paranoid pathology.*

(b) *Need for and modes of self-protection.* The paranoid patient's strong feeling of need for protection against the externalized threat is likely to be expressed through imagery that in one way or another emphasizes protection. The *mode* of protection specified or implied may, however, vary considerably. Sometimes the emphasis may be on concealment, protecting walls and flight. Then, such images as shields, armor, masks, the shells of turtles or crabs, and crouching or fleeing figures may prevail. Sometimes the mode of self-protection may be megalomanic in theme. This expansive mode may be expressed through such images of status, omnipotence or omniscience as coats of arms, emblems, idols, gods, prophets, crowns, thrones, sceptres, kings and queens, monuments, and persons famous for their achievement, wisdom, goodness, power, or supernatural attributes (Christ, Madonna, Socrates, Buddha, Shakespeare, Washington, Lincoln, Teddy or Franklin Roosevelt, Napoleon, Stalin, the Kaiser). Sometimes the need for protection may be stated through emphasis on failure of defense and on victimization rather than on modes of warding off attack. In these instances, such imagery as mangled butterfly wings, a bombed building, and a person being tortured on a rack may come to the fore.

Images explicitly or implicitly emphasizing self-protection will usually be somewhat less specific to paranoid pathology than those pertaining to the experience of external threat. This does not mean that these images are never vehicles for the expression of powerful paranoid attitudes—they frequently are. It only means that in themselves these images are not peculiar to predominantly paranoid contexts. Many of these protective images may, for example, be conspicuous in the setting of a strong authoritarian orienta-

---

* Phobic tendencies often express themselves in a similar but more moderate, modulated fashion, i.e., in seeing ugly, unpleasant, "weird" things without ascribing hostile intent in a conspicious way; see also p. 211.

tion. While one major aspect of the authoritarian orientation is a special readiness for superego projection and an implicitly paranoid orientation toward authority figures, the authoritarian orientation is not in itself a crystallized paranoid syndrome. Still, frequent or dramatic use of the imagery of self-protection (or its failure) should certainly raise the question of noteworthy paranoid pathology.

*(c) Impulse problems.* In the realm of disturbing impulses, we may expect must less specificity of paranoid reference than in the aforementioned experiences of threat and need for self-protection. This is because paranoid pathology of any magnitude implies significant general psychic regression. This regression will be manifest not only in formal primitivization of thought and perception, but also in a coming to the fore of various pregenital (oral, anal, phallic-aggressive, homosexual, etc.) impulse representations. Unless constrictive suspiciousness limits the Rorschach content to banalities, Rorschach test imagery should reflect this regressive release of primitive impulse representation.\* Those impulses which are crucial in the development of the paranoid disorder may be represented in the test imagery, but they may not be singled out for special emphasis and clearly indicated to be pathogenic. They may merely take their place along with other archaic expressions of impulse. There is no clear evidence as yet that one or another type of pregenital content prevails in the records of paranoid patients, and certainly no content that neatly fits the theory that paranoid pathology is primarily a defense against homosexuality [3].

Also, an increase in the imagery of infantile psychosexuality is hardly peculiar to paranoid pathology. This is because some regression occurs in all psychiatric syndromes, even though to different degrees. The chief exception to this generalization concerning regressive content seems to be the occurrence of one or a few striking (absurd, bizarre, confabulated) images with clear sexual, homosexual and/or anal implications in an otherwise banal, cautiously constricted record. In this instance, paranoid pathology is strongly suggested—although obviously not simply by the instinctual content.

*Under any conditions, the use of the impulse aspect of content for diagnostic purposes is risky.* The following considerations indicate why we cannot trust diagnosis by content alone. (1) Within each diagnostic category, the degree of general psychic regression varies from one case to the next, and this significantly influences the type of imagery that appears in the Rorschach record. (2) For various reasons, one type of archaic material may be more weakly defended against than another in one case and therefore may come to expression more frequently in the Rorschach content, while another dynamic pattern and corresponding imagery emphasis may

---

\* Numerous examples of images pertaining to these pregenital impulses will be found in Chapter 4 on the thematic analysis of content.

prevail in the next case. (3) Simultaneous or alternating operation of other defenses, other forms of pathological solution, and other drive problems than those pertaining to the pathology in question may lead to great inter-individual variation in psychosexual content emphasis among patients in the same diagnostic group. (4) There is great overlap among diagnostic groups in the impulses with which their members are struggling. While there are some diagnostic differences in the *intensity* and *patterning* of these impulse problems, the Rorschach record cannot be relied on to clarify these quantitative and configurational diagnostic differences.

Thus, in paranoid records, imagery with homosexual implications may or may not prevail. The same applies to phallic, anal, and oral imagery. Sometimes the paranoid patient's imagery may emphasize particularly hostile, devouring, *oral* themes (webs, teeth, jaws, fangs, poison, engulfing figures, and the like). Sometimes the imagery may be predominantly *anal* (rear ends, dirt, figures facing away or seen from the rear, etc.). At times it may be predominantly *phallic-aggressive* (huge penises, arrowheads, spears, cannons, etc.). And sometimes it may be specifically *homoerotic* (sex reversals, blurring or exaggeration of sex differences, lipstick and women's adornment in the records of men, masculine imagery in the records of women, etc.) As a rule, unless the imagery is cautiously banal, mixtures of all of these and of images pertaining to other infantile, archaic impulses may be expected in the content of severely paranoid records.

Consequently, we are safest when we restrict our handling of the pregenital Rorschach content to (a) identifying the dominant themes in the imagery, and (b) estimating the rawness, archaic conception and over-elaborateness of these themes. The first of these two interpretive approaches will help define the impulse problems that are pressing or against which defenses are weak at the moment; these impulses need not be the most crucial in the case dynamics, however, and cannot be used for the diagnosis of paranoid pathology. The second interpretive approach will help assess the prevailing degree of regression, defensive failure and general departure from reality.

### B. Case Studies

We have considered many possible forms of appearance of defensive projection in test responses—in formal scores, in test attitudes and behavior, and in thematic aspects of imagery. The following Rorschach records are presented as typical of pathological use of projection. Each patient to be discussed showed prominent paranoid features clinically. However, each relied heavily on defensive projection in a different ego context. Each had a distinctive pattern of overall defensive and adaptive strategy of which projection was only one aspect, though a major aspect. Each patient differed from the next in the extent of his general regression, weakness of defense and adaptability, impairment of reality testing and autistic excesses. Consequently, each Rorschach record will teach us something new about or illustrate further aspects of projective defense. The clinically encountered variety of paranoid contexts is not, of course, exhausted by these cases. Ten times this number would come closer to accomplishing that task. But these cases do stake out a large part of the paranoid territory and that is all that can be reasonably attempted in a work of this sort. Also, other forms of appearance of pathological projection have been and will be frequently singled out for comment in the case studies focused on other defensive operations.

### Case 1

The first case is that of an apparently well-functioning, 34-year-old, rising business man, married, the father of three children, and Catholic. He has a B.A. in political science and an IQ of 130, very superior range. This man was tested and studied psychiatrically in conjunction with his wife's psychiatric treatment. His wife had developed some mixed neurotic symptoms in response to a situation of acute marital maladjustment, and study of the husband was recommended to clarify the nature of this maladjustment. Under these circumstances, this man could be expected to be especially defensive during the examination. This is because, in spite of all reassurances to the contrary, he could hardly avoid the feeling that the crux of the examination was to decide whether he or his wife was "in the wrong."

Clinically, this man was distinguished by striking rigidity and narcissistic self-absorption. His personal adjustment seemed poor. He had strong political interests and aspirations, and the high point of his life had been his active participation on behalf of a presidential candidate a number of years earlier. During and after this presidential campaign, he identified himself strongly with his favored candidate, adopting various of this candidate's personal idiosyncrasies. The Rorschach record provides a good illustration of apparently nonpsychotic and nondisabling grandiose character trends.

CARD I   REACTION TIME: 3".   TOTAL TIME: 1' 30".

*1. (W F— A) The back of a frog or something swimming in the water.*

*2. (Ws F— Design) Or a design of some sort like a snowflake.*

*3. (W F∓ A) A water animal.*

*... (Very fidgety) Other things?*

*(If they occur to you.)*

*4. (W ChF At) Conceivably an x-ray of the skeleton of some sort of animal. I see the bone structure. [What made it look like an x-ray? You see two shades there. It looks like bone structure. There's a light and dark. A bone running up the center. It looks like the x-ray of a person's spine. I don't know. Of course, it isn't. It reminds me of x-rays I've seen.*]

. . . *You want more? (That's up to you.) I could think of a million things.*

His previous question ("Other things?") and the present one ("You want more?"), considered together with the circumstances under which he is being tested, suggest rather an attitude of effortful, grudging compliance than an ingrained submissive orientation. He seems to be saying he will do what the tester asks of him but he will not volunteer very much.

    *5. (W F— Geog) It could be an archipelago of islands.*

(a) High aspirations are indicated by his giving five *W* in a row and nothing else. It is consistent with this inference that he says after #4, "I could think of a million things." It is also noteworthy that all five responses are vague in form and that he misses the popular response to this card. These two findings suggest that his high aspirations probably exceed by far his analytic, integrative and imaginative capacities. It is in line with this inference that in #5, after saying he can "think of a million things," he thinks merely of a million islands, so to speak, and then quickly peters out. (b) The persistent vagueness in these responses gives them a noncommittal quality that may well express paranoid evasiveness. Severe vagueness is not uncommon in paranoid records.

    *Of course, I've been told all this is ink, blotted. That's about it.*

Here he becomes cautious, as he did during inquiry into #4 ("Of course, it isn't."). He may well be implying that he is "wise" to the tester. He may be inclined to vacillate between boastful, pompous grandiosity and self-protective caution. This vacillation, or what might better be described as putting brakes on his expansive tendencies, runs through the entire record and indicates some capacity on his part to take distance from his expansiveness and to stay in contact with reality. It is almost always a close call though.

CARD II     REACTION TIME: 10″.     TOTAL TIME: 1′ 10″.

    *1. (W C Paint) It doesn't look like much of anything to me, unless a kid spilled some water colors or something.*

Unable to form a good *W* but apparently driven to give a *W* regardless of quality, he turns out this shoddy response and externalizes the responsibility for the shoddiness by blaming the response on "a kid." Cautiousness is again evident.

    *That's about all I see (30″).*
    *(Take your time.)*

That the card, perhaps because of the red color, perhaps because of the potential sex responses, is anxiety-arousing is also evident in his haste to give it up. He has to be urged to keep working on it.

    *2. (D F+ Ad P) Two dogs' heads here, Scotties.*

This is his first adequate response and his first *D*. It is, however, an easy, popular one. He has yet to live up to the promise of his emphasis on *W*.

    *3. (DS C'F Hole) (Nervous laugh) A big hole in the ground (middle space and surrounding dark areas). [What made it look like a big hole in the ground? Well because it was light in the center and dark around the outside. Black and white: a hole (impatient, sarcastic tone).]*

(a) True to his high aspirations, he makes this a "big" hole. His sarcasm and impatience in inquiry appear to be further expressions of defensiveness or pompousness; that is, he seems either irritated that he should be bothered by such obvious, petty questions or hostile in response to a fear that the questions may be "tricky" or may show him up. (b) The image possibly states an anal theme.

*That's all.*

CARD III     FAILURE.     TOTAL TIME: 1' 25".

> *. . . Nothing (45"). (Take your time.) Still nothing (not even looking at card). (You're not looking at the card.) (Looks briefly and shakes head) No.*

The grudging compliance noted in Card I abruptly vanishes here. On the face of it, his rejection of this card is surprising. First of all, Card III is rarely rejected. Also, to anticipate, he gives a total of 34 responses to the other nine cards, a total that is relatively high for a record with a card rejection in it. Finally, his high ambitions appear to be such as to work against admission of inadequacy through rejection of a card. He was quite inadequate in handling Card I but that did not stop him from giving five *W* to that card.

One explanation suggests itself: he saw something he did not want to reveal. Several considerations support this explanation. (1) In view of the circumstances under which he was being tested, the patient must have felt he was "on trial." (2) The high aspiration and poor quality of performance noted thus far (and conspicuous throughout the remainder of the record) suggest grandiose character trends, which in turn suggest reliance on paranoid defense. Reliance on paranoid defense would certainly add to his feelings of being "on trial." (3) Finally, we have already noted a cautious, ungiving attitude in his manner of responding. Perhaps he saw blood in the red areas; perhaps he saw a huge spider or crab in the black area; perhaps he saw the popular human figures with mixed sex characteristics. Perhaps he saw nothing, but quickly, preconsciously sensed the beginning development of a response, such as one of these, and hastened to reject the card. In this last case we would have an instance of paranoid anxiety's being stimulated by fear that repressive defense will fail.

An additional paranoid aspect of this rejection of Card III is his refusing even to look at the card when urged to—very likely out of intense fear of what he sees or preconsciously recognizes he might see.

CARD IV     REACTION TIME: 3".     TOTAL TIME: 1' 30".

> *1. (W F+ Ad P) It looks like a bearskin or a—yeah—an animal skinned. [Bearskin? I've often seen them stretched out on the floor. It reminded me of an animal skin stretched out as a rug. How did it look like one? It had a head and four legs. Anything else? It was shaggy possibly. If it were straight lines it wouldn't be a skin. What do you mean about the straight lines? The edges are rounded.]*

This is the second adequate response in the record and again it is only a banal, "perceptual" one.

> *2. (W F— Emblem) Possibly a coat of arms.*

This response suggests special sensitivity to social status in interpersonal relationships, a sensitivity quite in keeping with the suggestions of grandiose aspirations.

*3. (W F— Obj) A shield; a crest (#2) or a shield.*

(a) In content, this response suggests the same trend as has been evident in his tendency toward card rejection and in his test verbalizations, namely, the need for an outer defensive wall. (b) Note the return of noncommittal vagueness in this and in #2.

*4. (W F∓ A) This way again it looks like another sea animal. Here are the tentacles (lower sides), the eyes (on lower middle), the feet (upper sides). Possibly the type that swims.*

It should be noted that he has regained the faltering grandiose stride evident in Card I. On Cards II and III, following five poor *W* on Card I, he tended to want to drop out of the test situation altogether. Now, on Card IV, he comes back with four straight *W*, one banal and three poor in quality. In this last response, he throws in at the last moment a very weak, almost absurd pseudo-specificity—"possibly the type that swims."

CARD V     REACTION TIME: 5″.     TOTAL TIME: 1′

*1. (W F+ A P) A butterfly.*

*2. (W F± Obj) A Flying Wing maybe. It would be a lousy Flying Wing but . . . .*

Further cautiousness is evident in (1) his restricting his second response to a variation on the very compelling first, (2) his criticism of this response, and (3) his introducing it with a "maybe" to boot.

*3. (W F∓ Geog) Maybe another island.*

On still another card he has given only *W* responses, the first banal, the second a variation of the banal first response, and the third noncommittal and vague.

*That's all.*

CARD VI     REACTION TIME: 1′ 40″.     TOTAL TIME: 2′ 25″.

*Jeez! All these look alike to me! Absolutely nothing to me! I don't see anything. To me it's just a variation of all these other ones. (How do you mean variation?) Well, there's a line down the center and these tentacles, lines or sticks protruding. A rough edge; no straight edges.*

(a) A rigid defensive outlook is suggested by this irritable verbalization. Presumably all of the situations (cards) have in common a threat to his need for self-concealment, status and achievement. (b) We must still ask why this extreme attitude appears on this card and why the reaction time increased to nearly two minutes. The hypothesis of shading shock is not compatible with the fact that he responded to Card IV with ease though not with quality. Possibly we are seeing an anxious reaction to the potential sexual implications of Card VI, and his unwillingness to go into such matters with the tester (and therapist) who are strangers and probably biased in his wife's favor. This possibility matches those suggested on Cards II and III.

*1. (De F∓ Geog) Like a coast line or something like that (indicates all of outside edge).*

This is an abortive *W* and of poor quality.

*To me it's nothing mechanical. (What do you mean?) To me it's just the same as all the others. (Anything else it might look like?)*

His implicit need to find something mechanical, i.e., with straight edges and clearly articulated form, indicates great intolerance of external ambiguity, vagueness, amorphousness. It may also reflect his retreat from personal (sexual) matters. This man has been functioning much below his intellectual level (total IQ 130) in response to these inkblot stimuli, producing mostly poor form and vague content. Here he seems to indicate a feeling that he is best able to stay mobilized and function efficiently if the situation in which he is operating is clear-cut and impersonal—like a machine. Not only that, but he disparages what is not safely "mechanical."

> 2. *(W F+ Ad P) Roughly it looks as though you took an animal and skinned him, put it up on the wall or on the floor or something.* [Animal skin? *It was the same as the other (reference to IV-1). The same reasons.* Anything else? *No.*]

(a) Again he seems to be defensively irritable and evasive in inquiry. (b) Again he has given nothing but *W* to a single card, even though the first response, for technical reasons, is scored *De.* (c) Again—in the "roughly" remark—he is cautious about an obvious response.

CARD VII    REACTION TIME: 4".    TOTAL TIME: 1' 50".

> 1. *(WS F± Geog) This might be an inlet . . . boats, ships come into.*
>
> 2. *(D F+ A (P) ) There might be two animals or creatures sitting on either side, looking at each other (upper ⅔). Here is the face and eyes.*
>
> 3. *(W ChF Cl) It could be clouds.* [Clouds? *They were round, broken-up sections. Cumulus clouds look like that, particularly if you're above them and you look down at them. If you're over water, you might get that silhouette. Those are slightly fuller: nimbus, I guess, with rain in them.* Fuller? *They have depth, three dimensions.*]
>
> 4. *(W Ch Sea) Or water. I mean the black could be water versus the white. It could be an inversion.* [Water? *Water, if you're over water, is like clouds: several colors, shades. It is shaded according to depth.*]

(a) It may be related to the suggestions of grandiose trends that in inquiry into #3 and #4 he visualizes himself as being *above* the clouds and the water. (b) In these two responses he also introduces an air of specificity about images that are intrinsically vague (see IV-4).

> 5. *(W F— Design) Maybe a design, a book cover or something, nouveau art or something. Anything could be that, I guess.*

(a) This time his whipping boy is the modern artist. On Card II it was the sloppy kid. The responsibility for the vagueness of his production is again externalized. In general, still running true to form, four of the five responses he gives to this card are *W*. High aspirations are relentlessly expressed. Again, the only adequate response is the popular response, the others being vague. Even the popular response is changed from a human being to a noncommittal "creature." Of 22 responses thus far in the record, 18 are *W*, one appeared to be an abortive *W*, and only three are *D*. Also, of the 22 responses, only six are adequate and these are all essentially banal and even so are cautiously expressed. The rest are vague, inadequate generalizations. His response to color, shading and lack of clear structure is consistently diffuse and inadequate though pretentious.

(b) Note, however, how his frank conclusion of this response—"Anything could be that"—belatedly introduces an element of control and distance from the most arbitrary aspects of his responsiveness (see end of Card I).

*That's about all.*

CARD VIII     REACTION TIME: 5″.     TOTAL TIME: 2′ 25″.

   1. *(W C Coral) Well this might be in the Coral Sea. Coral is that color.* He is still driven to *W* despite the difficulty of attaining *W* on Card VIII. To begin with, as on Card II, he produces only a vague *C* response.

   2. *(W C Design) It might be patches of dyes. You stretch them out if you're going to run a thousand yards of blankets. You bring out various tints on the piece of paper.*

(a) Another vague response embracing the entire card. (b) The essential artificiality of color in this response should be noted as well as the fact that of the three color responses thus far in the record, all have been *pure C* and two (II-1 and this one) have been artificial. (c) The reference to "a thousand yards" of material also has an expansive quality—two yards should bring out the pattern as well as a thousand. It is reminiscent of the "big hole" on Card II and the "million more" remark on Card I.

   3. *(D F+ A P) These two look exactly like animals. <> <> Two little mice or something. Not mice; maybe. . . . A big mouse is a what? Not a woodchuck. . . . Sort of that type.*

(a) Another adequate response but still a banal one. (b) His dissatisfaction with the smallness of the mouse image is noteworthy. He expands it to a "big mouse"—an image that apears to contain a nice condensation of his inadequate and grandiose self-images.

   4. *(D F+ Plant) ∧ This little section could be the crown of a tree (upper gray).* [Tree? *As a kid, you know, you draw a point at the top and the branches come down.* Anything else? *No.*]

(a) Another adequate but banal response. (b) "Crown" of a tree is a significant choice of metaphor in view of the grandiose context which has been developing. (c) In inquiry, the kid is dragged in again to take the blame for the response's inadequate aspects. (d) Although the patient had a chance to give an *FC* response, he did not, indicating the very weak adaptiveness that is already suggested by the diffuse color responses and by the many rigid, arbitrary aspects of his responses and test attitudes and behavior.

   5. *(D F+ At) It looks like the spinal column again (usual middle area).*

Another relatively accurate but quite ordinary response. It speaks for at least a minimum of flexibility that he could relax and lower his ambitions enough to give three adequate *D* responses to this card which is so conducive to *D* and so prohibitive of adequate *W*. While an element of flexibility is suggested by this relaxation, the quality of his responses remains definitely mediocre. He consistently aspires to much more than he can achieve.

*That's all.*

CARD IX   REACTION TIME: 15″.   TOTAL TIME: 2′ 15″.

*1. (D CF Sea) These two green things look like bodies of water down in the tropics or Pacific. [Bodies of water? The color primarily, I guess, and the shore line. From an airplane it would look like that.]*

(a) Another diffuse, narcissistic use of color—a *CF* that, in inquiry, is barely saved from being a *pure C.* (b) As in VII-3 and VII-4, he is looking down on things.

*2. (D CF Cl Fluid) The pink (lower red) looks like a pink cloud. [Cloud? Because cumulus is described in Navy books as looking like sheep or bolls of cotton. Anything else? They were blue; the color and form. They weren't blue, were they? What do you think? They were pink? Did you think of them as pink? A cloud could be pink in sunset. Did you think so originally? No.]*

(a) Still another vague, narcissistic use of color. The response is scored *CF* even though he finally rejects the color, because twice previously he has described the cloud as colored. (b) Fluidity is evident in inquiry when suddenly he thinks of the clouds as blue. This fluidity raises the question of disorganization but his spontaneous recovery in this instance is reassuring.

*3. (D C Bl) The red (orange) might be a stain of meat wrapped up in a piece of paper, like blood in a package of meat comes spread out.*

(a) Another vague, narcissistic use of color. (b) This is the first image in the record with clear hostile implications—"blood." He promptly attempts to neutralize these hostile implications, however: it is only a harmless blood stain on a piece of paper. Still, the type of blood referred to has putrid, gory connotations that retain some of the hostile quality.

*4. (W CF Design, Coat of Arms) The whole thing again could be some screwy design: not quite a coat of arms but some water color monstrosity of some nature.*

(a) Like Card VIII, Card IX is difficult to organize into an adequate *W.* A suggestion of some flexibility on the patient's part is contained in the fact that his first three responses to this card are *D,* even though all three are essentially unformed. Apparently unable to relax entirely and give only *D,* however, the patient reverts to a *W* and now blames its inadequacy on the designer. (b) His reference to a coat of arms restates the theme of status consciousness (see IV-2). (c) His disdainful style of verbalization suggests grandiosity.

*This has good symmetry: it's centered, has round figures, triangles and straight stalks. This is the only symmetrical one I've seen . . . or noticed. If the lines were straight, there would be geometric figures, but with a little art to them; not as a mathematician would draw them. That's about all.*

(a) The search for structure and order suggested on Card VI particularly is again brought to mind by his clinging to the symmetry of this card and by his quite arbitrary efforts to mold the amorphous areas into precise geometric figures. (b) The reference to geometric figures is also reminiscent of the arbitrary geometric forms (abstract shapes, letters, punctuation marks, etc.) that are almost always distinctively paranoid in connotation. (c) His reference to lack of symmetry in the previous cards is also quite arbitrary, but again, as in the case of the fluid cloud response to this card and the "art" rationalization of the geometric figures, it is quickly and spontaneously corrected ("or noticed"). This man apparently tends strongly toward fluid and arbitrary thinking and barely holds himself in check.

CARD X      REACTION TIME: 3″.      TOTAL TIME: 3′.

*1. (D F+ A P) Here are two crabs (side blue).*

Card X is also difficult to organize into an adequate *W*. Again he shows at least a little flexibility by beginning with a *D* response. The response is, however, obvious and easy.

*2. (W CF Design) This thing could be a dress pattern. They print them this way. They let the ink run any which way.*

(a) He quickly falls back to another inadequate, vague *W* and narcissistic color (*CF*). His inadequate handling of the color and form is now blamed on women's fashions. (b) His reference to women's clothing, like the reference to material on Card VIII and his general emphasis on designs, suggests an alertness to decorative, feminine matters that is commonly encountered in the records of homosexual men or men with strong conscious or unconscious homosexual tendencies. We have here an intimation of such tendencies. This intimation ties in with the suggestions of difficulty with sex responses on previous cards. (c) At the same time, these various design responses emphasize the overall "design of things"—a grandiose, though relatively empty, gesture.

*3. (W C World Symbolic, Peculiar) Maybe the world, the world's ideas: a lot of goddam twists—Communist reds, Republican blue, amateur green. It's all screwed up, no real sense of direction or ethical pattern, a conglomeration instead of a direction. Of course, the whole thing has some symmetry. It was made that way by putting ink on paper and folding it down the middle so it would come out the same on both sides. It looks like a pretty mess without anything very important. It's not important. It looks like hues of opinion and confliction and no real sense of right and wrong. That's drawing it out. If you were just dreaming but not looking at it, it might look like that.*

(a) This response is the crowning "achievement" of his record. It is obvious that a deep, disturbing sense of chaos and impotence is liberated by the dazzling variety of scattered forms and colors on this card. He at once transforms this disturbance into a response that is grandiose, self-righteous, full of Olympian scorn and disgust. It is a response that externalizes responsibility for his subjective sense of chaos and his vague, inadequate handling of the card's colors and lack of structure. An inner sense of confusion is projected wholesale into the outer world. Malignant potentialities are suggested, particularly by his shifting his conceptual level from realistic color symbolism (the red and the blue) to metaphoric color symbolism (amateur = inexperienced = "green").

(b) Again. however, he steps on the brakes in the nick of time, indicating that he remains this side of psychosis. His first attempt at control is his shift of emphasis to the card's symmetry, but this effort is inadequate and gives way to further arrogance and disdain. However, at the very end he takes responsibility for the response, renounces it, and saves it from being considered a *Confabulation*: he labels the response a far-fetched elaboration and hardly related to what he actually sees before him. Note, however, that he does not renounce his sentiments. He rejects only the applicability of these sentiments to this stimulus. It is implied that he is able to keep the worst of his grandiose, self-righteous, scornful sentiments to himself, or at least to require some more or less adequate reality pretext to express them. His hold on reality is not a sure one but he maintains it.

(c) His rigid, moralistic forcing of things into his conception of "right" and "wrong" is also strikingly authoritarian in social orientation.

## SUMMARY OF SCORES

R: 34                    EB: 0–11.5

| W | 23 | F+ | 9 | A | 7 | W% | 68 |
|---|----|----|---|---|---|-----|----|
| D | 10 | F− | 6 | Ad | 3 | D% | 29 |
| De | 1 | F± | 2 | Obj | 2 | DR% | 3 |
| S | 0+2 | F∓ | 4 | At | 2 | | |
| s | 0+1 | CF | 4 | Plant | 1 | F% | 62–62 |
| | | C | 5 | Geog | 4 | F+% | 52–52 |
| | | C'F | 1 | Design | 5 | | |
| *Qualitative* | | ChF | 2 | Sea | 2 | A% | 29 |
| Symbolic | 1 | Ch | 1 | Cl | 2 | H% | 0 |
| Fluid | 1 | | | Coat of | | P | 6+1 |
| Peculiar | 1 | | | Arms | 1+1 | P% | 18–21 |
| | | | | Misc | 5 | | |

In the end he has given 34 responses of which 23 or 68% are *W*. He has given 21 pure form responses (62%) of which only 11 or 52% are adequate, and all of which are trite, vague or poor in quality. He has given no *M, FC, F(C), FC'* or *FCh* and no *Human* content. In short, there are no responses in this record that would indicate sensitivity, adaptiveness, capacity for self-confrontation, empathy, genuine imaginativeness or good control of affect and anxiety. He has instead given 4 *CF*, 5 *C*, 1 *C'F*, 2 *ChF* and 1 *Ch*—all indicating considerable narcissism, impulsiveness, diffuse anxiety, and special vulnerability to external emotional influence and to mood.

The distribution of scores, like the total thematic analysis of responses, suggests a very poorly integrated, narcissistic, unadaptive, insensitive, unimaginative, anxious man who has extremely high, implicitly grandiose aspirations. Not only is he unable to rise above the obvious in trying to reach his goals, but he often desperately turns out inferior, shoddy, empty, blown-up responses. To top this off, thematic analysis adds that he consistently externalizes the responsibility for his inadequacies in a self-righteous manner and sneers at the world onto which he has projected wholesale his own sense of chaos and helplessness. Yet, he seems able to keep some distance from the most arbitrary or defensive aspects of his responsiveness. Thematic analysis also suggests that he may well have withheld responses suspiciously (if for no other reason than to defend himself against the clinical examination), that his tolerance of anxiety, emotional stimulation and ambiguity is quite low, and that underlying anxiety over sex and homosexuality may well be acute.

*Case 2.*

This is the record of a 45-year-old, married, childless, Jewish physician with an IQ of 125. His clinical diagnosis was "recurrent depression and hypomania with strong paranoid features in a compulsive, narcissistic character." At the time of testing, he was moderately depressed and extremely suspicious. The record is of interest in showing both the paranoid and the cyclic features.

CARD I    REACTION TIME: 10".    TOTAL TIME: 2' 5".

> 1. (W FCh± A P 3-Peculiar) *Well, it looks like a bat with . . . perhaps . . . which is perhaps in a not alive state, showing signs of deterioration. I can't say much more about it now.* [Which were the signs of deterioration you were referring to? *The variation in the coloration of the object, and the detached pieces.*]

(a) The opening theme is that of deterioration, death and disintegration. This theme, as well as its especially significant position as the first communication to the tester, suggests a deeply depressed, despairing view of himself. In effect, he seems to be saying, "I'm a goner." (b) The stilted, peculiar verbalization—"in a not alive state"—obviously is designed to avoid the word *dead*. In the Rorschach situation, avoidance of "dangerous" words, such as *dead*, suggests pathology that is paranoid in form and psychotic (magical) in quality and degree. Obsessional patients may avoid words that are "unclean," and pollyannish patients may avoid words that are "unpleasant," but in both cases the verbalizations will be appropriate and not peculiarly stilted. (c) Similarly peculiar and suggestive of psychosis is his reference in inquiry to the bat as "the object." (d) The *now* in "I can't say much more about it now" gives this verbalization a peculiarly guarded, paranoid tone. The *now* also indicates an unverbalized premise about time and communication, and an assumption that the tester knows this premise. The possibility must be considered that we are observing an altered state of consciousness in which the assumptions underlying communication are not the usual, relatively realistic ones.

> . . . *(Anything else?)*
> 2. (W F— Art Peculiar) *Well it might be . . . an impressionistic painting. . . . Some sort of symbolism that isn't quite clear to me.* [Did the painting seem to represent something? *I couldn't make any real object out of it.*]

(a) His reference to unclear symbolism also has a paranoid tone. Cards VIII, IX and X are multi-colored and difficult to organize into *Whole* responses. Consequently they often elicit implicitly or explicitly pretentious and critical comments about the incomprehensibility of modern art, surrealism, or—God's gift to the Philistines—Dali. This patient's verbalization not only occurs in an unusual place (on Card I), but it in no way shares the spirit of these scoffing remarks. This patient seems to be expressing a genuinely baffled feeling, a feeling that reinforces the impression just recorded of an altered state of consciousness. It is as if he has the feeling that things are going on about him that have hidden or obscure meanings and that he cannot quite get hold of or penetrate into these meanings. If this is his feeling, it has paranoid psychotic implications. (b) Thus, strong, if not extreme, depressive and paranoid trends, accompanied by peculiar variations of conscious experience, are already suggested by the first two responses to the test. The patient may well be dominated by feelings of confusion and unreality, and by fears of being destroyed by inner and outer forces.

*I think I'm through.*

CARD II    REACTION TIME: 45″.    TOTAL TIME: 2′ 10″.

*1. (D F∓ A Peculiar) Well this again looks to me like a . . . representation of some winged object (dark areas).*
"Winged object" is a peculiar verbalization (see I-1).

*2. (D CF Bl Peculiar) Here I think perhaps it might be . . . I'm reminded at least of blood (all red), but I can't connect the two (#1 and #2). [Blood? Principally the color, and the smooth but irregular outline of the forward patches. Anything else? It was sort of like a splash of blood.]*

(a) Note how he cautiously changes "it might be" to a much more non-committal "I'm reminded at least. . . ." (b) His inability to "connect the two" —the blood and the winged object—may be looked at from several points of view which are not mutually exclusive. (1) This is a failure of an integrative attempt, and, in view of the content, suggests defensive instability with respect to hostile impulses. The integration could only lead to an anxiety-arousing image of a bleeding creature. Presumably, the threat in this image would derive from the depressive (self-directed hostility) or paranoid (projected hostility) trends already suggested, or both. Hence, the need to stave off the image and his subsequent difficulty in integrating the separate elements. (2) He may well be assuming that he should give *W* responses only. This could reflect very high aspirations and possibly even a megalomanic self-concept. Megalomanic trends could be expected in view of the accumulating evidence of paranoid pathology. (3) Paranoid persons often seem to assume that there are "relationships" between the blots or between parts of the blots. These "relationship ideas" possibly stem from an underlying assumption that there are hidden meanings in the cards they must discover. This patient's verbalization in this instance is only mildly suggestive of such a paranoid assumption, but it fits well with a similar implication in I-2. (4) His experience of integrative difficulty may also reflect some of the baffled, confused conscious experience noted twice on Card I.

*3. (DS C'F Pit Peculiar) I just looked at it with not a very comfortable feeling about it. [What about it made you uncomfortable? I think it was the darkness with . . . a hollow in the middle. Did that suggest anything to you? Sort of a pit.]*

(a) His spontaneous verbalization reinforces the impression of a peculiarly altered state of consciousness. He seems at a loss to make sense of much of his conscious experience.

(b) Dynamically, the response appears to express another instance of defensive weakness. His spontaneous verbalization, in which he expresses only a feeling, suggests partial failure of repression: the idea of the "pit" may have been blocked off from consciousness, but not securely enough to obstruct the unpleasant affect associated with the idea. Then, in inquiry ("the darkness"), the emotional tone of the response emerges more clearly. In particular, his spontaneously expressed discomfort may have been due to increased awareness of depressive feelings (see II-2). Finally, the pit image emerges clearly. This image does not appear to be primarily depressive, however. It is not in the usual imaginal vocabulary of depressives. It suggests, on one level, fear of the "snake pit," that is, "going crazy," and losing control of impulses. On another level, this image suggests paranoid fears of being trapped or engulfed.

(c) Whatever his particular fear, it seems clear by now that this patient feels beset by dangers. Whereas in the disintegrating bat of I-1, the threat seemed to be perceived as an internal one and therefore suggested depressive rather than paranoid pathology, in this pit response the threat seems to be at least partly externalized and suggests paranoid rather than depressive pathology. Yet, the earlier depressive response seemed to contain paranoid elements, the present paranoid response apparently has depressive elements, and other responses have been suspected of having paranoid and/or depressive elements. It is likely, therefore, that the patient oscillates between the paranoid and depressive positions. Clinically, this is not an uncommon finding. Simultaneous or alternating depressive and paranoid solutions are often encountered clinically.

> *That's all.*

CARD III     REACTION TIME: 25".     TOTAL TIME: 2'.

> *1. (W M± H (P) Peculiar, Confabulation tendency) I see here two grotesque figures, more or less symmetrical, with a union between their anterior parts (lower middle). It suggests a Siamese-like effect.* [What sort of figures did you mean? *More like caricatures.* Of what? *Not anything special. Looked like a masquerade or buffoonery.* Do you mean to imply it looked like people? *That's right.* Did you make out the sex of the figures? *They were more like men.*]

(a) The "union between their anterior parts" formulation is a peculiarly stilted verbalization of the sort already noted (see I-1). It too therefore suggests paranoid pathology.

(b) Note the repeated cautiousness—"grotesque," "more or less symmetrical," and the doubly redundant "suggests a Siamese-like effect."

(c) In content, a union of the "anterior parts" of two men has striking homosexual overtones. The occurrence of stilted and extremely cautious verbalization at this point suggests that the patient feels threatened by this homosexually-toned image. Support for this inference is found in the patient's dismissing the response as grotesque and not to be taken seriously ("buffoonery"), and his becoming evasive in inquiry and reluctant to specify that these are people or men. For a man of his intelligence, this basically popular response is easy enough to form and to be specific about. We must therefore ask why he was so uneasy about it. To answer this question we must assume he feels his defensive position is threatened. This is the same line of reasoning we followed in discussing Card II, with respect both to his trying to relate the blood to the flying creature, and to his handling of the pit image.

> *I don't seem to be able to tie in the red elements here and it doesn't seem to bother me at this point (nervous laugh). That's all I can make out of that.*

Again he tries to establish relationships between everything and again he fails (see II-2). His need to specify that the integrative failure does not bother him now and his anxious laughter suggest that he *is* still bothered by it but trying to deny his anxiety. Otherwise he would probably not have mentioned it at all and he probably would not have laughed. Thus, a new defensive operation appears on the scene: denial. If indications of denial increase in quantity or intensity in the record, it will suggest that hypomanic as well as depressive mood swings are likely to occur (see Chapter 8 on denial).

CARD IV     REACTION TIME: 28".     TOTAL TIME: 1' 50".

> 1. *(W FCh± Ad (P)) Well this looks to me like it might be the pelt of an animal with a rather peculiar position of the head end (lower middle) down between what could be taken to be the legs (lower sides). I'm not sure what kind of an animal it is but. . . . I can't suggest a name for it. . . . I'm through with that one.* [Pelt? *Well, seeing the animal head and then the symmetrical appearance of the lateral projections and the ruffled appearance to it made me think it might be a pelt.* Ruffled? *I think that was the difference in light and shadow, light and dark.*]

(a) This perceptual organization of Card IV is occassionally encountered. Its most striking aspect is its anal perspective. Almost the entire figure is the rear end of an animal, and the upper middle is likely to be the anus. (Inquiry should have established this clearly, but experience with this image of an animal with its head between its legs strongly supports the assumption of anal perspective.) Anal emphasis frequently reflects homosexual tendencies, but just as frequently it seems to pertain more directly to the anal fixations and regressions commonly found in obsessional and paranoid pathology.

(b) If it is seen at all, this bent-over animal is usually thought to be alive. The patient's weaving the anal perspective into the popular "animal skin" response *and thereby devitalizing it* might well be a defensive maneuver designed to minimize or deny pressing—perhaps projected—anal temptations. His inability to specify the kind of animal that it is, even though this image ordinarily presents no such problem, also seems to reflect intensified defensive (in this respect, repressive) operations.

(c) Characterizing the position as "peculiar" seems to be another statement of his perplexity. Part of the background of his apparently altered state of consciousness and its associated perplexity seems by now to be the following: rigid defensive operations, including projection, introjection, denial and repression, seem frequently unable to stave off expressions of threatening content, but do limit the resulting eruptions to forms that are fragmented, abortive, vague, distorted or otherwise difficult to grasp. His paranoid tendency to externalize inner experience probably leaves him feeling then that he is surrounded by complex, elusive, peculiar phenomena.

> . . . *(Anything else?) I don't see anything else.*

CARD V     REACTION TIME: 50".     TOTAL TIME: 1' 50".

> 1. *(W F+ A P) Well here again all I can make out of this is perhaps a badly drawn winged creature. This may be in flight . . . And that's all I can say about that one.* [What sort of creature? *I'm not certain what kind it is but again I get the impression of a bat.*]

(a) He externalizes responsibility for what he considers the inadequacy of the figure—it is "badly drawn." This is a mild instance of projection but one

commonly encountered in the records of paranoid persons. The "normal" paranoid subject discussed first in this chapter used this device frequently. (b)
Criticism of this popular figure and vagueness in naming it ("creature"), both
suggest unusual guardedness of response. (c) His verbalization in inquiry points
again toward a peculiarly vague and uncertain variation of conscious experience

CARD VI     REACTION TIME: 80".     TOTAL TIME: 2' 35".

> 1. (DS F— Geog Confabulation tendency, Peculiar) Well as I look
> at the larger part of this sketch (lower D), this part may look very
> much like it could be a . . . a . . . island or small, a small island lying in
> a vast expanse (surrounding white) . . . and . . . I'm not able to tie
> any other into this diagram with it. [What made it look like an island?
> Well mostly the fact that it was surrounded by the white, I think, as
> though it might be a deserted island with water around it—I mean a
> desert island rather. Why a desert island particularly? There doesn't
> seem to be anything on it.]

(a) This is an unusual image. Thematically, it suggests feelings of smallness,
emptiness and loneliness. On the one level, his slip in inquiry—"deserted" substituted for *desert*—supports the inference of loneliness. On another level, the
slip suggests feelings of having been abandoned and of great dependence on
others. He seems to be saying, "I am alone; I have been abandoned; I am
empty, barren and insignificant by myself." This is a classical depressive statement. In fact, to a great extent it would be this miserable feeling and self-
concept that would need covering over by the grandiose trends suggested by
his striving to achieve *W* responses. (b) Looked at from the point of view of
thought organization, the response has a confabulated aspect, particularly in
its reference to the "vast expanse" around the island and to the "smallness" of
the island. There is almost a dream-like quality in this response. Confabulation
bespeaks noteworthy autistic features. Thus, in its formal aspect, the response
suggests autistic, grandiose features, while in content it suggests depressive
features—the former possibly defending against the latter.

> 2. (D FCh± Plant) But I suppose we could say that that was a rather
> free interpretation possibly of a tree; foliage on it (upper D).

He again externalizes responsibility for the inadequacy of his response and
even so is exceptionally cautious: "I suppose," "we could say," "rather free
interpretation" and "possibly" add up to far more qualification than response.
This overcautiousness is in striking contrast to the dreamy loss of distance
from his image in #1. This shifting between strict and inadequate reality
testing characterizes the functioning of many paranoid patients.

> That's all.

CARD VII     REACTION TIME: 10".     TOTAL TIME: 1' 30".

> 1. (W ChF Cl) This looks to me like a cloud formation. That's sug-
> gested by the sort of foamy texture to the drawing.
>
> 2. (D F+ Hd P) And the clouds sometimes do take that formation,
> similar to a head (upper ⅓). [What sort of head? A human head.]

Note how he cautiously avoids spontaneously specifying the kind of head and
in inquiry does not volunteer any more than the acceptable minimum.

> I think that's all.

CARD VIII     REACTION TIME: 40".     TOTAL TIME: 1' 50".

*1. (D F+ A P.) Well I see two reddish-pink figures here that look like rodents.*

*2. (DS F∓ Arch Confabulation) This (upper gray-green and middle blue) could represent a house. And the empty spaces in it (between blue and gray-green) could be significant of the fact that the rodents (#1) have partially eaten into it. [What made it look like a house? The idea of gables here (upper gray-green); the house here (middle blue).]*

We have here a full-blown confabulation that confirms our earlier suspicions. As a confabulation, particularly in such a cautious, constricted record, it has a clear paranoid implication. Yet, its content is depressive. In this respect it is very much like the deserted or desert island in VI-1. It is depressive in the theme of the house (his home? himself? both?) being destroyed by oral-devouring creatures (his impulses? others in his life?). Also, the same theme of deterioration and disintegration as was suggested by the dead bat in I-1 seems to be restated here. Apparently the painful threat of collapse and disintegration eats away at this man.

*That's all.*

CARD IX     REACTION TIME: 35".     TOTAL TIME: 1' 50".

*1. (W C Art) Well this could be a very good attempt I would say at modernistic, impressionistic painting.* [Did it seem to represent something? *Nothing especially.* What made it look modernistic? *It was nonobjective; at least that's my impression of it. It seemed like a nice color composition.*]

*That's all I can see in it. (Take your time.) It just looks rather pleasing. I rather like the design and the pastel-like colors; they're soft and pleasing. That's all.*

(a) This is a pseudo-response masking a failure. The responsibility for the inadequate form is externalized via his rationalization of the response as "modern art." (b) His positively toned references to the soft pastels have a quality of feminine sensitivity. If it were well integrated into his character structure, this feminine sensitivity could be an asset in that it would give some warmth and tenderness to this otherwise cold, rigid, cautious person. It should be noted, however, that he did not really make good use of this sensitivity. He could not impose form, let alone good form, on the blot and he could not give the art any representational significance.* We must conclude that there is significant adaptive and defensive weakness in this response. His sensitivity of feeling is probably not well integrated into his character structure and probably clashes seriously with his rigid efforts at control. In him, this clash may derive from a prejudice that warmth and delicacy of feeling are "feminine," fear of homosexual tendencies, and a defensive need to repudiate whatever smacks of womanliness (see III-1, IV-1). In short, sensitivity may be for him a disorganizing affect.

CARD X     REACTION TIME: 30".     TOTAL TIME: 2'.

*1. (W CF Spring Confabulation) This . . . suggests . . . to me spring, springtime with budding (side blue) and . . . flowers (side yellow)*

---

* No comment on nonobjective art outside the Rorschach test is implied.

*... water (middle blue) ... greenery (upper and lower green) ...*
*... ... A certain sort of exuberance to it. ... A feeling of newness*
*in it, beginning a new thing; sprouting and symmetrical orderliness.*
*That's all.* [*(Card shown.)* Where did it look like it was budding?
*The shoots here (projections on side blue).* Where was the water?
*I think of this as a lake (middle blue). (Card removed.)* What gave it
the quality of exuberance? *I think the variation of the forms and the*
*... variation in color ... and the multiplicity of themes in the drawing.*
And the newness? *Some of the forms are sort of reaching out and*
*that's what gave me the feeling of budding and sprouting.*]

(a) This response is essentially one massive denial, with hypomanic coloring,
of all the suspicious and depressive problems previously expressed. Instead of
death, deterioration and destruction, this response is bursting with vitality and
wholesomeness. Instead of a projected sense of threat, mistrustfulness, and
feelings of inner inadequacy and disintegration, there is order and optimism. It
is as if he has turned over a new leaf on Card X.

(b) But the appearance of the denial is abrupt. Nothing in the previous
responses prepared us for it, except perhaps the minor denial of anxiety at the
end of Card III. Not only is the response abrupt, it is physiognomically confabulated, and it includes elements of *pure C, absurd F—* and autistic handling
of size relationships. Altogether, it seems to reflect desperate, emergency defensive measures that are inherently unstable and out of touch with reality. If
such a response were part of a generally more colorful, impressionistic record,
and if, following this response, the patient settled down and gave good *D, F+*
*FC+, Popular* and near-popular responses, we might possibly take a more
sanguine view of the response. We might regard it then as reflecting a tendency
toward intense enthusiasm and exuberance and we might assume it emanated
from a working, even if somewhat hypomanic, adjustment. In this case, however, we see no evidence of real integration or internal consistency. In fact,
we see the direct antithesis of the emotional tone that pervades the rest of the
record. The previously conspicuous, rigid controls appear to have collapsed,
his gloom and apprehensiveness have vanished, and the patient is autistically
at one with the world.

### SUMMARY OF SCORES

R: 16        EB: 1–3.5

| W | 8 | F+ | 3 | A | 4 | W% | 50 |
|---|---|---|---|---|---|---|---|
| D | 8 | F− | 2 | Ad | 1 | D% | 50 |
| S | 0+3 | F∓ | 2 | H | 1 | | |
| | | M | 1 | Hd | 1 | F% | 44–69 |
| | | CF | 2 | Plant | 1 | F+% | 43–64 |
| *Qualitative* | | C | 1 | Geog | 1 | | |
| Confabulation | 2 | C'F | 1 | Art | 2 | A% | 31 |
| Confab. tend. | 2 | FCh | 3 | Misc | 5 | H% | 12 |
| Peculiar | 9 | ChF | 1 | | | P | 4+2 |
| | | | | | | P% | 25–38 |

We may conclude, therefore, that this man is probably psychotic and that
his psychosis is characterized by cyclic and paranoid features, as well as by
peculiar variations of conscious experience. He clearly appears to shift

among three major positions: depression with its reliance on defensive introjection, suspicious and grandiose paranoid autism with its reliance on defensive projection, and hypomanic exuberance with its reliance on defensive denial. From the point of view of defense and adaptation, each position he assumes seems to be desperate and extreme. This is a far cry from the well integrated, moderate forms of expression of these defensive operations in the records of normal persons. Accompanying these shifts of defensive position appear to be vague, perplexed feelings and an unstable hold on reality despite rigid efforts to remain safely realistic.

The score patterns tend to support this picture. In addition to the scores in the *Qualitative* column that reflect the patient's autistic tendencies of psychotic degree, the following features stand out: (1) white space is used relatively often (three times in major ways, even though these are scored "additional"); (2) the only color used is weakly formed or unformed; (3) the $F\%$ and $F+\%$ are relatively low; (4) $M$ is essentially absent; (5) there is a noteworthy emphasis on chromatic and achromatic color and on shading. Together, these score patterns suggest that at present this is a relatively poorly controlled, anxious, moody, negativistic, narcissistic man whose reality testing is inadequate and who is defensively trying to avoid free fantasy, self-confrontation and spontaneous self-expression.

In many respects, it should be mentioned, his scores are like those of the primarily repressive patients discussed in Chapter 7—low $R$, low $M$, $EB$ weighted on the side of *sum C,* and low $F\%$. Also, qualitative analysis in this case indicates the presence of major repressive efforts. But qualitative analysis further indicates that projection, introjection and denial are far more pathological in this case than repressive efforts. In fact, the repressive efforts may be sparing him further disorganization. This total defensive configuration is not brought out by the scores. Moreover, the low $F+\%$ is not specific to paranoid or cyclic pathology. The $W$ and $S$ scores, while relatively high, are not extreme. And while $R$ is relatively low, there is no extreme restriction of response (including card rejections) to suggest his severe paranoid guardedness. Only total thematic analysis indicates the breadth and depth of this patient's pathology.

*Case 3*

This is the record of a 22-year-old, single, Jewish, male college student and cocktail lounge musician, with an IQ of 120. He was tested at a time when, clinically, he appeared to be in the budding stage of an acute paranoid schizophrenia. Classical secondary symptoms, such as delusions, were not yet florid, but they seemed to be developing. Premorbid schizoid character features and a tendency toward excessive drinking were also noted. His immediate fears centered around the dangers of "blacking out," "going insane" and attacking women. His intense ambivalence towards his girl friend was conscious. He also worried that he "overidentified" himself with her—a fantasy with very thinly veiled homosexual components. The patient was tested hurriedly in response to unavoidable time pressure, and necessary inquiry into some responses had to be omitted.

CARD I    REACTION TIME: 4".    TOTAL TIME: 1′ 50″.

    *1. (W F+ A P) A bat. That's about all I see is a bat (15"). (Anything else?) It's an approximation of a bat; it just suggests one to me.*

(a) After one obvious response, he is ready to quit. Among the reasons why someone might want to quit so soon are the following: strong repressive policy; overt rebellious negativism; paranoid cautiousness; depressive inertia with its implicit negativism and demandingness; ingrained sullen passivity; and a state of acute anxiety. (b) Particularly when applied to popular responses, such a verbalization as "an approximation" suggests compulsive meticulousness or paranoid cautiousness.

    *2. (Drs F± (Hd) Fluid, Peculiar) It might be a face in here (entire middle area). [What sort of face did you have in mind? Face? . . . Oh! It had two large eyes which were triangular (upper middle spaces), a small dot for the nose (usual center "buckle"), and the other two white spaces below look like jowls although they're white—they look like something hanging from the face. The face of a what? It seemed like a mask of some sort; something artificial, obviously.]*

(a) Fluidity of thinking is suggested by his initially puzzled response to inquiry —"Face?". He quickly recovers his orientation, however. (b) The mask concept brought out in inquiry suggests concern with concealment or dissembling, but in itself is not sufficient for even a tentative conclusion to this effect, because the mask image is rather commonly elicited by this card. But when he describes the mask as "something artificial, obviously," he gives the response a self-expressive stamp and a definitely mistrustful tone.

    *3. (D F— Hd) These could be other faces here with a long nose (each side, facing out).*

    *4. (Dd F+ Hd Peculiar) These might be two hands reaching out in the other direction (upper middle), without the rest of this. [What did you mean by "reaching out in the other direction"? Into the board itself. How do you mean? Not pointing at me but toward you, holding the . . . (holds card vertically); just for a second.]*

(a) The "in the other direction" comment is an inadequate communication that is peculiarly schizophrenic. It assumes that a previous idea about direction—*this* direction—has already been communicated. As in the previous case, an altered state of consciousness may underlie this unrealistic assumption.

(b) The response takes on a paranoid aspect in his introduction of a three-dimensional quality. This three-dimensional quality is to be distinguished from reference to two-dimensional representation of depth by the use of shading and perspective. Objects, animals or persons *coming out of* or *going into* the cards appear to possess a vividness that almost brings these percepts to life. As a rule, such vividness is achieved only when pathological projection is at work and the line between fantasy and reality blurred. This patient's going on to specify the direction of movement of the figure in terms of the tester (another man) and himself increases the projective quality of the response. This personalized organization of space is also to be distinguished from merely locating the response on the card with respect to the tester and the patient as two poles in space, as in, "The head was the part that was nearer to you." In the present response, a percept has not only achieved life-like vividness, but apparently has done so in terms of the two real figures in the test situation. His suggested identification with the figure on the card underscores the pathological loss of distance from his own fantasies. Again it is indicated that he is experiencing peculiar alterations of consciousness.

(c) On one level, the response's content might be stating the theme of some reaching out on his part toward the tester. Whether this reaching out would be hostile, supplicating, homosexual, or some combination of these is unclear.

(d) Finally, a quality of preservation of reality testing is again suggested (see I-2), this time by his saying that it looked like reaching hands "just for a second." Qualifying verbalizations such as this one, when they pertain to peculiar or bizarre responses, usually imply that the autistic idea is not fully crystallized and is somehow experienced as unreal or tentative. These qualifications also suggest that the patient may be shifting in and out of the normal waking state of consciousness.

> *Am I supposed to search? (That's up to you.) I don't think I could exhaust it in a few hours (as he rejects card).*

The patient makes a feeble gesture with respect to his potential productivity. A significantly high level of ambition and, in context, possibly even grandiose tendencies are suggested.

CARD II     REACTION TIME: 4".     TOTAL TIME: 1' 5".

> *1. (DS F— Ad Fluid) It looks like a cat of some sort—a cat's face, that is (all but upper red). [(Card shown.) Show me the face. Except for the red projecting things up there (upper red). I got two views of the mouth: later I thought it was here (middle space) but at first I thought it was down here some place (lower red). (Card removed.) What made the lower part look like a mouth? I didn't think of the mouth specifically. I was just looking at the whole thing. I suppose when I looked again I chose the center piece because it was more appropriate.]*

(a) Inquiry into this response reveals perceptual fluidity, the mouth shifting from the lower red to the center space. Persons not characterized by fluidity of thinking and perception sometimes change their minds about the perceptual organization of a response but tend to do so somewhat deliberately and not with a tone of passive experience of changing perceptual organization. The latter quality seems to obtain in this instance and the potentiality for feelings of unreality is thereby suggested (see also end of discussion of I-4). (b) Note, however, that at the end of the inquiry he takes a firm grip on the change and accepts responsibility for it. Again, noteworthy preservation of reality testing is suggested. (c) That it is a mouth around which the fluidity centers suggests that oral (dependency, demand) conflicts may be particularly acute. His fleeting impression in I-4 of hands reaching toward the tester also had a possible supplicating implication. The fluidity in that response may well parallel the fluidity in this. If we are on the right track, we should (and do) encounter further indications that experience or expression of oral tendencies is especially threatening to him and especially disruptive of functioning (see IX-6).

> 2. (D F+ Ad P) Two dogs' heads with their noses approaching each other.

The "approaching each other" description is unusually tentative for this popular response. If these figures are seen at all, their noses are typically touching or jointly supporting something. Acute anxiety concerning intimacy and contact with others is suggested (see VII-1 below).

> 3. (D F— Ad) This looks like the tail of some animal here. I don't . . . (lower red).

An anal theme is suggested.

> 4. (Dr F± Hd Peculiar, Confabulation tendency) I can't make anything out of this (upper half of upper red) unless they just might be fingers. [What made it look like fingers? I was just groping. It was the only thing I could make it look like. How did it look like that? The top part: in shape. Anything else? No, except it might be pointing, directing something.]

Pointing fingers usually express a paranoid theme. The theme may be that of being accused (implied superego projection), being the accuser (implied id projection), ability to read signs and portents in the environment (implied omniscience), or having a mission to lead or control (implied omnipotence). The last of these paranoid themes is suggested by his confabulatory response to inquiry—"directing something."

CARD III        REACTION TIME: 5″.        TOTAL TIME: 2′ 15″.

> 1. (D M+(H) (P) Peculiar) Looks like two humans bending over in sort of a dance of some sort. That's the large shape. Looks like they're bending. Their heads don't look like heads at all.

(a) Persons who see the human figures but are dissatisfied with the head area as a human head usually point out that that area looks like a bird head or animal head or simply criticize the head as a weak part of the human response. His rejection of the head area as a head of any sort, though tentative, is peculiarly cautious and goes beyond what the typical compulsive patient might say. He repudiates these heads again in #4, below. (b) Also, he cautiously avoids stating the sex of the figures, suggesting thereby some doubt as to whether these are men or women. In turn, this doubt and its being kept secret imply both strong anxiety associated with homosexual tendencies and a guarded, possibly paranoid defense against this threat. (Of course, we need more direct evidence of these trends.) In #4, below, he returns to this problem of sexual identity, indicating significant instability of defense in this area.

> 2. (D FM+ A) Looks like something falling (upper red). Looks like a monkey or an ape, falling from a . . . .

(a) The initial vagueness of this response—"something falling"—points to the presence of a defensive problem. Only afterwards does the image take form. Faltering repressive efforts are particularly suggested by this.

(b) The theme of falling may refer to a subjective fear or actual experience of his own decompensation—his having lost his grip, so to speak.

> 3. (D F+ A) That center piece (middle red) could be a butterfly, I

*suppose.* [What made it look like that? *The wings; the center piece is a little too long but. . . .* Anything else? *The symmetry.*]
*That's about all.*
4. *(Dr F— Sex 2-Peculiar) Those figures (#1, P) are in some sort of costume. The possibility of a sexual note over here (points to projection on usual thigh).* [What did you mean by "a sexual note?" *It looks like a penis, on both.* Did it seem to be any particular sort of costume? *I suppose they had some sort of dancing pose and parts of their shape looked irregular, so I . . . . The heads are incongruous though; they weren't human. I don't know even if they were heads.*]

(a) Two male figures in a dance with their penises showing—his final version of the first response—has definite homosexual implications. In all likelihood, this patient's need to avoid alluding to this theme underlay his delayed reference to the penis and his peculiarly guarded way of verbalizing the penis—"the possibility of a sexual note over here." (b) That he did not withhold the response altogether, despite his anxiety about it and defensive delay in elaborating it, may bespeak some preservation of adequate reality testing and some efforts to ward off extreme paranoid mistrust (see also I-2, I-4, II-4). On the other hand, his "frankness" could merely reflect serious failure of repressive defense and consequent crowding of consciousness by normally unconscious fantasies, feelings and wishes (see #2). (c) Because we have an image strongly suggestive of homosexual tendencies does not mean, however, that we are necessarily on the right track so far as our inference of paranoid pathology is concerned. For one thing, too many records of non-paranoid patients have homosexual indications of one sort or another; for another, this record has had (and will have) too many indications of other infantile, primitive, libidinal and aggressive tendencies, particularly oral tendencies (see II-1) but also anal (see II-2), to be considered simply indicative of acute homosexual conflict. All we can say with any confidence is this: among other things it is likely that the patient feels threatened by homosexual impulses against which his defenses seem inadequate. (d) "I don't know even if they were heads" restates the passive, perplexed attitude that accompanies his externalizations.

CARD IV    REACTION TIME: 8″.    TOTAL TIME: 1′ 50″.

1. *(D F+ Ad) An animal's head, possibly a cow or a bull (lower middle).*

His giving alternatives—cow or bull—suggests uncertainty or ambivalence concerning the masculine-feminine dimension of his identifications or relationships, and a corresponding homosexual trend of note (see III-4).

2. *(D F+ Hd Peculiar) Possibly two large feet, pointing outwards, wearing ragged pants (lower sides).* [Ragged? *The pointed edges, and I think as soon as I decided they were feet, I had to make use of all the irregularities.*]

(a) Emphasizing the bigness of these feet often implies subjective feelings of smallness. (b) "Ragged pants" indicates preoccupation with fall and decline. As in the falling ape of III-2, we seem to have here a combination of strength (bigness) and failure. Concern with the decline of a powerful external figure is suggested by both images. This concern is more strongly suggested than concern with his own decline because the patient appears to feel small with respect to this image and not identified with it. (c) His passive feeling of compulsion—"as soon as I decided . . . I had to"—again suggests a peculiar variation of conscious experience. An overvalent theme seems to "take over" and lead to certain thought processes which the patient passively observes and, at best, weakly rationalizes.

> That's about all I can. . . .
>
> 3. (D F± Ad Peculiar) This is some sort of nose of some animal, elephant-style (upper side projection). It's not too clear.

(a) Long noses are frequently emphasized in the records of homosexual men and probably represent awe or fear regarding the phallus, perhaps particularly the paternal phallus. In dreams, the nose is often used as a symbol for the phallus. Also, it is not rare that this area is seen as a phallus. The emphasis in this response on length (see also I-3) could be the counterpart in implicit sex terms (big penis) of this patient's previous emphasis on physical size (big boots). Particular feelings of sexual inadequacy as well as general feelings of personal inadequacy could be implied. (b) Inasmuch as the area in question is clearly articulated, "It's not too clear" seems to mean "I'm not too clear." His very choice of words suggests a readiness to externalize responsibility.

> That's about all.

CARD V     REACTION TIME: 8".     TOTAL TIME: 1' 15".

> 1. (W F+ A P Peculiar) An insect of some sort, possibly a bat—another bat. It could be an insect or a bat, I suppose. The wings seem to be pointing slightly inward, like before (I-4), toward you.

(a) His repetition of the response in his second sentence indicates a ruminative proclivity that could be the obsessive counterpart of the compulsive meticulousness suggested in I-1 (see also III-1 and IV-2, inquiry). The stimulation of special ruminativeness at this point may derive from anxiety associated with his need to choose between a potentially threatening bat and an essentially innocuous insect (see also the ape vs. monkey alternative in III-2 and the cow vs. bull alternative in IV-1).

(b) The three-dimensional quality and the wings pointing specifically toward the tester have the same malignant, paranoid implications elaborated in connection with the reaching hands in I-4. This response is particularly paranoid in that the card was flat on the desk at the time the verbalization was delivered, so that, if anything, the wings were pointing toward the floor.

(c) The patient's experiencing the wings as pointing toward the tester indicates an interpersonal significance in the response—in particular, the possibility that the bat is an externalization of himself and that something of his relationship to the tester is stated through this image. Whereas in I-4 the implications of reaching hands were ambiguous, here the bat probably partakes of such threatening qualities usually associated with bats as eerie, dirty, vampirish, grasping, enveloping, and evil. If this line of reasoning is correct, the patient is preoccupied with and feels threatened by as well as guilty about his hostile, demanding impulses toward the tester and the real life figure(s) for whom the tester stands.

CARD VI     REACTION TIME: 17".     TOTAL TIME: 1' 25".

> 1. (D F± Ad) They all look like animals of some sort. This seems to be a comic cat's head viewed from the top, looking down on it, with the ears sticking out (upper D).

*2. (D,W F+ Ad P Fluid, 2-Peculiar) The rest of it (lower D) looks like a rug to me, an animal's rug. I guess the whole thing could be the rug and this (upper D) could be the head. [Rug? The way it was lying there. It reminds me of the way . . . I've seen a few bear, bearskin rugs and they seem to lie there that way.* Anything else? *Then when I added the head to it again, it still looked like it. There were a few things on the side I couldn't fit in. It reminds me of something else.* What does it remind you of? *If I had thought of them in themselves (reference to lower side projections) . . . (shrugs).]*
*That's about all.*

In addition to "animal's rug," the final two remarks in inquiry are peculiar communications. At first they definitely stimulate the expectation that he has seen something specific and then they disappoint this expectation. This may well be an instance of precarious—but in this instance still successful—repressive blocking of an image (see III-2, III-4).

It is noteworthy that the patient has gotten through six of the Rorschach cards, giving 10 *Peculiar* and 4 *Fluid* verbalizations, and one *Confabulation tendency*, but no *Confabulations, Contaminations, pure C, M—* or other major schizophrenic indications. Moreover, of his 18 responses thus far, 14 are of good form, yielding an $F+\%$ of 78% and an indication of generally fairly well-maintained reality testing. From this we may infer that he is probably not in a chaotic schizophrenic state and that his contact with reality and adaptive resources have been preserved to a significant extent. It is particularly paranoid psychotics who can give this picture. In the next two cards, this relatively smooth surface will be shattered and will never be fully restored, although partial recovery will be evident in Cards IX and X and will indicate significant resiliency.

CARD VII    REACTION TIME: 20″.    TOTAL TIME: 2′ 20″.

*1. (D FM± (H) P Fluid, Confabulation) Somehow these look like two figures (upper ⅔). They seem to be looking at each other, possibly in a comic manner. Each standing on one foot, it seems (base of middle ⅓). Now suddenly this one on the right, it looks like it's facing in the opposite direction (away from center) and the one on the left seems to be approaching it or chasing it. And then they interchange. (What do you mean?) The one on the right looks like it's going in two directions. Now I can make the left one look that way, look in the opposite direction. That's about all I see. Now I can make them go in either direction.* [What sort of figure did you have in mind? *One way it looked like a dog (facing outwards).* The other way? *The other way it's hard to say.* What do you think? *Possibly an animal mimicking a human.* Any particular animal? *No.]*

This response is one of the two high points of the record (see also VIII-4, 6, 7). In it is an intricate pattern of defensive projection, a statement of a sick interpersonal orientation, a losing struggle to maintain contact with external reality, and an autistic, megalomanic method of solving his conflicts.

The response starts off in a light, positively-toned vein, and is more or less conventionally elaborated. Up to his "in a comic manner" description, his adaptive and defensive operations appear to be effective. "Each standing on one foot" is perceptually somewhat arbitrary and marks the beginning of the response's invasion by autism. Abruptly, the perceptual organization of the response and its emotional tone change—"Now suddenly . . . it looks like it's facing in the opposite direction"—suggesting that defensive failure is occurring. Clearly, it is as if he is passively watching a puppet show when in fact he is the one who is manipulating the strings. This peculiar variation of conscious experience appears to involve externalization in pure form. What is inside—his fantasy, feelings and intentions—is experienced as altogether outside. This goes far beyond the moderate degree of externalization that is inherent in almost all projective test responses. Note in this regard how he begins the response with "somehow."

The origin of the above change in perceptual organization and emotional tone —from a presumably playful, mutual approach of the figures to unilateral pursuit and flight—may well be the anxiety stimulated by the fantasy of mutual approach. If we remember the hands reaching toward the tester in I-4, the peculiarly tentative approach of the dogs in II-2, the homosexual overtones in III-1 and III-4, the bat wings reaching toward the tester in V-1, and if we bear in mind the schizophrenic's characteristically intense anxiety concerning human relationships, we see one probable source of this anxiety: intimacy brings the danger of experiencing and expressing impulses and feelings that would destroy the object, the relationship and the self. Dynamically, the sequence thus far seems to be: approach, impulse stimulation (hostile? oral? homosexual?), anxiety, projection of unacceptable impulse, and flight. He goes on to say, "And then they interchange," meaning that the fleeing figure is now approaching again. Content-wise this suggests vacillation in attitude between approach and flight. From the standpoint of projection, however, the drama is still pathologically externalized.

At this point—the reversible direction of the figure on the right—the patient appears to make a new autistic maneuver to conquer the anxiety presumably stimulated by the initial response and coped with thus far via the fluid perceptual organization and unstable emotional tone of the response. He says, "Now I can make the left one look . . . in the opposite direction." He explicitly takes over the puppet strings; that is, he transforms the passive experience into one of active control. And yet his verbalization indicates that he does not take his share of the responsibility for the original drama. It suggests rather that he feels he is intervening in an external reality situation or at least intervening in a process which is basically directed by external forces. Thus, his control seems to be primarily autistic control. The content of this exercise of autistic control amounts to a statement that he can decide what will take place "out there": mutual approach, mutual flight, himself being pursued or himself being the pursuer. There is a megalomanic undercurrent to this assumption of power—a grandiose, counterphobic denial of the initial paranoid anxiety (see also II-4).

We seem to be watching the development of a defensive, megalomanic overlay on top of intense paranoid anxiety. One form of paranoid pathology compensates for the other. While his final solution is essentially autistic, it indicates that ways of mastering intense anxiety are available to him and could well act as stabilizing forces. The stability would be quite precarious, though. The realistic, adaptive response that opened the drama on this card should not be forgotten, however, and neither should the general adequacy of form and form level in his test responses thus far. In view of the extreme paranoid lengths to which this patient can go, his appreciation of and responsible handling of reality requirements are impressive. He is by no means altogether overwhelmed by or enmeshed in autism.

CARD VIII     REACTION TIME: 15″.     TOTAL TIME: 5′.

*1. (D F+ A P Peculiar) I can't decide whether these are rats or . . . yeah, probably rats. They're just sort of hanging there.*

(a) "Just hanging there" suggests feelings of precariousness mixed with a passive, helpless orientation. It is reminiscent of the falling ape in III-2. (b) The spatial concreteness in this response also suggests the altered state of consciousness we have encountered numerous times in this record.

*2. (D F± At) This looks like some sort of skeletal arrangement (usual ribs, middle).*

*3. (S F± Ad) A face right over here (middle space); the end of this long bar (midline segment) becomes its nose.*

*4. (Dr F∓ A Fluid, Peculiar) Now it looks like these rodents over here (#1) are trying to catch something that looks like a small animal (sides of upper gray-green) It (the small animal) should end right over here (part way in).*

*5. (D (C)F Geog) This reminds me of part of a relief map possibly (middle blue). [What made it look like a relief map? Just the different shades. It looked like, reminded me physically of the way a relief map looks with the higher parts and lower parts.]*

*6. (DS F— A Contamination, Confabulation) This gets complicated. At the same time as the two animals (#1, P) seem to be trying to catch this object and that object (#4, sides of upper gray-green) with their left front claws, the top part (all upper gray-green) looks like some insect overseeing the whole thing, with its head the part I described before (#3, middle space). This one could be expanded as far as I am concerned to a little drama of some sort. The rats are being fooled into believing they are chasing small objects but they've merely got a small portion of this larger animal on top—which is just waiting, I suppose.*

*7. (D F∓ Object Confabulation) Now these two rats might be fighting over this center piece in here (middle blue) which seems to be torn (in the middle); not fighting but pulling on it from both ends. It's torn about two-thirds down from the top.*

In #4, #6 and #7, we come to the second high point of the record. The three responses will be discussed together. To begin with, there is a chase (see VII-1): the rodents are trying to catch something. The theme of smallness—"small animals"—is introduced again (see IV-2). Then, the response's first clearly autistic element intrudes: a peculiar conceptual shift occurs as a result of which the gray-green extensions cannot be kept separate from the gray-green center mass; the small animals then "become joined with the rest of this." This autistic turn (and peculiar variant of conscious experience) forewarns of the defensive and adaptive failure that emerges clearly in #6. Note too that the animals, although originally merely passively "hanging there" (#1), are now actively pursuing. This change of content is reminiscent of the autistic change from approach to flight and then back to approach in VII-1. This reversal appears to be crucial to the subsequent development of the response.

Next, in #6, the gray-green area changes from small animals to an implicitly huge (conceptually contaminated) insect hovering over the chase. This image of a huge, hovering, observing figure may state a megalomanic or persecutory paranoid theme or both. That this change is externalized and passively experienced, as was the change in VII-1, is evident when the patient says, "This gets complicated." He talks as if he had no control over the drama, as if it were sweeping him along with it. It is this contrast between his actual passive observation of his projections on the one hand and his fantasied active mastery in the content of the projections on the other that indicates we are dealing with autistic control and not real control and effective adaptation. The patient appears to gain some distance from this response when he says, "This one could be expanded as far as I am concerned to a little drama of some sort." This verbalization is another indication of some preservation of reality testing (see end of discussion of VII-1, and also II-1). The hovering insect now changes into a "larger animal" that has in effect set a trap for the pursuing animals. Thus far the sequence seems to have been: passive helplessness ("hanging there") which autistically changes to active pursuit (of the small animals) which introduces megalomanic and/or fearful fantasy (the huge, overseeing insect or animal) and paranoid fear of falling into a trap ("being fooled").

It is difficult to say where this patient's identification lies in this complex response. The hanging animals response suggests a self-representation but then so do the hovering insect, the small animals being chased, and the chasing animal that is being "fooled." It is most likely that the response involves multiple self-representations, and that, in accord with his emotional reactions to what has already become conscious, the patient fluidly alters his fantasy (and identifications) as he goes along. Our decision about where his primary identification lies is less important, however, than our clarifying the major themes or modes of relationship he is concerned with. His position might change in relationships, for example, from one extreme to the other and yet the *mode* of relationship, such as tyrannical-submissive or strong-weak, might not change at all. In this case, the themes and relationships, as well as the formal aspects of thought and perception, are paranoid throughout. A trap set by a huge, hovering figure is florid paranoid fantasy.

There is one final development of the response. The patient drops the trap fantasy abruptly, works away from the most hostile implications of the response, and moves closer to reality again. The animals are now merely fighting over an object. In fact, they are not quite fighting over it—they are just pulling on it and tearing it. While feelings of being torn by external (projected) forces may well be expressed in this image, the response is purged of its most threatening and unrealistic aspects.

In these responses we have seen paranoid thinking not merely in the form of arbitrary inference and arbitrary relationships, as we did in the case of the previous patient with cyclic and paranoid features. This is live drama. It is more alive, in fact, than the vivid, three-dimensional quality of I-4 and V-1. Finally, it should be stated that at the appointment's termination the patient volunteered that the test had become interesting and enjoyable only "when the drama came in." He was referring to his autistic responses to Cards VII and VIII. In view of the threatening nature of the content of his projections, this final verbalization suggests the presence of pathological surface blandness. The meaning of the blandness would seem to lie in the reassurance he gains through his autistic manipulation of his fearful, paranoid fantasies. This is more than simple denial or counterphobic assertiveness. To a significant degree, autistic mastery appears to have replaced realistic mastery and seems now to provide the patient with a superficial sense of relief.

CARD IX    REACTION TIME: 12".    TOTAL TIME: 3' 15".

*1. (D F∓ (Hd) Peculiar) Two heads at the top, facing each other (upper orange, "gargoyle" organization).* [What sort of heads did you mean? *They're not natural human or animal. . . .*]

*I can't make up my mind which to approach first; I see so many things.*

*2. (Ds F— Hd) Two faces in the green, facing outward (nose is outer tip, eye is space in green). They remind me of Ed Wynn. This might be a goatee (side bump), although he doesn't have one.*

*3. (D F∓ At) The center piece looks sort of like the spinal column (midline).*

*4. (Dr F— Hd) A face right in here, facing directly downward, in the center, with a long nose coming out irregularly only on one side (around lower end of midline).*

This is the fourth long nose (see I-3, IV-3, VIII-3).

*5. (Drs FC'∓ (Hd)) A face in here (lower middle space); two eyes, longer than they are wide. It looks like a mask of some sort. There seem to be two teeth coming out, the white spots (tiny spaces between green areas).*

(a) The inclusion of teeth is unusual in this response. (b) The mask suggests concern with concealment or dissembling again (see I-2).

*6. (D F+ Hd) I was about to, this suddenly looks like a baby's head on either side (outer sections of pink).* [Why a baby particularly? *I guess . . . it just looked like one. I can't say why. Sort of fuzzy hair, a few curls coming out—not curls, a few strands.* Anything else? *Mostly the top part of the head and the shape.*]

(a) Infant, fetus, embryo, chick and similar content often reflect strong oral, passive, regressive wishes. This particular response is too frequently seen for this inference to stand by itself here, but in view of related indications in I-4, II-1, IV-1, V-1, VIII-1, VIII-4, VIII-6, and the unusual teeth in IX-5, this inference need not stand by itself. (b) Note again the peculiarly passive perceptual experience expressed in "this suddenly looks like," and the externalization of inner processes this implies.

CARD X    REACTION TIME: 8".    TOTAL TIME: 2' 50".

*1. (D F+ A P) These looked like spiders at first (side blue).*

Again a peculiarly passive experience of perceptual change—"at first." The presence of so many of these indications of an altered state of consciousness strongly suggests the occurrence of feelings of unreality.

*2. (D F± A) Two animals arguing with each other (upper gray). They might be birds; here's the tail.*

*3. (D F(C)+ A Peculiar) Caterpillars in the green at the bottom (usual).* [Caterpillars? *There were ruffles on the skin, the way cater-*

*pillar skin is curled up when they are in motion—compressed.* Anything else? *No.* Sure? *And the lengthy shape.*]

4. *(DS F— Hd Absurd) I could imagine a face here. I don't see all of it. The nose in the middle (middle of middle blue), the eyes are somewhere in the space above it (above middle blue). Just part of it; a portion.* [Did you make out parts other than the nose? *Just a portion of the face: the nose and cheeks (middle blue) and the top part seemed to be sockets. Of course, it's all white. There could be eyes in that area.*]

It is impressive how this arbitrarily organized face relies so much on the eyes which aren't there at all. Here is another striking projection—paranoid not only in form (arbitrary) but in content ("eyes") as well.

*There's so much here I can't stay long enough with one to decide what it is.*

A feeling of excitement is conveyed in this preface to the fifth response. His attitude is that of being passively swept along, as it was in his grand paranoid fantasies on Cards VII and VIII and elsewhere.

5. *(D F± A Peculiar) This might be a dog here, running—on the right only—running to the right of the paper but with the head straight up (side gray). It could be a dog on the left side but there's no eye in it.*

(a) Emphasizing dissimilarity of *content* on the right and left sides of the cards—regarding sexual identity, emotional tone, physical characteristics, etc.—may as a rule be regarded as a form of expression of more or less serious paranoid projection. With infrequent exceptions, it takes some breakdown of the distinction between fantasy and external reality and consequent gross externalization of fantasy to make the formal and emotional differences between the right and left that sharp. Ordinarily it also takes at least some paranoid mistrust to care that much about such minor discrepancies. The content of such projected differences is, of course, often revealing of crucial conflicts, each side possibly representing one horn of a basic dilemma. In contrast, merely pointing out uninterpreted physical differences between the right and the left may simply reflect a ruminative or overmeticulous mode of functioning. (b) Note his preoccupation with the eye in this response (see #4).

6. *(D F∓ A Fluid) This could be a little toad (lower middle, usual rabbit).* [Toad? *It had two feet projecting behind it (rabbit ears). I was thinking of a tadpole but a tadpole only has one tail. Aside from that, it looked like a tadpole or a toad.*]

7. *(D F+ Ad P) Or a face, a rabbit's face, between the two caterpillars (lower middle).*

*That's all.*

The score summary reflects many of the trends that have emerged in the total thematic analysis. The *Qualitative* scores alone are sufficient to indicate autistic features of psychotic degree. The general constriction that is frequently encountered in acute paranoid schizophrenic records is suggested by the $F\%$ of 85%–97%, the $EB$ of 2–0 and the $A\%$ of 54%. The paranoid emphasis in his psychosis is also suggested by his emphasis on *Space* responses. In this context, an emphasis on $S$ usually implies pathological suspiciousness. His relative withdrawal from real objects is suggested by the absence of color responses. His passive and somewhat confused approach to situations appears to be reflected in his achieving only 2-to-3 $W$ out of 39 $R$. Also relevant to the low $W$ is the qualitative suggestion that his grandiose trends express themselves more in fantasies and delusions or near-delusions of control and mastery than in extremely high aspirations. His is a different sort of expansiveness than that of the first subject studied in this chapter. His relative blandness is suggested, in context, by the presence of only two unimpressive shading responses—a $(C)F$ on Card VIII and an $F(C)$ on Card X.

SUMMARY OF SCORES

R: 39    EB: 2–0

| W | 2+1 | F+ | 12 | A | 12 | W% | 5–8 |
|---|-----|----|----|---|----|----|-----|
| D | 29 | F− | 8 | Ad | 9 | D% | 74 |
| Dd | 1 | F± | 8 | (H) | 2 | DR% | 18 |
| Dr | 6 | F∓ | 5 | Hd | 8 | | |
| S | 1+3 | M | 1 | (Hd) | 3 | F% | 85–97 |
| s | 0+3 | FM | 2 | Obj | 1 | F+% | 61–63 |
| | | F(C) | 1 | At | 2 | | |
| | | (C)F | 1 | Geog | 1 | A% | 54 |
| *Qualitative* | | FC′ | 1− | Sex | 1 | H% | 21–33 |
| Confabulation | 3 | | | | | P | 8+1 |
| Confab. tend. | 1 | | | | | P% | 21–23 |
| Contamination | 1 | | | | | | |
| Peculiar | 16 | | | | | | |
| Fluid | 5 | | | | | | |
| Absurd | 1 | | | | | | |

On the adaptive, preserved side are: (1) his $F+\%$ of 61%–63%, which is no worse than borderline so far as overall impairment of reality testing goes; (2) his $R$ of 39, which reflects somewhat more tolerance for self-expression and therefore somewhat less severe or better controlled constrictive suspiciousness than is typically encountered in acute paranoid schizophrenics; (3) his $P$ of 8+1, which indicates preserved interest in and responsiveness to conventional, clear-cut aspects of external reality; (4) the absence of *pure C* and an *EB* weighted on the *M* side. In this general schizophrenic context, these findings concerning $M$ and color suggest that blunting of affect and dilapidation of internal controls or capacity to delay impulse have not yet become prominent. They therefore suggest that the psychosis is probably in an early phase or has been held in such a phase.

Altogether, the picture that emerges is that of a deeply withdrawn, passively oriented young man in an early, acute phase of a predominantly paranoid schizophrenic psychosis. He still shows noteworthy preservation of ego functions such as reality testing and delay of impulse, but his defensive and adaptive position is quite weak and unstable, and peculiar alterations in his state of consciousness seem to occur frequently. He apparently attempts to achieve calm and stability by extreme projection and by grandiose manipulation of fearful paranoid fantasy as if it were external reality. The boundaries between fantasy and reality appear to be very fluid. Such calm and stability as he achieves in this autistic way do not appear to be securely maintained. Intense underlying anxiety in interpersonal relationships and a tendency to flee from relationships are repeatedly suggested. To him, contact and intimacy between people appear to be matters chiefly of pursuit and flight, traps and devouring. In typical schizophrenic fashion, he is likely to be characterized by highly mobile transferences—as evident in the extent to which the content of some of his responses seems to be invaded by impulses and feelings toward the tester. As the patient experiences it, these impulses are likely to represent some combination of homosexual, devouring, and evil tendencies. Feelings of smallness and helplessness appear to be prominent and may be associated on the one hand with the strong passive, regressive tendencies that are also indicated, and on the other hand with compensatory, defensive grandiosity. In all likelihood he is relying extensively on defensive regression from hostility to passivity in his relationships. It is also suggested that he may be preoccupied with the decline of a powerful figure—perhaps his father-figure—and that he may be feeling "torn apart" by externalized conflict.

## Case 4

This is the Rorschach record of a 30-year-old, unmarried, Protestant woman, an unemployed college graduate with an IQ of 122. Her clinical diagnosis was "chronic paranoid schizophrenia in partial remission." Several years previous to testing, she had an open paranoid schizophrenic break in which delusions about hostile foreign agents and being raped figured prominently. Since that break, she has been drifting in and out of jobs, psychiatric hospitals and her parental home. The patient was not a psychiatric patient at the time of testing. She came asking for vocational counselling and not for psychiatric evaluation or treatment.

CARD I    REACTION TIME: 6″.    TOTAL TIME: 1′ 55″.

1–2. (Ws FC′∓ Ad Confabulation, 5-Peculiar, Self-reference; W FCh+ A P Fluid, Contamination, Peculiar) Oh, it looks like a tiger staring at me (#1). And it also looks like a bat-like thing—just the outlines (#2). Sort of whiskers over there (upper middle projections; reference to #1). I don't know, sort of a tiger or a cat. Well, it's fiercer than a cat. A very fierce Tabby: the way it's staring at me. [What made the tiger look fierce? The light, the eyes: on first look it looked tigerish. The V-shaped, pointed, light spaces might have been fiery eyes (upper middle spaces) and maybe teeth (lower middle *spaces). And then if you look closely at the inner section (middle D) it looks like an insect body (reference to #2), feelers (upper middle) and wings (sides) and the white space (inside) is just space. It is almost microscopic; one of those x-rays: you see animal-like inner channels and various things, you know, down the center.]*

(a) In "a tiger staring at me" we have a clear, simple, blandly unabashed verbalization of a paranoid projection. Moreover, the *Confabulation* and *Self-reference* in the response, the patient's bland lack of ado about its fearful content, and her giving it as the first response in the record, all suggest that the patient has been psychotic for some time and is in a superficial way at home with her paranoid ideas, unconsciously threatening though their content may be.

(b) The tiger image suggests that in this instance it is oral-aggressive, devouring intent that is being projected. After #2, she returns to this image and tries to minimize its threatening theme by changing the tiger into a domesticated cat, but she achieves only a condensation that is almost a contamination—"a very fierce Tabby." This appears to be an instance of a double defensive failure, the first failure being the clear emergence of the threatening "tiger" material in projected form, and the second failure being her inability to deny the threatening material via the cat image. Her emphasis in inquiry on the animal's eyes underscores the paranoid projection. Her emphasis on the animal's teeth underscores the oral-aggressive content implications.

(c) The whiteness of the eye spaces is autistically interpreted to be the light in the tiger's eyes and this in turn is autistically elaborated to suggest fiery qualities. Such indications of thought disorder as these are numerous throughout the test. For the most part, these indications will not be commented on unless they relate directly to major projections. It should not be overlooked, however, that her verbalizations are consistently fluid and scattered and sometimes virtually incoherent.

(d) In inquiry into #1, she irrelevantly introduces #2, mixing up and implicitly contaminating the bat and the insect, and also the x-ray plate and the microscopic slide.

(e) It is possible that just as she apparently tried to change the threatening tiger into an innocuous cat in #1, in #2 she may be attempting to transform the potentially threatening bat into an innocuous insect.

> 3. *(W F— A Peculiar) Going the other way: a peculiar animal, with the head there (lower middle).*

By "going the other way," the patient means visualizing the head at the bottom instead of at the top.

> *(Peculiar:) It doesn't remind me of any particular terrain. (Peculiar:) It is definitely insect-like or animalistic. Something about the formation of the thing: it has a strange form, less haphazard than just a landscape. Anything else you want (offhand manner)? (Anything else you think of?) I'm kind of stuck on that.*

(a) "Animalistic" is probably a neologism in this instance. Although "animalistic" is a word, it is relatively rare and probably unknown to this patient, and, in any event, its meaning is irrelevant to the response. Her verbalizations continue to be scattered and often do not quite communicate anything.

(b) At the end, when she asks, "Anything else you want?" she seems to convey the attitude that has already been inferred from her changing the bat to an insect and the tiger to a cat: minimization of the fearfulness that results from her paranoid projections of hostility. Apparently she covers her paranoid anxiety with a superficially brash, ready-for-anything, counter-phobic manner toward the objects of her paranoid projections. The success of this maneuver gives the impression of schizophrenic blandness. There may also even be a grandiose aspect to this question—"Anything else you want?"— in its possible implication that she will be able to do whatever the tester might ask her. When the tester turns the question back on her, he prompts her to acknowledge that she is unable to respond further. The first patient discussed in this chapter used a similar maneuver, boasting explicitly that he could see many ("a million") things and putting it up to the tester whether the tester wanted more from him. That patient was also unable to deliver anything substantial when further response was left up to him. A similar turn of events took place at the end of Card I in the third case discussed. Brash or grandiose verbalizations like "Anything else you want?" should be distinguished from such submissive, authoritarian questions as "Is that enough?" and "Do you want me to go on?".

CARD II     REACTION TIME: 7".     TOTAL TIME: 1' 50".

> 1. (WS F— Ad Fluid, 4-Peculiar, Absurd) They all look like upside-down cat-Tabbies. That red (musing). . . . This is definitely an upside-down Tabby cat. [What made it look like a cat? I don't know; again the eye businesses. Where were the eyes? The cat was facing the other way (i.e., seen upside down); the eyes were nearer (to the patient). (Patient is asked to point out eyes on card; she searches.) . . . There aren't any eyes. Well, here are the eyes (upper tip of middle space) and that's just the nose (rest of middle space). There is no forehead.]

(a) "They all" is a grossly premature generalization that suggests poorly integrated grandiosity. (b) The eye emphasis in inquiry and the fluid perception of the eyes indicate both the paranoid problem again and the anxiety associated with her paranoid orientation but denied in her superficial manner. With respect to this denial of anxiety, note how nonchalantly—and arbitrarily —she improvises facial features at the end of inquiry.

> 2-3. (D F+ Ad P; D FC— Food Peculiar) Or it could be two little bears (#2). I know: profiles of two little bears with their noses sticking up in the air or holding something jointly. Their paws are in twin bottles of jam, I don't know, at the bottom (#3). Or little dogs, puppies. [Jam? It was red.]
> What these two things at the top are (upper red) I wouldn't know. (Peculiar:) It's quite symmetrical, too symmetrical to be much more interesting (laugh). I can't think of anything else beside that.

Unable to respond further to the card, the patient projectively blames her inability on the symmetry of the card and glibly affects boredom.

CARD III     REACTION TIME: 1".     TOTAL TIME: 2' 30".

> 1-2. (D M+ H P Peculiar; D C/F Dec) Oh these look like two ballet dancers doing some kind of dance of some kind (#1). The red stuff (middle and upper red, #2) just seems to be a decoration for the ballet dancers.

*(Peculiar:) Why are these things always so symmetrical? It bothers me! It isn't any picture! I want to play around with it like this (card turning).*

*3. (W F∓ A Confabulation tendency, 2-Peculiar) < ∨ That (all black) looks like a huge, horrible bug upside down—a tarantula (silly laugh). It looks dreadful, spidery: half a spider going into something. (Into something?) About to take something; the claws are out in front (P legs).*

The projected oral aggressive impulses inferred from the tiger image in I-1 are more clearly expressed in this tarantula response, particularly in the "about to take something" remark. Again, however, the patient apparently attempts to minimize this fearful image: it is only "half a spider" and she laughs (inappropriately) as she describes her horror of it. (b) Reference may be made in this image to an engulfing, poisonous, destructive mother-figure.

*4. (D F∓ Obj 2-Peculiar) They (#1) are just sort of leaning away from something, carrying a bucket, a joint bucket, balancing the bucket (laugh). That's good!*

This bit of silliness is a clear display of inappropriate affect.

CARD IV     REACTION TIME: 25".     TOTAL TIME: 1' 45".

*Oh my word! A uniformity about these. (2-Peculiar:) This has a strange similarity to the first two beforehand, the first two. . . .*

As noted in the previous chapters, one of the chief implications of vexed reference to uniformity is that a common defensive problem is posed by all the Rorschach cards. This patient goes on, however, to comment on "a strange similarity" to the other cards. She thereby indicates a growing, if not already crystallized, belief that there is a hidden, meaningful connection between the cards. This is a typical paranoid belief. It indicates that the tester is being woven into the paranoid patient's delusions.

*1. (W FCh— Ad Confabulation, 2-Peculiar, Self-reference, Fluid, Irrelevant) Actually, it seems like the skull of a steer—one of the skulls of steers in a desert. [Where did you see that? It's looking at me in the opposite direction. The underpainting, the light parts, suggest that it was looking in the opposite direction. Was it the whole blot? No, just something quick, something light about the way it was done.]*

(a) Images like a steer skull in a desert, connoting death from lack of food and water, commonly express feelings of oral deprivation. There has been a strong oral emphasis in each card thus far: the fierce tiger-cat on I, the bottles of jam on II, the tarantula on III, and now the parched skull on IV. (b) In inquiry, she again emphasizes eyes in her self-reference—"looking at me." The self-reference underscores the paranoid (being watched) implication of the eye response. (c) Her reasoning and verbalization are thoroughly bizarre, and her response to the second question in inquiry irrelevant. Apparently she was expecting to be asked the usual "Anything else?".

*2-3. (D (C)F Plant Peculiar; Dd F(C)+ Ad Fabulized Combination, Confabulation tendency, 3-Peculiar, Irrelevant) And then it has a separate, has peculiar qualities like an overturned leaf (lower side gray), except it has a peculiar snout-like thing at the top that looks like a head (upper middle). It is very vague though. That's completely non-dimensional, idiotic, stupid! [What did you mean by "non-dimensional"? I don't know what I meant by that. It doesn't have any connection with anything: no form, substance or reality. It's sort of half of fits of everything. It isn't sort of fish, flesh—what is that game? —not animal, vegetable or mineral.]*

(a) The remainder of her responses to this card are so poorly integrated and verbalized as to be chaotic. (b) Note her externalization of responsibility in inquiry for her difficulty in coping with this card.

*4. (Dr ChC' Ad) It's slightly furry. [Furry? The middle part of the black part, before the leaves (#2) that are curled back. It looked like animal rugs. What gave it that look? The black, inky splotches.]*

*I can't think of a thing more to say about that.*

CARD V　　REACTION TIME: 50″.　　TOTAL TIME: 2′ 10″.

*Gracious! (Peculiar:) Why do these always meet? (Patient gives serious, detailed explanation of construction of inkblots.)*

A number of times now the patient has become preoccupied with the symmetry and the construction of the blots. This continues throughout the remainder of the test. Her perseverativeness in this regard, the lengths to which she goes, and her emphasis on *why*, considered together with the numerous paranoid indications throughout the record, all suggest that she suspects or is on the lookout for some trickery or hidden meaning in the symmetry. At the beginning of Card IV we already encountered one clear suggestion of a paranoid approach to gross resemblances among the blots.

*1. (DW F+ A (P) Contamination tendency, Self-reference, Fabulized Combination, Fluid, Peculiar) This looks like a flying gazelle, I guess (W). It's got ears like our dog, little collie's ears sticking up there (upper middle). [What did you mean by "flying gazelle"? I just said that. It looked like something flying. Maybe it was the ears: the ears were like a gazelle. Anything else? Not that I know of. What is a gazelle? Sort of a doe.]*

*2. (W FC'— Arch Contamination tendency, Fluid) Also, it might be a hut-like structure too: kind of a thatched affair, pointed, with a pointed roof; sort of a witch-like structure. [What made it witch-like? I don't know. It was black and kind of . . . sort of the general outline of the whole thing: a witch-like outline. What about the outline was witch-like? There were little things sticking down the middle, and it went up in a V. What about those little things? I don't know; I don't know; I just said it.]*

Witch imagery generally expresses a hostile, evil conception of the mother-figure. By virtue of its extremeness, the image usually seems to involve considerable projection of hostility. The tarantula image in III-3 should be remembered at this point, because in dreams the image of the spider has commonly been found to represent a hostile, destructive mother-figure.

*3. (W FC'— (Hd) Peculiar, 3-Fluid) It could be an Indian wig. That's what it mostly looks like: an Indian hair-do (laugh). [What made it look like that? The part, the way they stick their hair—maybe not an American Indian—one of those other Indians all over the place. You know: South Seas. Indian black hair. More a sense of simple medieval folk and not a war-dance Indian.]*

In the last sentence in inquiry, we have another instance of minimization of an aggressive theme (see I-1, I-2, III-3).

CARD VI    REACTION TIME: 1″.    TOTAL TIME: 45″.

*Oh for heaven's sake!*

The reader will have been impressed by now with the exclamations that have opened the patient's responses to the last three cards. Similar exclamations will also be found at the beginning of each of the next four cards. In the light of the patient's chaotic approach to the test, her peculiar, irrelevant verbalizations, and her blandness with respect to the content of her responses, these exclamations must be considered for the most part, if not entirely, instances of manneristic pseudo-responsiveness. A hostile caricature of "feminine emotionality" may also be involved.

> 1. *(W FCh+ Ad P 2-Peculiar) That definitely looks like the skin of an animal. A doeskin rug. [Skin? I don't know. Just the general outline. Anything else? No. It's faintly sort of an indeterminate color. What did you mean by "indeterminate?" Slightly mottled, shadowy, like some of these rugs you see on the floor.]*

This doe, considered together with the doe-gazelle in V-1, suggests that the patient attempts to maintain a self-concept emphasizing shy, gentle, graceful, feminine qualities. We must regard this self-concept as a defensive denial of the fierce, devouring, war-like and frightening self-concept suggested (and denied) by many of the images.

> *(Peculiar:) I can't think of a thing other to do with that. (Patient describes symmetry in fine detail.) I don't know. I can't think of anything else on that.*

The patient's relative unproductiveness on this card and her haste to give it up may well be based on a conscious or preconscious perception of the commonly seen penis at the top of the blot. That she specified the skin in #1 was that of a female animal—an unusual twist in this popular response—suggests that sexual fantasy and anxiety may be in the background of her response to this card.

CARD VII    REACTION TIME: 25″.    TOTAL TIME: 1′ 45″.

> *Oh heavens! Gracious! (Peculiar:) That's quite abstract, isn't it? (Patient expresses further preoccupation with how these "damn blots" are made.)*
> 1. *(W F+ (Hd) P Peculiar, Confabulation) Amazing things staring at each other: faces. Don't ask me what! Persons: their heads (upper ⅓), busts (middle ⅓), and rocks (lower ⅓)—these are similar to two rocks. They're staring at each other and they've got. . . . They look like nuts to me (laugh), goons (silly laugh).*

(a) At this point in the test analysis, her seeing "nutty" persons in the blots may be suspected of being an instance of projection of a sense of inner chaos and "nuttiness." (b) More silliness and other bits of inappropriate behavior occur here. (c) The "staring" theme recalls the earlier emphasis on eyes (see I-1, II-1, IV-1).

> *(Anything else?) I can't think of anything (wide, long, uncovered yawn). (Peculiar:) It's awfully gray and there's a lot of space around.*

CARD VIII    REACTION TIME: 22".    TOTAL TIME: 1' 40".

*Oh gracious! My word!*

*1. (D CF A) That's kind of a butterfly there (lower pink and orange).*
[Butterfly? *The bottom: the colors. The bottom: the red and flame colored thing.* Anything else? *Just the outline.*]

*2. (D CC'F Rock Peculiar) Then again it might be a rock with sunset, on the bottom (lower pink and orange).* [Sunset? *The sun must be hitting the rock from below; the other things (areas) gray out progressively toward the top (long, uncovered yawn).*]

(a) The CF butterfly and CF sunset-colored rock both convey the potentiality for spontaneous or impulsive expressions of warmth.

(b) Her uncovered yawns, her previous use of the word "damn," and other unrecorded but glaring instances of unladylike behavior, such as her sprawling out in her chair, indicate in content a need to shock by flouting social requirements, but in form they indicate considerable schizophrenic dilapidation. This behavior may also reflect withdrawal of interest as a defense against anxious and resentful reactions to the test and tester.

*3–4–5. (D,W F+ A P 2-Confabulation tendency, Peculiar, Fluid; D C'F Rock; D FC'+ Mt) And two beavers (P) climbing up some gray stone (middle blue) up to the top of the hill, up there (upper gray-green). I don't know. There's a butterfly there (#1) but then it doesn't get a butterfly if you think these are beavers. That couldn't be.* [Why couldn't it be a butterfly? *Well it could (as in #1) except the bear (#3) seemed to have legs on the butterfly and it couldn't be that. It's a rock (#2), an oversized rock, with colors on it. The other leg is on the gray rock (#4) and sort of forestry at the top (#5).* Forestry? *It looked like the peak of the hill of a kind.* In what way? *A forest at a great distance: sort of gray and slightly fuzzy.*]

While she rejects the absurd combination of the beaver leg on the butterfly, showing thereby some usable capacity to confront her notions with reality, the fact remains that the combination was her idea in the first place. This is an instance of tenuous but not broken contact with reality and of precarious control over autistic tendencies. It is the sort of response frequently encountered in settings of partial, precarious remission from a schizophrenic break. It is also commonly observed in incipient schizophrenic settings. In short, it is a *borderline schizophrenic* response more than anything else. The more the autistic responses in a record fit this pattern, the more likely it is that the patient is in a borderline schizophrenic condition—going in, coming out, or chronically maintaining a borderline position. In this case, the record is so full of clearly schizophrenic material that the presence of such a response as this merely indicates that this patient sometimes maintains a semblance of adaptiveness and reality testing, that she can question some of her externalizations, and that she may therefore be in a relatively quiescent phase of her psychosis. Her manner of communicating is too peculiar and chaotic for us to regard her as a schizophrenic character, i.e., as superficially relatively well organized but implicitly schizophrenic in her conception of relationships and in her basic methods of coping with problems. Once verbal communication is seriously invaded by autism, a deteriorative psychosis marked by open breaks must be suspected.

*That's about all.*

CARD IX    REACTION TIME: 35″.    TOTAL TIME: 3′ 30″.

*Gracious! (Peculiar:) An amazing thing! What in the world it looks like I wouldn't know!*

*1–2. (DS F(C)C′+ Obj; D CF Ldsc Confabulation, Peculiar) Sort of a fountain effect in the middle (midline and middle space). It might be almost forest-like (green): a green bank on one side (of the fountain). And what those things rearing up are, I wouldn't know (orange). It's fountain-like in the middle (#1); I don't know why. [Fountain? It had a gray haze; it would be coming up in the middle of a green canyon (#2). Was it all part of one scene? The green suggested the fountain. In what way? Something about its combination with green. It sort of fitted together. The fountain was quite clear, sort of separate from everything else. Forest-like? The green parts: sort of space, like going through a canyon with green growing in either side.]*

(a) Her characteristic sequence of reaction appears to be first to blurt out her difficulty in coping with new situations (card or specific area), speaking before she gives herself time to work something out; then she struggles to organize a response, and typically, as in the present instance, comes up with feeble form and poor synthesis of detail. Both her impulsive confession of difficulty and her meager proportion of subsequent success in responding adequately indicate seriously impaired capacity for delay of impulse and generally weak defensive and adaptive operations. (b) Both the arbitrary combination of fountain and canyon and the strong suggestion that she is symbolizing sexual intercourse give the image a contrived, surrealistic quality. "Surrealistic" imagery is not uncommon in the Rorschach records of chronic schizophrenics and schizophrenic characters who have already been in psychotherapy (as this patient has) or have read or talked about sexual symbolism. At least in their therapy, but apparently also in their Rorschach responses, these patients do tend to dish up "juicy" content with enough disguise (i.e., ego participation) to make it psychoanalytically "respectable" and perhaps even "intriguing." In such usually preconscious manipulation of "unconscious" content there seems to be a mocking toying with the therapist (or tester), sizeable resistance to genuinely free responsiveness, and a basic inability to work in other ways with other types of imagery. Despite their implicit or even explicit air of artificiality and control, these patients seem genuinely incapable of responding otherwise.

*3. (D M+ (H) Confabulation) These look like maybe some kind of giants at the top—these queer things, the orange color (points out the location). They're kind of rearing up. I don't know what they're doing. It looks like they had one, two hands, holding out their hands, either a long hand or huge elongated fingernails; jabbing with one hand and the other up. They seem to be talking about something. (Patient repeats much of this description.) They are arguing about something.*

(a) Hostile interaction is suggested by "giants," "rearing up," "elongated fingernails," "jabbing" and "arguing." Denial of this hostile interaction is suggested by "I don't know what they're doing," "holding out their hands," and "talking about something." Such chaotic intermingling of impulse and defense reflects this patient's shattered integration. There are many leaks in her dyke. (b) The long fingernails give this hostile image a feminine quality and recall the witch concept in V-2 and the tarantula in III-3. Conceivably her mother-figure is the powerful (gigantic) and especially feared parental figure.

> *I don't know what all that rosy stuff at the bottom is. It (the blot) doesn't look like any whole thing to me.*
>
> *4. (s F— (Hd)) Just something that might suggest two eyes (slits in lower middle space). Not really eyes; just two apertures.*

Further emphasis on eyes (see I-1, II-1, IV-1, VII-1). Her rejecting the eye concept might reflect efforts to control her autistic, paranoid tendencies (see also VIII-3, IX-1). That she is fighting a losing battle is apparent everywhere in the test, including the three preceding responses to this card. These responses and their elaboration in inquiry are so poorly verbalized at points as to be almost incomprehensible.

CARD X     REACTION TIME: 35″.     TOTAL TIME: 3′ 50″.

> *That's very, quite a lot of fun, isn't it?! (Pleased tone) God only knows what. . . . Well. . . . (Patient describes symmetry again). . . .*

This positively-toned, opening verbalization and her favorable comment on the colors after #3 are further suggestions of relative stability and quiescence in this psychotic patient's present status (see VIII-2 and VIII-3, 4, 5).

> *1. (D F+ A Confabulation tendency) That could be a little mouse (side gray), two little mouse—er—mice flying at something (at the red).*

A minimized (small rodent) oral-attacking fantasy may be involved.

> *2-3. (D FC+ A; D F+ Ad P Fabulized Combination) Two green caterpillars down here (lower green). They look like they're gnawing on the eyes of a rabbit (lower middle).*

Note (a) the overt orality and (b) the eye emphasis.

> *The colors are very pretty.*
>
> *4. (D FC— Geog Peculiar, Contamination tendency) Kind of . . . I don't know really . . . I don't know what the blue things are: like the Great Lakes on a map (side blue). [How was it like the Great Lakes on a map? Oh just the blue, forked things sticking out. It's a little more splashy than the Great Lakes.]*
>
> *5. (D F± Obj Confabulation tendency) And this looks like some kind of derrick affair or dredger, reaching down to something, digging for oil, trying to pull up something in the ground (all upper gray).*
>
> *6. (D F+ Arch) The Eiffel Tower almost, that thing at the top (all upper gray).*
>
> *7. (D CF Plant Po) A couple of stray leaves going off the end (lower outer orange).*
>
> *8. (D CF Plant) A lot of leaves, stray leaves (side yellow and upper green). It's sort of autumnal.*

(a) From the patient's tone of voice and expressive movements in giving #7, it was clear she regarded these as *stray* leaves because they were off to the side and bottom of the card.

(b) The thematic emphasis on decay in # 7 and # 8 recalls the steer skull in a desert in IV-1, the curling leaf in IV-2, the "awfully gray" comment at the end of Card VII, and the sunset in VIII-2, all indicating concern with decline, death and deterioration. In contrast to these, and presumably reflecting efforts at denial, is the image of growth and vitality in IX-1 and IX-2—the fountain in the green canyon. The patient is likely to be concerned with her personal decline and possibly with inner feelings of deadness.

> *(Confabulation; Symbolic:) It's funny how you try to make pictures out of these. It doesn't symbolize any great thing. It's all sort of vacant. It doesn't symbolize struggle or anything. If you just had a, one-half of it, it would be fine, but you always find something staring at it from the other side, staring at it in a mirror.* [Why did the symmetry interfere with its symbolizing something? *I kept trying to figure what it looked like. It didn't suggest. . . . This (card) seemed light and airy. It didn't suggest any dark purposes, deep struggles. If it had been just one-half of it, it might have been something different.*]

Only at the end of the test does the patient spontaneously and explicitly express some of her paranoid assumptions about the test. She elaborates these assumptions somewhat in inquiry. "It doesn't symbolize any great thing" indicates both a search for hidden meaning and a grandiose conception of that meaning (see beginning of IV and V). "It's all so sort of vacant" and "it doesn't symbolize struggle or anything" begin to suggest that she is dealing with a projected self-image of emptiness, blandness, possibly even deadness (see discussion of #7, above).

Thus far this verbalization at the end of Card X seems to express disappointment that she is devoid of inner greatness and inner substance. She goes on to suggest at least one important basis for her previously noted anxious response to symmetry: the idea of self-confrontation—"staring at it in a mirror." If self-confrontation is a particular source of anxiety, then her previous emphasis on emptiness and absence of struggle might well represent a turning away from self-confrontation and a defensive denial of a sense of inner turmoil and conflict. That is to say, her schizophrenic blandness may well involve defensive denial of inner experience, which may then foster a feeling of emptiness and deadness. Of course, we are dealing here with only one level of the schizophrenic's feeling of emptiness and deadness. Withdrawal of emotional investment in relationships, self-destructive emphases, and other schizophrenic wishes and phantasies seem to play an equally important if not more important role in this feeling.

Then, in inquiry, talking specifically about Card X, she indicates that its symmetry gives the card a "light and airy" quality, and that this quality prevented her perceiving "dark purposes, deep struggles" in it. In other words, it would appear at this point that the symmetry is regarded by her as an obstacle to her paranoid investigations. We must add, however, that this is the use to which she is putting the symmetry. It appears then that on the one hand symmetry is threatening to her (suggesting self-confrontation, among other things) and on the other hand symmetry (and perhaps also the bright hues and small, discrete shapes) is used by her for purposes of denial of conflict and even denial of paranoid projection.

We cannot be certain of any of these specific meanings of her response to symmetry, since the entire verbalization is poorly integrated and rambling, and since her verbalizations in general have an "off the beam" quality. That is to say, we cannot be certain on which level she is talking at any moment. On the whole, however, one would infer from this final verbalization that underlying paranoid assumptions and attitudes of psychotic proportions are present, but that at the moment these paranoid features are to some extent superficially denied. If this is so, we have further reason to think that the patient may be in a relatively quiescent phase of her schizophrenia (see VIII-2, VIII-3, 4, 5, and beginning of X). In retrospect, this conclusion would be in accord with her tendency to minimize the hostile, threatening aspects of other images (see I-1, I-2, III-3, etc.). It is as if she is saying that there probably are "dark purposes" to be uncovered but she cannot quite build up a convincing case for her suspicions at the moment and will even try to enjoy herself while she may. At best, of course, this could only be a partial and precarious "quiescence" or "remission." The patient may be temporarily in control of her most autistic tendencies and temporarily somewhat more successfully adaptive on this basis.

SUMMARY OF SCORES

R: 36          EB: 2–6.5 (7.5)

| W | 10+1 | F+ | 7 | A | 8 | W% | 28 |
|---|------|----|---|---|---|----|----|
| D | 22 | F— | 3 | Ad | 8 | D% | 61 |
| Dd | 1 | F± | 1 | H | 1 | DR% | 6 |
| Dr | 1 | F∓ | 2 | (H) | 1 | | |
| S | 0+2 | M | 2 | (Hd) | 3 | F% | 36–75 |
| s | 1+1 | FC | 3(2—) | Obj | 3 | F+% | 62–59 |
| DW | 1 | CF | 5 | Dec | 1 | | |
| | | C/F | 1 | Plant | 3 | A% | 44 |
| | | F(C) | 2 | Ldsc | 1 | H% | 3–15 |
| *Qualitative* | | (C)F | 1 | Geog | 1 | P | 6+1 |
| Fab. Comb. | 3 | FC′ | 4+1(3—) | Arch | 2 | P% | 17–19 |
| Confabulation | 7 | C′F | 1+1 | Misc | 3 | | |
| Confab. tend. | 6 | C′ | 0+1 | | | | |
| Contamination | 1 | FCh | 3(1—) | | | | |
| Contam. tend. | 3 | Ch | 1 | | | | |
| Peculiar | 46 | | | | | | |
| Fluid | 10 | | | | | | |
| Irrelevant | 2 | | | | | | |
| Self-reference | 3 | | | | | | |
| Po | 1 | | | | | | |
| Absurd | 1 | | | | | | |
| Symbolic | 2 | | | | | | |

On the whole, the summary of scores conforms to the chronic (for the moment somewhat stabilized) paranoid schizophrenic picture which has emerged from the qualitative analysis. There are 85 entries in the *Qualitative* column, almost every one indicating schizophrenic disorganization. Within and between responses she was almost continuously autistic. The low *F%*, the *EB* and the distribution of color responses indicate her strongly narcissistic, poorly controlled and essentially unadaptive orientation and behavior. The emphasis on the color side of the *EB,* as well as the heavy emphasis on *Ch* and *C'*, also suggests chronicity—assuming the diagnosis of schizophrenia has already been made.

The scores also suggest, however, the quality of quiescence or remission that has been commented on in the qualitative analysis. In particular, there is the obvious absence of *pure C,* the presence of 3 *FC* (even though 2 are of poor form), the moderately high number of *Popular* responses (6+1) and the borderline *F+%* of 62%–59%. The abundance of entries in the *Qualitative* column makes it clear that we are dealing with a well-established schizophrenia, but certain of the traditional scores do bring out the adaptability that is present, scanty and unreliable as it must be.

# 10. Obsessive-Compulsive Defensive Operations

REGRESSION, ISOLATION, REACTION FORMATION and undoing will be discussed in one chapter because they form a defensive syndrome that typifies the obsessive-compulsive character structure and neurosis. It would therefore be artificial as well as extremely cumbersome to attempt to present test records illustrating principally one or another of these four defensive operations. They work together like a team. This discussion will follow Freud [50] and Fenichel's summary [37].

## A. REGRESSION: GENERAL REMARKS

According to Freud, defensive regression is basic to the dynamics of the obsessive-compulsive syndrome [50]. Freud assumes the syndrome to originate in defense against the libidinal demands of the Oedipus complex and in reaction to the castration anxiety associated with these demands. The key aspect of this defense is complete or partial regression from the genital orientation of the phallic phase of psychosexual development to the earlier sadistic orientation of the anal phase. This anal-sadistic regression helps account for the obsessive-compulsive's hostile and "dirty" conception of sexuality on the one hand and for the harshness of his superego attitudes on the other. And, since sexuality is conceived in such obnoxious anal-sadistic terms, the already overstrict superego attitudes are stimulated all the more to insist on rigid, uncompromising defense against impulse. Reaction formations particularly are then emphasized, mere repression being unsatisfactory. That is to say, it is not enough under these conditions to give up fighting on one side; one must go over to the other side—the anti-instinctual side—"wholeheartedly." Thus, as Freud noted, the anal-sadistic regression helps account for the fact that obsessive-compulsive defense is especially intolerant and that which is defended against (the anal-sadistic orientation) is especially intolerable.

In unstable defensive settings, the unconscious, repudiated impulses tend to permeate ego activities more and more intensively and extensively. This may culminate in a deadlock of id and superego forces, a deadlock expressed in paralysis of action accompanied by endless doubting and rumination. The ambivalent obsessive-compulsive patient often finds it impossible to move in any direction—in thought as well as action—without creating painful tension: one way leads to intolerable anxiety, guilt and self-punishment, and the other way to intolerable instinctual renunciation.

The regressive aspect of the obsessive-compulsive clinical picture is complicated by the following four considerations. First, regression appears to be one aspect of every neurotic and psychotic solution. Hysterical vomiting, alcohol addiction, schizophrenic delusion, depression, all involve regressive alterations of instinctual (and social) orientation. Thus, it is not really the fact of regression that distinguishes the obsessive-compulsive; it is what he regresses to, namely, the anal-sadistic phase of psychosexual development. Second, some obsessive-compulsive patients appear never to have grown significantly beyond the anal-sadistic level, and their illnesses therefore cannot be said to reflect *principally* the consequences of psychosexual regression. That is to say, from the very beginning their conception of sexuality seems to have been primarily hostile and "dirty" and their superego attitudes overly severe. Also, regression presupposes significant fixation on the level toward which regression tends. Thus, what we call "regression" is probably always a matter of degree, of relative weights of fixation and regression. These relative weights vary from one regressed person to the next. The concept "regression" will be used from here on with this important qualification in mind.

Third, obsessive-compulsives often seem to rely on an auxiliary regression from the anal-sadistic level to the oral-dependent level in an effort to bolster other defenses against their frightening and guilt-laden destructive impulses. Either chronically or in crises, they may seek safety in a passive, submissive, inert role in which they do not have to be hostile and even deny any capacity to be hostile. Thus, not only anal but oral problems are likely to be conspicuous in the regressive aspects of the obsessive-compulsive picture.

The fourth and last complicating aspect of the obsessive-compulsive regression to be mentioned derives from the fact that ambivalence is a crucial aspect of the anal orientation. This ambivalence tends to spread out along the entire psychosexual ladder and to express itself in oral, anal and phallic problems and in the inevitable interpenetrations or overlap of these problems. This spread of ambivalence may be seen in intense inner struggle concerning activity versus passivity (supporting-dependent, generous-stingy, productive-unproductive), sadism versus masochism (cruel-victimized, rebellious-submissive, dirty-clean), and masculinity versus femininity (potent-impotent, rapacious-receptive, homosexual-heterosexual). If we also take into account the obsessive-compulsive's early inclination to seal off experience of affect and impulse, and the consequent serious interference with his learning effective means of mastery of impulse as he grows up, we see some of the basic reasons why indications of a great variety of immature psychosexual trends may be particularly striking in obsessive-compulsive settings.

In short, the complications surrounding the notion that defensive regression is the keystone of the obsessive-compulsive syndrome are that regression is not specific to this syndrome, some obsessive-compulsive syndromes appear to involve considerably more anal fixation than anal regression, secondary regression to orality may complicate the instinctual and interpersonal picture, and the ambivalence associated with the anal orientation may contribute to a diffuse emphasis on psychosexual conflict even though the anal conflict may be the one of primary significance.

## B. Regression: Test Expectations

In the test scores, themes and attitudes, we may expect to encounter patterns of psychic functioning which reflect the infantile psychosexual levels to which the obsessive-compulsive patient has regressed (or on which he has remained fixated). This expectation assumes that the patient has completed the major part of his regressive work and that his test responses will correspondingly pertain to the end results of regression rather than to regressive processes themselves. Actually, as will be described below and illustrated frequently in the case studies to follow, we often do encounter active regressive alterations of response either in response sequences or in modifications of single responses or test attitudes. But mostly we may expect to see reflections of the types of impulses reactivated by defensive regression and against which the other obsessive-compulsive defenses are directed. Mainly by secondary inference from these particular impulse-defense struggles will we be able to draw conclusions concerning the importance of defensive regression in the obsessive-compulsive test picture.

*Since various types of oral, hostile, homosexual and other charged images are encountered in all kinds of Rorschach records, while anal imagery is not, it will be particularly the obsessive-compulsive's anal thematic emphasis that will point specifically to pathological anal regression.* Illustrations of anal imagery, such as "anus," "feces," "tails" and "dirt," have been presented in Chapter 4 on thematic analysis (see p. 132) and will not be duplicated here. Typically, however, the anal thematic emphasis should be accompanied by oral, sadistic, homosexual and other pregenital themes. This breadth of psychosexual reference will reflect the previously mentioned secondary oral regression, the pervasive sadistic component of the anal regression, and the obsessive-compulsive's diffusely ambivalent, generally immature psychosexual orientation. The hostile emphasis may appear particularly in sado-masochistic themes (see pp. 132–3), "superego," authoritarian and guilt themes (see pp. 133 and 134), oral themes (see pp. 131–2), phallic themes (see pp. 135–6), and/or clear-cut anal images with hostile implications such as "bleeding rectum," "talons in the anus," "messy splattering," and "flaming tail of a jet plane." In addition, representation of oral-dependent tendencies (see p. 131) and homosexual tendencies (see pp. 135-7) may be expected. More about these imagery emphases and corresponding test attitudes will be discussed in connection with the other obsessive-compulsive defenses, especially reaction formation and particularly reaction formation that is being invaded by the repudiated impulses (see pp. 345-54).

In addition to these indications of established regressive defense in the obsessive-compulsive setting, we may also expect at least some instances of regressive shifts within responses or response sequences. These shifts will occur from sexual or hostile themes to themes of weakness, innocence, oral-dependence and the like. Although they do not necessarily always have just this significance, the following response sequences and response alterations may serve to illustrate regressive shifts: "Two devils. . . . They could also look like clipped French poodles" (Card III, $P$); "A crab with long claws. . . . It could be a carrot" (Card IX, orange); "Up here is a female sex symbol. . . . A frog's mouth, with thick lips" (Card IV, upper middle); "A vagina. . . . A rectum" (Card VIII, lower middle); "It looks like two people fighting. . . . They also resemble two children in party costumes playing patty-cake" (Card II, $W$).

Regressive shifts may occur in test attitude rather than in sequences or inner alterations of imagery. Criticism of the test may be followed by exaggerated compliance and relatively spontaneous self-assertion may be hastily followed by apology. The regressive alteration of test attitude and behavior may also follow the appearance of a threatening image. For example, "That's all. . . . I mean I think that's all I can find"; "An explosion. . . . Do you want me to go on?" "It looks like a penis. . . . This one doesn't look like much of anything"; "These darn blots are all so symmetrical. . . . Do you want me to go on mentioning the symmetry?"

In addition to all of these indications of regressive defense, we may also expect to encounter pathological doubting in test attitudes and behavior. This is because, as was previously mentioned, extreme doubting is the resultant in consciousness of the ambivalence inherent in the anal-sadistic, regressive alteration of psychic functioning. Doubting, with its implied goal of balancing all considerations, reflects the obsessive-compulsive patient's precariously balanced instinctual position. The doubting may be reinforced by the reaction formations of conscientiousness and orderliness, the latter demanding thoroughness and continuous review of thoughts, feelings and actions anyway. Isolation and intellectualization may also increase doubting by blocking affective experience and thereby working against any sense of emotional conviction, and, in the case of intellectualization, facilitating seeing so many sides to each question that even a sense of intellectual conviction is precluded. When the obsessive-compulsive defenses against sadistic tendencies begin to be invaded by these very tendencies, the doubting may be intensified because then it may also serve as an aggressive weapon, that is, it may be used to challenge others relentlessly and to interfere with effective communication or activity in a group.

As indirect manifestations of the obsessive-compulsive patient's defensive regression, we are therefore likely to encounter tedious, excessively ruminative, implicitly hypercritical re-working of both the perceptual and verbal aspects of his responses, inability to commit himself to responses, and resorting instead to extensive reservations and qualification. For example, "It might possibly suggust a bat, but, of course, it isn't exactly like one: at first glance it just makes you think of one."* Also, "Actually . . . the front part of it—if that's the front—the front of the butterfly (previous response)—I don't know if it's a butterfly—it looks like a crab or butterfly." In addition, because the doubter is so concerned with balance, he is likely to become especially concerned with the symmetry and asymmetry of the inkblots, and his verbalizations should reflect this concern.

Finally, along with "anal" content, regressive alterations of imagery and attitudes, and pathological doubting, we may expect to encounter at least some instances of anally and/or sadistically colored verbalization; for example, "This is disgusting!" "It's messy . . . not neat!" "Are you allowed to tear it into its parts?" "That's torturing it out." As defenses weaken, we may expect more of these regressive (or fixated) impulse expressions to stand out in choice of words and metaphor.

### C. Isolation (and Intellectualization): General Remarks

Isolation refers to a fragmentation of conscious experience that either keeps apart ideas that belong together emotionally or keeps apart ideas and the affects corresponding to them. The crucial connections between ideas or between ideas and feelings are buried. In final analysis, it appears that the idea is isolated from the threatening impulse of which it is a derivative. The emotional charge relevant to the idea is displaced or repressed so that calmness may prevail where affect is appropriate and *vice versa*. For example, the isolating employee may have a "neutral" (actually frustrating) chat with his superior only to find himself flooded with anger upon leaving his superior's office, and he may remain unaware that there is any meaningful connection between the two. Another example: an analysand may talk first about a problem he has in getting along with his wife and then may drift over into talking about his mother (actually, discussing a similar problem he has had with her), but may see and "feel" no con-

* At its extreme, or in clearly paranoid contexts, this cautiousness may also reflect suspicious guardedness.

nection between the two. Also, on the basis of isolation, ideas may become conscious that would otherwise be subjectively intolerable and strictly tabooed. Such ideas may involve death wishes against loved ones, suicidal fantasy, physically sadistic fights, and the like. As the isolator experiences it, these ideas "pop into mind for no reason at all," or, if he is a psychologically sophisticated intellectualizer, he may speculate that he is "probably" angry and that it is "probably" for this or that reason, but he will have no subjective experience of anger and no conviction as to what he is angry about.

The normal prototype of isolation is logical thinking [50]. In logical thinking, emotional associations are eliminated in the interest of achieving objectivity. Obsessive-compulsive neurotics often caricature the logical thinker. They attempt to retreat from the world of impulse and emotionally-toned interpersonal relationships to a world principally of words and abstractions. This retreat we refer to as *intellectualization*. While intellectualization is often spoken of as a specific defense, it must be remembered that basically it is one form of expression of defensive isolation. It is a variant of isolation in that it rests on the strategy of precluding the experience of affect without restricting perception, memory and self-awareness.

Intellectualization is a common form of isolation, however, and deserves separate attention. Within the normal range, intellectualization takes its place, along with the other defensive operations, as a partial trend the expression of which is kept in some balance with appropriate implementation of id impulses and release of affect. When it reaches pathological proportions, intellectualization aims to substitute logic, knowledge and "objectivity" for *all* impulse and feeling. Rigid and pervasive rationalizing, and unrealistic, asocial, unproductive immersion of oneself in theoretical problems or systems may then be conspicuous.

Whether normally limited or pathologically extended, defensive intellectualization may also be a powerful asset in the cultivation of one's intellectual potential, in creative and analytic thought, and in comprehension and mastery of the world around one. In addition, defensive intellectualization merges into adaptive, realistic, possibly conflict-free emphasis on intellect which is not at all defensive even though this emphasis may have originated in defensive conflict. There is good reason to assume the existence of relatively autonomous, sublimated or even originally conflict-free areas of intellectual functioning [69, 70]. The most meaningful approach to defense in the realm of intellectual functioning seems to be to ask of any intellectual act to what extent it is subordinated to defensive aims and to what extent it is genuinely adaptive. Ultimately, these are matters of degree or relative emphasis, even if it is difficult in specific cases to make estimates one way or the other.

It must also be emphasized that intellectual accomplishment is strongly, though ambivalently, supported by many segments of our culture. Intellectualization may therefore be a particularly well-reinforced defensive operation, for it not only greatly facilitates intellectual mastery of important segments of the surrounding world, it may also be especially encouraged and rewarded by others. All this in addition to helping solve crucial intrapsychic conflict. *For all these reasons, it is necessary to think of intellectuality as a complex organization of trends only one aspect of which is defensive intellectualization.*

Actually, isolation and its variant, intellectualization, appear to lead in two directions. In one direction, they may lead to intense investments in matters that are relatively remote from the immediate give-and-take of interpersonal relationships. Studying mathematics, designing an experiment or writing a book tends to remove one from the emotional stimulations, gratifications and tribulations of daily interpersonal relationships and concrete action. It seems that ordinarily these pursuits cannot be carried on successfully unless sufficiently long periods of emotional, social and physical "abstinence" are possible; and these abstinent periods will be the more possible the stronger the capacity for defensive isolation. Of course, by displacement and by mature, sublimated investment in thought and achievement, the intellectual, creative process can itself become a source of intense and adaptive emotional stimulation, release and gratification.

The other direction in which isolation and intellectualization may lead is that of expanding the boundaries of internal awareness. In this respect, these defenses work in a direction opposite to that of repression and denial, the latter defenses tending to restrict consciousness. With the help of strong defensive isolation and intellectual detachment—keeping things apart in order to prevent their stimulating intolerable affect or instinctual expression, and dealing with concrete problems only in abstract, theoretical terms —it becomes possible to tolerate awareness of many aspects of one's life or behavior that would be extremely distressing otherwise. We see this in extreme form in "detached" obsessional symptoms that seem to express nakedly the most tabooed impulses—toward murder, suicide, perversion, and the like. In well-functioning obsessive personalities, we often see a more normal form of this expanded self-awareness in their keen reflectiveness, capacity for self-exploration, and intense interest in preparatory and peripheral elements of thought processes or what might be called the associative texture of thought. Refined awareness of their own thought processes stands out in these persons.

This second, self-observant direction in which isolation and intellectualization may lead is important to bear in mind when we try to understand obsessive phenomena both clinically and in tests. It is not unawareness of complex patterns of motivation and feeling that distinguishes the obsessive-compulsive person. In this awareness he often excels. He is distinguished instead by his fight against the subjective experience of the impulses and feelings of which intellectually he may be only too well aware. This is one main reason why the obsessional neurotics have been said to be the most instructive of the neurotic patients and the least tractable. Sooner or later in treatment, they may be seemingly aware of everything and anything about themselves, including even their own relative affectlessness. They may communicate it all in fine detail and in beguiling abstractions. Yet, somehow they just may not "feel" things and may not change for the better. To such a patient his analysis may remain, in one basic respect, an intellectual problem. He may behave as if it is not his life with which he is concerned, but merely a problem in psychodynamic, epistemological or semantic theory.

## D. ISOLATION: TEST EXPECTATIONS

For simplicity of presentation, the general expectations concerning isolation will be reviewed first and then those pertaining to intellectualization, so far as these can be separated. On the basis of the foregoing considerations, we could certainly expect of those who rely heavily on isolation a general approach to the Rorschach test that is designed above all to prevent experience of affect and impulse. This approach should be apparent in use of locations and determinants, in themes in the content, and in test attitudes and behavior. We might encounter efforts to make a "detached" intellectual affair of the response process, and indications in the content and manner of response of a nonpsychotic expansion of the boundaries of internal awareness.* The pattern that is the prototype or "ideal" for the isolator should therefore include the following features.

### 1. Scores

#### a) Locations:

(1) Dr% high (greater than 20%).† The isolating value of preoccupation with small detail derives from at least five factors: (a) preoccupation with small detail decreases the impact of the larger colored and shaded areas; (b) it precludes any hierarchy of importance among responses, the large and small all being given equal attention and major issues thereby being obscured; (c) it reduces the emotionally complex stimuli to easily manipulable proportions; (d) it tends to limit the content possibilities to *parts* of things, persons or animals—parts ordinarily being mostly innocuous, static, affectless affairs, while things carry the danger of

* A distinction is implied here between the failure of defenses, especially repression, in some psychotic conditions and normal or neurotic hyperalertness to internal processes, particularly thought processes.

† For scoring criteria, see Rapaport [118].

clearly expressing affect and impulse. In this respect, the *Dr* emphasis literally keeps apart what belongs together, and this is the keynote of isolation as a defense; (e) such impulse and affect as creep into the *Dr* may be conceived on a small emotional scale by the patient, paralleling the response's small physical scale.* To see, for example, a tiny red speck as "a drop of blood" is certainly less stimulating or expressive of hostility— in the patient's conscious experience—then to see a large red area as "a gush of blood."

*b) Determinants:*

(1) *High F% (greater than 75%) and high extended F% (95%–100%).*† The use of form implies emphasis on intellectual control. Where a defense is erected against spontaneity, as in the case of isolation, a high *F%* is ideal. Defensive isolation is less rigid if only the *extended F%* is high, since this pattern implies that some experience of the sort represented by movement, color and shading responses is tolerable. The *F%* is often raised by a very high *Dr%*, the tiny responses lending themselves poorly to determinants other than form. Therefore, if the *D* and *W* responses freely involve use of determinants other than form, more flexible defense is suggested. For this reason, if there are many tiny detail responses, it is instructive to recompute the *F%* omitting the tiny detail responses. The *F%* may also be pulled down if defensive isolation is failing or was weak to begin with, and if, as a result, impulses and affects are more or less out of hand.

(2) *High F+% (greater than 85%) and extended F+% (greater than 90%).*‡ One typical ideal of the isolating person is to be the utterly objective, realistic, emotionally unswayed observer. Accordingly, accuracy of percepts is ordinarily especially highly valued by him. There must be nothing impulsive or impressionistic about his responses. Hence his striving for consistently perfect form in the Rorschach test. The *F+%* will not be very high if the effectiveness of the defensive structure is reduced or was low to begin with. Again, if there are many tiny detail responses, the *F+%* should be recomputed eliminating these responses, since they may drastically lower the *F+%* (below 65%) without implying fundamental impairment of reality testing. The *F+%* that is seriously lowered by many trivial, inadequate *Dr* of the "face" variety frequently reflects a striving

---

* See pp. 238 and 354 for the possible role of denial and undoing, respectively, in such responses.

† The *extended F%* is the per cent of total responses made up by all responses with a primary form element, i.e., F, M, FM, Ms, FC, F(C), FC', FCh.

‡ The *extended F+%* is the *F+%* computed on the basis of the form level of all the responses included in the *extended F%*, namely, F, M, Ms, FC, F(C), FC', FCh. See Rapaport for further discussion and scoring criteria [118].

for productivity that is not backed up by either genuine ability and imaginativeness or freedom in the use of such assets. If the $Dr$ are over-elaborate, paranoid hyperalertness may well be involved.

(3) *High M (greater than 3 or 4).* * $M$ seems to be related to capacity for delay of impulse and for interposing thought and reflection between impulse and action. It also seems to involve capacity for self-awareness and ego-syntonic emotional investment in fantasy. Indirectly, these trends reflected in $M$ may be promoted or at least supported by reliance on defensive isolation. Isolation may neutralize the dangers in these imaginative, introspective activities. It may act like the safety catch on a loaded gun and thereby allow $M$ images to gain the conscious representation they might otherwise have to be denied.

(4) *Low sum C; minimal use of C', (C), and Ch.* The use of color and shading reflects the experience of affect of various sorts and of anxiety, and also the degree of acceptance of, yielding to or being overwhelmed by impulse and affect. Color and shading therefore have no place in the ideal Rorschach pattern of rigidly isolating persons. At best, some $F(C)$, $FC'$, $FCh$ and $FC$ (in small areas) will be acceptable to these persons. These responses will indicate that under conditions of strict control and limited scope, experience of feeling is permissible and tolerable. At times, as indications of the isolator's efforts to force or simulate the affect he cannot spontaneously experience but considers himself called upon to express, we may encounter some $F/C$ (artificial, reflected or gratuitous colors) and abortive $FC$ (e.g., "a bear but it's the wrong color"). Some shading of a delicate, subtle sort may appear as a reflection of the successful isolator's introspective facility; in these instances the tone of the response should be detached or intellectually intrigued.

As defenses fail, or if they were weak to begin with, color and shading responses should tend to increase, especially those in which form is vague, fragmentary, arbitrary or absent.

## 2. Thematic Analysis

The model of the machine in this era often has particular appeal to the obsessive-compulsive, isolating person, as it no doubt had to his parents originally. The machine after all is a controlled, affectless, smoothly operating, regulatory, utilitarian, productive construction. Therefore, objects (machines or their products) could well be emphasized in the Rorschach content of the isolating person. For example, a governor (Card X, usual

* See Rapaport for scoring criteria [*118*]. These criteria are relatively strict, so that each $M$ counts for much more than it would, for example, if Klopfer's scoring were employed.

"wishbone" in upper center) would be particularly appealing in this regard. The number of objects seen would also be increased by the isolator's need to find geometric precision in the generally vague, irregular and disorderly blots: the clean edge, the round contour, the neat joint could be greatly reassuring to a person requiring order and symmetry in life around him as he does in his instinctual life. Similarly, stress may be put on machine-like human precision, as in "A dance team: thin, wiry, exact performers; they so perfectly do the same thing in opposite directions together" (Card III). Less often, images of subjective feelings of coldness, such as icicles and snowmen, might also appear as representations of the severe isolator's concern with his congealed affective state. Or emphasis might fall on human figures, such as statues, that are not warm, flesh-and-blood beings.

### 3. Test Attitudes and Behavior

In his manner of relating himself to the tester, to the inkblots and to his responses, the isolating patient should strive to be detached and objective throughout. In addition, because of the frequent relationship between isolation and expanded self-awareness, he may manifest noteworthy awareness of the course of his thought processes. This awareness will become evident in his describing the formative phases of his responses and their changing quality once they are formed, and in the many doubts and qualifications he has concerning his responses. In verbalizing this associative texture, his attitude is likely to be that of a passive observer and noncommittal commentator.

In extreme form, this expanded self-awareness will take on a highly self-absorbed, narcissistic quality. It will be as if the test and tester merely provide a pretext for the patient to hold further communion with himself. The patient's thoughts about thoughts will become a wall between himself on the one side and the tester and the test stimuli on the other.

Thus, the ideal pattern of the rigidly isolating patient includes a high $Dr\%$, a high $F\%$ and $F+\%$, an *Experience Balance* that is relatively strong on the $M$ side and relatively weak on the *sum C* side, minimal use of shading and color generally, emphasis on objects in the content, and a detached, introspective, self-absorbed manner of taking the test.

### E. INTELLECTUALIZATION: TEST EXPECTATIONS

When intellectualization is the particularly emphasized form of expression of isolation, the ideal or model test pattern changes somewhat from that described for isolation although the essentials remain the same. The following additional trends in response should be evident.

*1. Scores*

*a) R*

(1) *R should ordinarily be high (greater than 40).* Intellectualization fosters transformation of the test situation into one of intellectual challenge purely, and into an occasion for the exhibition of intellectual virtuosity. One form of expression of intellectual virtuosity is quantity of ideas. The intellectualizing patient generally would have the wherewithal for a very high $R$ since intellectualization and the good endowment with which it is usually associated foster breadth, if not depth, of interests, pleasure in playing with ideas, and conceptual and perceptual agility.* These trends facilitate the accumulation, the ready availability and the facile modification of imagery, all of which are conditions of a high $R$ of any quality. The high productivity could also be fostered by isolation of affect *per se*. The patient who isolates and intellectualizes effectively but not with extreme rigidity would be relatively unthreatened by the *temporary regression in the service of the ego* previously discussed as a basis for Rorschach productivity (see pp. 78–82). He could therefore let ideas spill out relatively freely. In fact, under ordinary conditions, he is more than likely to enjoy it. The repressive patient, in contrast to the isolating, intellectualizing patient, is driven to low $R$ since his powers of isolation are ordinarily weak, his range of reference is limited by his repressive restriction of interests, and he therefore fears each spontaneous thought and fantasy because of its closeness to home and its readily felt charge of affect or anxiety. The inference is compelling, even if highly speculative, that besides its defensive significance and especially if it is made up of many trivial $Dr$ (faces, etc.), high $R$ may well have the expulsive, diarrheic significance of barraging the tester with valueless intellectual excrement.

(2) *R could be low (less than 20).* If the emphasis on intellectualization is on broad perspectives, *Weltanschauungen,* supreme generalizations, $R$ can be low. This type of responsiveness has been referred to as "quality ambition," its ideal form of expression being one "perfect" $W$ for each card, and in the end an $R$ of 10 and a $W$ of 10. Actually this ideal is rarely even approximated in American culture, the patient ordinarily giving a number of $D$ and $Dr$ in addition to his prized $W$. The closer the patient comes to this "quality" ideal, the more of an intellectual virtuoso or arty poseur he is likely to be in his life role, and the more we should be on the lookout for latent, if not overt, grandiosity (see pp. 281–2). Conceivably, an anally conceived approach to the test, involving megalomanic over-

---

* Genetically, intellectualization appears to be fostered by good endowment and rewarded early precocity [*68*].

valuation of one's products, each one having to be monumental, may also be involved in the association of low $R$ and high $W$.

*b) Locations.*

(1) *High W (greater than 10–15).* This trend would reflect the high intellectual ambitions described in the preceding paragraph.

(2) *Low W (less than 6).* If the intellectualizing takes a pedantic, querulous form, $W$ may be held down, since most $W$, even the popular ones, require a certain impressionistic freedom for abstraction. This is a freedom the pedantic person does not allow himself. But intellectualization may also be strong in the absence of any $W$, even without pedantry; $W$ may be kept low by passive or depressive trends in the intellectualistic setting.

(3) *High Dr% (greater than 20%).* This trend would occur on the basis of two trends already mentioned: the isolating value of preoccupation with tiny detail and the demonstration of virtuoso productivity.

(4) *High S (greater than 5%–10%).* Overinterpretation of $S$ could be facilitated by a need to leave no stone unturned, no angle unexplored, no alternative unelaborated. The empty spaces would therefore be interpreted as readily as the inkblots. This approach would be additionally fostered by the fundamental ambivalence of the obsessive-compulsive person, which ambivalence is expressed in intellectual functioning in dichotomous emphases, in doubt and the need for balancing opposites (the black against the white), and in hypermeticulousness (all details are equally important). This will be discussed further in the following section on "reaction formation."

## 2. Thematic Analysis

Above all, the variety of content categories introduced should be impressive. The general rationale of this expectation has been considered in the earlier paragraph on high $R$ as an expression of intellectualizing efforts. Especially content that implies special knowledge in the arts and/or sciences may be expected in intellectualistic settings. Of course, to some extent the utilization of acquired knowledge and demonstration of current interests are inevitable. People do "find" in the inkblots what matters to them, and broad interests do foster a wealth of factual reference in any thoughtful performance. The arts-and-science emphasis will be defensive to the extent that it is based on the strategy of transforming the test into a "range of information" test.

Distinguishing defensive and non-defensive demonstration of intellectual attainment is often difficult. It will be helped along by the defensive intellectualizer's exaggerated striving for historical, anthropological, esthetic and scientific specificity. By "exaggerated" is meant persistent, ruminative, gratuitous, verbose, time-consuming and trivial striving for specificity. Relentless naming of bones, gods, geologic periods, geographic areas, centuries of the French court, Indian tribes, artists, and animal species should be watched for in this regard—at least, among American subjects. The test results as a whole and the results of other valuable clinical tests, such as the Wechsler-Bellevue Scale and the TAT, will also help distinguish defensive from non-defensive variety of content reference.

Thematic analysis should also reveal a tendency toward abstract or arty versions of emotional expression.* The affect or impulse in these responses is remote from concrete expression. For example, the red on Card II will be "symbolic of conflict"; Card III will be a "Danse Macabre"; etc. This remoteness of affect should not be confused with the evasive, hollow, responsibility-externalizing interpretations of the blots (especially Cards VIII, IX, X) as incomprehensible modern art or surrealism.

### 3. Test Attitudes and Behavior

The rigidly intellectualizing patient will tend to define the test situation as a school examination. He will relate himself to the tester as teacher, to the test as examination of academic achievement and *IQ,* and to his responses as passing or failing, high-graded or low-graded test answers. Speed, clarity, quantity, meticulousness, methodical approach, originality and whatever else might earn one an *A* in school will be emphasized. The cards may then be worked on for long periods of time and even systematically rotated and "exhausted" from each angle. Each response may be carefully documented and criticized. The goal of precision, elegance and complexity of verbalization (sometimes or often going to artificial, stilted, even icy extremes) may be steadily evident. All reassurance by the tester to the contrary, that the Rorschach test is not *that kind* of test, will not relieve this patient's examination anxiety.

Schachtel has instructively discussed these test attitudes—and most of the test attitudes we shall consider in this chapter—from the point of view of the authoritarian orientation they imply (see pp. 41–3). There is little question that these test attitudes imply an authoritarian orientation (severe superego problems), but they may also be regarded from the point of view of defensive operations, as may the authoritarian orientation itself.

### F. Reaction Formation: General Remarks

Reaction formation refers to the unconsciously determined overemphasis on conscious attitudes and impulses that are the opposite of particularly threatening, unconscious ones. For example, impulses to be dirty and dis-

* Undoing may also contribute to this; see pp. 354–5.

orderly may be opposed by the reaction formations of exaggerated cleanliness and orderliness; cruel impulses may be opposed by tenderness; passive-feminine wishes in a man may be opposed by exaggerated masculinity. It should be noted that in combating certain instinctual impulses, reaction formation may impress other instinctual impulses into its service; for example, homosexual tendencies may be reacted against through exaggerated heterosexuality.*

It is perhaps reaction formation more than any other defense in this syndrome that underscores the severe superego pressures besetting the obsessive-compulsive patient. The obsessive-compulsive typically reacts with guilt to expression of instinctual derivatives even if this expression is in socially acceptable form. The guilt may be mostly unconscious but it will be widespread and often powerful. Reaction formations against tabooed impulses therefore may be seen in part as representing a knuckling under to superego pressure and a steady attempt to exonerate the self.

Reaction formation reinforces other defenses, such as repression and denial. That is to say, not only is the objectionable impulse kept unconscious by repression and/or denial, but the repudiation of the impulse is made into a personal and even a social "cause." Sometimes this may reach the point of fanaticism. Necessity is made into a virtue—an age-old human trick. If firmly established, reaction formation may also decrease the individual's need to rely on other defenses. With respect to denial, for example, the far-reaching denials of the sort that have been described in Chapter 8 may become less necessary. This is because reaction formation keeps the self "in the clear"; to one and all (and one's superego too) it demonstrates that one is on the "right side." Reaction formation thereby makes it possible for the individual to cope directly and consciously with material the existence of which he otherwise would have to deny by avoidance and by distorted perception of reality.

Because it allows active, conscious contact with derivatives of the tabooed material, reaction formation also makes possible some unconscious gratification of the defended against impulses. For example, hypercleanliness may be secretly experienced as a continuous playing with dirt. This consideration, in turn, indicates that reaction formation is peculiarly vulnerable to "invasion" by the defended against impulse. Extreme reliance on reaction formation against hostility generally becomes itself an indirect avenue for the expression of hostility: one can be too clean, too consci-

---

* Actually, neither heterosexuality nor homosexuality, activity nor passivity, sadism nor masochism, etc., should be regarded simply as an expression of an instinctual impulse. Each is itself a complex of instinctual tendencies and their derivatives, of ego aptitudes and attitudes that limit, direct and implement these, and of general defensive requirements.

entious, too sincere, too tender or too saintly for anyone else's comfort. Ultimately, exaggerated reaction formations are relentlessly demanding, accusing, guilt-provoking, and personally and socially stultifying.

Reaction formation is also characterized by the personality change it usually entails. It is typically not a defense on which the ego falls back at certain times of acute instinctual threat. Reaction formation assumes a constant instinctual danger. Once reaction formation is well developed, it involves a continuous on-guard orientation against the rejected impulses. It is an ever-watchful, ever-active mode of defense. It is this rigidity that gives away the defensive aspect of reaction formation to the observer and indicates to him that he is not dealing with a mature, secure attitude or value. Because it blocks appropriate channels of discharge, this rigidity facilitates breakthroughs or infiltrations by the rejected impulses, and these also help identify the defensive aspects of the reaction formations. The classical instances of compulsive handwashers with dirty genitals illustrate this problem.

Reaction formations commonly take pseudo-sublimated, socially highly valued forms such as generosity, tenderness, sincerity, orderliness, conscientiousness, meticulousness, manliness or femininity, bravery and altruism. The social rewards won by these reaction formations inevitably increase the tenacity with which people cling to them. That is to say, more than a defensive function is served by reaction formation. Generosity, tenderness, etc., are valuable means of interpersonal relationship and social gratification. This consideration also helps account for the intractability of obsessive-compulsive neurotics in therapy, reaction formation being a major aspect of their defensive strategy. In the patient's eyes, the therapist seeking to bring to consciousness the impulse repudiated by the reaction formation becomes the devil's advocate. In the obsessive-compulsive setting, therefore, reaction formation combines with isolation of affect to create a powerful deterrent to personality change.

The pseudo-sublimated forms of reaction formation are often difficult to distinguish from genuine sublimation. Actually, we seem to be dealing with a continuous transition from one to the other, the more socially oriented, adaptive forms merging into sublimation, and the more egocentric, rigid, all-pervasive forms representing primarily defensive reaction formation. In addition, in the course of personality development, behavior patterns and values that originate in reaction formation seem capable of attaining some autonomy from this conflictful origin. They may acquire reliability and durability that are not significantly altered by the ordinary, non-critical vicissitudes of defense [115].

Granting these considerations concerning our dealing with a continuum rather than a dichotomy, and granting also the notion of relative autonomy, some distinction is still often possible between primarily defensive reaction formations and primarily sublimated behavior patterns. Perhaps the major criteria for this distinction are the pervasiveness, egocentricity and rigidity of the behavior pattern in question. Tenderness that admits of no acknowledged anger, even in the face of clear provocation, generosity that admits of no acknowledged self-interest, even in states of great need, independence that admits of no reliance on others, even in overwhelming crises, and conscientiousness that takes no heed of real requirements and the actual expectations or reactions of others, all are qualities so rigid, egocentric and pervasive that they label themselves "reaction formation."

Reaction formation is especially clearly indicated if at the very time subjective experience (and possible expression) of anger, self-interest, reliance on others or casualness are most to be expected and most fitting, we encounter instead emphasis on their defensive opposites, namely, more and more sweetness, self-sacrifice, asceticism or perfectionism. In addition to pervasiveness, egocentricity, and rigidity, a useful criterion for the difference between the pseudo-sublimated and the truly sublimated is the way others tend to react to the behavior pattern in question. The more reaction formation is involved, the more frustrating and irritating that behavior will tend to become. This criterion assumes that the interpersonal relationship is at least moderately intensive, since brief or superficial contact with defensive reaction formations may be quite misleading.

In this regard it might be added that even doubting, which was considered in the earlier section on regression to be a pathological consequence or expression of anally-rooted ambivalence—even doubting seems to have forms that are transitional to sublimation or are primarily sublimated in nature. These forms would include critical zeal that was flexible and productive in intent and not relentlessly picayune or inappropriate; they would also include a capacity for constructive, relativistic re-examination of ideas that are ordinarily taken for granted or held to be absolute.

### G. Reaction Formation: Test Expectations

Since reaction formations vary in their content, their forms of expression in the Rorschach test, as in daily life, will vary with this content. Tenderness, conscientiousness, doubting, toughness, self-sufficiency and/or numerous other emphases in thought and behavior should be evident. At the same time, we should expect more or less clear-cut manifestations of the underlying rejected impulses—sadism, disorderliness, narcissism and the like.

For purposes of this presentation, reaction formations will be broken down into two general classes: those directed primarily against dependent needs and those directed primarily against hostility.

*1. Reaction Formation against Passivity*

Only one form of expression of this type of reaction formation will be discussed here. It will illustrate many of the phenomena that may be expected where passivity is rigidly warded off. Certain men with compulsive character structure are characterized by repudiation of anything tender, feminine and dependent about themselves, be it by hyper-masculinity or by exaggerated, hard-headed, hard-driving, earthbound practicality. They regard free fantasy and creativity as "woman's business" or for "weaklings," i.e., as activities of the scorned, parasitic, passive, frivolous set. This outlook is the same one that affirms, "Those who can, do; those who can't, teach." These men are typically characterized by rigidity, grumpiness, few words, lack of psychological mindedness, pompous dignity and considerable fear of tenderness, intimacy and freedom.*

Reaction formation against passive needs is *one* of the key themes of these adjustments. When seen as patients, these men frequently are in crises over passive, dependent needs. These crises may have been stimulated by increasing age or by sudden impairment of physical function (threat of blindness, for example), and the threat of passivity (among other things) they entail, or by their having assumed business or family obligations beyond their emotional means. Often, they have lost their usual drive and efficiency and have begun to decompensate into a state of anxiety and depression which they desperately try to stave off. They dare not let themselves go. Being a patient is therefore a matter of great shame to them; it is a public admission of needfulness. Accordingly, taking tests, which is one form of admitting imperfection and need for help, is humiliating. Because it opens up the psyche, psychological testing, like psychiatric history-taking or treatment, also threatens their desperate efforts to subdue their anxiety, depression and underlying feelings of need. All the more reason for resenting psychological examination and treatment.

These men, as patients, should (and do) therefore meet the Rorschach test situation with what Schachtel has called *the resistence definition* [131]: sullen, irritable rejection of the situation, at best covered by the flimsiest compliance and affability. The Rorschach test stimuli being vague, formless and disorderly, and the Rorschach test response involving creativeness, imagination, letting oneself go, the entire situation will be incompatible with the maintenance of their ideal self-concept and image of the world. Accordingly they should give few responses, emphasize the obvious *W* and *D,* use few determinants other than form, restrict their content to the most banal, be impatient with the formlessness and fuzziness of the cards, and

* Patterns of reaction formation against passivity also occur in women and are not necessarily entirely different from those discussed here, but will not be considered at this time.

resent the tester for violating their reserve and sense of privacy. These are also the men, other than psychopaths, who would tend to offer the tester a cigarette or a light, engage the tester in conversation about himself, patronize him, and the like—all to minimize their own emotionally needy position. Some, however, will strive to deny passivity through the test itself, that is, by driving themselves to give as many responses as possible.

With increasing decompensation of defenses, patients of this type will become more and more anxious, depressed and emotionally labile. Accordingly, they should more and more use shading and color in their responses, their responsiveness should decrease, and their criticism of the test and oblique or direct berating of the tester should increase.

Viewed in psychosexual terms, this pattern is likely to involve considerable anal and oral hoarding, efforts to prevent the draining away of inner substance, and avoidance of anally-conceived explosions of rage.

## 2. Reaction Formations against Hostility

Test manifestations of these reaction formations are more varied and complex than those of reaction formations against passivity. As previously described, the patient should generally emphasize in his behavior and thinking various forms of conscientiousness, compliance and "sincerity."

### a) Scores.

(1) *R high (greater than 40)*. Reaction formation against hostility in an obsessional setting should have an elevating effect on *R*, provided that inhibition and rigidity are not extreme. This is because the patient is likely to assume that the more responses he gives, the "better" he is morally, that is, the more obedient, dutiful and "considerate" he is. If we remember the additionally facilitating effect on *R* of defensive isolation and intellectualization, we see why high *R* is typical in obsessive-compulsive cases. One form of conscientiousness—the one that aims both at economy and thoroughness—may, however, underlie a moderate *R*. In this instance, the patient will define the task as one in which he should take account only of the "essentials" of each card. This approach will culminate, for example, in the patient's systematically giving one *W* and maybe one, two or three large *D* responses to each card, depending on its overall compactness and its number of large, discrete areas, and finally about twelve *D* responses to Card X, one to each of its major, discrete areas. This will be a more realistic approach than the driven productivity behind the very high *R*, but it too may express a rigid, overmethodical conscientiousness that is a manifestation of reaction formation against hostility.

(2) *Locations.*

(a) *Do responses present*. A perfectionistic, meticulous, conscientious approach to the cards should include an unwillingness to be carried along by total impressions, the parts of which, upon closer inspection, will undoubtedly be uneven in quality or accuracy. Usually accepted parts of common responses should then be eliminated because they are not up to the conscientious patient's high standards. Such patients will see, for example, only the head of the popular men on Card III, or only the leg. *Do* is also related to defense by isolation in somewhat the same way as *Dr* is: the patient fragments a perception and deals with only part of it, thereby preventing the response from being complete enough to carry a significant emotional impact. It is probably not simply a matter of perceptual meticulousness or limited integrative or empathic capacity that the two sets of figures that are most commonly given the *Do* treatment are the popular figures on Card III and the orange figures on Card IX. The bisexual aspects of the former and the claw-like or dueling aspects of the latter are probably sufficiently threatening to stimulate increased defensive, *Do*-producing meticulousness in persons so disposed. The frequent rejection of the upper red on Card II as the heads of the two human figures may be another instance of this *Do*-tendency, the red heads frequently suggesting tabooed anger, blood and violence.*

(b) *Dr high (greater than 20%)*. The striving for many responses on a conscientious basis ordinarily leads to many *Dr. Dr* is further increased by the need for conscientious attention to detail and thoroughness, by the intention of leaving no pebble unturned.

(3) *Determinants.*

(a) *FC, F(C), FC', FCh high (several or more of each); less controlled color and shading responses essentially absent*. Exaggerated emphasis on responses indicating striving for rapport, compliance, tact, altruism, manners, exaggerated love of Humanity or Nature or Life, and the like, should be emphasized as part of the total expression of reaction formation against hostility. Often it is clear that the overconscientious patient brings color and shading into his responses just to be thorough and dutiful. He takes account of color and shading just as he takes account of *Dr* and *S*—they are there and he is not one to have the audacity to ignore them. But ideally, form will not be sacrificed to global color and shading impressions. In fact the introduction of *C* and *C'* into form responses may be in the nature of "afterthoughts," "possible but not necessary" determinants, or gratuitous, artificial or feebly rationalized combinations.

(b) *F+% high*. The conscientious, perfectionistic approach should foster striving for order and accuracy in reaction against impulses

* Possibly a masochistic need to deny the potentially "merry" aspects of these red heads (clowns, party costumes, dancing, revelry, etc.) may also contribute to the dropping of these areas from the response.

to be sloppy, disorderly and careless. Hence, a high $F+\%$. Many $Dr$ may, however, lower the $F+\%$.

### b) Thematic Analysis.

Benign and neutral imagery should prevail in the ideal record's content. Such imagery seldom does prevail, however, because we are dealing after all with a defense that is especially vulnerable to "invasion" by the defended against impulse and because *in patients* pent-up hostility is likely to be especially pressing and this defense is more than likely to be weak or failing. Also complicating the thematic picture are the high correlations between emphasis on reaction formation, isolation and intellectualization, the latter two allowing basically objectionable images considerably more expression than could otherwise be tolerated. Actually, in pathological cases, we typically encounter a scrambled set of indications of success and failure of these defensive operations—in the thematic analysis as in the scores and test attitudes. Therefore, hostile imagery may well be conspicuous, but it should be defensively minimized and prettied up or else it should be found side by side with ostentatiously benevolent, gentle and controlled imagery. Stress may fall on images like puppet and parrot which combine submissive, "trained" qualities with "naughty," provocative qualities, and on "duty"-laden images like "A map; something you'd see in a text book in school from which you'd have to memorize something."

### c) Test Attitudes and Behavior

The patient is likely to be particularly helpful. He may spontaneously point out his responses, especially once inquiry has indicated that the tester is interested in the location of the responses. After a while, he may *spontaneously* give inquiry into his responses, repeatedly volunteering such information as, "The form but not the color makes it look like that," or "Just the head." In addition, he may spontaneously and repeatedly turn the card around so that the tester can see the responses right side up. The tempo of verbalization may be carefully adjusted to the tempo of the tester's writing. Each question asked by the tester may be considered seriously and answered thoroughly. Meticulousness may reach the point where even the "best" popular responses, such as that on Card VIII, are criticized and where frequent use is made of such qualifications as "looks a little bit like," "has the quality of," and "it could sort of suggest." These patients need to prove to the tester and ultimately to their own superego "judge" that they are really "good," "dutiful," "responsible," "innocent" people.

This entire pattern of defensive indications should be both exaggerated and disrupted as the reaction formations are invaded by the underlying hostility. The conscientiousness and helpfulness may become increasingly burdensome to the tester, as described in Chapter 2. For example, on Card III, "The two top right and left pieces don't mean anything. I can find something in them if you want me to. (Long pause.) Do you want me to? (Tester says that is up to the patient; another long pause follows.) That's all." Or the patient might overmethodically and perseveratively search for the same response on each card, such as "a map," and dwell at length on why certain cards *do not* look like maps.

Among the scores, as hostility invades the reaction formations, $S$ may become prominent (greater than 5%–10% of $R$): the underlying negativistic, rebellious, stubborn impulses of persons characterized by rigid reaction formations against hostility frequently find expression through $S$. In this respect, high $S$ stands in opposition to the general indications of exaggerated conscientiousness and to the emphasis on adaptive responses described in the preceding discussion. $R$ and $Dr$ may increase greatly, quantity replacing quality. Perfectionistic manipulation of responses and of verbalization of responses may become quite vexing to the tester. For example, "These look like fierce little—er—small—er—little animals," and, toward the autistic, inappropriate extreme, "This head in particular looks like a dog's head and on the other side it looks like a lamb's head. The left looks like a dog and the right looks like a lamb head. The dog looks like a cocker spaniel and the lamb looks like a lamb." The obeisance to superego pressures may turn into superficial gestures of conscientiousness that no longer preclude "disorderly" and "irresponsible" test reactions. Pseudo-responsiveness may increase in the form of empty talk about the physical properties of the cards and the details of responses, while only a small proportion of the total verbalization may deal with scorable responses. Thus, either high $R$ or low $R$ may result from hostile impulses and demanding attitudes invading the defense. Spontaneous criticism of responses may increase greatly in frequency with little effort being expended to improve the responses by alterations of perceptual organization and/or content.

In general, with increasing defensive failure, more and more effort will be put into defensive operations, like money being poured into failing stock. The defensive failure and the increasing desperation of the patient will also become evident in: (a) increased color and shading responses with the form elements vague, arbitrary, secondary or absent; (b) decreased $F+\%$; (c) increasingly hostile, anxious imagery (explosions, blood, monsters, devils, etc.) indicating fear of and guilt over underlying primitive, hostile impulses; (d) anal imagery breaking through the weakened defenses (anus, intestines, rear ends of animals, people bumping buttocks, bustles, big behinds, and, toward the extreme, bloody bowel movement, talons or teeth around an anus, feces, etc.); (e) increasingly aggressive implications in the patient's style of verbalization—"If you tear this (blot) apart. . . ," "I can torture more out of it. . . ," "If you chop it off here. . . ," etc.

## H. Undoing: General Remarks

Undoing is related to reaction formation. In reaction formation, as we have seen, an attitude is taken contradicting an original attitude. In undoing, a further step is taken: something positive is done which actually or "magically" is the opposite of something done before—in actuality or in imagination. The essential function of undoing is to set right again or atone for an act or thought that is tainted by a forbidden impulse. Often, the undoing consists of a repetition of the original act or thought with the hope that repeating the act or thought in a different emotional context will "prove" that the original unacceptable implication "doesn't count." Sometimes, like reaction formation, undoing may involve a reactive increase in the strength of a drive opposed to the original, forbidden drive. But whether by repetition (with repeated unconscious gratification) or by reactive increase of the strength of another impulse, undoing appears to be a condensed expression of impulse and defense. In this respect too undoing is like reaction formation.

## I. Undoing: Test Expectations

Clear simple instances of undoing are rare in test responses, even in the responses of severe obsessive-compulsive neurotics. Most likely the operation of undoing is hidden in the general synthesis of obsessive-compulsive defensive operations. The clearest instance of undoing we seem to encounter in test responses is that of following a "bad" response (from the point of view of content) with a "good" one; for example, changing an interpretation of a red area from blood to jam. Minimizing the content of a response is another possible form of expression of undoing; for example, "A bloody fight. Of course, it's only symbolic;" "A ferocious looking creature. It's very small, though;" and "A devil; a friendly sort of devil."

In test attitudes and behavior, undoing may be involved in the maddening obsessional tendency to repeat verbalizations with minor variations, with the air of getting the formulation just right. In this instance, the patient's implicit attitude seems to be that any flaw in expression or thought spoils the whole, and that the whole must be corrected. While from one point of view this is a manifestation of the reaction formations of conscientiousness and orderliness, and from another point of view a manifestation of regression to magical, ritualistic modes of thought characteristic of the anal level of personality organization, this manipulation of words may also have its atoning or undoing aspect. Another instance of undoing appears to be that of accompanying excessive or too rapid verbalization with apologies or with repeated questions whether the verbalization is excessive or too rapid.

Typically, to identify an instance of undoing in test results is difficult without the aid of extensive discussion with the patient. Also, undoing is not a defensive operation that overtly pervades behavior in the same way that reaction formation and isolation do. For these reasons, relatively little mention of undoing will be made in the following test analyses.

## J. Case Studies

Four obsessive-compulsive records will be presented, each illustrating the typical defensive operations previously described but each involving different contexts of ego organization and pathology. The first record is that of a well-functioning, apparently normal person, the second of a severe classical obsessive-compulsive neurotic, the third of a severe classical obsessive-compulsive neurotic with prominent psychotic trends, and the fourth of a chronic schizophrenic with vestiges of poorly integrated obsessive-compulsive tendencies. These four cases represent a rough sequence of increasing maladjustment and autism. The operation and form of appearance of the defenses will vary in accordance with the degree of maladjustment and autism prevailing. These variations will highlight the different major aspects of the complex obsessive-compulsive defensive operations.

In the case studies that follow, the introductory biographical material will be somewhat more detailed than it has been so far. In part, this increased detail reflects the rich texture of the obsessive-compulsive Rorschach records. This rich texture demands at least a general "feel" of the person being discussed. The relative increase in biographical detail is greatest in the first case to be discussed—the well-functioning, non-patient obsessive-compulsive man. This is because this man's record affords an excellent opportunity to study an effective adjustment at work in the Rorschach situation, and because it would therefore be well for the reader to know what sort of "normal" man this "normal" man seems to be clinically. It will become evident that his adjustment is certainly not an ideal one. Some clinicians would undoubtedly call him a "neurotic character" or something like that. Yet, there is no question but that he would easily qualify for inclusion in a normal control group in any psychological or psychiatric research project.

### Case 1

This is a 43-year-old physician who was seen for tests and psychiatric evaluation in connection with the treatment of his wife, a borderline schizophrenic woman with severe paranoid and sado-masochistic tendencies. This man had shown considerable self-reliance and resourcefulness throughout his life. From an early age he had been a brilliant, efficient, studious and pedantic person, with reading interests that tended toward the non-fictional in general and the scientific in particular. His development was also characterized by relatively poor social relationships and marked sexual inhibition. He appears to have always had a talent for ingeniously making provocative remarks and then being surprised at resentful reactions. He has also chronically had trouble complaining about things directly.

His relationship with his wife was thoroughly and mutually sado-masochistic. His wife constantly but unpredictably invited or demanded from him compassion, masochistic submission or sadistic assault. In the face of her provocativeness, he typically maintained a calm, detached, almost saintly air of tolerance and helpfulness, well knowing that this only provoked her more. At times, when his wife did succeed in breaking down his controls, he became mildly physically assaultive and also psychologically cruel in his criticism of her. Recently, this physician has become increasingly irritable and bored with his patients and fleetingly aware of suicidal impulses.

His wife, largely out of a paranoid need for self-justification, was active in bringing him for psychiatric examination. There was, however, some evidence to suggest that he was himself anxious to have this examination, that he hoped thereby to exonerate himself in anticipation of her becoming a hopeless, chronic, institutionalized psychotic. He said, upon beginning his examination, "I am here to see if I can regain enough strength to be able to hang on until she either completes her recovery or slips on into a severe enough paranoia to require permanent institutionalization." It is indicative of her orientation that although she insisted on his going for examination, she exacted a promise from him to discuss none of the details of their chronic conflict. It is indicative of his "kindness" that he made this promise and promptly broke it. And it points up his obsessive-compulsive rigidity that, in the midst of maintaining to the psychiatrist his love for and devotion to his wife, he could speak so pedantically of separation from her as "a wonderful surcease." He had a moderately active interest in psychiatry and it was noted that he demonstrated a good deal of intellectual insight into himself, his wife and their relationship. He made little effort, however, to carry this insight over into action. He was, for example, well aware of the complications introduced into the relationship by his surface passivity.

The diagnosis was "obsessive-compulsive character." In the staff conference, emphasis was put on his intense underlying sadistic impulses and the rigidity of his defenses against these, and on his subtle gratifications in his sado-masochistic relationship with his wife. Equal emphasis was, however, put on the strength, efficiency and in many respects "normality" of his adjustment.

Bearing in mind that he is a doctor whose adjustment is being examined by other doctors, his relative psychiatric sophistication, his intellectual insight into himself, his probably strong need to "exonerate" himself, and his consequently intensified need to present himself with his best defenses forward (particularly reaction formation against hostility in the form of cooperativeness, tenderness, understanding, and conscientiousness), we should expect to see this man at his "best" in test attitudes, if not in the scores and themes of his record as well. He should be out to prove he is a wonderful husband, a responsible and intelligent physician, and a model patient. His high intelligence is evident in his exceptionally high Total IQ of 145.

CARD I   REACTION TIME: 2″. TOTAL TIME (subject was interrupted) : 3′ 15″.
    *1. (W F+ A P) I'll start with a bat.*
As the opening verbalization, "I'll start with" sets a perfectly controlled, self-assured, productive tone to the response process.
    *2. (D F+ (H)) In the middle (middle D) there is an angel.*
The theme of innocence is introduced.
    *3. (Dr F— Plant) These seem to be leaves off to either side, outside (lower outer specks).*
    *4. (Dr Ch Cloud) Perhaps cloud effects (in side shading). [What made it look like clouds? The indefinite texture, I mean outline, and the irregular surface texture.]*
    *5. (Do F— Ad) I keep coming back to these wings (upper middle projections) and this head here (upper middle bumps) which seem to be disassociated from the torso (#2) below them. [Disassociated? It is separate from the basic angel figure (#2).]*
(a) Note the self-observant implication of "I keep coming back." (b) This dissociation of head from torso may symbolize need for defensive isolation: the head (intellect, reason, control) is out of touch with the body (instinct, passion, sensuality). The Do score would reflect this defensive operation. The relevance of this split to the angel image is not clear.
    *6. (D FM± Hd Do-tendency) Flattened heads here with arms projecting from them (upper side). [Any specific kind of head? I hadn't thought of it particularly. There are headdresses like that worn by women in French Indo-China.]*
"Flattened" is an implicitly sadistic description of the heads. He could have said, "The head is not fully pictured," or even, "The head is flat on top." Sadistic implications are commonly observed in the metaphors and style of wording of obsessive-compulsive persons. They appear to represent the expression through thought processes of the underlying anal-sadistic orientation characterizing these persons. Note, however, in inquiry, how in a cultured, intellectualistic way he "disposes of" the sadistic implications by attributing the flat shape to the French Indo-Chinese hair-do. His deft manipulation of knowledge may stand him in good stead adaptively as well as defensively.
    *I keep noticing this asymmetry down at the bottom.*
(a) Another instance of emphasis on self-observation. (b) In content, this ·verbalization probably expresses uneasiness at the card's "disorderly" imbalance

and an effort on his part to restore order, demonstrate his conscientiousness, and win the respect of the tester and the approval of his own superego. Imbalance or asymmetry is typically disturbing to the obsessive-compulsive, anally-oriented person because of his deep sense of ambivalence and of precarious balance of id and superego forces. In addition, the subject may be implicitly rebuking the tester for plopping him in this mess by calling attention to the "sloppiness" of his test.

> 7. (D F∓ A) It could be a dragon or a mythological bird, this part of the figure (upper side projection is wing and head is below that). [(While tracing:) That's standing on its head.]

Unlike the "hair-do" reference in #6, "mythological bird" is a relatively weak intellectualizing attempt to make a poorly formed response sound good.

> I find it hard to describe the darker material literally: sort of an amorphous mass. It just occurred to me that these might be exaggerated breasts (on torso contour of #2).

The "exaggerated breasts" description suggests that oral receptive needs may be strong in this man. But his choice of "exaggerated" as a description of the size of the breasts, rather than "large" or "emphasized," suggests either that he views women as not really nourishing (i.e., their feeding powers are exaggerated) or that he tries to minimize his own passive needs (i.e., the importance of being fed is exaggerated), or both. The late occurrence of his observation concerning the breasts and his pointed reference to this lateness both underscore the inference that he needs to minimize his interests and yearnings in this area.

> . . . (Anything else?) No. Not immediately. (Subject is interrupted and card removed.) I could probably work more on it. (Subject goes on to ask what quantity of responses is desirable, and volunteers to speed up his responses if speed is important.)

(a) He is apparently put in an obsessional dilemma by the tester's vaguely permissive and vaguely impatient—but still non-structuring—question, "Anything else?" On the one hand, he seems to want to comply with the possible implication that he may have given enough responses to this card already, but on the other hand he seems to want to go on to his limit, to do "his very best" before stopping. His solution to this dilemma is to make it clear that it is the tester and not he who is interrupting, that he is merely deferring to the tester's time needs, and that he for one is prepared to go on with Card I. Thus, superficially he is compliant in both respects and yet has shifted responsibility to the tester and the tester's "inadequate" instructions for any shortcomings in his responses.

(b) His insistence after the card has been removed that he could "work more on it" even suggests some resentment at being interrupted or hurried—resentment because the tester is interfering with the subject's effort to keep peace between himself and his superego dictates. As one might expect, the subject's reaction to his own implicit irritation at the tester is to fall back on further compliance, that is, increased reaction formation against the stimulated hostility. He next obligingly asks about the quantity and speed of responses that are desired. His compliance and search for rules are probably also determined by his wanting to be the good husband, obliging patient and responsible physician during the examination. His conception of "goodness" is the obsessive-compulsive one with authoritarian overtones.

(c) It should be noted, however, that there has been no serious disruption of response throughout this card and that even the suspected irritation and obsessional dilemma, if present, are smoothly and quickly handled by him. There has been no excessive verbiage, no prolonged doubting, no anxiety to speak of. This integratedness of response, particularly the facility with which French Indo-Chinese headdresses and mythological birds are invoked to take care of the presumed or actual intellectual and emotional complications of his responses, suggests that we are dealing with a relatively well-functioning, well-defended and, in his way, adaptable (although clearly predominantly obsessive-compulsive) person.

CARD II      REACTION TIME: 5″.      TOTAL TIME: 4′.

> *1. (D F(C)+ A) These red things could be butterflies, dancing, facing each other (upper red).* [What made it look like butterflies? *Those two red shapes there.* How did they look like them? *As if the bodies were toward the midline and the wings folded back, extending backwards. The pattern was somewhat suggestive of the pattern on butterflies' wings.* Anything else? *No.*]

A frolicsome and sensitive beginning which contains sufficient control and caution, however, to exclude the red color as a determinant.

> *2–3. (D FM+ A (P); D CF Blood) The large black masses: almost as if they were bears sparring. Their paws together and the other drawn far behind them. The red foot (lower middle), the feet in apposition might be red because they're bloody, but that's not my first impression. They don't look like they've been fighting that hard. If I had to explain the redness, I'd use something like that.* [Anything else to suggest sparring? *Their heads are curled over. They're in a perfect position to defend themselves against blows (to the head).*]

This is a key response in the record. At first we have a well-defended image: the bears are sparring, i.e., engaged in a playful, controlled, not really hostile interaction. Then, heralded by an intensification of intellectualizing detachment ("the feet in apposition"), a clearly hostile theme breaks through ("they're bloody"). He handles the bloody red in an uneasy, wavering and basically rejecting manner. Soon the bears are sparring again, the mechanism of denial having barred the blood from the image. Presumably to reinforce this unstable restoration of defense, the subject implicitly externalizes responsibility for the hostile theme, foisting it onto the tester: "If I had to explain the redness" appears to mean "For my part, I prefer to ignore the red and its disturbing potentialities. If you force me to pay attention to it, you will be responsible for what I say about it." Upon being brought back to this response in inquiry, the subject emphasizes the self-protective positions of the combatants, apparently further reinforcing his repudiation of the image's most hostile aspects. In addition, he may possibly be indicating an ideal of being aggressive without exposing himself to counter-attack. His emphasis on innocence (see I-2) and on compliance and conscientiousness (in test attitudes and behavior) suggests that reaction formation against hostility may be his defense against counterattack, while his flattened heads (see I-6) and bloody animals may represent his own sadistic, attacking impulses and a basically sado-masochistic conception of human relationships. But we should not overlook the spread of reference in this response from apparently deep-lying, threatening hostility to higher level strict control and effective, imaginative and realistic use of intelligence. "Sparring" is a fitting and perceptive characterization of these figures' interaction and he does rationalize the weak "head" part of the image rather well.

> 4. (S F+ A) The white area in the middle could be a manta, devilfish sort of thing; not perfect but suggestive (middle space).

Response I-7 involved a dragon and this response a manta, both images having noteworthy engulfing, destructive implications. The devilfish concept even suggests "evil" connotations.

> 5. (Dd F+ (Hd)) There are grotesque profiles on either side, somewhat like gargoyles (upper outer edge of dark).

Intellectualizing treatment of mediocre form.

> 6–7. (Do F+ Ad; Do F+ Ad) If I were to look at it from the side (subject tilts his head sidewise) I am sure I could. . . . That could well be one of these mythological creatures crouching (upper ½ of dark area). As a matter of fact it could be two of them (second one is lower ½ of dark area), back to back.

(a) "Crouching" again seems to introduce a hostile (ready to spring) theme, but this time the patient stifles the impulse aspect of the response by intellectualizing the animals as "mythological." (b) The back-to-back emphasis is a common form of appearance of anal preoccupation and orientation—a psychosexual orientation quite consistent with the general obsessive-compulsive personality picture developing thus far. (c) Note that he turns his head and not the card in a gesture of passive submission to fantasied restrictive authority.

> 8. (Do F± Coral) The red fingers here (long and short lower red projections) . . . I don't think I would. . . . These look almost like marine forms. [Marine forms? Those red projections. What about them? There are some sorts of coral that resemble that. I would have thought of a rigid form rather than something like a sea anemone. Coral? The irregularity.]

Note that color is not used. In II-1 and in this response including the red color could have added a genuinely warm quality. Instead he used color only in the hostile, eruptive "blood" response (II-3). The depth and sublimated nature of his conspicuous adaptive efforts are thrown into question by this pattern of handling color, and the presumed reaction formation aspect of these adaptive efforts is underscored.

> Probably I could work out other things but it would be pretty labored from here on.

A second uneasy, compulsively-toned relinquishing of a card (see end of Card I), but perhaps at the same time a piece of good self-evaluation.

CARD III    REACTION TIME: 15".    TOTAL TIME: 5' 30".

> 1. (D,W MC +̣ H P) These—the first thing I see—resemble two people in a very stylized, formal sort of. . . . It could be a dance; it could be some sort of a gesture. At first they looked almost like men in evening dress. As I look at it more closely, it's difficult to tell. They could well have goatees which would make them men, but there are projections that would be breasts or very badly cut jackets. The lower projections could be tails of the coat or genitalia. They seem to be wearing high-heeled gray shoes.

(a) As in the revealing sparring response (II-2, 3), and in contrast to his usually clever, effective handling of irregularities in his responses, poor integration of elements characterizes this response. This poor integration suggests defensive weakness at this point even though, with the help of ideas rendered available by intellectualization, the weakness masquerades as precision. (b) In particular, the mixed sex characteristics of the figure suggest strong and/or weakly defended against feminine tendencies. The subject behaves unanxiously, however, and like a physician absorbed in making a differential diagnosis or a scientist classifying a specimen. (c) The relationship between the figures is stiff, cold and affectless—"stylized," "a gesture." The imagery of spontaneity, friendly engagement, cooperation and fun seems underemphasized in this man (see also II-2, 3 which could have been dancing, playing, etc.). In this we see another indication of a relative lack of depth in his adaptive, compliant manner. (d) The "badly cut jackets" may include another implicit transfer of responsibility to the impersonal test for what the subject takes to be an inadequacy in the response (see end of discussion of Card I). That is to say, it is not that the jackets *concept* is unsatisfactory; the *jackets* themselves are. In this lies the externalization of responsibility and a hint of rigid self-righteousness.

> 2. *(D F+ At) The red squiggles on the outside (upper red) look not unlike an x-ray appearance of the stomach with barium going down the esophagus, although one would certainly be suspicious of a stomach with such a white projection going into the shadows. (Suspicious?) Of a carcinoma, if it were smaller. [What made it look like barium? Otherwise one doesn't see the stomach in an x-ray.]*

(a) "Not unlike" is an indispensable phrase in compulsive lingo. On the other hand, "squiggles" is cute and suggests at least a superficial capacity for humor and playfulness (see also II-1). (b) Imperfection in the form is again explicitly pointed out and then fairly smoothly rationalized. (c) Thematically, the image conveys an oral emphasis, although it is cloaked in detached diagnostics.

> 3. *(D FC+ At) The middle red things: the first thing I thought of were kidneys but they are not in the proper relationship to each other; the curves are wrong. [Kidneys? The shape is roughly that, but of course the curves were reversed, but it is a paired, bean-shaped organ. Anything else? Well, the color, but. . . .]*

(a) Further meticulousness. (b) The inclusion of color in the response during inquiry is very tentative and sounds more as if he could not quite rule the color out than as if he wanted to rule it in. It would even be possible to score this response *F* instead of *FC*. Basic adaptive weakness is again suggested (see II-8, III-1). (c) In the two responses to this card following the first homosexually-tinged response, he has emphasized anatomy. Possibly this indicates a tendency to fall back defensively on the detached, diagnostic aspects of the medical role. His verbalization of #1 suggested the same tendency.

> 4. *(D F+ Food) It could be beans (middle red).*

Food images generally carry oral-receptive connotations (see #2).

> 5. *(D F— Ad) This gray thing in the middle (lower middle gray): I'm not familiar with creatures with lateral teeth but it makes me think of some sort of animal with teeth that project in that direction (demonstrates: horizontally). The mouth. And I should say that anything with a mouth like that could well be threatening to whatever would be small enough to be bitten by it.*

In this not well-integrated oral-aggressive response, we encounter in clear form a maneuver that will recur and that indicates an outstanding defensive technique of this man. Unable either to block the threatening image altogether or to eliminate the theme of threat from the response, he minimizes the threat by taking the size of the blot more or less literally. In the end, the image is that of a tiny creature and therefore nothing he need fear or feel guilty about. So far as hostility is concerned, he seems inclined to make molehills out of mountains. Defensive denial and counterphobic emphasis are involved in this danger-minimizing and guilt-denying mode of organizing the response. These are not the only defensive operations involved, however, since typical successful denial would have ignored the area or else made it into something "pleasant," and the typical, successful counterphobic image, while phobic in content (ghost, ape, monster, etc.), is conspicuously disparaged in the way it is conceived and handled; that is, it is gleefully or scornfully described as silly, from a comic strip, engaged in ridiculous activity or the like. If these were the chief defensive operations involved in the present response and if they were *not* successful, we would expect signs of fear or revulsion from the patient.

In addition to denial and counterphobic defense, we must therefore assume that defensive isolation is crucially involved in this response. Isolation is involved in that a threatening impulse representation comes to consciousness but is manipulated affectlessly and is ingeniously denied any direct relevance to the self. It has been suggested before that he copes with inadequacies in his responses by more or less resourceful intellectualization and externalization, invoking images of real but "imperfect" things to explain away the "imperfections" of his responses. It is further suggested now that he copes with originally inadequate defense against threatening image content with equally resourceful denial, counterphobic attitudes and isolation of affect. In effect, he dismisses the response as emotionally unimportant and even irrelevant to him.

The technique of literal use of size for defensive purposes has an underlying continuity with such already discussed responses as making the bloody fight in II-2, 3 into "sparring." As he presents it, the hostility in his images is sham, petty or otherwise nothing to worry about. Also, he does not entirely repudiate these hostile themes, this suggesting that so long as he can maintain a secure, defensively detached or "isolated" position, he can intellectually acknowledge bits of aggression. The coolness and quickness of his defensive operations in the area of hostility suggest again that on the whole he is (and feels) relatively secure in his defensive position and that he is therefore likely to be functioning relatively stably at present. On the other hand, he seems to have to devote much energy to keeping hostile themes under control; hence the major interpretive emphasis on defense rather than genuine adaptiveness.

> 6. *(D F± Obj) I still haven't decided what this dark mass the gentlemen in their stylized gesture are carrying (lower middle black). It might be one of those round-bottomed water buckets. It (the lower middle) doesn't give me much of any sensation.*

(a) More detached self-observation and more overconscientious—and stilted— communication to the tester. (b) "Gentlemen" probably emanates from his general deferential gentility that in turn reflects strong reaction formations against hostility.

> 7. *(S F+ Ad) Now I switch to the white: I see the head of a bird,*

*a crested bird with a bill (space between leg and arm of P; beak is by P hip).*

Further self-observation and conscientious reporting.

*I think that's probably about all I could get reasonably.*

That is to say, it will be on the tester's head if the tester asks him for more responses and gets poor ones from him.

*(The subject volunteers to point out each of his responses as he goes along, having noted the tester's interest in locations during inquiry into the responses to Cards I and II.)*

Having failed at the end of Card I to get rules about speed and quantity of response and/or not having gained the tester's overt approval by his previous anticipatory compliance, he now tries again, this time by offering to point out his responses as he goes along. It is clear by now that for reasons mentioned earlier this man is so overcompliant that he is watching the tester like a hawk for indications of what the tester is interested in, what the tester expects of him, how he can help the tester out, etc. To anticipate, it should be said now that without encouragement he points out verbally and/or with his finger almost every response in the remainder of the record.

CARD IV     REACTION TIME: 3″.     TOTAL TIME: 4′ 50″.

*1. (W M+ H Do-tendency) These tremendous feet attracted my attention at once (lower sides). The whole thing here as a matter of fact might be a clown in the perspective . . . as if he were sitting on a post (lower middle), above one, with his feet here and his arms so (upper sides), which would account for the central projection downward.*

"Tremendous feet" suggests subjective feelings of smallness and of danger of being overwhelmed. The implicit threat is quickly removed from the response both by making the figure a clown (a friendly, harmless, foolish figure) and by emphasizing that the feet are not really "tremendous" since this is a perspective view. As in the small threatening teeth of III-5, denial, counterphobic efforts and isolation all seem to be elements of this defensive operation. The final response is a sharp, well-organized, imaginative one. This man is obviously a highly intelligent, quick, agile, ingenious thinker, but he is also obviously a man who devotes far too much of his thinking to isolating affect, forestalling anxiety, and remaining a detached, utterly "rational" and "adaptive" being. What is a prime function of thought—the achievement and maintenance of relatively detached, rational adaptiveness—may, when it is invested with too much importance, become a symptom or a character defect. A good deal—though obviously not all—of this man's talent and energy seems to be going down the drain of neurotic defense.

*2. (Dr F+ Ad) This gray, shaped like a sharp V, is not unlike the proboscis of hemipteri, which are the June bugs, and homoptera (upper center). This other darker thing is also seen in that type of creature (upper midline).*

This area is fairly often seen as a vagina or at least as an enclosing rather than a protruding or intrusive form. His seeing it as a stinging and sucking instrument—even though defensively minimized via the insect image—leads to the speculation that he has an attacking and parasitic conception of women. In view of the strong oral and feminine emphasis in this record, such a conception of women is not unlikely.

> *3–4. (D F+ Ad; D F+ Ad) These dark—I was going' to say arm-like, yet the thing I thought of before arms was a swan's neck and head (upper sides; #3)—perhaps they could be serpents (#4), though serpents don't have such a pointed anterior extremity.*

These two responses are also highlights of this record. (a) Expressed as alternatives, the swan and serpent suggest alternate or layered self-images: the gentle, serene swan representing all that his already highly conspicuous isolation and reaction formations against hostility have suggested, and the biting, poisonous serpent representing the hostile, attacking (oral as well as phallic) underlying self-image. (b) The evil connotations of serpent also stand opposed to the innocent implications of the angel in I-2 and allied with the guilty implications of the devilfish in II-4. They underscore the importance of superego problems in this man's personality (see also III-5). (c) Note that of the two alternatives, he criticizes—i·e., gets defensively compulsive about—only the serpent. Also, "serpent" for snake is stilted, emphasizing further his defensive lack of spontaneity in handling this response, the threatening alternative. We have here a nice instance of how the same impulse-defense problems may be reflected both in content and in test attitudes.

> *5. (D F(C)+ Ad Do-tendency) Here are a couple of eyes here I just noticed, making a very set sort of dragon (lower middle) with projections at the ends of the supra-orbital region, and the projections a little further back perhaps ears, and very fine tusks. He has a nicely striped back of the head and neck. I'm looking down on him, as I see it.*

Another image with primitive, attacking, devouring connotations, this one dealt with again as if the subject were engaged in a differential diagnosis or in studying a laboratory specimen (see also III-1, 2, 3). By giving him a set of approved techniques and values for regarding dispassionately what is strange, horrible and threatening, his professional medical role or identity may be seen to serve the purposes of isolation of affect and counterphobic reassurance against frightening impulses.

> *6–7. (s F+ A; s F+ A) In the white I can see a couple of ducks (enclosed spaces between lower middle and lower sides). One has his head and neck under water (upper space), and the other (duck) has his head up (lower space).*

> *8. (s F± A) This could be a sea elephant (enclosed space, upper sides): the head up toward you; the back flippers here.*

> *I think that's enough.*

On first hearing, this sounds like a perfectly ordinary, innocuous way of terminating work on a Rorschach card, and yet it has an unusual ring. Explicitly or implicitly, subjects usually emphasize "That's all I can see." His verbalization— "that's enough"—suggests that there is no dearth of responses in his case, that he can meet all demands, but that he is stopping because he has met the tester's needs. He may well have anticipated being interrupted at any moment by the tester (see end of Card I) and may have been trying to beat the tester to the draw. It had been disturbing to him when he was interrupted earlier. This way, by actively interrupting, he is being compliant and conscientious and thereby making a defensive virtue out of what could otherwise be a somewhat painful necessity. In deciding what is "enough," however, he is also usurping the tester's function and thereby expressing in his defensive operations something of his unconscious, rejected hostile tendencies. In this fashion, fine differences in the tune of certain routine verbalizations often reflect highly individual conceptions of the test situation and response process.

CARD V    REACTION TIME: 30".    TOTAL TIME: 3' 50".

> 1. (D F± Ad Do-tendency) I started off to have an idea but it's hard to carry it out. I see the back half of animals like deer or antelope (side wing and projections), but it's hard to tell what happened to their front ends. They get lost in all this stuff (middle D). The back legs, the tail and the back part of the back are pretty clear.

(a) Further conscientiously reported self-observation. (b) The overt content is "anal" (back half) in emphasis (see II-6, 7). (c) When this image is seen, it is usually stated that a head-on collision of the animals has occurred. That this hostile, clashing theme has been at least sensed and blocked, if not consciously thought and censored out of the response, is suggested by his sudden "ineptness" in coping with the center details. For such an intellectually facile subject, this is a conspicuous falling off in smoothness and integratedness of response and suggests defensive threat and instability. Note also in this respect the relatively slow reaction time for Card V, and the delayed appearance of the popular response.

> 2. (W F+ A P Do-tendency) These are large, swept-back wings here —looking at the black. Clumsy wings; they wouldn't work well, I suspect. Tying in with the wings perhaps are a head like that of a vampire bat with very large ears extending away from me and that would tie in with the legs toward me. It would be a pretty punk sort of bat, I expect.

(a) A threatening, devouring image ("vampire") and again he resorts to minimization, emphasizing its "clumsy" and "punk" aspects. In III-5 he made the teeth small, in IV-2 he made the blood-sucking parts tiny, and here he defends himself against the threatening oral image by "grounding" the vampire bat. (b) It also appears from the internal sequence in this response that he may initially have tried to head off the vampire image by fragmenting the response and dealing only with the wing (clumsy, ineffective) areas. This Do-tendency may be an instance of defensive isolation at work in perceptual organization paralleling isolation in his imagery and test attitudes. (c) All this minimizing of the size and strength of what he sees begins to suggest that the subject may well need to deprecate himself and to conceive of himself as weak and inadequate (see IV-1); that is to say, his rigidly defensive handling of the aggressive potential in his images suggests that he might typically deal with himself in the very same way. At the same time, his criticisms remain externally oriented.

> This is too uniform in reflection. There isn't enough to make it have many meanings for me.

Card V usually elicits fewer responses than most of the other cards, so that his critique of the card has an acceptable, realistic foundation. It is nevertheless noteworthy that he makes it plain that it is not his inadequacy but the inkblot's.

Presumably this self-defensiveness would cover the inadequacy feelings referred to in #2.

> *3. (Dr FC'(C)— A) If I try hard, I can see a dark animal with a dark neck and a small dark head in this region (dark shading in outer half of wing; head is at upper inner corner): a crouching animal; not at all a massive-looking thing.*

A "dark . . . crouching animal" suggests impending attack. Characteristically, he minimizes the threat by negation and by minimizing its physical size—"not at all a massive-looking thing."

> *No. I don't see much in this really.*

This is a much more secure, less defensive way of giving up a card than "I think that's enough" (see end of Card IV).

CARD VI     REACTION TIME: 5".     TOTAL TIME: 5' 25".

> *1-2. (W FCh+ Dec; W FCh+ Dec) The first thing I think of here is a Navajo rug (#1) or a sand painting (#2). [Navajo rug? The bilaterality, the long slender pattern, and less a rug than a sand painting. Anything else to make it look like a rug? The uneven texture. Sand painting? They—more than rugs—are likely to be in patterns similar to that: an elongated, bilaterally symmetrical design. Anything else? The texture: it was a bit speckled, although a good one is amazingly uniform. It's not the sort of analysis that would bear up under very close scrutiny though.]*

His striving for precision during inquiry into these two responses is impressive.

> *3. (W FCh+ Ad P) The texture along here (along midline) is very like that of many reptiles. It could be a skin spread out to dry.*

This skin is rarely described as reptilian. Thematically, reptilian images (such as crocodile, poison snake, or even dragon) often seem to carry primitive, oral-aggressive and/or phallic-aggressive connotations (see IV-4).

> *4. (D F(C)+ At) This whole pattern down along the center (midline and surrounding area): the first thing it made me think of was a cross-section of the central nervous system and yet I thought it didn't match.*

Still carefully self-observing and self-observingly careful.

> *5. (D F∓ Sound) And so the next thing I thought of were oscillographic recordings of sound waves, which this could well be (entire middle area; especially upper D). In that latter case, this stuff (upper wings) would be a beautiful representation of random noise—the kind of thing that hurts your ears when you hear it over the radio. [(While tracing:) It peters out down here (around midline in lower D) into a bum recording.]*

Note in inquiry that it becomes a "bum recording" rather than a bum response. This suggests again that there must be a great deal of defensive self-righteousness in this man (see III-1 and after V-2).

> *I get many ideas and abandon them. Do you want them all? (It's up to you.)*

This verbalization appears to combine further self-observation, boasting (see his opening remark on Card I), and seeking of permission from authority (the tester) onto whom he displaces responsibility; that is to say, he apparently wants it clear that any poor responses from here on will be the tester's responsibility.

6. *(Dr`F+ Ad) Again we go back to the bats. These hooks are like claws by which they hang themselves (lower middle projections).*

7. *(D F— Geog) There is a remote resemblance to a distorted map of the United States (½ lower D), with Florida here (lower side projection) and Texas going off here (upper side projection) but that's pretty difficult to sustain.*

At first the map rather than the response is "distorted," i.e., inadequate, but at the end he does take responsibility for the response's inadequacies and, it should be emphasized on the positive side, his critical evaluation of his responses is usually quite sharp. He can be highly defensive without becoming unrealistic.

8–9. *(D F+ Sex; Dr F∓ Sex) One could get genital suggestions from a thing like this: the very obvious phallus (upper middle shaft) and the rather insignificant testes (lower middle tiny bumps).*

A cautious, noncommittal verbalization of a pair of sex responses—"one could get" and "genital suggestions." This defensiveness in giving sex responses suggests significant conflict and inhibition in the sexual area. Disturbance is also indicated (a) by his going on to treat the size relationship in a literal manner, this being much below his usual sophisticated and versatile conceptual level, and (b) by his idiosyncratic manner of verbalizing the size difference in question— "the very obvious phallus . . . rather insignificant testes."

The following speculation is one way of accounting for these disrupted aspects of the two sex responses: the subject feels on the one hand that he has little to give sexually ("insignificant testes," i.e., not much semen or sexual tension to be discharged) but on the other hand that he must deny this feeling and present himself as a potent masculine figure ("obvious phallus"). Possibly relevant to the "insignificant testes" theme as interpreted here are the inadequacy feelings suggested by the "tremendous feet" in IV-1, the "clumsy wings . . . punk bat" in V-2, and his remarking in VI-5 of the area below the phallic area that "it peters out down here." Possibly relevant to the present interpretation of the "obvious phallus" theme are his repeated efforts to demonstrate or at least emphasize verbally his adequacy and productivity, even when he may be having serious trouble responding.

10. *(Do F± Ad) Oh, here is an eagle; very much like a gargoyle (lower ½ upper wings).*

By intellectualization, a possible attacking image is immobilized.

CARD VII    REACTION TIME: 12″.    TOTAL TIME: 5′ 20″.

1. *(W M+ H P) The first thing I see (laugh) are a couple of teen-age girls talking, gesticulating. Their hair is dressed upward in an exaggerated upsweep, and to some extent drawn forward over their brows. Their arms are back. They are apparently wearing loose bolero jackets that hang back as their arms go back. They are sitting with their knees as close together as they can get and they could very well be squatting on their knees—which would account for the fact that they've got no legs.*

(a) His careful, knowledgeable attention to female attire and the emphasis on physical intimacy between the girls underscore the previous inference of significant feminine identification (see III-1). (b) "Squatting" may have an anal emphasis, an emphasis that is reinforced by the fact that he does not quite mean squatting and is therefore introducing the notion inappropriately. (c) The image is organized quite skillfully, however, indicating again his intellectual perceptiveness and resourcefulness.

> 2. *(Dr FCh+ Cg) Breaking it down, this part could be sort of a coonskin cap (upper projection). [Coonskin? I see those caps on little boys in our neighborhood. They have that fluffy, rough, cylindrical appendage on their caps, and if it were to stand up it would look like that.]*

(a) "Breaking it down" appears to reflect more than his characteristically conscientious reporting of the details of the response process. Like "flattened heads" in I-6, "breaking it down" is sadistically-tinged verbalization, though a less striking instance of that. (b) There may be an anal reference in this image of a raccoon's tail. (c) In both #1 and #2 he may be stressing a benevolent paternal orientation—for his own peace of mind and possibly to impress the clinical authorities with his "innocence" in the family crisis.

> 3. *(D F(C)+ Hd) Here is a face in this region (middle ⅓, facing out): a light eye, a nose projecting outward, the line of the mouth.*

> 4. *(D F∓ A) Hmm! Here are a pair of animals, again squatting on their haunches, facing outward, away from each other (lower ⅓); their paws; their heads tilted upward. The faces are very indistinct. The details of the features are quite obscure.*

As in VII-1, he seems to mean "squatting on their knees," and this use of the word *squatting* may therefore have important anal connotations.

> 5. *(Dr F± Hd) Here's a curiously distorted head, flattened posteriorly, like those of some, I think, African tribe where the heads are bound so there is no occipital bulge (side projection; face is on its lower edge). This one (left) is far better than this one on the other side (right) which is indistinct.*

Another well-intellectualized poor form and another implicitly sadistic image and style of verbalization (flattened, deformed heads).

> *I think that's about all.*

CARD VIII   REACTION TIME: 10". TOTAL TIME: (subject was interrupted) ; 7'.

> 1. *(D F+ A P) A couple of red lizards at either side.*

Due to time pressure, there was little inquiry into his responses from here to the end of the record. This is particularly unfortunate in view of his frequent naming of color as he gives his responses, e.g., "red lizards." From his spontaneous verbalizations it is unclear whether he meant only to locate responses by naming color or whether he somehow included the color in his responses. At times the color could fit, as in this red lizard response, but that does not establish the response as an FC. At times the color does not fit, as in the "green rabbit" of X-8, below. And at times the use of color is nonspecific, as in the "red band" in VIII-6, below. The fact that only certain of his responses include this color detail suggests that FC, F/C or FC arbitrary scores should be given, but to score this way without inquiry would be presumptuous in this inhibited context. The responses can only be scored F. Since responses like IX-3 (fungus, lichen) and X-9 (worm) could so easily have been color responses and were not, so far as inquiry could establish, it is likely that the $F$ score alone is valid in most of these questionable color responses. Qualitatively, however, these color references must be considered instances of abortive, shallow, and insubstantial efforts to use color in his responses, or, on the level of experience and behavior, to respond emotionally where he has no genuine, spontaneous feeling.

*I like the colors in this: I don't know why but. . . .*

(a) Only a strict intellectualizer would so promptly—defensively—need to know why he liked the colors. Non-isolating, unintellectualistic persons would take such an affective response for granted. The verbalization indicates his conscious remoteness from his own feelings. (b) Although he "likes" the colors, he presumably is unable to use them *in responses* on this card. Again, strictly surface adaptiveness is what seems to characterize him, and even that seems strained and overcautious. Despite the limitations on the depth, ease and spontaneity of his emotional responsiveness, which limitations reflect overreliance on defensive isolation, he may still be capable of a relatively consistent and effective facade of emotional involvement and warmth. His color naming indicates this facade a little bit, and his smooth, obliging manner of taking the test and meeting its serious challenges indicates it strongly. His defenses are rigid but effective and do not lead him away from reality, logic and social form.

*2. (D F+ At) This alternate black and white area towards the center of the figure makes me think somewhat of the vertebral column (usual ribs).*

*3. (D F∓ Ad) The black triangular business pointing toward you is rather like the skull of some fishes (upper gray-green).*

Making this relatively light gray-green area "black" may have depressive origins. The skull concept also could suggest depressive feelings.

*4. (D F+ At) The orange and red mass toward me is quite a bit like a cross section of the brain stem (lower pink and orange). As you see, I'm not much of a neurological anatomist (laugh). [Cross section? The general outline. It's about in the region of the cerebellar peduncles. Anything else? The bilateral pattern in it. I should hate to trace out the tracts in that.]*

This is aggressive pseudo-modesty, since he has absolutely no reason to think that the tester, who is not a physician, could see that he is "not much of a neurological anatomist." All sweetness, this physician is pulling medical rank on the psychologist. Here is pseudo-adaptive reaction formation (modest, self-critical conscientiousness) with a "return of the repressed" in it.

*5. (S F— Obj) Here's a hammer-shaped white figure on each side. As I look closely, it doesn't look hammerish, but I got that impression (space below middle blue is handle; space between legs of P is head of hammer).*

Possibly a poorly defended against sadistic (pounding) image, especially in view of its poor form, its pure space location, and his conscious need to reject it. It also represents good reality testing that he does reject it.

*6. (S F∓ Hd) I could, by really stretching a point a great deal, see a white head with one of these very long lantern jaws and a Grecian nose (space, facing into belly of P). I was going to say no forehead at all, but he could be wearing a red band around his forehead (leg of P)—which would take care of that.*

(a) This is the seventh pure *Space* response in the record. Altogether there are 9 *S*—about 12% of the 76 responses. This is strong emphasis on space and under- scores the hostile negativism that underlies and sometimes seems to invade his gentle, considerate manner. (b) Note how he first scalps the Greek (no forehead) and then ingeniously completes the head. This alteration of the image may involve defensive undoing, i.e., aggressing and then atoning or setting right again. His "which would take care of that" remark at end strongly suggests a feeling of relief at his quick-witted, perceptive restoration of wholeness. He often seems just one step ahead of his threatening sadistic impulses—but it is an important step.

> 7–8. *(Dr F(C)+ (Hd); D F— Food) Here's a very grotesque face —almost Hogarthian or like Pieter Breughel: a completely anencephalic head with an eye up toward the top, a prominent nose and a large mouth (outer edge of lower pink is eye and nose area; lower, curved edge of pink is mouth). It is engulfing this orange material (lower orange).*

(a) The face is brilliantly intellectualized, the initially poor face being trans- formed into a good likeness of a relatively esoteric work of art. (b) The oral theme of this image is striking. The amorphousness of what is being "engulfed," the intensity of the expression "engulfed," as well as the combination of the two responses (#7 and #8), indicate the power of his already conspicuous oral cravings and also the disruptive effect these cravings may sometimes have on his functioning (see III-5). Unlike the head structure, this aspect of the response is very poorly handled. (c) This is the fourth distorted head (see I-6, VII-5, VIII-6). This may relate in part to a deformed body image of himself or of someone important in his life. The common unconscious equation of head and phallus may be involved here, in which case these responses may pertain in part to castration fantasies and feelings of sexual inadequacy (see VI-8, 9). Their sadistic aspects cannot be ignored in any case. (d) On another level, deprecation of intellect in others (he obviously values his own highly) may be implied—the deformed head commonly being associated with impaired mentality.

> 9. *(Dd F+ Ad) A couple of dog heads on either side of the orange material (outer projections, lower orange). The top of the head is away from the center line of the figure, the snouts pointed away from each other.*
>
> 10. *(Dr F(C)± A) There seems to be a flying fish in this center, rather blue area; again, flying toward you (middle of middle blue). The wings are up in the back; the ventral surface is toward the midline.*

This subject has been pointing out his responses spontaneously almost from the very beginning of the test. His "toward me" and "toward you" verbalizations must be viewed as part of this overconscientious context, and do not take on the malignant paranoid implications they otherwise might. In this last respect, the themes of his images involving "toward me" and "toward you" localizations are not threatening, beseeching or otherwise emotionally charged, as they typically are in paranoid contexts.

> 11. *(Dr F(C)∓ A) I see a small frog here in the darker blue with the two dark eyes (lower inner corner, blue).*
>
> *I have a feeling I should see something in this dark, double, central outline (upper midline) and yet it has no specific meaning for me. It's so clear-cut.*

CARD IX    REACTION TIME: 12″.    TOTAL TIME: 5′.

> *1. (D F∓.Ad) Well I see two orange heads, of most grotesque creatures (orange, usual "gargoyles"). I get the impression that they are rather friendly—that is, not menacing—animals, with curious projections from their snouts (upper projections to center).*

Further minimization of hostility, this time involving negation—"friendly—that is, not menacing" (see V-3). It is significant that he implicitly equates "friendly" and the negation "not menacing." This equation underscores both the reaction formation aspect of his adaptiveness and the basic sado-masochistic conception of human relationships previously inferred (see II-2).

> *2. (s F+ Ad) This white area (enclosed space, upper orange): I can see an animal; something like a dog barking or baying; his mouth wide open; an exaggerated snout on it (toward center); a rather ludicrous figure.*

An oral-aggressive image ("barking"), again minimized ("ludicrous").

> *3. (D (C)F Plant) This green area, in its almost amorphous general pattern, makes me think of some sort of fungus (all green). It would have to be a lichen or something of that sort.* [What made it look like fungus or lichen? *The uniform texture; the somewhat brokenly irregular outline; the bracket appearance projecting outward from the central support; the full outline.* Anything else? *No. Just that I was trying to see something. It's really not a good representation. Some of these are pretty labored.*]

It would have been easy to use the green color in this response and yet he could not allow himself the liberty of an essentially benign *CF* (see II-1, II-8). Note in this regard his anxious, defensive reaction in inquiry to the weak form (that is, poor control) in the response which he had tried so hard to patch up into something specific. Note too his one, two, three, four manner of responding in inquiry.

> *4. (Dr F+ Ad Do-tendency) Then I see an animal's head at the extreme lateral parts of the green area, an animal which appears to be completely composed and yet could perhaps be dealt with with more respect than these orange things I spoke of (#1). It's suggestive of a cat-like or leonine face, head.*

A composed though frightening animal, he implies, suggesting thereby an inner sense of how he sugar-coats or at least masks his intense hostility, and suggesting also how well isolated his thoughts are from the threatening hostile feelings and impulses to which they refer.

> *5. (D F+ Hd) I can see a distorted, rather ill-defined face on the left hand part of the lower red area. It's not strictly symmetrical so it doesn't show on the other side. A chinless sort of sub-human kind of face.*

Rather than acknowledge a defect in his response (as he sees it), he weaves his criticism into the response. The content of the image, that is, the content he introduces in rationalizing what he regards as the defects of this head response, appears to combine connotations of weakness ("chinless") and primitive impulse ("sub-human").

> *There isn't much more in this for me.*

CARD X     REACTION TIME: 15".     TOTAL TIME: 7'.

*This is a gay affair.*

Maybe so, but he uses no color in his responses to this card other than *F/C* and this occurs only once and relatively late at that (#7). In all likelihood, he feels the gaiety but responds to this feeling with excessively cautious control. He seems as afraid to be happy as to be aggressive (see II-1). Freedom of feeling of any sort probably threatens his entire obsessional system of defense and is probably rarely possible.

> *1–2. (D F+ A (P); D F+ A Fabulized Combination) This blue thing at either side is a creature with many extremities. It is apparently pursuing the green object which has the most superficial resemblance to leaping goat or antelope (upper green). But I keep seeing the blue object as being no larger than is actually shown there, so the goat or antelope would have to be very tiny.*

Like the minimized oral-aggressive insect image in III-5, this is a dramatic, almost autistic instance of his falling back on literal use of size for defensive purposes. By implication, the minimized threat is again oral-aggressive.

> *3. (D F+ A) I see a couple of things that almost look like scorpion fish, in this muddy-colored region up above (upper gray), with pectoral fins down below them almost like precursors of four legs, which of course they are (further description).*

"Scorpion" has an aggressive implication, only this is defensively and cleverly transferred into a scorpion fish. This man's biological erudition is given a thorough work-out in this threatening, defense-stimulating test situation.

> *4. (Dr F+ Obj) The thing there and on either side (upper middle gray) looks like drawings that Kipling made of the post which supported the door beneath which the 'Stute Fish hid. That's one of the Just So stories.*

In the story to which he refers (according to my subsequent investigations) the 'Stute Fish was being pursued by a devouring whale. Again therefore he seems to be defensively minimizing a hostile, oral image and stripping it of fear and affect—only this time the major defensive work has already been done by Kipling.

> *5. (D F+ Obj) This yellow thing looks quite a bit like a flyball governor, reduced to its bare essentials (upper middle orange).*

The image of the governor has enormous appeal to persons, like the obsessive-compulsives, who greatly fear their impulses and feelings and desperately strive to maintain control.

> *6. (D F+ A) I think the red thing is some kind of marine worm (all red). I've seen things similar to that. Not so much a worm as a large hydra.*

Hydra has oral-engulfing implications, but a large hydra is still a tiny, unfrightening thing (see III-5, X-1, 2).

> *7. (D F/C+ A) The yellow thing (middle yellow): protoplasm, an ameboid outline. It could well be a pair of yellow amebae. [Why did you refer to the amebae as yellow? Because it was printed in yellow. You get accustomed to various dyes used in microscopy, and colors per se have no meaning. Did you see it as dyed or did you mention color*

just to indicate where it was on the card? *Mostly to indicate where they were.*]

Even this feeble use of color has to be minimized. In inquiry there is a nice verbalization of the meaning of the F/C score: "colors per se have no meaning."

> *8–9. (D F+ Ad P; D F+ A Fabulized Combination) There's a light green rabbit here, his ears pointing toward you (lower middle). On either side of the midline he appears to have large green worms attached to each eyeball (lower green).* [Worms? *They were somewhat segmented and elongated cylindroids. The J-shaped distinct ends, caudal ones: one doesn't see it very often, but it isn't rare.* Anything else? *It would be hard to account for it as anything else.*]

(a) His invoking the shape of the tail end as a determinant of the response, even though he acknowledges that this particular shape is uncommon, gives the response a distinctly anal emphasis. (b) "Cylindroids" is another of the many instances of his precise, "diagnostic," well-intellectualized approach to the test.

> *There is a lot of movement in this. It's not all a static affair.*

Despite his apparent efforts to maintain a rigidly controlled, precise, emotionally "isolated" position, the inkblot is exciting to him. However, he cannot do more than express this diffuse feeling in measured words.

> *10–11. (D F+ A Confabulation tendency; D F∓ A) There's a grayish creature here (side gray) attempting to flee out from the middle, and particularly on the left side it appears to be having its head engulfed by this yellow amorphous mass (side yellow), which is somewhat fishlike. I have no feeling of menace about this. It's just a perfectly normal big-fish-eat-the-little-fish sort of problem.*
>
> *12. (s F∓ Hd) I can, by trying hard, make this (space, facing into back of middle yellow "dog") a rather grotesque humanoid face, but really I've exhausted it.*

The Confabulation tendency in #10 lies particularly in "attempting to flee from the middle." As in the "anencephalic head . . . engulfing this orange material" (VIII-7, 8), but more flagrantly, an oral-aggressive fantasy seems to be getting out of hand here. The breakdown of defense is accompanied by the emergence of some autism. The subject quickly recovers, however, draws a conventional oral moral from the picture, and defensively negates and denies any and all threat or "menace" in this picture.

Even in his denial ("perfectly normal") he gives away his conception of the whole world as one in which sado-masochistic, devouring relationships are the rule (see II-2, IX-1). Rather soon afterwards he defensively gives up the card ("I've exhausted it"), indicating thereby continuing anxiety despite his defensive operations in #10 and #11 (see also end of Card IV).

Confabulations represent a breakthrough of primary process thinking in a performance which is presumably carried out mainly on a fairly high level of secondary process thinking or at least culminates on such a level. In the Confabulation, there is more regression of the level of psychic functioning than is called for or explainable by the temporary creative "regression in the service of the ego" required for imaginative response to the inkblots. Confabulations typically involve a severe breakdown of the distinction between fantasy and external reality and are thereby closely related to or are one form of expression of pathological externalization, i.e., paranoid projection. Also, Confabulations must ordinarily be assumed to occur involuntarily and in spite of defensive efforts. Consequently, Confabulation *tendencies,* even though they are actually only uncrystallized or mild Confabulations, are cause for concern whenever they are encountered. They suggest that bizarre proclivities may be present and not strictly in hand, although not out of control.

We must remember, however, that there is only one Confabulation tendency in this record of 76 responses and no other indications of formal thought disorder. Fabulized Combinations, of which there are two in this record, are not specifically autistic in implication. They are often encountered in nonpsychotic settings, perhaps most often in obsessive-compulsive settings among these. Ordinarily, if malignant autistic developments are under way, and if the Rorschach record remains quantitatively and qualitatively dilated, as in the case of an $R$ of 76 and a wide variety of locations, determinants and content being called into play, many signs of thought disorder will be present. We are likely to encounter Peculiarities, other Confabulation tendencies, Fluidities, *pure C,* arbitrary use of color, and the like, if not full-blown Confabulations and Contaminations and instances of clear-cut Autistic Logic. Therefore, we may say of this subject only that he is open to an occasional, relatively autistic response which is not malignant and from which he is able to recover rather quickly.

The theme of his Confabulation tendency—flight from and falling into the clutches of devouring figures—suggests that paranoid projection of his apparently intense oral-aggressive impulses is likely to characterize the form and content of his autistic responses. Presumably, this would occur when his prominent reaction formations were unable to contain these impulses adequately (see VIII-7, 8).

### Summary of Scores

R: 76        EB: 4–1.5(2)

| | | | | | | | |
|---|---|---|---|---|---|---|---|
| W | 7+1 | F+ | 33 | A | 22 | W% | 9–11 |
| D | 40 | F— | 6 | Ad | 19 | D% | 53 |
| Dd | 2 | F± | 6 | H | 3 | DR% | 29 |
| Dr | 13 | F∓ | 9 | (H) | 1 | | |
| S | 4 | M | 3 | Hd | 5 | F% | 71–96 |
| s | 5 | FM | 2 | (Hd) | 3 | F+% | 72–77 |
| Do | 5+6 | FC | 1 | Obj | 4 | | |
| | | F/C | 1 | Cg | 1 | A% | 54 |
| | | CF | 1 | Dec | 2 | H% | 11–16 |
| *Qualitative* | | F(C) | 7+1(1—) | Plant | 2 | P | 7+2 |
| Fab. Comb. | 2 | (C)F | 1 | At | 5 | P% | 9–12 |
| Confab. tend. | 1 | FC′ | 1+1(1—) | Sex | 2 | | |
| | | FCh | 4 | Food | 2 | | |
| | | Ch | 1 | Misc | 5 | | |

Outstanding obsessive-compulsive indications in the summary of scores are the $R$ of 76, the 5+6 *Do,* the *DR%* of 29%, the relative emphasis on $M$ in the EB of 4–1.5(2), and the high *extended F%* of 96%. These indicate his ideationally active, meticulous, pedantic, overcontrolled, affect-isolating approach to situations and relationships. His strong emphasis on *FC,*

*F/C, F(C), FC'* and *FCh*—there are 14 such responses or nearly 1/5 of *R* —indicates great emphasis on tact and adaptiveness. But (a) only one of these 14 "adaptive" responses is a real *FC*, (b) his total of three color responses is strikingly low for his *R* of 76, (c) he basically rejects the color in all three of his color responses (blood on II, kidneys on III, and amebae on X), and (d) his two real uses of color both refer to blood (II and III). These observations combine to indicate that his conspicuous attempts to be adaptable and tactful are bound to be relatively forced, shallow, inhibited, cerebral and predominantly defensive rather than maturely adaptive. Moreover, the 9 *S+s* responses suggest that strong hostile, negativistic impulses underlie his conspicuous reaction formations against hostility. The relatively low full *M* (3) and high *A%* (54%) for a man with his very superior *IQ* and high *R* probably reflect the limiting effects of his rigid obsessive-compulsive defensive orientation.

On the whole, we have a picture of an exceptionally able, quick thinking, well-informed, logical, intellectually efficient man whose assets are so tied up in defensive operations that relatively little is left free for creative, imaginative thought and adequate spontaneity and fun. On the other hand, there is little evidence of severely disrupted general functioning. With all its limitations, this appears to be a working adjustment. Reality testing generally remains quite sharp, and defensive operations, though rigid, seem mostly successful in forestalling disruptive anxiety, rage and possibly low mood as well.

This man's entire orientation appears typical of the obsessive-compulsive person—hostility and passivity prevailing on the impulse side, rigid reaction formations against these along with isolation and intellectualization prevailing on the defensive side, and hidden, pervasive self-justification and conspicuous reaction formation substituting almost entirely for genuine adaptability. Although again and again the defended-against impulses show through his defensive operations, and anxiety shows through his cool rationalistic manner, the impulses and anxieties rarely get out of hand. If they threaten to break through, they are usually quickly and cleverly minimized, negated or otherwise stripped of threatening implications. While his intellectual maneuvers of this sort are impressively smooth and clever, he appears to be much less smooth in his social, emotional functioning, in the latter department being extremely detached and inhibited, and sometimes even somewhat out-of-tune and arbitrary.

The antitheses of active-passive, rebellious-submissive, and masculine-feminine that reflect the obsessive-compulsive's intense ambivalence on all psychosexual levels are strongly suggested by these test results. It is noteworthy, however, that the predominant hostile content in the record is oral rather than anal.

On first thought, in line with psychoanalytic theory's emphasis on anal-sadistic regression in the dynamics of the obsessive-compulsive person, one might have expected anal-aggressive imagery to prevail over oral-aggressive imagery in this record. The present finding, which, incidentally, is not unusual in obsessive-compulsive records, appears to be due to at least two factors, one general and one specific. In general, it is apparently difficult to give nonbizarre, clearly anal Rorschach responses. Except for preoccupation with tail parts of animals and objects (animal tails, hind quarters, tail of jet plane, etc.), anal imagery of any directness or obviousness is uncommon. In fact, strong emphasis on clearly anal imagery, such as rectum, feces and defecation, usually involves severely autistic elements within the anal responses or at least in the record as a whole. Also, direct, obvious oral and genital responses, whether hostile or erotic, seem to outnumber anal responses by far in Rorschach records in the general population. These findings may reflect the fact that in ordinary social relationships there are many types of references to (or images of) orality and genitality that are more or less acceptable while this is not true for anality. Hence, fewer anal images in general and a significant correlation between anal emphasis and autism (i.e., severe defensive and adaptive impairment). It may be that experience fosters and our culture permits a wider variety of symbolizations of oral and genital trends than anal trends. It may also be that what we encounter in the usual obsessive-compulsive record is a split representation of the anal-sadistic regression, some images emphasizing anal preoccupation and others an underlying, primarily sadistic conception of all impulses and interpersonal relationships. This split emphasis seems to characterize the present record, there being a number of responses indicating preoccupation with rear ends (which must be weighted heavily since they do not come to expression easily) and many responses betraying the underlying sadistic orientation, whether expressed in the imagery of orality, anality or genitality, in sado-masochistic imagery without clear psychosexual referents, or in general test attitudes and style of verbalization.

In addition to these general considerations, the individual factor that may help account for this record's relative underemphasis on anal-sadistic themes may be the relative "normality" of this man. The obsessive-compulsive persons to be considered next are all psychiatric patients and are in fact more openly "anal" in their Rorschach records. This implies that defenses in this crucial instinctual area are being well-enough maintained by this subject to keep anal emphasis, particularly anal-sadistic emphasis, inconspicuous in his Rorschach responses. Finally, his implicit partial resistance against the entire examination may have increased his conscious, preconscious and unconscious censoring efforts in this taboo realm.

## Case 2

.The next record is that of a 24-year-old, single, male, unemployed, wealthy, socially aristocratic Latin American, a college graduate with an IQ of 134. His diagnosis was "obsessive-compulsive neurosis, severe, in a schizoid personality." His case abstract reads: "The patient has been pre-occupied with dirt and sin since childhood. During the past eight years his preoccupation has been obsessional. During the past three years the obsessions have been disabling. The obsessional content is filth, disease and intestinal parasites." Rituals, hand washing, and magical thoughts about contamination and decontamination are prominent. The patient has also been obsessively preoccupied with homosexual tendencies, with a few impulsive homosexual acts during adolescence, and with masturbation; in these preoccupations and acts, anal-erotic components have been explicit.

The patient had a strict education in a Jesuit school where great emphasis was put on sin and the tortures of hell. This education has been a dominant force in his life, manifesting itself in obsessions about instinctual renunciation and the completeness or sacrilegiousness of his confessions. This education contrasted with his home atmosphere which was worldly, cynical and both corrupt and inconsistent in its social and religious values. His college years, spent in the United States, were characterized by his falling in with a group of free-thinking and radical students and quickly, though only superficially, abandoning his Jesuitic convictions. Since graduating, two years ago, he has been idle, except for traveling planlessly and being relatively promiscuous sexually.

This case is of special interest in that full-blown, classical obsessive-compulsive neuroses are infrequently seen these days, although the mechanisms and tendencies that are so dramatic in these neuroses are, in more or less subtle form, important in a wide variety of character problems and mixed and uncrystallized neuroses. The case is also interesting because of (a) the prominence of severe but "corrupt" superego dictates, that is to say, superego dictates so poorly integrated that, depending upon opportunistic rationalizations and moral gestures, they seem inconsistently to encourage and reward, prohibit and punish, and tolerate and ignore problematic instinctual expressions; (b) the open appearance in consciousness—despite the presence of crystallized obsessions and compulsions—of normally unconscious instinctual representations; and (c) the relatively clear-cut impact of his cultural (aristocratic) and religious (anti-"sin") background on the language and imagery of his Rorschach responses, symptoms and character structure.

The patient took this test once before. No doubt this experience influences the present record in significant—though elusive—ways. Nevertheless, the main lines of character structure and psychopathology are rarely, if ever, obscured by superficial familiarity with this test, particularly if the tester carries out the convergent analysis of scores, themes and test attitudes recommended here.

CARD I    REACTION TIME: 35″.    TOTAL TIME: 5′.

*Any time limit?*

Arrogance and humbleness seems to be condensed in this question. On the one hand, the question is submissively authority-oriented, but on the other hand it carries the implicit boast that the patient can go on for a long time. Ordinarily patients begin the test with worry about being able to produce responses at all.

*1. (W M± H) The two figures close to the center line look somewhat anthropomorphic, human (center D). The whole thing looks like a scene, part of the set of a dramatic production. Fantastic costumes on the two figures: they are hooded; the hands on the right and left are up in the air; they seem to have great big wings like bats (sides). I have no idea what they are doing. Their heads are close together. [What sort of dramatic production did you mean? Heavy Germanic, romantic, overly dramatic, operatic almost.]*

(a) "Anthropomorphic" is a strained, artificial, overly intellectualized verbalization. (b) The potentially threatening, hostile image—hooded, bat-winged figures —is stripped of affect, minimized, even ridiculed by his making it into ponderous Wagnerian dramatics. (c) His beginning his responses with an *M* as a determinant, with cultured and well-intellectualized content, and with an affect-mocking, defensively isolating attitude is triply obsessive-compulsive.

*. . . (Anything else?)*

*2. (D M+ H Peculiar) These two bigger portions look like two little girls or adolescent girls (side D). They have little caps flying behind them or perhaps their hands like this (clasped) and the other hand in back. They are playing a game or pulling at something. They have big behinds. [Why little or adolescent? Partly the dress, as I imagine it—girlish; partly the proportion of the heads and the height; partly the expression on the faces—if they were faces.]*

(a) These side figures, if seen as human, are rarely thought of as anything but adult figures. This image may therefore represent a regressive repercussion of the previous hostile, threatening response—minimized though that response was. That is to say, his turning at once to thoughts of playful, harmless little girls may represent a characteristic tendency to retreat from hostility to a passive, feminine, childish role. Note, however, how the alternative theme of "pulling" seems to intrude a hostile note again. (b) Specific references to "behinds" are uncommon and occur almost always within markedly obsessive-compulsive records, that is, in records of persons with marked anal problems and preoccupation. In this response, the "big behinds" reference underscores the anal aspects of the presumed regressive sequence from #1 to #2. (c) It is slightly peculiar and indicative of extreme emotional detachment, when, in inquiry, he so blithely refers both to the expression on the faces and his doubt that they looked like faces. This cavalier indifference to fact has elements of provocative, rebellious intellectual "slovenliness" that stand in marked contrast to his usual (see below) carefulness.

*3. (De F— Hd) In all of these things—every bit of outline you can make a face out of. There's no end to it (look of mixed boredom and dismay). [(Card shown.) Show me the face. I didn't see any at the time. (Patient proceeds to find three different, tiny faces.)]*

Possibly an oblique expression of awareness of an inclination to get bogged down in trivia—to his own annoyance and boredom.

*Look at it one way? (That's up to you.) V . . . (Do you think of other things?) Millions of things. I don't know how to go about it. . . . (For instance?)*

Here (and throughout the test) the patient needs prodding. He sits in thoughtful silence and thereby tends (in fact as well as in fantasy) to push the tester into the role of a demanding, driving, impatient person. At the same time he indicates that he is overwhelmed with impressions—a specifically obsessional experience that is related to the "no end to it" remark in I-3.

*4. (Dr F± Ad) This top part looks like the head of a bear (lower middle); a long, thick neck.*

*5. (Dr F∓ Anal) This here looks like somebody's behind (upper middle bumps).*

One anal response (I-2) is striking enough; two anal responses and the fact that both are among his opening communications are extremely impressive. These responses leave little doubt that anality is exceptionally important in this man's personality and illness. This conspicuous anal material well matches the obsessive-compulsive ego picture that is also evolving. In addition, it provides a clear contrast to the record of the previous well-functioning obsessive-compulsive subject.

*That's enough for one, I think.*

This self-assured, implicitly boastful and presumptuous taking over the test situation closely matches the arrogant aspect of his very first verbalization— "Any time limit?"

CARD II    REACTION TIME: 25″.    TOTAL TIME: 4′ 10″.

*1. (W MC'+ H P) This way it looks like the caricature of not an ordinary child—but like a child you would find in comic books or pictures, partly stylized. Perhaps not a child at all. They have longish, pointed, hook noses and a funny kind of hat. Of course, the black part which could make the body and the clothing sort of looks like academic gowns of some sort—which doesn't go very well with faces of gay children. The hands are against the other. I know what they could be: little men on a needle (reference to a toy). [What made it look like academic gowns? Partly the fact that they were black, ill-fitting, loose.]*

(a) Like the side figures in I-2, these figures are almost always seen as adult figures. A defensively regressive image of himself as a child—boy or girl—is again strongly suggested. His uncertainty that this is a child supports this inference. (b) He freezes the image's gay affect by making it stylized, that is, lacking in spontaneity and utterly controlled. Note too that like the people standing together in I-1, these are people in some sort of interaction, but that again he cannot specify what sort of interaction it is. He may be suppressing or repressing an image of hostile interaction—this card often stimulates such images—but his stylizing the image's gaiety suggests that he may be trying to avoid *any* affect or connotation of interpersonal intimacy. In view of his aristocratic background, the stylized gaiety may refer to past training and cultural atmosphere, but we must remember that now it is the patient who is imposing the stiffness, formality and artificiality. By now stylization is probably an internalized mode of adjustment and source of problems. (c) "Little men on a needle" is a toy and therefore a regressively-oriented image of innocence or harmlessness, like the girls in I-2 and the earlier children image in this response. At the same time, however, the image has its authoritarian, sado-masochistic aspects in its stress on people being both controlled and impaled. (d) The black academic gowns that clash with gaiety may contain an oblique reference to his somber, guilt-stimulating Catholic education.

*2. (S F+ A) The white part in the middle looks like a rayfish.*

Possible engulfing (oral) and/or stinging (phallic-aggressive) implications.

*3. (DS F— Ad) Oh yes, this white outline (middle space) with the center black here (upper middle) and the red for eyes (upper red) looks like a sort of rodent: a rabbit possibly. [Why a rabbit? It has puffed cheeks.]*

"Puffed cheeks" suggests stuffing food. The response's bad form may reflect reduction of intellectual efficiency associated with the disturbing theme of greedy orality.

*Do you want more? (That's up to you.)*

See opening and closing remarks on Card I for similar verbalizations with mixed haughty and submissive implications. This question, in addition, tends to externalize responsibility for his responses and to emphasize the tester's "demandingness" (see after I-3).

*4. (D F(C)± Plant) V . . . This upper part might look like a cross section of fruit, of an apple perhaps (lower red without projections). [Cross section of apple? It seems to be the part where the seeds are. The outline isn't very clear. I think also the different shadings of color.]*

All four responses elicited by Card II tended to suggest passive, regressive and/or oral themes—toy, engulfing, stuffing and, in the present response, womb or food.

CARD III    REACTION TIME: 20".    TOTAL TIME: 4'.

*1. (W M+ H P) These look very clearly like two human shapes here. They look like some sort of waiters. They seem to be lifting a heavy object, like a heavy caldron (lower middle). They have funny-looking faces; long necks. Strangely enough, they seem to have high-heeled shoes.*

(a) "Human shapes," like "anthropomorphic" in I-1, puts considerable emotional distance between him and the human content of the image. Defensive isolation is prominently at work in this record. Later (see below, particularly after #2), in his reference to the formal greeting, he strips the people of spontaneity and affect, as he did the people in II-1. Moreover, in referring to the men as funny-looking, comic and "little" (see also inquiry to #2 and after #3), he strips them of dignity, adulthood and effectiveness, as he has all the human figures thus far (I-1, I-2, II-1). Along with heavy reliance on isolation, a haughty, mocking orientation to people may be implied. (b) At the same time, the childhood imagery involved in this apparently condescending orientation may well express tendencies of his own to regress to passivity and ineffectiveness in order to avoid hostility in relationships. In line with this is the 'oral theme of this image—waiters and caldron (see II-2 and II-3). (c) His reference to the high-heeled shoes on men represents an integrative failure—a mild one in view of its frequency in the general population, but one suggesting that we be on the alert for other clues to feminine identification—of which there will be many.

> 2. (D F+ Cg Peculiar) The red thing in the middle, of course, looks like a bow tie. [How was it like a bow tie? It looks like a bow, any bow. How? You see a knot in the middle and two symmetrical wings on the sides. Anything else? But when I looked at it, I thought of it in connection with the two little men: if they were waiters, they would be wearing bow ties.]

At the end of inquiry he attempts a peculiarly forced integration of ideas. In full-blown form this could be a Confabulation or Contamination, but his verbalization indicates that basically he maintains adequate distance from the attempted integration. He does not say this is the bow tie of the waiters or that it is the bow tie that makes them look like waiters.

> They (#1) could also be, each one, carrying sort of odd-shaped luggage of some sort, and they would be saying good-bye or hello in a formal, stilted fashion—comically so, exaggerated. . . . (Anything else?) A design, anyway (reference to #1); very pretty.

Not satisfied with defining these as people on the outer edge of a pseudo-relationship, he winds up his defensive rejection of affect and interpersonal interaction by making this a design. Only then does he seem free to experience affect, particularly esthetic pleasure. Ironic humor and esthetic sensitivity may be the chief forms of whatever freedom of emotional expression he has retained.

> 3. (D F± A) < Each one of these red spots seen sideways looks like an unfinished drawing of a rooster or pheasant; more a rooster (upper red).

The rooster in dreams and popular metaphor commonly is an image of phallic-aggressive, potent masculinity. The concept of an unfinished rooster is therefore strikingly similar in implication to the concept of half-a-man, that is a child, an ineffective person, a castrate. This image is directly in line with the reasoning concerning the disparaged men in III-1, but is more telling.

> ∨ < ∧ These two little waiters (#1) or whatever they are have chicken-like faces, rooster-like faces, heads: a beak and a little crest.

A rooster with a "little crest" appears to be a disparaging as well as aggression-minimizing response. In particular, as in the unfinished rooster of #3, minimized phallic-aggressiveness and regressive "little boy" castratedness seem to be implied here.

CARD IV    REACTION TIME: 22".    TOTAL TIME: 6' 45".

> 1. (W FCh+ Ad P) ∨ ∧ This looks—either way—like an animal pelt on the wall. The outline could be rough and broken the way it is here, and the texture of the paint, of the color, is what adds to the impression that it's a pelt.

Note his spontaneously conducting inquiry. This involves compliance, conscientiousness and considerateness "above and beyond the call of duty." Persistent, spontaneous inquiry and other forms of anticipatory compliance are typically encountered in the setting of a submissive authoritarian orientation, an orientation which involves prominent reaction formations against hostility and regression to an overtly passive role. Much more of this submissive, defensive behavior will be seen throughout the remainder of the test.

> *2. (D F+ Ad) This section here looks like a head of some sort of beastie, some kind of fantastic looking . . . (lower middle D). Looking towards me; seen from above; looking upwards also. [Why did you say "beastie"? That had a slightly ironic connotation. It looked comical.]*

Another disparagement of a potentially hostile image (see I-1, III-3, and elaboration of III-1 after III-3). Again and again and again in this record, as in the previous record, hostile images are formed—only to be disposed of by minimization, negation, ridicule, doubting, criticism. In his battle against his unconscious but ever-pressing hostile impulses, there is no rest for the markedly obsessive-compulsive person.

> *There is a very definite mood to this one, but I can't quite place it: probably partly the blackness, partly the expression in this beastie's face here (#2). If it were a drawing, it would be dramatic from the artist's point of view: the whole outline is so broken. It's a liberal, daring drawing and very excellent design. It's not dramatic in the sense of the other picture (reference to I-1).*

From his references to the blackness, the beast and the broken outline, the mood he cannot place would seem to be one of gloom, fear and/or hostility. Instead of allowing the feeling to materialize, he repudiates the role of a participant ("it would be dramatic from the artist's point of view," i.e., not his own) and intellectualistically adopts the position of art critic. In a safely detached manner, he extols the picture's affect ("dramatic") and his projected hostility and rebelliousness ("broken" and "liberal, daring"). In I-1 he took the position of detached, mocking drama critic to cope with an apparently highly emotional, possibly frightening image. In III-1 (especially as elaborated after III-2) he also seemed to seek safety and some emotional freedom in the detached esthetic position. The previous subject, the well-functioning physician, seemed to fall back on his impersonal, diagnostic, medical role for similar defensive reasons. Isolation of affect appears to be the primary defense mechanism involved in such pedantic operations, but in these responses we actually seem to be dealing with larger configurations of drives, affects, defenses, abilities, values, etc., in short, with total ego identities. The doctor and the art critic are two of a wide variety of identities that may serve as foci for the integration of personality.

> *3. (Dd F(C)+ Plant) The upper part looks like something I've seen —I don't know what—sort of a cross section of a flower, an orchid. Just the very upper part (upper middle).*

A reproductive theme may be expressed in this image (see II-4).

> *4. (Dr F+ A) These clear sections look like two dogs, lying (inner ½ of lower side gray). I'm fascinated looking at them.*

His pleasure in the creative process may well derive from the esthetic role he stresses.

> *5. (Dr F(C)+ (Hd)) A rather beautiful face (in upper right shading, facing outwards). It has a rather classic expression. It could be a mask*

*also because it stops here (i.e., back half of head is missing). There is almost a smile.*

(a) Like the previous two responses, this response is sensitive and perceptive. In addition, it is clearly esthetically elaborated. Judging from all three responses, as well as from the entire tone of the record, this is certainly not a crude, callous, unfeeling person, even though he does stifle spontaneity and warmth. More than likely he is characterized by elegant, delicate, subtle, esthetically-toned feeling in those areas where he lets himself feel things at all. (b) Making the face a mask suggests mistrust of attractive appearances—probably in himself as well as in others—as well as a need to strip this originally pleasant experience of affect (see I-1, II-1, III-1). In this last regard, note how he picks up and stresses the remoteness of affect in the image—"almost a smile."

*6. (s F— (Hd)) This thing looks like wooden sculpture you might put in front of ships (space within upper side projection).*

*7. (De F— Hd) V . . . < . . . V . . . There's a face every quarter of an inch (vague, bored pointing).*

CARD V    REACTION TIME: 5″.    TOTAL TIME: 5′.

*1–2–3. (W F+ A P; Do F+ Ad Fabulized Combination; Dr F— At Fabulized Combination) This is something in flight, something with a capital S. Whatever it is has long ears and a tail that spreads in two like some birds do. I wouldn't think of it as a bird. Again some kind of prehistoric animal, although the outline of the top of the wings looks like a bat's. The head: you have so many rabbits in these things. It seems in flight. Looking at it from above, because I can see vaguely the outline of the vertebrae, the vertebral column.*

*Fabulized Combinations* are common in obsessive-compulsive records. They appear to reflect one absurd length to which isolation-based detachment can go, namely, a passive, relativistic feeling that anything is possible, almost no matter how senseless, and that the world around and within one is not meaningfully integrated or amenable to integration. In this respect, *Fabulized Combinations* stand in superficial contrast to, but in basic unity with, the fragmented *Do* and tiny *Dr* responses that also occur frequently as expressions of obsessive-compulsive isolating efforts.

*. . . (Anything else?)*

Further prodding required.

*4–5. (D M+ H; D F+ A Fabulized Combination) Oh yes, I remember from before (from previous testing), one of my favorites. It's really quite pretty. Two children, one on each side, reclining (outer ⅔ of wings). You must have heard that before. It's very striking. The age is something between eight and twelve or fourteen, between eight and fourteen. You can't see how large they are. They have no feet, actually. There is, of course, a figure in between (middle D). We can keep on calling it a rabbit if we wish (see #2), an elf-sized rabbit. The children seem to be asleep, taking a nap. For some reason, possibly because of the rabbit, I think of them as being out in the country. Their arms are like this (folded) as if they are embracing an object that I can't see.*

(a) This is not the first truly positive affect expressed in connection with an image (see IV-5), but it is the most vivid. The emphasis is on childhood and particularly on passivity ("reclining . . . asleep . . . out in the country") and on harmlessness ("elf-sized"). The incidental remark about the missing feet introduces further stress on incompleteness (see III-3). The role of the small, passive, pre-sexual or castrated child seems to appeal to him greatly (see I-2, II-1, III-3).

   . . . (Anything else?) . . . No.

CARD VI    REACTION TIME: 10".    TOTAL TIME: 4' 30".

   *1. (D F+ Obj) The top part of it looks like the top part of a totem pole, with whiskers (upper D).*

   *2. (Dr F(C)± Ad Peculiar) The very top of it looks like an embryo —of any kind of animal (upper tip.)* [Embryo? *The nose and mouth are not clearly defined. It had big eyes. It looked curiously dead, though an embryo. I take it I'm doing this the right way, Dr. Schafer?*]

   *3. (Dr F— Plant) Here again is this big cross section of a fruit (base of upper D).*

   *4. (Dr FCh(C)+ Plant) The whole thing or this middle part looks like the cross section of a watermelon (around midline in lower D).* [What made it look like that? *Again the shadings, colors; almost an outline; all the seeds.*]

(a) Responses 2, 3, and 4 bring out clearly the preoccupation with wombs and reproduction that was first suggested in the earlier cross section of a fruit (II-4; see also IV-3). Connotations of ovary, womb, pregnancy and birth pervade these images. This reproductive preoccupation probably involves more than passive regressive wishes, since such wishes ordinarily appear to find sufficient expression in more obvious oral imagery (e.g., seeing all types of food, open mouths, breasts, etc.). His preoccupation with reproduction may also pertain 1) to feminine identification and wishes to be impregnated, and/or 2) to oedipal preoccupation with the mother figure's insides and her sexual and reproductive functions. The present material does not identify the major implications of reproduction in this patient's mind.

(b) His peculiar detachment in "curiously dead" (#2) indicates defensive isolation hard at work, particularly since the death theme in this image is quite morbid and ultimately hostile. Perhaps it pertains to death wishes against siblings; perhaps in especially primitive, regressed form it expresses inner feelings of weakness, deprivation and/or emotional isolation verging on lifelessness. In any event, his going on in inquiry to ask for reassurance about his way of responding, considering that this is his twenty-sixth response to the test, strongly suggests that he has failed in his attempt to isolate this image's morbid, hostile affect, that he has become anxious and possibly guilty ("the right way" has moral overtones), and that he has consequently shifted his position regressively in the direction of doubt, passive submissiveness and externalization of responsibility. It is at this point that he promotes the tester, who was known to be a *Mister* at that time, to the rank of *Doctor*. Such promotions usually involve unconscious irony or teasing, but in this presumed context of defensive regressiveness, the promotion seems mostly to reflect the patient's need for a strong authority figure on whom he can lean, i.e., at least a doctor.

   *5. (Dr FC'(C)± (H)) This lighter colored part (#3 and #4) could be two ghosts, ghost-like figures. . . . Not necessarily. . . . They are hooded. . . . A white, light material.* [Ghosts? *Again the business of the place where the seeds are developing or already are (meaning the area of #3 and #4); and the outline.* Anything else? *No.*]

This juxtaposition of generative (#3, 4) and degenerative (#5) images is reminiscent of the dead embryo in #2. His handling of this theme is again anxious and uncertain.

< ∨ ∧ *This one is very unpromising. Also a very unusual picture.*

6. *(D FC'∓ Obj) This part (all upper D) could also be some sort of monument; the base here. It is rather neatly drawn.* [What made it look like a monument? *It looks like a rather crude monument made of cement with a primitive design for the base. Only the base I could see clearly. It was slightly cross-like: I didn't mention that (the cross) because the totem pole (#1) interfered, and the arms of the cross looked rather feather-like (#7, below). It was made of white cement.*]

(a) Inquiry brings out this response's poor integration and points thereby to a special defensive problem. There seems to be a triple repudiation of the Church in this response—the Cross is crude, the Cross is rejected in favor of the pagan totem pole, and the Cross is a flimsy, feathery affair. In view of his strict Catholic upbringing, such a response as this probably represents, in one respect, scornful rejection of religious belief, and, in a more intimate respect, rebellion against external and internalized (superego) parental authority and values. Note how impersonally the response is given (as in the esthetically-toned "neatly drawn" remark), reflecting his defensive isolation, but note too the remarks preceding this entire response, particularly, "This one is very unpromising": he might then have already sensed and tried to head off the formation of this threatening, rebellious, pagan image.

(b) In view of the fact that this patient comes from a worldly, aristocratic family, it is easily conceivable that this scornful and/or rebellious treatment of the Church reflects his internalization of "corrupt" or inconsistent parental attitudes toward religion and religious ritual. In other words, the patient may not be rebelling against an internally consistent parental and superego position. Possibly, like the parents, he may be playing it both ways, sinning freely and yet being haunted by guilt.

(c) Although cultured, intelligent, perceptive and sensitive, this patient often strikingly lacks the smooth integrative facility of the previous well-functioning subject. In this response we see how obsessional meticulousness, ruminativeness and doubt result from the disruption of response. This patient's breakdowns of integrative facility and the content in connection with which his breakdowns occur, both imply impairment of defensive and adaptive operations, and this in turn implies that neurotic symptoms are likely to be present.

7. *(D F(C)+ Ad) These things coming out are feather-like (upper wings).*

(a) Further delicacy of response. (b) Here there emerges only a fragment of the concepts evolved in connection with #6 but unverbalized until inquiry into that response.

8. *(De F− Hd) The usual quota of faces inside and on the outline (vague, bored pointing).*

Bored obsessive productivity. He seems to feel forced to give this trivial, evasive kind of response, though devaluating it all the while. He is considerate enough not to impose on the tester the obligation of carefully recording each' face in detail. The tester accepts this "gift."

> 9. *(De F— Geog) The outline (of lower D) has the quality of a map.* [Anything beside the outline? *I wonder. Perhaps the outline clearly defined in relation to the white, and also I immediately thought of the shapes of some islands—of Scotland, for instance.* Anything else? *It looked like islands.*]

CARD VII      REACTION TIME: 3".      TOTAL TIME: 4'.

> 1. *(D FM+ Hd P) Here are two little old ladies; the top (upper ⅔). Old ladies: I remember describing them as old ladies, having feather affairs in back (upper projections). They could be great big combs. These are not the type of ladies who would wear combs. They are a little stooped. I imagine them in a type of drawing I dislike: a comic book. I distrust the expression of their faces. Although the others are all double like this, these look like twin old ladies.* [What about the expression on their faces did you have in mind? *They look bewildered perhaps, the way old ladies sometimes do; perhaps having a mild lady-like, old lady-like argument.* Why bewildered? *The head, the neck is a little stooped.*]

(a) From the point of view of defense, the most notable aspect of this response is its open expression of feeling—annoyance, dislike and distrust (see also end of this card). Apparently he is not as successful in staving off affect—particularly hostile affect—as he would like to be. Emotional involvement is plain. His response seems self-righteous, mistrustful, scornful and condescending (see discussion of III-1). (b) This attack on older women, especially women who implicitly are aristocratic ("lady-like") and wearing Spanish dress, suggests particular hostility and suspicion directed toward the mother-figure. In inquiry he indicates that it is particularly the inept, trivial and affected aspects of the mother-figure that rile him.

> . . . *(Anything else?)*
>
> 2. *(S F± Ad,Dec) The white part of it here is rather pretty. It could be a sea shell.*
>
> 3. *(S F± Obj,Dec) It could be a completely opened fan.*
>
> 4. *(S F± Obj,Dec) If you follow it (middle space) all the way up and cut it here, it looks like a glass, one of the heavy Steuben glasses or cups; very heavy.*

Very likely in response to the critical theme of the opening response, he gives three thematically split responses in a row ( # 2, 3, 4) and then irritably gives up the card. These three responses are thematically split in that each is a pure *S* in location, suggesting that the hostile, rebellious, mistrustful affect expressed by him in the first response may be silently continuing to dominate his perceptual approach to the blot, but, at the same time, the content of each *S* response is more or less elegant, sensitively feminine, or oral in implication, suggesting a reactive need to regress from hostility to a passive, feminine, and also snobbish, esthetic position. At least, these inferences are in line with similar sequences observed previously in the test (see I-2, III-1, III-3, after IV-2, V-4, VI-2).

*This one I find relatively uninteresting because I'm annoyed at the type of design of the ladies (#1).*

Note how by stressing that the blot is "uninteresting" he displaces his annoyance to the intellectual and esthetic sphere and simultaneously externalizes the responsibility for his difficulty.

CARD VIII    REACTION TIME: 45".    TOTAL TIME: 3' 30".

*1. (D F+ A P) Very plainly two animals here on each side, bears, on their four feet.*

*2. (D F(C)+ Obj) This greenish-bluish portion in the middle looks like two crossed flags (middle blue). Strangely enough both seem to be waving in different directions. [Flags? Again the outline, and it looked like two crossed flags. You almost see the folds: that's why it's waving.]*

His concern with the direction of waving of the two flags probably stems from obsessive sensitivity to ambivalence and contradiction—perhaps especially with regard to conflicting loyalties.

*3. (Dr F⇌ Ad) This top part looks like sort of the head and claws of a lobster (around tip of upper gray). The head is especially clear; the eyes that pop out.*

*. . . (Looks up and smiles) No hints from you?*

At this point in the test he can't mean this question. His smile and his obvious tone of not expecting an answer betray that this is an anxious social gesture of some sort, perhaps to establish contact with the tester in a teasing but implicitly dependent manner.

*4. (D F(C)C+ Plant) This lower portion could be some sort of flower, lily-like flower (lower pink and orange). [Lily? The outline especially. I could see petals. The color also, perhaps.]*

(a) "Lily-like flower" has a feminine aspect in its specificity, but his tentative introduction of color as a determinant indicates the careful restraint he exercises over warm, spontaneous feelings. His femininity seems to be cool and refined.
(b) This is his first color response. Its lateness and tentativeness highlight his tendency to avoid spontaneous affective response.

CARD IX    REACTION TIME: 45".    TOTAL TIME: 5' 20".

*∨ ∧ (As he turns card right side up:) This way? (Did the other way seem better?) Maybe. It could be a base here (lower pink).*

This suggests a search for "a solid base" as protection against feelings of precarious control and emotional imbalance.

*1. (Dr FC(C)+ (Hd)) On each side, here and here, I see two faces with eyes (usual animal profile in green-orange shading). They could be from little Chinese jade sculpture; possibly because of the color; possibly also because of the stylized expression, mask-like. They also seem bearded, the way Oriental sculpture usually is.*

(a) This response is a "gem" of isolation—through the *dehumanizing* implications of sculpture, through cultural, geographical and probably temporal *remoteness,* through the stiffness of *stylization,* through the *subdued, contemplative* connotations of Chinese elders, through the *emptiness* and implied *affect-simulation* of a mask (see also IV-5), and through the *smooth, cool hardness* of green jade. Here is a masterpiece of overcontrol masquerading as an *FC,* supposedly an indication of socially well-modulated affect. In this case we must assume that the identity of the thoughtful esthete is the means by which affect may be rendered cool enough and controlled enough to be consciously experienced (see also III-1, especially after III-2; his comments after IV-2; IV-5; VII-2, 3, 4; VIII-4). (b) The mode of response represents further anticipatory compliance in the form of spontaneously conducting inquiry.

> 2. *(Drs F— Ad) This central portion should be of some importance (lower middle space). It looks like a worse kind of beastie than the other one (IV-2); a menacing one. The other one looked sad. Tusks here (dark inner green); eyes here (white slits).*

A phobically-tinged response (see also the ghosts in VI-5).

> 3. *(D M+ H) Two figures here with pointed caps (orange). They look vaguely like monks or. . . . They seem to be doing some kind of work. They have robes on. Of course the pointed caps are not monk-like. They seem to be pointing to one another with these hands, if they are hands, and with the other hand working at something.*

Being abstinent, peaceful and industrious ("doing some kind of work"), the monk is a figure *par excellence* of self-discipline and self-denial in the realm of sex and hostility. In these respects, the monk therefore probably offers an appealing identity solution to this patient who seems so afraid of feeling and impulses and who apparently has such strong passive-regressive tendencies. His strict Catholic rearing and the culture in which he grew up would offer particular (though ambivalent) support to this religious model of instinctual control and adaptiveness.

> 4. *(D F≠ A) I can't make much out of this red part here (lower red) —the sections seem to be separate, not much connection—unless they were little, fat, turkey-like birds with great big tails (lower red; outer part is tail).*

Further prominent anal emphasis (see I-2, I-5). His emphasis on fatness suggests an oral (gluttonous) theme as well.

> *This is quite rich, like I ought to be able to see more, but. . . .*

Here for a change is frank admission of difficulty. The verbalization suggests that his aristocratic, self-righteous arrogance is not an altogether impenetrable affair.

CARD X    REACTION TIME: 35″    TOTAL TIME: 9′.

> 1-2. *(D FM+ (H),Sex Peculiar; D F— Discharge Confabulation tendency) Oh yes, here's two newly-born babies, fetal almost, before being born (pink). Something is coming out of their mouth, something gooey (middle blue). It could be just before being born. I see little sexual organs also down here (pink projection to middle yellow), and something (middle yellow) coming out also of the sexual organs as well as out of the mouth. [Fetal? Partly, I suppose, the faces: very —not expressionless faces—but not alive enough, and the fact that there wasn't much of a body to them. And the possible association*

> *with this thing that came out of the mouth which could be . . . the placenta?* Did that thing coming out of the penis look like anything specific? *'I don't think I thought about it in detail. There was just something gooey; some unpleasant stuff.*]

(a) Further preoccupation with reproduction (see VI-2). (b) In inquiry, the oral, passive-receptive fantasy associated with the fetus emerges clearly, the middle blue being conceived as the placenta going into the mouth of the fetus. (c) The "unpleasant," "gooey" discharge from the penis suggests a "dirty," anal conception of semen—a conception common among anally-regressed obsessive-compulsive neurotics (see also X-5 below). (d) In another respect, the response seems to bespeak a conception of infancy as a period of dirty, gooey excretions—a conception also common among obsessive-compulsive neurotics, whose regressive, anal fantasies concerning the insides of the body and instinctual expression are saturated with shame and disgust.

> *This is crammed full of things.*

> *3–4. (D F+ A; Dr F± Plant) Two little animals glaring at each other (base of upper gray). They have multiple legs coming right on out of the torso. There are numerous antennae-like projections on their heads or outstretched kind of claws. If there were not such a clear expression of hostility, they could be said to be gnawing at a tree-like affair (upper gray shaft).*

These animals are commonly said to be hostile so that the aggressive theme cannot be made much of in itself. The "gnawing" concept does point up the oral-aggressiveness in this image.

> *5. (D F∓ Sex Peculiar) The whole figure (all upper gray) looks like something indecent. . . . (What do you have in mind?) Do I have to mention these things or could you fill in? (It will be more helpful if·you say everything that occurs to you.) It looks like the male sexual organ.* [What made it indecent? *Not only because it looked like sexual organs, but because it looked like indecent sexual organs, as if it were in a turgid state, shall we call it?* Could you explain further why it was indecent? *It was embarrassing to mention to you: especially the fact that it wasn't a child's sexual organ; also the position in which it was—looked at from below.*]

Inquiry elicits what is most likely a submissive homosexual fantasy—that of an erect penis which he is looking at from below. Without the "looked at from below" remark, the response might also convey general disgust with sex. The patient reacts to this image with shame and disgust—"indecent" and "embarrassing." To judge from his remarking "especially the fact that it wasn't a child's sex organ," a basic source of appeal of the child figure—a prominent figure in his imagery—would seem to be the clean, decent sexlessness of his child-concept. In line with this, in the fetus of #1, he had emphasized that "there wasn't much of a body," that its face was relatively expressionless, and that its penis was "little." Thus, much of his regressive orientation seems to be toward the passive (orally-fed), impulse-free and affect-free (bodiless, expressionless, sexless) infantile state. Yet, as was also suggested by #1, his apparently dominant anal conception of infancy may make this passive-regressive solution unacceptable to him. If this is so, he would be torn—as he seems to be—between accepting and rejecting regressive tendencies. In this state, he would be ripe for or already suffering from neurotic symptom formation, neurotic symptoms typically representing partial yielding to anxiety-provoking and guilt-provoking impulse and partial repudiation of and self-punishment for such impulse.

>6. (D F+ A P) These two blue things could be, just on first impression, crabs (side blue).

An overmeticulous handling of a popular response.

>7. (D F+ A) Perhaps these other spots could also be crabs (side gray).

>8. (D F∓ Plant) These could also be daisy-like flowers with petals (side blue).

Further feminine floral specificity.

>9–10. (D F+ Ad (P); D F− Discharge Fabulized Combination) This one (lower middle) is quite fascinating. It has a face here of a locust; insect-like anyway (usual rabbit head). It is difficult to account for the two green things streaming down from the eyes (usual worms).

"Locust" introduces a devouring, parasitic theme.

>11. (D FC(C)+ A) They could be two—not worms—these things that eat up the leaves of trees (lower green). What do you call them? . . . Larva. [Larva? One thing: the color—they were green. They were segmented. They had a soft, round shape.]

Another parasitic image.

>12. (D CF Food) These things also look like scrambled eggs, from above (middle yellow). [Scrambled eggs? The color, for one thing. Now I realize the bigger portion isn't white· The shape; the yolk.]

(a) Another oral image. (b) Since he can see the yolk, it is the response that is scrambled, not the egg. (c) This is his only CF and even it tends towards an FC.

>This is interminable (calmly said).

Note the passive, detached position he takes with respect to his own thought processes—a peculiarly obsessive phenomenon.

>13. (D Ms± H Confabulation tendency) Very curious figures (side gray): they seem to be flying away. [Kind of figure? I thought it would be feminine for some reason. They had large bellies and there was something feminine about the position of the arms. They seem to be insane, hysterical figures flying away. Not floating; rushing away. I couldn't make out if the yellow part (outer yellow) was wings or hair of some sort.]

This striking, almost confabulated image suggests that the patient tends to view women as extremely excitable and vulnerable to complete loss of control (see also VII-1 for a milder version of this theme). His apparent distaste and scorn for this poor control—and his fear of it—probably corresponds to feelings he has about his own evidently strong feminine tendencies. Note, however, his conscious, isolation-toned detachment—"curious figures."

>14–15. (S F− Ad; D FC∓ Cg) The face of some animal, anthropomorphic animal. The shape of the head is like a cat (lower middle space), especially the ears (space between middle blue and pink). I'm thinking of the white space. A blue bow (middle blue); eyes (middle yellow) which used to be the scrambled eggs (#12). These two

*(lower green) would be nostrils going down, but in cats they go up more.*

More anticipatory compliance in the form of spontaneous inquiry.

*I could probably see a great many more things.*

He terminates the test as he began it—with a boastful statement of his intellectual versatility and productivity.

SUMMARY OF SCORES

R: 60          EB: 8–2(3)

| | | | | | | | |
|---|---|---|---|---|---|---|---|
| W | 5 | F+ | 13 | A | 11 | W% | 8 |
| D | 30 | F− | 12 | Ad | 12 | D% | 50 |
| Dd | 1 | F± | 6 | H | 7 | DR% | 38 |
| Dr | 13 | F∓ | 5 | (H) | 2 | | |
| De | 4 | M | 6 | Hd | 4 | F% | 60–98 |
| S | 5+1 | FM | 2 | (Hd) | 3 | F+% | 53–69 |
| s | 1+1 | Ms | 1 | Obj | 5 | | |
| Do | 1 | FC | 3+1 (1∓) | Cg | 2 | A% | 38 |
| | | CF | 1 | Dec | 0+3 | H% | 18–27 |
| | | F(C) | 7+4 | Plant | 6 | P | 7+1 |
| *Qualitative* | | FC' | 2+1 (1−) | Sex | 1+1 | P% | 12–13 |
| Fab. Comb. | 4 | FCh | 2 | Discharge | 2 | | |
| Confab. tend. | 2 | | | Anal | 1 | | |
| Peculiar | 5 | | | Misc. | 4 | | |

The summary of scores is consistent with the picture that has emerged in thematic analysis, namely, that of a severe obsessive-compulsive neurosis: R is relatively high (60); the DR% is high (38%); the EB is heavily weighted on the M side (8–2 or 8–3); the *extended F%* is very high (98%) and, correspondingly, the emphasis in the color and shading responses is strongly on controlled, compliant adaptiveness (14–20 FC, F(C), FC' and FCh and only 1 CF) and particularly on cautious adaptiveness (only 3–4 FC compared to 11–16 F(C), FC' and FCh). At the same time, the relatively high number of S+s responses (6+2 or 10%–13% of R) indicates significant negativistic, rebellious tendencies underlying his defensive overadaptiveness (reaction formation against hostility). The 1 Do and 4 *Fabulized Combinations* also are in line with the diagnostic impression. The *extended F+%* (69%), when corrected by omitting the mostly weak Dr, De and s responses, is adequately high (80%); we do not therefore have evidence of severe general impairment of reality testing.

The 5 *Peculiar* and 2 *Confabulation tendencies* suggest that the neurosis is severe to the point of the patient's tending toward autistic excesses. Some borderline psychotic tendencies are to be expected in any severe neurosis, perhaps particularly in the magically-inclined obsessional neurosis, and should not be used for a diagnosis of "borderline psychosis." The latter diagnosis requires evidence of more pervasive and/or dramatic autistic tendencies than are evident in this case. The cases to follow illustrate the more or less borderline or fully psychotic forms of obsessionality.

In summary of the qualitative and score analyses, this patient appears to be relying heavily on the obsessive-compulsive defenses of isolation, intellectualization and reaction formation against hostility. Noteworthy conscientiousness, detachment, inhibition, and mocking retreat from affect and spontaneity are indicated. Impulses to be dirty, disorderly, rebellious, negativistic, and "pagan" appear to underlie, clash with and break through this outwardly submissive and overcompliant orientation and his aristocratic, snobbish delicacy of feeling and refinement of taste. Feelings of shame and disgust result. Among other things, this clash may well reflect the cultural clash between the strict anti-instinctual stress of his religious education, the cynical and decadent values of his family, and—what has not been mentioned so far—the tempting but frightening and morally objectionable primitive, lower-class Indian and Spanish models of passionate, tempestuous, even violent relationships.

Also conspicuous is regressive turning away from the adult, male, heterosexual role toward the role of the weak, passive, presexual or feminine castrate. Through this latter role, which in its most adaptive form is that of the sensitive, reflective but critical and snobbish esthete, he appears able to experience and tolerate affect if it is limited in quantity and cool and refined in quality. Through the esthetic role he also seems able to avoid, minimize, camouflage or legitimately express his intense hostility.

It appears that this patient has no workable model of response. Neither the submissive, docile, feminine role nor the sadistic, voracious, phallic-aggressive role seems subjectively tolerable or acceptable to him, and he seems unable to conceive of other modes of response. Most likely he is torn between the antitheses of submissive-autocratic, vulgar-aristocratic, conscientious-irresponsible, productive-parasitic, kind-violent, faith-atheism. These ambivalences combined with his weakness of defense appear at times to drive him toward autistic solutions, even though on the whole his coping with the instability among impulse, defense and adaptation remains within the neurotic range. His repressive defenses, particularly with respect to fantasies concerning homosexuality, dirt, sadism and reproduction, seem to be in serious jeopardy. Most of all he seems busily and very anxiously engaged in staving off and minimizing hostility in one form or another. A severe obsessional neurosis appears to have developed in response to these conflicts, anxieties and ego limitations and impairments.

## Case 3

This is the record of a 24-year-old, single, male physicist with an IQ of 133. His diagnosis was "obsessive-compulsive neurosis, severe, with paranoid trends in a markedly schizoid personality." The possibility of an underlying paranoid schizophrenic process was seriously considered in the clinical differential diagnostic discussion, but it was felt his defenses and his hold on reality, though weak, were well enough preserved to rule out the schizophrenic diagnosis at that time. Although chronically intellectualistic and obsessionally interested in systems of measuring time and space, only recently had he become obsessional (and autistic) to the point of severe social and occupational incapacity.

His thinking was characterized by extreme circumstantiality and meticulousness, by inability to set up hierarchies of importance and relevance, and by a great need, as he put it, "to break each new item of information down into its most basic parts and compare each of the parts with all of the other basic pieces of information in my memory (etc.)." Extreme sexual naivete stood in contrast to very active curiosity in many fields of knowledge. Troubled by his extreme need to isolate affect, the patient said of his therapeutic goal, "I want to live like a human being . . . not like a machine."

In much clearer form and with much greater frequency than in the previous case, autistic forms of expression of obsessional tendencies will be conspicuous in this patient's Rorschach test responses. This means that the obsessive-compulsive defensive operations will often be caricatured, inappropriate to the immediate situation, and less successful in warding off expressions of defended-against impulses—particularly negativism, demandingness, disorderliness and sadism. The inner structure of these defensive operations should therefore be clearer.

CARD I    REACTION TIME: 5".    TOTAL TIME: 2' 40".

*1. (W F+ A P Peculiar) That resembles a bat more than anything else I could think of. That's just the overall of it.*

*2. (Drs F∓ (Hd)) I could possibly get the idea of a face in the middle, I suppose, more than anything else. You could see the whole face if you wish: those empty spaces the eyes and mouth (inner spaces), with the nose sticking down over it (lower middle "legs"). [Any particular kind of face? I suppose some, something Indian.]*

His verbalization of this response contains a neat string of cautious, conscientious, doubt-laden hedging: ". . . possibly . . . the idea of . . . I suppose . . . more than anything else . . . if you wish."

*Am I supposed to keep pulling out . . .? I could torture it into a butterfly or a bat (#1). It resembles a bat more than a butterfly: these two. . . . Nothing else about the darned thing. I could invent things if you wished me to, but it would be purely imaginative.*

(a) Note the sadistic metaphor in his "pulling out" and especially in his "I could torture it into" verbalizations. This verbal imagery probably reflects intense sadistic impulses underlying his boyish tone and his cautious, conscientious, submissive authoritarian manner. In this vein, "the darned thing" may represent an attack on the test and tester disguised as wholesome juvenile expletive. (b) His doubt-laden handling of even this popular response is noteworthy. (c) By saying, "I could invent things if you wished me to," he is apparently playing up his compliance and at the same time maneuvering to put responsibility on the tester for demanding more responses and for any "faults" in subsequent responses. This verbalization may also express some awareness of the border between reality and fantasy, and thus may be a positive indication as well.

CARD II     REACTION TIME: 28″.     TOTAL TIME: 3′ 45″.

> *(Peculiar:) Where do the colors come from (musing tone)? The overall impression: I don't think I get much of anything out of that.*

He is struck by the colors, judging by his peculiar rhetorical question, but can do nothing with them now, nor can he throughout his responses to this card. Following the initial impact of color, he tries to be systematic in his manner of approach by concentrating on an "overall impression," but fails in that respect too (see below). It is implied that he is likely to have much trouble in coping with affect and impulse, perhaps especially hostility, and that he may characteristically attempt to retreat from emotional experience to an "affectless," overmethodical position. The present success of this maneuver is likely to be limited, judging from the poorly organized or fragmented responses (#1, 2 and 3) that follow.

> 1. *(S F— Hd Do-tendency) It faintly resembles a mouth, but only very faintly (middle space).* [What made it look like a mouth? *The hole, I guess.* Anything else? *Not much else. It's not the shape of a mouth; just the hole and the fact that it was symmetrical.* Anything else? *No.*]

Thematically, this is an intensely oral image. Since the image is a gross, poor form, his emphatic near-rejection of it reflects adequate reality testing at this point. At the same time, his criticizing the response very likely stems directly from the threat to defensive stability posed by so open and disruptive an expression of need or impulse. In other words, this seems to be an instance of anxiety-induced, defensively-motivated sharpening of reality testing following the breakthrough of a powerful, crude impulse representation.

> 2. *(Dr F+ Ad Do-tendency) I'm not too sure of this thing. You could get feet out there if you wanted to (lower inner projections, upper red). I don't know if it would be clawing or running.* [What kind of feet did you mean? *Oh that thing! Some small animal like a cat or a dog.*]

(a) His alternative characterizations of these feet suggest inner indecision about whether to attack ("clawing") or flee ("running"). (b) From a defensive point of view, his spontaneous verbalization disclaims responsibility for the image—"I'm not too sure . . . you could get . . . if you wanted to." Also, in inquiry, he defensively minimizes the hostility and anxiety in the image by making it a small, essentially unthreatening animal—a cat or dog. (c) Note also the actually small physical scale of the image (tiny projections) and his *Do*-ish fragmentation of the red area—both aspects of the response probably representing the consequences of defensive isolation. Thus, in attitude, in perceptual organization and in content, this response is strikingly defensive. Only his reference to "clawing" and the initial impact of the red color give clues to the source of this defensiveness, namely, retreat from emotional experience in general and hostility in particular.

*I'm not too sure what I make out; that's probably why I mumble. (Patient has been mumbling and has been urged to speak louder.)*

(a) Persistent mumbling has a significant aggressive, demanding aspect, despite the mumbler's typical subjective experience that he is mumbling only out of fear, uncertainty or modesty. Mumbling implicitly demands that the listener hang on every word uttered by the mumbler, and, if it is good mumbling, thwarts the listener even then. (b) This patient's responsiveness to this card has thus far been altogether disturbed, beginning with a defensively weak, perceptually gross, powerfully oral $S$ $F-$ response, going on to a defensively weak, perceptually fragmented, hostile and fearful response, and involving mumbling all the while. As inferred from his opening flustered response, the patient must be threatened by this blot. At the same time, his form level remains satisfactory throughout—the $F-$ of the first response being spontaneously rejected by him and the remaining responses (#s 2, 3, 4) being F+. In other words, although threatened, highly defensive and precariously integrated, he is not going to pieces here.

*3. (Do F+ Hd) I get chins sticking out here, a chin and a nose (upper outer edge, dark area). I'm stretching to get those.* [What kind of face did you mean? *Of an Indian.*]

(a) The second perceptually fragmented response in a row. (b) The second Indian image (see I-2). Indian images frequently are representations of rebellious, defiant impulses.

*I don't know. I observe these stripes here (in dark shading) but they don't suggest anything to me. These two darned things sticking down (lower red projections): . . .*

His "darned things" remark is probably another juvenile attack on the test and tester (see after I-2). Throughout the test this patient continues to use "darned" and other all-American-boy expletives such as "gee," "gosh," and "hey." In view of his generalized flight from affect, these exclamations seem to represent more a peculiar, manneristic pseudo-responsiveness than any genuine emotional spontaneity or lability.

*4. (D F+ A) The whole thing (lower red) reminds me of a Luna moth I was introduced to this summer. It has some awfully big tails on it.* [Moth? *It was a fairly large thing; the hind wings. I don't know the technical name. It came out in a tail; it looked like a tail between wings.* Anything else? *No. Especially since the Luna moth is bright green and not red. It was mainly the form, the symmetrical wings and the body in the middle and the tail.*]

(a) His repetitive emphasis, especially in the first response to inquiry, on the moth's hind parts suggests anal preoccupation. (b) Note too his overcautious, earthbound—i.e., form-bound—exclusion of color.

*Not much else that stands out.*

CARD III     REACTION TIME: 20″.     TOTAL TIME: 5′ 30″.

> *Good night!*

This boyish dismay seems to be another pseudo-spontaneous reaction (see after II-3).

> 1. *(D F+ At) Well (nervous laugh), the general shape of these things on the side (upper red) seem to me something like that in a biology book of the stomach and—what is it?—the esophagus. Is that the tube going up?* [What made it look like a stomach? *That definitely was from a biology book: the stomach with the long tube; the same general shape.* Anything else? *No.*]

(a) The oral emphasis in this image is quickly removed to the safety of a medical book diagram. (b) Even then, no color, not even artificial color, is elicited in inquiry.

> 2. *(Do F+ Ad) I don't know, I might be able to torture this half into a face, the face of a duck (P head).*

(a) Further sadistic metaphor—"torture this" (see after I-2). (b) Note how, in his meticulousness, all he can accept of the popular human figure is the face and then only as a duck face.

> 3. *(D ChF Geog) The idea of a contour map, possibly, from the lights and darks; almost as if it were a picture of a mountain range or island or something like that (all dark).*

> 4. *(D F+ A Do-tendency) Down at the bottom it looks like a fish tail (P foot) but the rest of it (of P leg) doesn't look much like a fish. The rest of it might look like a fish at that. It's got a fin on top. I wouldn't know what kind: maybe an eel.*

It is probably no accident that at first this doubt-laden, near-*Do* settles on the tail—i.e., anal—end of the fish (see II-4).

> 5. *(s F∓ Geog) Along with the contour map (#3), here's a little lake in the darned island (tiny space within P hip area).*
>
> *(Confabulation tendency, Peculiar:) I don't know whether the inkblot suggests this or the idea of an island but it (#3 and #5) reminds me of the movie "King Kong" and the location in it.* [What made you think of the "King Kong" location? *You got me there. I don't know, except possibly it was a small island and I seem to remember it had mountains in it (in the movie).*]

(a) Like the implicitly hostile Indian heads in I-2 and II-3, this association to King Kong probably relates to fantasies of destruction by savage, primitive forces and the subduing of these forces by civilized man. In turn, such fantasies reflect concern with mastery of impulses he must view as formidable, primitive and hostile. Judging from the unintegrated way this association pops out, defense and control in this realm are likely to be shaky. The hostile theme is defensively kept quite remote, however, Indians and King Kong being dangerous in far off places and far off times or else mere products of literary and Hollywood fantasy.

(b) While this response's theme suggests the content of a basic conflict, its very poorly rationalized introduction of the King Kong fantasy represents pathologically loose thinking. This loose association suggests that the impact of intense conflict may result in perceptions being autistically overelaborated and peculiarly rationalized (small inkblot, therefore "small island"). To the credit of his reality testing, however, the patient obviously maintains some distance from this overelaboration.

> (Peculiar:) I'm getting this all out of one side—the left—of the card. I haven't seen anything on the right that reminds me of anything. They don't even remind me of what the left does. Oh. possibly the fish (#4).

In view of the essential identity of the two sides of the blot, his using only the left side suggests magical thinking about *right* and *left*. Magical thinking about direction is especially clear and common in obsessive-compulsive neurotics, although it seems to occur in the unconscious thinking of many, if not all, of us. Particular concern with *right* and *left* has been found to pertain to a need for balance or symmetry within and around one as magical insurance against losing control of impulses. Also, *left* tends to take on weak, unacceptable, evil, unconscious implications while *right* tends to take on strong, acceptable, good and conscious implications. It is, however, unusual for this *right-left* sensitivity to come out clearly in the Rorschach test, partly because of the patient's waking state and partly because of the inkblots' almost perfect symmetry. This patient's split use of *right* and *left* is therefore scored *Peculiar,* i.e., more or less autistic. It is one thing to have an unconscious tendency, and quite another to express it in the Rorschach test.

> 6. (D F± At) Those globs in the middle might represent some body organs (middle red). They might be kidneys—or what I don't know; I'm not that familiar with anatomy. [Body organs? Gosh, you got me! I think it just reminded me of a picture I saw in a biology book in college or high school. How was it like such a picture? Possibly because it was symmetrical. Anything else? No.]

(a) Still no color, not even artificial chart-color. (b) The complete inhibition of *M* and color is striking in Cards II and III. This finding might well be another aspect of the cautiousness and perfectionism, the *Do* fragmentations, the ruminativeness, and the anal, rebellious, sadistic themes suggested by his images and verbalizations. All these features point toward rigid obsessive-compulsive defensive operations and the likelihood of a severe obsessive-compulsive neurosis. The peculiar forms sometimes taken by his defensive operations suggest that autistic trends complicate this neurotic picture.

> Nothing else right now.

CARD IV    REACTION TIME: 2".    TOTAL TIME: 4' 45".

> 1–2. (D ChF Food; D ChF At 2-Peculiar) The first thing I think of is a walnut (upper ½, without projections). There again the general symmetry of the darned thing, I guess. Where it's folded, it's more pronounced (midline); it's more prominent than a walnut, of course, or in a pecan or anything like that. [Walnut? There were different lights and shadows on the thing, sort of suggesting the different indentations. On the same theory I could have called it a huge brain. I never thought of that. Gory (nervous laugh)! Why gory? I should think so. How so? I'm not too sure. Possibly it was unreal; something you don't see every day. I saw it only once, after an accident.]

(a) In one respect the walnut image is oral, pertaining to food. In another respect it implies concern with outer protective covering and with vulnerability (the hard shell removed and the soft inner meat exposed). The inference concerning vulnerability is 'supported when, during the inquiry, he suddenly thinks of a brain in a destructive, even though "accidental," context (the hard, protective skull having been split open). (b) His peculiarly literal emphasis on the hugeness of the brain suggests that he sets high value on intellect and intellectualization. His entire approach to the test is in line with this inference.

> 3. *(Do F+ Ad (P)) I'm not too sure whether I have the next impression right: something hanging on the wall. I don't know if it's a bearskin or the skin of an animal or what. You might get feet out of these (lower sides), if that was the case. I wouldn't call these hands (upper sides). That (lower middle) wouldn't fit in. Whatever it is, you would be looking at it from the back. This line down the middle would suggest the backbone. Also, something about the so-called feet suggest turning into the card.* [What made it look like a skin? *I don't know. Just something about it seemed to be stretched out. Something you would expect to find on a floor, a rug.* Anything else? *You could see feet on it.*]

(a) His verbalization and handling of detail are unduly cautious for this popular response (see also after I-2). This suggests extreme meticulousness and perfectionism. (b) Usually, people do not spontaneously specify that this is a view of the back. His doing so suggests anal preoccupation (see II-4, III-4).

> 4. *(D F+ Cg) It could be shoes too (each side), except for the tongue-like thing (upper side projection).*
>
> *I'm trying to look at the other parts. I haven't thought of anything for them yet.*

Throughout the test, in typical obsessive-compulsive style, he anticipates inquiry and more or less keeps the tester posted on his progress in an overly conscientious manner but also in an implicitly tedious and demanding way. As the patient knows, these verbalizations must be recorded in detail and therefore easily become drains on the tester's time, effort and interest. Patients being tested should not be too helpful; that is to say, it is by no means necessarily a favorable sign when the patient is very helpful. Great helpfulness often represents pseudo-adaptive submissiveness and covert demandingness and provocativeness that are typical parts of the obsessive-compulsive character picture with its anal-sadistic orientation, severe superego pressures, and resulting authoritarian attitudes, rigid reaction formations against hostility and oblique expressions of hostility. A moderate amount of spontaneous and compliant helpfulness is quite another thing.

> 5. *(W F— A Do-tendency) There is a vague resemblance to a frog, very vague (indicating whole blot); more looking up at the head region of the object (upper middle). This seems to be something I see the whole thing on. Most of the others. . . . It's one object, whatever it is. It doesn't look like a head or the back of a head at the top (rejection of #4).* [Did you mean a whole frog at first? *No. I was trying to look at the head of the object; just the head (repudiates original response).*]

(a) His ruminative, doubt-laden shifts of attitude toward this response are impressive. The *Do-tendency* score reflects his fragmentation of this image. (b) Note how he introduces another back view.

> 6. *(Dr F∓ Ad) You just take this part and turn it around, you get ears, a beak—maybe a rooster, some fowl (upper middle).*

CARD V     REACTION TIME: 5″.     TOTAL TIME: 5′.

> 1. *(W F+ A P Peculiar) Well, there'd be a Luna moth again. More like it than the other one (II-4). Tails. I almost see a bat but it doesn't look like a bat because the wings are bent back this way and a bat I associate straight out when flying. The whole trouble with the thing is that it extends too far on the side. (Patient repeats explanation spontaneously why it's not quite a bat or a butterfly.) I don't think it would have enough muscle power to flap with such big wings.*

(a) Further emphasis on the tail (see II-4, III-4; also IV-3 and IV-5). (b) Tedious, overconscientious attention to accuracy reduces the tester to summarizing in parentheses. (c) Note that this hypermeticulousness centers around rejecting the bat possibility in favor of the moth possibility. Possibly this represents defensive efforts to reject the hostile in favor of the harmless (see also after I-2). In the end, the bat image is still with him, however, and now, by making the bat too weak to work its wings, he "grounds" the bat and renders it harmless. In this compulsively developed image there seems to be a statement similar to what we have observed in the two preceding obsessive-compulsive records—intrusion of hostility into an image followed by either defensive denial and isolation (minimizing the aggressive implications of the image) or defensive regression (emphasizing smallness, weakness, passivity and ineffectiveness), or both. This patient may at present think of himself as weak and helpless, but rather than take this self-concept at face value and regard it as highly pathogenic in its own right, we should bear in mind his need to regress from strength and to stay weak in his efforts to stave off intense, frightening hostile impulses. His plight is more complicated than real or fantasied weakness or discouragement.

> 2. *(Dr F± Ad) A little goose's neck sticking out; an awfully long neck, though; the neck and head and bill (lower side projection).*
>
> 3. *(D F+ Food) What the thing above is. . . . What kind of leg: a drumstick (upper side projection).*

Another oral image (see II-1, II-2, IV-1).

> 4. *(D F∓ Obj Peculiar) Or a piano leg (upper side projection). I haven't quite decided on that (between drumstick and piano leg).*

This is an inappropriate instance of doubting.

> *Hey! Here's a lot of . . . I've forgotten the word . . . symmetry: there's a big section where it's not symmetrical (detailed comparison made here of base of upper middle).*

All naivete, he obliquely criticizes the tester's materials for being asymmetrical. Moreover, he makes this minor detail "a big section." This is of a piece with his artificially juvenile "darned" this and "darned" that. It is likely that his temporary forgetting the word "symmetry" (or "asymmetry") at this point reflects a defensive retreat from the hostility in this verbalization. His concern with symmetry would also reflect obsessional need for balance and control.

> 5. *(Dr F— Ad) Hey! Right here it reminds me of another picture in a biology book (end of upper side projection). I forget whether it's a sponge or a hydra, growing out from rock. The sort of feathery stuff at the end reminds me of heads I associate with the darned animal.*

The sponge or hydra is a small-scale—i.e., well-defended—engulfing image (see II-1 for a weakly-defended devouring image).

> 6. *(De F— Obj) Saw teeth there (upper middle: center of its left, outer edge).*

On one level, saws, pliers, cleavers, scissors and similar attacking, cutting or ripping-off objects often refer, in Rorschach responses as in dreams, to castration anxieties.

> 7. *(Do F± Ad) I can't decide on these: horns or rabbit's ears or what (upper middle projection).*

This alternative—horns vs. rabbit's ears—appears to reflect the same vacillation between hostility (tearing, goring horns) and defensive reaction formation and regression (timid, weak rabbit) as has been evident in the "clawing or running" feet in II-2 and the weak bat in V-1.

> 8. *(s F+ Obj Peculiar) A very regular looking arrowhead down into them (tiny space into upper middle; "them" refers to the horns or ears in #7). That's another thing that puzzles me.* [What puzzled you about it? *I couldn't fit it (the arrowhead) into anything. It was there. It didn't seem to belong there. It was out of place.* Out of place? *The main thing looked like a moth (#1). I was looking for something you would find on an animal.*]

(a) The arrowhead is commonly a phallic-aggressive image. (b) A sadistic fantasy is implied when he says "down into them," that is, a fantasy of the arrowhead penetrating the skull between the ears. His immediate expression of doubt and the elaboration of his doubt in inquiry suggest obsessional defensive retreat from this sadistic fantasy (see also the gory brain in inquiry into IV-1; both responses seem to imply violence done to the brain). (c) There is also an incipient paranoid tone in "It didn't seem to belong there. It was out of place." He disclaims—i.e., projects responsibility for—his response too much.

> *It's also dark in the middle: shadows or contrasts. I might get something out of that but it's all very dark in the middle.*

His emphasis on the darkness "in the middle" suggests feelings of inner confusion, but this may be only the defensive aspect of the thought. "Dark" may also or instead stand for dark (i.e., evil, hostile) inner purposes. From this material we cannot know, but either or both possibilities would well fit the picture of personality and pathology that has been steadily developing.

CARD VI     REACTION TIME: 15".     TOTAL TIME: 5′ 40".

> 1. *(D F+ Obj Peculiar) That's a funny looking thing, like something I expect to find on a totem pole—I don't know exactly what yet. This upper part (upper D) looks like a totem pole. Quite frequently at the tops they have things like arms and wings at the top. It could*

*be an Indian variety of wing. It doesn't suggest a wing I would find*
*in any living animal (nervous laugh).*

Note in this and in the following response how the patient experiences preparatory phases of the formation of responses, and also how he reports this experience in a passive, detached way. Both aspects of response are specifically
obsessive and seem to reflect the expanded self-awareness that is apparently
based on good capacity for defensive isolation and intellectualization.

   *2. (Do F(C)± Ad) Whatever this is (upper tip) it will suggest some-*
   *thing soon. I'm thinking in terms of a head. This triangular arrange-*
   *ment of dots: two eyes and a head, but I'm not sure. Like on the*
   *ground, like a snake and I'm above it. I can't figure it out.*

The snake theme, the *Do* location, the image's slow development, his uncertainty about the response, his initial preoccupation with the upper area, all
suggest an anxious and rejecting reaction to the phallic quality of the upper
projection. Presumably, his anxious, rejecting reaction would be based on a
hostile, destructive conception of the phallus (see also the arrowhead and its
doubt-laden, rejecting treatment in V-8).

   *3. (Dr F± A) These darned things (laugh). . . . (What were you*
   *thinking?) Some kind of bird; possibly a woodpecker (light spots on*
   *midline).*

Like the hydra in V-5, this appears to be a small-scale, innocuous, well-defended-
oral-aggressive image.

   *4. (D ChF Dec Peculiar) Some kind of regularity about this thing.*
   *I don't know; you almost expect to find it in a pattern made in a*
   *weave shop (middle of lower D).* [What made it look woven? *It*
   *seemed to have a pattern.* Anything else? *Partly the half-tone, the*
   *dark and light and another color. It looked like they (the two sides)*
   *seemed parallel to each other almost.*]

Here, his compulsive need for precision asserts itself conspicuously within an
image rather than, as is more usual, in test attitudes and behavior. But note
also his overmeticulous, overcautious final verbalization in inquiry—"looked
like . . . seemed . . . almost."

   *5. (W F— Obj Peculiar) Suppose you stood it up on end (stands*
   *card on end): you might get a fountain out of it, a cross section of*
   *a fountain. It might not make a bad one at that. It's a lot better than*
   *that thing the E—— Company (the one he works for) showed the*
   *kids in their exhibition, I'll tell you that!*

(a) In this response, in the guise of conscientious attention to accuracy, he
simultaneously attacks his employer and defensively justifies—if not glorifies—
himself. Additional defense is thrown up by his immature manner that is
pathetically (and regressively) "harmless." (b) The peculiar literalness or
loss of distance in his needing to stand the card on edge suggests the three-
dimensional vividness of perception of the blots that often has paranoid implications (see also V-8 for paranoid trend).

   *Gee, I still think it looks something like tapestry (#4). The fact that*
   *it is in half-tone. . . . The photograph of the inkblot does it—lines*
   *running through it that are introduced in the half-tone process. That's*
   *another thing that made it look man-made, whatever it is.*

His ruminative clinging to the formal regularity and to the chemical, impersonal process suggests that he is deriving much compulsive reassurance from them (see also #7 below).

> 6. *(s F∓ Obj) I've noticed these two white blotches (tiny inner spaces at base of lower side projection). I haven't been able to think of anything yet. Possibly an old-time gun, but not much resemblance to it.*

(a) Like the arrowhead in V-8 and the snake head in VI-2, this seems to be another phallic-aggressive image that is defensively minimized ("old-time" or collector's item rather than dangerous weapon) and even so must be defensively rejected (in the guise of perfectionism). (b) His acute attention to such tiny areas as these and those of the arrowhead in V-8 and the "lake" spaces in III-5 suggests paranoid hyperalertness. That these are all white spaces underscores this inference (see also #5 and V-8).

> 7. *(Dr F(C)∓ Sex 2-Peculiar) I suppose I could see a couple of balls and a penis there, if I wished to. I wasn't thinking along those lines. I was thinking along artificial lines (lower middle tiny bumps are "balls"; dark shading above them is penis). [(As he traces response during inquiry:) I tortured it out of it. It really doesn't look like it. I wasn't thinking along those lines.]*

First he speaks with utter obsessive detachment (isolation) and denial of responsibility—"I suppose I could see . . . if I wished to." Then he essentially berates himself for having strayed from the straight and narrow compulsive path and having thought a human (not artificial, mechanical) thought. Conceivably, the previous suggestions of rigid defensiveness and intense hostility in his conception of sex (see #6) account for his being defensive and anxious now. In inquiry, using sadistic metaphor ("I tortured it"), just as to begin with he used a "dirty" word to express his response ("balls"), he utterly repudiates the sexual line of thought. Thus, he is being hostile and "dirty" in test attitude and behavior even while rejecting a hostile and "dirty" image. Also, in inquiry, in one breath he swears he was not thinking of stuff like that and yet admits he actually "tortured" it out with little help from the blot. In this he is strikingly unaware of the glaring self-contradiction that simultaneously expresses and rejects objectionable impulse representation.

Altogether, it is as if he is actually fighting it out with his drives—championing his mechanical, compulsive defenses and denying sexual and hostile drives or interests. This struggle is generally acute in obsessive-compulsive neuroses, but, like the *right-left* ambivalence on Card III, the transparent appearance of the struggle within Rorschach test responses and behavior indicates great defensive instability. In turn, this transparency suggests the danger of psychotic developments, a suggestion supported by the relatively conspicuous and numerous —though usually moderate—peculiarities in this record. The latest addition to this string of peculiarities is "a couple of balls"—an inappropriately casual verbalization of the number of testicles one is likely to envision together.

CARD VII     REACTION TIME: 18″.     TOTAL TIME: 6′ 15″.

> 1. *(Dr F∓ Obj) That just there (lower middle) reminded me of one of those mechanical music things they used to have in merry-go-rounds. I forget the name: calliope or what. . . .*

(a) Further mechanical, compulsive imagery (see VI-4 and remarks following VI-5). (b) This image also suggests childhood play, a suggestion consistent with his immature "gee," "hey," "gosh" and "darned" manner.

> 2. *(WS C'F Cave DW-tendency, Autistic Logic) An unusual looking' thing. Something about it makes me think of the lines to a cave of some sort. I've never been in one. It's lighter colored than most of the rest (of the cards). It made me think first of icicles and then a cave. Maybe it doesn't look too much like it but maybe that's why I hit upon something I wasn't too familiar with and hit upon that rather than something I was familiar with.* [What made it look like a cave? *You got me. It was just an initial impression of mine.* Think about it for a minute. *The only thing I could think of was the light color and a lot of points—stalactites or stalagmites sticking up in the air.* Could you explain your reasoning about its being unfamiliar? *I was trying to explain to myself why I should think of a cave, because I've never been in one.* And? *All the projections sticking up from it probably could suggest stalactites or stalagmites or icicles or something like that. It wasn't too clear a picture in my mind. Well, I just pulled it out of my hat almost.* But what was the explanation you had in mind? *It was more or less of a double negative. It didn't look like anything I was familiar with and caves are something I'm not familiar with.*]

This is the most autistically rationalized—and perceptually disorganized—response in the record. It strongly indicates the potentiality for bizarre departures from reality testing and conventional logic. Two facts must be remembered, however: (1) the record as a whole has not been flagrantly psychotic, even though many moderate peculiarities of thought, affect and verbalization have been encountered. In other words, the patient has remained marginally faithful to reality, even though the record's quantitative dilation has offered many opportunities for him to confabulate, contaminate and to introduce bizarre, archaic, morbid content into his responses; (2) the Rorschach test ordinarily tends to highlight weakness of reality adaptation and defenses. It follows from these two considerations that this autistic response, which more or less stands by itself in this record, represents the patient's functioning at its lowest level rather than its typical level. For the most part his functioning seems borderline psychotic and not fully psychotic.

> 3. *(W ChF Ldsc) It might possibly have some aspects of looking down on a forest from an airplane. It might possibly, although it's a thing I've never done.*

See after #4 for basis of *ChF* score.

> 4. *(s F± Obj) A little arrowhead again (location not recorded; F± was scored at time of response). A slightly different shape of one (compared to V-8), not so obvious—on either side· It's made of a light material.*

Another minimized ("little," "light") phallic-aggressive image (see V-8, VI-6).

> *The half-tone might have something to do with it, with the forest (#3): it gives the sense of a lot of little things and might have been. . . .*

More ruminativeness.

> *5. (Do F(C)— Ad) Here (shading in lower inner corner of lower ⅓), very small, it looks possibly like the face of a dog—a dog with what dictionaries love to call pendulous ears (further detailed description of dog).*

Dictionaries or the patient?

> *6–7. (Dr F+ Arch 2-Peculiar; Dr F∓ Arch Peculiar) These two things sticking up, right at the edge, could be lighthouses (on P forehead). It wouldn't make too much sense. It could be a tower of some kind, some sort of observation tower. I can't think for myself if it would be for observations of sightseers or forestry service. They get use out of the tower. The idea of something sticking up in the air: it could be a radio antennae or antennae—that's this one (on left). Maybe some kind of temple or monument (on right). (Further rumination about the two sides.) Down in the back here (small projection on the outside of #6), these others might be domes such as the national capitol or the N—— state capitol.*

(a) In these two responses, his vacillation between a tower for sight-seeing and one for forestry service, his differing interpretations of identical areas on the right and on the left of the card (see also the verbalizations preceding III-6), and his lengthy rumination and overspecificity about these tiny areas are all obsessional in style *but also more or less autistic.* (b) The antithesis of pleasure and duty—one that plagues the obsessive—seems to be implied in the sight-seeing and forestry alternative. (c) The domes in #7 and the temple and monument in #6 have grandiose overtones that probably relate to the paranoid suggestions already encountered (see V-8, VI-5, VI-6).

CARD VIII     REACTION TIME: 22″.     TOTAL TIME (patient was interrupted): 4′ 20″.

> *Oh (laugh) look at the pretty colors!*

This is a strong though both childish and effeminate response to color for a young man of 24. He never really gets control of this spontaneous response (see especially #3, 4, and 6 below; see also the disruptive effects of color inferred on Card II).

> *1. (W F— A) That overall impression is something or other. Some sort of crab, I believe, looks like that; not with those colors though. [What made it look like a crab? It was a particular kind of crab. I don't remember the name. How did it look like that? That kind has a lot of little horns or bony places on his body.]*

An arbitrary form response that suggests anxiety behind his pleased opening remark. Significantly, he makes no more than a gesture toward using color in this response.

> *2. (D F+ A P) A very good impression of an animal here. A very good impression. You don't need to do much imagining to see that. I don't know what kind: the dog family; a wolf maybe.*

Some recovery of control and reality testing—but with a good deal of help from the inkblot, i.e., from this compelling *P.* Note how pleased and reassured he is with this very realistic animal form (see after VI-5, VI-7). He is obviously uncomfortable with his "imaginings" or fantasy life.

> ' 3. *(D C Sand Peculiar) Sort of a pretty thing (orange): the colors at the bottom suggest sand to me, beach.* [What made it look like beach or sand? *The color.* Anything else? *It was fairly extensive.*]

(a) Once he begins using color, the responses are unformed, i.e., affectively poorly controlled. (b) "A pretty thing" has feminine overtones; so does "quite pretty" in the next response (see also the opening remark on this card).

> 4. *(D C Sunset) I can even get a sunset out of that. It looks quite pretty (lower pink and orange).* [Sunset? *There again the color: the reds and the yellows looked very pretty.* Anything else? *No.*]

> 5. *(S F+ Emblem) I suppose it's fair to let the spaces remind you of something. These two remind me of what doctors have—a couple of serpents around a stick. I don't know the right name (upper middle space; usual rib area).*

(a) Note his defensively cautious and compliant but intrinsically negativistic use of space. (b) The concept "fair" is inappropriate to this situation and suggests at least neurotic preoccupation with moral issues. (c) There have been a number of instances of word-finding difficulty so far, including *esophagus* in III-1, *symmetry* after V-4, *calliope* in VII-1, and now *caduceus* (see also IX-1, below). While each of these difficulties may have its own content significance—in this instance it is conceivable that anxiety associated with the phallic-aggressive symbol and/or with the patient-doctor relationship is the disruptive force—recurrent verbal difficulty of this sort reflects severe inefficiency of ego functioning. It is not unusual to encounter word-finding difficulty, along with slight word distortion and misuse, in the records of persons recovering from and "sealing over" a recent psychotic break and in the records of chronically poorly integrated patients.

> 6. *(D C Sea) This center blot (middle blue) has a greenish tint. It reminds me of the waters around Bermuda. They actually were as advertised—for once.*

Lest the reader think the patient was unbending and cracking a joke about advertising, it should be said that his remark about advertising was dead serious and somewhat irritated.

> 7. *(D F— A) Now I'm getting more into the realm of speculation. The upper one (upper gray) might possibly represent a frog in the position of jumping maybe.* [Frog? *You could get the impression of a small body and long legs sticking out.* Anything else? *No.*]

In a weak way, good reality testing is involved here.

> *So far this really heavy thing down the middle (upper midline) hasn't suggested anything.*

He may be having trouble with the phallic and club-like qualities of this form, as well as with his fantasy of it as "heavy"; that is, he may be precariously repressing a "big penis" response. His need to emphasize his weakness in the next response is in line with this highly speculative inference (but see also his difficulty with the presumed phallic imagery in V-8, VI-2, VI-6, VI-7, and VIII-5).

> 8. *(Dr F+ Hd Peculiar) This might be quite revealing. This gives the impression of a hand pulling himself up on a bar (orange projec-*

*tion and blue loop linking middle blue and lower pink). It's something I've never been able to do, even with practice—chinning.*

If a patient spontaneously makes a big point about something being "revealing," especially with no background of intensive therapeutic work, it is fairly safe to assume that what is being referred to is a well-defended and not directly revealing bit of behavior. In this instance, for example, the image and his self-reference emphasize his weak, implicitly harmless and unaggressive self-image. As we have had reason to surmise (see, for example, V-1, 6, 7), this weakness, however real it may be, usually cannot be fully understood unless passive, regressive defense against hostility is assumed to play a big part in its genesis and present prominence.

*I can observe how the red and the blue don't quite blend (further color description; patient interrupted).*

Conscientious and taxing attention to detail, continual ineffective handling of color, and possibly implicit criticism of the tester's "sloppy" test (see beginning of Card IX).

Card IX    Reaction Time: 40″.    Total Time (patient was interrupted): 4′ 10″.

*There's a case where the colors definitely clash. (Nervous laugh) That doesn't look pretty! That looks somewhat like a mess, I would say!*

To begin with, and especially after #3, below, he more or less openly responds with great anxiety and irritation to this card. The emphasis he puts on "clash," "mess," "revolting" and mixed-up colors suggests that to him this blot stands for loss of control, disorderliness and dirtiness, or, in other words, for experiences and behaviors that represent defensive failure and eruption of anally-conceived hostile and libidinal impulses. To this he reacts with the appropriate obsessive-compulsive defensive affect—disgust ("revolting")—but also with a bitter attack on the test (obliquely on the tester) for plunging him into this threatening situation. His defensive position seems so weak that the would-be warded-off impulses have relatively free access to expression when he feels threatened.

Even so, his efforts to contain and to minimize his irritation should not be overlooked: "doesn't look pretty" is cautiously oblique; "somewhat like a mess," "sort of revolting" and "I would say" undermine his emphatic stand; "I don't think they had any business" keeps the tester safely out of it.

Although not very successfully, he does slowly regain some composure as he goes on responding to this card. Unlike a repressive patient, he keeps responding in the face of stress. Anxiety tends to intensify defensive efforts; that is, it ordinarily prompts a repressive person to repress more, while it prompts an obsessive-compulsive person to engage in increased reaction formation and isolation in the form of compliance, conscientiousness, ambitious intellectual productivity, rationalizing and the like.

*1. (D (C)C/F Geog) I might be able to get some sort of landscape out of this (green). I mean looking down from a plane or a topological, I mean topographical map. (Patient explains at length that "topological" is a mathematical term.) [What made it look like a topographical map? You could sort of get the idea they filled in the shadows for the mountain ranges and so on.* Anything else? *The color, green, but that's about all. It resembled that even in the red portion but that would not. . . .* Do you mean you thought of it originally as a green landscape? *No, I don't think so.*]

(a) A weak attempt to regain control and manage the colors. He finally manages the colors by rejecting them altogether. An all-or-none orientation to affect is strongly suggested—and is to be expected in severely obsessive-compulsive neurotics. (b) Note his pedantic, overcompensatory correction of his topology-topography slip.

*So far it's sort of indefinite.*

*2. (S F— Geog) This white space has somewhat the same shape as the island of England (middle space).*

Another weak response. This time he avoids the colored areas.

*3. (S F± Obj) Maybe a bell (middle space).*

He is slowly regaining control, but still avoiding the colored areas.

*The thing is sort of revolting, if you ask me! (Peculiar:) I don't think they had any business in mixing the colors in that particular way!*

His defenses and controls weaken again as he is unable to sustain his blotting out of the disturbing, overlapping, shaded colors.

*4. (Dd F± Ad) Here you might get the tusks of an elephant, but I can't see the rest of the elephant (upper inner orange projections).*

(a) He again begins to regain control, but has to fall back on a relatively small, well-articulated area. (b) The image is likely to have oral and/or phallic-aggressive implications.

*5. (Dr F± Hd) I suppose you might say fingers here (streaks between green and lower red). That's sort of far-fetched, though.*

Another acceptable percept in a small—i.e., easily controlled, unthreatening—area.

*6. (D C(C) Blood) The color might possibly suggest blood around here—clotted or stained or something (orange). The heavy ring around the border might suggest that: a blood stain.*

(a) Except superficially, he is unable to articulate the color (affect) once he experiences it. (b) Unlike plain blood, which suggests a representation of hostility in general, blood *stain* suggests guilt over hostility; that is, it seems to imply concern with past aggressions and with "incriminating" evidence.

*7. (Dr F(C)— Letter) I've seen some Japanese symbols that look like that (in upper middle of lower red). They look almost like the Greek letter Pi, but spread too far apart. [Pi? It was that shape: the idea of the cross-bar and two things sticking down.]*

(a) Letters, geometric and other abstract forms, especially if they are of arbitrary form—as this one is—suggest paranoid proclivities (see also V-8, VI-5, VI-6, VII-7). The previous autistic responses in this record also suggest that paranoid reactions have fertile soil here. His background of mathematical interests and sophistication is relevant here as a source of this content, but it does not account for the formal arbitrariness of the response. In fact, this background underscores its arbitrariness.

(b) It will be instructive to pause at this point and scrutinize his extremely cautious, tenuous, doubt-laden, obsessional relationship to his responses. The first response to this card begins with "I might be able to get some sort of" and continues in inquiry with "you could sort of get the idea"; #2 "has somewhat the shape of"; #3 is "maybe"; #4—"you might get"; #5—"I suppose you might say" and "that's sort of far-fetched"; "The color might possibly suggest" #6, and of #7 "I've seen some . . . that look like that. They look almost like . . . but spread too far apart." In the end he has committed himself to nothing, has allowed no feeling of emotional participation in and conviction about his responses to develop, and has in effect kept the entire situation at arm's length if not at the length of a ten foot pole. This defensive rigidity is extreme to the point of implicit paranoid cautiousness. Clinically, latent paranoid suspiciousness is commonly encountered in the therapy of such obsessional patients. The scattered paranoid indications in this record are relevant here.

CARD X     REACTION TIME: 12".     TOTAL TIME (patient was interrupted): 4' 30".

*That should offer a lot of possibilities. All right: I'll start right here.* A much better controlled opening response than that at the beginning of Card IX and even that of Card VIII. This patient has some doggedness and resiliency, rigid and peculiar and remote as he may get.

*1. (D F+ Obj) The governor of a steam engine (upper center orange).* A prize obsessional image of mechanical control.

*2. (D F+ Ad P) Here's a face of some sort (lower middle): Bugs Bunny; I don't know (nervous laugh).* Bugs Bunny is a smart-alecky, voracious rabbit and not a harmless, timid one. Very likely this image appeals to this inhibited but irritable and latently defiant and sadistic patient, but the image's appeal seems to make him anxious, even though the image comes coated with comic and fictional sweetening. In the response itself, anxiety is suggested by his tacking on "I don't know" and laughing nervously. Perceptually, the response is obvious enough; the "I don't know" may well have a taking-it-back, undoing significance.

*3. (Dr FC+ Food) A fairly good walnut inside there (dark spot in middle yellow). It would be a fairly good one: the shell and not the inside—like it was the other time (IV-1). [Walnut? The color; the shape. By the shape I mean it is almost round, and still there are points sticking out diametrically opposite each other.]* Unlike IV-1, this walnut is an image of invulnerability—it has its hard shell—and is not an image of (shelled) vulnerability. He seems pleased by this restoration of outer walls—and geometric precision. He even finally gives an *FC*, also indicating his restoration of control, but it is a tiny *FC*, it is not very "hot" in color, and it is hopelessly outweighed by the 4 *pure C* on Cards VIII and IX.

*4. (D F+ A) These green spots (upper green) might possibly represent sheep; the legs are not enough pronounced; that horn. Maybe a goat in the process of butting.* Note the shift from the peaceful sheep image to the hostile, phallic-aggressive goat image (see V-1, V-7, and the remarks preceding VIII-8 as well as VIII-8 itself).

*5. (D F+ Ad) A couple of more faces with mouth and eyes (upper gray). I don't know what kind of an animal it might be; no existing animal, anyway.*

*6. (D F± Ad) This whole thing here might possibly resemble the wishbone, maybe (all lower middle green).*

An image with passive-receptive overtones.

*7. (D F(C)∓ Geog) The red things once again remind me of islands because the borders are so sharply defined (all red). Not so much an island as a map of an island. It is so sharply defined on that one side (along inner edge).*

His fastening on the definite outer boundary may tie in with the walnut-shell emphasis (see #3) and with his general search for geometric precision.

*I haven't got much out of the yellow as yet. I may not, because yellow never stands out so much from white for me as some of the other colors do. The blue I ought to be able to think of something for soon; not yet.*

Further conspicuously conscientious but unproductive and tedious keeping the tester posted on his progress.

*8. (D F— A) Possibly some sort of insect (side blue); I don't know what.*

This insect is scored *F—* because it is a mosquito (see after #9). "A magnified mosquito" is another minimized (denied) oral-aggressive image.

*9. (Dr F± Ad, Obj) You might possibly conjure up a horse's head (upper middle of side blue). That's not true, I don't think. A knight piece in a chess game.*

*I still think more in terms of an insect (#8): maybe a magnified mosquito, maybe.*

One version of this response is cerebral in theme—the chess game. In this respect, the image is related to the biology book emphasis in III-1, III-6 and V-5, the huge brain in IV-2, the dictionary reference in VII-5, the mathematical reference in IX-1, the Greek and Japanese reference in IX-7, and his pervasive search for and pleasure in mechanical, geometrically regular or precise objects and constructions (see VI-5, VII-6, VII-7, X-1). His intellectualizing takes him to matters remote from simple, immediate human passions. Some of these responses reflect his training and interest in physics and mathematics, of course, but the personality picture that has evolved adds a great deal to our understanding of why he may have made his professional choice, that is, why he may have in the first place developed these interests which are now being reflected in the test content. Abstract scientific interest may become a relatively autonomous, conflict-free, sublimated affair, but it lends itself very well to purposes of defensive isolation and intellectualization.

[See p. 410 for Score Summary.]

The summary of scores is clearly that of a very precariously integrated, at least borderline psychotic, obsessive-compulsive person. Considered together, the relatively high *R* of 64 and *DR%* of 39%, the very high *Do* of 5+4, the 8+2 *Space* responses and the *Object%* of 16%–17% suffice to establish the presence of extreme obsessive-compulsive trends. Implied by these scores are intellectual drive, hypermeticulousness to the point of fragmentation of the most obvious or ignoring of the most obvious, a search for and clinging to precision and balance and regularity (very likely involving idealization of the machine and its products), and underlying, stubborn, negativistic, rebellious tendencies.

SUMMARY OF SCORES

R: 64                    EB: 0–6.5(7.5)

| | | | | | | | |
|---|---|---|---|---|---|---|---|
| W | 7 | F+ | 21 | A | 11 | W% | 11 |
| D | 26 | F− | 10 | Ad | 14 | D% | 41 |
| Dd | 1 | F± | 10 | Hd | 4 | DR% | 39 |
| Dr | 16 | F∓ | 6 | (Hd) | 1 | Do% | 8–14 |
| De | 1 | FC | 1 | Obj | 10+1 | | |
| S | 4+1 | C/F | 0+1 | Geog | 5 | F% | 73–83 |
| s | 4+1 | C | 4 | At | 3 | F+% | 66–62 |
| Do | 5+4 | F(C) | 5 (4−) | Sex | 1 | | |
| | | (C)F | 1+1 | Blood | 1 | A% | 39 |
| | | C'F | 1 | Food | 3 | H% | 6–8 |
| *Qualitative* | | ChF | 5 | Nature | 5 | P | 4+1 |
| Peculiar | 20 | | | Arch | 2 | P% | 6–8 |
| Autistic Logic | 1 | | | Misc | 4 | Obj% | 16–17 |
| Confab. tend. | 1 | | | | | | |
| DW-tend. | 1 | | | | | | |

His precarious integration and autistic tendencies are evident in 1 *DW-tendency,* 20 *Peculiar,* 1 *Autistic Logic,* 1 *Confabulation tendency,* a borderline *F+%* of 66%–62%, 4 *pure C* as compared to only 1 *FC* and 1 additional *C/F,* the virtual absence of well-controlled and accurate color and shading responses generally, and, in context, the absence of *M.* His pattern of color and shading responses, considered in the context of the total record, suggests more than failing defense against and control of affect and impulse, with resulting intense anxiety, tenseness, moodiness and irritability. This pattern also suggests severe emotional withdrawal, minimal adaptive efforts, possibly some emotional inappropriateness and the potentiality for violent psychotic outbursts. Also, the relatively many *Space* responses suggest that his psychotic trends have paranoid coloring.

In this score analysis, we have surmised—or could have—much that became clear in the previous thematic analysis, such as the existence of extreme defensive instability and weakness, the pervasive invasion of functioning by underlying hostile impulses and emotional lability, and the relatively often autistic and emotionally inappropriate forms of appearance of his defensive intellectualizing, isolation, reaction formations and undoing. We could also have inferred that such symptoms as he has are likely to be thoroughly and openly "invaded" by the hostile, demanding, defiant impulses that were meant to be inhibited, deflected and disguised. We can surmise these trends from the scores, but in the previous thematic analysis we saw them in operation before our very eyes. And we saw plainly the great lengths he goes to in order to impress others and himself (his super-ego, presumably) with his juvenile innocence and harmlessness, as well as with his intense feelings of weakness and inadequacy.

One final consideration concerning the scores. The absence of $M$ and the emphasis on *sum C* in the $EB$ (0–6.5) are relatively infrequent, though not rare, in obsessive-compulsive records. We must ask what this reversal implies in this particular instance. It need not imply that ideational symptoms such as obsessions, doubting and pathological intellectualizing are probably absent. In this case, for example, both clinically and in qualitative Rorschach analysis, these symptoms are outstanding. $M$ may be absent on the basis of several factors: (a) impairment of integrative and imaginative functioning associated with pedantic, overmeticulous application of intel-lectual assets. This impairment is evident in this record in the high $Do$, high $DR\%$ and relatively few and only vague, arbitrary or banal $W$. The achievement of more than one or two $M$ requires more or less versatile and forceful integrative efforts; (b) turning away from genuine, penetrating self-confrontation and introspection. In his test attitudes this patient seems threatened and "revolted" by awareness of inner affective experience, and, as reflected in his imagery, he seems to be rejecting imaginative fantasy and to be searching instead for what is objective, concrete, regular and clear-cut; (c) the absence of $M$ may be related to the presence of obvious autistic trends. Autistic disruption of neurotic adjustment efforts often is reflected in parallel disruption of usual diagnostic patterns. Also, in this case, at least partly as a reflection of his psychotic trends, this patient's general intel-lectual efficiency appears to be severely reduced: his $F+\%$ is only 66%–62% and his + or ± responses are almost entirely mediocre in quality. His *S Caduceus* and *Dr Chinning* responses on Card VIII and his *Dr Walnut* on Card X are his best responses from the combined viewpoints of relative originality, accuracy and fineness of perception—and that is very little for a person with an $R$ of 64 and an $IQ$ of 133. In short, the third factor that may account for the complete absence of $M$, even of the easy popular $M$ on Card III, is the undermining of his assets by psychotic developments.

The explanation of the relatively high *sum C* appears to be the following: (a) ideally this patient's *sum C* approaches 0, reflecting his rigid efforts to repudiate and be free from affect and impulse; (b) his controls and defenses are weak, however, allowing more or less painfully experienced affect and impulse to push their way into conscious awareness and even behavioral expression, and being reflected in the Rorschach test in an emphasis on poorly controlled color responses; (c) his psychotic trends result in—or are expressed through—his poorly controlled reactions taking diffuse, primitive, arbitrary or inappropriate forms and hence coming to expression in *pure C* rather than *CF*.

But whatever the explanation of the reversed *EB,* it is impressive how even with a dramatic *EB* reversal and with much evidence that schizophrenic disintegration of the neurosis is probably taking place, the basic obsessive-compulsive defensive picture is preserved in many of the score patterns and throughout the qualitative aspects of the response process.

## Case 4

The next (and last) record is that of a 19-year-old, male college freshman with an IQ of 112. This IQ appears to have deteriorated from a level of at least 120. This patient's diagnosis was "schizophrenia, with prominent catatonic features, in a compulsive and schizoid personality." The record will illustrate extremely autistic forms of expression of obsessive-compulsive defensive operations in general and of conscientiousness in particular. This patient will go to extremes such as the previous relatively autistic obsessive-compulsive patient rarely approximated. Such conscientiousness as is evident will be mostly empty, profitless, self-absorbed and chaotic.

Impressive clinical evidence of this patient's autistically elaborated caricature of obsessive-compulsive tendencies—the clinical counterpart of what we shall encounter in his Rorschach record—is found in the following report on his hospital behavior during the examination period: "In his room at night he puts himself to various tests. For example, he must balance himself on the edge of the bed and reach a long way under the bedside table to 'pick up some dust.' If he fails, as he almost always does, it means that he is not 'sincere.' He spent an hour or two one night crouched in a very uncomfortable position beneath his wash basin, trying to pull the bath mat from under a chair and in a certain way. Failure meant that he 'couldn't take it.' When, rarely, he succeeds in passing such a test, it proves to him that he is so 'soft' and such a 'baby' that he devised too easy a task."

In addition, there was clinical evidence of compulsive rituals in connection with dressing, eating and studying, as well as of extreme, persistent self-depreciation, extreme shyness, and confusional and hallucinatory experiences. The schizophrenic aspects of the following Rorschach record will mostly be ignored except when they are integral aspects of obsessive-compulsive instinctual problems, superego pressures, and defensive operations.

CARD I     REACTION TIME: 5″.     TOTAL TIME: 3′.

*1. (W F+ A P) The first thing I see is a bat.*
*2. (Ws F± (Hd) Confusion, Confabulation) And kind of a face of a . . . devil, I'll say.* [What made it look like a devil? *It just did; I thought it was.* In what way? *It was kind of . . . fearful, I think.* What gave it that quality? *Kind of . . . eyes and . . . its kind of look, kind of weary look.* Do you mean weary or weird? *I guess I mean weird*

*(uncertain tone), terrifying.* Do you feel scared now? *Not too, but it just gave me that impression; a little bit scared, yes.*]

The devil is a powerful image of evil and guilt. The patient's subjective feeling of fright, brought out in inquiry, indicates the presence of pathological projection of hostility and/or guilt.

*3–4–5. (Do F∓ Hd; Dr F+ Hd; Do F— Hd Fluid, Peculiar, Contamination tendency, Confusion) This looks like you might see, here, here are the legs of two women there, kind of standing back-to-back (lower middle, usual legs), and yet not back-to-back: it's one woman facing in the opposite direction and you can just see her back, and yet you can see two heads (upper middle bumps). It's almost as if at first you could see two women together and yet it's only one.* [How much of the woman did you see? *The heads.* Didn't you see some of the body? *Not all of it: down to about here (chest); that's about all.* You didn't see other parts? *No. Just down to the waist.* No legs? *No. The legs look like one person standing, facing in the other direction.* How much of that person did you see? *The feet and the legs and . . . that's about all. In the middle, I couldn't see any legs but it must be the legs making up the middle part of the body. I didn't actually see it.*]

(a) The shifting and merging impressions in this set of three responses indicate pathological fluidity of thinking and fertile soil for the development of feelings of unreality and confusion (see Card X). (b) The back-to-back and facing away aspects of these images suggest noteworthy anality.

*6. (D F— (Hd) Peculiar) Here . . . I see some kind of face: eye and nose (all side, facing out). . . . The devil, I suppose; as well as here too I see a devil (other side).*

Another powerful image of evil and guilt.

*7. (Drs F+ (Hd)) Here I see a kind of, what would be a kind of a lantern, jack-o-lantern (vaguely outlines inner circle), with the eyes cut out (upper inner spaces) and. . . .*

Although not an unusual response, the jack-o-lantern may in this instance, by its Halloween connotation, continue the theme of supernatural evil and deviltry.

CARD II    REACTION TIME: 7".    TOTAL TIME: 5' 30".

*1–2. (W MC+ H P; D CF Fire) I see two clowns, dancing . . . and kind of holding hands. . . . Red caps. . . . Almost as if this were a fire, maybe (lower red). It looks like they're dancing over a fire.*

As one follows his verbalization, one sees how slowly and almost painfully the response is being pulled together from preparatory components. In non-obsessional settings these components tend to remain preconscious or unverbalized and to be quickly welded into a forceful total concept.

*3. (D F+ A P) I also see two dogs, two dogs of some sort, two dogs that are kind of touching noses. I guess not touching noses . . . not touching noses. . . .*

Note here, as elsewhere, the extremely doubt-laden, ruminative, slow-motion quality of the patient's handling of his impressions.

*4. (D F+ A 2-Peculiar) And this is some kind of turkey maybe (lower red). It looks like a turkey, this red here . . . kind of blending in with the black, with the dogs (#3), the feet of the dogs, the legs of the dogs. . . . And these are the feathers here (irregular edges) and the head (in lower middle) and it's facing me, looking at me, and the legs here (lower projections).* [Turkey? *It had feathers and a head. I suppose I just have Thanksgiving in my head (date of test is November 26th). First I thought it was something else.* What was that? *I've forgotten.* Anything else to make it a turkey? *The shape of it, the general shape of it.*]

Further peculiar, obsessional manipulation of words is evident in "with the dogs, the feet of the dogs, the legs of the dogs." This inappropriately labored grasping after just the right formulation suggests extreme reliance on reaction formation against hostility in the form of hyperconscientiousness and meticulousness. In fact, the verbalization suggests that to the patient every thought and action must seem so potentially evil—i.e., invaded by primitive sadistic and libidinal impulses—that the least flaw must be carefully eliminated (see also discussion of III-1 below).

5. *(S F+ Obj) This might be a kind of a top, that you spin (middle space) . . . with this too (upper middle dark).*

CARD III     REACTION TIME: 10″.     TOTAL TIME: 5′.

1. *(W FM± (H) (P) Confabulation, 2-Peculiar) I see two ducks warming themselves over a fire . . . and they're kind of animated ducks, animated ducks. . . . I mean they're not real. You don't see ducks like. . . . They're not really ducks but the idea of ducks came into my head. . . . I get the impression that they are friends . . . and . . . over a fire, warming themselves over a fire . . . and. . . .* [Why did you think they were friends? *They look . . . kind of friendly. They look . . . as if they might be friends. . . . They look happy together.* What made them look happy? *They were both there at the fire together, warming their hands.*]

(a) Note how he struggles to achieve the best possible formulation for the ducks. After #4, below, he even gives the duck verbalization one more going over. These slow, halting, repetitive verbalizations consume a great deal of time. They are thereby quite demanding of the tester's patience, interest, time and restraint. It was quite evident during the testing that the patient was desperately involved in these extreme obsessional ruminations. For the tester to intervene even in a matter-of-fact way would have certainly distressed the patient. Yet, however pathetic, this peculiar and extreme obsessional rumination cannot but stimulate a desire to intervene, a desire, moreover, more or less invaded by impatience and irritability. The therapeutic study of patient behavior of this sort makes it clear that in part the patient usually intends to stimulate negative feelings in the therapist. In short, this "sincere" behavior involves oversubmissive provocativeness. As a defense it is riddled by the impulses it was erected against. As discussed in Chapter 2, the tester, like the therapist, can learn to use his feelings toward a patient and toward his own work as clues to the understanding of the patient's behavior and attitudes.

(b) An important pathological aspect of this form of conscientiousness is that the patient is merely manipulating words and is not working to refine, elaborate, vary or otherwise do something more with the response itself. In this regard the patient appears to have withdrawn from relationships with real objects and to have substituted relationships with words and concepts. Up to a point, this substitution of thoughts for people is an aspect of defensive intellectualizing, normal or neurotic. But such defensive intellectualizing also should have its adaptive, reality-oriented aspects; that is, it should be to some extent a means of reaching people too, even if highly inhibited, or of being productive in some way. When, however, real objects, events, feelings and people disappear from the psychological scene and all that remains is empty verbalization, schizophrenic withdrawal must be inferred. At the same time, by going to extreme "compliant" lengths and yet remaining essentially unproductive in so doing, the patient is burlesquing conscientiousness and thereby mocking the tester and the authority figures for whom the tester stands.

(c) Thematically, the image suggests the same defensive remoteness from people as his style of verbalization. He substitutes animals for people, and even that is not enough—they must be unreal, "animated (cartoons)," etc. Only then is the idea of intimacy reintroduced. At this safe remove, expressing longing for closeness to others may be subjectively tolerable, but note (1) the gloomy implication that these are companions in a cold world, happy to find a little warmth anywhere, and (2) the confabulated nature of the happy, friendly theme. The implicit gloom and the confabulation suggest that little or no effective adaptive efforts are likely to accompany whatever yearnings are being reflected here.

> 2. (Drs F∓ (Hd) Confabulation) Here I . . . see the face of another devil (lower middle gray; eyes in spaces). . . . [Devil? It just . . . it just did. It was weird and . . . kind of . . . terrifying.]

This is the third devil (see I-a, I-6), and this one too, as brought out in inquiry, involves psychotic paranoid projection and consequent fear in the patient. These devil images must be seen in part as expressions of severe superego condemnation of instinctual impulses and their derivatives. The evil self-concept has been at least implicit in the records of all the obsessional patients considered in this chapter, but in this record—a schizophrenic record that is "wide open" in important respects—it emerges dramatically, even though in projected form primarily.

> 3–4. (D F— Smoke Fluid, Peculiar; D F+ A) And this is kind of smoke (middle red). Not smoke; a butterfly of some sort. . . . A butterfly . . . and. . . . I guess this is kind of smoke from the fire. . . . [Butterfly? The shape of it. Anything else? . . . No. What made it look like smoke? Nothing. It might be smoke if it (lower middle in #1) were a fire. It didn't particularly look like smoke. Smoke isn't red. I just thought it might be.]
>
> (Peculiar:) I get the impression that these are not real ducks (#1) but drawn up, animated, created. This is going. . . . A devil (#2). . . .

(a) Further insistance on the unreality or remoteness of the "friendly" figures.

(b) His mutterings are fragmented almost to the point of incoherence. They seem to make it clear that often he is less interested in communicating with words than he is in performing some kind of magic with them or settling some internal debate. At any rate, the test and tester fade far into the background at these moments of "conscientious review."

CARD IV     REACTION TIME: 20″.     TOTAL TIME: 4′ 40″.

> *1. (W F± A Peculiar, Confabulation tendency, Do-tendency) The first thing I see here is a lion-er-dragon, a dragon. . . . Here are the eyes (on lower middle D), nostrils here. . . . It's the kind of . . . that spits fire out of its. . . . And these are kind of wings (bottom of lower side). V . . . ∧ . . . These are the wings (all lower side), I think, and the legs (upper side projections), the legs, and that's about all. [What suggested a lion? It looked like a dragon. At first you said a lion: what about that? It was just the wrong word. What suggested that it spits fire? It just looked like it would. I mean, it looked like . . . it looked like it was . . . cartoons of such dragons.]*

(a) Inquiry into this response elicits practically nothing—a finding consistent with the tendency toward empty pseudo-responsiveness in this patient (see discussion of III-1). Inquiry into previous responses has also been relatively unproductive so far as determinants are concerned. The patient typically takes the position, "It just looks like it." The meaning of such unreflectiveness probably involves some combination of the following factors: (1) anxiety about the content of this particular response; (2) general, chronic anxiety about self-confrontation; (3) paranoid wariness with respect to communicating to others; (4) paranoid self-righteousness about his behavior; (5) negativistic, "disobedient" withholding of orally-conceived and/or anally-conceived inner contents; (6) impairment of reflective capacity as a result of regressive schizophrenic reorganization of thought patterns and relation to the self. The sixth and last of these factors may well be the resultant in schizophrenic thought patterns of the previous five factors. In any event, with all his earnest, labored conscientiousness, the patient does not really "come across" in inquiry, just as he is usually unproductive in his spontaneous ruminations.

(b) Note how in his image he makes the already unreal dragon doubly unreal, i.e., a cartoon dragon. In III-1, he seemed to withdraw from intimacy; here he withdraws from hostility.

> *. . . (Anything else?) . . . I just. . . .*
>
> *2. (D F+ Cg Do-tendency) This looks like a shoe here (bottom of lower side), a boot (all of lower side). . . .*

CARD V     REACTION TIME: 25″.     TOTAL TIME: 4′.

> *1. (W F± A (P)) Here I see some kind of vulture. That's all. . . . Here's the head and kind of a beak (upper middle).*

The vulture is a classic oral-aggressive image. In addition, it probably carries powerful implications of low esteem or shame—the vulture being a carrion eater. The fire-spitting dragon in IV-1, while similarly oral-aggressive, was far more mighty and awesome. This variation on the bat-butterfly-bird theme is quite unusual and therefore all the more significant. Inquiry may well have established that he saw the lower or upper middle projections as an open beak.

> *. . . (Anything else?)*
>
> *2. (D F+ Ad) This looks like the leg of . . . of . . . the leg and tail of some animal (side projections). . . . It looks like the tail of a lion or something like that . . . and this too (other side). . . .*

Tail images ordinarily have anal connotations. This being the tail of a lion—

a powerful, hostile beast—it suggests the theme of anal aggression, a theme that would be closely related to the obsessional tendencies already evident.

    ⋏ *And this (lower middle) is something. I don't know . . . (traces upper edge). . . . That's about all. (What were you thinking just then?) I was looking at the wings (of #1).*

CARD VI    REACTION TIME: 10″.    TOTAL TIME: 6′.

    *1. (D F∓ Hd Peculiar) Two faces together, back-to-back (each half of lower D, facing out). . . . Two faces. . . . Fear on them . . . and . . . this is, and yet kind of laughing; another face laughing, funny. . . . [What made it look like fear on them? I suppose it just did. How? I think the . . . look, the general appearance . . . the look, the general appearance. . . . It just might look like it, that it was . . . yeah. What about the laughing? Yes. . . . No. . . . The fact that the mouth was opened made it look like it was laughing . . . the fact that the mouth was opened.]*

(a) The mixture of fear and laughter probably expresses unstable efforts to deny intense anxiety by "good humor." In this obviously schizophrenic context, such good humor might well appear as silliness (see also III-1). If we compare this image with those reflecting successful counterphobic efforts, such as "a comic version of Dracula" on Card IV (from another record), we see how the latter involve psychically well-coordinated manipulation of objects so as to eliminate their terrifying aspects, while the former—the fearful and laughing face of the present response—is internally contradictory and is concerned only with manipulating the inner affect. This difference may well derive from the schizophrenic withdrawal from real objects. In other words, schizophrenic inappropriate affect, such as silliness and blandness, might well involve autistically elaborated remnants of, substitutes for, or caricatures of normal or neurotic counterphobic operations. (b) The back-to-back emphasis probably has an anal implication.

    *2. (D F± Obj, A Do-tendency, Peculiar) And also this is kind of a totem pole (midline and upper D). I get that impression too. And these are the eyes of some owl or something (upper tip). It looks like an owl, the whole thing (upper D). It might be an owl, a bird of some sort; feathers (too), not just the head. This is a figure on a totem pole. The feathers joining the totem pole, attached to the totem pole. This whole thing is a totem pole.*

Note again his extremely ruminative, circumstantial, sterile verbalization and his labored integrative efforts.

    *3. (DS F— Obj Absurd) Also this is kind of a chest of drawers (lower D) with . . . one drawer open on each side of it (lower side projections) and some kind of a gap here (lower middle space), perhaps where one drawer had been taken out. I think perhaps where one drawer had been taken out.*

Drawers are inner containers that are filled and emptied. Physiognomically, they lend themselves especially well to representation of anal fantasy. In particular, the "open drawer" theme suggests anal concern with exposure of one's inner contents, while the "missing drawer" theme suggests anxiety about being robbed of one's inner contents. His usual ungivingness in inquiry may involve these particular anxieties (see discussion of IV-1). Apparently the intensity of his anxiety in this realm is such as to cause a marked drop in form level and dramatic primitivization of perceptual organization, i.e., simultaneously seeing three views of one bureau.

> *4. (D F+ Obj) And this might be some kind of bedpost (midline and upper shaft).*
>
> *(Fabulized Combination:) And maybe this face here (#1) is kind of on to the totem pole (#2) too.*

This arbitrary combination may reflect efforts to transform the laughing, fearful faces of #1 into wooden, unfeeling and remote figures (see III-1, IV-1).

CARD VII    REACTION TIME: 3".    TOTAL TIME: 8'.

> *1. (D F− Hd Absurd) Thumbs up (upper projection is index finger, side projection is thumb).*
>
> *2. (W M+ H P) Two clowns dancing.*
>
> *Thumbs up is what I see (#1). Not thumbs up, but like . . . this finger is (index finger). . . . They're dancing (#2).*

(a) Bearing in mind that it comes from an apparently utterly withdrawn, disorganized, guilt-stricken and frightened young man, the perceptually arbitrary "thumbs up" image strongly suggests one of two content interpretations: either this is a desperate effort to shake off the heavy atmosphere of guilt and evil by using superficial denial (see III-1 and especially VI-1), or it is a pseudo-submissive caricature of the "wholesome" ideals of good cheer, perseverance and achievement. The image may even express both trends; that is to say, the patient may not see any other way of dealing with his sense of evil and danger than by playing up optimistic cliches and ideals based on denial and simultaneously burlesquing these to express how much he despises and mistrusts them. Soon, after the good cheer in #2 ("clowns"), he begins obsessionally to tear down this response—"Not thumbs up, but (etc.)"—and by the time he reaches #4, below, he is restating the theme of fear covered by good cheer (see VI-1). This sequence, as well as the inner structure of #4, reemphasizes the impression of considerable instability in this autistically counterphobic and counterdepressive defensive effort. (b) Pointing fingers— and this image ends up implicitly as an extended index finger—commonly have paranoid implications.

> *. . . > ∨ Can I turn it around? (If you wish.)*
>
> *3. (W M± H Peculiar) This—the reason (i.e., area) from which I think somebody was dancing—here I see two clowns, two girls, dancing girls (lower ⅓ is hair; face is along outer edge of lower ⅓) . . . and here I saw the two dancing clowns (#2).*
>
> *4. (Drs F− (Hd) Absurd, Do-tendency, 2-Peculiar) Here I see eyes (nose of popular head in upper ⅓), a nose (chin of popular head), and a mouth (space below chin). . . . Fear . . . and yet kind of . . . laughing at each other. . . . Funny, yeah. . . . ∨ . . . ∧ . . . [The face of a what? The devil, I suppose.]*

Again fear and laughter are combined inappropriately (see VI-1), but this time the theme of evil intrudes as well.

CARD VIII    REACTION TIME: 3″.    TOTAL TIME: 6′ 30″.

> *1. (D F+ A P) The first thing: two animals here. And then. . . .
> Two animals here. . . .*
>
> *2. (D F— Plant Autistic Logic, 3-Peculiar, Fluid) These are rocks
> (lower pink and orange). Not rocks but something; moss; not moss;
> moss; some kind of fertilization, growth, land or something.* [What
> made it look like a growth or something? *The fertilization thing.* What
> about it? *I just felt that the animal (#1) was. . . . It was barren and
> kind of wild because the animal was wild.* Do you mean the wild animal
> made it look like wild terrain? *Yes: if the animal was wild, therefore
> the terrain would be wild.* Any other reason? *The shape, I guess.*]

Note the peculiar obsessional indecision and wording with respect to the rocks,
moss, etc., and also the fluid and grim shift of emphasis from "growth" to
"barren."

> *3. (Ds F— Ad Absurd) And this is a rooster (blue and gray). At
> least, I get the impression. . . . And there are the eyes (oval spaces
> between blue and gray) and the beak (around upper heavy midline).*
> [Rooster? *The beak and the eyes; just the head.*]
>
> *These two are animals here (#1) and they're kind of . . . looking
> across this way (at each other). < (Contamination:) If I look at it
> this way > . . . then it's kind of looking down in the water and seeing
> the other's reflection. . . .*
>
> *4. (D C Water Peculiar) Maybe this is water (blue). I get the impres-
> sion that that's a reflection.* [Water? *The fact that it was blue and
> the fact that it was a one-animal-reflected idea.*]
>
> *5. (DWs F— (Hd) Peculiar) . . . ⋁ . . . And if I turn it this way, it
> looks like the faces of. . . . (Of what?) A devil . . . here. . . . The
> eyes and the nose here . . . (same configuration as #3 at first and
> then, as he traces, it changes to a W).*

This is the fifth devil, the fourth having appeared in VII-4.

CARD IX    REACTION TIME: 60″.    TOTAL TIME: 6′ 20″.

> *This one I haven't seen. . . . I don't remember. . . . Oh yes, I do. . . .
> (Peculiar:) I think I only had this once when I had the others. It
> isn't as familiar as the others; the other I had twice. . . .*

This is the third time the patient has taken the Rorschach test in recent years.

> *1. (D F(C)+ Obj 2-Peculiar, Confusion) This is a candle here (mid-
> line), and this is the base (lower red), and this (upper tip of midline)
> is the flame here, I think, although it's not red, not orange, or reddish
> orange, although it's not orange . . . although it's not reddish orange.
> . . . And this is wax, I think. . . .* [What made it look like a candle?
> *Nothing, except there was a flame. It might be some kind of a lamp
> (see #3 below) that would give light. I had in mind the idea that
> it was a candle (#1) and . . . the idea of the candle and then I
> thought it might be in the picture, it might be a lantern (#3). . . .
> Yes. . . . There was a candle (#1) and this (#3) might be some-
> thing else that would give  light.* Lantern? *It might be giving off
> light.*]

The supreme, autistic mockery of obsessional conscientiousness emerges in his debate about the best way to formulate the color of the candle's flame. It is particularly significant that his deliberations are inherently empty: he is merely debating what color the flame area is *not* rather than what color it *is*—it is not red or orange, etc. (see III-1). True, he is concerned with the real color of candle flame, but the negative form of this preoccupation and its dragged-out quality are out of touch with the realities of the immediate situation.

> 2. (Ds F— Ad Absurd) *This might be a whole . . . some kind of face of an animal (all green); the eyes here (spaces in green).*

> 3. (Ws FC'— Obj Contamination) *And here is kind of, it almost looks like. . . . I'm trying to make it out, make it into a . . . make it into a kerosene lamp (green and orange) . . . and this is kind of a glass here (middle space). . . .*

See inquiry in #1, above, for the basis of scoring the C' and the *Contamination*.

> 4. (s F— Ad) *And here are the eyes of something (slits in lower center). It looks like a. . . . I don't know what it would be. . . .*

Again and again he "thwarts" the tester by leading him up to the edge of a response and then trailing off into silence or rumination. The inference of hostile, thwarting intent is justified by the consideration that blocking or severe repressive and suppressive efforts would lead to no comments at all or to "I don't know" reactions. Some thwarting intent seems required to bring about this demanding and ultimately annoying style of (non-)communication. Of course, agonizing inner struggles must also play a big part in these fragmented, unfinished responses as in the drawn-out, ruminative responses.

> *This (lower red) is the base of the whole candle (#1).*

CARD X     REACTION TIME: 25".     TOTAL TIME: 10'.

> 1. (D F+ A P) *I see two crabs.*

> 2. (D M+ H Confabulation, Peculiar) *It (red figure) looks like. . . . These look like two people that are . . . that are looking at each other with fear; not fear, but kind of hatred; (they are) mean. . . . And as if they were fighting or about to fight, challenging each other. . . .* [What made it look like hatred? *They looked . . . looked . . . mean. . . . They looked mean.* In what way? *Just the general effect, expression.* Can you say any more about it? *Well, they looked mad.* What made it look like they were challenging each other? *They were just looking mean at each other.*]

(a) Here the alternation is not between fear and laughter as it has been previously (see VI-1, VII-4); it is between fear and hatred or between fear and fighting. One layer of projection appears to be peeling off and we seem to be getting closer to underlying affect and impulse.

(b) The confabulation of fear and hatred in this response involves pathological projection. Reliance on this archaic mechanism in connection with this hostile theme suggests intense and subjectively intolerable hostility in the patient's relationships. This has been implied in previous images and in his general manner of taking the test. Often, however, an image like this one relates to important external figures in conflict, most likely the parents. Such responses as that to Card I, for example, of a person being torn in two by two other persons (middle area torn by side areas) tend to express the same theme, along with the subjective feeling of intolerable inner conflict of loyalties.

This reference to external figures in conflict does not invalidate the previous assumption that the patient is projecting hostility onto others. It means only that so far as conflict does exist between important real-life figures, it provides good reality support for such projection. Hertzman's discussion of the representation of external figures in human content in the Rorschach test is especially relevant here [75].

> *3-4-5-6 (D F— A Absurd, 2-Confusion; D F∓ A; D F— A Absurd; D F— A Absurd, 2-Fluid) And these look like some kind of winged animals; not winged animals; . . . maybe . . . well . . . winged animals. Perhaps some kind of sea. . . . Well, winged animals, yeah (vague pointing around card including side gray, side yellow, lower outer orange and lower red). (What did you start to say about the sea?) Sea things, sea beasts.* [How many animals did you see altogether? *First I got the impression there were three but now (with card before him) I see only two.*]

From this point on the patient is almost totally incapable of dealing with the blot. He becomes quite arbitrary and confused in his responses. This may be a delayed reaction to the bright colors of this card. It is relevant to note that on Card VIII, after the first adequate response, the next four are either $F-$ or *pure C*, and on Card IX, after the first adequate response, the next three are $F-$. Such a consistent falling off in quality of response has not occurred on any card previous to VIII. The adequacy of his first responses to these last three cards may indicate merely a very fragile front of realistic, moderately adequate responsiveness, while the inadequacy of the responses that follow gives away the patient's extremely autistic and confused state. It is also possible, however, that the particularly severe deterioration of response quality following #2 on this card is in reaction to the theme of that response. This response is the first in the record involving open hostility and fighting. We have seen what an extremely conscientious, superficially aggression-denying manner the patient has been frantically and pathetically trying to maintain. Bearing these defensive efforts in mind, we can understand why the open appearance of hostility would be so threatening to him and so disruptive. A third possibility, and the most likely, is that the rapid and severe deterioration of level of response to Card X represents a combined drastic reaction to both the colors and the disturbing hostile second response. Apparently his fragile front could not withstand this double assault.

> *7. (D F— A Confusion) This (upper center orange) look like a bird here or a butterfly, an insect, a beast, yeah.*
>
> *(Fluid:) These are crabs here . . . crabs here (same as #1 but offered as new response). . . .*
>
> *8. (D F— A Confusion) And this is a . . . something (all lower green); I don't know; bird, beast. . . .*
>
> *Can I turn it around? ∨ Here I see it a little bit differently. ∧ . . . ∨ . . .*
>
> *9. (D F— Cliffs) Kind of cliffs, I can see here (red).*
>
> *10. (D F± A Peculiar) Two birds here (middle blue): hawks of some sort, holding hands, touching wings. They're touching wings, touching claws, holding hands, touching claws, yeah. . . .* [Birds? *The general shape, the wings.* Anything else? *No.*]

(a) As in the candle verbalization in IX-1, the patient goes to fantastic lengths in trying to define his meaning exactly. The combinations of the elements *holding, touching, hands, wings* and *claws* are almost completely exhausted before he lets go of this response. (b) It is noteworthy that the hawk image has oral-aggressive thematic connotations. Thus, the contact, particularly of claws, could represent another image of hostile interaction. This in turn could have spurred on his autistically obsessional floundering. The inappropriate interpolation of "holding hands" may represent a thin overlay of "friendliness," denying the hostility (see III-1, VII-1).

> *(Fluid:) Here's . . . wings: a winged animal, a creature here (same response as #8).*
>
> 11. (D F— A Absurd) *More of them here (middle yellow), or something living in the rocks, something like that.*
> *(Fluid:) Crabs here (same response as #1). I get the impression of crabs.*

### SUMMARY OF SCORES

R: 48         EB: 4.5–2.5(3)

| | | | | | | | |
|---|---|---|---|---|---|---|---|
| W | 9 | F+ | 12 | A | 16+1 | W% | 17 |
| D | 30 | F− | 18 | Ad | 4 | D% | 62 |
| Dr | 4 | F± | 5 | H | 4 | | |
| S | 1+2 | F∓ | 4 | (H) | 1 | DR% | 12 |
| s | 1+6 | M | 4 | Hd | 5 | | |
| Do | 2+4 | FM | 1 | (Hd) | 6 | F% | 81–96 |
| DW | 1 | FC | 0+1 | Obj | 6 | F+% | 44–50 |
| | | CF | 1 | Cg | 1 | | |
| | | C | 1 | Plant | 1 | A% | 42–44 |
| *Qualitative* | | F(C) | 1 | Fire | 1 | H% | 17–33 |
| Fab. Comb. | 1 | FC′ | 1− | Smoke | 1 | P | 6+2 |
| Confabulation | 4 | | | Water | 1 | P% | 12–17 |
| Confab. tend. | 1 | | | Cliffs | 1 | | |
| Peculiar | 24 | | | | | | |
| Contamination | 2 | | | | | | |
| Contam. tend. | 1 | | | | | | |
| Autistic Logic | 1 | | | | | | |
| Absurd | 9 | | | | | | |
| Confusion | 7 | | | | | | |
| Fluid | 7 | | | | | | |

In the summary of scores, the patient's obsessional tendencies are suggested by the moderately high *R* of 48, the *EB* of 4.5–2.5 with its emphasis on the *M* side, the 2+4 *Do,* and the relatively high *F%* of 81%–96%. From the *Qualitative* scores, the *DW* and the low *F+%* of 44%–50% particularly, and to a lesser extent from the distribution of color responses, there is no question but that we are dealing with a severely schizophrenic young man. As a whole, the picture implied by the test scores is that of a relatively inhibited schizophrenic who in some ways shows noteworthy preservation (*M* of 4.5, *P* of 6+2) and whose preservation of integration, poor as it is, most likely is sustained by fragments of a premorbid obses-sional adjustment or by a partial one that was never consolidated.

These latter inferences from the scores concerning the integrative con-tribution of the obsessional trend are supported by the preceding qualitative analysis. According to the qualitative analysis, one of the patient's out-standing character features is obsessional defense, particularly conscientious-ness and meticulousness as forms of expression of reaction formation against hostility. However, his performance is a far cry from that of the well functioning obsessive man first discussed in this chapter. Where that man brought intellectualization, isolation and reaction formation to bear against hostility and passivity, he tended to do so by ambitious and genuine productivity, and also by clever rationalization and reconciliation of anxiety-induced inadequacies and contradictions in his responses. In the present case we see only an empty shell and a grim parody of that smooth obsessive-compulsive performance. Far-reaching decompensation and withdrawal appear to have led to the appearance of obsessive-compulsive defense in such regressive, inappropriate, ineffectual, inconsiderate and frustrating forms as halting, fragmented, incomplete thoughts and verbalizations, sterile manipulation of words rather than productive manipulation of ideas and objects, and doubt-laden flounderings and paralysis of the yes-no-yes-no-etc.-etc. variety. Over all this hovers a sense of inner and (by projection) surrounding evil together with fear of superego condemnation and punish-ment. We see here not only the *reductio ad absurdum* of obsessive-com-pulsive defense, particularly reaction formation, but the shambles and desolation of an adjustment effort that has failed totally.

# 11. Retrospect and Prospect

WE HAVE COVERED A GREAT DEAL OF TERRITORY since beginning these explorations in Rorschach theory and interpretation. With ego processes as our chief point of reference, we have considered many intricacies of the interpersonal test relationship, the response process, the analysis of content, the criteria for sound interpretation, and theoretical and practical problems in interpreting types, strengths and total personality contexts of major defensive operations. But even as explorations these are grossly incomplete, and before proceeding any further it will be worthwhile to pause and survey quickly the ground we have not covered. Such a survey will be useful both as a necessary reminder of the need for caution in this area and as a review of major themes in this book.

First and foremost it must be emphasized that we have been dealing with relatively few aspects of psychoanalytic theory and observation. We have paid more than passing attention only to those psychoanalytic contributions that most obviously promise to enrich our work with tests. In this connection it should be added that a number of the conceptions used here are not free from differences of interpretation and valuation in the psychoanalytic literature. The systematizing efforts of Fenichel, Hartmann, Kris, and Rapaport, among others, bear witness to the fact that contemporary Freudian psychoanalysis is not a static, thoroughly developed and integrated body of hypotheses and observations.

Also, the preceding discussions often merely touched on complexities of response and interpretation that require considerable additional clarification. These complexities pertain, for example, to the relation between the processes of artistic creation and Rorschach response and to the relation between communication in therapy and communication in the test situation. Further, the demonstration of defensive operations in the case studies tended to call attention away from the Rorschach response's theoretically and diagnostically significant *spread of emotional and ideational reference* from the highly developed levels of psychic functioning to the primitive, although the observation that responses often include such a spread obviously influenced all the interpretations offered. We do not yet have precise criteria for identifying and comparing these levels of psychic functioning in Rorschach responses; the same may be said for shifts of level within individual responses and between responses. The nature of these

spreads and fluctuations of psychic level would be clarified by studying
more closely and systematically than we have the relation between instances of thought disorder or other response disruption on the one hand
and the dominant response content and test attitude of the moment on the
other.

The case studies too are incomplete in certain important respects. For
reasons presented earlier, scores were kept in the background of the
analyses. Individual scores, sequences of scores and summarized score
patterns, while not ignored, were not integrated into the interpretive
process as much as possible—and desirable. Also neglected were the *real*
interaction between patient and tester, as it evolved through the administration of a battery of tests, and its possible effects on test performance.
Discussion in this realm was restricted mainly to the patient's neurotically
or psychotically elaborated fantasies concerning the tester-patient interaction. In addition, many of the interpretations in the case studies were
tentative, highly speculative, uncertain. Often they raised rather than
answered questions, and sometimes they were left hanging. Finally in this
connection, certain qualitative aspects of each Rorschach record were
ignored in order to develop a clear analysis of the major impulse, defense,
and adaptation problems under discussion. In short, the case studies are
not *and were not meant to be* demonstrations of total Rorschach analysis.

The case studies were also not meant to be demonstrations of recommended clinical testing practice. As already indicated, each patient studied
in this book was originally given a battery of tests, including, in addition to
the Rorschach test, at least the Wechsler-Bellevue Intelligence Scale and
the Thematic Apperception test. In each clinical test report, equally important interpretations were derived from the other tests as from the
Rorschach test, and in many vital respects integrated interpretation of all
the tests clarified, confirmed, amended and significantly extended the
interpretations of the Rorschach record alone. *The Rorschach test does not
tell all.* However, it was not possible for me at this time to undertake theoretical and clinical expositions of the Wechsler-Bellevue Scale and the
TAT that would parallel the one presented here for the Rorschach test;
nor was it possible to take up the many subtle problems involved in integrating the results of a battery of tests.* For these reasons, the results
of the entire test battery administered to the patients studied in this book
were not presented, analyzed and integrated with the Rorschach findings.

To me this is an especially disturbing omission. I have always worked
with a battery of tests and believe deeply in the necessity and advantages

* I have discussed some aspects of these problems elsewhere [*135*]. Rapaport's
basic contributions [*117, 118*], Stein's [*140*] and Holt's [*78*] extended case
studies, and Holt's recent theoretical contribution [*77*] are valuable theoretical
and clinical references bearing on the Wechsler-Bellevue Scale and/or TAT.

of this approach to clinical testing and test research.* As we have seen, the psychoanalytic conception of psychic functioning is one that extends from relatively advanced, articulated, realistic, stable and autonomous ideational and emotional processes (functioning in terms of the "secondary process") to archaic, diffuse, autistic processes charged with intense, highly mobile impulse and affect (functioning in terms of the "primary process").† From this theoretical conception of a continuum of levels of psychic functioning follow certain requirements for studying personality and psychopathology with tests. Specifically, we need tests that tap processes on various psychic levels. As Rapaport has pointed out [110], tests of "quasi-stable" intellectual functions, such as the sub-tests of judgment, information, concept formation, concentration, and visual-motor coordination in the Wechsler-Bellevue Scale, have a definite place in a psychoanalytically-oriented test battery. Patterns of past intellectual achievement, of current problem-solving methods, and of verbalization, as these are elicited by a standardized intelligence test, almost always illuminate important dimensions of personality, especially if they are approached with relevant concepts from psychoanalytic ego psychology. Beyond establishing general intellectual level, these cognitive patterns reflect established defensive and adaptive policies, characteristic rigidity, flexibility or looseness of ego integration, and the degree to which controls and defense are undermined and the ordinarily impersonal, detached intellectual functions are neurotically or psychotically invaded by primitive impulse representations, conflict, and narcissistic preoccupation.

As for the TAT, its inclusion in a battery of tests no longer needs any detailed explanation. Suffice it to say that it is a personalized, semi-structured test situation which normally does not reach the primitive levels to which the Rorschach test can penetrate, but which does get below the relatively autonomous levels of functioning on which intelligence tests concentrate. As a result of its intermediate position, the TAT often conveys more directly than the other tests discussed here the patient's characteristic mode of functioning in everyday situations that are personal, not routinized, immediately meaningful, and potentially or actually conflictful. In this formalistic, structural respect, as much as through revealing story content, the TAT makes a basic contribution to any test battery—and could have added greatly to the case studies in this book. Also, like the Wechsler-Bellevue Scale protocols, the TAT protocols would have often yielded interpretations which converged with those derived from the Rorschach protocols alone. These interpretations would have increased the depth, soundness and convincingness of the Rorschach interpretations pre-

---

* See in this regard *The clinical application of psychological tests* [134].
† See pp. 78–82 for fuller discussion of these concepts.

sented here. Unfailingly, this is the way it works out in daily clinical practice.

So much for the omissions and other limitations of this presentation. More shortcomings could be specified, and all would lead to the correct conclusion that this book is no more than *an introductory exploration* of psychoanalytic interpretation in Rorschach testing.

Yet, introductory and exploratory as this presentation is, its theoretical and interpretive analyses carry definite implications for the interpretation of test results in daily clinical practice and for clinical research with psychological tests. The implications for clinical interpretation have been detailed throughout this book; here, only some summary remarks concerning research will be presented. One implication for research is well-known in the clinical field: it is the researcher's obligation to recognize and respect the structural and dynamic complexity of human psychic functioning and its expression in test responses. This means that comparing individuals or groups simply in terms of their Rorschach scores and score averages, even with the help of Cronbach's "pattern tabulation" [25], or of multiple regression equations [38], can never do justice to the processes shaping the individual Rorschach record. Score analysis is *minimal* analysis. It has a place in Rorschach research but is not synonymous with it. This last point applies as well to "sign" analysis, since that is essentially score analysis.

To supplement these limited treatments of Rorschach data, we need research designs that embrace rather than skirt the complexities of psychic functioning, that is, designs that simultaneously take account of scores, content themes, and test attitudes and behavior. One way to meet these complexities I have pointed out elsewhere [135]. It is to use *interpretations* as our research units rather than scores alone or, as is becoming more common, content alone.* This total quantitative and qualitative approach takes into account the fact that similar interpretations may be arrived at on the basis of different specific indicators. It also recognizes that interpretations often must be couched in terms of several variables simultaneously, such as particular impulse-defense combinations. So long as the patterns of specific indicators used are explicitly defined and thus subject to modification in the light of validation studies, and so long as our experimental analyses of test protocols and clinical data are carried out "blind" or with other necessary safeguards, we will be dealing with scientifically testable propositions while remaining appropriately complex and flexible.

---

* The *Q-technique* rests on the use of interpretations as units for research, but it is suitable only for gross comparisons. Also, this technique implicitly rests on the theoretically unacceptable conception of personality as a collection of traits that stand in no hierarchic relation to each other either conceptually or motivationally.

There is another major implication for research to be spelled out. It is a corollary of this book's basic presupposition that theory centrally determines the tester's selective perception, conceptualization and hierarchic organization of test results; it also reflects this book's psychoanalytic orientation. This research implication is that we would do well to define our research problems more systematically than we ordinarily have in terms of current psychoanalytic conceptions and questions concerning personality and psychopathology.* Too often, Rorschach research "starts from scratch," as if nothing were known about this or that clinical group and about the Rorschach test, and also as if no relevant theory were extant. Its design is then "exploratory," that is, it compares two or more groups in terms of all possible variables (scores, usually) instead of specific variables chosen in advance on the basis of a definite hypothesis that integrates theory, clinical observation and previous Rorschach research. The statistically significant precipitates of this "naive," exploratory analysis are then rationalized so as to "support," "refute," or "extend" current descriptive or dynamic conceptions of the groups in question. Clearly, this buckshot research design is dictated more by the Rorschach test scoring scheme than by psychological considerations. Although it has added significantly to our general orientation to Rorschach results, particularly when carefully defined and selected clinical samples have been used, as in *Diagnostic psychological testing* [117, 118], this type of study has also inevitably yielded many ambiguous and contradictory findings.

In order to illustrate how a systematic orientation to psychoanalytic theory and observation could influence research design, two areas of Rorschach investigation will be considered briefly: the study of schizophrenia and the study of personality change. Ideally, test research in these areas should employ a battery of tests. Also, it is not meant to be implied in the following that tests are the only, the best, or the simplest ways of studying the illustrative problems. The point in this regard is merely that if the Rorschach test (and other tests) can be shown to be sufficiently sensitive to the relevant structural and dynamic variables—as I have attempted to show here—there is every reason to enlist their aid in research in these areas.

*The study of schizophrenia* with the Rorschach technique—or with any clinical technique—is almost inevitably fascinating and instructive. In the past, Rorschach research in this area has tended to remain instrument-centered [7, 106, 121, 139, 143]; that is to say, it has focused on variables traditionally assumed to be involved in each of the Rorschach scores and

* Although oversimplified in conception, Aranson's study of "homosexual" content in the Rorschach records of paranoid patients is one of several recent studies illustrating a psychoanalytically-oriented Rorschach research design [3]; see also Bolgar [16] and De Vos [27].

score patterns, and has not been concerned from the beginning with variables most emphasized in current psychodynamic conceptions of and questions about schizophrenia. Not that the traditional score significances are irrelevant or unimportant, but they can be subordinated to major dynamic and structural variables, as was done in this book in the introductory sections of the chapters on the defense mechanisms. It is not, for example, the typical or average *sum C* or *A%* of the schizophrenic that should be our sole or primary concern. In fact, it has been shown that what is typical, even in the scores, depends on the type and the stage of the schizophrenic process [118]. Instead of asking about score averages first and then effortfully improvising *ad hoc* explanations of significant trends in order to link them up with clinical and theoretical thought, if that is attempted at all, we might do better to ask first about defenses in schizophrenia, for example, or alterations of self-concept, regression from object relationships, and archaic superego pressures as they appear in this or that type and stage of schizophrenia. At present, we can tentatively specify gross patterns of scores, content, and test attitudes that we think correspond to some of these variables. These patterns might be tried out, revised and reapplied. In this way, we might investigate how far we can relate the fluctuations in schizophrenic thought between the poles of primary process thinking and secondary process thinking to the waxing and waning of threatening impulse representations in fantasy and in interpersonal relationships. We might more precisely identify and elaborate early indications of the failure of normal and neurotic defense and subsequent reliance on archaic, autistic defense. Diffusion and negative definition of the self-concept are outstanding aspects of schizophrenic failure to achieve or maintain ego identity; through total thematic Rorschach analysis, these pathological trends might be better defined and articulated.

All along these lines of investigation it would be necessary and desirable to clarify the ways in which and the extent to which schizophrenic Rorschach phenomena are abortive or hypertrophied forms of such normal psychic phenomena as dreams, daydreams, fluctuations of concentration efficiency, sporadic defensive ineffectiveness, momentary or circumscribed loss of clarity about one's social role or about the line between fact and fantasy. It has been one basic assumption of this entire presentation that the processes underlying Rorschach responses are more or less continuous with processes underlying these normal dream, daydream, etc., phenomena on the one hand and their schizophrenic variants on the other. Thus, the Rorschach medium seems to lend itself especially well to a comparative study of the normal and the schizophrenic ego. For example, with respect to the "temporary regression in the service of the ego" that has been held to pave the way for creative, self-expressive Rorschach responses, we might investigate to what extent and in what ways this regression corresponds to and differs from the extensive regressive alteration of psychic functioning characterizing schizophrenic disorders. Kris, in his studies of art, has paved some of the way for such comparative analyses [92].

Comparisons and distinctions of this sort are much needed. They may help us understand the ability of some persons to maintain a borderline or latent psychotic position without serious or prolonged lapses into bizarreness and without evident progressive deterioration [89, 138]. These comparative ego analyses could also increase our comprehension of both the "sealing over" process following some psychotic breaks, and the capacity many schizophrenics seem to have, as seen in therapy and in hospital behavior, to manipulate others by deliberately, probably preconsciously, exaggerating their autistic tendencies at some times and minimizing them at other times. Therapeutic and prognostic criteria might simultaneously be refined.

Theoretical and clinical problems of this sort have been pushed into the foreground in recent years by increased interest in psychoanalytic psychotherapy with schizophrenics [30, 56, 108, 109, 151, 152]. Of course, these problems must be studied primarily within therapy and real life situations if their understanding is to have adequate depth and breadth, but this does not mean that the use of sensitive auxiliary techniques, such as Rorschach testing, is superfluous or pretentious.

*Turning now to the systematic investigation of personality change* with the Rorschach test, we must first note that it may be carried out best in longitudinal studies of development and in studies of the effects of psychotherapeutic techniques. Only the latter will be considered here. Such investigations of personality change would benefit significantly, according to the main theses of this book, by being organized around specific psychological questions rather than simply around Rorschach scores on the one side and therapists' unqualified estimates of "improvement" or "continuation in treatment" on the other [4, 23, 100, 122, 123]. Concerning the effects of treatment, such questions might include, How much general relaxation of defensive efforts seems to have occurred? What sorts of content have gained freer access to consciousness as a result of lightened or lifted repressions? How much anxiety is associated with the appearance of this formerly repressed material in conscious awareness? Has anxiety tolerance increased in this regard? These are questions that concern any psychoanalyst or psychotherapist in evaluating the course or outcome of intensive treatment, and, as has been demonstrated earlier, there are a series of Rorschach indications concerning repression and unconscious content that can help answer these questions. Or, to shift away from alterations in repressive operations, there are such pertinent questions to direct at Rorschach results as, How have the guilty (or weak, cruel, grandiose, etc.) aspects of the patient's self-concept been altered? Or, How accurately does the Rorschach imagery anticipate the content of early, middle and late associations and dreams in psychoanalysis, and how well do major test attitudes and behavior forecast outstanding transference and resistence problems in treatment?

The answers to these and other relevant questions will require careful, traditional score analysis, wherever this is appropriate, but they will also require study of dominant structural and dynamic themes in the patient's test imagery, attitudes and behavior. On the whole, we may expect the answers to these psychological questions concerning personality change to lie in *configurations* of test data before, during and after treatment. Again, it is not implied that Rorschach research in this area will or can completely or most easily answer the many unsettled questions concerning therapeutic processes. The results of this research may, however, help sharpen our therapeutic recommendations and facilitate our conceptual organization of the complicated processes involved in the course and outcome of therapy.

It is worth mentioning in this regard that re-tests often seem to lag far behind overt behavior in reflecting change for the better. While it is certainly possible that the Rorschach test is insensitive to some basic personality changes, and also possible that we underestimate the significance of some small Rorschach changes, we must still be prepared to consider whether major shifts in clinical behavior may not derive from quantitatively small but qualitatively significant shifts in the balance of id, ego-defensive, ego-adaptive and superego forces, and the repercussions these have on the patient's external life situation.* Important theoretical problems regarding therapy, adaptation, and Rorschach interpretation overlap here. In the interaction of theory and application in such research, as in the previously described study of schizophrenia, the psychoanalytic rationale of the Rorschach response process and the principles of Rorschach interpretation are bound to be improved by modification, articulation and extension.

Obviously, these remarks on research into schizophrenia and the effects of therapy are very general and incomplete. They illustrate an orientation toward clinical research using tests and are not meant to outline specific experimental designs. Admittedly, implementing ideas of this sort will be no easy task. Difficult problems in conceptualization, validation, and establishment of reliability will have to be faced, but these are problems inherent in all qualitatively complex clinical investigation. Psychoanalysis as a system of hypotheses, concepts and observations is a big system and a subtle one; it demands appropriate breadth of test rationale and refinement of research design. Such rationale and research will be powerful allies in coping with the elusive, ever-changing, sometimes overwhelming psychological phenomena and professional responsibilities in daily clinical work.

* See in this regard Freud's late statement on this subject in "Analysis Terminable and Interminable" [52].

# Bibliography

1. Alden, P. and Benton, A. L.: Relationship of sex of examiner to incidence of Rorschach responses with sexual content. *J. proj. Tech.*: 1951, *15*, 231–234.
2. Allen, R. M.: The influence of color in the Rorschach test on reaction time in a normal population. *J. proj. Tech.*: 1951, *15*, 481–485.
3. Aranson, M.: A study of the Freudian theory of paranoia by means of the Rorschach test. *J. proj. Tech.*: 1952, *16*, 397–411.
4. Auld, F. and Eron, L. D.: The use of Rorschach scores to predict whether patients will continue psychotherapy. *J. consult. Psychol.*: 1953, *17*, 104–109.
5. Baer, A.: Le test de Rorschach interpreté du point de vue analytique. *Revue Française de Psychoanalyse:* 1950, *14*, 455–503.
6. Barnouw, A. J.: *The fantasy of Pieter Breughel.* New York: Lear Publishers, 1947.
7. Beck, S. J.: *Personality structure in schizophrenia.* New York: Nervous and Mental Disease Monograph, 1938.
8. ———: *Rorschach's test. Vol. I. Basic processes.* New York: Grune & Stratton, 1944.
9. ———: *Rorschach's test. Vol. II. A variety of personality pictures.* New York: Grune & Stratton, 1945.
10. ———: Trends in orthopsychiatric therapy. II. Rorschach F plus and the ego in treatment. *Amer. J. Orthopsychiat.*: 1948, *18*, 395–401.
11. ———: *Rorschach's test. Vol. III. Advances in interpretation.* New York: Grune & Stratton, 1952.
12. Bergler, E.: *The basic neurosis.* New York: Grune & Stratton, 1949.
13. Bergman, M. S.: Homosexuality on the Rorschach test. *Bull. Menninger Clinic:* 1945, *9*, 78–83.
14. Berman, Leo: Countertransference and attitudes of the analyst in the therapeutic process. *Psychiatry:* 1949, *12*, 159–166.
15. Blake, R. R. and Ramsey, G. V. (ed.): *Perception, an approach to personality.* New York: Ronald Press, 1951.
16. Bolgar, H.: Consistency of affect and symbolic expression: a comparison between dreams and Rorschach responses. Unpublished; read at 1953 meeting of American Orthopsychiatric Association.
17. Booth, G.: Organ function and form perception. *Psychosom. Med.*: 1946, *8*, 367–385.
18. Brenman, M.: On teasing and being teased: and the problem of "moral masochism." In *The psychoanalytic study of the child*, Vol. VII, 264–285. New York: International Universities Press, 1952.
19. ———, Gill M., and Knight, R. P.: Spontaneous fluctuations in depth of hypnosis and their implication for ego functions. *Int. J. Psychoanal.*: 1952, *31*, 22–33.

20. Brown, F.: An exploratory study of dynamic factors in the content of the Rorschach protocol. *J. proj. Tech.:* 1953, *17,* 251–279.

21. Bruner, J. S.: Perceptual theory and the Rorschach test. *J. Pers.:* 1948, *17,* 157–168.

22. Buker, S. L. and Williams, M.: Color as a determinant of responsiveness to Rorschach cards in schizophrenia. *J. consult. Psychol.:* 1951, *15,* 196–202.

23. Carr, A. C.: An evaluation of nine nondirective psychotherapy cases by means of the Rorschach. *J. consult. Psychol.:* 1949, *13,* 196–205.

24. Crandall, V. J.: Induced frustration and punishment-reward expectancy in thematic apperception stories. *J. consult. Psychol.:* 1951, *15,* 400–404.

25. Cronbach, L. J.: "Pattern tabulation": a statistical method for analysis of limited patterns of scores, with particular reference to the Rorschach test. *Educ. psychol. Measmt.:* 1949, *9,* 149–171.

26. Deri, S.: *Introduction to the Szondi test.* New York: Grune & Stratton, 1949.

27. De Vos, G.: A quantitative approach to affective symbolism in Rorschach responses. *J. proj. Tech.:* 1952, *16,* 133–150.

28. Dubrovner, R. J., Van Lackum, W. J., and Jost, H.: A study of the effect of color on productivity and reaction time in the Rorschach test. *J. clin. Psychol.:* 1950, *6,* 331–336.

29. Due, F. O. and Wright, M. E.: The use of content analysis in Rorschach interpretation. I. Differential characteristics of male homosexuals. *Rorschach Res. Exch.:* 1945, *9,* 169–177.

30. Eissler, K.: Remarks on the psychoanalysis of schizophrenics. *Int. J. Psychoanal.:* 1951, *32,* 139–156.

31. Elizur, A.: Content analysis of the Rorschach with regard to anxiety and hostility. *Rorschach Res. Exch.:* 1949, *13,* 247–284.

32. Eriksen, C. W. and Lazarus, R. S.: Perceptual defense and projective tests. *J. abnorm. soc. Psychol. Suppl.:* 1952, *42,* 302–308.

33. Erikson, E.: Studies in the interpretation of play: I. Clinical observation of play disruption in young children. *Genet. Psychol. Monogr.:* 1940, *22,* 557–671.

34. ———: Hitler's imagery and German youth. *Psychiatry:* 1942, *5,* 475–493.

35. ———: *Childhood and society.* New York: Norton, 1950.

36. ———: Sex differences in play configurations of preadolescents. *Amer. J. Orthopsychiat.:* 1951, *21,* 667–692.

37. Fenichel, O.: *The psychoanalytic theory of neurosis.* New York: Norton, 1945.

38. Ferguson, G. A.: Approaches to the experimental study of the Rorschach test. *Canad. J. Psychol.:* 1951, *5,* 157–166.

39. Filmer-Bennett, G.: Prognostic indices in the Rorschach records of hospitalized patients. *J. abnorm. soc. Psychol.:* 1952, *47,* 503–506.

40. Fine, L. G.: Rorschach signs of homosexuality in male college students. *J. clin. Psychol.:* 1950, *6,* 248–253.

41. Frank, L. K.: *Projective methods.* Springfield, Ill.: C. C Thomas, 1948.

42. Freud, A. (1936): *The ego and the mechanisms of defense.* New York: International Universities Press, 1946.

43. Freud, S. (1900): The interpretation of dreams. In *The basic writings of Sigmund Freud,* 179–549. New York: Modern Library, 1938.

44. —— (1904) : Psychopathology of everyday life. In *The basic writings of Sigmund Freud,* 33–178. New York: Modern Library, 1938.

45. —— (1911) : Formulations regarding the two principles in mental functioning. In *Collected papers,* Vol. IV, 13–21. London: Hogarth, 1946.

46. —— (1911) : Psychoanalytic notes upon an autobiographical account of a a case of paranoia (dementia paranoides). In *Collected papers,* Vol. III, 387–470. London: Hogarth, 1946.

47. —— (1915) : Repression. In *Collected papers,* Vol. IV, 84–97. London: Hogarth, 1946.

48. —— (1922) : Certain neurotic mechanisms in jealousy, paranoia, homosexuality. In *Collected papers,* Vol. II, 232–243. London: Hogarth, 1946.

49. —— (1925) : Negation. In *Collected papers,* Vol. V, 181–185. London: Hogarth, 1950.

50. —— (1926) : *The problem of anxiety.* New York: Psychoanalytic Quarterly Press, 1936.

51. —— (1927) : Fetishism. In *Collected papers,* Vol. V, 198–204. London: Hogarth, 1950.

52. —— (1937) : Analysis terminable and interminable. In *Collected papers,* Vol. V, 316–357. London: Hogarth, 1950.

53. —— (1938) : Splitting of the ego in the defensive process. In *Collected papers,* Vol. V, 372–375. London: Hogarth, 1950.

54. Fromm, E.: *Escape from freedom.* New York: Farrar and Rinehart, 1941.

55. Fromm, E. O. and Elonen, A. S.: The use of projective techniques in the study of a case of female homosexuality. *J. proj. Tech.:* 1951, *15,* 185–230.

56. Fromm-Reichman, F.: *Principles of intensive psychotherapy.* Chicago: University of Chicago Press, 1950.

57. Gero, G.: The concept of defense. *Psychoanal. Quart.:* 1951, *20,* 565–578.

58. Gibby, R. G.: Examiner influence on the Rorschach inquiry. *J. consult. Psychol.:* 1952, *16,* 449–455.

59. Gill, M.: The psychodynamics of paranoid delusions. Unpublished.

60. Gitelson, M.: The emotional position of the analyst in the psychoanalytic situation. *Int. J. Psychoanal.:* 1952, *33,* 1–10.

61. Goldfarb, W.: A definition and validation of obsessional trends in the Rorschach examination of adolescents. *Rorschach Res. Exch.:* 1943, *7,* 81–108.

62. Goldstein, K. and Rothman, E.: Physiognomic phenomena in Rorschach responses. *Rorschach Res. Exch.:* 1945, *9,* 1–7.

63. Gorlow, L., Zinet, C. N., and Fine, H. J.: The validity of anxiety and hostility Rorschach content scores among adolescents. *J. consult. Psychol.:* 1952, *16,* 73–75.

64. Gross, A.: The secret. *Bull. Menninger Clinic:* 1951, *15,* 37–44.

65. Gurvitz, M. S.: World destruction fantasies in early schizophrenia: a Rorschach study. *J. Hillside Hosp.:* 1952, *1,* 7–20.

66. Hammer, E. F. and Piotrowski, Z. A.: Hostility as a factor in the clinician's personality as it affects his interpretation of projective drawings (H-T-P). *J. proj. Tech.:* 1953, *17,* 210–216.

67. Harrower-Erickson, M. R. and Steiner, M. E.: *Large scale Rorschach techniques.* Springfield, Ill.: C. C Thomas, 1945.

68. Hartmann, H.: On rational and irrational action. In *Psychoanalysis and the social sciences,* Vol. I (G. Roheim, ed.), 359–392. New York: International Universities Press, 1947.

69. ——: Comments on the psychoanalytic theory of the ego. In *The psychoanalytic study of the child,* Vol. V, 74–96. New York: International Universities Press, 1950.

70. ——: Ego psychology and the problem of adaptation. In *Organization and pathology of thought* (D. Rapaport, ed.), 362–396. New York: Columbia University Press, 1951.

71. —— and Kris, E.: The genetic approach in psychoanalysis. In *The psychoanalytic study of the child,* Vol. I, 11–29. New York: International Universities Press, 1945.

72. ——, ——, and Loewenstein, R. M.: Comments on the formation of psychic structure. In *The psychoanalytic study of the child,* Vol. II, 11–38. New York: International Universities Press, 1946.

73. ——, ——, and ——.: Notes on the theory of aggression. In *The psychoanalytic study of the child,* Vol. III-IV, 9–36. New York: International Universities Press, 1948.

74. Hertz, M.: Suicidal configurations in Rorschach records. *Rorschach Res. Exch.:* 1948, *12,* 3–58.

75. Hertzman, M. and Pearce, J.: The personal meaning of the human figure in the Rorschach. *Psychiatry:* 1947, *10,* 413–422.

76. Hobbs, N. et al.: *Ethical standards for psychologists.* Washington, D. C.: American Psychological Association, 1953.

77. Holt, R. R.: The Thematic Apperception Test. In *An introduction to projective techniques* (H. A. Anderson and G. L. Anderson, ed.), 181–229. New York: Prentice Hall, 1951.

78. ——: The case of Jay: interpretations and discussion. *J. proj. Tech.:* 1952, *16,* 444–475.

79. ——: Implications of some contemporary personality theories for Rorschach rationale. In Klopfer, B., Ainsworth, M. D., Klopfer, W. G. and Holt, R. R. *Developments in the Rorschach technique: Vol. I, technique and theory;* Chapter 15. New York: World Book Company, 1954.

80. Hutt, M. L., Gibby, R. C., Milton, E. O., and Pottharst, K.: The effect of varied experimental "sets" upon Rorschach performance. *J. proj. Tech.:* 1950, *14,* 181–187.

81. Janis, M. G. and Janis, I. L.: A supplementary test based on free associations to Rorschach responses. *Rorschach Res. Exch.:* 1946, *10,* 1–19.

82. Joel, W.: Interpersonal equation in projective methods. *Rorschach Res. Exch.:* 1949, *13,* 479–482.

83. Kimble, G. A.: Social influence on Rorschach records. *J. abnorm. soc. Psychol.:* 1945, *40,* 89–93.

84. Klatskin, E. H.: An analysis of the effect of the test situation upon the Rorschach record: formal scoring characteristics. *J. proj. Tech.:* 1952, *16,* 193–199.

85. Klein, G. S.: The personal world through perception. In *Perception, an approach to personality* (R. R. Blake and G. V. Ramsey, ed.), 328–355. New York: Ronald Press, 1951.

86. Klopfer, B. and Kelley, D.: *The Rorschach technique.* Yonkers-on-Hudson, New York: World Book Co., 1942.

87. Knight, R. P.: Introjection, projection and identification. *Psychoanal. Quart.:* 1940, *9,* 334–341.

88. ——: The relationship of latent homosexuality to the mechanism of paranoid delusions. *Bull. Menninger Clinic:* 1940, *4,* 149–159.

89. ——: Borderline states. *Bull. Menninger Clinic:* 1953, *17,* 1–12.

90. Korner, A. F.: Theoretical considerations concerning the scope and limitations of projective techniques. *J. abnorm. soc. Psychol.:* 1950, *45,* 619–627.

91. Kris, E.: On preconscious mental processes. In *Organization and pathology of thought* (D. Rapaport, ed.), 474–493. New York: Columbia University Press, 1951.

92. ——: *Psychoanalytic explorations in art.* New York: International Universities Press, 1952.

93. Kutash, S. B.: The Rorschach examination and psychotherapy. *Amer. J. Psychother.:* 1951, *5,* 405–410.

94. Lazarus, R. S.: The influence of color on the protocol of the Rorschach test. *J. abnorm. soc. Psychol.:* 1949, *44,* 506–516.

95. Lewin, B.: *The psychoanalysis of elation.* New York: Norton, 1950.

96. Lindner, R.: The content analysis of the Rorschach protocol. In *Projective psychology* (L. E. Abt and L. Bellak, ed.), 75–90. New York: Knopf, 1950.

97. Lord, E.: Experimentally induced variations in Rorschach performance. *Psychol. Monogr.:* 1950, *64* (10), No. 316.

98. Machover, K.: *Personality projection in the drawing of the human figure.* Springfield, Ill.: C. C Thomas, 1949.

99. Meyer, B. T.: An investigation of color shock in the Rorschach test. *J. clin. Psychol.:* 1951, *17,* 367–370.

100. Muench, G. A.: An evaluation of non-directive psychotherapy. *Appl. Psychol. Monogr.:* 1947, No. 13.

101. Murphy, G.: *Personality, a biosocial approach to origins and structure,* 331–478. New York: Harper, 1947.

102. Murray, H. A.: *Explorations in personality.* New York: Oxford University Press, 1938.

103. Nunberg, H.: The synthetic function of the ego. *Int. J. Psychoanal.:* 1931, *12,* 123–140.

104. Pascal, G. R., Ruesch, H. A., Devine, C. A., and Suttell, B. J.: A study of genital symbols on the Rorschach test: presentation of a method and results. *J. abnorm. soc. Psychol.:* 1950, *45,* 286–295.

105. Phillips, L. and Smith, J. G.: *Rorschach interpretation: advanced technique.* New York: Grune & Stratton, 1953.

106. Piotrowski, Z. A.: Experimental psychological diagnosis of mild forms of schizophrenia. *Rorschach Res. Exch.:* 1945, *9,* 189–200.

107. ——: A Rorschach compendium; revised and enlarged. *Psychiat. Quart.:* 1950, *24,* 549–596.

108. Pious, W. L.: The pathogenic process in schizophrenia. *Bull. Menninger Clinic:* 1949, *13,* 152–159.

109. ——: Obsessive-compulsive symptoms in an incipient schizophrenia. *Psychoanal. Quart.:* 1950, *19,* 327–351.

110. Rapaport, D.: Principles underlying non-projective tests of personality. *Annals N. Y. Acad. Sci.:* 1946, *66,* 643–652.

111. ———: The theoretical implications of diagnostic testing procedures. *Congrès International de Psychiatrie, Paris, Rapports:* 1950, *2,* 241–271.

112. ———: On the psychoanalytic theory of thinking.' *Int. J. Psychoanal.:* 1950, *31,* 161–170.

113. ——— (ed.) : *Organization and pathology of thought.* New York: Columbia University Press, 1951.

114. ———: States of consciousness, a psychopathological and psychodynamic view. In *Problems of consciousness: transactions of the second conference, March 19–20, 1951, New York, N. Y.* (H. A. Abramson, ed.). New York: Josiah Macy, Jr. Foundation, 1951.

115. ———: The autonomy of the ego. *Bull. Menninger Clinic:* 1951, *15,* 113–123.

116. ———: Projective techniques and the theory of thinking. *J. proj. Tech.:* 1952, *16,* 269–275.

117. ———, Schafer, R., and Gill, M.: *Diagnostic psychological testing.* Vol. I. Chicago: Year Book Publishers, 1945.

118. ———, ———, and ———: *Diagnostic psychological testing.* Vol. II. Chicago: Year Book Publishers, 1946.

119. Reik, T.: *Masochism in modern man.* New York: Farrar and Rinehart, 1941.

120. Reitzell, J. M.: A comparative study of hysterics, homosexuals and alcoholics using content analysis of Rorschach responses. *Rorschach Res. Exch.:* 1949, *13,* 127–141.

121. Rickers-Ovsiankina, M.: The Rorschach test as applied to normal and schizophrenic subjects. *Brit. J. med. Psychol.:* 1938, *17,* 227–257.

122. Rioch, M. J.: The use of the Rorschach test in the assessment of change in patients under psychotherapy. *Psychiatry:* 1949, *12,* 427–434.

123. Rogers, L. S., Knauss, J., and Hammond, K. R.: Predicting continuation in therapy by means of the Rorschach test. *J. consult. Psychol.:* 1951, *15,* 368–371.

124. Rorschach, H.: *Psychodiagnostics.* Bern: Hans Huber; New York: Grune & Stratton, 1942.

125. Rosen, E.: Symbolic meanings in the Rorschach cards. *J. clin. Psychol.:* 1951, *7,* 239–244.

126. Sanders, R. and Cleveland, S. E.: The relationship between examiner personality variables and subjects' Rorschach scores. *J. proj. Tech.:* 1953, *17,* 34–50.

127. Sappenfield, B. R. and Buker, S. L.: Validity of the Rorschach 8–9–10 per cent as an indicator of responsiveness to color. *J. consult. Psychol.:* 1949, *13,* 268–271.

128. Sarason, S. B.: The test situation and the problem of prediction. *J. clin. Psychol.:* 1950, *6,* 387–392.

129. Schachtel, E. G.: The dynamic perception and the symbolism of form: with special reference to the Rorschach test. *Psychiatry:* 1941, *4,* 79–96.

130. ———: On color and affect: contributions to an understanding of the Rorschach test. *Psychiatry:* 1943, *6,* 393–409.

131. ———: Subjective definitions of the Rorschach test situation and their effect on test performance. *Psychiatry:* 1945, *8,* 419–448.

132. ———: Projection and its relations to character attitudes and creativity in the kinesthetic responses. *Psychiatry:* 1950, *13,* 69–100.

133. ——: Some notes on the use of the Rorschach test. In S. and E. Glueck, *Unraveling juvenile delinquency*, 363–385. New York: Commonwealth Fund, 1950.

134. Schafer, R.: *The clinical application of psychological tests.* New York: International Universities Press, 1948.

135. ——: Psychological tests in clinical research. *J. consult. Psychol.:* 1949, *13,* 328–334.

136. ——: Review of *Introduction to the Szondi test* by S. Deri in *J. abnorm. soc. Psychol.:* 1950, *45,* 184–188.

137. ——: Content analysis in the Rorschach test. *J. proj. Tech.:* 1953, *17,* 335–339.

138. Shapiro, D.: Special problems in testing borderline psychotics. Unpublished.

139. Sherman, M.: A comparison of formal and content factors in the diagnostic testing of schizophrenia. *Genet. Psychol. Monogr.:* 1952, *46,* 183–234.

140. Stein, M. I.: *The Thematic Apperception Test: an introductory manual for its clinical use with adult males.* Cambridge, Mass.: Addison-Wesley Press, 1948.

141. Stotsky, B. A.: A comparison of remitting and non-remitting schizophrenics on psychological tests. *J. abnorm. soc. Psychol. Suppl.:* 1952, *47,* 489–496.

142. Sullivan, H. S.: Conceptions of modern psychiatry. *Psychiatry:* 1940, *3,* 1–117.

143. Thiesen, J. W.: A pattern analysis of structural characteristics of the Rorschach test in schizophrenia. *J. consult. Psychol.:* 1952, *16,* 365–370.

144. ——: Assessment of current trends in psychodiagnosis. Unpublished; read at 1953 meeting of American Psychological Association.

145. Vorhaus, P. G.: The use of the Rorschach in preventive mental hygiene. *J. proj. Tech.:* 1952, *16,* 179–192.

146. Walker, R. G.: A comparison of clinical manifestations of hostility with Rorschach and MAPS test performance. *J. proj. Tech.:* 1951, *15,* 444–460.

147. Wallen, R.: The nature of color shock. *J. abnorm. soc. Psychol.:* 1948, *43,* 346–356.

148. Warner, S. J.: An evaluation of the validity of Rorschach popular responses as differentiae of ambulatory schizophrenia. *J. proj. Tech.:* 1951, *15,* 268–275.

149. Wechsler, D.: *The measurement of adult intelligence* (3d ed.). Baltimore: Williams and Wilkins, 1944.

150. Werner, H.: *Comparative psychology of mental development.* New York: Harper, 1940.

151. Wexler, M.: The structural problem in schizophrenia: therapeutic implications. *Int. J. Psychoanal.:* 1951, *32,* 157–166.

152. ——: The structural problem in schizophrenia: the role of the internal object. *Bull. Menninger Clinic:* 1951, *15,* 221–234.

153. Wheeler, R. M.: An analysis of Rorschach indices of male homosexuality. *J. proj. Tech.:* 1949, *13,* 97–126.

154. Wyatt, F.: Content analysis in the Rorschach test. Unpublished; read at 1952 meeting of American Psychological Association.

# Subject Index

*Numerous references to a wide variety of psychological trends are scattered through the case studies in Chapters 7–10; except in special instances, these remarks will not be individually indexed.*

Absurd form, 179
Adaptation
  definition, 47–48, 163–164
  effectiveness of, 116, 171–185, 358–359
  and ego identity, 157–158
  in response process, 78–82
Addiction, 55
Administration of Rorschach test, 15, 17, 18–19, 75–76, 190
Adult role, rejection of, 137
Age differences, 124–125
Aggression. *See* Hostility
Aging, concern over, 137
Ambition, 232, 291–300
Ambivalence, 333–334, 344
Anality
  in content, 132, 136, 137, 375–376, 379
  in definition of responses, 44
  in obsessive-compulsives, 332–336
Anxiety, 108, 161–162, 196
Anxiety hysteria. *See* Phobic
Aptitudes of tester, 69–71
Authoritarian orientation
  in attitude and behavior, 41, 48–49, 51, 60–61, 62, 345
  in content, 133–134, 288–289
  and tester's role, 22–23
Autism. *See* Borderline psychosis, Hypomania, Paranoid, Primary process, Schizophrenia, Thought disorder
Autonomy. *See* Ego autonomy

Borderline psychosis, 16, 54, 66, 194, 265, 391–392, 403, 411–412. *See also* Schizophrenia

Castration anxiety, 96, 125, 136, 137, 332
Character structure, 145
Children, 15–16
Cognitive style, 90, 114–115
Color
  magical use of, 253, 254
  research into, 1
Competitive definition of test situation, 41–42, 51
Compliance, 350–354, 358, 363, 364–365
Compulsive, 52–53, 72, 281, 349. *See also* Obsessive-compulsive
Condensation, 85
Confabulation
  in hypomania, 254
  in paranoid pathology, 285–286
  primary process thinking in, 373–374
Conflict-free functioning. *See* Ego autonomy, Sublimation
Conscientiousness, 350–354, 412–423. *See also* Reaction formation
Consciousness
  changes in states of, 84, 105–106, 300–307, 307–320
  expansion of, 183, 338
  flooded by unconscious content, 183, 194, 202
Content analysis
  age differences in, 124–125
  cultural differences in, 125–126
  diagnostic differences in, 126, 287–290
  "psychoanalytic symbolism" in, 52
  research into, 1
  sex differences in, 125

# Author Index

3
4
5
6 n
7 o
8 p
9 q
0 r
1 s
82 t